FREE Test Taking Tips DVD Offer

To help us better serve you, we have developed a Test Taking Tips DVD that we would like to give you for FREE. **This DVD covers world-class test taking tips that you can use to be even more successful when you are taking your test.**

All that we ask is that you email us your feedback about your study guide. Please let us know what you thought about it – whether that is good, bad or indifferent.

To get your **FREE Test Taking Tips DVD**, email freedvd@studyguideteam.com with "FREE DVD" in the subject line and the following information in the body of the email:

a. The title of your study guide.

b. Your product rating on a scale of 1-5, with 5 being the highest rating.

c. Your feedback about the study guide. What did you think of it?

d. Your full name and shipping address to send your free DVD.

If you have any questions or concerns, please don't hesitate to contact us at freedvd@studyguideteam.com.

Thanks again!

FTCE Elementary Education K-6 Study Guide

FTCE Elementary Education Exam Prep and Practice Test Questions for the Florida Teacher Certification Exam [3rd Edition]

TPB Publishing

Written and edited by TPB Publishing.

ISBN 13: 9781628457070
ISBN 10: 1628457074

Table of Contents

Quick Overview

As you draw closer to taking your exam, effective preparation becomes more and more important. Thankfully, you have this study guide to help you get ready. Use this guide to help keep your studying on track and refer to it often.

This study guide contains several key sections that will help you be successful on your exam. The guide contains tips for what you should do the night before and the day of the test. Also included are test-taking tips. Knowing the right information is not always enough. Many well-prepared test takers struggle with exams. These tips will help equip you to accurately read, assess, and answer test questions.

A large part of the guide is devoted to showing you what content to expect on the exam and to helping you better understand that content. In this guide are practice test questions so that you can see how well you have grasped the content. Then, answer explanations are provided so that you can understand why you missed certain questions.

Don't try to cram the night before you take your exam. This is not a wise strategy for a few reasons. First, your retention of the information will be low. Your time would be better used by reviewing information you already know rather than trying to learn a lot of new information. Second, you will likely become stressed as you try to gain a large amount of knowledge in a short amount of time. Third, you will be depriving yourself of sleep. So be sure to go to bed at a reasonable time the night before. Being well-rested helps you focus and remain calm.

Be sure to eat a substantial breakfast the morning of the exam. If you are taking the exam in the afternoon, be sure to have a good lunch as well. Being hungry is distracting and can make it difficult to focus. You have hopefully spent lots of time preparing for the exam. Don't let an empty stomach get in the way of success!

When travelling to the testing center, leave earlier than needed. That way, you have a buffer in case you experience any delays. This will help you remain calm and will keep you from missing your appointment time at the testing center.

Be sure to pace yourself during the exam. Don't try to rush through the exam. There is no need to risk performing poorly on the exam just so you can leave the testing center early. Allow yourself to use all of the allotted time if needed.

Remain positive while taking the exam even if you feel like you are performing poorly. Thinking about the content you should have mastered will not help you perform better on the exam.

Once the exam is complete, take some time to relax. Even if you feel that you need to take the exam again, you will be well served by some down time before you begin studying again. It's often easier to convince yourself to study if you know that it will come with a reward!

Test-Taking Strategies

1. Predicting the Answer

When you feel confident in your preparation for a multiple-choice test, try predicting the answer before reading the answer choices. This is especially useful on questions that test objective factual knowledge. By predicting the answer before reading the available choices, you eliminate the possibility that you will be distracted or led astray by an incorrect answer choice. You will feel more confident in your selection if you read the question, predict the answer, and then find your prediction among the answer choices. After using this strategy, be sure to still read all of the answer choices carefully and completely. If you feel unprepared, you should not attempt to predict the answers. This would be a waste of time and an opportunity for your mind to wander in the wrong direction.

2. Reading the Whole Question

Too often, test takers scan a multiple-choice question, recognize a few familiar words, and immediately jump to the answer choices. Test authors are aware of this common impatience, and they will sometimes prey upon it. For instance, a test author might subtly turn the question into a negative, or he or she might redirect the focus of the question right at the end. The only way to avoid falling into these traps is to read the entirety of the question carefully before reading the answer choices.

3. Looking for Wrong Answers

Long and complicated multiple-choice questions can be intimidating. One way to simplify a difficult multiple-choice question is to eliminate all of the answer choices that are clearly wrong. In most sets of answers, there will be at least one selection that can be dismissed right away. If the test is administered on paper, the test taker could draw a line through it to indicate that it may be ignored; otherwise, the test taker will have to perform this operation mentally or on scratch paper. In either case, once the obviously incorrect answers have been eliminated, the remaining choices may be considered. Sometimes identifying the clearly wrong answers will give the test taker some information about the correct answer. For instance, if one of the remaining answer choices is a direct opposite of one of the eliminated answer choices, it may well be the correct answer. The opposite of obviously wrong is obviously right! Of course, this is not always the case. Some answers are obviously incorrect simply because they are irrelevant to the question being asked. Still, identifying and eliminating some incorrect answer choices is a good way to simplify a multiple-choice question.

4. Don't Overanalyze

Anxious test takers often overanalyze questions. When you are nervous, your brain will often run wild, causing you to make associations and discover clues that don't actually exist. If you feel that this may be a problem for you, do whatever you can to slow down during the test. Try taking a deep breath or counting to ten. As you read and consider the question, restrict yourself to the particular words used by the author. Avoid thought tangents about what the author *really* meant, or what he or she was *trying* to say. The only things that matter on a multiple-choice test are the words that are actually in the question. You must avoid reading too much into a multiple-choice question, or supposing that the writer meant something other than what he or she wrote.

5. No Need for Panic

It is wise to learn as many strategies as possible before taking a multiple-choice test, but it is likely that you will come across a few questions for which you simply don't know the answer. In this situation, avoid panicking. Because most multiple-choice tests include dozens of questions, the relative value of a single wrong answer is small. As much as possible, you should compartmentalize each question on a multiple-choice test. In other words, you should not allow your feelings about one question to affect your success on the others. When you find a question that you either don't understand or don't know how to answer, just take a deep breath and do your best. Read the entire question slowly and carefully. Try rephrasing the question a couple of different ways. Then, read all of the answer choices carefully. After eliminating obviously wrong answers, make a selection and move on to the next question.

6. Confusing Answer Choices

When working on a difficult multiple-choice question, there may be a tendency to focus on the answer choices that are the easiest to understand. Many people, whether consciously or not, gravitate to the answer choices that require the least concentration, knowledge, and memory. This is a mistake. When you come across an answer choice that is confusing, you should give it extra attention. A question might be confusing because you do not know the subject matter to which it refers. If this is the case, don't eliminate the answer before you have affirmatively settled on another. When you come across an answer choice of this type, set it aside as you look at the remaining choices. If you can confidently assert that one of the other choices is correct, you can leave the confusing answer aside. Otherwise, you will need to take a moment to try to better understand the confusing answer choice. Rephrasing is one way to tease out the sense of a confusing answer choice.

7. Your First Instinct

Many people struggle with multiple-choice tests because they overthink the questions. If you have studied sufficiently for the test, you should be prepared to trust your first instinct once you have carefully and completely read the question and all of the answer choices. There is a great deal of research suggesting that the mind can come to the correct conclusion very quickly once it has obtained all of the relevant information. At times, it may seem to you as if your intuition is working faster even than your reasoning mind. This may in fact be true. The knowledge you obtain while studying may be retrieved from your subconscious before you have a chance to work out the associations that support it. Verify your instinct by working out the reasons that it should be trusted.

8. Key Words

Many test takers struggle with multiple-choice questions because they have poor reading comprehension skills. Quickly reading and understanding a multiple-choice question requires a mixture of skill and experience. To help with this, try jotting down a few key words and phrases on a piece of scrap paper. Doing this concentrates the process of reading and forces the mind to weigh the relative importance of the question's parts. In selecting words and phrases to write down, the test taker thinks about the question more deeply and carefully. This is especially true for multiple-choice questions that are preceded by a long prompt.

9. Subtle Negatives

One of the oldest tricks in the multiple-choice test writer's book is to subtly reverse the meaning of a question with a word like *not* or *except*. If you are not paying attention to each word in the question, you can easily be led astray by this trick. For instance, a common question format is, "Which of the following is...?" Obviously, if the question instead is, "Which of the following is not...?," then the answer will be quite different. Even worse, the test makers are aware of the potential for this mistake and will include one answer choice that would be correct if the question were not negated or reversed. A test taker who misses the reversal will find what he or she believes to be a correct answer and will be so confident that he or she will fail to reread the question and discover the original error. The only way to avoid this is to practice a wide variety of multiple-choice questions and to pay close attention to each and every word.

10. Reading Every Answer Choice

It may seem obvious, but you should always read every one of the answer choices! Too many test takers fall into the habit of scanning the question and assuming that they understand the question because they recognize a few key words. From there, they pick the first answer choice that answers the question they believe they have read. Test takers who read all of the answer choices might discover that one of the latter answer choices is actually *more* correct. Moreover, reading all of the answer choices can remind you of facts related to the question that can help you arrive at the correct answer. Sometimes, a misstatement or incorrect detail in one of the latter answer choices will trigger your memory of the subject and will enable you to find the right answer. Failing to read all of the answer choices is like not reading all of the items on a restaurant menu: you might miss out on the perfect choice.

11. Spot the Hedges

One of the keys to success on multiple-choice tests is paying close attention to every word. This is never truer than with words like almost, most, some, and sometimes. These words are called "hedges" because they indicate that a statement is not totally true or not true in every place and time. An absolute statement will contain no hedges, but in many subjects, the answers are not always straightforward or absolute. There are always exceptions to the rules in these subjects. For this reason, you should favor those multiple-choice questions that contain hedging language. The presence of qualifying words indicates that the author is taking special care with his or her words, which is certainly important when composing the right answer. After all, there are many ways to be wrong, but there is only one way to be right! For this reason, it is wise to avoid answers that are absolute when taking a multiple-choice test. An absolute answer is one that says things are either all one way or all another. They often include words like *every*, *always*, *best*, and *never*. If you are taking a multiple-choice test in a subject that doesn't lend itself to absolute answers, be on your guard if you see any of these words.

12. Long Answers

In many subject areas, the answers are not simple. As already mentioned, the right answer often requires hedges. Another common feature of the answers to a complex or subjective question are qualifying clauses, which are groups of words that subtly modify the meaning of the sentence. If the question or answer choice describes a rule to which there are exceptions or the subject matter is complicated, ambiguous, or confusing, the correct answer will require many words in order to be expressed clearly and accurately. In essence, you should not be deterred by answer choices that seem excessively long. Oftentimes, the author of the text will not be able to write the correct answer without offering some qualifications and modifications. Your job is to read the answer choices thoroughly and completely and to select the one that most accurately and precisely answers the question.

13. Restating to Understand

Sometimes, a question on a multiple-choice test is difficult not because of what it asks but because of how it is written. If this is the case, restate the question or answer choice in different words. This process serves a couple of important purposes. First, it forces you to concentrate on the core of the question. In order to rephrase the question accurately, you have to understand it well. Rephrasing the question will concentrate your mind on the key words and ideas. Second, it will present the information to your mind in a fresh way. This process may trigger your memory and render some useful scrap of information picked up while studying.

14. True Statements

Sometimes an answer choice will be true in itself, but it does not answer the question. This is one of the main reasons why it is essential to read the question carefully and completely before proceeding to the answer choices. Too often, test takers skip ahead to the answer choices and look for true statements. Having found one of these, they are content to select it without reference to the question above. Obviously, this provides an easy way for test makers to play tricks. The savvy test taker will always read the entire question before turning to the answer choices. Then, having settled on a correct answer choice, he or she will refer to the original question and ensure that the selected answer is relevant. The mistake of choosing a correct-but-irrelevant answer choice is especially common on questions related to specific pieces of objective knowledge. A prepared test taker will have a wealth of factual knowledge at his or her disposal, and should not be careless in its application.

15. No Patterns

One of the more dangerous ideas that circulates about multiple-choice tests is that the correct answers tend to fall into patterns. These erroneous ideas range from a belief that B and C are the most common right answers, to the idea that an unprepared test-taker should answer "A-B-A-C-A-D-A-B-A." It cannot be emphasized enough that pattern-seeking of this type is exactly the WRONG way to approach a multiple-choice test. To begin with, it is highly unlikely that the test maker will plot the correct answers according to some predetermined pattern. The questions are scrambled and delivered in a random order. Furthermore, even if the test maker was following a pattern in the assignation of correct answers, there is no reason why the test taker would know which pattern he or she was using. Any attempt to discern a pattern in the answer choices is a waste of time and a distraction from the real work of taking the test. A test taker would be much better served by extra preparation before the test than by reliance on a pattern in the answers.

FREE DVD OFFER

Don't forget that doing well on your exam includes both understanding the test content and understanding how to use what you know to do well on the test. We offer a completely FREE Test Taking Tips DVD that covers world class test taking tips that you can use to be even more successful when you are taking your test.

All that we ask is that you email us your feedback about your study guide. To get your **FREE Test Taking Tips DVD**, email freedvd@studyguideteam.com with "FREE DVD" in the subject line and the following information in the body of the email:

- The title of your study guide.
- Your product rating on a scale of 1-5, with 5 being the highest rating.
- Your feedback about the study guide. What did you think of it?
- Your full name and shipping address to send your free DVD.

Introduction

Function of the Test

In order to become a certified teacher in the state of Florida, a candidate must pass the Florida Teacher Certification Examinations (FTCE). In 2001, the No Child Left Behind Act began the administration of the FTCE. These exams are part of a teacher's certification process in the state of Florida. The Bureau of Educator Certification (BEC) determines the specific exams that a candidate needs to take to teach and become certified in Florida. The required tests depend on certifications that a candidate holds in other states or countries, his or her change of career status, and whether the candidate graduated from a teaching institute in Florida. In order to determine which tests to take, a candidate must submit an application to the BEC, whom will then determine a candidate's testing requirements.

The Elementary Education K-6 Exam assesses content knowledge and pedagogy in four subtests: Language Arts and Reading, Social Science, Science, and Mathematics. All four subtests must be passed in order to successfully pass the Elementary Education exam. Test takers who are attempting the exam for the first time are required to take all four subtests. On subsequent attempts, any or all subtests can be attempted in one testing appointment.

Test Administration

After the BEC determines which tests a candidate needs to take, an applicant can then register for a test. Admission tickets are sent via email and must be presented at the test appointment along with proper identification. Test sites are available throughout the state of Florida as well as nationwide. Appointments can be made year-round.

A candidate must report to the test site 30 minutes before the appointment time on the admission ticket in order to complete pre-administration activities, such as an identity verification procedure, which includes a photo and palm scan. If a candidate wears glasses, a visual inspection is conducted, but the candidate's glasses will not be handled or touched. All personal items are kept in a secure storage area and a candidate receives an erasable notepad and pen. Then, a tutorial is given on how to take a computer-based test, as well as a test agreement and waiver. These processes need to be completed in 5 minutes. If the waiver is not accepted within 5 minutes, the candidate will be required to wait 31 calendar days before a retest, and he or she will not be given a refund. Breaks for the restroom are counted as part of the test time, unless scheduled breaks are provided; test takers attempting at least three subtests are allowed a 15-break. Candidates with disabilities need to complete an Alternative Testing Arrangements Request Form. The form must be submitted to FTCE customer service as soon as possible because test appointment cannot be made until approval.

Test Format

The FTCE Elementary Education is a computer-based exam. A reference sheet is provided for the math subtest. The breakdown of the number of questions and allotted time for each of the four subtests is provided in the table below:

Test	Number of Questions	Allotted Time
Subtest 1: Language Arts and Reading	60 multiple-choice questions	65 minutes
Subtest 2: Social Studies	55 multiple-choice questions	65 minutes
Subtest 3: Science	55 multiple-choice questions	70 minutes
Subtest 4: Mathematics	50 multiple-choice questions	70 minutes

It is important to note that the exam may include evaluation questions that the administrators use to assess for future inclusion. These questions are unscored.

Scoring

A minimum scaled score of 200 on each of the four subtests is required to achieve a passing score on the FTCE Elementary Education exam. Candidates wishing to take a retest must wait 31 calendar days after the most recent attempt before reattempting the exam. Scores are posted to a candidate's online account on Tuesdays after 10:00p.m. Eastern Standard Time on the score report date, which is within 4 weeks after the test date. As long as the test is not under current revision or getting redeveloped, the unofficial passing status will be displayed on the computer screen upon completion prior to leaving the testing site. Otherwise, a candidate will just receive a receipt of test completion until scores are released.

Language Arts and Reading

Reading Process

Emergent Literacy

English language literacy can be categorized into four basic stages:

- Beginning
- Early Intermediate
- Intermediate
- Early Advanced

Beginning Literacy
This stage is commonly referred to as **receptive language development**. Educators can encourage this stage in literacy development by providing the student with many opportunities to interact on a social level with peers. Educators should also consider starting a personal dictionary, introducing word flashcards, and providing the student with opportunities to listen to a story read by another peer, or as a computer-based activity.

Early Intermediate Literacy
When a child begins to communicate to express a need or attempt to ask or respond to a question, the child is said to be at the early intermediate literacy stage. Educators should continue to build vocabulary knowledge and introduce activities that require the student to complete the endings of sentences, fill in the blanks, and describe the beginning or ending of familiar stories.

Intermediate Literacy
When a child begins to demonstrate comprehension of more complex vocabulary and abstract ideas, the child is advancing into the intermediate literacy stage. It is at this stage that children are able to challenge themselves to meet the classroom learning expectations and start to use their newly acquired literacy skills to read, write, listen, and speak. Educators may consider providing students with more advanced reading opportunities, such as partner-shared reading, silent reading, and choral reading.

Early Advanced Literacy
When a child is able to apply literacy skills to learn new information across many subjects, the child is progressing toward the early advanced literacy stage. The child can now tackle complex literacy tasks and confidently handle much more cognitively demanding material. To strengthen reading comprehension, educators should consider the introduction to word webs and semantic organizers. Book reports and class presentations, as well as continued opportunities to access a variety of reading material, will help to strengthen the child's newly acquired literacy skills.

<u>Phonological Awareness</u>
Well before children are able to read and write, they begin to develop basic listening skills and gradually begin to imitate and produce the sounds they hear. Since language is used to communicate one's needs, react to situations, share experiences, and develop an understanding of the surrounding world, these beginning stages form the foundation of a child's literacy development. Before a child reaches the

preschool years, they begin to develop the ability to recognize and manipulate the sounds in their environment.

Generally speaking, **phonological awareness** is the ability to identify and manipulate specific units of oral language, including words, syllables, onsets, and rimes. The beginning stages of phonological awareness occur when a child is able to listen to and understand the words that people speak and read and when they are further able to recognize the various sounds within these words. Phonological awareness is also defined as the ability to sound out various words by connecting the sounds heard to familiar sounds and to manipulate those sounds in order to create new sounds and words. A child is demonstrating phonological awareness when they are able to do the following:

- Appropriately recognize and apply words that rhyme—*cat, bat, sat*
- Identify initial letters—the *c* in *cat*
- Identify middle letters—the *a* in *cat*
- Identify ending letters—the *t* in *cat*
- Separate simple words into their individual sounds or phonemes—c/a/t *cat*

There are many strategies educators can use to strengthen a child's phonological awareness. One effective strategy to strengthen a child's awareness of word units is clapping out the number of syllables in a word. Familiar and enjoyable songs, such as "Bingo," help children to identify individual phonemes within a word and strengthen their spelling skills, listening comprehension, and rhythm. Other strategies may include word games that challenge children to think of rhyming words or words that share the same initial, middle, or ending sounds. Creating fun and engaging ways for children to strengthen their phonological awareness will build the framework for future literary success.

Automatic Word Recognition of High-Frequency Sight Words

Beginning readers enter primary school years with many challenges involving literacy development. Tackling the alphabetic principle and phonemic awareness helps children to recognize that specific sounds are usually comprised of specific letters, or a combination thereof, and that each letter or combination of letters carries a specific sound. However, these young readers are also faced with the challenge of sight word mastery. **Sight words** do not necessarily follow the alphabetic principle and appear quite often in primary reading material. Some sight words are decodable, but many are not, which requires the additional challenge of memorizing correct spelling. Some of these non-decodable sight words include words such as *who, the, he, does*, and so on. There are approximately one hundred sight words that appear throughout primary texts.

The goal for primary teachers is to help emergent readers to recognize these sight words automatically, in order to help strengthen reading fluency. One effective instructional approach is to provide children daily opportunities to practice sight words in meaningful contexts and to establish a clearly visible, large print word wall that children can freely access throughout the day. Dr. Edward William Dolch was a well-known and respected children's author and professor who, in the late 1940s, published a list of sight words he believed appeared most frequently in children's literature for grades kindergarten through second grade. Now known as the Dolch Word List, these sight words are still widely used in primary classrooms throughout the United States. Organized by grade and frequency, the Dolch Word List consists of 220 words in total, with the first one hundred known as the "Dolch 100 List." Dr. Edward Fry, a university professor, author, and expert in the field of reading, published another commonly used high-frequency word list approximately a decade later. Although similar in many ways to the Dolch List, the Fry Word List primarily focuses on sight words that appear most frequently in reading material for third to ninth grade. Other high-frequency word lists now exist, but the Dolch and Fry word lists are still widely used in today's elementary classrooms. The debate, however, is whether to teach high-frequency sight words in isolation or as part of the integrated phonics program.

Unlike many sight words, **decodable words** follow the rules of phonics and are spelled phonetically. They are spelled precisely the way they sound—as in words like *dad* and *sit*. When a child has mastered his or her phonics skills, these decodable words can also be easily mastered with continued opportunities to practice reading. Activities involving segmenting and blending decodable words also help to strengthen a child's decoding skills. Some educators will find that it is beneficial to integrate lessons involving decodable words and high-frequency sight words, while others may see a need to keep these lessons separate until children have demonstrated mastery or near mastery of phonemic awareness. Some activities that encourage the memorization of sight words and strengthen decoding skills involve the use of flash cards, phonemic awareness games, air writing, and card games, such as *Bingo* and *Go Fish*.

Both Dolch and Fry word lists are organized according to frequency and grade level. It is widely accepted that educators follow a cumulative approach to reading instruction, introducing high-frequency sight words that are also phonetically decodable. Should words appear in the lesson that are not phonetically decodable, educators may wish to use this as an opportunity to evaluate the children's phonemic awareness skills and determine whether or not students are ready for lessons that integrate non-decodable sight words. For instance, an educator might challenge a student to study the parts of the non-decodable sight word by asking whether or not there are parts of the word that are phonetically decodable and parts that are not. This approach gives students the opportunity for guided word study and acts as a bridge between phonemic awareness skills and sight word memorization.

Determining what lists of words to introduce to students varies greatly and depends on an initial and ongoing spelling assessment of each child to determine his or her current spelling and reading levels. Effective instructional approaches also involve the intentional selection of words that demonstrate a specific spelling pattern, followed by multiple opportunities to read, spell, segment, and blend these word families. Students will benefit the greatest with ongoing formative and summative assessments of their decoding skills as well as their ability to apply their word knowledge to and memorize non-decodable sight words.

With the reinforcement of high-frequency word walls, daily opportunities to read, write, and engage in meaningful word games and activities, children will gradually begin to develop their reading and spelling skills and learn to become more fluent and capable readers.

When students are invited to become word detectives, the study of root words and affixes is of prime importance. There are several instructional approaches to the study of root words and affixes, including a multi-sensory guided approach in which children can physically pull apart the affixes to be left with the root word and then manipulate the root word by playing with a variety of suffixes and prefixes.

The following table begins with the original word containing both a prefix and suffix. The word is pulled apart into its individual components—root, prefix, and suffix. Then, it is given a new prefix and suffix to form a new word, carrying a completely new meaning:

Original Word	Root Word	Prefix	Suffix	New Prefix	New Suffix	New Word
inactive	act	in	ive	De	ate	deactivate
disbelieving	believe	dis	ing	Un	able	unbelievable
unbearable	bear	un	able	For	ing	forbearing

Effective instruction for root, prefix, and suffix study should involve the active exploration of words, with ample opportunity for children to read the words in meaningful context. Typically, a formal study of root words and affixes is introduced by the 4th grade, but it may be introduced earlier, depending on the students' understanding of basic phonics and spelling patterns. It is important for educators to keep in mind that new vocabulary terms, verb forms, plurals, and compound words may present a challenge for some students.

A formal study of root words, prefixes, and suffixes strengthens a child's knowledge of word meanings, expands vocabulary knowledge, and advances his or her understanding and application of various spelling patterns. Children will learn more about how affixes affect the spelling of the root word and can completely alter its meaning, which ultimately strengthens their ability to read, write, and spell accurately and effectively. As children become familiar with various affixes, they will begin to decipher the meaning of unfamiliar words that share the same affixes and roots.

Concepts of Print

Print awareness aids reading development, as it is the understanding that the printed word represents the ideas voiced in spoken language. Print awareness includes the understanding that:

1. Words are made of letters; spaces appear between words and words make sentences.

2. Print is organized in a particular way (e.g., read from left to right and top to bottom, read from front to back, etc.), so books must be tracked and held accordingly.

3. There are different types of print for different purposes (magazines, billboards, essays, fiction, etc.).

Print awareness provides the foundation on which all other literacy skills are built. It is often the first stage of reading development. Without print awareness, a student is not likely to develop letter-sound correspondence, word reading skills, or reading comprehension skills. For this reason, a child's performance on tasks relevant to their print awareness is indicative of the child's future reading achievement.

The following strategies can be used to increase print awareness in students:

1. *An adult reads aloud to students and shared reading experiences*. In order to maximize print awareness within the student, the reader should point out the form, function, orientation, and sounds of letters and words.

2. *Shared readings also build one-to-one correspondence*. **One-to-one correspondence** is the ability to match written letters or words to a spoken word when reading. This can be accomplished by pointing to words as they are read. This helps students make text-to-word connections. Pointing also aids **directionality**, or the ability to track the words that are being read.

3. *Use the child's environment*. To reinforce print awareness, teachers can make a child aware of print in their environment, such as words on traffic signs. Teachers can reinforce this by labeling objects in the classroom.

4. *Instruction of book organization can occur during read-alouds*. Students should be taught the proper orientation, tracking, and numbering conventions of books. For example, teachers can differentiate the title from the author's name on the front cover of a book.

5. *Let students practice*. Allowing students to practice book-handling skills with wordless, predictable, or patterned text will help to instill print awareness.

Recognizing Uppercase and Lowercase Letters

Among the skills that are used to determine reading readiness, letter identification is the strongest predictor. **Letter recognition** is the identification of each letter in the alphabet. Letter recognition does not include letter-sound correspondences; however, learning about and being able to recognize letters may increase student motivation to learn letter sounds. Also, the names of many letters are similar to their sounds, so letter recognition serves as a gateway for the letter-sound relationships that are needed for reading to occur. Similarly, the ability to differentiate between uppercase and lowercase letters is beneficial in determining where a sentence begins and ends.

To be fluent in letter identification, students should be able to identify letter names in and out of context with automaticity. In order to obtain such familiarity with the identification of letters, students need ample experience, acquaintance, and practice with letters. Explicit instruction in letter recognition, practice printing uppercase and lowercase letters of the alphabet, and consistent exposure to printed letters are essential in the instruction of letter recognition.

Research has revealed that the following sequencing guidelines are necessary to effectively promote letter naming and identification:

1. The initial stage includes visual discrimination of shapes and curved lines.

2. Once students are able to identify and discriminate shapes with ease, then letter formations can be introduced. During the introduction of letter shapes, two letters that share visual (*p* and *q*) or auditory (/a/ and /u/) similarities should never be presented in back-to-back.

3. Next, uppercase letters are introduced. Uppercase letters are introduced before lowercase letters because they are easier to discriminate visually than lowercase letters. When letter formations are first presented to a student, their visual system analyzes the vertical, horizontal,

and curved orientations of the letters. Therefore, teachers should use think-alouds when instructing how to write the shape of each letter. During think-alouds, teachers verbalize their own thought processes that occur when writing each part of a given letter. Students should be encouraged to do likewise when practicing printing the letters.

4. Once uppercase letters are mastered, lowercase letters can be introduced. High-frequency lowercase letters (*a, e, t*) are introduced prior to low-frequency lowercase letters (*q, x, z*).

5. Once the recognition of letters is mastered, students need ample time manipulating and utilizing the letters. This can be done through sorting, matching, comparing, and writing activities.

Invented Spellings and Understanding of Phonetic Principles

When children begin to learn the various letter-sound correspondences, their phonemic awareness begins to overlap with their awareness of orthography and reading. One of the widely accepted strategies to employ when introducing children to letter-sound correspondences is to begin with those correspondences that occur the most frequently in simple English words. In an effort to help build confidence in young learners, educators are encouraged to introduce only a few letter-sound combinations at a time and provide ample opportunities for practice and review before introducing new combinations. Although there is no formally established order for the introduction of letter-sound correspondences, educators are encouraged to consider the following general guidelines, but they should also keep in mind the needs, experiences, and current literacy levels of the students. The following is intended as a general guide only:

1. a	6. n	11. g	16. l	21. x
2. m	7. c	12. h	17. e	22. v
3. t	8. d	13. i	18. r	23. y
4. p	9. u	14. f	19. w	24. z
5. o	10. s	15. b	20. k	25. j
				26. q

As a generally accepted rule, short vowels should be introduced ahead of long vowels, and uppercase letters should be mastered before the introduction of their lowercase counterparts.

Spelling conventions in the English language are primarily concerned with three areas: mechanics, usage, and sentence formation.

Mechanics

For primary students who are just beginning to master the alphabetic principle, educators should first concentrate on proper letter formation, the spelling of high-frequency words and sight words, and offer classroom discussions to promote the sharing of ideas. When children begin to write in sentences to share their thoughts and feelings in print, educators may consider the introduction of an author's chair, in which students read their writing out loud to their classmates.

Although the phonetic spelling or invented spelling that primary students employ in these early stages may not be the conventional spelling of certain words, it allows primary students to practice the art and flow of writing. It works to build their confidence in the writing process. This is not the time for educators to correct spelling, punctuation, or capitalization errors, as young learners may quickly lose interest in writing and may lose self-confidence.

One strategy to employ early on to help students with proper spelling is to ensure there is an easily accessible and updated word wall that employs high-frequency words and sight words. Students should be encouraged to refer to the word wall while they write.

Usage

Usage concerns itself with word order, verb tense, and subject-verb agreement among other areas. As primary children often have a basic knowledge of how to use oral language effectively in order to communicate, this area of spelling conventions may require less initial attention than the mechanics of spelling. During read-aloud and shared reading activities, educators may wish to point out punctuation marks found in print, model how to read these punctuation marks, and periodically discuss their importance in the reading and writing process.

When children begin to engage in writing exercises, educators may wish to prompt self-editing skills by asking if each sentence begins with a capital and ends with a period, question mark, or exclamation point.

Sentence Formation

Verbs, nouns, adverbs, and adjectives all play significant roles in the writing process. However, for primary students, these concepts are fairly complex to understand. One instruction approach that may prove effective is to categorize a number of simple verbs, nouns, adverbs, and adjectives on index cards by color coordination. Educators can then ask one child to choose a noun card and another student to choose a verb card. The children can then face the class and read their words starting with the noun and then the verb. The students can even try reading the verb first followed by the noun. A class discussion can follow, analyzing whether or not the sentences made sense and what words might need to be added to give the sentence more meaning.

The Processes, Skills, and Stages of Word Recognition that Lead to Effective Decoding

It is believed that literacy development is the most rapid between birth and 5 years of age. From birth until around 3 months, babies start to recognize the sounds of familiar voices. Between 3 months and 6 months, babies begin to study a speaker's mouth and listen much more closely to speech sounds. Between 9 months and 12 months, babies can generally recognize a growing number of commonly repeated words, can utter simple words, respond appropriately to simple requests, and begin to attempt to group sounds.

In the toddler years, children begin to rapidly strengthen their communication skills, connecting sounds to meanings and combining sounds to create coherent sentences. The opportunities for rich social interactions play a key role in this early literacy development and help children to understand cultural nuances, expected behavior, and effective communication skills. By age 3, most toddlers can understand many sentences and can begin to generalize by placing specific words into categories. In the preschool years, children begin to develop and strengthen their emergent literacy skills. It is at this stage that children will begin to sound out words, learn basic spelling patterns, especially with rhyming words, and start to develop their fine motor skills. Awareness of basic grammar also begins to emerge with oral attempts at past, present, and future verb tenses.

There are many factors that influence a child's language acquisition. A child's physical age, level of maturity, home and school experiences, general attitudes toward learning, and home languages are just some of the many influences on a child's literacy development. However, a child's *language acquisition* progresses through the following generalized stages:

Stage	Examples	Age
Preproduction	does not verbalize/ nods yes and no	zero to six months
Early production	one to two-word responses	six to twelve months
Speech emergence	produces simple sentences	one to three years
Intermediate fluency	simple to more complex sentences	three to five years
Advanced fluency	near native level of speech	five to seven years

While this applies to language acquisition in one's home language, the very same stages apply to English language learners (ELLs). Since effective communication in any given language requires much more than a mere collection of vocabulary words that one can accurately translate, paying particular attention to each stage in language acquisition is imperative. In addition to vocabulary knowledge, language acquisition involves the study and gradual mastery of intonation, a language's dialects—if applicable—and the various nuances in a language regarding word use, expression, and cultural contexts. With time, effort, patience, and effective instructional approaches, both students and educators will begin to see progress in language acquisition.

Second language acquisition does not happen overnight. When educators take the time to study each stage and implement a variety of effective instructional approaches, progress and transition from one stage to the next will undoubtedly be less cumbersome and more consistent. In the early stages of language acquisition, children are often silently observing their new language environment. At these early stages, listening comprehension should be emphasized with the use of read alouds, music, and visual aids. Educators should be mindful of their vocabulary usage by consciously choosing to speak slowly and to use shorter, less complex vocabulary. Modeling during these beginning stages is also very effective. If the educator has instructed the class to open a book for instance, they can open a book as a visual guide. If it is time to line up, the educator can verbally state the instruction and then walk to the door to begin the line.

During the **pre-production stage**, educators and classmates may assist ELLs by restating words or sentences that were uttered incorrectly, instead of pointing out errors. When modeling the correct language usage instead of pointing out errors, ELL learners may be less intimidated to practice their new language.

As students progress into the **early production stage**, they will benefit from exercises that challenge them to produce simple words and sentences with the assistance of visual cues. The educator should ask students to point to various pictures or symbols and produce words or sentences to describe the images they see. At the early production and speech emergent stages, ELL students are now ready to answer more diverse questions as they begin to develop a more complex vocabulary. Working in heterogeneous pairs and small groups with native speakers will help ELL students develop a more advanced vocabulary.

At the **beginning and intermediate fluency stages**, ELLs may be asked questions that require more advanced cognitive skills. Asking for opinions on a certain subject or requiring students to brainstorm and find ways to explain a given phenomenon are other ways to strengthen language proficiency and increase vocabulary.

When a child reaches the **advanced fluency stage**, he or she will be confident in social and academic language environments. This is an opportune time to introduce and/or increase his or her awareness of idiomatic expressions and language nuances.

World-Class Instructional Design and Assessment (WIDA) is a consortium of various departments of education throughout the United States that design and implement proficiency standards and assessments for English language learners and Spanish language learners. Primarily focusing on listening, speaking, reading, and writing, WIDA has designed and implemented English language development standards and offers professional development for educators, as well as educational research on instructional best practices. The five English language proficiency standards according to WIDA are as follows:

English Language Proficiency Standards—WIDA
1. Within a school environment, ELL students require communication skills for both social and instructional purposes.
2. Effective communication involving information, ideas, and concepts are necessary for ELL students to be academically successful in the area of Language Arts.
3. Effective communication involving information, ideas, and concepts are necessary for ELL students to be academically successful in the area of Mathematics.
4. Effective communication involving information, ideas, and concepts are necessary for ELL students to be academically successful in the area of Science.
5. Effective communication involving information, ideas, and concepts are necessary for ELL students to be academically successful in the area of Social Studies.

According to WIDA, mastering the understanding, interpretation, and application of the four language domains—listening, speaking, reading, and writing—is essential for language proficiency. Listening requires ELL students to be able to process, understand, interpret, and evaluate spoken language. Speaking proficiently allows ELL students to communicate their thoughts, opinions, and desires orally in a variety of situations and for a variety of audiences. The ability to read fluently involves the processing, understanding, interpreting, and evaluating of written language with a high level of accuracy, and writing proficiency allows ELL students to engage actively in written communication across a multitude of disciplines and for a variety of purposes.

Since language acquisition involves the ELL students, their families, their classmates, educators, principals and administrators, as well as test and curriculum developers, WIDA strives to ensure that the

English Language Proficiency Standards reflect both the social and academic areas of language development.

Blending, Segmenting, Substituting, and Deleting Phonemes, Syllables, Onsets, and Rimes

The ability to break apart a word into its individual phonemes is referred to as **segmenting**. Segmenting words can greatly aid in a child's ability to recognize, read, and spell an entire word. In literacy instruction, **blending** is when the reader connects segmented parts to create an entire word. Segmenting and blending practice work together like pieces of a puzzle to help children practice newly-acquired vocabulary. Educators can approach segmenting and blending using a multi-sensory approach. For example, a child can manipulate letter blocks to build words and pull them apart. An educator may even ask the child to listen to the word being said and ask him or her to find the letter blocks that build each phoneme, one at a time:

/m/ /u/ /g/

/b/ /a/ /t/

/r/ /u/ /n/

Once children are able to blend and segment phonemes, they are ready for the more complex skill of blending and segmenting syllables, onsets, and rimes. Using the same multi-sensory approach, children may practice blending the syllables of familiar words on a word wall, using letter blocks, paper and pencil, or sounding them out loud. Once they blend the words together, students can then practice segmenting those same words, studying their individual syllables and the letters and sounds that create the words. Educators may again read a word out loud and ask children to write or build the first syllable, followed by the next, and so on. The very same practice can be used to identify the onset. Children can work on writing and/or building this sound followed by the word's rime. Word families and rhyming words are ideal for this type of exercise so that children can more readily see the parts of each word. Using words that rhyme can turn this exercise into a fun and engaging activity.

Once children have demonstrated the ability to independently blend and segment phonemes, syllables, onsets, and rimes, educators may present a more challenging exercise that involves **substitutions** and **deletions**. As these are more complex skills, children will likely benefit from repeated practice and modeling. Using word families and words that rhyme when teaching this skill will make the activity more enjoyable, and it will also greatly aid in a child's overall comprehension.

Substitution and Deletion Using Onset and Rime				
Word	**Onset Deletion**	**Rime Deletion**	**Onset Substitution**	**Rime Substitution**
run	un	r	fun	rat
bun	un	b	gun	bat
sun	un	s	nun	sat

Word families continued:

Substitution and Deletion Using Phonemes		
Word	**Phoneme Substitution**	**Phoneme Deletion**
sit	sat	si
bit	bat	bi
hit	hat	hi

Substitution and Deletion Using Syllables		
Word	**Syllable Substitution**	**Syllable Deletion**
cement	lament or, cedar	ce
moment	statement, or motive	mo
basement	movement, or baseball	base

Selecting and Applying Instructional Methods for the Development of Decoding Skills

Age-appropriate and developmentally appropriate instruction for phonological and phonemic awareness is key to helping children strengthen their reading and writing skills. Phonological and phonemic awareness, or PPA, instruction works to enhance correct speech, improve understanding and application of accurate letter-to-sound correspondence, and strengthen spelling skills. Since skill-building involving phonemes is not a natural process but needs to be taught, PPA instruction is especially important for children who have limited access and exposure to reading materials and who lack familial encouragement to read. Strategies that educators can implement include leading word and sound games, focusing on phoneme skill-building activities, and ensuring all activities focus on the fun, playful nature of words and sounds instead of rote memorization and drilling techniques.

Instruction of phonics skills and sight words for students with reading difficulties, disabilities, or special needs should be streamlined, systematic, and explicit. Focus should be committed toward essential skills and the highest-frequency sight words. Phonics skills and sight words that are lacking and words that are often misspelled need to be targeted through remediation and routine practice. Concepts and tasks should be supported through the employment of a variety of concrete examples. Visual, auditory, kinesthetic, and tactile techniques, such as the multisensory writing strategies previously discussed, will help to promote spelling and mastery of new sight words.

Instruction of phonics skills, sight word knowledge, and the spelling of single-syllable words can also be differentiated for ELLs and speakers of nonstandard English. For these students, teachers ought to capitalize on the transfer of relevant knowledge, skills, and similar words from a student's primary language into the English language. In this way, extra attention and instructional emphasis can be applied toward the teaching of sounds and meanings of words that are nontransferable between the two languages.

Advanced learners benefit from phonics skills, sight word knowledge, and spelling of single-syllable words of increased complexity. The breadth of current knowledge and skills ought to be extended for advanced learners, and instruction should occur at a faster pace.

Phonics instruction and word-recognition exercises involve a number of skills, including print awareness, alphabetic knowledge, phonological and phonemic awareness, the alphabetic principle, decoding, the memorization of high-frequency words, and reading practice. As language acquisition is highly complex, there seems to be some debate in the educational field regarding the best instructional approaches for ELL students and emerging readers. Some educators argue that phonics should be taught in isolation and not in context, while others stress the need for a more integrated approach. When faced with what instructional approach to implement, educators who take the time to learn about each child's home language, literacy development, and exposure to the English language will be in the best position to decide on whether a student would benefit from an isolated phonics approach or one that is more integrated. The following are the three different instructional approaches to phonics:

Synthetic Phonics

Educators implement an explicit approach, teaching individual letter-sound correspondence and helping students to blend letters into words.

Embedded Phonics

Educators teach letter-sound correspondence during the reading of a text.

Analogy-Based Phonics

Educators teach students to use parts of words that they already know to help decode words that they don't know. Analogy-Based phonics involves the use of story time, tutoring in small groups, and various language-based activities. Educators share various books and stories with decodable words with students and provide opportunities for children to spell words and write simple sentences with letter-sound correspondence.

The amount of time allotted for phonics and word recognition instruction varies greatly from classroom to classroom. Educators who pay particular attention to the ages of the ELL students and their current level of English language proficiency will be in the best position to decide on an appropriate approach to phonics instruction. However, generally speaking, younger ELL students in the primary grades will benefit from explicit practice with phonemic awareness and the alphabetic principle. Exposure to print awareness will increase in complexity as the child progresses in his or her understanding and application of phonemic awareness skills. Decoding practice, exposure to word families, spelling patterns, onsets and rimes, and structural analysis—including affixes and root words—should be gradually introduced as the child becomes more able to read simple words and simple sentences independently.

When working with ELL students, educators must be sensitive to each child's background knowledge, home language, and experiences involving literacy. In order to become proficient in the English language, ELL students must develop a clear understanding of the relationship that exists between letters and sounds in the English alphabetic system, and this may be in complete opposition to the rules they have already mastered in their home language. For example, some languages use the same or similar alphabet as English, but some of the phonemes might be pronounced differently, causing confusion. The English language may also have letter combinations that do not exist in the student's home language, adding to the confusion. Complicating matters even further, some languages do not utilize an alphabetic writing system, such as the Chinese language, which is **logographic,** relying on characters that represent a word or idea, rather than relying on letters to produce a sound. Therefore, a formal study of phonics is critical to ELL students' literacy development.

One approach for educators to consider is the highlighting of similarities and differences between the student's home language and that of English. For instance, many **cognates** exist between English and Spanish that can act as a bridge to strengthen a child's English language acquisition. Since cognates share the same or similar meaning, spelling, and pronunciation in two different languages, ELL students can quickly add these new words to their vocabulary inventory. Some effective approaches to integrate cognate awareness into lessons include read alouds, student reading activities, and word sorts.

As children read aloud, ELL students are encouraged to raise their hand when they think they've come across a cognate. The reading can momentarily stop while the class discusses the similarities and differences between the pronunciation, spelling, and meaning of each cognate. During a student reading activity, ELL students are encouraged to locate two, three, or more cognates they encounter in their reading and to write them down in their notebooks. These cognates can then be added to the classroom's word wall and further explored. In pairs, students can be given a number of cards with Spanish and English cognates. The students then sort the cards appropriately and discuss their meaning, spelling, and pronunciation. These approaches not only build vocabulary knowledge and confidence for ELL students by actively including their home language in lessons, but they also help to build social bonds in the classroom. Since language acquisition is also very social, when children develop and strengthen positive friendships within and outside the classroom, language acquisition will likewise develop and strengthen. Other effective classroom approaches to help ELL students with phonics and word-recognition skills include the use of word walls and posters throughout the classroom.

As children progress with their phonemic awareness skills, educators may introduce word studies by helping children classify and sort words according to the same or similar spelling patterns. Word study increases children's vocabulary and acts as a bridge from reading to writing as children transfer their newly-acquired words into print. Introducing children to a variety of reading and writing genres and formats will also help to strengthen their reading and writing skills. For example, learning to follow recipes provides children with opportunities to read and engage in hands-on activities to demonstrate their understanding by following a recipe's steps. Personal journals continue to be an effective practice that stimulates creative writing and helps children to express their thoughts and opinions in writing, without worrying too much about grammar, spelling, and punctuation. Personal journals can also be used as reading practice as children pick and choose sections to read aloud to the entire class, in pairs, or in small groups.

It is important for educators to recognize that some written languages are not read from left to right, and some are not even read from top to bottom. Therefore, it is also important for educators to teach print conventions and book awareness, including the direction in which the words in books are read and how to handle and hold a book. These lessons can be taught explicitly or may be simply modeled by the educator during shared reading time.

The Components of Reading Fluency

Word recognition occurs when students are able to correctly and automatically recognize and read a word. Phonics and sight word instruction help with the promotion of accurate and automatic word identification and word recognition. Once students are able to readily identify and recognize words, their attention is not devoted toward the dissection of word interpretation, and they can focus on the meaning of the text, supporting reading comprehension skills.

Phonics instruction stresses letter-sound correspondences and the manipulation of phonemes. Through phonics instruction, students learn the relationships between the letters and symbols of written language and the sounds of spoken language. It is through the application of phonics principles that students are able to decode words. When a word is **decoded,** the letters that make up the printed word are translated into sounds. When students are able to recognize and manipulate letter-sound relationships of single-syllable words, they are able to apply such relationships to decode more complex words. In this way, phonics aids reading fluency and reading comprehension.

Sight words, sometimes referred to as **high-frequency words**, are words that are used often but may not follow the regular principles of phonics. Sight words may also be defined as words that students are able to readily recognize and read without having to sound them out. Students are encouraged to memorize words by sight so their reading fluency is not deterred through the frequent decoding of regularly- occurring irregular words. In this way, sight word recognition aids reading fluency and reading comprehension.

Accuracy, Rate, and Prosody

In order to understand the objectives of RICA's Domain 3, the following three key indicators of reading fluency must be understood:

- *Accuracy* refers to the correct reading and pronunciation of words.
- *Reading rate* refers to the speed at which an individual reads within a given amount of time, often measured in words per minute.
- *Prosody* refers to the appropriate use of expression, intonation, emphasis, and tone when reading.

As word recognition increases, readers become less taxed with the interpretation of a text; thus, reading fluency and comprehension improve. When students read too quickly or too slowly for their skill level, they may lose reading comprehension. As accuracy and fluency increase, students begin to read aloud with appropriate prosody, and reading becomes a natural process.

Choosing and Applying Instructional Methods for Developing Reading Fluency

Vocabulary

Vocabulary consists of the bank of words that children can understand and apply fluently in order to communicate effectively. A strong vocabulary and word recognition base enables children to access prior knowledge and experiences in order to make connections in written texts. A strong vocabulary also allows children to express ideas, learn new concepts, and decode the meanings of unfamiliar words by using context clues. Conversely, if a child's vocabulary knowledge is limited and does not steadily increase, reading comprehension will be negatively affected. If children become frustrated with their lack of understanding of written texts, they will likely choose to only read texts at their comfort level or refuse to read altogether. With direct instruction, educators introduce specific words to pre-teach before reading, or examine word roots, prefixes, and suffixes. Through indirect instruction, educators ensure that students are regularly exposed to new words. This engages students in high-quality conversations and social interactions and provides access to a wide variety of challenging and enjoyable reading material.

Morphology

The study of **morphology** generally deals with the structure and formation of words. A **phoneme** is the smallest unit of sound that does not necessarily carry meaning. Essentially, phonemes are combined to form words, and words are combined to form sentences. Morphology looks at the smallest meaningful part of a word, known as a **morpheme**. In contrast to a phoneme, a morpheme must carry a sound and a meaning. Free morphemes are those that can stand alone, carrying both sound and meaning, as in the following words: *girl, boy, man*, and *lady*. Just as the name suggests, **bound morphemes** are bound to other morphemes in order to carry meaning. Examples of bound morphemes include: *ish, ness, ly*, and *dis*.

Semantics

Semantics is the branch of linguistics that addresses meanings. Morphemes, words, phrases, and sentences all carry distinct meanings. The way these individual parts are arranged can have a significant effect on meaning. In order to construct language, children must be able to use semantics to arrange and rearrange words to achieve the particular meaning they are striving for. Activities that teach semantics revolve around teaching the arrangement of word parts (morphology) and root words, and then the teaching of vocabulary. Moving from vocabulary words into studying sentences and sentence structure leads children to learn how to use context clues to determine meaning and to understand anomalies such as metaphors, idioms, and allusions.

There are five types of semantic relationships that are critical to understand:

- **Hyponyms** refer to a relationship between words where general words have multiple more-specific words (hyponyms) that fall into the same category (e.g., horse: mare, stallion, foal, Appaloosa, Clydesdale).
- **Meronyms** refer to a relationship between words where a whole word has multiple parts (meronyms) that comprise it (e.g., horse: tail, mane, hooves, ears).
- **Synonyms** refer to words that have the same meaning as another word (e.g., instructor/teacher/educator, canine/dog, feline/cat, herbivore/vegetarian).
- **Antonyms** refer to words that have the opposite meaning as another word (e.g., true/false, up/down, in/out, right/wrong).
- **Homonyms** refer to words that are spelled the same (homographs) or sound the same (**homophones**) but mean different things (e.g., there/their/they're, two/too/to, principal/principle, plain/plane, (kitchen) sink/ sink (down as in water)).

Syntax

With its origins from the Greek word, "syntaxis," which means arrangement, **syntax** is the study of phrase and sentence formation. The study of syntax focuses on the ways in which specific words can be combined to create coherent meaning. For example: the simple rearrangement of the words, "I can run," is different from the question, "Can I run?" which is also different from the meaningless "Run I can."

The following methods can be used to teach syntax:

- Proper Syntax Modeling: Students don't need to be corrected for improper syntax. Instead, they should be shown ways to rephrase what they said with proper syntax. If a student says, "Run I can," then the teacher should say, "Oh, you can run how fast?" This puts syntax in place with conversational skills.
- Open-Ended Sentences: Students can complete open-ended sentences with proper syntax both orally and in written format, or they can correct sentences that have improper syntax so that they make sense.
- Listening for Syntax: Syntax is auditory. Students can often hear a syntax error before they can see it in writing. Teachers should have students use word cards or word magnets to arrange and rearrange simple sentences and read them aloud to check for syntax.
- Repetition: Syntax can be practiced by using songs, poems, and rhymes for repetitive automation.

Pragmatics

Pragmatics is the study of what words mean in certain situations. It helps to understand the intentions and interpretations of intentions through words used in human interaction. Different listeners and different situations call for different language and intonations of language. When people engage in a conversation, it is usually to convey a certain message, and the message (even using the same words) can change depending on the setting and the audience. The more fluent the speaker, the more success she or he will have in conveying the intended message.

The following methods can be used to teach pragmatics:

- When students state something incorrectly, a response can be given to what they intended to say in the first place. For instance, if a student says, "That's how it didn't happen." Then the teacher might say, "Of course, that's not how it happened." Instead of putting students on defense by being corrected, this method puts them at ease and helps them learn.
- Role-playing conversations with different people in different situations can help teach pragmatics. For example, pretend playing can be used where a situation remains the same but the audience changes, or the audience stays the same but the situations change. This can be followed with a discussion about how language and intonations change too.
- Different ways to convey a message can be used, such as asking vs. persuading, or giving direct vs. indirect requests and polite vs. impolite messages.
- Various non-verbal signals can be used to see how they change pragmatics. For example, students can be encouraged to use mismatched words and facial expressions, such as angry words while smiling or happy words while pretending to cry.

Strategies to Help Read New and/or Difficult Words

Children who are developing reading fluency and comprehension skills can become frustrated when presented with unfamiliar words in a given text. With direct phonics instruction, educators can teach children to decode words and then use context clues to define the words while reading. If children have a strong enough understanding of language structures, including nouns and verbs, educators can ask them to consider what part of speech the unknown word might be based on and where it might fit into the sentence. Other useful strategies involve **self-monitoring**, in which children are asked to think as they read and ask themselves if what they have just read makes sense. Focusing on visual clues, such as drawings and photographs, may give children valuable insight into deciphering unknown words. Looking for the word in another section of the text to see how it relates to the overall meaning could give a clue to the new vocabulary word. Spelling the word out loud or looking for word chunks, prefixes, and suffixes, as well as demonstrating how to segment the unknown word into its individual syllables, may also be effective strategies to employ.

One of the most valuable strategies, however, for helping children to read and understand new words is **pre-teaching**. In this strategy, educators select what they evaluate to be the unfamiliar words in the text and then introduce them to the class before reading. Educators using this method should be careful not to simply ask the children to read the text and then spell the new words correctly. They should also provide clear definitions and give the children the opportunity to read these words in various sentences to decipher word meaning. This method can dramatically reduce how often children stop reading in order to reflect on unknown words. Educators are often unsure as to whether to correct every mispronounced word a child makes when reading. If the mispronounced word still makes sense, it is sometimes better to allow the child to continue to read, since the more the child stops, the more the child's reading comprehension and fluency are negatively affected.

Instructional Methods and Strategies for Increasing Vocabulary Acquisition Across the Content Areas

Vocabulary knowledge is an indicator and predictor of comprehension. If students find a match between a word within a text and a word that they've learned through listening and speaking, they are likelier to recognize and understand the meaning of the word in the written context. As the students will spend less time decoding and interpreting the word, they are likelier to read fluently and with comprehension. In contrast, if students cannot connect a written word to a word within their speaking or listening vocabulary, their fluency and comprehension may be interrupted. This proves to be true even if the student is able to correctly pronounce the word.

Word-Analysis Skills

Phonics and decoding skills aid the analysis of new words. **Word analysis** is the ability to recognize the relationships between the spelling, syllabication, and pronunciation of new and/or unfamiliar words. Having a clear understanding of word structure, orthography, and the meaning of morphemes also aid in the analysis of new words.

However, not all words follow predictable phonics patterns, morphology, or orthography. Such irregular words must be committed to memory and are called sight words.

Phonics skills, syllabic skills, structural analysis, word analysis, and memorization of sight words lead to word recognition automaticity. **Word recognition** is the ability to correctly and automatically recognize words in or out of context. Word recognition is a prerequisite for fluent reading and reading comprehension.

Reading competence of multisyllabic words is accomplished through phonics skills that are accompanied with a reader's ability to recognize morphological structures within words. **Structural analysis** is a word recognition skill that focuses on the meaning of word parts, or morphemes, during the introduction of a new word. Therefore, the instruction of structural analysis focuses on the recognition and application of morphemes. **Morphemes** are word parts such as base words, prefixes, inflections, and suffixes. Students can use structural analysis skills to find familiar word parts within an unfamiliar word in order to decode the word and determine the definition of the new word. Identification and association of such word segments also aids the proper pronunciation and spelling of new multisyllabic words.

Similarly, learning to apply phonics skills to longer and more complex words relies on a reader's ability to recognize syllable structures within multisyllabic words. **Syllabic analysis**, or **syllabication**, is a word analysis skill that helps students split words into syllables. **Syllables** are phonological units that contain a vowel sound. Students may be intimidated by long, multisyllabic words. Helping students break up multisyllabic words into morphological units (structural analysis) and phonological units according to syllable types makes longer words appear as a connected series of smaller words. The identified syllables can then be blended, pronounced, and/or written together as a single word. This helps students learn to decode and encode the longer words more accurately and efficiently with less anxiety. Thus, syllabic analysis leads to the rapid word recognition that is critical in reading fluency and comprehension.

The following table identifies the six basic syllable patterns that should be explicitly taught during syllabic instruction:

Basic Syllable Patterns		
Name of Syllable Type	Characteristics of Syllable Type	Examples
Closed	A syllable with a single vowel closed in by a consonant.	lab, bog, an
Open	A syllable that ends with a single vowel. Note that the letter *y* acts as a vowel.	go, me, sly
Vowel-Consonant-Silent *e*	A syllable with a single vowel followed by a consonant then *e*.	like, rake, note, obese
Vowel Teams	A syllable that has two consecutive vowels. Note that the letters *w* and *y* act as vowels.	meat, pertain, bay, toad, window
R-controlled	A syllable with one or two vowels followed by the letter *r*.	car, jar, fir, sir, collar, turmoil
Consonant *le (-al, -el)* Also called final stable	A syllable that has a consonant followed by the letters *le*, *al*, or *el*.	puddle, stable, uncle, bridal, pedal
Other final stable syllables	A syllable at the end of words can be taught as a recognizable unit such as *cious, age, ture, tion*, or *sion*.	pension, elation, puncture, stumpage, fictitious

Context Clues

Reference materials are the most obvious way students can independently learn the definition and pronunciation of new vocabulary terms.

When using **contextual strategies**, students are introduced to new words indirectly within a sentence or paragraph. Contextual strategies require students to infer the meaning of a word by utilizing semantic and contextual clues.

The use of appositives and parenthetical elements can be very effective contextual strategies. **Appositives** are words or a group of words that add meaning or define a term that directly precedes them. An example of a sentence that includes apposition is: "Strawberries, heart-shaped and red berries, are delicious when eaten right off of the vine." In this sentence, the definition of strawberries ("heart shaped and red berries") directly follows the term and is introduced with and closes with a comma. **Parenthetical elements** are specific types of appositives that add details to a term but not necessarily a definition. For example: "My cat, the sweetest in the whole world, didn't come home last night." In this sentence, the parenthetical element ("the sweetest in the whole world") further describes the cat but does not provide a definition of the word "cat."

Structural analysis skills are beneficial in the pronunciation of new words. When readers use **structural analysis**, they recognize affixes or roots as meaningful word parts within a word. When a new word doesn't contain parts that are recognized by a student, the reader can use phonic letter–sound patterns to divide the word into syllables. The word parts can then be combined to yield the proper pronunciation.

Word maps are visual organizers that promote structural analysis skills for vocabulary development. **Word maps** may require students to define or provide synonyms, antonyms, and pictures for given vocabulary terms. Alternatively, **morphological maps** may be used to relate words that share a common morpheme.

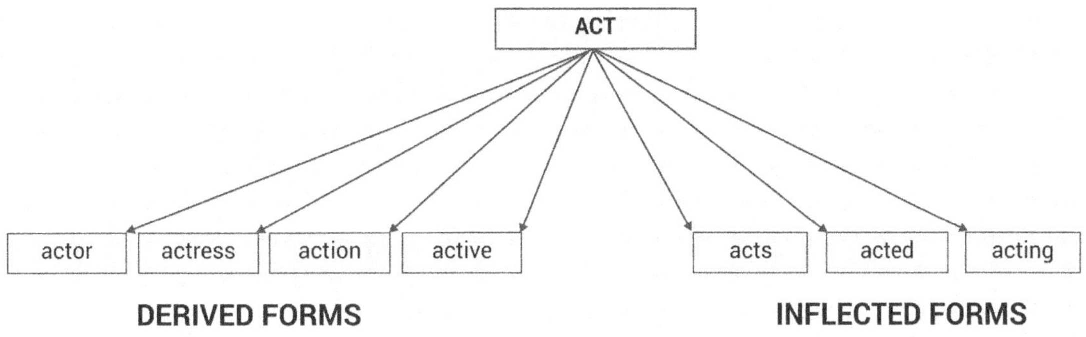

Similarly, **word webs** are used to compare and classify a list of words. Word webs show relationships between new words and a student's background knowledge. With the main concept placed centrally within the word web, secondary and tertiary terms stem off from this central concept.

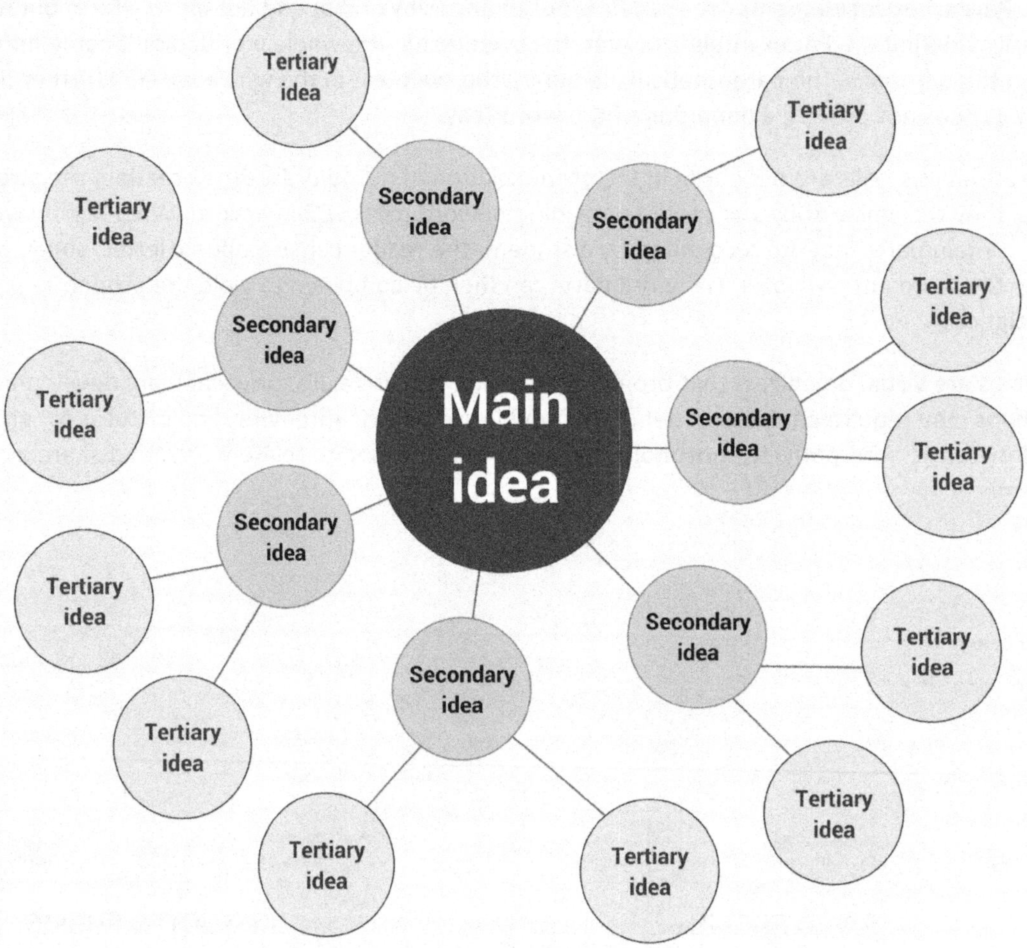

The table below identifies additional ways in which teachers can help students independently define unfamiliar words or words with multiple meanings:

Strategy	**Examples**
By Definition: Look up the word in a dictionary or thesaurus. Helps students realize that a single word can have multiple meanings.	Her favorite fruit to eat was a date. He went on a date with his girlfriend.
By Example: Invite students to offer their own examples, or to state their understanding following your own examples.	A myth is a story attempting to explain a natural phenomenon, such as the story of Prometheus to understand fire.
By Synonym: Understand that words have many different meanings. Some words are better synonyms than others.	She was very happy that day; her face was *radiant* with joy.
By Antonym: Teach student to look for words that have opposite meanings if the context of the sentence calls for its opposite.	Hannah was not happy that day; she was, in fact, very *depressed*.
By Apposition: **Apposition** is when the definition is given within the sentence.	The mango, a round, yellow, juicy fruit with an enormous seed in the middle, was ripe enough to eat.
By Origin: Identify Greek and Latin roots to figure out meanings of words.	In the word *hypertension*, the root "*hyper*" is a Greek word meaning "above" or "over."
By Context: Identifying what a word means by the surrounding text.	Water evaporates when it becomes hot, and the liquid turns into gas.

Instructional Methods and Strategies for Facilitating Students' Reading Comprehension

Organizational/Explanatory Features

Using and understanding references is imperative in developing reading comprehension skills. Pre-teaching a lesson on understanding references can be helpful, or a teacher may even incorporate this skill into teaching some broader comprehension skills. Prior to teaching from the basal reader, or prior to each story in the basal reader, a teacher should address the table of contents at the beginning of the textbook. This teaches students to use the table of contents frequently and allows them to find parts of a story that they will be reading on their own. When teaching from nonfiction texts, such as social studies or science, instruction should be provided on using the index to identify and locate specific information to answer comprehension questions. Both nonfiction and fiction texts can be used to teach how to use the glossary to locate boldfaced and important vocabulary. It is often most beneficial to identify and teach new vocabulary prior to reading a piece, so that students gain a deeper understanding of the text as they read it for the first time.

Typographic Features

Understanding changes in the appearance of text will help students easily identify important information. Pointing out boldfaced words during reading instruction tells students these may be important words in the understanding of the text, and that new vocabulary may be present. Boldfacing or italics may help students identify when a thought or topic is changing or being brought to attention. Color-coding may be used when comparing or contrasting different parts of the text. During reading comprehension instruction time, it is important to point out when these changes occur. It is also helpful to try to find text of this nature to use in small group or whole group instruction. Text with these types of typographic features assist students on their path to reading comprehension.

Graphic Features

Graphics always help interpret a story or text. Younger learners rely on pictures to help tell the story, while older students use diagrams, maps, and charts to aid in understanding texts. Even for adults, graphic features assist with visualizing the text being read. Charts and diagrams help organize information into more clear and concise patterns. Maps help understand specific places and locations. Illustrations help visualize a fictional story. Furthermore, illustrations with captions help visualize nonfiction and fiction texts, particularly when paired with captions that provide an explanation of why the illustration is important.

Independent Reading

Independent reading strategies promote healthy reading for pleasure and enjoyment. Hopefully, these strategies promote a lifelong love of reading. Students should be given daily, independent reading time in the classroom. Teachers phrase this time as **D.E.A.R.** or "Drop Everything and Read" time. Typically, this time can be incorporated into a teacher's reading block. It is suggested that students have about 20 minutes of D.E.A.R. time daily. Students can read a book from home, the library, or one selected from the variety of books found within the classroom.

Promoting Independent Reading

Teachers are required to have a classroom library. Some schools require a certain number of books or filled bookcases within a classroom. The library center should also contain more than just books. The classroom library should be an inviting environment for students. Small lamps make the area warmer—like home rather than school—and provide extra light for reading. Furniture—such as beanbag chairs, pillows, and small chairs—allow students to get comfortable, rather than reading at their desk. Not only is the environment important, but the reading center must also be an organized, designated space. If books are disorganized in the classroom library, students may be deterred from using the space appropriately, simply because they cannot find what they are looking for, or out of shear frustration. Organizing books by theme or genre helps students search for the books they desire. For students in younger grades, books should be grouped in plastic tubs using picture and word category labels like "animals" or "holidays." This organization method is especially helpful to those learning to read.

A listening center is also another helpful space in the classroom library. In the listening center, students listen to stories that are played through a sound device (like a CD or MP3 player) and follow along in the text. A teacher can switch the book out weekly to match a theme in the classroom, or can leave a "free choice bin" for students to choose what they would like to listen to. Again, listening to the story will encourage and emphasize reading strategies, such as voice and pacing.

Having a bookshelf with the teacher's or students' text selections may encourage readers to select a good book quickly. Some students enjoy re-reading a book from a teacher read aloud; therefore, placing it in the "teacher's pick" area may encourage developing readers to pick it up. Students also like to follow their classmates. Therefore, teachers should have a section where students can place a book that students can recommend to their friends. For older students, brief recommendation sheets can be filled out by the students. These sheets briefly list a few of a book's main themes so that potential readers can see if they are interested in reading the book. Reading from basal readers and school texts do not necessarily encourage reading for pleasure, as they are texts that are chosen by the school and instructor. For this reason, silent reading time is so important. Silent reading time gives students options and a chance to make their own choices. Students can choose the book and the appropriate reading pace when reading independently.

Promoting Family and Community Involvement in Literacy Activities

The following are strategies for promoting purposeful and independent reading of a wide variety of texts:

- Promote independent reading of narrative, literary, expository, and informational texts.
- Teach students how to select books that are at appropriate reading levels.
- Use students' personal interests to help motivate them to read independently.
- Provide structured reading opportunities in class.
- Encourage independent reading at home.
- Monitor students' independent reading.

In addition to teacher read-alouds, as discussed earlier, students should have approximately twenty minutes per day to read independently. This time should be structured and occur at predictable times each day or throughout the week. Students should be encouraged to read a variety of texts at this time (narrative, literary, expository, and informational texts). Students also should read independently.

In order to benefit from independent reading, students must read texts that are appropriate for their assessed reading level. Therefore, students should be aware of their reading levels and be able to select texts that coincide with this level. For students in primary school, the **five-finger test** can be used in the text-selection process. The five-finger test asserts that if a student has trouble with five or more words on a randomly selected page, then the book is above that student's reading level. For older readers, the teacher can group texts into levels and/or categories, from which students can select based on their personal interests.

In order for independent reading time to be effective, students should be accountable for what is read. A great assessment tool is to have each student give an oral report of one book that they have read during the marking period. Students should be given nightly reading homework as well. Teachers may require students to log the number of minutes read each night. Such reading logs should require parents to sign next to the number of minutes a night a child has read.

Essential Comprehension Skills

Topic, Main Idea, and Supporting Details Purpose

Topics and main ideas are critical parts of any writing. The **topic** is the subject matter of the piece, and it is a broader, more general term. The **main idea** is what the writer wants to say about that topic. The topic can be expressed in a word or two, but the main idea should be a complete thought.

The topic and main idea are usually easy to recognize in nonfiction writing. An author will likely identify the topic immediately in the first sentence of a passage or essay. The main idea is also typically presented in the introductory paragraph of an essay. In a single passage, the main idea may be identified in the first or the last sentence, but will likely be directly stated and easily recognized by the reader. Because it is not always stated immediately in a passage, it's important to carefully read the entire passage to identify the main idea.

Readers should also remember that when most authors write, they want to make a point or send a message. This point or message of a text is known as the **theme**. Authors may state themes explicitly, like in *Aesop's Fables*. More often, especially in modern literature, readers must infer the theme based on text details. Usually after carefully reading and analyzing an entire text, the theme emerges. Typically, the longer the piece, the more themes the reader will encounter, though often one theme dominates the rest, as evidenced by the author's purposeful revisiting of it throughout the passage.

The main idea should not be confused with the thesis statement. A **thesis statement** is a clear statement of the writer's specific stance, and can often be found in the introduction of a nonfiction piece. The main idea is more of an overview of the entire piece, while the thesis is a specific sentence found in that piece.

In order to illustrate the main idea, a writer will use **supporting details** in a passage. These details can provide evidence or examples to help make a point. Supporting details are most commonly found in nonfiction pieces that seek to inform or persuade the reader.

A reader should carefully examine the author's supporting details to be sure they are credible. The reader needs to consider whether the supporting details provide evidence of the author's point and whether they directly support the main idea. Readers might find that an author has used a shocking statistic to grab their attention, but that the statistic doesn't really support the main idea, so it isn't being effectively used in the piece.

Point of View

The **point of view** is the position the narrator takes when telling the story in prose. If a narrator is incorporated in a drama, the point of view may vary; in poetry, point of view refers to the position the speaker in a poem takes.

First Person

The first person point of view is when the writer uses the word "I" in the text. Poetry often uses first person, e.g., William Wordsworth's "I Wandered Lonely as a Cloud." Two examples of prose written in first person are Suzanne Collins' *The Hunger Games* and Anthony Burgess's *A Clockwork Orange*.

Second Person

The second person point of view is when the writer uses the pronoun "you." It is not widely used in prose fiction, but as a technique, it has been used by writers such as William Faulkner in *Absalom, Absalom!* and Albert Camus in *The Fall*. It is more common in poetry—e.g., Pablo Neruda's "If You Forget Me."

Third Person

Third person point of view is when the writer utilizes pronouns such as him, her, or them. It may be the most utilized point of view in prose as it provides flexibility to an author and is the one with which readers are most familiar. There are two main types of third person used in fiction. **Third person omniscient** uses a narrator that is all-knowing, relating the story by conveying and interpreting thoughts/feelings of all characters. ***In third person limited,*** the narrator relates the story through the perspective of one character's thoughts/feelings, usually the main character.

Purpose

Expository texts typically share information about a given topic. *Persuasive texts* aim to convince readers to think or act a certain way, and *procedural texts* generally give step-by-step or "how-to" instructions in a given discipline. *Nonfiction narratives* tell a true story, perhaps to inspire, educate, bring awareness to a subject, or simply chronicle an important historical event. In order for students to become independent readers and draw their own conclusions about what they read, it is critical that they learn to discern the **author's purpose**.

One obvious approach to teaching children how to reveal an author's purpose is to simply ask children why they think the author wrote this information. These types of open-ended class discussions allow children to express their ideas, explore theories, and consider what others have to say on the subject. Educators can record various answers and then ask the children to return to the text as detectives, looking for clues that support each theory.

Another approach to uncovering the author's purpose is for students to take a closer look at the written structure of the text and the vocabulary usage. For example, is the text's structure written in chronological order, simply listing events as they occurred? Does the text open up with a problem that is then resolved? Is the author using cause/effect or compare/contrast vocabulary? Learning about the structure of the text gives great insight into the author's purpose.

When children develop reading fluency, they are able to read a text with minimal to no errors, with consistent speed, and with appropriate expression, and they learn to connect with what they are reading on a personal level. As children read through an informational text, educators may ask how the students are feeling. Did they begin feeling one way and end up feeling another by the end of the text? When children examine their own personal feelings with regard to what they have read, they will be in a better position to explore the author's purpose.

Once children have had several opportunities to explore the author's purpose using a variety of informational texts, prompting them to write their own informational texts will help them to develop and strengthen a better understanding about writing with a purpose. Perhaps they can write a procedural text that lists the steps in how to ride a bike, or they can write a persuasive paper to try to convince their teacher that extra free time during the school day stimulates learning.

Learning to identify an author's purpose connects children with their reading on a deeper level. Instead of believing everything they read, they will begin to understand that there are many reasons why authors write, and they will further understand that they possess the ability to draw their own conclusions and make their own decisions on any given topic.

Inferences

Although related to predictions and the finding of factual information, **inferences** refer to the ability to make logical assumptions based on contextual clues. People of all ages make inferences about the world around them on a daily basis but may not be aware of what they are doing. Even young children may infer that it is likely cold outside if they wake up and their bedroom is chilly or the floor is cold. While being driven somewhere on the highway and a child notices a person at the side of the road with a parked car, that child will likely infer that the individual is having car problems and is awaiting some assistance. Therefore, the challenge for educators is not necessarily teaching children how to infer, but rather demonstrating how this skill they already use can be transferred into the study of various texts.

One effective introductory strategy may be to set up scenarios within the classroom and challenge the children to infer what is happening. For instance, the educator may arrive at school pretending to have a cold without saying anything. By placing a personal box of tissues on the desk along with a nasal spray and frequently sneezing, the teacher is challenging the students to infer that he or she not feeling well.

Once the children begin to understand that making inferences is indeed similar to detective work by collecting key evidence, the educator can now introduce more inanimate objects like photographs, pictures, or diagrams void of explanatory language. The children's task would be to study the visual aids to try to infer what the subject is about. Educators can assist the children initially by asking questions aloud, modeling how to arrive at a logical inference. For example, the teacher might hold up a picture of a school in which all children are gathered in the playground and grouped according to their classes. Upon closer examination, the children might spot a fire truck parked at the side of the road and may infer that the school had a fire drill or an actual fire.

As the children progress in their ability to infer based on picture clues, it is time to transfer their new skill to texts. Educators may wish to begin with inference challenges in which students are prompted to write short stories about specific events—without directly mentioning the event. For instance, if a child is interested in swimming, they may write about the ideal temperature of the water, backstroke, freestyle, full laps, and so on without ever mentioning the word *swimming*. Other children in the class will then be prompted to read the short story and infer what the text is about. The children must examine the clues in the text, make an inference, and support the inference with evidence from the text:

> In the second paragraph, it says that the water was relatively warm, so it was easy to finish a full lap. This must mean that the person was swimming in the water.

The more initial practice children receive before moving into more complicated texts, the most success they will have in making accurate inferences and, in turn, the more fun they will have acting as text detectives.

Using Multiple Representations of Information for a Variety of Purposes

Authors of informational texts will often employ the use of visual or graphic aids in strategic locations throughout the text in order to strengthen the reader's understanding of the topic at hand. Visual aids can provide an overview of key information, illustrate relationships among important text elements, and summarize the main idea. Visual aids are generally colorful and catch students' attention; they help to simplify what could be potentially complicated information. There are a multitude of visual aids that are frequently used in informational texts, including models, graphs, charts, tables, maps, drawings, photographs, and time lines. Some visual aids also involve a side bar, which defines key vocabulary necessary to understand the topic.

In most instances, children merely need to look at the visual aid to make an instant connection. The implementation of graphic aids in writing reduces instructional time and strengthens comprehension. During read alouds and guided reading sessions, educators may wish to model how to extract meaning from visual aids by connecting the graphic to specific elements in the text. Before reading begins, educators have students skim through the pages to find the visual aids and predict what the text may be about based on the text's graphics. Therefore, visual aids may often help students to identify the text's main idea.

The time it requires to read and process the written text is considerably longer than the time it takes to derive meaning from the graph. Helping students to identify and derive meaning from visual aids will help to strengthen their reading comprehension skills and overall literacy development.

Strategies for Developing Critical-Thinking Skills

Metacognitive strategies ask the student to decode text passages. In part, they require the student to preview text, be able to recognize unfamiliar words, then use context clues to define them for greater understanding. In addition, meta-cognitive strategies in the classroom employ skills such as being able to decode imagery, being able to predict, and being able to summarize. If a student can define unfamiliar vocabulary, make sense of an author's use of imagery, preview text prior to reading, predict outcomes during reading, and summarize the material, he or she is achieving effective reading comprehension. When approaching reading instruction, the teacher who encourages students to use phrases such as *I'm noticing*, *I'm thinking*, and *I'm wondering* is teaching a meta-cognitive type strategy.

Pre-Reading Strategies

Pre-reading strategies are important, yet often overlooked. Non-critical readers will often begin reading without taking the time to review factors that will help them understand the text. Skipping pre-reading strategies may result in a reader having to re-address a text passage more times than is necessary. Some pre-reading strategies include the following:

- Previewing the text for clues
- Skimming the text for content
- Scanning for unfamiliar words in context
- Formulating questions on sight
- Making predictions
- Recognizing needed prior knowledge

Before reading a text passage, a reader can enhance his or her ability to comprehend material by **previewing the text for clues.** This may mean making careful note of any titles, headings, graphics, notes, introductions, important summaries, and conclusions. It can involve a reader making physical notes regarding these elements or highlighting anything he or she thinks is important before reading. Often, a reader will be able to gain information just from these elements alone. Of course, close reading is required in order to fill in the details. A reader needs to be able to ask what he or she is reading about and what a passage is trying to say. The answers to these general questions can often be answered in previewing the text itself.

It's helpful to use pre-reading clues to determine the main idea and organization. First, any titles, sub-headings, chapter headings should be read, and the test taker should make note of the author's credentials if any are listed. It's important to deduce what these clues may indicate as it pertains to the focus of the text and how it's organized.

During pre-reading, readers should also take special note of how text features contribute to the central idea or thesis of the passage. Is there an index? Is there a glossary? What headings, footnotes, or other visuals are included and how do they relate to the details within the passage? Again, this is where any pre-reading notes come in handy, since a test taker should be able to relate supporting details to these textual features.

Next, a reader should **skim** the text for general ideas and content. This technique does not involve close reading; rather, it involves looking for important words within the passage itself. These words may have something to do with the author's theme. They may have to do with structure—for example, words such as *first, next, therefore*, and *last*. Skimming helps a reader understand the overall structure of a passage and, in turn, this helps him or her understand the author's theme or message.

From there, a reader should quickly *scan* the text for any unfamiliar words. When reading a print text, highlighting these words or making other marginal notation is helpful when going back to read text critically. A reader should look at the words surrounding any unfamiliar ones to see what contextual clues unfamiliar words carry. Being able to define unfamiliar terms through contextual meaning is a critical skill in reading comprehension.

A reader should also **formulate any questions** he or she might have before conducting close reading. Questions such as "What is the author trying to tell me?" or "Is the author trying to persuade my thinking?" are important to a reader's ability to engage critically with the text. Questions will focus a reader's attention on what is important in terms of idea and what is supporting detail.

Along with formulating questions, it is helpful to make predictions of what the answers to these questions and others will be. **Making predictions** involves using information from the text and personal experiences to make a thoughtful guess as to what will happen in the story and what outcomes can be expected.

Last, a reader should recognize that authors assume readers bring a **prior knowledge** set to the reading experience. Not all readers have the same experience, but authors seek to communicate with their readers. In turn, readers should strive to interact with the author of a particular passage by asking themselves what the passage demands they know during reading. This is also known as making a text-to-self connection. If a passage is informational in nature, a reader should ask "What do I know about this topic from other experiences I've had or other works I've read?" If a reader can relate to the content, he or she will better understand it.

All of the above pre-reading strategies will help the reader prepare for a closer reading experience. They will engage a reader in active interaction with the text by helping to focus the reader's full attention on the details that he or she will encounter during the next round or two of critical, closer reading.

Strategies During Reading

After pre-reading, a test taker can employ a variety of other reading strategies while conducting one or more closer readings. These strategies include the following:

- Clarifying during a close read
- Questioning during a close read
- Organizing the main ideas and supporting details
- Summarizing the text effectively

A reader needs to be able to **clarify** what he or she is reading. This strategy demands a reader think about how and what he or she is reading. This thinking should occur during and after the act of reading. For example, a reader may encounter one or more unfamiliar ideas during reading, then be asked to apply thoughts about those unfamiliar concepts after reading when answering test questions.

Questioning during a critical read is closely related to clarifying. A reader must be able to ask questions in general about what he or she is reading and questions regarding the author's supporting ideas. Questioning also involves a reader's ability to self-question. When closely reading a passage, it's not enough to simply try and understand the author. A reader must consider critical thinking questions to ensure he or she is comprehending intent. It's advisable, when conducting a close read, to write out margin notes and questions during the experience. These questions can be addressed later in the thinking process after reading and during the phase where a reader addresses the test questions. A reader who is successful in reading comprehension will iteratively question what he or she reads, search text for clarification, then answer any questions that arise.

A reader should **organize** main ideas and supporting details cognitively as he or she reads, as it will help the reader understand the larger structure at work. The use of quick annotations or marks to indicate what the main idea is and how the details function to support it can be helpful. Understanding the structure of a text passage is sometimes critical to answering questions about an author's approach, theme, messages, and supporting detail. This strategy is most effective when reading informational or nonfiction text. Texts that try to convince readers of a particular idea, that present a theory, or that try to explain difficult concepts are easier to understand when a reader can identify the overarching structure at work.

Post-Reading Strategies

After completing a text, a reader should be able to **summarize** the author's theme and supporting details in order to fully understand the passage. Being able to effectively restate the author's message, sub-themes, and pertinent, supporting ideas will help a reader gain an advantage when addressing standardized test questions.

A reader should also evaluate the strength of the predictions that were made in the pre-reading stage. Using textual evidence, predictions should be compared to the actual events in the story to see if the two were similar or not. Employing all of these strategies will lead to fuller, more insightful reading comprehension.

Inference refers to the reader's ability to understand the unwritten text, i.e., "read between the lines" in terms of an author's intent or message. The strategy asks that a reader not take everything he or she reads at face value but instead, add his or her own interpretation of what the author seems to be trying to convey. A reader's ability to make inferences relies on his or her ability to think clearly and logically about the text. It does not ask that the reader make wild speculations or guess about the material but demands that he or she be able to come to a sound conclusion about the material.

An author's use of less literal words and phrases requires readers to make more inference when they read. Since inference involves **deduction**—deriving conclusions from ideas assumed to be true—there's more room for interpretation. Still, critical readers who employ inference, if careful in their thinking, can arrive at the logical, sound conclusions the author intends.

Questioning has immeasurable value in the reading process. Answering questions about a text gives purpose for reading to students and focuses them on reading to learn information. Similarly, generating questions about a text for others to answer enables a student to analyze what is important to learn in the text and glean summarizing skills. Keeping s's Taxonomy in mind, teachers can scaffold students toward increased critical thinking capabilities. Bloom's Taxonomy shows the hierarchy of learning progressing through the following stages:

- Remembering
- Understanding
- Applying
- Analyzing
- Evaluating
- Creating

Teaching a Variety of Informational and Literary Texts

It is important for students to be exposed to a variety of texts, reading materials, and resources. To become well-rounded readers, teachers should provide students with expository texts in addition to the classroom textbooks. Key characteristics of informational and expository texts include informative facts about a specific topic. Since these are nonfiction texts, diagrams or other graphic aids may be used to assist in understanding the text. Other forms of informational text include news articles, research journals, educational magazines with informational text, and websites. These texts can be used in small groups or can be introduced in whole group instruction, and then further explored in small intervention groups.

Fact-based understanding and the use of textual evidence is imperative in expository and informational texts. Students should be able to compare and contrast two different texts and identify problems and solutions as well as cause and effect. Graphic organizers arranged chronologically can help students take notes when covering nonfiction texts. Students need to have the correct order of events in a nonfiction piece in order to identify the cause of an event, as well as the effect it had on problems and solutions. At times, students may need to compare and contrast two texts to identify the similarity of facts, the differences in reported facts, or note any bias from the author. Using knowledge of writing standards and instruction can aid students' understanding of informational text. When comprehending an informative text's objective, students should utilize their prior knowledge of the topic, prior writing assignments, and concluding sentences in the text. This is another example of how reading comprehension and writing go hand-in-hand in the learning process, and how writing and language become important to student comprehension.

Although independent reading is important for students to cultivate a love of reading, reading in the content areas is another way to stimulate reading skills while also learning about other subjects at the same time. **Content areas** are main subject areas like Math, English, Social Studies, and Science. Reading in the content areas is the idea that reading is an integral part of each and every subject and not simply a practice all by itself. The **three-phase model of reading** is a set of steps that depicts the stages before, during, and after reading. This model is used to identify reading strategies for content-area reading:

- **Pre-Reading**: In the pre-reading stage, students construct background information, make predictions, connect to personal life, and activate prior knowledge and experience. During this stage, activities that can take place include setting a purpose, developing vocabulary, studying of high-frequency words, and the use of graphic organizers.

- **During Reading**: In this stage, students return to the purpose of the text, find the main idea, identify details, find the organizing structure of the text, and draw conclusions. This stage allows students to speculate about the text, express their opinions, connect to other text, question and critically analyze the text, question the author, and interpret character behavior.

- **Post-Reading**: In the post-reading stage, students will summarize the text, learn to retell the information, connect to personal life, and discuss or interpret the motivation of the author. This stage includes making judgments, dealing with graphic organizers, illustrating or acting out a storyline, and connecting to the ideas used in other texts.

This model of reading is an important tool to use when teaching in the content areas because it goes beyond reading for pleasure and encourages students to think critically about whatever subject they may be reading about. In a Social Studies text, this model of reading will help students to draw upon their prior knowledge of Social Studies by discussing the event beforehand, actively read to find the purpose and details embedded within the text, and finally summarize the text and analyze the events that have just been learned through the reading phase.

Effective and Responsible Practices in Communication with Children

The foundation of a child's academic, social, and emotional success in any classroom lies directly in the educator's ability to use effective communicative interactions. DAP, or Developmentally Appropriate Practice, was designed by researchers who took into consideration what is known about how children develop, as well as what is known about effective early education instruction. Classrooms with effective communication techniques will generally see enthusiastic, engaged children. DAP focuses on these 10 basic principles that aim to help educators build an effective foundation of communication:

- Acknowledgement
- Encouragement
- Immediate and beneficial feedback
- Modeling
- Demonstrating
- Challenging
- Questioning
- Providing effective assistance
- Providing valuable information
- Giving appropriate directions

Acknowledgement

Students are not simply little subjects for educators to enlighten. They are intellectual, social, and emotional beings worthy of recognition and appreciation. Acknowledgement of students begins with understanding where they are coming from and the experiences they bring with them. When a teacher considers prior knowledge before beginning instruction, they are being considerate of the student's time and intellect. They are acknowledging that the student already has the capacity for learning and brings valid experiences and aptitudes that are useful for assimilating new information. The teacher doesn't waste time re-teaching what students have already mastered. Review is necessary, of course, but not to the extent that there is a risk of losing student engagement and interest.

Students come to learn at various stages of intellectual development. In the early stages, there is a duplicity of black-and-white thinking. Multiplicity should come next, where there is some understanding of opinion and perspective. Finally, learning to value evidence and validity helps students understand topics at various levels of complexity. When teachers take this into account, they are acknowledging the students' individuality and honoring their learning needs.

Significant differences exist in the way teaching and learning is conceptualized for various cultures. Values for particular types of learning, the beliefs about best practices, and the role of the teacher/student relationship may be strikingly different from culture to culture. The value of learning itself is a bridge for multicultural connection. When teachers recognize and celebrate cultural differences, they are acknowledging the students at the level of their individual identity.

The social trends and expectations of students and teachers grow and change over generations. The topics and ways that students are learning and teachers are teaching are likely quite different from what they were even a decade ago. Educators cannot expect students to learn the same way from generation to generation. Awareness of generational differences acknowledges the student and his or her perception of the world.

Encouragement

Ideally, students come into classrooms hopeful and willing to take risks. With this in mind, teachers have to develop the kind of classroom that fosters participation and motivation. Here are some ways that teachers can encourage classroom participation:

- Students should be praised. This helps them know they are at the center of learning. They need to feel cared for and valued. Positive behavior should be rewarded and progress acknowledged.
- Students should be allowed to have some control in their lives. Choices should be offered and mistakes forgiven.
- Excellence should be expected from students. High but realistic expectations should be held for them. The effort they put forth should be respected. The learning process, over the end product, should be valued.
- Children should be allowed to be children. There should be much activity and collaboration.
- The fun of learning should be shown to students. They should be encouraged by taking part in the planning of field trips, guest speakers, and other extraordinary activities.
- Students should be made aware of how learning relates to their lives. Teachers should teach to the interests of the students and understand where they are coming from.
- Clear and simple lessons should be presented at a pace they can all follow. Teachers should communicate clearly and enunciate understandably so students do not have to struggle to follow along. Teachers should regularly check on the students' level of understanding.
- A pleasant and comfortable environment free from obvious distractions should be created.

Immediate and Beneficial Feedback

Students need to know what they are doing well and what needs improvement. There should be no mystery about the learning targets. They need a positive self-image fostered by repeated success. Feedback should be positive and specific. Giving clear and effective feedback communicates to the student that her or his work is worthwhile, and that someone cares enough to review and consider it.

Informal feedback is part of formative assessment and should let students know where they are in the learning process and what they should do next. They should be able to formulate a plan for improvement and a vision of the next success they can achieve. Informal feedback is often oral and interactive.

Formal feedback is driven by objectives and rubrics that students should be given prior to a learning task. This gives them a clear goal for the activity and outlines expectations. Formal feedback should be presented in writing or another tangible format. Formal feedback is often summative in nature and may or may not be tied to grades and final assessments.

Feedback strategies are variable. Individualized adjustments can be made regarding timing, amount, mode, and audience. The timing may be immediate or delayed and given frequently or infrequently. Feedback might describe progress on many points or just a few, and it may go into great detail or be generalized. It may be oral, written, or demonstrative. It might be addressed to the individual, a small group, or the entire class. Feedback content is also infinitely variable. Feedback might focus on the work itself, the process, or the student's self-regulation but never on the student personally. Feedback comparisons might be criterion-, norm-, or self-referenced. It may function as a description of the work or an evaluation of the work but should not be judgmental. It can be both positive and negative, but any negative comments should be accompanied by suggestions for improvement. Feedback should be understandable to the student and developmentally appropriate. In some cases, feedback can be too specific so that it becomes difficult for a student to apply it to other situations. It can also be overly general, which does not give the student enough information to help with correction. Finally, feedback should communicate respect, activate motivation, and inspire thought.

Modeling, Explaining, and Demonstrating

In order to learn to read and write well, all children need effective modeling and demonstration. Educators often are content to assign reading and writing tasks and ask students to answer questions about the task in lieu of quality direct interactive instruction.

Modeling is when teachers engage in the activity of reading or writing and the children observe and imitate the procedures and strategies. Children can pick up many skills by simply watching and attempting to copy adult behaviors. Reading aloud is one of the most powerful strategies for teaching in the classroom. When being read to, students are given a model for how reading should sound and how stories are constructed. Talking about the reading selection during and after reading models an appropriate response to text. It also fosters comprehension strategies that children need in order to become effective readers. Writing down main points of the reading selection and taking notes models a function of writing. Designating a time each day for reading aloud highlights the importance of reading. High-quality literature with rich text and content should be chosen to read in the classroom. This models the evaluation of literature and the selection of quality reading material. Response groups should be formed so children have a model for collaboratively comprehending text. Modeling is an essential component of any classroom. However, modeling is not sufficient to give children enough information about how to accomplish the tasks that readers and writers actually need to be proficient.

Explanation is also a key component of classroom instruction. Adults in classrooms spend much time explaining reading and writing methods to students. Unfortunately, students often miss key messages because their attention span isn't long enough to follow wordy explanations. Explanations often involve specialized vocabulary that students may not be able to use to comprehend the instruction. Giving excellent explanations is an essential skill for teachers. Seeing teachers and other children model reading and writing and being told how to read and write is still not sufficient for teaching literacy to many struggling learners. This is where **demonstration** comes into play.

Demonstration is when a teacher not only models and explains how to do a task but also engages in thinking through the task with the students. Effective teachers narrate their thinking processes when modeling a strategy. An effective demonstration includes opportunities for the student to try the strategy with immediate feedback from the teacher. Demonstration is teaching and learning in real-time. Effective demonstration occurs in four steps: preparation, presentation, application, and evaluation.

During **preparation**, a teacher puts the students at ease with the impending learning task. He or she assesses students for prior knowledge of the information. Explaining the importance of the learning task is essential. This step may include an attention-getter or motivational strategy. Finally, preparation includes getting the students ready to observe, ensuring they can see and hear well and have appropriate note-taking supplies.

During **presentation,** the teacher tells, shows, illustrates, explains, questions, and models the task. By carefully and patiently narrating the process step-by-step, stressing key points and learning goals, the teacher presents all information and models all skills needed.

Application is guided practice. It includes students attempting the task and then having the teacher give them immediate feedback. Repetition is often used to solidify the skills. The teacher's job is to narrate the steps taken, to ask questions for a measure of understanding, and to prevent errors.

Evaluation is following up with the learning that occurred during the demonstration. The teacher reviews the objectives and evaluates whether they were covered effectively. Checking for readiness and making sure the students know how to get help if they need it are parts of this step.

Challenging and Questioning

Educators are constantly asking questions. This is because questioning serves a wide range of functions in the classroom. Teachers ask questions to involve and engage students in a lesson. Questions increase interest and motivation. A teacher asks questions to assess prior knowledge and readiness for learning. Questioning can help check for completion of learning tasks. It is key for developing critical thinking skills. Questions might be asked to review or assess mastery of learning goals. Asking questions stimulates independent and collaborative learning and invites insight and forethought.

When questioning, it is important to consider how many questions to ask. During the lesson, it is vital to know when the questions are the most appropriate. Will the questions lend meaning to the instruction? Will the questions cause students to focus on all the information presented or only on the parts that help them answer the question? Will the questions lead away from the topic? It is also important to consider how much wait-time to give students to answer the question before the teacher elaborates or asks a new question. Typically, students need to be afforded at least three seconds to formulate an answer to a question. The way a teacher responds to answers is just as important as the questions themselves. The teacher can affirm a correct response, probe the student for more information, or redirect him if the answer is wrong or misinterpreted.

It can be difficult for teachers to give lessons at the appropriate level of difficulty in a classroom of students who are at varying levels of academic readiness. How does a teacher reach a student who is struggling and one who is above grade level in the same lesson? Knowing the appropriate challenge level is essential for learning in the classroom. If a lesson is too challenging, some students will give up. Conversely, if a lesson is not challenging enough, some students will get bored.

There are many strategies that teachers can use to differentiate lessons for varying challenge levels including:

- Allowing choices
- Integrating technology
- Allowing collaboration
- Accommodating pace

- Assessing prior knowledge
- Encouraging goal setting
- Providing creative teaching
- Allowing independent learning
- Allowing students to explore their interests
- Using self-assessment

Providing Effective Assistance and Valuable Information

Students need assistance and guidance in a classroom; however, knowing how much help to offer is always a balancing act. If teachers give too much assistance, they end up doing the work for students, who then do not learn. If teachers do not offer enough assistance, students become lost, overwhelmed, and do not learn. What does the right amount of help look like for each student? Giving effective assistance to students is a foundational teaching strategy. The goal is to help students become as self-motivated and autonomous as possible.

Autonomy in the classroom begins with establishing clear and consistent classroom procedures. Students should be taught how the classroom runs and how to manage themselves. If a student knows what to do to solve simple problems such as sharpening pencils, teachers do not need to waste valuable teaching time with disruptions. Educators can continue to build autonomy by allowing freedom of choice and giving students some power.

Related to autonomy is the concept of self-motivation. Teachers can help students become self-motivated learners by making learning individualized and accessible to all. Instruction should be differentiated for levels of readiness, for personal interests and aptitudes, and for varied learning styles and multiple intelligences. Offering students choices of learning activities and methods of assessment helps individualize education. Educators should have knowledge of the Universal Design for Learning, which promotes differentiation through considering the following three premises:

- Content should be presented in multiple ways: visual, oral, kinesthetic, etc.
- Students should be able to show their learning in multiple ways: writing, speaking, drawing, acting, etc.
- Engaging students should occur in multiple formats: videos, technology, group work, etc.

Teachers can also foster self-motivation by holding high expectations of students and giving them a sense of competence. When adults expect excellence from students, the students often rise to the occasion. Care must be taken that expectations are developmentally appropriate and attainable, but they should always stretch students to the top of their capabilities. Giving students a sense of competence means learning effective praise techniques. It is best to praise effort (something students can control) over intelligence (something out of their control). Students will gain a sense that they learn through their own hard work.

Giving Appropriate Directions

One of the biggest obstacles to learning is when students do not understand or cannot remember the directions they are given. Present directions in auditory and visual formats and assess for understanding by having students retell them to each other or to the teacher.

Some tips for teachers to give good directions include:

- Providing directions in story form. Students can often remember stories, since they are typically more interesting and therefore, better than other forms of communication for multi-step directions.

- Starting with *"when I say go,"* which gets them to listen for all the directions before moving, then telling students what they're *"going to"* do for each step of the process. Students create pictures of themselves doing the steps in their mind's eye and assume they can do it without help.

- Being silly! Throwing in some funny character voices, different facial expressions, or random silly instructions for things they should do between steps of the real task adds interest and increases the desire of students to listen more closely.

- Asking students to speak up if they don't understand all the steps. Teachers should inform students that they want to know of any questions before the students begin the task, rather than find out in the middle of the activity that the students didn't hear or understand all the instructions at the beginning. This makes students responsible for knowing what to do.

- Begin with requiring students to only do a few things at a time. However, as they get used to working with provided instructions, they will be able to take on much more lengthy activities and remember more directions.

Literary Analysis and Genres

Characteristics and Elements of Literary Genres

Genre is a method of categorizing literature by form, content, style, and technique. When selections of literature share enough characteristics and literary elements, they are classified into the same genre. Genre is more than just a categorization system, though; genre identifies literature by its communicative purpose. Authors write to accomplish any of a variety of social purposes: to inform, to explain, to entertain, to persuade, to maintain relationships, and so on. All types of texts fall into one of the following five genres: fiction, nonfiction, poetry, drama, and folklore. Each of these has a variety of subgenres. A particular piece of writing may fall into more than one genre or subgenre.

A variety of texts must be used to teach literature and reading. Folklore and poetry both have aspects to enhance comprehension. Poetry teaches lyrical reading and emphasis; it is written with specific structure and rhythm. There are many types of poetry, such as ballads, lyrics, couplets, epics, and sonnets. Poetry teaches students about adhering to punctuation while reading and allows students to read with pauses. A great teaching strategy to employ with poetry lessons is the use of blank poetry books that students can use to take notes and create their own specific poems. Poetry contains similes, personification, and onomatopoeia; therefore, poems are a great way to teach imagery and figurative language.

Drama, or plays, can emphasize voice, and gives students the option to take on a role of a character. One way to teach drama is to divide students into groups and host a reader's theater. Students and teachers have a lot of fun preparing to present a play in front of the class. Prose text covers a wide range of literature from novels, to folklore, to biographies. Developing a unit dedicated to the various types of folklore (short stories, tall tales, myth, legend, and fantasy) can be creative and fun for students. Autobiographies, biographies, and historical fiction can help teach facts. Providing students with the opportunity to research a person in history and present the findings to the class develops comprehension, presentation, speaking, writing, and research skills.

Reading is fundamental to learning. Reading nurtures imagination, critical thinking, communication skills, and social competence. Many children are drawn to the allure of reading and often their attention is captivated by a certain type of book or books about a particular personal interest. It is important to introduce them to an eclectic selection of text types. Cultural knowledge, a more intricate worldview, and a host of new vocabulary can be built through the experience of diverse literature. Reading a wide range of writing styles brings students into contact with many characters and lifestyles. Reading varied texts sparks different emotions in a child and teaches a variety of means of expression. In this way, children deepen social and emotional skills. In short, reading a wide variety of texts produces a well-rounded education and prepares children for their experience of the world.

Fiction

Fiction is imaginative text that is invented by the author. Fiction is characterized by the following literary elements:

- **Characters:** the people, animals, aliens, or other living figures the story is about
- **Setting:** the location, surroundings, and time the story takes place in
- **Conflict:** a dilemma the characters face either internally or externally
- **Plot:** the sequence and the rise and fall of excitement in the action of a story
- **Resolution:** the solution to the conflict that is discovered as a result of the story
- **Point of View:** the lens through which the reader experiences the story
- **Theme:** the moral to the story or the message the author is sending to the reader

Historical Fiction

Historical fiction is a story that occurs in the past and uses a realistic setting and authentic time period characters. Historical fiction usually has some historically accurate events mixed and balanced with invented plot and characters.

Science Fiction

Science fiction is an invented story that occurs in the future or an alternate universe. It often deals with space, time travel, robots, or aliens, and highly-advanced technology.

Fantasy

Fantasy is a subgenre of fiction that involves magic or supernatural elements and/or takes place in an imaginary world. Examples include talking animals, superheroes rescuing the day, or characters taking on a mythical journey or quest.

Mystery and Adventure

Mystery fiction is a story that involves a puzzle or crime to be solved by the main characters. The mystery is driven by suspense and foreshadowing. The reader must sift through clues and distractions to solve the puzzle with the protagonist. **Adventure stories** are driven by the risky or exciting action that happens in the plot.

Realistic and Contemporary Fiction

Realistic fiction depends on the author portraying the world without speculation. The characters are ordinary, and the action could happen in real life. The conflict often involves growing up, family life, or learning to cope with some significant emotion or challenge.

Nonfiction Literature

Nonfiction literature is text that is true and accurate in detail. Nonfiction can cover virtually any topic in the natural world. Nonfiction writers conduct research and carefully organize facts before writing. Nonfiction has the following subgenres:

- **Informational Text:** This is text written to impart information to the reader. It may have literary elements such as charts, graphs, indexes, glossaries, or bibliographies.
- **Persuasive Text:** This is text that is meant to sway the reader to have a particular opinion or take a particular action.
- **Biographies and Autobiographies:** This is text that tells intimate details of someone's life. If an author writes the text about someone else, it is a **biography**. If the author writes it about himself or herself, it is an **autobiography.**
- **Communicative text:** This is text used to communicate with another person. This includes such texts as emails, formal and informal letters, and tweets. This content often consists of two-sided dialogue between people.

Drama

Drama is any writing that is intended to be performed in front of an audience, such as plays, and TV and movie scripts. Dialogue and action are central to convey the author's theme. **Comedy** is any drama designed to be funny or lighthearted. **Tragedy** is any drama designed to be serious or sad.

A drama, or a play, is almost exclusively delivered as a dialogue and performed live on a stage. The audience observes the story unfolding as opposed to reading it in a book. The actors or actresses in a drama follow written scripts, which are divided into acts and further divided into scenes. The only written material generally given to the audience is the cast of characters, which lists all the character names with an accompanying brief description of their role in the play. This is the only written assistance the audience will receive, so it is imperative that they read through the cast of characters and then carefully follow each scene in the play to understand the story.

Stage directions in a drama refer to the directions or descriptions given to the actors in each scene. They are often presented in italics or in parentheses to differentiate the directions from the dialogue. Stage directions may tell actors where to stand, what direction to face, how to deliver lines, and whom to address.

Poetry

This is text that is written in verse and has a rhythmic cadence. It often involves descriptive imagery, rhyming stanzas, and beautiful mastery of language. It is often personal, emotional, and introspective. Poetry is often considered a work of art.

Generally speaking, **rhyme** goes hand and hand with the study of poetry and involves the repetition of similar sounds. Sounds may rhyme at the end of every two or more lines, referred to as **end rhyme**, or may even rhyme in the middle of a line, referred to as **internal rhyme**.

The following offers examples of both:

> I went to school *today*,
>
> Not wanting to leave the *house*,
>
> And as I passed the *day*,
>
> I remained as quiet as a *mouse*.
>
> In rain or *shine*, your house or *mine*,
>
> We'll meet *again*, my dear *friend*.

The first poem demonstrates the example of end rhyme. The second example demonstrates internal rhyme.

Meter is the rhythm of the syllables within a poem. Each type of meter equates to the specific number of syllables and, possibly, the way the syllables are stressed. There are five basic meters: *iambic*, *trochaic*, *spondaic*, *anapestic*, and *dactylic*. Recognizing the meter within poetry helps readers understand the poem's rhythm and guides the reader in how to read the poem with the poet's intended emphasis. Meter also helps poets develop and maintain the structural elements within the poem.

Folklore

Folklore is literature that has been handed down from generation to generation by word of mouth. Folklore is not based in fact but in unsubstantiated beliefs. It is often very important to a culture or custom. The following are some common types of folklore:

- **Fairy Tales:** These are usually written for children and often carry a moral or universal truth. They are stories written about fairies or other magical creatures.
- **Fables:** Similar to fairy tales, fables are written for children and include tales of supernatural people or animals that speak like people. They often are built around a moral lesson.
- **Myths:** These tales are often about the gods, include symbolism, and may involve historical events and reveal human behavior. Sometimes they tell how historical things came about.
- **Legends:** Exaggerated and only partially truthful, these are tales of heroes and significant events.
- **Tall Tales:** Often funny stories and sometimes set in the Wild West, these are tales that contain extreme exaggeration and were never true.

Literary Response and Analysis Skills

Structural Elements of a Plot

There are five main structural elements of a plot:

1. **Exposition:** This is where the author introduces characters and establishes the setting.
2. **Rising Action:** This is where the conflict starts to develop and complications may form.
3. **Climax:** This is when the conflict is at its highest moment.
4. **Falling Action:** This is where characters make choices that will determine the end result.
5. **Resolution:** This is how the story ends and overall the outcome.

Characters

When readers compare and contrast characters, it is important that they ask themselves three questions:

1. Why compare/contrast characters?
2. What is compared/contrast between characters?
3. How are they the same/different?

Setting

Evaluating the relevance of the setting impacts a text's direction. For example, how is the storyline affected by the time and location of the story's events?

Recurring Themes

Texts may carry recurring themes like acceptance, courage, loyalty, man versus nature, family, and life. There are many themes that may overlap in a variety of texts. It is important for teachers to remember to coordinate texts with recurring themes in order for students to clearly understand the intent or message.

Literary Devices

Inferential reading and comprehension skills, such as figurative language, involve some abstract understanding of the text. Students must first gain comprehension of the text, and then use their inference skills to further break down the text. Students must understand characters' feelings as well as the reason for the setting. Again, identifying theme is a difficult skill to teach. When introducing a new text, teachers should provide students with a list of common themes to pick from. Figurative language and literary devices can help identify the theme. **Figurative language** includes metaphors, similes, personification, and hyperbole. **Literary devices** include imagery, symbolism, irony, and foreshadowing. These two tools help readers interpret the author's theme or purpose in texts.

Whereas **literal language** is the author's use of precise words, proper meanings, definitions, and phrases that mean exactly what they say, **figurative language** deviates from precise meaning and word definition—often in conjunction with other familiar words and phrases—to paint a picture for the reader. Figurative language is less explicit and more open to reader interpretation.

Some examples of figurative language are included in the following graphic.

	Definition	Example
Simile	Compares two things using "like" or "as"	Her hair was like gold.
Metaphor	Compares two things as if they are the same	He was a giant teddy bear.
Idiom	Using words with predictable meanings to create a phrase with a different meaning	The world is your oyster.
Alliteration	Repeating the same beginning sound or letter in a phrase for emphasis	The busy baby babbled.
Personification	Attributing human characteristics to an object or an animal	The house glowered menacingly with a dark smile.
Foreshadowing	Giving an indication that something is going to happen later in the story	I wasn't aware at the time, but I would come to regret those words.
Symbolism	Using symbols to represent ideas and provide a different meaning	The ring represented the bond between us.
Onomatopoeia	Using words that imitate sound	The tire went off with a bang and a crunch.
Imagery	Appealing to the senses by using descriptive language	The sky was painted with red and pink and streaked with orange.
Hyperbole	Using exaggeration not meant to be taken literally	The girl weighed less than a feather.

Figurative language can be used to give additional insight into the theme or message of a text by moving beyond the usual and literal meaning of words and phrases. It can also be used to appeal to the senses of readers and create a more in-depth story.

Poetic Devices

Rhyme is the poet's use of corresponding word sounds in order to create an effect. Most rhyme occurs at the ends of a poem's lines, which is how readers arrive at the **rhyme scheme**. Each line that has a corresponding rhyming sound is assigned a letter—A, B, C, and so on. When using a rhyme scheme, poets will often follow lettered patterns. Robert Frost's *"The Road Not Taken"* uses the ABAAB rhyme scheme:

Two roads diverged in a yellow wood,	A
And sorry I could not travel both	B
And be one traveler, long I stood	A
And looked down one as far as I could	A
To where it bent in the undergrowth;	B

Another important poetic device is **rhythm**—metered patterns within poetry verses. When a poet develops rhythm through **meter,** he or she is using a combination of stressed and unstressed syllables to create a sound effect for the reader.

Rhythm is created by the use of **poetic feet**—individual rhythmic units made up of the combination of stressed and unstressed syllables. A line of poetry is made up of one or more poetic feet. There are five standard types in English poetry, as depicted in the chart below.

Foot Type	Rhythm	Pattern
Iamb	buh Buh	Unstressed/stressed
Trochee	Buh buh	Stressed/unstressed
Spondee	Buh Buh	Stressed/stressed
Anapest	buh buh Buh	Unstressed/unstressed/stressed
Dactyl	Buh buh buh	Stressed/unstressed/unstressed

Poetic Structure

Poetry is most easily recognized by its structure, which varies greatly. For example, a structure may be strict in the number of lines it uses. It may use rhyming patterns or may not rhyme at all. There are three main types of poetic structures:

- **Verse**—poetry with a consistent meter and rhyme scheme
- **Blank verse**—poetry with consistent meter but an inconsistent rhyme scheme
- **Free verse**—poetry with inconsistent meter or rhyme

Verse poetry is most often developed in the form of **stanzas**—groups of word lines. Stanzas can also be considered **verses**. The structure is usually formulaic and adheres to the protocols for the form. For example, the English **sonnet** form uses a structure of fourteen lines and a variety of different rhyming patterns. The English **ode** typically uses three ten-line stanzas and has a particular rhyming pattern.

Poets choose poetic structure based on the effect they want to create. Some structures—such as the ballad and haiku—developed out of cultural influences and common artistic practice in history, but in more modern poetry, authors choose their structure to best fit their intended effect.

Selecting Multicultural Texts

Awareness of multicultural education is vital in the fast-changing demographics of United States education. Multicultural education seeks to ensure that all students have a fair and equal chance at education. Educators should keep in mind the importance of teaching various historical perspectives and an awareness of global issues and cultural consciousness. Educators should always seek to display cultural sensitivity when implementing activities or assigning multicultural texts.

In addition to different cultures, multicultural education also seeks to include all those who are considered to be in underrepresented groups, such as girls, students of different ethnicities, and students with disabilities. Taking assessment of the students in the classroom and their various needs are essential in developing a multicultural curriculum.

There is a multitude of options to choose from for educators looking to incorporate multicultural reading in their classrooms. Below is a brief list of possible texts that deal with multicultural sensitivity:

Preschool:

- I Love Saturdays y Domingos by Alma Flor Ada
- *Wild Berries* by Julie Flett
- "My People" by Langston Hughes
- Niño Wrestles the World by Yuyi Morales
- *Cradle Me* by Debby Slier
- *Pecan Pie Baby* by Jacqueline Woodson
- The Twins' Blanket by Hyewon Yum

Ages Five to Seven:

- *Little Roja Riding Hood* by Susan Middleton Elya
- Honey, I Love, and Other Poems by Eloise Greenfield
- Take Me Out to the Yakyu by Aaron Meshon
- Shades of Black: A Celebration of Our Children by Sandra L. Pinkney
- *Jingle Dancer* by Cynthia Leitich Smith
- What Can You Do With a Paleta? by Carmen Tafolia

Ages Seven to Nine:

- My Name is Maria Isabel by Alma Flor Ada
- *Shin-chi's Canoe* by Nicola Campbell
- The Year of the Book by Andrea Cheng
- *Crouching Tiger* by Ying Chang Compestine
- The People Could Fly: American Black Folktales by Virginia Hamilton
- *Wings* by Christopher Myers
- *Rickshaw Girl* by Mitali Perkins
- *Indian Shoes* by Cynthia Leitich Smith
- Diego Rivera: His World and Ours by Duncan Tonatiuh

Ages Nine to Twelve:

- The Birchbark House by Louise Erdrich
- Inside Out & Back Again by Thanhha Lai
- Where the Mountain Meets the Moon by Grace Lin
- *Ninth Ward* by Jewell Parker Rhodes
- Star in the Forest by Laura Resau
- *Boys without Names* by Kashmira Sheth
- *The Composition* by Antonio Skarmeta
- *One Crazy Summer* by Rita Williams-Garcia

Appropriate Techniques for Varying Students' Response to Texts

When educators introduce a text within a classroom, there are a few ways to identify and evaluate appropriate techniques for students to respond to that text. Giving students a chance to respond to readings helps them feel included in the classroom setting and inspires them to administer focus into the reading and instruction. Below are a few different techniques to incorporate student response to text in the classroom.

Think-Pair-Share

Think-pair-share is a reading response technique that educators use to allow every student a chance to voice their ideas. After the teacher reads a few pages of a text, the teacher asks the students to think about a concept that was just read, or may have the students compare those few pages with another text that was read before in class. After the students think about their ideas, they turn to a partner and share their ideas with their partner. The teacher goes around the room and asks each of the students what their ideas were. This technique allows all children to share their ideas to each other and the teacher, and does not put pressure on the students less reluctant to share in front of a group. This technique also motivates students to think about a topic independently as well as build oral communication skills.

Reading Response Journals

Educators use reading response journals in order to increase reading comprehension amongst their students. These journals give students the freedom and confidence to respond to the text in their own way, enhancing their reading capacity as well as writing capacity. Journals can be anything from a few papers sewn together to a store-bought notebook. Some teachers have students write or take notes as they read, and some teachers use the letter format. The letter format is where students write a letter to the author or character in their journal. This facilitates student response to text and allows them to critically think about the content they've read.

Evidence-Based Discussion

Evidence-based discussion is a strategy used in the classroom to facilitate student response to a topic using objective data to back up that response. For example, let's look at a class of fourth graders. The students are given a topic with a research question, and then they are asked to do some research on that topic and focus on the research question. The students go to the library and write down facts and examples they learn about their topic on note cards. Once they come back to class, they share their responses with the class one at a time using the information they've gathered from the library. Evidence-based discussion provides students with the ability to confidently share their ideas with facts and allows students to participate in a discussion where they built upon one another's ideas.

Think-Alouds

A teacher "think-aloud" is a great strategy to promote the development of comprehension skills and eventually transfer these skills to written language. Students who are allowed to stop periodically throughout the text to verbalize what they have read score significantly higher on standardized testing. Teacher read-alouds help promote listening comprehension skills because students can listen without having to decode the text. Students can freely take notes and outline what they hear, and can listen for reading strategies, such as word and voice emphasis. In small intervention groups, a teacher can read aloud shorter texts to help teach reading comprehension. Rather than having students read aloud during smaller group work, teachers can help promote comprehension by simply having students listen to books catered to their reading level, and then having think-alouds in small groups. Students can complete graphic organizers or comprehension worksheets during listening comprehension time.

Language and the Writing Process

Developmental Stages of Writing

Developmental stages of writing are stages students go through when learning to write fluently. Not all students will be on the same stage as their peers. The developmental stages of writing are fluid, and the stages have been merged over the years.

Below is a list of stages that are the most common in writing development.

- Scribbling: Younger students use scribbling to express their ideas. This is a mock-writing stage, and represents a random assortment of lines and marks on paper. These marks may resemble drawing, although students at this stage do not have the coordination to form letters.
- Letter-Like Symbols: At this stage, students write symbols that look similar to letters and numbers. Spacing between letters is non-existent at this stage.
- Strings of Letters: In the strings-of-letters stage, students begin to write capital letters side-by-side without spacing, although the letters usually do not form actual words. Students at this stage are becoming aware of the sound-to-symbol relationship.
- Beginning Sounds Emerge: Though students may not use spacing in this stage, they start seeing the differences between letters and words.
- Consonants Represent Words: At this stage, the letters may have spaces between them, and the writing, though it may still be illegible, begins to look like small sentences strung together. Uppercase and lowercase letters may be mixed together.
- Initial, Middle, and Final Sounds: Student writing at this stage is legible. Familiar words may be spelled out, such as names of family members or pets. Most words are written the way they sound, instead of the way they are actually spelled.
- Transitional Phases: At this stage, writing is legible and looks more like conventional spelling.
- Standard Spelling: Students at this stage in their writing spell most words correctly and understand that root words, compound words, and contractions can be used in other similar wording.

Like with any complicated processes, writing development begins with the simplest form of indiscernible scribbles and progresses to fully formed words and, finally, to clearly written sentences and paragraphs. This is actually a complicated cognitive process that takes time and instruction to improve.

With very young students, emphasis can focus on simply making letters clear. After all, letters and word formation are the starting blocks of written language. The next phase in development can focus on actually creating words and making sure they are spelled correctly. When students are at the sentence development stage, grammar and linguistic rules become a priority. The foundations of the English language need to be firm in order for students to have good writing. When students have progressed to more advanced levels and are composing fully formed sentences with a specific purpose, it's time to incorporate content-related feedback.

Feedback at all levels of writing development is crucial; this is how students will learn to correct mistakes and strengthen growing skills. Instructor feedback must be clear while also being sensitive to the students' struggles or backgrounds. Differentiated instruction may be required to bolster students' writing skills. A good starting point for overall writing instruction is to introduce students to the stages of writing an original piece.

The goal with the stages of writing is to build on the previous work. The prewriting stage is the time for students to just write down ideas and plan on how they will approach the topic at hand. The actual writing stage then dovetails on this fluidly because the student already has a framework of what the writing will focus on and how they will present information. In addition to practicing physical writing, these stages focus on critical-thinking and planning skills and may lessen the student's stress before they write and receive feedback. Feedback on the initial writing, or first draft, is key. The instructor should be able to assess any difficulties and then steer the student toward improving their writing in the revision stage. After revisions, instructors should examine how effective their feedback was in helping the writing improve overall.

Stages of the Writing Process

Writing Skills Development

Children who receive regular and consistent encouragement to write and whose environment is rich with writing materials and resources will be more apt to strengthen their writing proficiency. Research suggests that at least an hour a day of writing practice, including skilled instruction, is necessary. Writing projects should be chosen that also involve the subjects of science, social studies, reading, or mathematics to give students well-rounded views of the purposes for writing. Piece by piece, students practice writing skills in all subjects, and collectively it should add up to more than an hour a day.

POWER Strategy for Teaching the Writing Process

The POWER strategy helps all students to take ownership of the writing process by prompting them to consciously focus on what they are writing.

The POWER strategy is an acronym for the following:

- Prewriting or Planning
- Organizing
- Writing a first draft
- Evaluating the writing
- Revising and rewriting

Prewriting and Planning

During the Prewriting and Planning phase, students learn to consider their audience and purpose for the writing project. Then they compile information they wish to include in the piece of writing from their background knowledge and/or new sources.

Organizing

Next, students decide on the organizational structure of their writing project. There are many types of organizational structures, but the common ones are: story/narrative, informative, opinion, persuasive, compare and contrast, explanatory, and problem/solution formats. Often graphic organizers are an important part of helping students complete this step of the writing process.

Writing

In this step, students write a complete first draft of their project. Educators may begin by using modeled writing to teach this step in the process. It may be helpful for beginning writers to work in small groups or pairs. Verbalizing their thoughts before writing them is also a helpful technique.

Evaluating

In this stage, students reread their writing and note the segments that are particularly strong or need improvement. Then they participate in peer editing. They ask each other questions about the piece. The peers learn to provide feedback and constructive criticism to help the student improve. Scoring rubrics are a helpful tool in this phase to guide students as they edit each other's work.

Revising and Rewriting

Finally, the student incorporates any changes she or he wishes to make based on the evaluating process. Then students rewrite the piece into a final draft and publish it however it best fits the audience and purpose of the writing.

6+1 Traits Strategy for Teaching Writing

6+1 Traits is a model for teaching writing that uses a common language to explain the standards for what good writing looks like. Students learn to evaluate whether these expectations have been met in their own writing and then edit, revise, and rewrite accordingly. The 6+1 Traits are the characteristics that make writing readable and effective no matter what genre of writing is being used. The 6+1 Traits are as follows:

- Ideas
- Organization
- Voice
- Word choice
- Sentence fluency
- Conventions
- Presentation

The Ideas Trait

This trait is the content of the writing. This is where students learn to select an important topic for their writing. They are taught to narrow down and focus their idea. Then they learn to develop and elaborate on the specific idea. Finally, they investigate and discover the information and details that best convey the idea to others.

The Organization Trait

This trait teaches students how to build the framework for their writing. They choose an organizational strategy or purpose for the writing and build the details upon that structure. There are many purposes for writing, and they all have different frameworks. However, there are commonalities that students can learn to effectively organize their writing so it makes sense to the reader. Students learn to invite the reader into their work with an effective introduction. They are taught how to create thoughtful transitions between ideas and key points in their writing and how to create logical and purposeful sequencing of ideas. Finally, students are taught how to create a powerful conclusion to their piece that summarizes the information but leaves the reader with something to think about. Many students are inclined to jump into their writing without a clear direction for where it is going. The organization trait teaches them to plan and purpose their writing toward excellence.

The Voice Trait

This is the trait that gives the writing a sense of individuality and connection to the author. It shows that the writing is meaningful and that the author cares about it. It is what makes the writing uniquely the author's own. It is how the reader begins to know the author and what she or he "sounds like." Students learn to recognize "voice" in some writing samples and find their own "voice" to apply to their work. Students are taught to speak on an emotional level directly to their readers. Students experiment with matching their style to the audience and the purpose of the writing. Students are taught to enjoy taking risks and putting their personal touch into their work.

The Word Choice Trait

This trait gives writing a sense of functional communication through precise language that is rich and enlightening. If the work is narrative, the words create images in the mind's eye; if the work is descriptive, the words clarify and expand thoughts and ideas. If the work is persuasive, the words give new perspective and invite thought. Students learn not only to choose exceptional vocabulary, but also to hone their skills for using ordinary words well. Students are taught to describe things using striking language. They learn to use exact language that is accurate, concise, precise, and lively.

The Sentence Fluency Trait

When sentences are built to fit together and move with one another to create writing that is easy to read aloud, the author has written with fluency. Students learn to eliminate awkward word patterns that otherwise would encumber the reader. Sentences and paragraphs start and stop in precisely the right places so that the writing moves well. Students are taught to establish a flow, develop a rhythm, and give cadence to their work. They edit their sentences to vary the structure and length. Educators can teach fluency through reading aloud beautifully written examples and contrasting them with less fluent work.

The Conventions Trait

Here the focus changes from creation of the piece to preparation for the reader. Instead of revision that the first five traits teach, this trait teaches editing skills. The students learn to make their writing clear and understandable through the use of proper grammar, spelling, capitalization, and punctuation. Students are taught the differences between revision and editing. They learn basic editing marks and symbols. Teachers can assist students to learn conventions through guided editing and regular practice. Expectations for correctness need to be kept developmentally appropriate. If immediate correctness is expected, students may shy away from experimenting and taking risks.

The Presentation Trait

This trait focuses on the final appearance of the work. Presentation is not a concern during the process of the other six traits, nor must perfect presentation be expected for every work a student does. Students are taught to make their work inviting and accessible to the reader of the end product. They learn to show they care about their writing when it is neat and readable. Students are taught about uniform spacing, legible handwriting, appropriate use of fonts and sizes, and how to use bullets, numbers, headings, charts, graphs, and pictures to help make the work visually appealing. Students are taught about the publishing process and are given opportunities to showcase their finished products.

Purposeful Writing

Purposeful writing practices have a significant effect on writing development. Purposeful writing refers to intentional writing practices for the purpose of communicating. Through learning to write well, students can begin to use writing as a method of thinking through issues and solving problems. They become more adept with questioning and investigation. Students learn to accurately convey and critique information. They can more readily express real or imagined experiences to others. Through the varied writing purposes, students learn to focus on what the audience understands, while at other times, they focus on the topic and what information they are trying to impart. Other situations call for focus on their own thinking and feelings.

Writing as a whole becomes more effective and accessible as students glean skills for writing with purpose. Some of the writing purposes are as follows:

- Letter writing
- Poetry and Songs
- Creative and Narrative writing
- Informative writing
- Opinion writing
- Persuasive writing
- Compare and Contrast writing
- Explanatory/Expository writing
- Problem and Solution writing

Modes of Writing

Opinion/Argument

In the early elementary grades, students begin to write simple **opinion pieces**. Acting as a precursor to argumentative and persuasive writing, opinion pieces allow children to express how they feel on a certain subject based on preferences, express their likes and dislikes, and use personal knowledge, without relying too heavily on supporting evidence. Educators encourage children to write opinion pieces with the use of personal journals as well as reflective pieces, connecting personal experiences to various stories read.

In the middle school years and beyond, students will be required to write **argumentative** or **persuasive** pieces of writing, which must involve logical and relevant proof for a claim or an assertion. Regarded as a more sophisticated form of writing, argumentative or persuasive writing works to change the point of view of the readers or ignite a call-to-action response. This form of writing does not shy away from contradicting points of view but, instead, brings them to light and then works to disprove or discredit each opposing claim. Some examples of argumentative or persuasive writing include essays, reviews, and letters to the editor.

Informative

Informative writing comes in many forms, including directions, instructions, definitions, summaries, and more. **Informative writing** works to relay information and advance the reader's understanding of a given subject. If written correctly, the vast majority of informative writing is written in third person to distance the author from relying on personal bias, instead relying on objective facts, historical evidence, and statistics.

Narrative

Almost always written in first person, **narratives** include autobiographies, memoirs, and even fictional stories. Their general purpose is to entertain readers, but some also focus on morals, values, or life lessons. By conveying personal experiences on a given subject or by opening up one's life to the audience, narrative writers create a more intimate connection with readers.

Selecting the Appropriate Mode of Writing for a Variety of Occasions, Purposes, and Audiences

Effective writing, whether for the purpose of persuading, entertaining, or advancing a reader's knowledge, must be well planned and organized. In order to create a powerful piece of writing, authors must adhere to specific structural designs, apply a functional and logical order to their writing, and employ key elements.

The following chart outlines three types of writing and their respective purposes, the structural elements unique to each type of writing, and some examples of subgenres:

	Opinion/Persuasive	**Narrative**	**Informative**
Purpose	To persuade, influence, or prompt a call-to-action response	To entertain or to share a moral when writing fictional narratives To share factual information when writing nonfiction narratives	To convey information and advance a reader's knowledge of a given topic
Key components	Opening statement and point of view Well organized paragraphs with supportive evidence and/or examples Strong concluding statement that reinforces point of view	Fictional narratives: plot, characters, setting, point of view, tone Nonfictional Narratives: introductory paragraph Body: including details and descriptions of events and individuals Conclusion	Introduction Headings and Subheadings Body Conclusion Works Cited
Subgenres	Speeches, letters, reviews, advertisements, essays	Fictional narratives: folktales, fantasy, science-fiction, mystery, drama Nonfictional narratives: autobiographies, biographies, memoirs	How-to books, cookbooks, instructional manuals, textbooks

Aristotle's Rhetorical Triangle is perhaps the best visual representation to demonstrate the importance of effective writing. Three key areas require the writer's full attention and should be balanced accordingly throughout the writing process:

Ethos refers to the writer's credibility: What are the writer's qualifications regarding the subject of the writing? Is the author using an objective or subjective approach? Are the sources, evidence, and examples in the writing relevant and credible?

Pathos refers to the writer's ability to engage and connect with the intended audience: What details and imagery does the author use to ignite and excite the emotions, imagination, values, and beliefs of the audience?

Logos refers to the validity of the author's message: Is the author's message clearly discernible? Is it logical and well organized?

Each of these three areas are critical to the quality of the writing and require the author's full attention and consideration throughout the writing process, from the preliminary stages to the final published work. Writers are tasked with the responsibility of choosing appropriate language to connect with an audience and choosing a style that maintains interest, which helps the audience understand the writer's purpose and accept the writer's intent. Did the writer succeed, for instance, in entertaining, informing, or persuading the audience?

Instructional Methods for Teaching Writing Conventions

Educators must first be masters of the English language in order to teach it. Teachers serve several key roles in the classroom that all require that they know the conventions of grammar, punctuation, and spelling. Teachers are communicators. They must know how to structure their own language for clarity. They must also be able to interpret what the students are saying to accurately either affirm or revise it for correctness. Teachers are educators of language. They are the agents of change from poor-quality conventions to mastery of the concepts. Teachers are responsible for differentiating instruction so that students at all levels and aptitudes can succeed with language learning. Teachers need to be able to isolate gaps in skill sets and decide which skills need intervention in the classroom.

Teachers are evaluators. They are responsible for making key decisions about a student's educational trajectory based on their assessment of the student's capabilities.

Teachers also have great impact on how students view themselves as learners. Teachers are models. They must be superb examples of educated individuals. Just like with any other subject, people need a strong grasp of the basics of language. They will not be able to learn these things unless the teachers themselves have mastered it.

Teachers foster socialization; socialization to cultural norms and to the everyday practices of the community in which they live is of utmost importance to students' lives. These processes begin at home but continue early in a child's life at school. Teachers play a key role in guiding and scaffolding students' socialization skills. If teachers are to excel in this role, they need to be adept with the use of the English language.

When learning to speak, listen, read, or write in any language, students are tasked with multiple challenges. The study of the English language is no exception. The conventions of Standard English are complex and require comprehensive study and continual practice.

Parts of Speech

Words within the English language play very unique roles in the formation of coherent sentences. Each English word is categorized into a specific part of speech that carries a unique function. For instance, in order to create simple English language sentences, writers are required to incorporate a noun and a verb. However, when sentences become more complex, additional parts of speech are required. The following chart outlines the parts of speech, along with a brief description of their function within an English sentence and concrete examples.

Part of Speech	**Function**	**Examples**
Noun	Identifies a person, place, or thing—can be concrete or abstract	Love, thought, man, woman, child, school, home, integrity, America
Pronoun	Replaces a noun	He, she, it, they
Verb	Depicts an action or state of being	Run, jump, fly, is, are
Adjective	Modifies nouns	Great idea, interesting thought, tall girl
Adverb	Modifies verbs, other adverbs, and adjectives	He has an extremely shy demeanor. She quickly ran away. They walked very clumsily together.
Preposition	Almost always combined with other key words in a sentence in order to indicate a time, location, or movement	At nine o'clock, beside the nightstand, toward the door
Conjunction	Connects words, clauses, or sentences, with related meaning	She and I have similar tastes in food. The teacher handed us the assignment, but we refused to accept it. The dogs ran and played, while the cats sat and stared.
Interjection	Brief exclamations that are added to sentences for emphasis or effect	Wow! I had no idea you could sing! "Boo!" she screamed, as she jumped out from behind the door.

Although an explicit approach to teaching the various parts of speech plays an integral role in the primary grades, it is equally as important that a child learns to recognize these parts of speech when reading and gradually learn to apply them to writing tasks. Being able to recognize and appropriately use various parts of speech demonstrates a growing command of the English language and its conventions.

Correction of Errors

Usage and mechanics are often mistakenly used as interchangeable terms in the educational field. In writing, **usage** refers to a student's ability to choose appropriate words that clearly express an idea, thought, or opinion, or accurately summarize information. Therefore, usage is a very important component of learning to be an effective writer. **Mechanics** involve the writer's ability to use capitalization, ending punctuation, apostrophes, and commas properly. For writing to be both coherent and fluent, mechanics play an important role. **Spelling** is a little less complicated to understand, as it refers to the student's ability to spell decodable and non-decodable words accurately. Learning how and when to correct errors in usage, mechanics, and spelling can be a source of frustration for educators, but it need not be. By creating a logical balance and manageable plan for correcting student writing, educators will help children to be more effective, lifelong writers. The key is balance.

Traditionally, English language educators have focused a great deal of evaluation and feedback on correcting mistakes in usage, mechanics, and spelling alone. Although it is widely accepted that these components are necessary in order to write fluent and coherent sentences, too much focus on correcting these areas—and not enough attention paid to the creative side of writing—may have a negative impact on the writing process.

For example, instead of emphasizing or highlighting every spelling error, educators should ensure that their corrections reflect the task. In other words, if children are given a writing assignment that must incorporate their spelling words, they will undoubtedly expect the educator to correct and evaluate how well they spelled these key words. However, since the assignment also asked the children to use a creative approach to this writing assignment, educators would be doing students a disservice if they did not also offer praise and feedback on the children's writing creativity.

Developing a writing checklist with well-defined goals and sharing this checklist with the class helps educators keep the correction process clear and specific, and it provides children with the opportunity to self-correct and edit their work prior to submission. Using a standardized system of symbols that helps children focus on spelling, capitalization, or word choice is also an effective strategy. Displaying these symbols in a readily accessible place in the classroom will allow them to self-correct and help their peers with the correction process.

For writing to be meaningful and for students to advance in their writing skills, educators should follow a balanced approach to correcting student work with frequent, timely, and appropriate feedback that reflects the task.

Sentence Types

When children begin to connect letters to words and, gradually, words to sentences, those sentences are generally very simple, consisting of one subject and one verb. However, as children advance in their writing fluency, it is paramount to introduce more complex sentences.

Simple sentences are sentences that consist of one subject and one verb:

> I run.
>
> She eats.
>
> They play.

At this stage, educators may prompt children to add some more detail to the simple sentences with adjectives or adverbs:

> I run *quickly*.
>
> She eats *very well*.
>
> They play *together*.

Compound sentences contain two independent clauses connected by a conjunction:

> I run, but she runs marathons.

I run is an **independent clause**. *She runs marathons* is another independent clause. Each clause could be a complete sentence that stands on its own. However, they are connected with the coordinating conjunction, *but*.

Complex sentences are structures in which two clauses exist, but one clause is **dependent** on the other—that is, it cannot form a sentence in its own right and requires the assistance of the independent clause in order for the sentence to be coherent. Here's an example:

> Although he passed the exam, he remained very sad.

He remained very sad is an independent clause, but *Although he passed the exam* is not, as it is dependent on the second part of the sentence in order for the sentence to be coherent.

Compound-complex sentences are structures that employ two or more independent clauses along with at least one dependent clause:

> Though I preferred long distance running, I started speed walking, and I enjoyed it very much.

Though I preferred long-distance running is a dependent clause that relies on the independent clause *I started speed walking*. The second independent clause is *I enjoyed it very much*, making this sentence compound-complex.

English Used in Stories, Dramas, or Poems

Register

Despite the fact that a standardized form of English is used in published academic and scientific language, several varieties of spoken and written English also exist. There are differences in how one speaks at home, with friends, to teachers, and to colleagues. In each social setting, a person's **register**—his or her level of formality—will likely change in order to appropriately address the audience. Written registers also vary, depending on a number of factors. For instance, when writing a research paper for professional purposes, formal language will be used, but when writing a letter to a friend, a person is more apt to employ a more casual register. The following statements indicate differences in register:

> Call me back when you get this message.
>
> I look forward to hearing back from you at your earliest convenience.

Although both statements express the writer's desire to further communicate with the receiver of the message, the degree of formality, the register, is strikingly different.

Dialect

A language also has several dialects, which are dependent on a great many factors. **Dialects** have specific grammatical rules and patterns that often differ from the standard rules of the language. For instance, within Britain, Canada, and the United States, there are several dialects of the English language. One need only travel from Newfoundland, in eastern Canada, to Louisiana, in the southern United States, to witness a striking difference in how the English language is spoken.

Written dialects and registers also exist. They vary, based on the type of written work, when it was created, where it was written, by whom it was written, for what purposes, and for what audience it was intended. Authors of dramas, stories, and poetry employ the use of dialect for a multitude of reasons. For instance, when authors wish to develop a clear picture of the setting and characters within a drama, dialect plays a significant role. Here are some examples of dialect:

> "Bess, you is my woman now . . ."—from George Gershwin's opera, *Porgy and Bess*

> "That ain't no matter."—from Mark Twain's novel, *Huckleberry Finn*

With the careful and skillful placement of written dialect, the author conveys the character's personality, situation, and social class.

Instructional Methods for Teaching Writer's Craft Across Genres

Current trends in education have recognized the need to cultivate writing skills that prepare students for higher education and professional careers. To this end, writing skills are being integrated into other subjects beyond the language arts classroom. The skills and strategies used in language arts class, then, should be adaptable for other learning tasks. In this way, students can achieve greater proficiency by incorporating writing strategies into every aspect of learning.

To teach writing, it is important that writers know the writing process. Students should be familiar with the five components of the writing process:

1. *Pre-writing*: The drafting, planning, researching, and brainstorming of ideas
2. *Writing*: The part of the project in which the actual, physical writing takes place
3. *Revising*: Adding to, removing, rearranging, or re-writing sections of the piece
4. *Editing*: Analyzing and correcting mistakes in grammar, spelling, punctuation, formatting, and word choice
5. *Publishing*: Distributing the finished product to the teacher, employer, or other students

The **writing workshop** is possibly the most common approach to teaching writing. It is an organized approach in which the student is guided by the teacher and usually contains the following components:

- *Short lesson* (~10 min) in which the teacher focuses on a particular aspect of the writing process—e.g., strategies, organization, technique, processes, craft—and gives explicit instructions for the task at hand
- *Independent writing time* (~30 min) in which the student engages in the writing activity and works through the process while receiving help from the teacher, writing in his/her own style on either a chosen topic or one assigned, and engaging with other students
- *Sharing* (~10 min) in which the student shares a piece of his or her work, either in a small group or as a class, and gains insight by listening to the work of other students

Another common strategy is **teacher modeling,** in which the student views the teacher as a writer and is therefore more apt to believe the teacher's instruction on the subject. To be a good writing teacher, the teacher must be a good writer. Therefore, it is important that the teacher practice his or her own writing on a somewhat regular basis through blogging, journaling, or creative writing, in order to keep his or her skills sharp. The following are some strategies for teacher writing:

- *Sharing written work*: This strategy is a good audio and/or visual learning technique. The teacher should frequently share personal writing with students so that the student recognizes the instructor as having authority on the subject. Many teachers also encourage feedback from the students to stimulate critical thinking skills.
- *Writing in front of students*: This strategy is very effective as a visual learning technique as the students watch as the teacher works through the writing process. This could include asking the students to provide a question or topic on which to write and then writing on blackboard or projector.
- *Encouraging real-world writing*: This is a kinesthetic teaching strategy in which the teacher urges students to write as frequently as possible and to share their written work with other students or an authentic audience. Teachers may also find it beneficial to show students their own blogs and other online media to demonstrate exactly how it's done. Students may also choose to model their writing after a published author, imitating his or her style, sentence structure, and word choices to become comfortable with the writing process.

Finally, a good thing for a student to have is a **writer's notebook,** which contains all the student's written work over the course of the curriculum, including warm-up assignments, drafts, brainstorming templates, and completed works. This allows the student to review previous writing assignment, learn from their mistakes, and see concrete evidence for improvement. Depending on the age group, many of the assignments could be performed on a word processor to encourage computer literacy.

Identifying Strategies for Teaching Writing Tasks

There are over thirty research-proven strategies for teaching all components of the writing process through a variety of different tasks, the most comprehensive of which will be covered in this section.

Evidence shows that the most effective strategy for teaching writing is to have the students use the process-writing approach, in which they practice planning, writing, reviewing, editing, and publishing their work. Students should be taught how to write for a specific audience, take personal responsibility for their own work, and participate in the writing process with other students, such as a discussion-like setting where they can brainstorm together. Additionally, specific goals should be assigned, either classroom wide or to fit individual needs, through activities that encourage attention to spelling, grammar, sentence combination, and writing for specific audiences.

- For pre-writing, students should also be exposed to the process of generating and organizing ideas before they set pen to paper, such as being given a specific topic and considering many different aspects associated with that topic using a brainstorming web or mindmap, visually dividing a project into main topics and subtopics. Teachers can help students by encouraging them to explore what they already know about a subject, topic, or genre. They can then illustrate how to go about researching and gathering information or data by using teacher modeling to access a variety of resources. Another research-based strategy is to require students to analyze and summarize a model text through writing, which encourages them to condense a composition into its main ideas and, in doing so, allows them to understand how these ideas were expressed and organized.

- To teach the actual act of writing, **freewriting** is an effective writing warm-up activity as it requires nothing more than for the student to continually write uninterrupted for an allotted amount of time. One of the most common problems many students encounter is being uncertain what to write or how to begin. Freewriting creates a space in which the student does not have to worry about either of those things—they simply need to write. For this particular strategy, a teacher should avoid assigning a particular topic, genre, or format, nor should the student be encouraged or required to share what they have written so that they may write freely and without fear of judgment. After the allotted time for freewriting is up, students can then read back over what they have written and select the most interesting sentences and ideas to expand upon in a more organized piece of writing.

Another form of instruction is **discipline-based inquiry**, which encourages students to analyze writing models in a particular mode to better grasp the characteristics of that style. For example, before assigning students a persuasive writing assignment, an instructor would first give several samples of persuasive passages to students and ask them to read the texts carefully, paying attention to components such as diction—what kind of emotional or connotative language the writer uses to subtly influence readers' opinion, supporting arguments—how the writer integrates objective data to support a subjective argument, and organization—how the writer presents the information and argument. By focusing students' attention on a specific writing mode, the instructor allows students to use their analytical and observation skills to formulate an idea about the prominent characteristics of a particular mode of writing.

In **Self-Regulated Strategy Development** (SRSD), instructors progressively instill independent skills in students by first prompting students for their prior knowledge about a subject, building on that background knowledge, instructing them more deeply in strategies related to the learning objective, and then practicing the strategy enough times so that it becomes an embedded habit in students' learning process.

Finally, encouraging students to write with one another in a collaborative setting is a good way to enhance revision, editing, and publishing skills by learning, discussing, and writing for each other. By giving constructive feedback to their peers, students learn how to recognize and apply standards of effective writing, and they also become more skilled at troubleshooting and making corrections when problems occur in the writing process.

Interpreting and Applying Research to Writing Challenges

Teaching writing to many students can be challenging as they all possess individual needs, individual learning styles, and individual emotional responses to feedback. There is no one way to teach writing that will address the needs of every student, and the techniques may vary between genres, topics, and audiences. However, teachers should keep in mind the five fundamental criteria, which research has shown to be most effective.

The most important way a student learns is by doing—being given as many opportunities to write as possible. Activities such a pre-writing, writing on prompts, peer revision, and writing in groups should be implemented as often as possible in many different types of subjects.

A welcoming, encouraging, and judgment-free atmosphere is the most conducive environment for learning how to write, where students can feel comfortable in engaging in activities, sharing what they have written, brainstorming ideas, providing feedback to peers, and giving/receiving mutual respect.

Feedback should be specific and individualized—teachers must provide sufficient time to students to help them reach their writing goals and improve on their weaknesses, while also being mindful of students' responses to criticism. At the same time, teachers should give students the tools they need to self-evaluate their own writing and identify areas of improvement.

Strategies for teaching writing should be varied and comprehensive. Teachers should be able to adjust their pedagogical techniques to meet individualized needs while still maintaining the fundamental approaches to teaching all elements of the writing process.

Learning is often achieved through writing—not only of the writing process, but of all subjects in general. Keeping a reflective journal of what they have learned at school encourages students to learn the material as they must make sense of it through writing it down. Having a student write on a historical event or a scientific theory provides the same advantage. Writing skills learned in a language arts class can and should be utilized in other subject areas.

While there are many challenges to teaching a range of students, each student can have his or her learning needs met if the teacher utilizes all five of these methods in his or her instructional approaches.

High-quality writing takes more than simply good writing skills and a knowledge of vocabulary. High-quality writing takes a lot of planning, writing, and revising in order to meet the standards of the audience. Many factors go into high-quality writing, but some major ones, including content, voice, and word choice, are listed below:

Content

The **content** of a piece of writing includes the ideas, structure, language, and effect of a particular text. Content begins with a writer being able to effectively brainstorm and research their topic in order to obtain credibility as an author. Thorough research of a topic and proper citation is the first step in creating good content. Organization of the text is also important to high-quality content, as is knowledge of vocabulary and sentence structure. Finally, good writing content will have an intended effect on the audience, whether that be persuading the audience to act or informing them of how something is done.

Voice

The voice an author selects is also important to note. An author's **voice** is that element of style that indicates their personality. It's important that authors move us as readers; therefore, they will choose a voice that helps them do that. An author's voice may be satirical or authoritative. It may be light-hearted or serious in tone. It may be silly or humorous as well. Voice, as an element of style, can be vague in nature and difficult to identify, since it's also referred to as an author's tone, but it is that element unique to the author. It is the author's "self." A reader can expect an author's voice to vary across literary genres. A nonfiction author will generally employ a more neutral voice than an author of fiction, but use caution when trying to identify voice. Do not confuse an author's voice with a particular character's voice.

Word Choice

An author's choice of words—also referred to as **diction**—helps to convey his or her meaning in a particular way. Through diction, an author can convey a particular tone—e.g., a humorous tone, a serious tone—in order to support the thesis in a meaningful way to the reader.

Connotation is when an author chooses words or phrases that invoke ideas or feelings other than their literal meaning. An example of the use of connotation is the word *cheap*, which suggests something is poor in value or negatively describes a person as reluctant to spend money. When something or someone is described this way, the reader is more inclined to have a particular image or feeling about it or him/her. Thus, connotation can be a very effective language tool in creating emotion and swaying opinion. However, connotations are sometimes hard to pin down because varying emotions can be associated with a word. Generally, though, connotative meanings tend to be fairly consistent within a specific cultural group.

Denotation refers to words or phrases that mean exactly what they say. It is helpful when a writer wants to present hard facts or vocabulary terms with which readers may be unfamiliar. Some examples of denotation are the words *inexpensive* and *frugal*. *Inexpensive* refers to the cost of something, not its value, and *frugal* indicates that a person is conscientiously watching his or her spending. These terms do not elicit the same emotions that *cheap* does.

Authors sometimes choose to use both, but what they choose and when they use it is what critical readers need to differentiate. One method isn't inherently better than the other; however, one may create a better effect, depending upon an author's intent. If, for example, an author's purpose is to inform, to instruct, and to familiarize readers with a difficult subject, his or her use of connotation may be helpful. However, it may also undermine credibility and confuse readers. An author who wants to create a credible, scholarly effect in his or her text would most likely use denotation, which emphasizes literal, factual meaning and examples.

Literacy Instruction and Assessments

Different Types of Assessments

Formal and Informal Assessments

Formal assessments, such as selected-response questions, are a useful and quick way to grade students as opposed to free response assessments. However, informal assessments are an even quicker and more frequently used method of assessing students. Informal assessments can be conducted after a modeled lesson and before independent practice. The use of individual whiteboards and a few quick selected response questions prepared before the lesson is a helpful tactic for teachers to quickly survey which students grasped the concepts and which students need additional reinforcement. Those who still need to master the skill can then be efficiently identified and grouped together for a small reteach.

Demonstrating Ability to Interpret Results

When using the results from formal assessments addressing multiple skills, it is important to group students according to ability for the particular skill of interest from the assessment and not just on the overall score. However, the overall score may be beneficial for grouping with regards to pacing and complexity of questions.

Results of Assessments

Grouping students should be continuous and change daily, or at least weekly. Each student's needs change from concept to concept. Assessments must be ongoing and frequent. Results from these ongoing assessments should be the driving force behind the grouping of students. Lessons and groups should be adjusted to the needs of the students.

Oral and Written Methods for Assessing Students' Progress

Entry-level assessments, progress monitoring, and summative assessments need to be administered in order to determine students' print awareness, letter recognition, and alphabetic principle knowledge to identify misconceptions that can be remediated in future lessons. Formal and informal assessment methods are as follows:

- **Print awareness** is easily assessed through observation. Teachers can give students a book and ask them to demonstrate their tracking and orientation knowledge. Similarly, teachers can ask students to identify parts of a book, such as its title or page numbers.

- The **Concepts About Print (CAP) test** assesses a student's print awareness. The CAP test is administered one-on-one, typically at the beginning and middle of a student's kindergarten year. During the CAP test, the teacher asks a student questions about a book's print. The teacher records the student's responses to the questions asked on a standardized rubric. This helps to identify specific areas of weakness for each student in terms of print awareness. These areas can then be reinforced and retaught in future lessons.

Planned Observations

"**The Observation Survey**" created by Marie Clay, can be beneficial in the assessment of a student's letter recognition and alphabetic principle knowledge. The Observation Survey includes six literacy tasks:

1. Letter Identification
2. Concepts About Print
3. Writing Vocabulary
4. Hearing and Recording Sounds in Words
5. Text Reading
6. Word Test

During such assessments, a student may be asked to identify a letter's name, its sound, rhyming pairs, isolated initial/final phonemes, blending of compound words/syllables, and word segments, or to add or delete phonemes in words. Similarly, teachers can say a letter and ask students to write that letter on a sheet of paper. The teacher records student responses. In this way, the teacher can identify the skills that have not yet been mastered by a single student, small group, or entire class. The teacher can then use any of the aforementioned strategies to reinforce those skills within individuals, small groups, or whole-class instruction.

Analyzing Assessments to Guide Instructional Decisions and Differentiate Instruction

Whether an instructor uses informal or formal assessment, **data** will be produced from the assessment. This data, both written or gained through observation, is highly valuable in diagnosing whether to change teaching methods in order to accelerate students' reading skills development. Data-driven instruction guides reading improvement for all students simply because the data provides clear indications of where students are facing reading challenges or demonstrating strengths.

Differentiated instruction acknowledges that, while a group of students may be learning the same subject, the way each student learns and processes the subject is different. This technique looks at the different learning methods and reading areas that students respond best to in order to effect change.

Therefore, an educator can then tailor, or differentiate, lessons to build on these skills and expedite the learning process. Differentiated instruction is divided into interest-based and ability-based instruction.

Much of a student's performance is based on their interest in the subject at hand. Sometimes a student may show difficulty reading because he or she isn't engaged in the material. One way to encourage reading growth is to allow students to choose their learning activities. This will give students ownership over their own education, enabling them to have fun while learning and to use specific activities they feel help them improve their reading abilities. For example, students more interested in visual activities may find reading more beneficial than listening to oral reading exercises.

Ability-based differentiation focuses on three core focus areas that determine reading proficiency and build skill. The first area of focus examines students' conceptual understanding of reading. If a teacher uses vocabulary or reading comprehension exercises in class, they will be able to examine how students are performing and modify instruction to address any confusion. This can also indicate students' preferences as well. The second differentiation looks at how students analyze and use the reading. Instructors must look at how students respond to questions and whether their interpretation is accurate. The final differentiation looks at how students evaluate and perform reading, creating a reaction that responds to the reading. The third differentiation looks at interpretation with the added step of using this knowledge to write or say something without being prompted that involves the reading. Identifying issues in one of these areas will narrow down where more emphasis must be placed to improve reading skills. Each reading area will affect the other two; improving one differentiated area will impact the others.

Analyzing and Interpreting Students' Formal and Informal Assessment Results to Inform Students and Stakeholders

Assessments are useful for identifying which students may be struggling with certain criteria as well as the specific areas of difficulty. This information can be used to inform students, their parents, and stakeholders, as well as inform teachers as to how to best modify instruction. Assessments can also indicate how well the material is being presented or provide vital clues on how to modify an individual student's instruction to help them grasp the content better. Generally, two types of assessments are used: informal and formal.

Informal assessments are not planned and lack a typical format or timeline. They can be as simple as watching and listening to how the students respond to answers in class or perform classwork. Observation is key. The instructor should be perceptive to how students not only respond to reading and language concepts but also to how they are interpreting them. If a student isn't understanding something such as a cultural reading concept, it may indicate that a more in-depth explanation is required. This will help the teacher adapt the instruction to enable the student to self-correct his or her own performance.

Formal assessments are partially based on observation, but are planned and implemented with the design to see how students respond to specific stimuli. They give a clearer indication of where students' weaknesses lie or whether they are on point in grasping the material. There are two primary methods for conducting formal assessments. The most conventional is a simple pencil-and-paper test in which students read prewritten questions and respond to them in writing. These physical answers provide a direct window into what the students know and how their reading comprehension is progressing.

Performance assessments are a little less concrete but can provide a lot of insight into the student's mind-set and reactions that are more three-dimensional than a written assessment. This method does not use written responses, but instead analyzes students' performance in response to reading questions or activities. When giving performance assessments, it's important to bear in mind key questions: Does the student understand what they just read, did they seem uncomfortable when presenting their answer, and how accurate was their response? From here, new teaching strategies can be implemented, or the instructor can identify ways to provide specialized assistance to boost students' skills.

Evaluating the Appropriateness of Assessment Instruments and Practices

Most research has already been done to evaluate the effectiveness of certain strategies of formative and summative assessments. Because there are innumerable approaches to the art of teaching, the only real way one can evaluate a strategy's effectiveness is to monitor how the students improve over time with any given approach. If one strategy does not seem to show much improvement, then a different one should be used. Because each student has individual needs, a teacher may need to utilize several different techniques tailored to the needs of each student.

- To monitor student process, the following approaches should be considered:
- Asking questions in the classroom during and after a lecture
- Cultivating a classroom environment that encourages student questions
- Circulating around the classroom and engaging in one-on-one conferences during in-class assignments
- Giving periodic quizzes
- Leaving sufficient time for questions at the end of a lecture
- Assigning and collecting homework and returning the corrected material immediately
- Giving midterms and final exams
- Conducting regular reviews of student progress through the above methods and adjusting teaching strategies accordingly

Another strategy to assess student knowledge and identify areas in need of development is to create a K-W-L chart in preparation for a lesson that introduces a new topic. First, students are prompted for what they already know (K). Then, they are asked to consider what they want to know (W). The instructor may then choose to adjust the lesson by spending less time on areas that students are already proficient in and by spending more time on areas that students want to know more about. Finally, after the lesson, students can be asked to reflect on what they learned (L). A K-W-L chart lets students know that they are active participants in their own learning.

It is almost as important to provide feedback and evaluate a student's skill level as it is to teach. Most classes utilize both formative and summative assessments as a grading template. Although assessment and grading are not the same thing, assessments are often used to award a grade. A **formative assessment** monitors the student's progress in learning and allows continuous feedback throughout the course in the form of homework and in-class assignments, such as quizzes, writing workshops, conferences, or inquiry-based writing prompts. These assessments typically make up a lower percent of the overall grade. Alternatively, a **summative assessment** compares a student's progress in learning against some sort of standard, such as against the progress of other students or by the number of correct answers. These assessments usually make up a higher percent of the overall grade and come in the form of midterm or final exams, papers, or major projects.

One evidence-based method used to assess a student's progress is a rubric. A **rubric** is an evaluation tool that explicitly states the expectations of the assignment and breaks it down into different components. Each component has a clear description and relationship to the assignment as a whole. For writing, rubrics may be **holistic,** judging the overall quality of the writing, or they can be **analytic,** in which different aspects of the writing are evaluated, e.g., structure, style, word choices, and punctuation.

Rubrics can be used in all aspects of a curriculum, including reading comprehension, oral presentations, speeches, performances, papers, projects, and listening comprehension. They are usually formative in nature, but can be summative depending on the purpose. Rubrics allow instructors to provide specific feedback and allow students to understand the expectations for an assignment.

An example of an analytic rubric is displayed below:

Name ________________________ **Date** ________________________

Essay Rubric	**4** **Mastery**	**3** **Satisfactory**	**2** **Needs Improvement**	**1** **Poor**
Writing Quality	-Excellent usage of voice and style -Outstanding organizational skills -Wealth of relevant information	-Style and voice of essay was interesting -Mostly organized -Useful amount of information	-Inconsistent style and voice -Lacked clear organization -Small amount of useful information	-No noticeable style or voice -Virtually no organization -No relevant information
Grammar Conventions	-Essentially no mistakes in grammar -Correct spelling throughout	-Minor amount of grammar and spelling mistakes	-Many errors in grammar conventions and spelling	-Too many grammatical errors to understand the meaning of the piece

Another research-proven strategy is **conferencing,** in which students participate in a group discussion that usually involves the teacher. Students learn best when they can share their thoughts on what they've read or written and receive feedback from their peers and instructors. For writing, conferencing is frequently done in the revision stage. Through discussion, students are also able to enhance their listening and speaking skills. Conferences can be done in a one-on-one setting, typically between a student and instructor, or in a small group of students with guidance from the instructor. They are useful in that they provide an atmosphere of respect where a student can share his or her work and thoughts without fear of judgment. They increase motivation and allow students to explore a variety of topics and discussions. Conferences also allow the instructor to provide immediate feedback or prompt students for deeper explanations of their ideas. The most successful conferences have these characteristics:

- Have a set structure
- Focus on only a few points—too many are confusing or distracting
- Are solution based

- Allow students to both discuss their thoughts/works and receive/provide feedback for others
- Encourage the use of appropriate vocabulary
- Provide motivation and personal satisfaction or pleasure from reading and writing
- Allow a time where questions can be asked and immediately answered

Rubrics and conferencing are both methods that provide useful **feedback,** one of the most important elements in the progress of a student's learning. Feedback is essentially corrective instruction delivered in writing, either verbally or non-verbally. Research has shown that the following techniques are the most effective when giving feedback:

Being Specific

For a student to know exactly how he or she is doing, feedback should be directed towards specific components of a student's writing, listening, or speaking skills, not a holistic overview. For example, writing "Excellent!" on a student's paper or homework is not useful information as it's unclear what was done well. A paper should provide useful comments throughout the body of the work, for example, "Wording is confusing here," or "Great use of adjectives." However, instructor comments should not overwhelm the student's writing; they should be used to focus their attention on specific areas of success or improvement. This encourages the student to keep doing what he or she is doing well and work on what needs improvement without being overwhelmed.

Being Sensitive

Giving feedback is precarious in nature as it entirely depends upon the emotional and mental states of the receiver. Some students do well with "tough love," while others may be discouraged and disheartened to see a slew of comments on their paper. Teachers should pay attention to how a student reacts to feedback. As a general rule, feedback should focus more on the positives so as not to damage self-esteem, while teaching students new techniques for self-correction, instead of simply criticizing what they've done. Also, it's important to try and be aware of the types of feedback each student responds the most effectively to, for example, providing oral feedback for students who don't read well.

Being Prompt

Feedback should be presented sooner rather than later, so that students will not have time to repeat mistakes they are unaware of that may become habitual. Studies have shown that students who are given immediate feedback display a greater increase in performance than those who were given feedback later in the term. As soon as the action has happened, it is important give the appropriate praise or critique so that the student associates the feedback with the action.

Being Explicit

It is important to explain the purpose of the feedback before it is given so that a student does not feel controlled, too closely examined, or competitive. This can cause the learner to feel self-conscious and discourage him or her from performing his or her best. The importance of feedback and how it is meant to improve on a personal skill set should be explained to the student.

Being Focused

Teachers should try and keep the feedback in alignment with the goal the student is expected to achieve. Too much feedback, especially if it is unrelated to the goal, can be overwhelming and distracting from the purpose of the assignment or paper.

Here are some other tips to consider when giving feedback:

- Teachers should be aware of their body language and facial expressions when giving feedback—a frown or grimace can be very discouraging, even if the written feedback was mostly positive.
- It's conducive to concentrate on one thing at a time. If a student submits a paper with a lot of errors, for example, it may be helpful to identify a prevalent pattern of error and work through strategies to correct it so that student does not feel overwhelmed.
- Using effective rubrics can make all the difference—letting students know exactly what is expected will provide them with a basis on which to model their techniques and skills.
- Students should be educated on giving feedback. This can be demonstrated by example and through instruction how to give feedback in a positive, constructive way and correct any behavior that trends toward disrespect or excessive competition. Students should also provide feedback to the teacher as well.
- Teachers should not give the same comments to every student, but make them personal.
- When offering criticism, teachers should always offer tips for how the student can improve.
- It's important to avoid personal comments, e.g., "You're so smart!" or "Math isn't your best subject." Rather, the comments should focus on the writing: e.g., "The organization of this paper is clear."
- Students shouldn't be compared to each other, e.g., "Look how perfectly Victor composed this sentence!" This can galvanize the students into competing with one another.

Selecting Appropriate Classroom Organizational Formats for Specific Instructional Objectives

Flexible Grouping and Addressing Changing Needs

Another way to differentiate instruction is the use of groups and collaboration in going over or learning the reading material. In class, there are two forms of grouping instruction: teacher-based and student-based. A well-balanced and flexible learning environment will incorporate both types of grouping exercises to help students approach reading from multiple angles and practice problem-solving and critical-thinking skills. Students also strengthen social skills through flexible grouping.

Teacher-based grouping is organized by the instructor. This is the best method for introducing students to new material and exploring key concepts. Instructors may also choose to break the class up into small groups to provide instruction and work with students individually while the class is working. The goal here is to monitor students directly and provide differentiated instruction when necessary. This is the more variable of the two groupings and provides a more direct line for teacher intervention. However, students can also grasp concepts by interacting with their peers.

Student-based grouping focuses on students dictating the way the group is formed, essentially freeing the teacher to observe how they are interacting with others and approaching reading topics. Students can be given the option to form their groups independently or simply opening the class to a group discussion. This is different from actually lecturing because it allows students to talk about the reading subject among themselves as opposed to just listening and learning from the instructor. Posing questions for the class is a great way for students to learn correct answers and ask questions through simple conversation. Student-based groups are also excellent for school projects, allowing group members to pool their knowledge for success.

Flexible grouping relies on utilizing both teacher-based and student-based groupings throughout the instructional period. Using one more than the other isn't necessarily unbalanced, but the instructor should try to incorporate both groupings in order to broaden the students' experience. The teacher's choice in using either method should also relate to how they are implementing differentiated teaching methods. Educators can combine the use of grouping to suit activities and lessons for all areas in which students may be facing difficulties in order to boost confidence and clarify material.

Response to Intervention Process (RTI) is a process designed to help struggling students catch up through intervention and monitoring in a general education classroom. Students who suffer from undiagnosed reading disorders, attention issues, or even ESL students struggling to learn the language may begin to fall behind the rest of the students in reading skills. RTI is an informal intervention process done by the school that focuses on utilizing research and technology to help the student "catch up" to the rest of the class. The school's RTI teams will review assessments taken of each child in the classroom to determine which students need these instructional interventions. Teachers track students through **progress monitoring**, a process that measures whether or not the interventions are making a difference.

Although there are various ways to do RTI, it is usually set up as a three-tier system of support, also known as **multi-tier system of supports** (MTSS). The tiers below are in order of least intense to most intense:

Tier 1: High-Quality Classroom Instruction, Screening, and Group Interventions

In Tier 1 interventions, the entire classroom is assessed using **universal screening**, where everyone's skillset is measured in a general education classroom by using methods that have been proven to be effective. Students who receive Tier 1 support are generally divided into small groups based on their skill level. Many students receive Tier 1 support because their math or reading skills are not quite at grade level. Progress of Tier 1 instruction is monitored, and many students are able to effectively catch up to grade level.

Tier 2: Targeted Interventions

Tier 2 interventions are for students who do not yet reach the potential of Tier 1 intervention. **Targeted interventions** give more detailed attention to the student who is struggling in addition to the regular classroom instruction. Since targeted interventions are done in addition to the regular classroom instruction, they are sometimes conducted during extracurricular activities or electives.

Tier 3: Intensive Interventions and Comprehensive Evaluation

The third tier of the RTI process is **intensive intervention**. Intensive interventions are often done one-on-one or in small groups with other special-needs children. Usually only one or two students in a classroom will need this kind of instruction, so one-on-one help is more readily available for this tier.

Methods for the Diagnosis, Prevention, and Intervention of Common Emergent Literacy Difficulties

Depending on where diagnostic data indicates areas of students' difficulty, reteaching certain material is a promising starting point to help students overcome their reading issues. This isn't a step backward in instruction; it's an alteration. Differentiated instruction offers opportunities for students to relearn reading principles in ways that best fit them individually.

If students are having reading difficulties, the lessons can be modified to be clearer or address the specific areas of difficulty. Sometimes, this means teaching the material in a different way entirely. Recalling the areas of differentiated instruction, there are many components of reading skills and understanding. If a student is having difficulty in one area, such as reading analysis, building on his or her conceptual knowledge and performance/evaluation reading skills could help connect the gaps in his or her analysis. For example, instead of just reading and responding to questions, students might grasp the material better through the use of simple logic. Breaking down sentence context and discussing the reading, rather than just asking questions and giving answers, can help bridge the gap in understanding, thus allowing students to draw further insight from the reading.

Considering what kind of activities improve which aspects of reading is also important. If students have phonetic problems, instructors should introduce activities that analyze the different aspects of words, as well as sounding out words, to build familiarity with English vocabulary and structure. To strengthen reading comprehension, incorporating activities that help students visualize what they read will help. Instructors should encourage students to paraphrase and summarize texts to examine their strengths and weaknesses as well. This will help the instructor identify what kind of differentiation may be necessary. Instead of shying away from challenging areas, it's important to modify lessons to help students approach the material with better focus and a renewed interest.

Student engagement will be instrumental in improving reading skills. Again, differential instruction encourages not only differentiated lessons and activities based on student ability, but also on interest. Having students design their own reading activities allows them to expand their skill sets while becoming eager to learn more. Activities such as synonym association for vocabulary words or even physically drawing out a given sentence will engage reading comprehension, analysis, and replication skills. Further assessments should be done to gauge the effectiveness of the new instruction methods.

Communication and Media Literacy

Characteristics of Penmanship

While most adults perceive handwriting as second nature, it is actually a complicated skill to master within the course of child development. This mastery includes: letter formation, sizing, alignment, spacing, speed and fluency, and overall legibility.

- **Letter Formation**: Letter formation refers to the practice of constructing accurate letters, shapes, and numbers using horizontal and vertical lines, circles, curves, intersecting lines, dots, and diagonal lines.
- **Letter Sizing**: Letter sizing refers to a student's ability to properly write within a designated space while maintaining an appropriate dimension for the letters, shapes, and numbers that are being recorded; this skill ensures that students are not writing extremely huge or small letters that do not account for the spatial parameters of the paper.
- **Letter Alignment:** Letter alignment refers to whether students have a sense of where one word/number/shape ends and another word/number/shape begins; it is a skill that ensures that students are constantly using the bottom handwriting lines as a baseline for each letter, number, or shape.
- **Letter Spacing**: Letter spacing simply means a student's ability to leave the appropriate amount of space between lines.
- **Speed and Fluency**: Speed and fluency refers to the increase in automatic accuracy and the decrease in time it takes for a student to write; speed and fluency can only be enhanced if all of the previous categories are mastered; additionally, students need to enhance their tactile skills, visual motor integration, and fine motor coordination.
- **Legibility**: Legibility is a category that encompasses all previously-mentioned categories; it refers to the overall ability for other people to recognize the formation, sizing, alignment, spacing, and fluency of a student's writing; a student's speed should not sacrifice legibility.

Listening and Speaking Strategies

Understanding Effective Delivery of a Speech or Presentation

Good public speakers all have several characteristics in common. It is not enough to simply write a speech, but it must also be delivered in a manner that is both engaging and succinct. The following qualities are inherent to good public speaking.

Confidence is possibly the most important attribute a speaker can have. It instills trust in the listener that the person knows what he or she is talking about and that he or she is credible and competent. Confidence is displayed by making brief eye contact—about 2-3 seconds—with different members of the audience to demonstrate that the speaker is engaged. It is also displayed in his or her tone of voice—strong, light-hearted, and natural. A nervous speaker can easily be identified by a small, quivering voice. Confidence is also conveyed by the speaker facing the audience; turning one's back may demonstrate insecurity.

Authenticity is another quality of an effective speaker, as it makes a person more relatable and believable to the audience. Speeches that are memorized word-for-word can give the impression of being inauthentic as the monologue does not flow quite naturally, especially if the speaker accidentally fumbles or forgets. Memorizing speeches can also lead to a monotonous tone, which is sure to put the audience to sleep, or worse, a misinterpreted tone, which can cause the audience to stop listening entirely or even become offended. Therefore, speeches should be practiced with a natural intonation and not be memorized mechanically.

Connection with the audience is another important aspect of public speaking. Speakers should engage with their listeners by the use of storytelling and visual or auditory aids, as well as asking questions that the audience can participate in. Visual and auditory aids could range from an interesting PowerPoint presentation to a short video clip to physical objects the audience can pass around to a soundtrack. The use of appropriate humor also allows the audience to connect with the speaker on a more personal level and will make the speech sound more like a conversation than a one-sided lecture. Speakers who are passionate about their subject inspire their listeners to care about what they're saying; they transfer their energy into the audience. This level of connection will encourage their listeners to want to be there.

Succinctness and **purposeful repetition** ensures that the audience's attention remains focused on the message at hand. Repeating the overall point of the speech in different ways helps listeners remember what the speaker is trying to tell them, even when the speech is over. A speech that is longer than necessary will cause listeners to become bored and stop absorbing information. Keeping the speech short and sweet and leaving more time for questions at the end will ensure that the audience stays engaged.

There are many different styles a speaker can utilize, but the most important thing speakers should keep in mind is maintaining a connection with the audience. This will help ensure that the audience will remain open and focused enough to hear and absorb the message.

Evaluating the Advantages and Disadvantages of Different Media

Each visual aid has its advantages and disadvantages and should be used sparingly to avoid distracting the audience. Visual aids should be used to emphasize a presentation's message, not overwhelm it.

Microsoft PowerPoint is currently the most commonly used visual aid. It allows for pictures, words, videos, and music to be presented on the same screen and is essentially just a projection of a computer screen, allowing easy and quick access to all forms of media as well as the Internet. However, a PowerPoint presentation should not be overwhelmed with information, such as text-heavy slides, as audience members will spend more time reading the slides than listening to the speaker. Conversely, they may avoid reading it entirely, and the presentation will serve no purpose. A PowerPoint presentation that uses too many animations and visual elements may also detract from the presence of the speaker.

Handouts are a great way for the audience to feel more involved in a presentation. They can present lots of information that may be too much for a PowerPoint, and they can also be taken home and reviewed later. The primary disadvantage of handouts is that the audience may choose to read rather than to listen, thus missing the main points the speaker is trying to make, or they may decide not to read it at all. The best handouts are those that do not contain all the information of a presentation, but allow for the audience to take notes and complete the handout by listening or asking questions.

Whiteboards and **blackboards** are excellent for explaining difficult concepts by allowing the audience to follow along with a process and copy down their own version of what is being written on the board. This visual aid is best used to explain concepts in mathematics and science. The main problem with the board, however, is that there can be limited space, and if the presenter runs out of room, he or she will have to erase the content written on the board and will be unable to refer back to it later. He or she may also have to wait for the entire audience to write the information down, which slows down the presentation.

Overhead projectors are wonderful in that a speaker can use a prepared transparency and draw images or add words to emphasize or explain concepts. They can also erase these additions but still keep the original content if they wish to alter their method to fit the audience or provide further explanations. Similar to PowerPoint presentations, overhead projections should limit the amount of text to keep the audience focused on listening.

Physical objects are a useful way to connect with the audience and allow them to feel more involved. Because people interact with the physical world, physical objects can help solidify understanding of difficult concepts. However, they can be distracting if not properly introduced. If they are presented too early or are visible during the presentation, the audience will focus on the objects, wondering what purpose they may serve instead of listening to the speaker. Objects should instead be hidden until it is time to show them and then collected when they are no longer useful.

Videos are a great way to enliven a presentation by giving it sound, music, flow, and images. They are excellent for emphasizing points, providing evidence for ideas, giving context, or setting tone. The major issue with videos is that the presenter is unable to speak at this point, so this form of media should be used sparingly and purposefully. Also, overly-long videos may lose the audience's attention.

Effective public speakers are aware of the advantages and disadvantages of all forms of media and often choose to utilize a combination of several different types to keep the presentations lively and the audience engaged.

Presenting Information Clearly, Concisely, and Logically

All information should be presented with a clear beginning, middle, and end. Distinct organization always makes any work more clear, concise, and logical.

For a presentation, this should involve choosing a primary topic and then discussing it in the following format:

- Introducing the speaker and the main topic
- Providing evidence, supporting details, further explanation of the topic in the main body
- Concluding it with a firm resolution and repetition of the main point

The beginning, middle, and end should also be linked with effective transitions that make the presentation flow well. For example, a presentation should always begin with an introduction by the speaker, including what he/she does and what he/she is there to present. Good transitional introductions may begin with statements such as *For those who do not know me, my name is...*, *As many of you know, I am...* or *Good morning everyone, my name is ____, and I am the new project manager.* A good introduction grabs the attention and interest of the audience.

After an introduction has been made, the speaker will then want to state the purpose of the presentation with a natural transition, such as *I am here to discuss the latest editions to our standard of procedure...* or *This afternoon, I would like to present the results of our latest findings.* Once the purpose has been identified, the speaker will want to adhere to the main idea announced. The presenter should be certain to keep the main idea to one sentence as too much information can confuse an audience; an introduction should be succinct and to the point.

Supporting information should always be presented in concise, easy-to-read formats such as bullet points or lists—if visual aids are presented during the presentation. Good transitions such as *Let's begin with...* or *Now to look at...* make the presentation flow smoothly and logically, helping listeners to keep ideas organized as they are presented. Keeping the material concise is extremely important in a presentation, and visual aids should be used only to emphasize points or explain ideas. All the supporting information should relate back to the main idea, avoiding unnecessary tangents.

Finally, a firm conclusion involves repeating the main point of the presentation by either inspiring listeners to act or by reiterating the most important points made in the speech. It should also include an expression of gratitude to the audience as well as transition to opening the floor for questions.

Instructional Methods for Developing Listening and Speaking Skills

Identifying Techniques to Use in Collaborative Discussions

Effective oral communication requires the ability to express oneself clearly and diplomatically. It is imperative to teach students from a young age the value of respecting oneself and others, as well as the ability to keep an open mind during discussion and not to make things personal. Students should also be taught to keep the flow of discussion in alignment with the topic at hand and to listen actively as well as speak.

Age-appropriate Topics

Keeping topics **age-appropriate** is one way to stimulate productive conversation. It is important to consider the breadth of knowledge that an individual or group is likely to have. One of the primary objectives of conferencing in an academic setting is to challenge students into thinking critically. Choosing topics that are too advanced or beyond the realm of their knowledge would be an act in futility as they do not have the appropriate tools to engage in conversation. Similarly, topics that are too simple will not be beneficial as they will not be challenging. When choosing a topic, teachers should consider the average age of students, their vocabulary, their reading and writing skills, and life experiences they are likely to have.

Facilitating Appropriate Discussion Behavior

Once an appropriate topic has been chosen, discussions should be monitored to facilitate appropriate behavior. It is very important to stress that all perspectives will be welcome and respected and to make sure that student inquiries and responses are in alignment with that principle. The following are suggestions for facilitating appropriate discussion behavior in a group setting:

1. Cultivating an environment of inclusion and mutual respect

- Students should introduce themselves and be encouraged to address each other by name. "Icebreaker" games are an effective way to get students to know each other before engaging in any discussions.

- Allowing enough time for students to think about the topic and thoughtfully contribute to the discussion will encourage inclusion.

- The use of insulting or disrespectful language, tone, or body language should not be permitted.
- Students should be made aware of differences in cultural and social perspectives.
- Students should be encouraged to be mindful of the language they are using.
- Teachers should not make assumptions on how students will respond or behave based on their cultural, racial, or religious backgrounds.
- Everyone should have a chance to speak—e.g., teachers should not show favoritism towards a particular student or set of students or allow more tenacious students to dominate the discussion.
- Particular perspectives or ideas should not be verbally or nonverbally discouraged. Instead, students should be encouraged to think critically about what is being discussed and what they are saying.
- It's important not to rush students or make any student feel as though his or her comments and ideas are not important.
- Facilitators should not display a sense of superiority.

2. Keeping discussions productive

- Teachers should be explicit about the expectations or goals of the discussion and guide students back towards the topic if they get off track.
- Demonstrating what disrespectful behavior looks like at the start of the discussion can help establish clear expectations. Students should be reminded not to take things personally or to identify with any emotions they may experience from the discussion and, instead, approach the topics with logic.
- Ideas or counterarguments should be related to personal experiences or backed with evidence. Students should validate each other's ideas first before arguing in a respectful way, such as "I respect what you are saying," or "I understand where you are coming from."
- Stereotyping and sweeping generalizations should be identified when used and subsequently avoided.
- If a student goes off on a tangent, he or she should be guided back to the primary topic or purpose by asking him/her to summarize what he/she is saying.
- If the discussion becomes heated or emotional, students should be encouraged to explore the real issue that is causing the emotions. The teacher might say, "I think there is a greater issue here that we should discuss openly and respectfully." Alternatively, students can be asked if they would like to take break and resume the discussion later. A teacher may also wish to bring up the differing values that are being displayed in the conference in an unbiased way so that students can recognize what they're truly arguing about.
- It's important that teachers avoid arguing with a student if the student attacks them. Acknowledging this kind of behavior only validates it.

3. Encouraging participants/guiding the flow of discussion

- For shy students, it's helpful to call on them by name and ask if they have any thoughts/feedback, while being nonjudgmental if they admit they don't know or don't have anything to say.
- Asking questions and requesting examples when students make a comment or present an idea helps guide the discussion flow.
- Writing student comments down and asking for other participants to elaborate on them will encourage more participation.
- Depending on the exercise, giving the students a topic or asking a student to present one will elicit participation.
- For students who have trouble participating in large groups, breaking up discussion into smaller groups will help them feel more comfortable.

Ensuring Accountability

One of the most challenging things about group discussions is ensuring that the students have prepared for it. For a discussion to be as productive as possible, students should be held accountable for completing their due preparation, such as homework, pre-class readings, or research. This can be done in numerous ways, such as by requiring the students to complete an at-home assignment and submit it electronically by midnight the previous night or on the day before. This assignment could be worth a significant grade to encourage students to complete it, and it could be in the following forms: responding to a question on an online discussion board, completing quizzes in reading comprehension, or answering true or false questions.

To ensure accountability during the discussion, students should be encouraged to participate by asking questions and asked to elaborate when something is unclear. Letting them take notes and leaving plenty of time for the formulation of thoughts and follow-up questions will increase accountability. After the discussion has ended, passing out a handout that students can fill out or having them summarize the discussion online are two beneficial strategies for accountability.

Evaluating the Effectiveness of Strategies for Effective Discussions

To increase student participation in discussion, teachers should consider the following strategies:

- Asking students what they know about the topic and writing their responses on the white or blackboard, which creates an outline of what the students do and don't know as well as increases their self-esteem.
- Having an anonymous question box where students can write down questions that can be read before or during the discussion, being careful not to react negatively to any questions, verbally or non-verbally, so as not to damage self-esteem
- Allowing students to teach each other, proven as the most effective way to learn something is to teach someone else what has been learned—e.g., writing their own tests or homework, conducting one-on-one conferences

- Dividing the class into smaller groups if students seem non-responsive, which helps shy students feel less intimidated and more comfortable in smaller settings

- Allowing students to work together, which encourages them to interact with others and allows them to feel more comfortable with doing so when it comes time for group discussion

- Asking students to create a topic to get them to initiate the conversation

- Using games to make the discussion fun and motivate students to participate

The effectiveness of these strategies will depend entirely on the class. Teachers should use the assessment tools discussed previously to determine whether the techniques have been effective and adjust the teaching style accordingly.

Many of the above strategies can be used for one-on-one discussions as well. The most important things to keep in mind in keeping a student engaged and comfortable during a one-on-one discussion are as follows:

- Asking follow-up questions
- Clarifying any unclear or obscure questions or statements
- Never making the student feel unintelligent or inadequate
- Being as reassuring as possible, particularly if a student expresses insecurity in his or her abilities
- Being patient and allowing time for the student to sort out thoughts and ask necessary questions

Selecting and Evaluating a Wide Array of Resources for Research and Presentation

Identifying Relevant Information During Research

Relevant information is that which is pertinent to the topic at hand. Particularly when doing research online, it is easy for students to get overwhelmed with the wealth of information available to them. Before conducting research, then, students need to begin with a clear idea of the question they want to answer.

For example, a student may be interested in learning more about marriage practices in Jane Austen's England. If that student types "marriage" into a search engine, he or she will have to sift through thousands of unrelated sites before finding anything related to that topic. Narrowing down search parameters can aid in locating relevant information.

When using a book, students can consult the table of contents, glossary, or index to discover whether the book contains relevant information before using it as a resource. If the student finds a hefty volume on Jane Austen, he or she can flip to the index in the back, look for the word marriage, and find out how many page references are listed in the book. If there are few or no references to the subject, it is probably not a relevant or useful source.

In evaluating research articles, students may also consult the title, abstract, and keywords before reading the article in its entirety. Referring to the date of publication will also determine whether the research contains up-to-date discoveries, theories, and ideas about the subject, or whether it is outdated.

Evaluating the Credibility of a Print or Digital Source

There are several additional criteria that need to be examined before using a source for a research topic.

The following questions will help determine whether a source is credible:

Author

- Who is he or she?
- Does he or she have the appropriate credentials—e.g., M.D, PhD?
- Is this person authorized to write on the matter through his/her job or personal experiences?
- Is he or she affiliated with any known credible individuals or organizations?
- Has he or she written anything else?

Publisher

- Who published/produced the work? Is it a well-known journal, like National Geographic, or a tabloid, like The National Enquirer?
- Is the publisher from a scholarly, commercial, or government association?
- Do they publish works related to specific fields?
- Have they published other works?
- If a digital source, what kind of website hosts the text? Does it end in .edu, .org, or .com?

Bias

- Is the writing objective? Does it contain any loaded or emotional language?
- Does the publisher/producer have a known bias, such as Fox News or CNN?
- Does the work include diverse opinions or perspectives?
- Does the author have any known bias—e.g., Michael Moore, Bill O'Reilly, or the Pope? Is he or she affiliated with any organizations or individuals that may have a known bias—e.g., Citizens United or the National Rifle Association?
- Does the magazine, book, journal, or website contain any advertising?

References

- Are there any references?
- Are the references credible? Do they follow the same criteria as stated above?
- Are the references from a related field?

Accuracy/Reliability

- Has the article, book, or digital source been peer reviewed?
- Are all of the conclusions, supporting details, or ideas backed with published evidence?
- If a digital source, is it free of grammatical errors, poor spelling, and improper English?
- Do other published individuals have similar findings?

Coverage

- Are the topic and related material both successfully addressed?
- Does the work add new information or theories to those of their sources?
- Is the target audience appropriate for the intended purpose?

Identifying Effective Research Practices

The purpose of all research is to provide an answer to an unknown question. Therefore, all good research papers pose the topic in the form of a question, which they will then seek to answer with clear ideas, arguments, and supporting evidence.

A **research question** is the primary focus of the research piece, and it should be formulated on a unique topic. To formulate a research question, writers begin by choosing a general topic of interest and then research the literature to determine what sort of research has already been done—the **literature review**. This helps them narrow the topic into something original and determine what still needs to be asked and researched about the topic. A solid question is very specific and avoids generalizations. The following question is offered for evaluation:

> *What is most people's favorite kind of animal?*

This research question is extremely broad without giving the paper any particular focus—it could go any direction and is not an exceptionally unique focus. To narrow it down, the question could consider a specific population:

> *What is the favorite animal of people in Ecuador?*

While this question is better, it does not address exactly why this research is being conducted or why anyone would care about the answer. Here's another possibility:

> *What does the animal considered as the most favorite of people in different regions throughout Ecuador reveal about their socioeconomic status?*

This question is extremely specific and gives a very clear direction of where the paper or project is going to go. However, sometimes the question can be too limited, where very little research has been conducted to create a solid paper, and the researcher most likely does not have the means to travel to Ecuador and travel door-to-door conducting a census on people's favorite animals. In this case, the research question would need to be broadened. Broadening a topic can mean introducing a wider range of criteria. Instead of people in Ecuador, the topic could be opened to include the population of South America or expanded to include more issues or considerations.

The Ethical Process for Collecting and Presenting Authentic Information While Avoiding Plagiarism

Identifying the Components of a Citation

Citation styles vary according to which style guide is consulted. Examples of commonly-used styles include MLA, APA, and Chicago/Turabian. Each citation style includes similar components, although the order and formatting of these components varies.

MLA Style

For an MLA style citation, components must be included or excluded depending on the source, so writers should determine which components are applicable to the source being cited. Here are the basic components:

- Author—last name, first name
- Title of source

- Title of container—e.g., a journal title or website
- Other contributors—e.g., editor or translator
- Version
- Number
- Publisher
- Publication date
- Location—e.g., the URL or DOI
- Date of Access—optional

APA Style

The following components can be found in APA style citations. Components must be included or excluded depending on the source, so writers should determine which components are applicable to the source being cited. The basic components are as follows:

- Author—last name, first initial, middle initial
- Publication date
- Title of chapter, article, or text
- Editor— last name, first initial, middle initial
- Version/volume
- Number/issue
- Page numbers
- DOI or URL
- Database—if article is difficult to locate
- City of publication
- State of publication, abbreviated
- Publisher

Chicago/Turabian Style

Chicago/Turabian style citations are also referred to as note systems and are used most frequently in the humanities and the arts. Components must be included or excluded depending on the source, so writers should determine which components are applicable to the source being cited. They contain the following elements:

- Author—last name, first name, middle initial
- Title of chapter or article—in quotation marks
- Title of source
- Editor—first name, last name
- Page numbers
- Version/volume
- Number/issue
- Page numbers
- Date of access
- DOI
- Publication location—city and state abbreviation/country
- Publisher
- Publication Date

Citing Source Material Appropriately

The following information contains examples of the common types of sources used in research as well as the formats for each citation style. First lines of citation entries are presented flush to the left margin, and second/subsequent details are presented with a hanging indent. Some examples of bibliography entries are presented below:

Book

- MLA
  Format: Last name, First name, Middle initial. *Title of Source*. Publisher, Publication Date.
  Example: Sampson, Maximus R. *Diaries from an Alien Invasion*. Campbell Press, 1989.
- APA
  Format: Last name, First initial, Middle initial. (Year Published) *Book Title.* City, State: Publisher.
  Example: Sampson, M. R. (1989). *Diaries from an Alien Invasion. Springfield, IL*: Campbell Press.
- Chicago/Turabian
  Format: Last name, First name, Middle initial. *Book Title*. City, State: Publisher, Year of publication.
  Example: Sampson, Maximus R. *Diaries from an Alien Invasion. Springfield, IL*: Campbell Press, 1989.

A Chapter in an Edited Book

- MLA
  Format: Last name, First name, Middle initial. "Title of Source." *Title of Container*, Other Contributors, Publisher, Publication Date, Location.
  Example: Sampson, Maximus R. "The Spaceship." *Diaries from an Alien Invasion*, edited by Allegra M. Brewer, Campbell Press, 1989, pp. 45-62.
- APA
  Format: Last name, First Initial, Middle initial. (Year Published) Chapter title. In First initial, Middle initial, Last Name (Ed.), *Book title* (pp. page numbers). City, State: Publisher.
  Example: Sampson, M. R. (1989). The Spaceship. In A. M. Brewer (Ed.), *Diaries from an Alien Invasion* (pp. 45-62). Springfield, IL: Campbell Press.
- Chicago/Turabian
  Format: Last name, First name, Middle initial. "Chapter Title." In Book Title, edited by Editor's Name (First, Middle In. Last), Page(s). City: Publisher, Year Published.
  Example: Sampson, Maximus R. "The Spaceship," in *Diaries from an Alien Invasion*, edited by Allegra M. Brewer, 45-62. Springfield: Campbell Press, 1989.

Article in a Journal

- MLA
  Format: Last name, First name, Middle initial. "Title of Source." *Title of Container*, Number, Publication Date, Location.
  Example: Rowe, Jason R. "The Grief Monster." *Strong Living*, vol. 9, no. 9, 2016, pp 25-31.
- APA
  Format: Last name, First initial, Middle initial. (Year Published). Title of article. *Name of Journal, volume*(issue), page(s).
  Example: Rowe, J. R. (2016). The grief monster. *Strong Living, 9*(9), 25-31.
- Chicago/Turabian:

Format: Last name, First name, Middle initial. "Title of Article." *Name of Journal* volume, issue (Year Published): Page(s).
Example: Rowe, Jason, R. "The Grief Monster." *Strong Living* 9, no. 9 (2016): 25-31.

Page on a Website

- MLA
  Format: Last name, First name, Middle initial. "Title of Article." *Name of Website*, date published (Day Month Year), URL. Date accessed (Day Month Year).
  Example: Rowe, Jason. "The Grief Monster." *Strong Living Online*, 9 Sept. 2016. http://www.somanylosses.com/the-grief-monster/html. Accessed 13 Sept. 2016.
- APA
  Format: Last name, First initial. Middle initial. (Date Published—Year, Month Day). Page or article title. Retrieved from URL
  Example: Rowe, J. W. (2016, Sept. 9). The grief monster. Retrieved from http://www.somanylosses.com/ the-grief-monster/html
- Chicago/Turabian
  Format: Last Name, First Name, Middle initial. "Page Title." *Website Title*. Last modified Month day, year. Accessed month, day, year. URL.
  Example: Rowe, Jason. "The Grief Monster." *Strong Living Online*. Last modified September 9, 2016. Accessed September 13, 2016. http://www.somany losses.com/ the-grief-monster/html.

In-Text Citations

Most of the content found in a research paper will be supporting evidence that must be cited in-text, i.e., directly after the sentence that makes the statement. In-text citations contain details that correspond to the first detail in the bibliography entry—usually the author.

- MLA style - In-text citations will contain the author and the page number (if the source has page numbers) for direct quotations. Paraphrased source material may have just the author.
  - According to Johnson, liver cancer treatment is "just beyond our reach" (976).
  - The treatment of liver cancer is not within our reach, currently (Johnson).
  - The narrator opens the story with a paradoxical description: "It was the best of times, it was the worst of times" (Dickens 1).
- APA Style - In text citations will contain the author, the year of publication, and a page marker—if the source is paginated—for direct quotations. Paraphrased source material will include the author and year of publication.
  - According to Johnson (1986), liver cancer treatment is "just beyond our reach" (p. 976).
  - The treatment of liver cancer is not within our reach, currently (Johnson, 1986).
- Chicago Style - Chicago style has two approaches to in-text citation: notes and bibliography or author-date.
  - Notes – There are two options for notes: endnotes—provided in a sequential list at the end of the paper and separate from bibliography—or footnotes provided at the bottom of a page. In either case, the use of superscript indicates the citation number.
    - Johnson states that treatment of liver cancer is "just beyond our reach."[1]
    - 1. Robert W. Johnson, Oncology in the Twenty-first Century (Kentville, Nova Scotia: Kentville Publishing, 1986), 159.
  - Author-Date – The author-date system includes the author's name, publication year, and page number.

- Johnson states that treatment of liver cancer is "just beyond our reach" (1986, 159).
- Research shows that liver cancer treatment is not within our reach, currently (Johnson 1986, 159).

Integrating Information from Source Material

It can be daunting to integrate so many sources into a research paper while still maintaining fluency and coherency. Most source material is incorporated in the form of quotations or paraphrases, while citing the source at the end of their respective references.

There are several guidelines to consider when integrating a source into writing:

- The piece should be written in the author's voice. Quotations, especially long ones, should be limited and spaced evenly throughout the paper.
- All paragraphs should begin with the author's own words and end with his or her own words; quotations should never start or end a paragraph.
- Quotations and paraphrases should be used to emphasize a point, give weight to an idea, and validate a claim.
- Supporting evidence should be introduced in a sentence or paragraph, and then explained afterwards: According to Waters (1979) [signal phrase], "All in all, we're just another brick in the wall" (p.24). The wall suggests that people are becoming more alienated, and the bricks symbolize a paradoxical connection to that alienation [Explanation].
- When introducing a source for the first time, the author's name and a smooth transition should be included: In Pink Floyd's groundbreaking album The Wall, Roger Waters argues that society is causing people to become more alienated.
- There should be an even balance between quotations and paraphrases.
- Quotations or paraphrases should never be taken out of context in a way that alters the original author's intent.
- Quotations should be syntactically and grammatically integrated.
- Quotations should not simply be copied and pasted in the paper, rather, they should be introduced into a paper with natural transitions.
- As argued in Johnson's article...
- Evidence of this point can be found in Johnson's article, where she asserts that...
- The central argument of John's article is...

Current Technology for Use in Educational Settings

Different technological tools serve different functions. To function in the developing world, students need to learn and understand **digital literacy**—the knowledge, dexterity, and critical thinking skills involved in using technology to create, evaluate, and present information. The best techniques for instructing students on choosing and using technological tools involve educating them on the advantages and disadvantages of each, demonstrating how to use them, breaking down their different aspects, assigning students homework or projects in which they will utilize different technological resources, and instructing them on when it is appropriate to use each kind. The most common types of tools used for communication are as follows:

- Smartphones/apps
- Email
- Microsoft Office
- iMovie
- Skype
- Twitter
- Facebook
- Instagram
- Google Drive
- Various blogging websites
- Online bulletin boards
- Wikis

A good way to introduce students to varying technological tools is by using them in the classroom. It would be helpful to teach students how to use a PowerPoint presentation, for example, by giving a PowerPoint presentation. If a student asks a question to which the teacher does not know the answer, they can discover the answer together by using a reliable source on the Internet, projecting the process on the board, so that they can see exactly how it's done. Students can also receive homework and updates on school and classroom events through a personal blog or class bulletin board the teacher has designed so that they may become familiar with using online communication. Students can also be assigned to use personal blogs to practice and improve their writing skills.

The most effective method for learning new skills is a hands-on approach. Students can be educated on the pros and cons of each technological tool, but the best way for them to learn is to allow them to find out for themselves by assigning projects and asking them to give the reasoning behind choosing a specific tool. For example, they may be asked to do a project on some aspect of the Revolutionary War by choosing a media format. Ideas may include the following:

- Doing a presentation
- Filming and editing a video re-enactment of a great battle
- Writing a script in Microsoft Word or in a Google doc and having classmates act it out
- Creating Facebook statuses from the viewpoints of the forefathers in modern colloquial language
- Having a "Twitter war" between the British and the Colonials
- Asking various people to participate in a collaborative Wiki or Google Doc in which many people give their versions of aspects of the Revolutionary War
- Writing a blog narrating life as a soldier

- Posting photos of the signing of the Declaration of Independence

Students can then give their presentations to the classroom so that students can learn about the topic through different presentation styles.

Another way to engage students in using technology is to have them communicate with each other through the various methods of communication—e.g., starting a class Google Doc, creating a classroom Facebook group, or using a discussion board. This is also an excellent opportunity to encourage students to use Standard English through all methods of communication to enhance their writing skills and instill a sense of professionalism, which they will need throughout their lives.

For example, requiring that all students use complete sentences, proper spelling, and grammar through Facebook, Twitter, or blogs associated with homework or projects will encourage them to do so in their daily lives as well. Another example is requiring that students select tweets from their favorite celebrities or politicians, analyze their meaning and purpose, correct their grammar and spelling, and re-tweet them in the correct way. There are countless ways in which technology can be used in the classroom to enhance students' understanding of digital communication; all it requires is a little creativity.

Evaluating Technology-Based Strategies

It is hard to find a technological tool that will not be useful for students to explore. The more a student engages with the numerous different types of technology, the more digitally literate that student will become. Each type is effective and brings value to the table in its own way. When evaluating the effectiveness of a specific technology-based strategy, it's important to consider how this method is enhancing the student's digital literacy, as well as their critical thinking and communication skills. It is also necessary to evaluate the technology itself by asking relevant questions:

- Is it appropriate for the average age of the students in the classroom?
- Is it user friendly?
- Does it work consistently?
- Are there multiple ways to get help on learning how to use it?
- Are there trouble-shooting options?
- Does it have good reviews?
- Is it relevant to the content of the curriculum?
- Does it support and align to the learning objective?
- Is it more distracting than it is useful?
- Is it a tool that is/will be used often in the real world?
- Can it be used for more than one project or assignment?

One very effective teaching strategy is *collaborative learning*, in which two or more students work together to develop a project, work through an idea, or solve a problem. This method allows for students to play off each other's strengths and different experiences and learn how to communicate with their classmates to achieve goals. Technology can be used for collaborative learning in Google Drive, Skype, Google Hangouts, Neapod, Padlet, and Periscope, in creating PowerPoint presentations together, or by conducting surveys with websites like Survey Monkey.

Another effective teaching method is **discussion,** in which students are given a topic or create a topic themselves and then use technology to engage in discourse. This can be done via discussion boards, such as ProBoards or Boardhost, or done live through programs such as Skype or Hangouts. Discussion strategies are extremely effective for enhancing communication skills and digital literacy.

A third method is **active learning**, in which the student engages in activities such as reading, writing, or teaching the subject to another student. Blogging is a great way to encourage active learning as it provides a medium through which students can reflect on what they've learned and respond to comments posted by the teacher or other students. Most of the suggestions made in the previous section—making presentations, creating video re-enactments, writing scripts, having mock Twitter or Facebook comment wars—are all forms of active learning. These types of activities solidify events, ideas, and skills in a student's mind in a way that memorization or flashcards do not as they utilize many different types of thinking and interaction.

One method that a teacher may employ depending on the class and circumstances is **distance learning**. Distance learning is any type of teaching method in which the student and teacher are not in the same place simultaneously. Many professors utilize distance learning through different kinds of technologies, including a live virtual lecture, computer simulations, interactive discussions, and virtual/audio learning environments. These strategies have their advantages in that one teacher can teach a large number of students and multiple locations, and students can communicate with fellow classmates across the globe.

Auditory learning is a strategy in which a student learns through listening. This typically happens via recorded lectures that can be downloaded as podcasts onto a classroom website, discussion board, or some other audio-simulated learning environment. **Visual learning** is learning through watching, in which ideas and concepts are illustrated through images, videos, or by observing a teacher complete a task, explain a concept, or solve a problem. This can be achieved through recorded videos, cartoons, virtual lectures, or by sitting in the classroom. Additionally, **kinesthetic learning** is active learning through physical interaction with an object or actively solving a problem, as opposed to passively listening or watching.

Every student has a different learning style which is unique to them—some learn better through listening while others learn better through doing. The best teaching methods employ all different learning strategies so that all the senses are engaged and every student has a chance at learning material based on their individual learning needs. Technology offers educators the tools do that.

A student may be exposed to a plethora of technology, but this does not mean that she or he necessarily knows how to use it for learning. The teacher is still responsible for guiding, monitoring, and scaffolding the students toward learning objectives. It is critical that educators teach students how to locate credible information and to reliably cite their sources using bibliographies. Platforms and apps for online learning are varied and plentiful. Here are some ideas for how to use technology for writing instruction in the classroom:

- Use a projector with a tablet to display notes and classwork for the group to see. This increases instructional time because notes are already available rather than having to be written in real-time. This also provides the ability to save, email, and post classwork and notes for students and parents to access on their own time. A student can work at his or her own pace and still keep up with instruction. Student screens can be displayed for peer-led teaching and sharing of class work.

- More technology in class means less paperwork. Digital drop-boxes can be used for students to turn in assignments. Teachers can save paper, keep track of student revisions of work, and give feedback electronically.

- Digital media can be used to differentiate instruction for multiple learning styles and multiple skill levels. Instead of using standardized textbook learning for everyone, teachers can create and collect resources for individualizing course content.

- Inquiry- and problem-based learning is easier with increased collaborative capabilities provided by digital tools.

- Digital textbooks and e-readers can replace hardback versions of text that are prone to damage and loss. Students can instantly access definitions for new words, as well as annotate and highlight useful information without ruining a hardbound book.

- Library databases can be used to locate reliable research information and resources. There are digital tools for tracking citation information, allowing annotations for internet content, and for storing internet content.

- Mobile devices may be used in the classroom to encourage reading and writing when students use them to text, post, blog, and tweet.

- PowerPoint and other presentation software can be used to model writing for students and to provide a platform for presenting their work.

- Students can create a classroom blog, review various blog sites, and use blogs as they would diaries or journals. They can even write from the perspective of the character in a book or a famous historical person.

- Web quests can be used to help guide students on research projects. They can get relevant information on specific topics and decide what pieces to include in their writing.

- Students can write about technology as a topic. They can "teach" someone how to use various forms of technology, specific learning platforms, or apps.

- Students can create webpages, make a class webpage, and then use it to help with home-school communication.
- Online feedback and grading systems can be used. There are many to choose from. This may allow students to see the grading rubric and ask questions or receive suggestions from the teacher.
- Students and teachers can use email to exchange ideas with other schools or experts on certain topics that are being studied in the classroom.
- Game show-style reviews can be created for units of study to use on computers or on an overhead projector.
- A wiki website can be created that allows students to collaborate, expand on each other's work, and do peer editing and revision.
- Publishing tools can be used to publish student work on the web or in class newspapers or social media sites.

Practice Questions

1. When children begin to negotiate the sounds that make up words in their language independently, what skill/s are they demonstrating?
   a. Phonological awareness
   b. Phonemes
   c. Phoneme substitution
   d. Blending skills

2. What is phonics?
   a. The study of syllabication
   b. The study of onsets and rimes
   c. The study of sound-letter relationships
   d. The study of graphemes

3. Word analysis skills are NOT critical for the development of what area of literacy?
   a. Vocabulary
   b. Reading fluency
   c. Spelling
   d. Articulation

4. What area of study involves mechanics, usage, and sentence formation?
   a. Word analysis
   b. Spelling conventions
   c. Morphemes
   d. Phonics

5. How do the majority of high-frequency sight words differ from decodable words?
   a. They do not rhyme.
   b. They do not follow the Alphabetic Principle.
   c. They do not contain onsets.
   d. They contain rimes.

6. Reading fluency involves what key areas?
   a. Accuracy, rate, and prosody
   b. Accuracy, rate, and consistency
   c. Prosody, accuracy, and clarity
   d. Rate, prosody, and comprehension

7. When students study character development, setting, and plot, what are they studying?
   a. Word analysis
   b. Points of view
   c. Literary analysis of fictional texts
   d. Fluency

8. The author's purpose, major ideas, supporting details, visual aids, and vocabulary are the five key elements of what type of text?
   a. Fictional texts
   b. Narratives
   c. Persuasive texts
   d. Informational texts

9. When students use inference, what are they able to do?
   a. Make logical assumptions based on contextual clues
   b. Independently navigate various types of text
   c. Summarize a text's main idea
   d. Paraphrase a text's main idea

10. Story maps, an effective instructional tool, do NOT help children in what way?
   a. Analyze relationships among characters, events, and ideas in literature
   b. Understand key details of a story
   c. Follow the story's development
   d. Read at a faster pace

11. Which text feature does NOT help a reader locate information in printed or digital text?
   a. Hyperlink
   b. Sidebar
   c. Glossary – just a dictionary
   d. Heading

12. Read the following passage to answer the question below:

> *He is a kind and generous man who wants nothing more than the best for his community*, thought Michael as the board members discussed the nominees for head of council. Lana June, however, was far more critical. *He is just saying those things to get elected*, she thought.

What is the author's point of view?
   a. First person
   b. Third person limited
   c. Third person omniscient
   d. Objective

13. What do *quantitative*, *qualitative*, and *reader and task* measure?
   a. Text complexity
   b. Genres of writing
   c. Points of view
   d. Reading comprehension

14. Autobiographies and memoirs are examples of what form of writing?
   a. Fiction
   b. Narrative
   c. Informational text
   d. Research papers

15. Rating scales, student logs, and the POWER method are effective assessment practices for what area of literacy development?
    a. Reading
    b. Writing
    c. Spelling
    d. Listening

16. Which effective writing area engages and connects with the audience, igniting emotion?
    a. Ethos
    b. Logos
    c. Pathos
    d. Kairos

17. When children begin to leave spaces between words with a mixture of uppercase and lowercase letters, what developmental stage of writing are they demonstrating?
    a. Emergence of beginning sound
    b. Strings of letters
    c. Words represented by consonants
    d. Transitional phase

18. First-hand accounts of an event, subject matter, time period, or an individual are referred to as what type of source?
    a. Primary sources
    b. Secondary sources
    c. Direct sources
    d. Indirect sources

19. The following is an example of what type of sentence?

> Although I wished it were summer, I accepted the change of seasons, and I started to appreciate the fall.

    a. Compound
    b. Simple
    c. Complex
    d. Compound-Complex

20. Read the following sentence to answer the question below:

> The teacher directed the children's attention to the diagram, but the children couldn't understand the information.

This is an example of what type of sentence?
    a. Complex
    b. Compound
    c. Simple
    d. Compound-Complex

21. Read the following sentences to answer the question below:

Give me a shout back when you can.
Please return my call at your earliest convenience.

What is the main difference in these two sentences?

a. Point of view
b. Dialect
c. Accent
d. Register

22. What type of literary device is being used in this sentence?

I worked a billion hours this week!

a. Idiom
b. Metaphor
c. Hyperbole
d. Alliteration

23. What are the three tiers of vocabulary?

a. Conversational, academic, and domain-specific language
b. Informal, formal, and academic
c. Social, professional, and academic
d. Phonics, fluency, and rate

24. Volume, articulation, and awareness of audience help with what practice?

a. Effective instruction
b. Communication
c. Active listening
d. Oral presentations

25. Offering a presenter with undivided attention and asking relevant and timely questions are examples of what skill set?

a. Active listening skills
b. Effective speaking
c. Formal communication
d. Informal communication

26. What is the method called that teachers use before and after reading to improve critical thinking and comprehension?

a. Self-monitoring comprehension
b. KWL charts
c. Metacognitive skills
d. Directed reading-thinking activities

27. When a student looks back at a previous reading section for information, he or she is using which of the following?

a. Self-monitoring comprehension
b. KWL charts
c. Metacognitive skills
d. Directed reading-thinking activities

28. Which choice of skills is NOT part of Bloom's Taxonomy?
    a. Remembering and understanding
    b. Applying and analyzing
    c. Listening and speaking
    d. Evaluating and creating

29. When a student looks at a word and is able to tell the teacher that the letters spell C-A-T, but the student cannot actually say the word, what is the spelling stage of the student?
    a. Alphabetic Spelling
    b. Within Word Pattern Spelling
    c. Derivational Relations Spelling
    d. Emergent Spelling

30. Predicting, Summarizing, Questioning, and Clarifying are steps of what?
    a. Reciprocal teaching
    b. Comprehensive teaching
    c. Activation teaching
    d. Summative teaching

31. When a student asks, "What do I know?" "What do I want to know?" and "What have I learned?" and records the answers in a table, he or she is using which of the following?
    a. Self-monitoring comprehension
    b. KWL charts
    c. Metacognitive skills
    d. Directed reading-thinking activities

32. What technique might an author use to let the reader know that the main character was in a car crash as a child?
    a. Point of view
    b. Characterization
    c. Figurative language
    d. Flashback

33. A graphic organizer is a method of achieving what?
    a. Integrating knowledge and ideas
    b. Generating questions
    c. Determining point of view
    d. Determining the author's purpose

34. A student is trying to decide if a character is telling the truth about having stolen candy. After the student reads that the character is playing with an empty candy wrapper in her pocket, the student decides the character is guilty. This is an example of what?
    a. Flashback
    b. Making inferences
    c. Style
    d. Figurative language

35. What is the method of categorizing text by its structure and literary elements called?
   a. Fiction
   b. Non-Fiction
   c. Genre
   d. Plot

36. A reader is distracted from following a story because they are having trouble understanding why a character has decided to cut school, so the reader jumps to the next page to find out where the character is headed. This is an example of what?
   a. Self-monitoring comprehension
   b. KWL charts
   c. Metacognitive skills
   d. Directed reading-thinking activities

37. Phonemic Awareness, Phonics, Fluency, Vocabulary, and Comprehension are the five basic elements of what?
   a. Bloom's Taxonomy
   b. Spelling instruction
   c. Reading education
   d. Genre

38. A child reads the story Little Red Riding Hood aloud. He easily pronounces the words, uses an apprehensive tone to show that the main character should not be leaving the path, adds a scary voice for the Big Bad Wolf, and reads the story at a pace that engages the class. What are these promising signs of?
   a. Reading fluency
   b. Phonemic awareness
   c. Reading comprehension
   d. Working memory

39. A student is trying to read the word "preferred." She first recognizes the word "red" at the end, then sounds out the rest of the word by breaking it down into "pre," then "fer," then "red." Finally she puts it together and says "preferred." This student is displaying what attribute?
   a. Phonemic awareness
   b. Phonics
   c. Fluency
   d. Vocabulary

40. A class silently reads a passage on the American Revolution. Once they are done, the teacher asks who were the two sides fighting, why were they fighting, and who won. What skill is the teacher gauging?
   a. Orthographic development
   b. Fluency
   c. Comprehension
   d. Phonics

41. Poems are often an effective device when teaching what skill?
    a. Fluency
    b. Spelling
    c. Writing
    d. Word decoding

42. What allows readers to effectively translate print into recognizable speech?
    a. Fluency
    b. Spelling
    c. Phonics
    d. Word decoding

43. A teacher wants to help her students write a nonfiction essay on how the Pueblos built their homes. Before they write, she helps the students make clay from cornstarch and water, draw a plan for the house with a ruler, and build it using the clay and leaves from the schoolyard. These exercises are examples of what?
    a. Proficiency
    b. Collaboration
    c. Constructive writing
    d. Cross-curricular integration

44. A student has quickly written a story and turned it in without reading it. To help reinforce the POWER strategy, the teacher tells the student go back and read his story. This POWER stage is called what?
    a. Prewriting
    b. Evaluating
    c. Organizing
    d. Revising

45. During which stage of the POWER strategy are graphic organizers used?
    a. Pre-writing
    b. Organizing
    c. Writing
    d. Evaluating

46. A teacher wants his students to write a story over two weeks. They are instructed to write a draft the first day. On each of the following days, he asks the students to develop and edit the story for one of the following: ideas, organization, voice, word choice, sentence fluency, conventions, and presentation. What does this teaching technique incorporate?
    a. Ideas
    b. POWER strategy
    c. Cross-curricular integration
    d. 6+1 Traits

47. Which trait teaches students to build the framework of their writing?
    a. Conventions
    b. Word choice
    c. Ideas
    d. Organization

48. Which trait ultimately forms the content of the writing?
    a. Conventions
    b. Word choice
    c. Ideas
    d. Voice

49. Which trait is most commonly associated with giving individuality and style to writing?
    a. Voice
    b. Word choice
    c. Presentation
    d. Ideas

50. A teacher asks a student to describe a beautiful day. The student says the flowers were pretty, the air was warm, and animals were running. The teacher asks the student to specify how many flowers there were—just a few hopeful buds or an abundance of blossoms? Was the air still or breezy? How did it feel? The teacher is developing which trait in the student?
    a. Voice
    b. Word choice
    c. Organization
    d. Presentation

51. Writing practice for the sole purpose of communicating refers to what kind of writing?
    a. Persuasive
    b. Informational
    c. Narrative
    d. Purposeful

52. A second-grade student brings a book to read to a group. It is about a caterpillar counting its food each day of the week before becoming a butterfly. Realizing the group is very familiar with their days and numbers, the teacher uses the story to explore the "moral" of the story and proper nutrition. This is an example of what?
    a. Modeling
    b. Encouragement
    c. Acknowledgement
    d. Challenging

53. A student is struggling with reading, especially aloud. When it is his turn to read to the class, the teacher offers an easier book she knows the student likes and is very familiar with. When the student reads aloud well and with enthusiasm, the teacher praises him to the class, then gives a more challenging book the next time. What is this called?
    a. Acknowledgement
    b. Providing feedback
    c. Encouragement
    d. Effective assistance

54. Preparation, Presentation, Application, and Evaluation are the four steps of what?
   a. Demonstration
   b. Modeling
   c. Explanation
   d. Challenging

55. Students are asked to pretend to prepare a meal. At various classroom stations, they must draw a picture, engage in pretend play, or write a list of instructions: one for grocery shopping, cooking, and cleanup. The teacher helps each student choose which task to pair with which station, encouraging autonomy and self-motivation. This is an example of what instruction technique?
   a. Challenging
   b. Modeling
   c. Giving feedback
   d. Giving assistance

56. Throughout the day, a teacher used language priority, beginning each subject by asking students to volunteer five related words that start with the letter "P." Then, during a reading exercise, the teacher partnered with a small group to turn their words from the day into a cover illustration for a story. This is an example of what?
   a. Giving directions
   b. The Abecedarian Approach
   c. Developmentally appropriate practice
   d. Autonomy

57. Speaking, listening, reading, and writing are four essential elements of what?
   a. Developmentally appropriate practice
   b. The Abecedarian Approach
   c. Literacy development
   d. Task, purpose, and audience

58. A teacher is about to read a story. He tells the class they will be quizzed and need to pay attention. He instructs them to focus by clearing everything else from their desks, to look at his face for clues about the story's tone, and to think about the adjectives used to describe the characters to learn more about them. What skill is he teaching?
   a. Writing
   b. Reading
   c. Speaking
   d. Listening

59. Since teachers must be communicators, educators, evaluators, models, and agents of socialization, this is considered to be mastery of what?
   a. Conventions
   b. Spelling
   c. Speaking
   d. Listening

60. Synonyms, Antonyms, and Homonyms are examples of what?
   a. Syntax relationships
   b. Pragmatic relationships
   c. Semantic relationships
   d. Morphology relationships

Answer Explanations

1. A: Phonological Awareness refers to a child's ability to understand and use familiar sounds in his or her social environment in order to form coherent words. Phonemes are defined as distinct sound units in any given language. Phonemic substitution is part of phonological awareness—a child's ability to substitute specific phonemes for others. Blending skills refers to the ability to construct or build words from individual phonemes by blending the sounds together in a unique sequence.

2. C: When children begin to recognize and apply sound-letter relationships independently and accurately, they are demonstrating a growing mastery of phonics. Phonics is the most commonly used method for teaching people to read and write by associating sounds with their corresponding letters or groups of letters, using a language's alphabetic writing system. Syllabication refers to the ability to break down words into their individual syllables. The study of onsets and rimes strives to help students recognize and separate a word's beginning consonant or consonant-cluster sound—the onset—from the word's rime—the vowel and/or consonants that follow the onset. A grapheme is a letter or a group of letters in a language that represent a sound.

3. D: Breaking down words into their individual parts, studying prefixes, suffixes, root words, rimes, and onsets, are all examples of word analysis. When children analyze words, they develop their vocabulary and strengthen their spelling and reading fluency.

4. B: Spelling conventions is the area of study that involves mechanics, usage, and sentence formation. Mechanics refers to spelling, punctuation, and capitalization. Usage refers to the use of the various parts of speech within sentences, and sentence formation is the order in which the various words in a sentence appear. Generally speaking, word analysis is the breaking down of words into morphemes and word units in order to arrive at the word's meaning. Morphemes are the smallest units of a written language that carry meaning, and phonics refers to the study of letter-sound relationships.

5. B: Although some high-frequency sight words are decodable, the majority of them are not, so they do not follow the Alphabetic Principle, which relies on specific letter-sound correspondence. High-frequency sight words appear often in children's literature and are studied and memorized in order to strengthen a child's spelling and reading fluency. High-frequency sight words, as well as decodable words, may or may not rhyme and may or may not contain onsets and rimes.

6. A: Reading fluency involves how accurately a child reads each individual word within a sentence, the speed at which a child reads, and the expression the child applies while reading. Therefore, accuracy, rate, and prosody are the three key areas of reading fluency.

7. C: Literary analysis of a fictional text involves several areas of study, including character development, setting, and plot. Although points of view refer to a specific area of study in literary analysis, it is only one area. Word analysis does not involve the study of elements within a fictional text.

8. D: Informational texts generally contain five key elements in order to be considered informative. These five elements include the author's purpose, the major ideas, supporting details, visual aids, and key vocabulary. Narratives are accounts—either spoken or written—of an event or a story. Persuasive texts, such as advertisements, use persuasive language to try to convince the reader to act or feel a certain way. Informational texts strive to share factual information about a given subject in order to advance a reader's knowledge.

9. A: When a person infers something, he or she is demonstrating the ability to extract key information and make logical assumptions based on that information. The information provided is not direct, but implied. Being able to navigate a variety of texts independently has nothing to do with inference; it demonstrates a student's reading comprehension and fluency. Successfully summarizing and paraphrasing texts are advanced literacy skills that demonstrate a student's reading comprehension and writing proficiency.

10. D: Story maps are a specific type of visual aid that helps younger children develop a clearer understanding of a story being read. Story maps may represent the beginning, middle, and ending of a story, or they may be used to develop a clearer picture of each character's personality and traits, unfold the story's plot, or establish the setting.

11. C: Informational texts organized with headings, subheadings, sidebars, hyperlinks and other features help strengthen the reader's reading comprehension and vocabulary knowledge. A glossary defines terms and words used within a text.

12. C: Third person is a term used to refer to a specific point of view in literature. A third person omniscient point of view develops the point of view of each character within a given story and allows the reader to understand each character's feelings as well as their interpretation of a story's events. Third person limited only offers insight into one character, usually the main character. Character analysis is the intimate study of one character within the story—the character's physical characteristics, personality traits, and relationships to the story's elements and other characters. The story's plot refers to the story's main events; it usually reveals the problem and how it might be resolved. A genre of writing is the specific style of writing the author employs—fiction, non-fiction, mystery, narrative, or informational text.

13. A: These are all measures of a text's complexity. Quantitative measures determine a text's level of difficulty. There are several ways to measure this level of difficulty, some of which are sentence length, number of unfamiliar words, and even syllable count within words. Qualitative measures examine a text's attributes, including clarity of language, figurative versus literal language, and a text's overall meaning. Since each reader has unique background knowledge, skill set, and level of reading motivation, reader and task refers to how likely a reader is to engage in and comprehend a given text. Thus, all three of these components comprise a text's complexity. A genre of writing is simply the style of writing that the author employs. Authors will always reveal a given point of view in fictional writing. Sometimes, the author offers readers several points of view, and sometimes, the points of view are limited. Reading comprehension refers to how well a student demonstrates understanding or mastery of the text.

14. B: Narratives are personal accounts of a time period, event, or an individual, with the purpose of documenting, recording, or sharing such factual information. By contrast, fiction is a genre of writing that is fabricated. Informational texts are academic texts used to further a student's mastery of a given subject, and research papers are written reports students write to demonstrate their understanding of a given area of study that has been researched.

15. B: There are several effective assessments to evaluate a child's overall writing progress. Rating scales, student logs, and the POWER method are just some of these assessment methods. Although educators can create rating scales and student logs to assess and help students assess reading and spelling, the POWER method is specific to writing:

P—Prewriting

O—Organizing

W—Writing a rough draft

E—Evaluating

R—Revise and Rewrite

16. C: Pathos refers to the author's appeal to the audience or reader's emotions. Ethos refers to the level of credibility of a piece of writing. Logos refers to the author's appeal to the audience or reader's logic. Kairos refers to the most opportune moment to do something. Therefore, the correct answer is pathos.

17. C: There are eight developmental writing stages:

- Scribbling
- Letter-like symbols
- Strings of letters
- The emergence of beginning sounds
- Words represented by consonants
- Initial, middle, and final sounds
- Transitional phase
- Standard spelling

When children begin to leave visible spacing between words, even if those words are incorrectly spelled or if there is a mixture of upper and lower case letters, they are considered to be at the *Words represented by consonants* stage.

18. A: Firsthand accounts are given by primary sources—individuals who provide personal or expert accounts of an event, subject matter, time period, or of an individual. They are viewed more as objective accounts than subjective. Secondary sources are accounts given by an individual or group of individuals who were not physically present at the event or who did not have firsthand knowledge of an individual or time period. Secondary sources are sources that have used research in order to create a written work. Direct and indirect sources are not terms used in literary circles.

19. D: Since the sentence contains two independent clauses and a dependent clause, the sentence is categorized as compound-complex:

Independent clause: *I accepted the change of seasons*

Independent clause: *I started to appreciate the fall*

Dependent clause: *Although I wished it were summer*

20. B: Since the sentence contains two independent clauses connected by a conjunction, it is referred to as a compound sentence.

Independent clause: The teacher directed the children's attention to the diagram
Independent clause: The children couldn't understand the information
Conjunction: But

21. D: The first sentence is written quite informally and gives a clear impression that the exchange is on a socially relaxed level. The second sentence is written quite formally and gives a clear impression that the exchange is academic or professional in nature. Although both sentences carry the same message—to respond to the messenger as quickly as possible—the register, or level of formality, is very different.

Accent refers to the way in which certain words are pronounced by an individual and is usually dependent on where a person resides. Dialect refers to how groups of people from a specific geographical region manipulate their language. Point of view refers to a person's interpretation of or feelings toward an event. In literature, a point of view refers to a character's interpretation of or feelings toward an event.

22. C: When authors use hyperbole, they are using extreme exaggeration to strongly state a point or evoke a specific emotion in the reader. Idioms can be in the form of words, phrases, or sentences that are expressed figuratively, but they carry a literal meaning that readers must infer. Metaphors are literary devices that compare two unlike entities, as in "The United States is a melting pot." Alliteration is a poetic device that repeats the beginning consonant sound throughout a sentence or phrase strictly for entertainment—"The **b**all **b**ounced along the **b**lue **b**alcony."

23. A: The three tiers of vocabulary are as follows:

Conversational: informal, more relaxed
Academic: more professional, with vocabulary intended to challenge critical thinking skills
Domain-specific language: a unique vocabulary inventory that focuses around a given discipline or computer language

24. D: In order for oral presentations to be effective, the presenter's volume should match the size of audience and the location of the presentation. The presenter should also practice articulation—how clearly the words are being said. The third most important element of oral presentations is how well the presenter is engaging the audience. Making eye contact, moving around the room, and involving the audience, when appropriate, are all part of audience awareness skills.

25. A: Active listening skills are very important in all forms of communication, whether one is at home, among friends, in school, or at work. An active listener is one who pays close attention to what is being said, maintains eye contact, uses body language to indicate respect, asks relevant questions, and shares information that directly pertains to the subject.

26. D: Teachers use directed reading-thinking activities before and after reading to improve critical thinking and reading comprehension. Metacognitive skills are when learners think about thinking. Self-monitoring is when children are asked to think as they read and ask themselves if what they have just read makes sense. KWL charts help guide students to identify what they already know about a given topic.

27. C: Asking oneself a comprehension question is a metacognition skill. Readers with metacognitive skills have learned to think about thinking. It gives students control over their learning while they read. KWL charts help students to identify what they already know about a given topic.

28. C: Listening and speaking are not part of Bloom's Taxonomy. The six parts are remembering, understanding, applying, analyzing, evaluating, and creating.

29. D: During the Emergent Spelling stage, children can identify letters but not the corresponding sounds. The other choices are all fictitious.

30. A: Reciprocal teaching involves predicting, summarizing, questioning, and clarifying. The other choices are all fictitious.

31. B: KWL charts are an effective method of activating prior knowledge and taking advantage of students' curiosity. Students can create a KWL (*Know/Want to know/Learned*) chart to prepare for any unit of instruction and to generate questions about a topic.

32. D: Flashback is a technique used to give more background information in a story. None of the other concepts are directly related to going back in time.

33. A: Graphic organizers are a method of integrating knowledge and ideas. These include many different visual tools for connecting concepts to help students understand information.

34. B: Making inferences is a method of deriving meaning in writing that intended by the author but not explicitly stated. A flashback is a scene set earlier than the main story. Style is a general term for the way something is done. Figurative language is text that is not to be taken literally.

35. C: Genre is a means of categorizing text by its structure and literary elements. Fiction and non-fiction are both genre categories. Plot is the sequence of events that make a story happen.

36. A: Scanning future portions of the text for information that helps resolve a question is an example of self-monitoring. Self-monitoring takes advantage of a natural ability of students to recognize when they understand the reading and when they do not. KWL charts are used to help guide students to identify what they already know about a given topic. Metacognitive skills are when learners think about thinking. Directed reading-thinking activities are done before and after reading to improve critical thinking and reading comprehension.

37. C: The five basic components of reading education are phonemic awareness, phonics, fluency, vocabulary, and comprehension.

38. A: If a child can accurately read text with consistent speed and appropriate expression while demonstrating comprehension, the child is said to have reading fluency skills. Without the ability to read fluently, a child's reading comprehension (Choice *C*) will be limited.

39. B: Phonics is the ability to apply letter-sound relationships and letter patterns in order to accurately pronounce written words. Phonemic awareness is the understanding that words are comprised of a combination of sounds. Fluency is an automatic recognition and accurate interpretation of text. Vocabulary is the body of words known to a person.

40. C: Comprehension is the level of content understanding that a student demonstrates after reading. Orthographic development is a cumulative process for learning to read, with each skill building on the previously mastered skill. Fluency is an automatic recognition and accurate interpretation of text. Phonics is the ability to apply letter-sound relationships and letter patterns in order to accurately pronounce written words.

41. A: Poems are an effective method for teaching fluency, since rhythmic sounds and rhyming words build a child's understanding of phonemic awareness.

42. C: Phonics allows readers to effectively translate print into recognizable speech. If children lack proficiency in phonics, their ability to read fluently and to increase vocabulary will be limited.

43. D: Cross-curricular integration is choosing to teach writing projects that include the subjects of science, social studies, mathematics, reading, etc.

44. B: Students should carefully read what they've written during the Evaluating stage of the POWER strategy.

45. B: Graphic organizers are used during the Organizing stage of the POWER strategy. They help students to examine, analyze, and summarize selections they have read and can be used individually or collaboratively in the classroom. Graphic organizers may be sequencing charts, graphs, Venn diagrams, timelines, chain of events organizers, story maps, concept maps, mind maps, webs, outlines, or other visual tools for connecting concepts to achieve understanding.

46. D: 6+1 Traits is a model for teaching writing that uses common language to explain writing standards. The 6+1 Traits are the characteristics that make writing readable and effective no matter what genre of writing is being used. These seven traits are ideas, organization, voice, word choice, sentence fluency, conventions, and presentation.

47. D: Organization is the trait that teaches students how to build the framework of their writing. Students choose an organizational strategy or purpose for the writing and build the details upon that structure. There are many purposes for writing, and they all have different frameworks.

48. C: Ideas ultimately form the content of the writing. The Ideas Trait is one of the 6+1 Traits model and is where students learn to select an important topic for their writing. They are taught to narrow down and focus their idea before further developing it.

49. A: Voice is the primary trait that shows the individual writing style of an author. It is based on an author's choice of common syntax, diction, punctuation, character development, dialogue, etc.

50. B: Word choice is the trait that teaches the use of precise language. Teachers can enhance this trait in students by helping them to use exact language that is accurate, concise, precise, and lively.

51. D: Intentional writing practice for the purpose of communicating refers to purposeful writing. Students can use this as a method of thinking through issues and solving problems related to writing.

52. C: Considering prior knowledge before instruction is part of Acknowledgement. For teachers, it begins with understanding where students are coming from and the experiences they bring with them to the classroom. When a teacher considers prior knowledge before beginning instruction, they are being considerate of each student's time and intellect.

53. B: Providing feedback is a way to build positive self-image and encourage success. A positive self-image is fostered by repeated success. Giving clear and effective feedback communicates to the student that her or his work is worthwhile, and that someone cares enough to review and consider it.

54. A: Demonstration includes the four steps: Preparation, Presentation, Application and Evaluation. Demonstration is when a teacher not only models and explains how to do a task but also engages in thinking through the task with the students. Effective teachers narrate their thinking processes when modeling a strategy.

55. D: Autonomy and self-motivation are the goals of giving assistance. Students need assistance and guidance in a classroom; however, knowing how much help to offer is always a balancing act. If teachers give too much assistance, they end up doing the work for students, who then do not learn. If teachers do not offer enough assistance, students become lost, overwhelmed, and do not learn.

56. B: Conversational reading and language priority are premises of the Abecedarian Approach. Conversational reading involves a conversational-style of reading instruction in which the educator plays an active role by partnering in shared reading activities. By emphasizing language throughout the day, the language priority strategy creates endless occasions for meaningful conversations. Educators work to extend conversations from a variety of different angles, promoting higher cognitive thinking and engagement.

57. C: Speaking, Listening, Reading, and Writing are the four elements of literacy development. As social beings, children begin to recognize that with effective literacy skills, their social, emotional, and physical needs can be met, and their curiosity can be satisfied.

58. D: Four concepts that teach listening skills are focusing, looking, non-verbal cues, and verbal cues. Behaviors that enable good listening skills should not be expected. They need to be taught. Students need to learn the difference between what an excellent listener does and what poor listening behaviors are.

59. A: Teachers must master conventions because they are communicators, educators, evaluators, models, and agents of socialization. Teachers serve several key roles in the classroom. Students will not be able to learn properly unless their teachers have mastered these conventions.

60. C: Synonyms, Antonyms, and Homonyms are examples of semantic relationships. There are five types of semantic relationships, including the three noted in the question. The other two are Hyponyms and Meronyms.

Social Science

Effective Instructional Practices and Assessment of the Social Sciences

Instructional Delivery of Social Science Concepts

Teachers should strive to move beyond textbooks in the classroom, introducing students to a variety of primary and secondary sources. Written secondary sources can include professional monographs, popular histories, historical fiction, magazines, newspapers, and scholarly journals and articles. Written primary sources can include journals, diaries, newspaper clippings, government documents, context-specific literature, letters, biographies and autobiographies, folklore, and cultural mythology. Students should also be exposed to visual sources such as political cartoons, artwork, ads, signs, graphs, charts, tables, photographs, and videos. Students can also be introduced to relevant musical works. As digital archives and histories are becoming more relevant in 21st century classroom, it's important that students are exposed to computer-based resources.

Planning for Instruction of Social Science Concepts

Besides traditional lectures, textbook work, PowerPoints, and direct instruction, teachers can diversify pedagogical methods in their classrooms by incorporating inquiry-based practices, project-based learning, field work, role plays, sociodramas, skits, simulations, field trips, student-specific academic interventions, debates, and identity-based social-emotional learning activities into social science courses. The goal is to differentiate sources, instruction, and assessments so all students have access to social science content.

Assessing Social Science Concepts

Differentiated assessments are crucial for tailoring the educational environment for individual learning types. Teachers must be aware and sensitive to the neurodiversity in their classrooms. When designing social science assessments, teachers should keep in mind the unique learning types and cognitive skills of English Language Learners (ELLs), Section 504 students, Gifted and Talented (GT) students, and Special Education (SPED) students. In addition, teachers in K-6 social science classrooms must be sensitive to cultural. Whenever possible, social science teachers should make their materials and assessments personally and culturally relevant.

Students should be comfortable exploring and expressing their identities in social science classrooms. For students to excel at historical inquiry, it's important that they understand their own genders, sexual orientations, races, ethnicities, political affiliations, religious beliefs, and socioeconomic statuses to better understand how these categories drive the decisions of historical actors and even their peers. The social studies performance standards for the State of Florida act as a means for assessing the needs of each student; moreover, these standards encourage cultural diversity. They can be found on the CPALMS website at cpalms.org. Contrary to popular belief, these standards don't limit one's ability to implement varied assessments; rather, the standards were created as guideposts for implementing diverse assessments that account for the varied interests and skills present in every classroom. Whenever possible, use the official State of Florida's social studies standards for direction, and employ kinesthetic-, auditory-, oral-, written-, and visual-based assessments for every student. There are related benchmarks for each standard that can be used to guide assessment formation. Also try to vary assessments by incorporating design-thinking, inquiry-based learning, project-based learning, and student voice and choice. Inevitably, a good teacher will respond to student needs and concerns and offer alternative assessments without diminishing the crucial nature of the standards.

Learning Environments for Social Science

Besides direct classroom instruction, teachers can take students on field trips to different communities, historical sites, and museums. Teachers should introduce students to the notion that history exists in all settings, finding opportunities for students to carry out research projects, project-based learning, and experiential learning in surrounding communities. Students should recognize that all materials—buildings, streets, schools, antiques, common objects—possess some semblance of historical agency. Each material item has a unique biography. By "taking to the streets," students will be more prepared for interdisciplinary scholarship and field research in higher education. Students can also be encouraged to explore their own communities to collect formal and oral histories for the classroom.

History

Connections Between Causes and Effects

When examining the historical narratives of events, it is important to understand the relationship between causes and effects. A **cause** can be defined as something, whether an event, social change, or other factor, that contributes to the occurrence of certain events; the results of causes are called **effects**. Those terms may seem simple enough, but they have drastic implications on how one explores history. Events such as the American Revolution or the Civil Rights Movement may appear to occur spontaneously, but a closer examination will reveal that these events depended on earlier phenomena and patterns that influenced the course of history.

For example, although the battles at Concord and Lexington may seem to be instantaneous eruptions of violence during the American Revolution, they stemmed from a variety of factors. The most obvious influences behind those two battles were the assortment of taxes and policies imposed on the Thirteen Colonies following the French and Indian War from 1754 to 1763. Taxation without direct representation, combined with the deployment of British soldiers to enforce these policies, greatly increased American resistance. Earlier events, such as the Boston Massacre and the Boston Tea Party, similarly stemmed from conflicts between British soldiers and local colonists over perceived tyranny and rebelliousness. Therefore, the start of the American Revolution progressed from preceding developments.

Furthermore, there can be multiple causes and effects for any situation. The existence of multiple causes can be seen through the settling of the American West. Many historians have emphasized the role of manifest destiny—the national vision of expanding across the continent—as a driving force behind the growth of the United States. Yet there were many different influences behind the expansion westward. Northern abolitionists and southern planters saw the frontier as a way to either extend or limit slavery. Economic opportunities in the West also encouraged travel westward, as did the gradual pacification of Native American tribes.

Even an individual cause can be subdivided into smaller factors or stretched out in a gradual process. Although there were numerous issues that led to the Civil War, slavery was the primary cause. However, that topic stretched back to the very founding of the nation, and the existence of slavery was a controversial topic during the creation of the Declaration of Independence and the Constitution. The abolition movement as a whole did not start until the 1830s, but nevertheless, slavery is a cause that gradually grew more important over the following decades. In addition, opponents of slavery were divided by different motivations—some believed that it stifled the economy, while others focused on moral issues.

On the other end of the spectrum, a single event can have numerous results. The rise of the telegraph, for example, had several effects on American history. The telegraph allowed news to travel much quicker and turned events into immediate national news, such as the sinking of the USS Maine, which sparked the Spanish-American War. In addition, the telegraph helped make railroads run more efficiently by improving the links between stations. The faster speed of both travel and communications led to a shift in time itself, and localized times were replaced by standardized time zones across the nation.

The importance of grasping cause-and-effect relationships is critical in interpreting the growth and development of the Civil Rights Movement. Historical narratives of the movement often focus on charismatic individuals, such as Martin Luther King Jr., and they certainly played a key leadership role. Even so, elements of the movement had already emerged in previous decades through the growth of the National Association for the Advancement of Colored People (NAACP) and other organizations. Several factors proved critical to the formation of civil rights organizations during the 1950s. African American veterans returning from World War II, as well as those continuing to serve in the military, called for equal rights. Furthermore, the United States' role as a key member of the United Nations, which included African countries, required the federal government to take racial discrimination seriously.

A specific example in the Civil Rights Movement is the sit-ins during 1960, in which black and white students defied segregation policies in restaurants and other establishments. The wave is often thought to originate from spontaneous activism by students in Greensboro, North Carolina. However, there had already been other sit-ins, such as at Royal Ice Cream Parlor in Durham, North Carolina, in 1957. In fact, the sit-ins would not have spread as quickly without a preexisting network of activists across the nation, which in part stemmed from the growth of organizations through various local and national movements. By looking at such cases closely, it becomes clear that no event occurs without one—if not multiple—causes behind it, and that each historical event can have a variety of direct and indirect consequences.

One of the most critical elements of cause-and-effect relationships is how they are relevant not only in studying history but also in contemporary events. Much of the current political debate about social security and health care stems from FDR's New Deal in the 1930s, and at the time some people criticized the programs for being too extensive, while others argued that he did not go far enough with his vision. Current environmental concerns have their origins in long-term issues that reach back centuries. The United States' mixed history of global isolation and foreign intervention continues to influence foreign policy approaches today. Most of all, people must realize that events and developments today will likely have a number of consequences later on. Therefore, the study of cause and effect remains vital in understanding the past, the present, and the future.

Sequential Nature of Historical Events

Timelines are useful tools that teachers and students of history use to understand the sequential nature of events. Timelines are essential for listing events in chronological order. Knowing the chronology of events can help teachers and students understand relationships between events, and how historical context can affect human decisions. Often, in a social studies classroom, timelines assist students in understanding cause and effect. There are two basic types of chronologies that teachers can highlight for students: absolute chronology and relative chronology. Timelines are examples of absolute chronologies that arrange events in a specific order based on the dates that events occurred. Relative chronologies are less structured than absolute chronologies and merely list events in order without regarding specific dates.

Primary and Secondary Source Documents

Traditionally, historical documents have been separated into two major categories: primary sources and secondary sources. Understanding the features of each is crucial for building foundational historical inquiry skills in the K-6 classroom. Students must learn to deconstruct primary and secondary sources to gain a better understanding of historical context and personal perspective.

Primary sources contain firsthand documentation of a historical event or era. Primary sources are provided by people who have experienced an historical era or event. Primary sources capture a specific moment, context, or era in history. They are valued as eyewitness accounts and personal perspectives. Examples include diaries, memoirs, journals, letters, interviews, photographs, context-specific artwork, government documents, constitutions, newspapers, personal items, libraries, and archives. Another example of a primary source is the Declaration of Independence. This historical document captures the revolutionary sentiment of an era in American history.

Authors of secondary sources write about events, contexts, and eras in history with a relative amount of experiential, geographic, or temporal distance. Normally, secondary source authors aren't firsthand witnesses. In some cases, they may have experienced an event, but they are offering secondhand, retrospective accounts of their experience. All scholars and historians produce secondary sources—they gather primary source information and synthesize it for a new generation of students. Monographs, biographies, magazine articles, scholarly journals, theses, dissertations, textbooks, and encyclopedias are all secondary sources. In some rare instances, secondary sources become so enmeshed in their era of inquiry that they later become primary sources for future scholars and analysts.

Teachers and students alike must spend a great deal of time analyzing the relationships between primary sources, secondary sources, and their historical scopes. Juxtaposing primary sources with secondary sources helps teachers and students attain a deeper understanding of the material they are studying.

Cultural Contributions and Technological Developments

Cultural Contributions and Technological Developments in Africa

Between the 1500s and 1800s, over 12 million African slaves were shipped across the globe as free labor for agricultural markets. Slavery had a cultural impact not only on Africa, but also the entire globe, especially the developing colonies and nations of North and South America. The spread of African languages and cultures to the New World (called the African Diaspora) created an entirely new culture in the Americas.

Africa is also responsible for exporting important agricultural and animal domestication techniques, textile creation skills, and other technological advances to the rest of the world in antiquity. North Africans shared shipbuilding techniques with Greek and Roman civilizations, and they became leaders in mathematics and engineering. Ethiopians were the first to cultivate coffee and recognize its energizing properties. The Nile River Valley region is also believed to be one of the first to develop cotton as a textile and agricultural export.

Cultural Contributions and Technological Developments in the Americas

During the Age of Exploration, indigenous Americans taught European explorers how to cultivate such plants as maize (corn), beans, pumpkins, squash, cacao, beans, vanilla, sweet potatoes, peppers, peanuts, pineapples, sunflowers, gourds, plums, and tobacco. Native American agricultural techniques and harvesting technologies transformed the diets of people around the world. Native Americans also exported domestication techniques for turkeys and certain dog breeds, transforming the trade market for household and farm animals. Additionally, the Native American civilizations advanced studies in mathematics, engineering, and astronomy. In the United States, indigenous culture and mythology still pervades the national psyche even though many Native Americans were slaughtered by the colonial and revolutionary governments of the New World.

Revolution, in and of itself, is also one of the greatest exports of the Americas. The American Revolution, the first of its kind in the New World, became a focal point of later revolutions. Today, many revolutionary forces still look to the American Revolution for inspiration.

Cultural Contributions and Technological Developments in Europe

Much of the West's political and philosophical heritage is owed to the Greek and Roman civilizations of European antiquity. The Greeks established democracy, and the Romans established the framework of republicanism. During the Enlightenment, these classical values helped shape the revolutionary sentiments of the Founding Fathers of the United States. Christianity is another essential European export. Europe adopted the religion during Late Antiquity and the Middle Ages. Eventually, Christianity was dispersed throughout the world during the Age of Exploration. During the Enlightenment and Age of Exploration, Europe also became a leader in science, mathematics, and technology, thanks in part to the influences of North Africa, the Middle East, and the Arab world. Europeans became expert shipbuilders and explorers, refining such exploratory tools as the astrolabe and compass.

Cultural Contributions and Technological Developments in the Middle East

The Middle East has always been a hub of early civilization. Middle Easterners helped develop early mathematical principles (number systems, algebra, geometry) as well as advanced mathematics (trigonometry and calculus). Likewise, Middle Easterners were leaders in engineering and architecture during Late Antiquity and the Middle Ages. Their architectural styles influenced European and American buildings. The Middle East is also the epicenter of monotheistic religion, as the original home of Judaism, Christianity, and Islam.

Cultural Contributions and Technological Developments in Asia

Asia was responsible for dispersing gunpowder, silk, fireworks, tea, and spices throughout the world during the Age of Exploration. Following the success of overland travels across the Silk Road in the 1200s and 1300s, Europeans began to develop a fascination with the Far East. This Orientalism drove explorers to find faster sea routes to China and Japan. In many ways, the Far East's grip on the European consciousness is, perhaps, the driving force of the Age of Exploration.

Significant Historical Leaders and Events that have Influenced Eastern and Western Civilizations

In the years following World War II, the U.S. and Soviet Union arose as the two dominant world forces. But because the countries had very different political systems—democracy (the U.S.) and Communism (the Soviet Union)—a feeling of mistrust developed between the two. This was heightened by the fact that both countries had developed nuclear weapons. This became known as the Cold War. The Soviet Union introduced Communism into Eastern Europe, which it had occupied since World War II. This led to the formation of the North Atlantic Treaty Organization (NATO) between Western Europe, Canada, and the U.S. in defense of Soviet hostility. The Soviet Union countered by creating the Warsaw Pact.

Slavery

Slavery was an issue for America from its early days when Africans were brought to Virginia to work in the tobacco fields. In the 1800s, the Underground Railroad was a secret network of tunnels and safe houses that helped slaves escape slavery in the South and gain freedom in the North. Escaped slave Harriet Tubman was its most famous "conductor." Slave owners and abolitionists bitterly debated slavery, and southern leaders began to threaten secession. Slavery became the major focus of the 1860 presidential election, particularly since the South was convinced that Abraham Lincoln would abolish slavery if elected. Lincoln won the election, which only further increased tensions. Southern states began to secede in late 1860. By February 1861, they had formed the new nation of the Confederate States of America, electing Jefferson Davis as their president in November of that year.

Civil War

In April 1861, Confederate soldiers fired upon a Union-held ship seeking to reinforce Fort Sumter in Charleston, South Carolina. This signaled the beginning of the Civil War and divided the U.S. into the North (Union) and South (Confederates). The two sides battled for four years, and the smaller Confederate Army surprised the Union Army with their tenacity. The Confederate Army claimed various victories throughout Virginia from 1861-1863 under the leadership of General Robert E. Lee. These victories included the Battle of Bull Run, Fredericksburg, and Chancellorsville. The turning point was the Battle of Gettysburg in Pennsylvania, which resulted in 51,000 troops on both sides being killed, wounded, or declared missing. The Confederate Army suffered a loss of one-third of its soldiers. In 1864, Union General William T. Sherman marched through Georgia, burning Atlanta and devastating much of the landscape. In 1865, he then moved through the Carolinas to Richmond, Virginia where General Lee, who was facing the determined assaults of future president Ulysses S. Grant, surrendered. Five days later, John Wilkes Booth shot President Lincoln who was watching a play at Ford's Theatre in Washington, D.C.; Lincoln died the next morning.

Reconstruction

During the Reconstruction period following the Civil War, the North and South continued to wage power and economic struggles. Many African Americans from the South moved north and west to seek more fair treatment. The American frontier provided opportunities for immigrants and others seeking new prospects. Many people made their way west, farming the land and finding jobs in industries such as mining, forestry, and oil. This forced Native Americans to fight for their land or pick up and move to reservations. In the 1876 conflict known as **Custer's Last Stand**, Colonel George Custer's troops were killed by a group of Sioux Indians led by Chiefs Crazy Horse and Sitting Bull. This defeat angered the U.S. government and caused them to increase their efforts against the Indians, which put an end to the Indian Wars. The introduction of the railroad in the mid-nineteenth century provided many jobs and allowed people and goods to travel the vast landscape of North America at a much quicker pace.

Industrial Revolution

Author Mark Twain deemed the period of business and industrial growth from 1876 through the turn of the twentieth century as the **Gilded Age** since it appeared shiny and golden on the surface, but was fueled by undercurrents of corruption led by big businessmen known as robber barons. They controlled many of America's booming new industries, including steel (Andrew Carnegie), steamships and railroads (Cornelius Vanderbilt), oil (John D. Rockefeller), and banking (J.P. Morgan). None of the U.S. Presidents during this period were particularly strong leaders and practiced a hands-off approach to business. High tariffs were another issue supported by businesses and Congress. In 1890, Congress passed the McKinley Tariff, named after future President and then Representative William McKinley. This tariff raised duties over 48 percent on average.

U.S. Expansion

The U.S. continued to seek out and acquire new lands, a tactic often referred to as **Manifest Destiny**. This practice led to the purchase of Alaska from Russia in 1867 and the annexation of Hawaii in 1898. The Spanish-American War in 1898 lasted just a few weeks, but helped Cuba gain its independence from Spain and helped the U.S. gain a strategic foothold in many distant locales that were formerly Spanish territories. These included Guam and the Philippines. Future president Theodore Roosevelt became a hero when his troops defeated the Spanish fleet at the Battle of San Juan Hill.

World War I

World War I began in 1914 when a Serbian assassin killed Archduke Franz Ferdinand of Austria, which prompted Austria-Hungary to declare war on Serbia. Due to protective alliances they had forged, other European countries soon joined the war. If one country was attacked, the country's allies were obliged to defend it.

Most Americans supported the Allies, particularly after German submarines sank the passenger ship *Lusitania* in 1915, killing 128 Americans. In 1917, news leaked that Germany was trying to turn Mexico against the U.S. As a result, President Woodrow Wilson declared war on Germany. American troops helped defeat the German army in September 1918. Fighting ended in November of that year after Germany signed a peace agreement. President Woodrow Wilson's plan for peace was the League of Nations, which was adopted as part of the Treaty of Versailles in 1919, but then rejected by the U.S. Senate.

Prohibition and The Great Depression

Prohibition (the 18th Amendment to the U.S. Constitution) was passed in 1919 and prohibited the production and sale of alcoholic beverages. This amendment fueled corruption since people made, sold, and transported liquor illegally. The 21st Amendment repealed it in 1933. Women had been campaigning for the right to vote since the 1840s, and these suffragettes used the outbreak of World War I to leverage their fight, stating they would help support the war if they were granted the right to vote. The 19th Amendment, which guaranteed women the right to vote in federal elections, was finally passed by Congress in 1919 and ratified the following year. On October 29, 1929 (referred to as Black Tuesday) the stock market crashed, marking the beginning of the Great Depression that lasted through the 1930s. President Franklin Delano Roosevelt's solution was the **New Deal**—a variety of new programs and laws to provide government funding to help rebuild America's economy.

World War II

In 1939, after Adolf Hitler began to invade and occupy several European nations, World War II broke out in Europe and many countries declared war on Germany. Germany aligned with Italy and Japan in 1940 to form the Axis Alliance. Their goal was to establish a German empire in Europe and place Japan in control over Asia. When Germany invaded the Soviet Union in June 1941, the Soviets immediately allied with Britain. The U.S. entered the war when Japan bombed Pearl Harbor in Hawaii on December 7, 1941. Battles raged in Europe and the Pacific, and the Allied forces won an important victory in June 1942 at the Battle of Midway. At this battle, the U.S. stopped the Japanese from advancing and prevented the invasion of Australia. In 1943, Axis troops in North Africa surrendered to the Allies, who then began to invade Italy, and finally France on June 6, 1944 (known as D-Day), which resulted in severe losses on both sides. In early 1945, President Roosevelt met with British Prime Minister Winston Churchill and Soviet director Joseph Stalin in Yalta, Crimea to plan their final assault on Germany and discuss postwar strategies. The Allies continued their attack, liberating Nazi death camps. This forced Hitler to commit suicide, and Germany surrendered in May. However, Japan did not yield, even after the capture of Okinawa in June. As a result, the U.S. dropped an atomic bomb on the Japanese cities of Hiroshima and then Nagasaki, forcing Japan to surrender in early September.

United Nations

Toward the end of World War II, a group of fifty nations (including the U.S. and the Soviet Union) formed the United Nations as a peacekeeping group. However, Communism still continued to spread throughout the world, including to Latin America, Africa, and Asia. When Communist North Korea invaded South Korea in June 1950, the U.N. sent a group of troops led by the U.S. to help South Korea. This action led to a three-year conflict that ended in a cease-fire in 1953. Although war was never officially declared and neither side won, the fighting showcased President Truman's hard stance against Communism.

Baby Boom

The 1950s were generally a prosperous time for Americans. Many Americans took advantage of college loan programs and the G.I. Bill, which gave military veterans a free education. Mortgage programs provided more affordable housing, which enabled many people to move to the suburbs. The population surged during this **baby boom**, labor unions helped workers increase their wages, and people were able to afford more expensive items, such as cars and television sets.

Civil Rights Movement

During this time, African Americans were still repressed, particularly in the southern U.S., and segregation was rampant in many public places. When the Supreme Court ruled that school segregation was illegal in 1954 in the revolutionary case **Brown vs. the Board of Education**, the Civil Rights Movement was set in motion. This movement continued throughout the 1950s and 1960s and included dozens of nonviolent protests, such as the Montgomery bus boycott in Alabama. The boycott was organized after Rosa Parks was arrested because she refused to give up her seat on the bus to a white man. The Southern Christian Leadership Conference (SCLC) was soon formed as a way to bring African Americans together to help fight segregation in a peaceful way. The Reverend Dr. Martin Luther King, Jr. was its first president. Dr. King and his supporters kept up the fight throughout the 1960s, staging sit-ins at segregated lunch counters, **Freedom Rides** on segregated buses, and marches and protests in segregated cities, such as Birmingham, Alabama. The demonstrations often ended in violence and police brutality, which served to aid the cause and led to the passage of the Civil Rights Act in 1964.

U.S. Conflicts

The Cold War between the U.S. and Soviets continued as both countries tried to assert their dominance through technological and military advances. This spawned events such as the creation of the Berlin Wall by the Russians in 1961, which was devised to separate the sector of Berlin they occupied from the area controlled by the Western allies (France, Britain, and the U.S.). The Cuban Missile Crisis in 1962 was sparked by the failed invasion of Cuba by the U.S. a year earlier. After the invasion, the Soviets placed nuclear missiles aimed at the U.S. in Cuba. However, when U.S. spy planes spotted them, President John F. Kennedy demanded the dismantling and removal of the missile sites, and as a concession agreed to go forward with the planned removal of U.S. missile sites in Turkey. A year later on November 22, 1963, President Kennedy was assassinated in Dallas by Lee Harvey Oswald.

Space Race

The Cold War prompted the **space race** between the U.S. and Soviets, each attempting to outdo the other with different space exploration milestones. In 1957, the Russians launched *Sputnik*, the first satellite, into space. This prompted President Eisenhower to establish the National Aeronautics and Space Administration (NASA) in 1958. Although the Soviets were also the first nation to send a human into space in 1961, the U.S. quickly caught up. President Kennedy vowed to land an American on the moon by 1969—a feat that was accomplished by astronaut Neil Armstrong on July 20, 1969.

Vietnam War

In 1954, rebels seized control of Vietnam from France. The country was split into two regimes with the northern part under Communist leadership. As the threat of communism continued to loom, the U.S. sent advisors and weapons to South Vietnam beginning in 1955. The U.S. got more directly involved in the 1960s during the presidency of Lyndon B. Johnson, who sent troops in great numbers to help South Vietnam win the fight. Many Americans opposed the war, which caused anti-war protests and unrest. A cease-fire was signed in 1973, and the last U.S. forces pulled out in 1975.

Women's Rights Movement

Women gained the right to vote in 1920, but still were not on equal terms with men in many areas. Suffragist leader Alice Paul had introduced the Equal Rights Amendment (ERA) in 1923 to help bridge this gap. Congress finally passed the ERA in 1972 and sent it to the states for ratification. However, not all states ratified the amendment, and to date only a total of thirty-five have ratified it, which is three less than the thirty-eight required to pass. In the controversial 1973 court case *Roe vs. Wade*, the Supreme Court gave women the right to legally obtain abortions within the first three months of pregnancy.

1970s and Watergate

U.S. diplomatic relations with the Communist nations of China and the Soviet Union improved a bit in the 1970s. President Richard Nixon paid visits to both countries in 1972. The Strategic Arms Limitation Talks (SALT I and II), negotiated between 1972 and 1979, resulted in limits on nuclear weapons for both the U.S. and Russia. In 1974, Nixon became the first and only U.S. president to resign from office as a result of the Watergate scandal. The scandal erupted when five of his staff members were caught stealing information from the Democratic Party headquarters in Washington, D.C. In 1973, a group of Arab nations tried to regain land seized by Israel in the 1967 Six-Day War. The U.S. was a main Israeli ally, and the Arab-controlled Organization of Petroleum Countries (OPEC) cut off oil shipments to the U.S. Because the U.S. was highly dependent on imports of oil from the Middle East, this energy crisis resulted in a huge surge in gas prices and long lines at the pumps.

The Reagan Years

In his role as U.S. president from 1980-1988, Ronald Reagan was against big government and supported industry deregulation, fewer social programs, lower taxes, and bigger military spending. A scandal referred to as the Iran-Contra Affair emerged during Reagan's presidency, involving the secret sale of weapons to Iran in exchange for American hostages. Profits from the sale were then sent to aid Nicaraguan Contras in their cause to overthrow the communist Sandinista government. Reagan opposed Communism and advocated **peace through strength**, building up the U.S. military and launching the Strategic Defense Initiative (SDI), also called **Star Wars**, designed to shield the U.S. from nuclear attack. Reagan worked with Soviet President Gorbachev to put controls on nuclear weapons after Gorbachev launched the policies of **glasnost** (political openness) and **perestroika** (economic restructuring). This led to the breakup of the Soviet Union, and the end of the Cold War.

Desert Storm

In 1990, Iraqi dictator Saddam Hussein invaded Kuwait in order to take possession of the tiny country's huge oil fields. A few months later, U.S. President George H.W. Bush launched Operation Desert Storm with a coalition of several Middle Eastern and European countries. This Gulf War started with air bombings and ended in a five-day ground war that drove Hussein out.

The Clinton Years

Democratic President William (Bill) Clinton was elected in 1992. Unlike Reagan, he supported social programs, although his plan for a national health care system never passed through Congress. He negotiated the North American Free Trade Agreement (NAFTA) with Canada and Mexico in 1993. In 1996, he was impeached for lying under oath about his relationship with a young White House intern, Monica Lewinsky, but the Senate did not think his crimes were severe enough to remove him from office.

1990s and Technology Boom

IBM had introduced personal computers in 1981, and the early 1990s marked the public adoption of the Internet, an interconnected communications network that changed the way people accessed information. The 1990s were also a time of violence. This violence included bombings on New York's World Trade Center in 1993 by an Islamic Fundamentalist group, the bombing of the Murrah Federal Building in Oklahoma City in 1995 by antigovernment extremists, race riots, and school shootings.

September 11th Terrorist Attacks

On September 11, 2001, terrorists led by Islamic fundamentalist Osama bin Laden hijacked four airplanes. Terrorists flew two planes into the World Trade Center in New York City, bringing down both buildings, and flew one plane into the Pentagon in Washington, D.C. The other plane crashed into a Pennsylvania field when passengers tried to overthrow the terrorists. The terrorist attack killed over three thousand people. This led President George W. Bush to wage a **war on terror** and resulted in bombing raids on various locations in Afghanistan where bin Laden and his al-Qaeda network were purportedly hiding. When Iraqi dictator Saddam Hussein defied terms of the truce agreed upon in 1991 after the Gulf War, Bush was convinced that the country possessed **weapons of mass destruction** (WMDs) and invaded Iraq in 2003.

Obama's Presidency

Barack Obama, America's first African American President, was elected in 2008. Fighting in the Iraq region continued between groups with differing political and religious views. Obama pulled U.S. troops from the region in 2011, but many have been trickling back into the country in efforts to help maintain order. In 2011, Obama gave the order to launch a raid on bin Laden's compound in Pakistan, which resulted in a group of Navy SEALs finding and killing the al-Qaeda leader. In December 2010, a revolution in Tunisia kicked off a series of democratic uprisings and protests throughout the Middle East. These uprisings are often referred to as the **Arab Spring**. The U.S. pledged support and military aid, but tensions continue to escalate particularly in Syria. The militant group Islamic State of Iraq and al-Sham (ISIS) has taken advantage of the Syrian civil war by launching a series of terrorist attacks there and in areas outside the Middle East. Domestically, one of Obama's pledges was to launch a health care reform plan providing affordable and accessible health care for all Americans. He signed the Affordable Care Act, sometimes referred to as **Obamacare,** into law in 2010.

The Causes and Consequences of Exploration, Settlement, and Growth on Various Cultures

Early Exploration

European exploration in North America dates back to around 1000 AD when Scandinavian Vikings, led by Leif Eriksson, first made their way to Greenland and then journeyed on to modern-day Newfoundland. They settled briefly in an area now known as L'Anse Meadows. However, clashes with the Native American people living nearby caused them to return to Greenland a few years later. The first permanent settlements in North America began after Italian sailor Christopher Columbus landed in the Caribbean in 1492. This was a significant breakthrough since most Europeans did not know that this huge landmass even existed. It initiated a period of discovery, conquest, and colonization of the Americas by the Europeans. Often referred to as the **Columbian Exchange**, this period allowed people who had been cut off from each other for 15,000 years to share knowledge, ideas, culture, food, plants and animals, technology, and religion; this led to significant changes and enhancements for both regions.

European Expansion and Influence

Other European cultures quickly followed, sending sailors across the Atlantic to find new passages to the East and lay claim to new lands. Explorers typically hailed from countries with a seafaring reputation. Spain, France, and England were the major forces, whereas Portugal, Holland, Russia, and Sweden played lesser roles. This merging of cultures had an unfortunate effect on the Native American people who were not immune to the diseases the new arrivals brought with them. Millions died from deadly diseases; others were killed or enslaved in territorial encounters when some Europeans sought to conquer the Indians. Over the next few centuries, this led to a 90 percent population decline among the Native Americans.

England and Spain waged the biggest struggle to claim the most land in North America. Spain took the initial lead in the early 1500s, exploring or establishing settlements in the southern portion of what is now the United States. Spain settled in present-day Florida, Texas, California, Arizona, New Mexico, Mexico, and a good portion of Central America and South America. Up until the 1840s, Spain, and later Mexico, controlled large expanses of the area now known as the southwestern United States.

Colonization

The British first established a presence in 1585 when Sir Walter Raleigh founded the Roanoke colony in what was then called Virginia, but later became North Carolina. It is now known as the **Lost Colony** because John White, the colony's leader, went back to England for supplies in 1587 and later returned to find that all of the colonists had mysteriously disappeared. In 1607, the British established their first permanent settlement in Jamestown, Virginia. In 1620, a group of approximately one hundred people sailed from England on the **Mayflower** and landed at a site they named Plymouth. Many were Pilgrims seeking religious freedom. They founded the first permanent European settlement in New England. Within seventy-five years, England had established thirteen British colonies along the east coast of North America, laying the foundation for the future United States of America.

French Influence

The French gained a stronghold in Canada in 1534 when Jacques Cartier sailed up the St. Lawrence River and claimed the territory for France. In 1608, French explorer Samuel de Champlain further explored the region and later founded Quebec. By 1673, France expanded their claim from Canada to the Gulf of Mexico when Father Jacques Marquette and Louis Joliet journeyed down the Mississippi River, naming the territory Louisiana after King Louis XIV.

The Ways that Individuals and Events Have Influenced Economic, Social, and Political Institutions in the World, Nation, or State

At the turn of the twentieth century, imperialism had led to powers, such as France, the United States, and Japan, to establish spheres of influence throughout the world. The combination of imperial competition and military rivalries led to the outbreak of World War I when Archduke Ferdinand of Austria was assassinated in 1914. The war pitted the Allies, including England, France, and Russia, against the Central Powers of Austria-Hungary, Germany, and the Ottoman Empire—a large Islamic realm that encompassed Turkey, Palestine, Saudi Arabia, and Iraq. The rapid advances in military technology turned the war into a prolonged bloodbath that took its toll on all sides. By the end of the war in 1918, the Ottoman Empire had collapsed, the Austrian-Hungarian Empire was split into multiple countries, and Russia had descended into a civil war that would lead to the rise of the Soviet Union and Communism.

The Treaty of Versailles ended the war, but the triumphant Allies also levied heavy fines on Germany, which led to resentment that would be accentuated by the Great Depression of the 1930s. The Great Depression destabilized the global economy and led to the rise of fascism, a militarized and dictatorial system of government, in nations such as Germany and Italy. The rapid expansion of the Axis Powers of Germany, Italy, and Japan led to the outbreak of World War II. The war was even more global than the previous conflicts, with battles occurring in Europe, Africa, and Asia. World War II encouraged the development of new technologies, such as advanced radar and nuclear weapons, that would continue to influence the course of future wars.

In the aftermath of World War II, the United Nations was formed as a step toward promoting international cooperation. Based on the preceding League of Nations, the United Nations included countries from around the world and gave them a voice in world policies. The formation of the United Nations coincided with the independence of formerly colonized states in Africa and Asia, and those countries joined the world body. A primary goal of the United Nations was to limit the extent of future wars and prevent a third world war; while the United Nations could not prevent the outbreak of wars, it nevertheless tried to peacefully resolve them. In addition to promoting world peace, the United Nations also helped protect human rights.

Even so, the primary leadership in the early United Nations was held by the United States and its allies, which contributed to tensions with the Soviet Union. The United States and the Soviet Union, while never declaring war on each other, fueled a number of proxy wars and coups across the world in what would be known as the Cold War. Cold War divisions were especially noticeable in Europe, where communist regimes ruled the eastern region and democratic governments controlled the western portion. These indirect struggles often involved interference with foreign politics, and sometimes local people began to resent Soviet or American attempts to influence their countries. For instance, American and Soviet interventions in Iran and Afghanistan contributed to fundamentalist Islamic movements. The

Cold War ended when the Soviet Union collapsed in 1991, but the conflict affected nations across the globe and continues to influence current issues.

Another key development during the twentieth century, as noted earlier with the United Nations, was that most colonized nations broke free from imperial control and asserted their independence. Although these nations achieved autonomy and recognition in the United Nations, they still suffered from the legacies of imperialism. The borders of many countries in Africa and Asia were arbitrarily determined by colonists with little regard to the arrangement of native populations. Therefore, many former colonies have suffered conflicts between different ethnic groups; this was also the case with the British colony in India, which became independent in 1947. Violence occurred when it split into India and Pakistan because the borders were largely based on religious differences. In addition, former colonial powers continue to assert economic control that inhibits the growth of native economies. On the other hand, the end of direct imperialism has helped a number of nations, such as India and Iran, rise as world powers that have significant influence on the world as a whole.

Additionally, there were considerable environmental reforms worldwide during the twentieth century. In reaction to the growing effects of industrialization, organizations around the world protested policies that damaged the environment. Many of these movements were locally based, but others expanded to address various environmental threats across the globe. The United Nations helped carry these environmental reforms forward by making them part of international policies. For instance, in 1997, many members of the United Nations signed a treaty, known as the **Kyoto Protocol**, that tried to reduce global carbon dioxide emissions.

Most significantly, the twentieth century marked increasing globalization. The process had already been under way in the nineteenth century as technological improvements and imperial expansions connected different parts of the world, but the late twentieth century brought globalization to a new level. Trade became international, and local customs from different lands also gained prominence worldwide. Cultural exchanges occur on a frequent basis, and many people have begun to ponder the consequences of such rapid exchanges. One example of globalization was the 1993 establishment of the European Union—an economic and political alliance between several European nations.

Charles Darwin

Charles Darwin is known as the Father of Evolution, and was a naturalist and geologist. Darwin collected samples and made extensive observations in his Voyage of the Beagle from 1831 to 1836. His most famous spot was the Galápagos Islands, where he discovered varying species of finches from island to island. His theory of natural selection proposed that organisms best suited to their surrounding environment were most likely to survive.

Mao Zedong

In China, Mao Zedong, the chairman of the Communist Party and leader of the People's Republic of China, attempted to quickly transform China into a Communist state through an ineffective and devastating economic program known as the **Great Leap Forward**, which abolished private ownership of property and featured collective communes. The Great Leap Forward caused a humanitarian disaster, resulting in tens of millions of deaths, due to inefficient economic planning under a poorly devised Communist system.

Mohandas Gandhi

Mohandas Gandhi became the leader of the Indian independence movement following the passage of the Rowlatt Act, which allowed the British colonial government to jail Indian protesters without a trial by jury. Returning World War I veterans and human rights advocates in India violently rejected the Rowlatt Act as a stumbling block to Indian self-government and a threat to Indian rights. In an act of defiance against the colonial British government in the spring of 1919, ten thousand Hindu and Muslim protesters flocked to Amristar, the capital city of the Punjab province in India. During this protest, British troops killed over four hundred Indians and injured over one thousand protesters. This controversial moment in history paved the way for Gandhi to emerge as the respected leader of Indian resistance. Unlike other revolutionaries at that time in history, Gandhi urged his followers to employ nonviolent noncooperation tactics against the British government. The former lawyer called upon the nonviolent principles of world religions to instill in his followers the principle of satyagraha ("truth force"). In the Western world, Gandhi's principle of satyagraha has become colloquially known as passive resistance or civil disobedience.

In the 1920s and 1930s, Gandhi launched a passive resistance campaign that combined peaceful marches with economic boycotts. These nonviolent means of resistance eventually led to the passage of the Government of India Act by the British Parliament in 1935, which offered Indians limited democratic elections and local self-government. This act, however, was not respected by the British government during World War II when it deployed Indian troops without the consent of local government officials. During this time, Gandhi pressed the Indian people to find peace during these controversial times. Nevertheless, in the postwar years, by 1947, Indians were becoming increasingly violent, not only with British officials, but also with each other. Muslims and Hindus grew increasingly at odds with one another in the postwar years. Despite all his passive efforts, Gandhi's hope for a united, independent India was only half realized: On July 16, 1947, the British government partitioned the Indian subcontinent into two countries, Pakistan and India. In 1948, Mohandas Gandhi's life was taken by a Hindu extremist who disliked his attempts to achieve equal treatment for both Muslims and Hindus. Gandhi's nonviolent ethos has, nevertheless, continued to reverberate through history, namely in the work of such civil rights advocates as Martin Luther King Jr. and Nelson Mandela.

Adolf Hitler

Adolf Hitler was an Austrian-born soldier who was awarded the Iron Cross on two occasions for his service in the German army during World War I. Following the end of the war, Hitler joined a small, right-wing political group that threatened to overturn the Treaty of Versailles, which placed sanctions on the postwar German military, government, and economy. Hitler also joined the group in vowing to destroy global Communism. As the group expanded, it became known as the National Socialist German Workers' Party, often abbreviated as "Nazis." Nazism became the German brand of fascism, promising to protect the middle and lower-middle classes from postwar sanctions and the global overreach of Communism. Like Benito Mussolini, the Fascist leader of Italy, Adolf Hitler had the ability to command and manipulate a crowd with his fiery speeches. His public-speaking skills eventually led to his assumption of the position as chosen *der Führer*—or "leader" —of the Nazis. A failed attempt to seize power in Munich in 1923 landed Hitler and many of his fellow Nazis in prison. While in prison, Hitler wrote his famous book *Mein Kampf* (*My Struggle*). This book served as the blueprint for Nazism, labeling Jews, Slavs, gypsies, and other groups as "subhuman" and calling for the eugenic creation of the Aryan race. By 1933, Hitler and his book *Mein Kampf* had gained so much popular support that he became chancellor of Germany, paving the way to World War II, the Holocaust, and the eventual fall of Nazism in Germany.

Nelson Mandela

Born to a royal family of the Xhosa-speaking South African Thembu tribe in 1918, Nelson Mandela became one of the premier civil rights activists in world history. In the 1940s, Mandela joined the African

National Congress party, joining fellow black leaders in South Africa in their fight against the white minority's oppressive regime. This regime had its roots in colonial practices that legitimized the oppression and marginalization of black and interracial South Africans. The white minority leadership created an apartheid system of social segregation. Mandela joined other revolutionaries in protests and armed conflicts, leading to his eventual imprisonment. Following his release from prison in 1990, Nelson Mandela continued his civil rights battle in the racially divided South Africa. He eventually helped end apartheid in South Africa, becoming the first black president in 1994. As president, he formed a multiethnic government, using his position of power to fight racial prejudice throughout the globe. He died in 2013 at the age of ninety-five.

Mother Teresa

Born Agnes Gonxha Bojaxhiu, Mother Teresa (1910–1997) became one of the most beloved religious figures and missionaries in the twentieth century. Recipient of the Nobel Peace Prize in 1979, Mother Teresa dedicated her life to helping the poor, the elderly, the sick, and the disabled in South Asia and the rest of the world. After joining the sisterhood in Ireland, she left the convent for missionary work in Calcutta, India. In 1948, she established the Order of the Missionaries of Charity in Calcutta. This organization established schools, refugee camps, hospitals, churches, and convents throughout the world. Clad in her iconic plain white sari with a blue border, Mother Teresa became famous for helping the downtrodden of the Third World. Millions lamented her death in 1997, knowing that they lost one of the most dedicated missionaries in modern history. Her work is as iconic as other social justice warriors such as Dr. Martin Luther King Jr. and Mohandas Gandhi.

Immigration and Settlement Patterns that have Shaped the History of the U.S.

Constant immigration meant that land prices in the eastern United States rose, and people sought new economic opportunities on the frontier where land was cheaper. The United States government tried purchasing land from Native Americans, but most refused to relinquish their territories. Native Americans continued to defend their land until Tecumseh was defeated in the War of 1812. This defeat helped secure the Northwest Territory, and more settlers began pouring in. After the Louisiana Purchase, Lewis and Clark paved the way for expansion into the Great Plains and further west.

Several important laws also stimulated western expansion during the second half of the 19th century. Congress passed the Homestead Act in 1862, which allowed citizens to claim 160 acres for only $1.25 per acre. The settler also had to live on the land for five years and make improvements. That same year, Congress also passed the Pacific Railroad Act, which supported the construction of a transcontinental railroad. The United States government provided land and financial support to railroad companies and the first transcontinental link was established in 1869. This facilitated trade and communication between the eastern and western United States.

As Americans poured westward, conflict again broke out between settlers and Native Americans. The discovery of gold in the Black Hills of South Dakota caused prospectors to flood into the area although the U.S. government had recognized the territory belonged to the Sioux. General George Armstrong Custer brought in troops to try and take possession of the Black Hills. This led to disaster when Custer and more than 250 soldiers died at the Battle of Little Big Horn in 1876.

The U.S. government continued its efforts to control Native American tribes. The Dawes Act of 1887 encouraged Native Americans to settle on reservations and become farmers in exchange for U.S. citizenship. Chief Joseph was a leader of the Nez Perce tribe who refused to live on a reservation and tried to flee to Canada. However, the U.S. captured Chief Joseph and his tribe and forced them onto a reservation. Reformers also required Native Americans to send their children to boarding schools where they had to speak English and dress like Caucasians instead of maintaining their traditional culture. The schools were often crowded, and students were also subjected to physical and sexual abuse.

In 1890, the Lakota Indians tried to preserve their traditional beliefs by performing a special ceremony called a Ghost Dance. U.S. government officials felt threatened and sent soldiers to try and disarm the Lakota. This led to the Massacre at Wounded Knee in 1890 where at least 150 Lakota, including many women and children, were slaughtered. It was the last major conflict between Native Americans and U.S. forces.

Cultural Contributions to Florida

The historical development of Florida can be broken into eight major categories: 1) Florida's prehistory, 2) exploration and colonization, 3) the 18th century, 4) American possession and Indian removal, 5) antebellum slavery and the Civil War era, 6) Reconstruction and railroads, 7) 20th century advances, and 8) postwar immigration and the allure of the Sun Belt.

Florida's Prehistory

Around 12,000 years ago, Florida's coastline extended further into the Atlantic Ocean and the Gulf of Mexico. In fact, the peninsula was twice as large as modern-day Florida. During this time, Florida's first inhabitants settled there after migrating from eastern Asia to North America. Following the Ice Age, these Paleo-Indians, as they are now called, altered their nomadic lives to accommodate the warmer climates. Around 700-500 BCE, the Paleo-Indians of Florida began creating more stable political and social institutions, adopting the technological and environmental changes spawned by the wider Agricultural Revolution. Natives began to cultivate corn in the northern half of modern-day Florida.

Exploration and Colonization (Pre-Statehood)

Juan Ponce de Leon became the first European explorer to arrive on the Florida peninsula. In 1513, the adventurer docked his ships at the modern city of St. Augustine, naming the land ***la Florida*** after the Feast of Flowers in his home nation of Spain. Attacks from the natives stifled any attempts at immediate colonization. Over twenty years later, Spanish explorer Hernando de Soto explored the Tallahassee region of Florida in search of treasure, but he did not establish a colony.

Between the 1550s and 1560s, Spanish and French settlers tried to establish colonies in Florida, but with little success. By the 1570s and 1580s, as colonization accelerated for the major European powers, Florida became a sought-after prize for the Spanish, French, and English. While English explorers like Sir Francis Drake successfully attacked Spanish forts, Spain remained the unassailable power of the Caribbean region. Even with English colonies sprouting in the north and French colonies expanding in the west, Spain held on to Florida throughout most of the 17th century.

18th Century

Florida fell into different colonial hands on several occasions during the 18th century. On several occasions, English colonists attacked Spanish forts and missions, including a failed siege on the Castillo de San Marcos at St. Augustine in 1740. Following the Seven Years' War of 1756-1763, Florida briefly became a British colony. Nevertheless, by 1781, Florida returned to Spanish control following the treaty that ended the American War for Independence. Throughout this time, Native Americans in Florida, specifically the Seminoles of Creek descent, fought for their homeland, adding to the conflict in the region.

American Possession and Indian Removal

In 1821, Spain ceded Florida to the United States government. President Andrew Jackson, who had already fought in the First Seminole War in 1818, had a vested interest in the region, establishing it a territory of the United States. The new territory diversified the United States, adding more Spanish colonists, African-American slaves, and Native Americans to the growing nation. In 1845, Florida gained admission into the union as the 27th state. As more Anglo-Americans moved to Florida in the antebellum period to establish plantations, many residents started to pressure the President to remove the lingering Native American tribes. Between 1835 and 1842, the U.S government waged a war with the remaining Seminoles. Jackson allocated millions of dollars to remove the Seminoles to Oklahoma (then called Indian Territory). Seminoles who resisted were forced onto confining reservations in Florida if they didn't accept relocation to Oklahoma.

Antebellum Slavery and the Civil War Era

Sometimes labeled the "Forgotten State of the Civil War," Florida remained tied to slavery in the antebellum and Civil War eras. Nearly half of the population in the antebellum period—almost 60,000 people—were slaves. Most Floridian plantation owners refused to accept abolition, leading to Florida's secession from the Union on January 10, 1861. Thousands of white residents joined the Confederate army, heading North for battle, as no decisive Civil War skirmishes were fought in Florida.

Reconstruction and Railroads

Farming remained vital to the agricultural economy of Florida during the Reconstruction era. During Reconstruction, white and black sharecroppers moved to Florida to develop the farming sector. Railroad construction provided access to the remote state, catalyzing citrus production and tourism. By the late 19th century, Florida became a major player in the American tourism industry as businessmen drained swamps for lavish hotels. By the time the Spanish-American War rolled around, Florida had become a key port state for the growing U.S. military.

Twentieth Century Advances

Thanks to the growth of the railroad, agricultural, and tourism industries, population and wealth were booming in Florida by the end of World War I. Yet a combination of local environmental disasters (hurricanes and the introduction of the Mediterranean fruit fly) and national economic disaster (the Great Depression) stifled economic growth in the late 1920s-1940s. Women gained the right to vote in this era, and by 1944, whites-only primary elections were outlawed in Florida. The expanding U.S. military industrial complex reached well into Florida, further diversifying the populace.

Postwar Immigration and the Allure of the Cold War Sunbelt

The U.S. Immigration and Nationality Act of 1965 transformed the ethnic fabric of the United States, eliminating many of the previous quotas on immigration from the Middle East and East Asia. Consequently, the Act helped to diversify states such as Florida during the Cold War. During this time, highway construction and the invention of air conditioning brought many to Florida. Northern laborers and retirees migrated to the Sunshine State to escape the harsh winters and economic desolation of the Rust Belt. This era also witnessed the desegregation of schools and the expansion of the universities in Florida. Community colleges and state university systems surrounded the burgeoning U.S. Space Program at Cape Canaveral. The arrival of the National Aeronautics and Space Administration in the 1950s and 1960s brought a sort of "brain boom" during the Cold War, which witnessed Florida becoming the home of immigrants seeking to aid in the ongoing space race with the Soviet Union. Tourist attractions such as Walt Disney World also brought millions of people to Florida. In this era,

Florida became home for Cuban, Caribbean, and Latin America refugees seeking escape from hostile governments.

Major Contributions of Classical Civilizations

There were a number of powerful civilizations during the classical period. Mesopotamia was home to one of the earliest civilizations between the Euphrates and the Tigris rivers in the Near East. The rivers provided water and vegetation for early humans, but they were surrounded by desert. This led to the beginning of irrigation efforts to expand water and agriculture across the region, which resulted in the area being known as the Fertile Crescent.

The organization necessary to initiate canals and other projects led to the formation of cities and hierarchies, which would have considerable influence on the structure of later civilizations. For instance, the new hierarchies established different classes within the societies, such as kings, priests, artisans, and workers. Over time, these city-states expanded to encompass outside territories, and the city of Akkad became the world's first empire in 2350 B.C. In addition, Mesopotamian scribes developed systemized drawings called pictograms, which were the first system of writing in the world; furthermore, the creation of wedge-shaped cuneiform tablets preserved written records for multiple generations.

Later, Mesopotamian kingdoms made further advancements. For instance, Babylon established a sophisticated mathematical system based on numbers from one to sixty; this not only influenced modern concepts, such as the number of minutes in each hour, but also created the framework for math equations and theories. In addition, the Babylonian king Hammurabi established a complex set of laws, known as the Code of Hammurabi, which would set a precedent for future legal systems.

Meanwhile, another major civilization began to form around the Nile River in Africa. The Nile's relatively predictable nature allowed farmers to use the river's water and the silt from floods to grow many crops along its banks, which led to further advancements in irrigation. Egyptian rulers mobilized the kingdom's population for incredible construction projects, including the famous pyramids. Egyptians also improved pictographic writing with their more complex system of hieroglyphs, which allowed for more diverse styles of writing. The advancements in writing can be seen through the Egyptians' complex system of religion, with documents such as the *Book of the Dead* outlining not only systems of worship and pantheons of deities but also a deeper, more philosophical concept of the afterlife.

While civilizations in Egypt and Mesopotamia helped to establish class systems and empires, other forms of government emerged in Greece. Despite common ties between different cities, such as the Olympic Games, each settlement, known as a polis, had its own unique culture. Many of the cities were oligarchies, in which a council of distinguished leaders monopolized the government; others were dictatorships ruled by tyrants. Athens was a notable exception by practicing an early form of democracy in which free, landholding men could participate, but it offered more freedom of thought than other systems.

Taking advantage of their proximity to the Mediterranean Sea, Greek cities sent expeditions to establish colonies abroad that developed their own local traditions. In the process, Greek merchants interacted with Phoenician traders, who had developed an alphabetic writing system built on sounds instead of pictures. This diverse network of exchanges made Greece a vibrant center of art, science, and philosophy. For example, the Greek doctor Hippocrates established a system of ethics for doctors called the Hippocratic Oath, which continues to guide the modern medical profession. Complex forms of literature were created, including the epic poem "The Iliad," and theatrical productions were also developed. Athens in particular sought to spread its vision of democratic freedom throughout the world, which led to the devastating Peloponnesian War between allies of Athens and those of oligarchic Sparta from 431 to 404 B.C.

Alexander the Great helped disseminate Greek culture to new regions. Alexander was in fact an heir to the throne of Macedon, which was a warrior kingdom to the north of Greece. After finishing his father's work of unifying Greece under Macedonian control, Alexander successfully conquered Mesopotamia, which had been part of the Persian Empire. The spread of Greek institutions throughout the Mediterranean and Near East led to a period of Hellenization, during which various civilizations assimilated Greek culture; this allowed Greek traditions, such as architecture and philosophy, to endure into the present day.

Greek ideas were later assimilated, along with many other concepts, into the Roman Empire. Located west of Greece on the Italian peninsula, the city of Rome gradually conquered its neighbors and expanded its territories abroad; by 44 B.C., Rome had conquered much of Western Europe, northern Africa, and the Near East. Romans were very creative, and they adapted new ideas and innovated new technologies to strengthen their power. For instance, Romans built on the engineering knowledge of Greeks to create arched pathways, known as aqueducts, to transport water for long distances and devise advanced plumbing systems.

One of Rome's greatest legacies was its system of government. Early Rome was a republic, a democratic system in which leaders are elected by the people. Although the process still heavily favored wealthy elites, the republican system was a key inspiration for later institutions such as the United States. Octavian "Augustus" Caesar later made Rome into an empire, and the senate had only a symbolic role in the government. The new imperial system built on the examples of earlier empires to establish a vibrant dynasty that used a sophisticated legal code and a well-trained military to enforce order across vast regions. Even after Rome itself fell to barbarian invaders in fifth century A.D., the eastern half of the empire survived as the Byzantine Empire until 1453 A.D. Furthermore, the Roman Empire's institutions continued to influence and inspire later medieval kingdoms, including the Holy Roman Empire; even rulers in the twentieth century called themselves Kaiser and Tsar, titles which stem from the word "Caesar."

In addition, the Roman Empire was host to the spread of new religious ideas. In the region of Israel, the religion of Judaism presented a new approach to worship via monotheism, which is the belief in the existence of a single deity. An offshoot of Judaism called Christianity spread across the Roman Empire and gained popularity. While Rome initially suppressed the religion, it later backed Christianity and allowed the religious system to endure as a powerful force in medieval times.

Geography

Six Spatial Elements of Geography

Spatial Terms

Earth is an incredibly large place filled with a variety of different land and water **ecosystems. Marine ecosystems** cover over 75 percent of the Earth's surface and contain over 95 percent of the Earth's water. Marine ecosystems can be broken down into two primary subgroups: **freshwater ecosystems**, which only encompass around 2 percent of the earth's surface; and **ocean ecosystems,** which make up over 70 percent. On land, **terrestrial ecosystems** vary depending on a variety of factors, including latitudinal distance from the equator, elevation, and proximity to mountains or bodies of water. For example, in the high latitudinal regions north of the Arctic Circle and south of the Antarctic Circle, frozen **tundra** dominates. Tundra, which is characterized by low temperatures, short growing seasons, and minimal vegetation, is only found in regions that are far away from the direct rays of the sun.

In contrast, **deserts** can be found throughout the globe and are created by different ecological factors. For example, the world's largest desert, the Sahara, is almost entirely within the tropics; however, other deserts like the Gobi in China, the Mojave in the United States, and the Atacama in Chile, are the result of the orographic effect and their close proximity to high mountain ranges such as the Himalayas, the Sierra Nevada, and the Andes, respectively. In the Middle Latitudes, greater varieties of climatological zones are more common due to fluctuations in temperatures relative to the sun's rays, coupled with the particular local topography. In the Continental United States, **temperate deciduous forest** dominates the southeastern portion of the country. However, the Midwestern states such as Nebraska, Kansas, and the Dakotas, are primarily **grasslands**. Additionally, the states of the Rocky Mountains can have decidedly different climates relative to elevation. In Colorado, Denver, also known as the "Mile High City," will often see snowfalls well into late April or early May due to colder temperatures, whereas towns and cities in the eastern part of the state, with much lower elevations, may see their last significant snowfall in March.

In the tropics, which are situated between the Tropics of Cancer and Capricorn, temperatures are generally warmer, due to the direct rays of the sun's persistence. However, like most of the world, the tropics also experience a variety of climatological regions. In Brazil, Southeast Asia, Central America, and even Northern Australia, tropical rainforests are common. These forests, which are known for abundant vegetation, daily rainfall, and a wide variety of animal life, are absolutely essential to the health of the world's ecosystems. For example, the **Amazon Rain Forest** is also referred to as "the lungs of the world," as its billions of trees produce substantial amounts of oxygen and absorb an equivalent amount of carbon dioxide—the substance that many climatologists assert is causing climate change or **global warming.** Unlike temperate deciduous forests whose trees lose their leaves during the fall and winter months, **tropical rain forests** are always lush, green, and warm. In fact, some rainforests are so dense with vegetation that a few indigenous tribes have managed to exist within them without being influenced by any sort of modern technology, virtually maintaining their ancient way of life in the modern era.

The world's largest ecosystem, the **taiga,** is found primarily in high latitudinal areas, which receive very little of the sun's indirect rays. These forests are generally made up of **coniferous** trees, which do not lose their leaves at any point during the year as **deciduous** trees do. Taigas are cold-climate regions that make up almost 30 percent of the world's land area. These forests dominate the northern regions of Canada, Scandinavia, and Russia, and provide the vast majority of the world's lumber.

Overall, it is important to remember that climates are influenced by five major factors: elevation, latitude, proximity to mountains, ocean currents, and wind patterns. For example, the cold currents off the coast of California provide the West Coast of the United States with pleasant year-round temperatures. Conversely, Western Europe, which is at the nearly the same latitude as most of Canada, is influenced by the warm waters of the **Gulf Stream**, an ocean current that acts as a conveyor belt, moving warm tropical waters to the icy north. In fact, the Gulf Stream's influence is so profound that it even keeps Iceland—an island nation in the far North Atlantic—relatively warm.

Use this graph to understand current patterns:

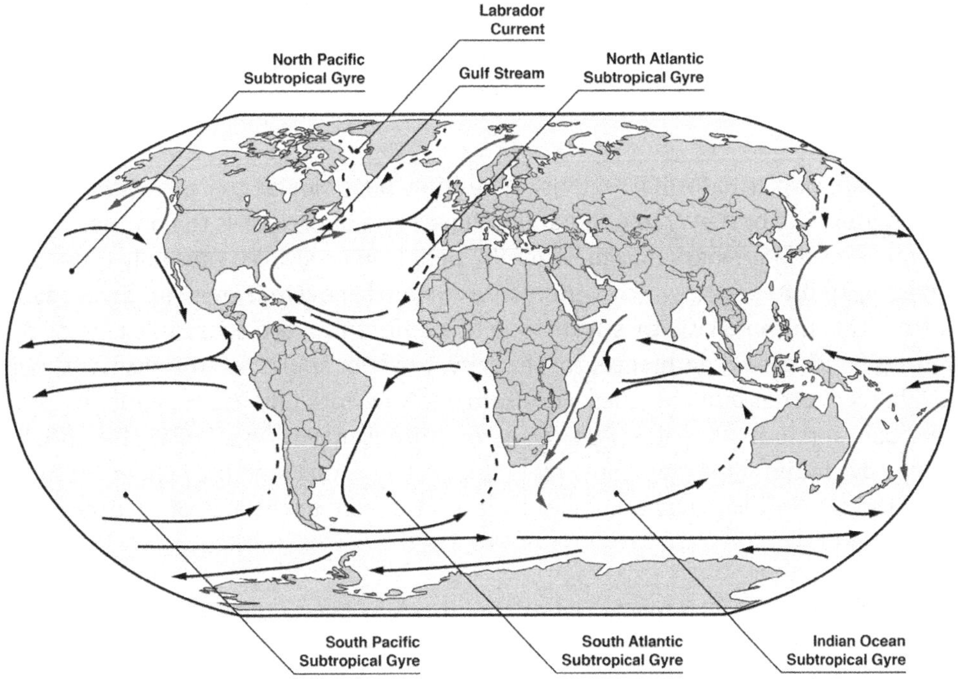

Places and Regions

Both absolute and relative location help humans understand their sense of place. Place is a simple concept that helps to define the characteristics of the world around us. For example, people may create **toponyms** to further define and orient themselves with their sense of place. Toponyms are simply names given to locations to help develop familiarity within a certain location. Although not always the case, toponyms generally utilize geographical features, important people in an area, or even wildlife commonly found in a general location. For example, many cities in the state of Texas are named in honor of military leaders who fought in the Texas Revolution of 1836 (such as Houston and Austin), while other places, such as Mississippi and Alabama, utilize Native American toponyms to define their sense of place.

Regions

Geographers divide the world into regions in order to more fully understand differences inherent with the world, its people, and its environment. Lines of latitude such as the Equator, the Tropics, and the Arctic and Antarctic Circles already divide the Earth into solar regions relative to the amount of either direct or indirect sunlight that they receive. Although not the same throughout, the middle latitudes generally have a milder climate than areas found within the tropics. Furthermore, tropical locations are usually warmer than places in the middle latitudes, but that is not always the case. For example, the lowest place in the United States—Death Valley, California—is also home to the nation's highest-ever recorded temperature. Likewise, the Andes Mountains in Peru and Ecuador, although found near the Equator, are also home to heavy snow, low temperatures, and dry conditions, due to their elevation.

Formal regions are spatially defined areas that have overarching similarities or some level of **homogeneity** or **uniformity.** Although not exactly alike, a formal region generally has at least one characteristic that is consistent throughout the entire area. For example, the United States could be broken down into one massive formal region due to the fact that in all fifty states, English is the primary language. Of course, English isn't the only language spoken in the United States, but throughout that nation, English is heavily used. As a result, geographers are able to classify the United States as a formal region; but, more specifically, the United States is a **linguistic region**—a place where everyone generally speaks the same language.

Functional regions are similar to formal regions in that they have similar characteristics, but they do not have clear boundaries. The best way to understand these sorts of regions is to consider large cities. Each large city encompasses a large **market area,** whereby people in its vicinity generally travel there to conduct business, go out to eat, or watch a professional sporting event. However, once anyone travels farther away from that **primate city**, they transition to a different, more accessible city for their needs. The functional region, or **area of influence**, for that city, town, or sports team transitions, depending upon the availability of other primate cities. For example, New York City has two primary professional baseball, basketball, and football teams. As a result, its citizens may have affinities for different teams even though they live in the same city. Conversely, a citizen in rural Idaho may cheer for the Seattle Seahawks, even though they live over 500 miles from Seattle, due to the lack of a closer primate city.

Physical Systems

Earth is a complex system of the atmosphere (air), hydrosphere (water), as well as continental land (land). All work together to support the biosphere (life).

The atmosphere is divided into several layers: the troposphere, stratosphere, mesosphere, and thermosphere. The troposphere is at the bottom and is about seven and a half miles thick. Above the troposphere is the 30-mile-thick stratosphere. Above the stratosphere is the mesosphere, a 20-mile layer, followed by the thermosphere, which is more than 300 miles thick.

The troposphere is closest to Earth and has the greatest pressure due to the pull of gravity on its gas particles as well as pressure from the layers above. 78 percent of the atmosphere is made of nitrogen. Surprisingly, the oxygen that we breathe only makes up 21 percent of the gases, and the carbon dioxide critical to insulating Earth makes up less than 1 percent of the atmosphere. There are other trace gases present in the atmosphere, including water vapor.

Although the stratosphere has minimal wind activity, it is critical for supporting the biosphere because it contains the ozone layer, which absorbs the sun's damaging ultra-violet rays and protects living organisms. Due to its low level of air movement, airplanes travel in the stratosphere. The mesosphere contains few gas particles, and the gas levels are so insignificant in the thermosphere that it is considered space.

Visible light is colors reflecting off particles. If all colors reflect, we see white; if no colors reflect, we see black. This means a colored object is reflecting only that color—a red ball reflects red light and absorbs other colors.

Because the thermosphere has so few particles to reflect light rays (photons), it appears black. The troposphere appears blue in the day, and various shades of yellow and orange at sunset due to the angle of the sun hitting particles that refract, or bend, the light. In certain instances, the entire visible spectrum can be seen in the form of rainbows. Rainbows occur when sunlight passes through water droplets and is refracted in many different directions by the water particles.

The hydrosphere, or water-containing portion of the Earth's surface, plays a major role in supporting the biosphere. In the picture below, a single water molecule (molecular formula H_2O) looks like a mouse head. The small ears of the mouse are the two hydrogen atoms connected to the larger oxygen atom in the middle.

Each hydrogen atom has one proton (positively charged, like the plus end of a magnet) in its nucleus (center), while oxygen has eight protons in its center. Hydrogen also has only one electron (negatively charged, like the minus end of a magnet) orbiting around the nucleus. Because hydrogen has only one proton, its electron is pulled more toward the oxygen nucleus (more powerful magnet). This makes hydrogen exist without an electron most of the time, so it is positively charged. On the other hand, oxygen often has two extra electrons (one from each hydrogen), so it is negatively charged. These bonds between the oxygen and hydrogen are called covalent bonds.

This charged situation is what makes water such a versatile substance; it also causes different molecules of water to interact with each other.

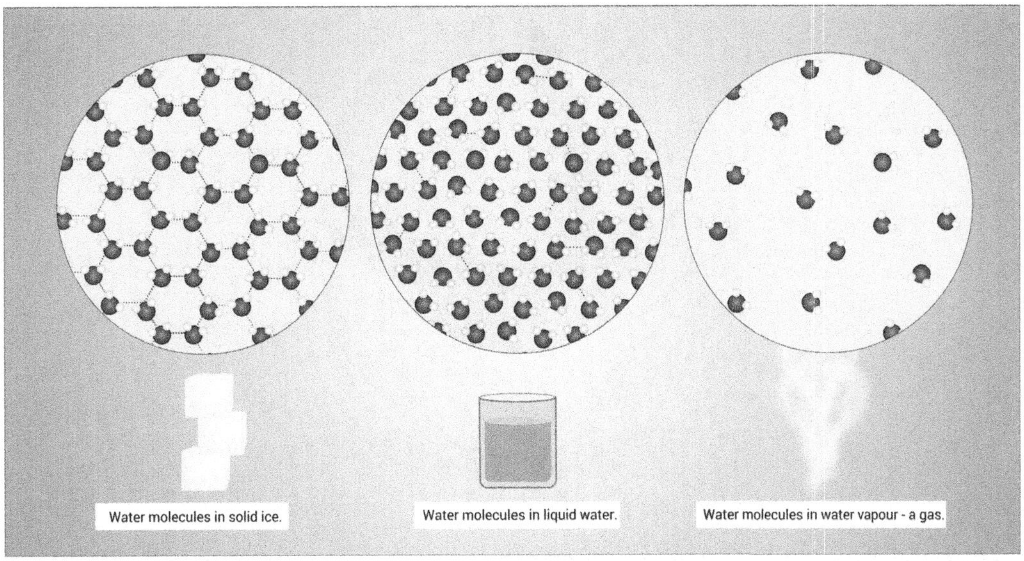

In a solid form (ice), water lines up in a crystal structure because the positive hydrogen atoms prefer to be next to the negative oxygen atoms that belong to other water molecules. These attractions are represented by the blue lines in the molecular picture of ice above. As heat is added and the ice melts, the water molecules have more kinetic energy and move faster; therefore, they are unable to perfectly arrange in the lattice structure of ice and turn into liquid. If enough heat is added, the water molecules will have so much kinetic energy they vaporize into gas. At this point, there are no bonds holding the water together because the molecules aren't close enough.

Notice how ice in its intricate arrangement has more space between the particles than liquid water, which shows that the ice is less dense than water. This contradicts the scientific fact that solids are denser than liquids. In water's case only, the solid will float due to a lower density! This is significant for the hydrosphere, because if temperatures drop to lower than freezing, frozen water will float to the surface of lakes or oceans and insulate the water underneath so that life can continue in liquid water. If ice was not less dense than liquid water, bodies of water would freeze from the bottom up and aquatic ecosystems would be trapped in a block of ice.

The hydrosphere has two components: seawater and freshwater (less than 5 percent of the hydrosphere). Water covers more than 70 percent of the Earth's surface.

The final piece of the biosphere is the lithosphere, the rocky portion of earth. Geology is the study of solid earth. Earth's surface is composed of elemental chunks called minerals, which are simply crystallized groups of bonded atoms. Minerals that have the same composition but different arrangements are called polymorphs, like graphite and diamonds. All minerals contain physical properties such as luster (shine), color, hardness, density, and boiling point. Their chemical properties, or how they react with other compounds, are also different. Minerals combine to form the rocks that make up Earth.

Earth has distinct layers—a thin, solid outer surface, a dense, solid core, and the majority of its matter between them. It is kind of like an egg: the thin crust is the shell, the inner core is the yolk, and the mantle and outer core that compose the space in between are like the egg white.

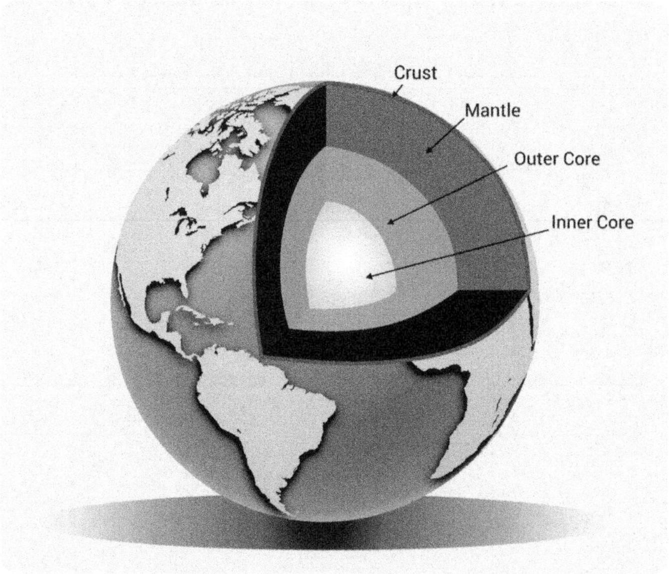

The outer crust of Earth consists of igneous or sedimentary rocks over metamorphic rocks (dense compacted rock underneath). The crust, combined with the upper portion of the mantle, forms the lithosphere, which is broken into several different plates, like puzzle pieces.

Human Systems

Migration is governed by two primary causes: **push factors**, which are reasons causing someone to leave an area, and **pull factors,** which are factors luring someone to a particular place. These two factors often work in concert with one another. For example, the United States of America has experienced significant **internal migration** from the industrial states in the Northeast (such as New York, New Jersey, Connecticut) to the Southern and Western states. This massive migration, which continues into the present-day, is due to high rents in the northeast, dreadfully cold winters, and lack of adequate retirement housing, all of which are push factors. These push factors lead to migration to the **Sunbelt,** a term geographers use to describe states with warm climates and less intense winters.

In addition to internal migrations within nations or regions, international migration also takes place between countries, continents, and other regions. The United States has long been the world's leading nation in regard to **immigration,** the process of having people come into a nation's boundaries. Conversely, developing nations that suffer from high levels of poverty, pollution, warfare, and other violence all have significant push factors, which cause people to leave and move elsewhere. This process, known as **emigration,** is when people in a particular area leave in order to seek a better life in a different—usually better—location.

Demography, or the study of human populations, involves a variety of closely related stimuli. First, economic factors play a significant role in the movement of people, as do climate, natural disasters, or internal unrest. For example, in recent years, millions of immigrants from the war-torn country of Syria have moved as far as possible from danger. Although people are constantly moving, some consistencies remain throughout the world. First, people tend to live near reliable sources of food and water, which is why the first human civilizations sprung up in river valleys like the Indus River Valley in India, the Nile River Valley in Egypt, and the Yellow River Valley in Asia. Second, extreme temperatures tend to push people away, which is why the high latitudinal regions near the North and South Poles have such few inhabitants. Third, the vast majority of people tend to live in the Northern Hemisphere, due to the simple fact that more land lies in that part of the Earth. In keeping with these factors, human populations tend to be greater where human necessities are easily accessible, or at least more readily available. In other words, such areas have a greater chance of having a higher population density than places without such characteristics.

Demographic patterns on Earth are not always stagnant. In contrast, people move and will continue to move as both push and pull factors fluctuate along with the flow of time. For example, in the 1940s, thousands of Europeans fled their homelands due to the impact of the Second World War. Today, thousands of migrants arrive on European shores each month due to conflicts in the Levant and difficult economic conditions in Northern Africa. Furthermore, people tend to migrate to places with a greater economic benefit for themselves and their families. As a result, developed nations such as the United States, Germany, Canada, and Australia have a net gain of migrants, while developing nations such as Somalia, Zambia, and Cambodia generally tend to see thousands of their citizens seek better lives elsewhere.

It is important to understand the key variables in changes regarding human population and its composition worldwide. Religion and religious conflict play a role in where people choose to live. For example, the Nation of Israel won its independence in 1948 and has since attracted thousands of people of Jewish descent from all over the world. Additionally, the United States has long attracted people from all over the world, due to its promise of religious freedom inherent within its own Constitution. In contrast, nations like Saudi Arabia and Iran do not typically tolerate different religions, resulting in a decidedly uniform religious—and oftentimes ethnic—composition. Other factors such as economic opportunity, social unrest, and cost of living also play a vital role in demographic composition.

Environment and Society

When gas prices are high, prices on virtually everything increase. After all, there are very few products that humans can buy that are not transported by either a gasoline- or diesel-powered engine. As a result, an increase in fuel prices leads to an increase in the price of food, goods, or other cargo. Recently, there has been considerable debate regarding the reliance on **nonrenewable resources** like oil, natural gas, and coal. These resources, which are also known as **fossil fuels,** are quite common throughout the world and are generally abundant, and cheaper to use than **renewable resources** like solar, wind, and geothermal energy. While solar energy is everywhere, the actual means to convert the sun's rays into energy is not. Conversely, coal-fired power plants and gasoline-powered engines, which are older technologies in use during the industrial revolution, remain quite common throughout the world. In fact, reliance on non-renewable resources continues to grow, due to the availability coupled with the existing infrastructure. However, use of renewable energy is increasing, as it becomes more economically competitive with nonrenewable resources.

In addition to sources of energy, nonrenewable resources also include anything that can be exhausted. These can include precious metals like gold, silver, and platinum, freshwater underground aquifers, and precious stones such as diamonds, emeralds, and opals. Although abundant, most nonrenewable sources of energy are not sustainable because their creation takes so long that they cannot be reproduced. Renewable resources are sustainable, but must be properly overseen so that they remain renewable. For example, the beautiful African island of Madagascar is home to some of the most amazing rainforest trees in the world. As a result, logging companies cut, milled, and sold thousands of them in order to make quick profits without planning how to ensure the continued health of the forests. As a result of severe deforestation on the island, mudslides became more and more common as the forests gradually shrank from widespread logging. In this case, renewable resources were mismanaged, and thus essentially became nonrenewable, due to the length of time for growth for the replacement of rainforest trees. In the United States, paper companies harvest pine trees to create paper; and because it can take almost twenty years for a pine tree to reach maturity, most of the companies utilize planning techniques to ensure that mature pine trees will always be available. In this manner, these resources remain renewable for human use in a sustainable fashion.

Renewable sources of energy are relatively new in the modern economy. Even though electric cars, wind turbines, and solar panels are becoming more common, they still do not provide enough energy to power the world's economy. As a result, reliance on older, reliable forms of energy continues, which has a devastating effect on the environment. Beijing, China, which has seen a massive boom in industrial jobs, is also one of the most polluted places on Earth. Furthermore, developing nations with very little modern infrastructure also rely heavily on fossil fuels, due to the ease in which they are converted into usable energy. Even the United States, which has one of the most developed infrastructures in the world, still relies almost exclusively on fossil fuels, with only ten percent of the required energy coming from renewable sources.

Uses of Geography

Two primary realms exist within the study of geography. The first realm, **physical geography**, essentially correlates with the land, water, and foliage of the Earth. The second realm, **human geography**, is the study of the Earth's people and how they interact with their environment. Like land and water on Earth, humans are also impacted by different forces such as culture, history, sociology, technological advancement and changes, and access to natural resources. For example, human populations tend to be higher around more reliable sources of fresh water. The metropolitan area of New York City, which has abundant freshwater resources, is home to nearly 20 million people, whereas Australia, both a continent and a country, has almost the same population. Although water isn't the only factor in this disparity, it certainly plays a role in a place's **population density**—the total number of people in a particular place divided by the total land area, usually square miles or square kilometers. Australia's population density stands at 8.13 people per square mile, while the most densely populated nation on Earth, Bangladesh, is home to 2,894 people per square mile.

Population density can have a devastating impact on both the physical environment/ecosystem and the humans who live within the environment/ecosystem of a particular place. For example, Delhi, one of India's most populated cities, is home to nearly five million gasoline-powered vehicles. Each day, those vehicles emit an enormous amount of carbon monoxide into the atmosphere, which directly affects the quality of life of Delhi's citizens. In fact, the problem of the smog and pollution has gotten so severe that many drivers are unable to see fifty feet in front of them. Additionally, densely populated areas within third-world nations, or developing nations, struggle significantly in their quest to balance the demands of the modern economy with their nation's lack of infrastructure. For example, nearly as many automobiles operate every day in major American cities like New York and Los Angeles as they do in Delhi, but they create significantly less pollution due to cleaner burning engines, better fuels, and governmental emission regulations.

Due to improvements in transportation and communication, the world has become figuratively smaller. For example, university students on the Indian Subcontinent now compete directly with students all over the world to obtain the skills employers desire to move their companies forward. Additionally, many corporations in developed nations have begun to **outsource** labor to nations with high levels of educational achievement but lower wage expectations. The process of opening the marketplace to all nations throughout the world, or **globalization,** has only just started to take hold in the modern economy. As industrial sites shift to the developing world, so does the relative level of opportunity for those nation's citizens. However, due to the massive amounts of pollution produced by factories, the process of globalization also has had significant ecological impacts. The most widely known impact, *climate change*, which most climatologists assert is caused by an increase of carbon dioxide in the atmosphere, remains a serious problem that has posed challenges for developing nations, who need industries in order to raise their standard of living, and developed nations, whose citizens use a tremendous amount of fossil fuels to run their cars, heat their homes, and maintain their ways of life.

Interpreting Maps

Geography is essential in understanding the world as a whole. This requires a study of spatial distribution, which examines how various locations and physical features are arranged in the world. The most common element in geography is the region, which refers to a specific area that is separate from surrounding ones. Regions can be defined based on a variety of factors, including environmental, economic, or political features, and these different kinds of regions can overlap with each other.

It is also important to know the difference between location and place. A location, defined either through its physical position or through its relation to other locations, determines where something is, and this characteristic is static. A place, on the other hand, describes a combination of physical and human elements in relation to each other; the determination of place is therefore changeable depending on the movement of individuals and groups.

Geography is visually conveyed using maps, and a collection of maps is called an atlas. To illustrate some key points about geography, please refer to the map below.

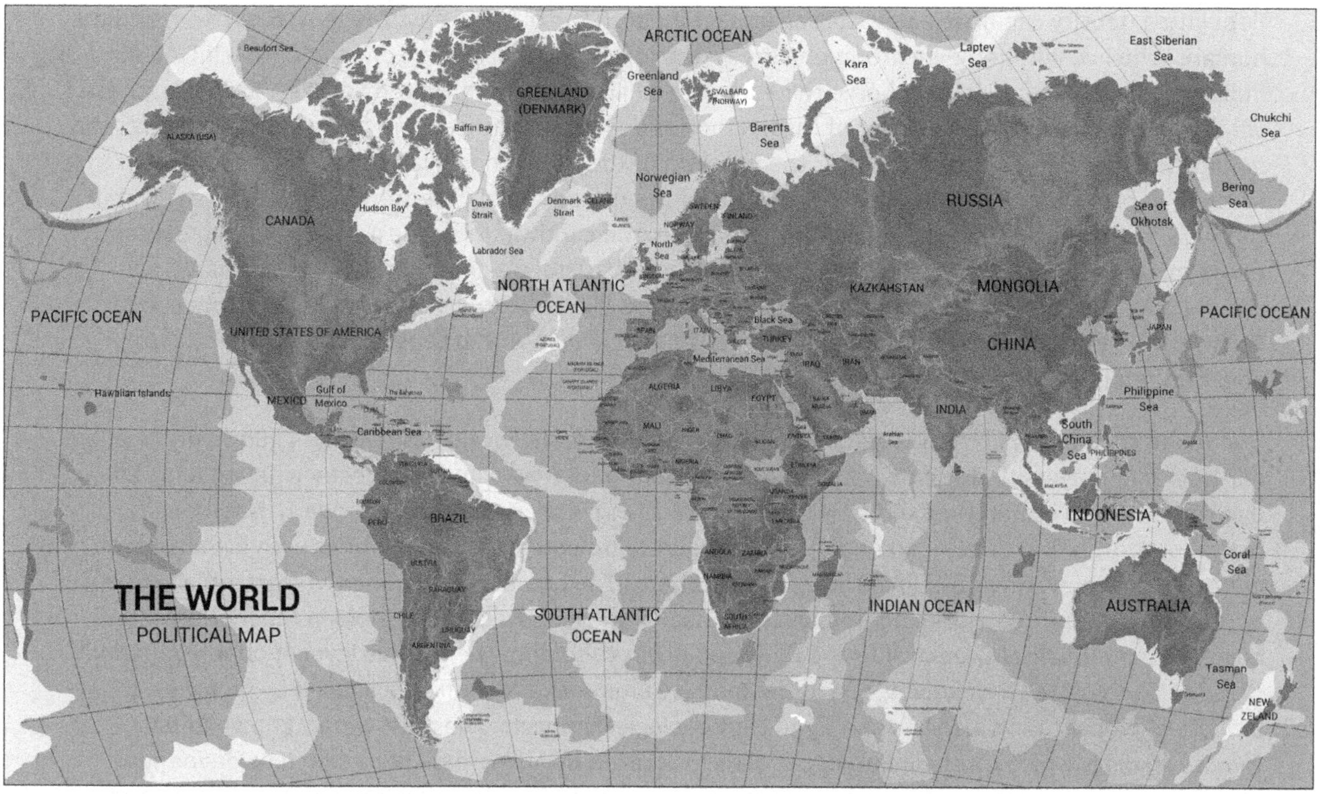

This is a traditional map of the world that displays all of the countries and six of the seven continents. Countries, the most common approach to political regions, can be identified by their labels. The continents are not identified on this map, with the exception of Australia, but they are larger landmasses that encompass most of the countries in their respective areas; the other five visible continents are North America, South America, Europe, Africa, and Asia. The seventh continent, Antarctica, is found at the South Pole and has been omitted from the map.

The absence of Antarctica leads into the issues of distortion, in which geographical features are altered on a map. Some degree of distortion is to be expected with a two-dimensional flat map of the world because the earth is a sphere. A map projection transforms a spherical map of the world into a flattened perspective, but the process generally alters the spatial appearance of landmasses. For instance, Greenland often appears, such as in the map above, larger than it really is.

Furthermore, Antarctica's exclusion from the map is, in fact, a different sort of distortion—that of the mapmakers' biases. Mapmakers determine which features are included on the map and which ones are not. Antarctica, for example, is often missing from maps because, unlike the other continents, it has a limited human population. Moreover, a study of the world reveals that many of the distinctions on maps are human constructions.

Even so, maps can still reveal key features about the world. For instance, the map above has areas that seem almost three-dimensional and jut out. They represent mountains and are an example of topography, which is a method used to display the differing elevations of the terrain. A more detailed topographical map can be viewed below.

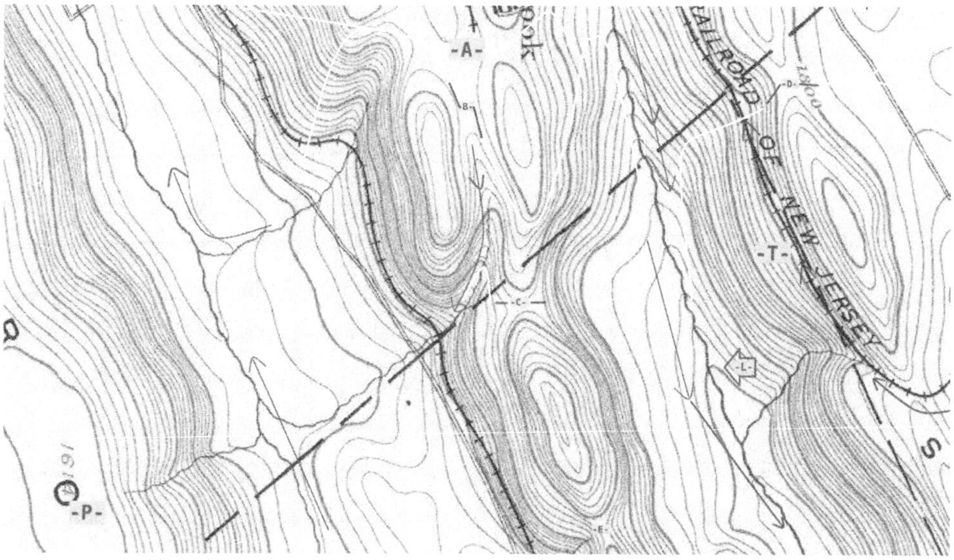

On some colored maps, the oceans, represented in blue between the continents, vary in coloration depending on depth. The differences demonstrate **bathymetry,** which is the study of the ocean floor's depth. Paler areas represent less depth, while darker spots reflect greater depth.

Please also note the many lines running horizontally and vertically along the map. The horizontal lines, known as **parallels**, mark the calculated latitude of those locations and reveal how far north or south these areas are from the equator, which bisects the map horizontally. Generally, with exceptions depending on specific environments, climates closer to the equator are warmer because this region receives the most direct sunlight. The equator also serves to split the globe between the Northern and Southern hemispheres.

Longitude, as signified by the vertical lines, determines how far east or west different regions are from each other. The lines of longitude, known as meridians, are also the basis for time zones, which allocate different times to regions depending on their position eastward and westward of the prime meridian. As one travels west between time zones, the given time moves backward accordingly. Conversely, if one travels east, the time moves forward.

There are two particularly significant longitude-associated dividers in this regard. The prime [Greenwich] meridian, as displayed below, is defined as zero degrees in longitude, and thus determines the other lines. The line, in fact, circles the globe north and south, and it therefore divides the world into the Eastern and Western hemispheres. It is important to not confuse the Greenwich meridian with the International Date Line, which is an invisible line in the Pacific Ocean that was created to represent the change between calendar days. By traveling westward across the International Date Line, a traveler would essentially leap forward a day. For example, a person departing from the United States on Sunday would arrive in Japan on Monday. By traveling eastward across the line, a traveler would go backward a day. For example, a person departing from China on Monday would arrive in Canada on Sunday.

Note the Prime Meridian:

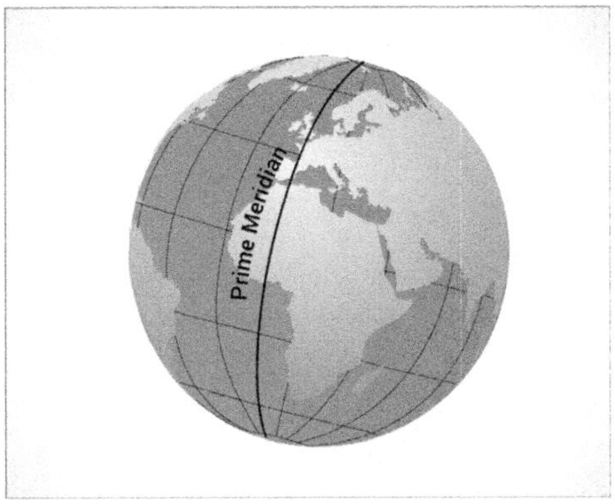

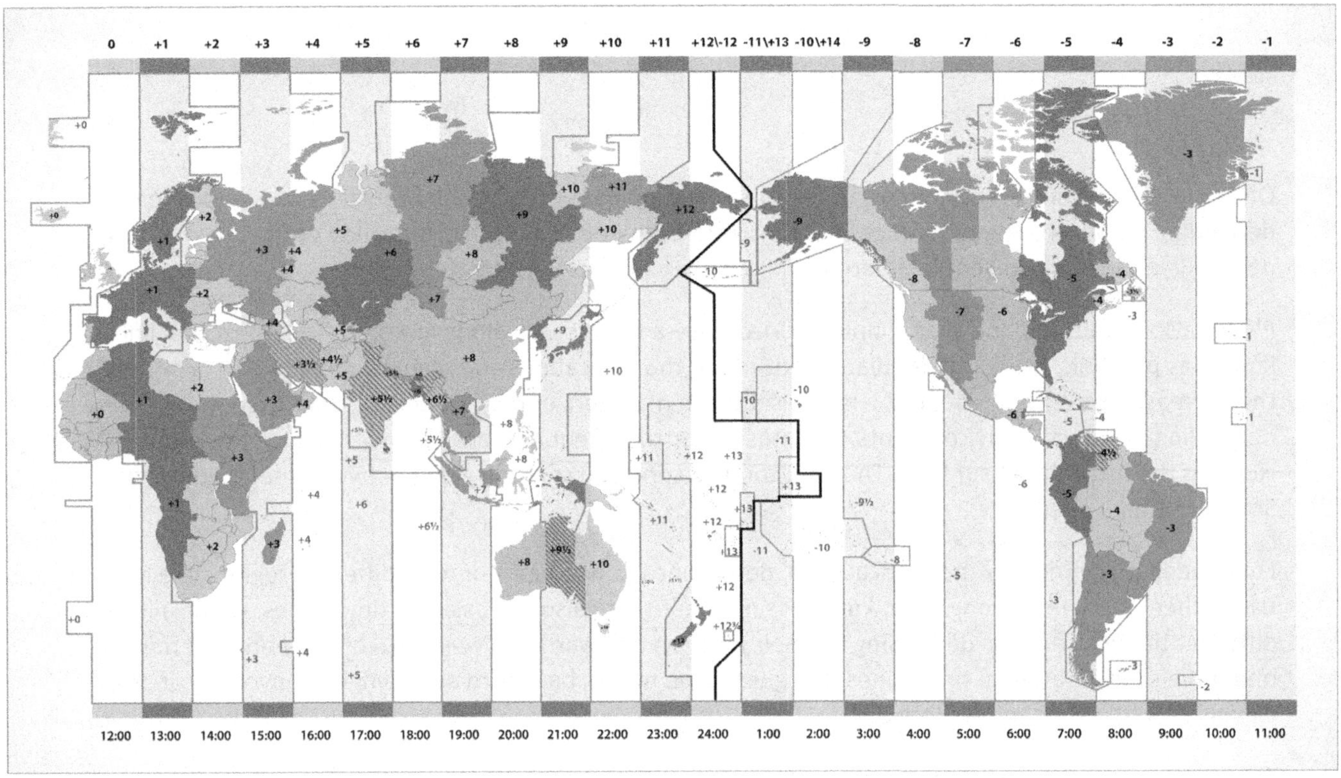

Although world maps are useful in showing the overall arrangement of continents and nations, it is also important at times to look more closely at individual countries because they have unique features that are only visible on more detailed maps.

For example, take the following map of the United States of America. It should be noted that the country is split into multiple states that have their own culture and localized governments. Other countries are often split into various divisions, such as provinces, and while these features are ignored for the sake of clarity on larger maps, they are important when studying specific nations. Individual states can be further subdivided into counties and townships, and they may have their own maps that can be examined for closer analysis.

Refer to this map for the previous point(s):

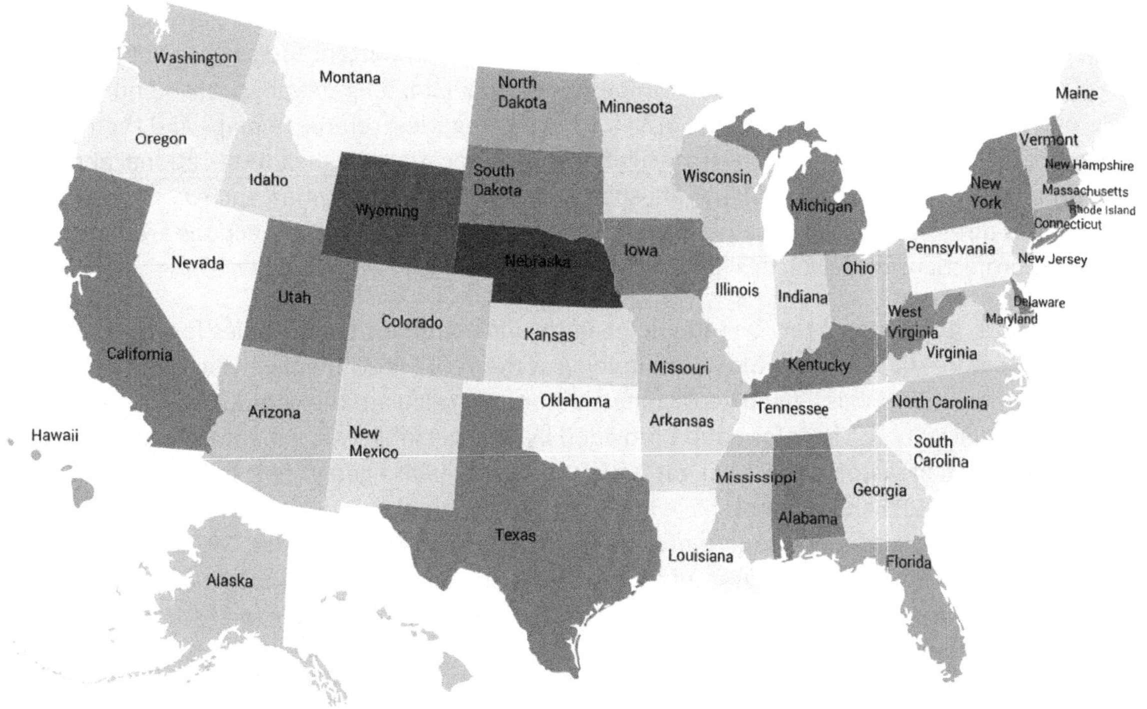

Finally, one of the first steps in examining any map should be to locate the map's key or legend, which will explain what features different symbols represent on the map. As these symbols can be arbitrary depending on the maker, a key will help to clarify the different meanings.

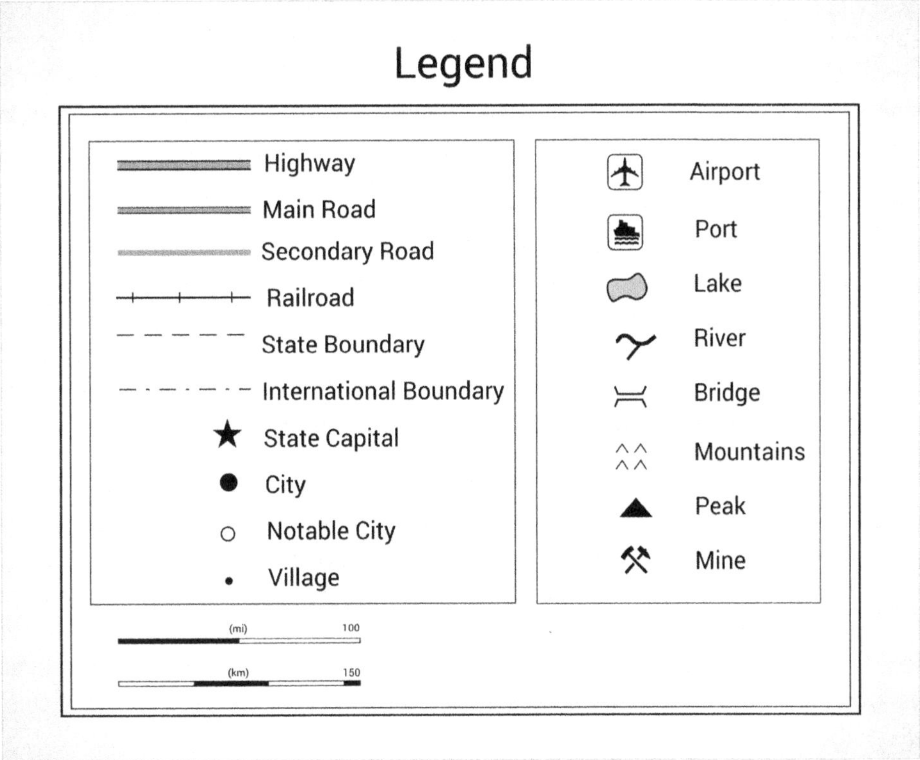

Tools and Technologies Used for a Spatial Perspective

Geographers must employ an array of tools and technologies to adequately analyze environments, cultures, and demographics from a spatial perspective. Maps are important tools because they offer 2D and 3D graphic images that display useful information for understanding the physical and human features of a region. Maps are usually separated into two categories: reference maps and thematic maps. Geographers use reference maps to designate specific locations, highlighting national and physical boundaries. Thematic maps designate spatial distributions of activities, such as weather and climate. Globes differ from maps because they are three-dimensional. Map projections are flat (two-dimensional) projections of the Earth's features.

In the early 2000s, geographers rely on satellite imagery and computer technologies for representing and analyzing features of the Earth. Global positioning system (GPS) technology, which was first implemented in the 1960s, has helped geographers accurately calculate the coordinates of a location via satellite-based trilateration. The information provided by GPS technology is enhanced further by the geographic information systems (GIS) that gather, store, and organize geographic information on computers. Together, GPS and GIS tools have helped usher geography into the 21st century, streamlining how humans acquire, process, and report information from a spatial perspective. GPS and GIS tools have not only influenced the work of scholars and geographers, but they have also dramatically altered how teachers and students approach learning in a social-studies classroom. Teachers and students now have GPS technology at their fingertips with the advent of smartphones, and one major challenge to the current paradigm in education will be finding ways to incorporate this technology into everyday social studies lessons.

Interaction of Physical and Human Systems

Humans have always interacted with nature, and humanity has been shaped by, and, in turn, reshaped environments. Using tools to accomplish things they cannot do on their own, humans have proven highly adaptable to different environments. However, the specific ecosystems have helped to shape human development as individuals and as groups. The earth is highly diverse and has many different ecosystems, each with its own flora and fauna. The specific resources available in different places have, therefore, influenced how humans develop.

Water, in particular, has proved vital in determining the course of human civilizations. As humans require water daily to survive, even more than they do food, proximity to water has always been of utmost necessity. Many human settlements originated adjacent to sources, and only in time expanded to other areas. Water is also essential for the growth of plants, which form a considerable portion of the human diet. In the wild, edible plants grow in places where they can thrive but may not be conveniently located for harvesting by humans. Therefore, humans gradually learned to grow plants themselves in places of their own choice. Humans also diverted water sources to new areas for themselves and to irrigate crops, thus transforming ecosystems.

Another important factor in the relationships between humans and nature has been the role of other animals. From small pests, such as weevils and rodents, to predators, including crocodiles and bears, many species of animals have often posed threats to humans, and conflict increased as humans expanded into environments inhabited by other creatures. On the other hand, animals are invaluable to humans because they can provide sustenance and clothing. This led to hunting and domestication of animal species. Domestication of both plants and animals involves humans breeding species to fit their own needs, which leads to new qualities that would normally not appear in the wild.

However, despite the considerable role that humans can play in altering environments, these changes have remained limited to local levels for much of human history. This does not mean that humans did not affect their ecosystems; some Native American tribes, for instance, used regular fires or hunting methods to maintain environments suitable for their needs. Even so, for much of human existence, nature was seen not simply as an obstacle but rather a power of its own right that was above human interference. Natural phenomena such as severe weather, diseases, and famine all kept human populations in check. Many pantheons of deities center on the gods' roles as arbitrary powers in the natural world, which reflects the lack of influence that humans had in the larger course of environmental changes.

Therefore, natural resources such as water and food were often seen as forces to be respected. Natural environments were recognized as vital regions, and alterations to fully exploit the resources were limited so that the resources could remain adequately sustainable. Riparian customs meant that water was the right of those with immediate access to it, and ownership changed accordingly with who lived nearby. However, increasing industrialization meant that natural resources such as water and lumber became resources that could be commoditized. In addition, appropriation gave water rights to those individuals or businesses that had first used the resource instead of being based on physical proximity.

Another instrumental change in the relationship between humans and nature is the increasing global connections worldwide. In many cases, earlier changes to environments occurred at local levels, with travel between different regions requiring considerable time and effort. The ability to travel around the world quickly has sharply altered that dynamic. Many local ecosystems, and the human cultures that developed accordingly, originated in separate circumstances that created unique plants and animals. Now products from one part of the world can be transported to entirely different environments and create new exchanges of goods. In some cases, the transferred species escape into the wild, and they often have traits for which the local environments are not prepared. This can result in invasive species that quickly grow and overpower native species.

A key symbol of artificial environments created by humans since early civilization has been the city, which is a human center of habitation that exists separate from the countryside around it. The creation of cities usually requires significant changes to the environment in which it is located, and the city must provide for the needs of residents without being compromised by nature. Yet the city has always remained connected to the rest of the world and to nature. Because a city generally lacks the capacity for agriculture and few natural resources are located within its confines, urban populations rely on resources from outlying areas for nourishment. The city, in turn, acts as a processing center for nearby settlements and offers rural workers and farmers the opportunity to sell their goods to a larger market.

Furthermore, the city, while an artificial construct, is still an environment in its own right. Although many species of animals have perished with the creation of cities, others, such as coyotes and pigeons, have adapted to urban life, thereby creating new ecosystems within cities. Natural connections within cities used to be stronger and more common because people would raise livestock within the city and regularly reuse garbage for livestock feed. While less hygienic, this helped stimulate natural cycles within the city. Recent efforts in many cities to create natural pockets, such as parks and community gardens, have also strengthened the ties between cities and the natural world. In a sense, the city reflects humanity's mixed relationship with nature as a whole: while humans continue to reshape the environment, they also remain linked to nature.

Ways in Which People Adapt to an Environment Through the Production and Use of Clothing, Food, and Shelter

All cultures throughout history have, to some degree, relied on clothing, food, and shelter for their survival.

The production and use of these goods are common practices among all civilizations, large and small. Moreover, all of these processes of production rely on the surrounding environment Clothing, food, and shelter have always derived from the resources of the environment. Food-gathering and production tills the land and reaps its harvests. The domestication of animals can occur only if adequate food sources are reaped from the environment to feed the animals. Likewise, clothing and infrastructure are produced from the plants and minerals of the environment:

Clothing

Since the First Agricultural Revolution, civilizations have relied on domesticated animals and crops to produce clothing. These groups use products from the environment, such as cotton or sheep's wool, to produce clothing. In many cases, the climate of the environment dictates the clothes that are worn. For instance, the Inuit and Yupik peoples of the Artic regions continue to wear heavy furs and animal skins to protect them from the cold. For centuries, humans have relied on these practices for survival.

Food

Food-gathering and agricultural production cannot be readily understood without considering the environmental changes (and damages) wrought by the process of planting, fertilizing, and harvesting crops. In essence, agriculture cannot exist without some alteration – positive or negative – of the natural environment. Agriculture has the power not only to shift the physical landscape of the globe, but also the social and cultural landscape. In any case, these agricultural shifts have natural geographic consequences. Throughout history, a demand for mass food production began to take its toll on the land, altering the physical geography of natural landscapes. The population growth brought on by new sedentary farming techniques inevitably transformed the landforms of the earliest "hearths of domestication." Food production flourished as a result of new farming techniques: terrace-building, irrigation, slash-and-burn deforestation, and the draining of wetlands. Together, these new techniques reshaped humanity's relationship with the land, establishing a human reliance on environmental factors.

- **Terraces**: While most early "hearths of domestication" emerged in fertile river valleys, some took hold on steep-sloping hillsides and mountainsides. The ancient Incas and Chinese, for example, established their agricultural dominance on seemingly inhospitable elevated slopes. In order to grow crops on these hillsides and mountainsides, ancient Incan and Chinese farmers cut terraces – stratified, flat farming plains – into their steep landscapes. These terraces helped shore up the hillsides and mountainsides, making them more hospitable for farming practices: the terraces prevented erosion by altering the natural flow of water and providing level plains to soak up moisture for soil fertility. In ancient China, terraces were created for rice fields that needed a lot of water to grow. Even in modern Southeast Asia, farmers still employ terraced rice farming practices, which allow the crop to grow in regions that, at first glance, are not necessarily ideal for agricultural practices. Similarly, in Machu Picchu today, the ancient Inca agricultural terraces, built centuries ago, are still functional. The Incas developed this stepped method of agriculture to avoid floods in lower elevations and mudslides at higher elevations. The sunken semi-circular terraces of Machu Picchu helped control mountainside water flow while simultaneously offering just the right amount of sun and soil for crops such as potatoes.

- **Irrigation**: Prior to the First Agricultural Revolution, nomads had to rely on natural flooding and growth to gather necessary plant materials to survive. With the technological advances of the First Agricultural Revolution, ancient civilizations turned to irrigation to plant life in even the most arid areas. Irrigation, by definition, is the process of redirecting of water via channels, ditches, canals, aqueducts, or other human-made systems. The Sumerians of Mesopotamia and the Egyptians of the Nile River Valley were some of the earliest irrigation engineers who dug canals, built dams and dikes, and constructed aqueducts in hopes of controlling floodwaters and sustaining new farming practices. Both civilizations built irrigation systems that cut through the alluvial soil of their respective riverbeds. The result was a set of complex water feeder systems that helped hydrate the burgeoning sedentary Sumerian and Egyptian populations. In ancient Mexico, the Mayan civilization embedded irrigation features into the landscape. Mayan laborers and farmers sought to channelize streambeds by constructing spillways and floodgates in the marshes of the Yucatan. The remnants of these human-made waterways can still be seen in the ruins and archaeological sites of Central and Southern Mexico.

- **Deforestation**: By around 3000 BCE, formerly nomadic groups, such as the Guarani people of the lowland river basins of South America, began to establish stable farming communities. Like other ancient civilizations, the Guarani people of the Paraguay and Parana river valleys began employing slash-and-burn deforestation techniques to make way for new crops such as corn, sweet potatoes, and cassava. Although the Guarani people continued to fish and hunt on the side, slash-and-burn farming became their most crucial source of nourishment. This process of slash-and-burn deforestation was carried out in the following capacity:

    - Thick jungle areas were slashed, or cut down, to make way for new sources of food.
    - The fallen forest materials were burned to open up the land even more.
    - The ash produced by the forest fires served as fertilizer for later crops.
    - The open land was tilled and ashed (using wood ash or burnt plant material to raise the pH so it was not too acidic) for new crops such as corn, sweet potatoes, and cassava.
    - The Guarani people moved on once the cleared soil became too arid due to over-farming.

  The Guarani people and other ancient civilizations would repeat this procedure, deforesting more plots of the jungle in the process. Slash-and-burn practices are still used today, and they threaten the persistence of rain forests in South America. These practices, which have their root in the First Agricultural Revolution, are still impacting the jungles of the Paraguay and Parana river valleys in the twenty-first century.

- **Draining Wetlands**: Recent archaeological evidence indicates that the Mayan civilization's irrigation system was used to drain the low-lying wetlands of Central and Southern Mexico. The Maya agricultural system, which churned out crops such as avocados and maize, depended upon a process of mucking out ditches, draining marshes, and tossing waterlogged, nutrient-rich soils into newly drained fields. This process of draining wetlands for crop use is still in use today, centuries after the Mayan collapse. The modern-day practice of draining wetlands, which is more malevolent than the ancient Mayan approach, threatens endangered marshlands across the United States and Mexico.

Shelter

Shelter is also dictated by the environment. One example is the ways in which the Inuit and Yupik peoples use ice and snow to create igloo shelters. Another example is how Native Americans in the Southwest used cliff-side caves and resources to create their pueblos.

Ways Tools and Technological Advances Affect the Environment

Technology and technological change cannot be readily understood if not analyzed through the lens of environmental change. All technological shifts have natural geographic consequences. For example, industrialization, agriculture, and urbanization have affected the environment are the forces behind climate change. Technology, however, is not wholly negative. In many ways, technological change has helped sustain larger global, national, and urban populations, which has allowed humankind to reach greater heights in terms of scientific advancement.

Reasons for the Movement of People

People migrate for a variety of reasons. Geographers typically categorize migration into two major groups: emigration and immigration. Emigration occurs when a person or entire group of people move *from* a location. Immigration occurs when a person or entire group of people move *to* a location. Immigrants and emigrants move for physical, cultural, economic, and political reasons. An immigrant is a person who comes from another country to the one currently being discussed, While an emigrant is a person who leaves their home country to settle elsewhere. Geographers traditionally separate reasons for migration into push and pull factors. Push factors encourage (or force) people to move from their homes. Pull factors attract people to a location. Political push factors include war, government-induced violence and intimidation, genocide, or oppression. Refugees are those pushed from their home country because of such political factors. Refugees are often forcefully expunged from their home states when new countries are formed or when national boundaries are redrawn. For example, the unification of North Vietnam and South Vietnam after the Vietnam War brought hundreds of thousands of Vietnamese refugees to the United States during the 1970s. Economic push factors include economic depressions or panics.

Other economic forces can be push factors. Deindustrialization in cities in the Industrial North (now called the "Rust Belt") during the 1960s-1980s pushed away many residents from industrial hubs like Buffalo, Cleveland, Chicago, and Milwaukee. In the 1840s, many Irish citizens were pushed from their homes due to a potato famine. During the Great Depression in the 1930s and 1940s, many from the American Heartland moved away from the economic conditions of the Dust Bowl. An extreme version of an economic push factor would be slaves brought to the Americas to enhance the Triangle Trade of the colonial era. Environmental push factors include flooding, natural disasters, droughts, nuclear contamination, and water contamination. In the Sahel region of North Africa, many have found new lands due to the intense droughts. Similarly, after Hurricane Katrina, many New Orleans residents had to relocate to Houston or Baton Rouge to find refuge from the environmental and economic devastation.

Political pull factors include the lure of democracy, safety, and liberty. In the late 19th and early 20th centuries, millions immigrated to the United States from Europe because they were enamored by freedom and opportunity. Some U.S. residents are moving to Canada because of its healthcare system. Some move to states like Texas because of the promise of no state taxes. Economic pull factors include job creation, higher wages, and low unemployment rates. In the United States, millions were drawn to the Sunbelt from the Rust Belt because industry moved South during the 1960s-1970s with the advent of new air conditioning technologies.

Environmental pull factors include hospitable climates, low chances of natural disasters, and outdoor aesthetics. Each year, thousands flock to Colorado to be closer to the outdoor activities associated with the Rocky Mountains. Many move to dry states like New Mexico and Arizona in order to escape inhospitable conditions for those suffering from respiratory ailments such as allergies or bronchitis.

The Impact of Transportation and Communication Networks on Economic Development

The globalization of the world economy has been catalyzed by the creation of transportation and communication networks. The interconnection of the world's economies has revolutionized how people acquire, absorb, and communicate knowledge. Technology—in particular, the Internet and social media—has enhanced the ways that people communicate. It has also transformed global economic development, creating what some geographers refer to as the global assembly line, a system of production built upon transnational economic development. The globalized efforts of transnational businesses—businesses that are not confined by national boundaries—have created complex systems of inequality across the globe. The global assembly line has increased industrialization in the Global South while catalyzing deindustrialization in the Global North. As a result, former industrial powerhouses in the North have suffered relative degrees of urban plight.

Meanwhile, developing urban areas in the Global South have become epicenters of low wages and exploitation. The current structure of the global assembly line still benefits developed countries despite their recent battles with deindustrialization. Meanwhile, developing sectors of the globe have witnessed some semblance of economic growth, but not without costs like environmental pollution and low wages for workers. The global assembly line has also forced many regions to the periphery, marginalizing their chances of reaping the benefits of the global economy. Industrializing nations such as Mexico are still struggling to create solid infrastructure, while remote rural regions of industrializing countries like India lack infrastructure altogether. The landscape of global economic development, therefore, continues to benefit the so-called former industrial powerhouses, such as the United States, Great Britain, Russia, Japan, and China.

Major Regions in the World, Nation, or State

North America

North America is comprised of Canada, the United States, and Mexico. All three are post-colonial nation-states that developed from the global changes in economics and politics during the 1700s and 1800s. Canada and the United States have long been described as developed nations, having gone through the process of industrialization, though they are now entering a new era of deindustrialized economics. A major aspect of the deindustrialized economy is the so-called information economy. This economy is built on information technology, computers, and fiber optics. Since the 1980s, Canada and the United States have relied heavily on the global retail economy and the information economy. Mexico, on the other hand, is traditionally considered to be a developing nation that relies on factory work and industrialization. Mexico is slowly becoming a major player in the global economy, thanks to beneficial trade deals such as NAFTA.

Latin America (Central America, the Caribbean, and South America)

The region known as Latin America is comprised of Central America, the Caribbean, and South America. The nations of these regions have close ties to the colonial period when they supplied the Spanish, French, English, and Portuguese crowns with crucial resources. Today, nations in this region enjoy their independence thanks to a series of revolutions beginning in the 1700s with the Haitian Revolution. Tourism and agricultural production continue to play a crucial role in the economic development of Latin America. Nevertheless, some nations have entered an era of intense industrialization. Brazil can now be considered one of the leading developing nations of Latin America. Other nations, such as Nicaragua and El Salvador, continue to be marginalized by global economics. Still other nations, such as Cuba, have entered a new era of economic relations following the end of diplomatic tensions with the United States.

Europe

Europe has entered a new era of socio-political development following the economic changes brought about by the European Union (EU). Traditionally a hub for colonialism, Europe has entered a post-colonial era of global economics, which reinvigorated the importance of regional economic relations. Created in 1999, the EU brought together several European nations under a common currency: the euro. The euro has not only brought about economic benefits, but also political benefits to marginal nation-states such as Greece. Nevertheless, the EU has been the subject of political debate, culminating in the recent Brexit, which legitimized the United Kingdom's decision to leave the European Union as of June 23, 2016. This decision makes the future of the region uncertain.

Russia

Previously the political epicenter of the communist Soviet Union, Russia has once again become a player in the global economy under the expansionist tactics of President Vladimir Putin. He has reinvigorated the Russian stronghold over former Soviet states and emphasized Russia becoming a self-sustaining powerhouse of energy resources. As tense relations with the United States and NAFTA threaten to reheat the Cold War, Russia aims to capitalize on resource booms in Siberia and the Caspian coast. Recent reports also indicate that Russia has its eyes focused on the resource-rich territory of the Arctic Circle. Historically, Russia continues to convey itself as an aggressive superpower that answers only to what is best for Moscow and its people.

Middle East

The Middle East has experienced a long history of conflict, as many nations vie for diplomatic supremacy in the region. The oil-rich countries of the Middle East are now, in many ways, facing their greatest conflict as the war in Syria and the growing power of ISIS threaten regional stability. Increased anti-Semitism and a renewed Israeli-Palestinian conflict threaten to undo decades of attempts at peaceful diplomatic relations. The Middle East continues to be one of the economic epicenters of an oil-dependent world, but growing income gaps, sporadic revolutions, and increased populations threaten the status quo. Russia and the West have renewed interest in the region as conflicts continue in Iraq, Afghanistan, and Syria. The spirit of Islam also seems to be at stake in the wake of ISIS's violent acts and the increasingly Islamophobic sentiment of the West. As Syrian, Iraqi, and Kurdish refugees scatter across the globe, they have been met, at times, with anti-Islamic fervor.

India and South Asia

Rampant urbanization has made India and South Asia a region wrought with overpopulation. India and South Asia have developed into hubs for industry and technology, but not without a cost. Billions of residents in the region are exposed to the devastating effects of pollution and poor infrastructure. Additionally, the income gap has widened, and the region has become relatively destabilized due to India's recent attempts at demonetization. Nevertheless, expect this region to continue to be an important sector of the global economy in the 21st century.

China

China and the Asia-Pacific region face their own industrialism and overpopulation issues. During the late 20th and early 21st centuries, China has joined Japan and South Korea as a global powerhouse in the region. Like India, China's struggles with overpopulation and industrial development come with struggles to maintain infrastructure and limit pollution. Yet, this rapid economic expansion has also made China a leader in private engineering and public works, as the nation rapidly develops high-rise skyscrapers and superhighways. The whole Asia-Pacific region, which includes Australasia, has become a magnet for wealth and economic development.

Government and Civics

The Structure, Functions, and Purpose of Government

The United States of America's government, as outlined by the Constitution, is designed to serve as a compromise between democracy and preceding monarchical systems. The American Revolution brought independence from Britain and freedom from its aristocratic system of governance. On the other hand, the short-lived Articles of Confederation revealed the significant weaknesses of state-based governance with limited national control. By dividing power between local, state, and federal governments, the United States can uphold its value of individual liberties while, nevertheless, giving a sense of order to the country.

While the federal government manages the nation as a whole, state governments address issues pertaining to their specific territory. In the past, states claimed the right, known as nullification, to refuse to enforce federal laws that they considered unconstitutional. However, conflicts between state and federal authority, particularly in the South in regard to first, slavery, and later, discrimination, have led to increased federal power, and states cannot defy federal laws. Even so, the Tenth Amendment limits federal power to those specifically granted in the Constitution, and the rest of the powers are retained by the states and citizens. Therefore, individual state governments are left in charge of decisions with immediate effects on their citizens, such as state laws and taxes. Like the federal government, state governments consist of executive, judicial, and legislative branches, but the exact configuration of those branches varies between states. For instance, while most states follow the bicameral structure of Congress, Nebraska has only a single legislative chamber. State governments have considerable authority within their states, but they cannot impose their power on other states, nor can they secede from the United States.

Local governments, which include town governments, county boards, library districts, and other agencies, are especially variable in their composition. They often reflect the overall views of their state governments but also have their own values, rules, and structures. Generally, local governments function in a democratic fashion, although the exact form of government depends on its role. Depending on the location within the state, local government may have considerable or minimal authority based on the population and prosperity of the area; some counties may have strong influence in the state, while others may have a limited impact.

Native American tribes are treated as dependent nations that answer to the federal government but may be immune to state jurisdiction. As with local governments, the exact form of governance is left up to the tribes, which ranges from small councils to complex systems of government. Other U.S. territories, including the District of Columbia (site of Washington, D.C.) and acquired islands, such as Guam and Puerto Rico, have representation within Congress, but their legislators cannot vote on bills.

Rights and Responsibilities of Citizenship in a Democracy

Citizens living in a democracy have several rights and responsibilities to uphold. The first duty is that they uphold the established laws of the government. In a democracy, a system of nationwide laws is necessary to ensure that there is some degree of order. Therefore, citizens must try to obey the laws and also help enforce them because a law that is inadequately enforced, such as early civil rights laws in the South, is almost useless. Optimally, a democratic society's laws will be accepted and followed by the community as a whole.

However, conflict can occur when an unjust law is passed. For instance, much of the civil rights movement centered around Jim Crow laws in the South that supported segregation between black and whites. Yet these practices were encoded in state laws, which created a dilemma for African Americans who wanted equality but also wanted to respect the law. Fortunately, a democracy offers a degree of protection from such laws by creating a system in which government leaders and policies are constantly open to change in accordance with the will of citizens. Citizens can influence the laws that are passed by voting for and electing members of the legislative and executive branches to represent them at the local, state, and national levels.

This, however, requires citizens to be especially vigilant in protecting their liberties because they cannot depend solely on the existing government to meet their needs. To assert their role in a democracy, citizens should be active voters and speak out on issues that concern them. Even with these safeguards, it is possible for systems to be implemented that inhibit active participation. For instance, many southern states had laws that prevented blacks from voting. Under such circumstances, civil rights leaders felt that they had no choice but to resist the laws in order to defend their personal rights. Once voting became possible, civil rights groups strove to ensure that their votes counted by changing state and national policy.

An extension of citizens' voting rights is their ability to run as elected officials. By becoming leaders in the government, citizens can demonstrate their engagement and help determine government policy. The involvement of citizens as a whole in the selection of leaders is vital in a democracy because it helps to prevent the formation of an elite cadre that does not answer to the public. Without the engagement of citizens who run for office, voters are limited in their ability to select candidates that appeal to them. In this case, voting options would become stagnant, which inhibits the ability of the nation to grow and change over time. As long as citizens are willing to take a stand for their vision of America, America's government will remain dynamic and diverse.

These features of a democracy give it the potential to reshape itself continually in response to new developments in society. In order for a democracy to function, it is of the utmost importance that citizens care about the course of politics and be aware of current issues. Apathy among citizens is a constant problem that threatens the endurance of democracies. Citizens should have a desire to take part in the political process, or else they simply accept the status quo and fail to fulfill their role as citizens. Moreover, they must have acute knowledge of the political processes and the issues that they can address as citizens. A fear among the Founding Fathers was the prevalence of mob rule, in which the common people did not take interest in politics except to vote for their patrons; this was the usual course of politics in the colonial era, as the common people left the decisions to the established elites. Without understanding the world around them, citizens may not fully grasp the significance of political actions and thereby fail to make wise decisions in that regard. Therefore, citizens must stay informed about current affairs, ranging from local to national or global matters, so that they can properly address them as voters or elected leaders.

Furthermore, knowledge of the nation's history is essential for healthy citizenship. History continues to have an influence on present political decisions. For instance, Supreme Court rulings often take into account previous legal precedents and verdicts, so it is important to know about those past events and how they affect the current processes. It is especially critical that citizens are aware of the context in which laws were established because it helps clarify the purpose of those laws. For instance, an understanding of the problems with the Articles of Confederation allows people to comprehend some of the reasons behind the framework of the Constitution. In addition, history as a whole shapes the course of societies and the world; therefore, citizens should draw on this knowledge of the past to realize the full consequences of current actions. Issues such as climate change, conflict in the Middle East, and civil rights struggles are rooted in events and cultural developments that reach back centuries and should be addressed.

Therefore, education is a high priority in democracies because it has the potential to instill generations of citizens with the right mind-set and knowledge required to do their part in shaping the nation. Optimally, education should cover a variety of different subjects, ranging from mathematics to biology, so that individuals can explore whatever paths they wish to take in life. Even so, social studies are especially important because students should understand how democracies function and understand the history of the nation and world. Historical studies should cover national and local events as well because they help provide the basis for the understanding of contemporary politics. Social studies courses should also address the histories of foreign nations because contemporary politics increasingly has global consequences. In addition, history lessons should remain open to multiple perspectives, even those that might criticize a nation's past actions, because citizens should be exposed to diverse perspectives that they can apply as voters and leaders.

Major Concepts in the U.S. Constitution and Other Key Documents and Speeches in U.S. History

With more than two hundred years of history, American leaders have produced a number of important documents and speeches. One of the most essential is the Declaration of Independence, which the Second Continental Congress ratified on July 4, 1776. Although many historians and politicians have drawn upon the words of the Declaration to demonstrate the American ideal of freedom, most of them focus on the preamble, which focuses on the necessity of fair government and the right to overthrow tyrants. The main body of the document consists of a set of grievances against King George III. Still, this document was instrumental in American history because it asserted American independence from Great Britain. Even so, it is important to note that the Declaration did not immediately lead to the United States; the document does not outline the government of the soon-to-be independent colonies, and independence would not become reality until Britain agreed.

The colonies' first blueprint for government was the Articles of Confederation, which was ratified in 1777. The document declared that the confederacy would be called the United States of America and that the individual states would have "a firm league of friendship" with each other. The emphasis on friendship and cooperation highlights how the confederation was a voluntary effort that states could follow or ignore as they saw fit. Still, the document also revealed the importance of obeying decisions made by Congress as a whole; while this was not very effective during the confederation period, the framework would live on to a degree in the following Constitution.

Much like the Declaration of Independence, the 1787 Constitution of the United States is most remembered for the preamble, which takes a more philosophical approach. However, the body of the Constitution is highly complex, and it covers the framework and responsibilities of the different branches of the federal government and the limits to state power. These details are very important and help to define the key institutions within the government. To resolve later issues not addressed in the Constitution, the fifth article in the document establishes a process to modify the government, and the first ten amendments are known as the ***Bill of Rights.*** Under the Tenth Amendment, powers not specifically allotted to Congress by the Constitution are reserved for the people and to individual states.

George Washington was the first president of the United States, and his administration set many precedents for the nation, particularly with his Farewell Address. In it, he noted the rise of regional feelings, and he urged citizens to uphold their duty to the nation above sectionalism because he felt that America was strongest when united. The issue of regional conflicts and national identity would become increasingly important in years to come, especially during the Civil War. Washington also argued against intervention in European affairs, and this warning would become the cornerstone for advocates of American isolation. On the other hand, his advice that political parties are detrimental to democracy failed to halt the development of the party system.

Washington's fears about sectional conflict were confirmed at the start of the Civil War, when the southern states violently seceded from the Union. As the president during that tumultuous time, Abraham Lincoln was seen by many to embody the Union as a whole. This can be demonstrated through his Gettysburg Address in November of 1863. After the difficult and bloody Battle of Gettysburg ended in a Union victory, crowds gathered for the dedication of the Soldiers' National Cemetery. Although he was not the main speaker of the event, Lincoln's short yet eloquent speech proved to be the most significant. Drawing upon the Declaration of Independence's assertion that "all men are created equal," he argued that the current war was a test of that ideal. More than that, he emphasized the importance of the United States as a whole and argued that it must endure as a Union for the sake of the world.

Earlier that year in January, Lincoln had already indicated his opposition to slavery through the Emancipation Proclamation. Although it was an executive order instead of a law passed by Congress, this document was not challenged by the courts and helped determine the objectives of the Civil War. The proclamation asserted that all slaves in Confederate territories were free. One must note that some southern states remained in the Union, and therefore, were not affected by this proclamation. Even so, the order helped establish a basis for later laws and amendments that would end slavery in the United States.

Another presidential attempt to set a new precedent for American policy was Woodrow Wilson's Fourteen Points, which were outlined in a speech he gave to Congress in 1918 after the United States had entered World War I. Wilson saw the United States as a protector of democracy in the world and said that we could reform world policy by fighting in the war. For instance, Wilson called for an end to private negotiations, which had contributed to the secret alliances behind the war. Most of all, he argued for nations to come together in an international body to determine world policies. The negotiations after the war only partially fulfilled Wilson's ambitions by creating a weak League of Nations, but his vision of U.S. involvement in global affairs would become a key aspect of American foreign policy.

Even as the United States began playing a more active role on the international stage of politics, internal issues such as civil rights remained important, as shown in Martin Luther King Jr.'s "I Have a Dream" speech. A leader in the civil rights movement, King gave his speech as part of the 1963 March on Washington. Drawing on Lincoln's past speech at Gettysburg, King argued that America's journey to true equality was not over yet. His references to biblical passages gave the speech a spiritual tone, but he also mentioned specific locations across the nation to signify how local struggles were tied with national consequences. By emphasizing his optimism, King's speech reflects not only civil rights activism but also the American dream of freedom and progress.

Legislative, Executive, and Judicial Branches

The federal government, which is in charge of laws that affect the entire nation, is split into three main branches: executive, judicial, and legislative. It is important to realize that the three segments of the federal government are intended to stand as equal counterparts to the others, and that none of them are "in charge." The executive branch centers on the president, the vice president, and the cabinet. The president and vice president are elected every four years. Also known as the commander-in-chief, the president is the official head of state and serves as the nation's head diplomat and military leader. The vice president acts as the president of the Senate in the legislative branch, while the president appoints members of the cabinet to lead agencies, including the Treasury and Department of Defense. However, the president can only sign and veto laws and cannot initiate them himself.

Instead, the legislative branch, specifically Congress, proposes and debates laws. Congress is bicameral because it is divided into two separate legislative houses. Each state's representation in the House of Representatives is determined proportionally by population, with the total number of voting seats limited to 435. The Senate, in contrast, has only two members per state and a total of one hundred senators. Members of both houses are intended to represent the interests of the constituents in their home states and to bring their concerns to a national level. Ideas for laws, called bills, are proposed in either chamber and then are voted upon according to the body's rules; should the bill pass the first round of voting, the other legislative chamber must approve it before it can be sent to the president. Congress also has a variety of other powers, such as the rights to declare war, collect taxes, and impeach the president.

The judicial branch, though it cannot pass laws itself, serves to interpret the laws. At the federal level, this is done through several tiers of judicial bodies. At the top, the Supreme Court consists of judges appointed by the president; these judges serve for life, unless they resign from their position or are removed by Congress for improper behavior. The Supreme Court's decisions in trials and other judgments rest on the justices' interpretations of the Constitution and enacted laws. As the Constitution remains fundamental to the American legal system, the Supreme Court's rulings on how laws follow or fail to uphold the Constitution have powerful implications on future rulings. Beneath the Supreme Court, there are a number of other federal judicial bodies—courts of appeals, district courts, and courts of special jurisdiction.

The U.S. Electoral System and the Election Process

As members of a democracy, U.S. citizens are empowered to elect most government leaders, but the process varies between branch and level of government. Presidential elections at the national scale use the Electoral College system. Rather than electing the president directly, citizens cast their ballots to select electors, who generally vote for a specific candidate, that represent each state in the college. Legislative branches at the federal and state level are also determined by elections, albeit without an Electoral College. In some areas, judges are elected, but in other states judges are appointed by elected officials. It should also be noted that the two-party system was not built into the Constitution but gradually emerged over time.

The Relationships Between Social, Economic, and Political Rights and the Historical Documents that Secure These Rights in the United States

The U.S. Constitution is a series of written rules defining the power of the U.S. government and the rights of U.S. citizens. Written in 1787 to create a stronger national government, it is the world's oldest working constitution. It gave Americans more rights than any other country had previously given its people. Collectively referred to as the Bill of Rights, the first ten amendments to the Constitution were added to protect the individual rights of U.S. citizens and to keep the federal government from wielding too much control. These are rights such as freedom of speech, freedom of religion, freedom of the press, and right to a fair trial. The Constitution has been amended twenty-seven times in order to accommodate changes and updates. Some of these amendments were made to be more inclusive to the wide range of American citizens. For example, the 14th Amendment, adopted in 1868, abolished slavery and stated that all citizens must be treated equally under Constitutional law and allowed the same protection within each state.

The Processes of the U.S. Legal System

The processes of the U.S. legal system have historically borrowed components from English common law, relying heavily on the role of judicial structures in dictating, developing, and monitoring laws, which are evaluated through the lens of the nation's principal federal governing document, the U.S. Constitution.

In the United States of America, all laws are developed at the federal and state levels. Additionally, local municipal jurisdictions can pass legal codes, so long as they do not interfere with the statutes established in state constitutions and the U.S. Constitution. Statutes can be defined as any law adopted by the legislative bodies of the federal and state governments. The state and federal courts assist in the process by enforcing these statutes and making addenda to these statutes.

Common Law: Common law is different than statutory law because of its focus on individual rights; all common laws are not covered by statutory law.

Federal Statutes: Federal statutes are federal laws enacted by Congress and supported by the U.S. Constitution. The process of making these statutes begins when the Senate or House of Representatives introduces a bill. After sending these bills through committees and subcommittees, which have to resolve differences between the bicameral legislature, the Senate and House approve a uniform version of the bill. This bill is then sent to the president, where it can be vetoed. The Senate and the House can overrule the veto with a two-thirds vote.

Below is a chart explaining the process of how a bill becomes law:

How does a bill become a law?

1. Every law starts with an idea

That idea can come from anyone, even you! Contact your elected officials to share your idea. If they want to try to make it a law, they will write a bill.

2. The bill is introduced

A bill can start in either house of Congress when it's introduced by its primary sponsor, a Senator or a Representative. In the House of Representatives, bills are placed in a wooden box called "the hopper".

Here, the bill is assigned a legislative number before the Speaker of the House sends it to a committee.

3. The bill goes to committee

Representatives or Senators meet in a small group to research, talk about, and make changes to the bill. They vote to accept or reject the bill and its changes before sending it to:

The House or Senate floor for debate

or

to a subcommittee for further research

4. Congress debates and votes

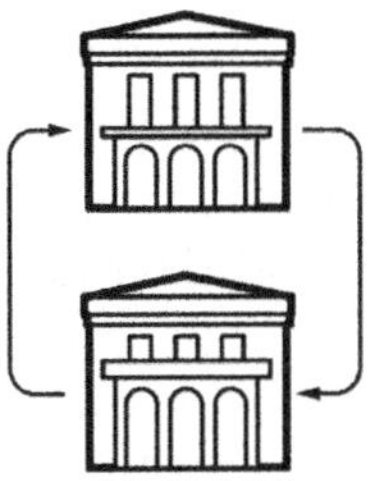

Members of the House or Senate can now debate the bill and propose changes or amendments before voting. If the majority vote for and pass the bill, it moves to the other house to go through a similar process of committees, debates, and voting. Both house have to agree on the same version of the final bill before it goes to the President.

The House uses an electronic voting system while the Senate typically votes by voice, saying "yay" or "nay".

5. Presidential action

When the bill reaches the President, he or she can:

Approve and Pass → **The bill is law**

The President signs and approves the bill. The bill is law.

Veto

The President rejects the bill and returns it to Congress with the reasons for the veto. Congress can override the veto with 2/3 vote of those present in both the House and the Senate and the bill will become a law.

Choose no action

The President can decide to do nothing. If Congress is in session after 10 days of no answer from the President the bill then automatically becomes law.

Pocket veto

If Congress adjourns (goes out of session) within the 10 day period after giving the President the bill, the President can choose not to sign it and the bill will not become law.

State Statutes: So long as the laws do not conflict with those established by federal statutes and the U.S. Constitution, state legislatures can also pass laws that reside in their jurisdiction or within their shared jurisdiction with Congress. The process for a bill to become a law in each state legislature is very similar to the ways in which bills become laws at the federal level.

The Roles of Courts: U.S. courts can enforce, interpret invalidate, and create laws.

- **Enforce**: If a law is infringed upon, undermined, or disregarded, the courts can oversee a suit to enforce the law.
- **Interpret**: If a definition, statement, or meaning within a law is not adequately defined, then the courts have the right to interpret that law, offering their own definitions, statements, and meanings within parameters of constitutionality.
- **Invalidate**: Using the U.S. Constitution as a "litmus test for legality," courts have the power to invalidate laws if they are deemed unconstitutional.
- **Create**: Courts can create "common laws" that focus on individual rights that are not protected under statutory law.

Types of Courts: There are two major types of federal and state courts, trial courts and appellate courts.

- **Trial Courts**: Any case is tried in a trial court.
- **Appellate Courts**: Trial decisions can be reviewed in appellate courts.

Levels of Federal Court: There are a total of thirteen judicial circuits within the federal court system of the United States of America. These circuit courts handle some appeals, such as patents and claims court cases. Each of the thirteen federal circuit courses has one appellate court, which is referred to as a Court of Appeals. Each federal circuit has lower levels of judicial districts. These districts vary in size, but can be as large as an entire state or as small as one city. The Supreme Court has the power to review all decisions made by the Court of Appeals.

Jurisdiction: Jurisdiction refers to the right each court has to review a particular question or case; for instance, the federal court has jurisdiction over federal cases and federal questions.

Criminal vs. Civil Cases: Criminal cases are a violation of criminal law, such as murder or arson. The defendant in these cases is tried and sentenced by a jury. Civil cases are not criminal infractions; they are legal suits over rights that are based on common laws or statutory laws.

Economics

Scarcity

Economies, by nature, have limited access to certain resources, which creates a conflict between supply and demand. Scarcity occurs when the demand for a product exceeds its availability. Scarcity in part depends on the choices of individuals as they determine which products they want more than others. Choices, in turn, are influenced by the perceived costs of pursuing certain options over others. The costs and benefits of specific choices often differ depending on the individuals' perceptions of the options. When people believe that a certain service's or product's benefits outweigh its necessary costs, they may choose to pay more for the desired benefits. It is important to realize that the laws of supply and demand are not absolute, and they may fluctuate depending on the situation.

Characteristics and the Importance of Currency

Currency describes the monetary unit that's commonly used within a nation or union of nations. Examples include the Indian rupee, the U.S. dollar, the Canadian dollar, the Japanese yen, the Swiss franc, the Russian ruble, the South Korean won, the Egyptian pound, the Norwegian krone, and the euro. Within each nation, these currencies maintain an absolute value. On a global scale, these currencies maintain a relative value, based on global economic development and prowess. Currencies are traded among nations in the global exchange, and their absolute and relative values can increase or decrease based on factors in global politics and economics.

Currency isn't confined to coins and paper notes. Credit is a component of national and global currency systems. Credit is a form of borrowing money to be repaid later, though it usually accrues interest over time. Loans—both secured (e.g., home loans and car loans) and unsecured (e.g., student loans, credit cards, and personal bank loans)—are examples of credit systems that affect national and global currency rates. Failure to pay back credit cards or loans typically leads to poor credit ratings, which may affect a person's ability to obtain more credit. In extreme cases, people who fail to pay off credit may have to file for bankruptcy. In the United States the main currency/financial institutions are stock markets, banks, credit unions, and the Federal Reserve System. Banks are owned by small groups of investors who hold or loan money based on the expectation that they'll earn a return on their investments. Stock markets are the overarching financial structure of the United States economy that serve as a mechanism for buying and selling company stocks; stock markets also describe significant increases and decreases in corporate finances. Credit unions are owned collectively by members rather than private investors. This means all information, responsibilities, and resources are shared. The Federal Reserve System is a central banking system that allows government officials and financial experts to consult and influence the creation of national, regional, and local banking policies. The Federal Reserve System maintains reserves of money to lend to banks.

The Role of Markets from Production Through Distribution to Consumption

Product Markets

Product markets are marketplaces where goods and services are bought and sold. Product markets provide sellers a place to offer goods and services to consumers, and for consumers to purchase those goods and services. The annual value of goods and services exchanged throughout the year is measured by the Gross Domestic Product (GDP), a monetary measure of goods and services made either quarterly or annually. Department stores, gas stations, grocery stores, and other retail stores are all examples of product markets. However, product markets do not include any raw, scarce, or trade materials.

As the Circular Flow Model below indicates, the role of a product market is quite different from the role of a resource market in a market economy. Both the resource market and product market interact with businesses and households, but their roles in buying and selling are reversed. **Resource markets** function with households selling resources and businesses buying these resources. The role of the product market is quite different: product markets function with businesses (i.e., stores, gas stations, grocery stores, and other retail stores) selling products and households buying these products. As the Circular Flow Model illustrates, consumption and expenditures are funneled into the product market via households, allowing revenue to flow to the businesses. Goods and services are filtered through the product market and into the households of consumers. Also, goods and services flow into the product market from businesses in exchange for revenue. This is different from resource markets where land, labor, capital, and entrepreneurial ability flow into the resource market from households as money and income (wages, rent, interest, profits) flow back into the households from the resource market. On the business side of resource markets, costs flow from the businesses to the resource market and resources flow from the resource market to the business.

Circular Flow Model

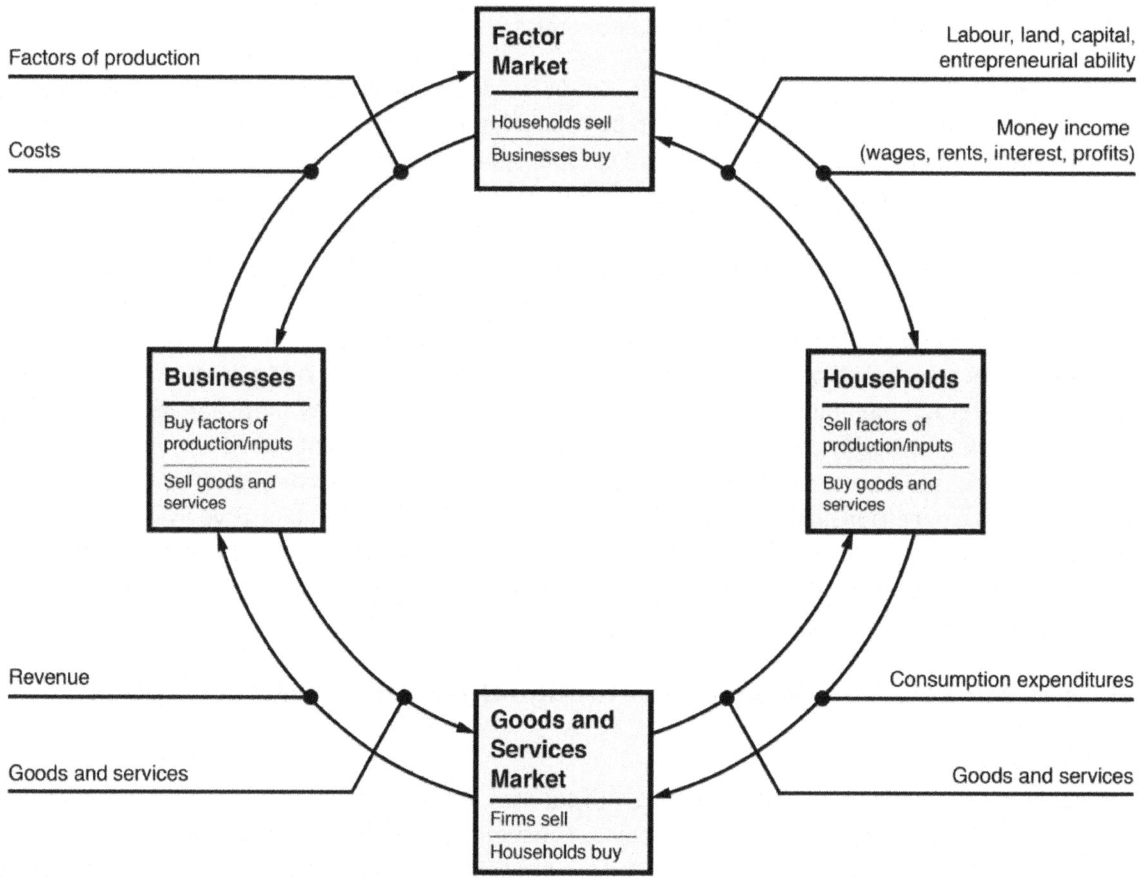

Factors to Consider When Making Consumer Decisions

Consumer economics is a term used to describe the ways in which consumers make decisions about their roles in a capitalist economy. The factors that consumers consider when buying goods and services include satisfaction and utility. Most consumers want to obtain as much satisfaction and/or utility from their purchase as possible; in colloquial terms, they "want the biggest bang for the buck." Consumers also have to consider the quantity of goods and services they are able to purchase at any given time, in accordance with the current price. This phenomenon is known as **demand.** When individual demand combines with aggregate demand, it is called **market demand.** Individual demands and market demands are also factors that consumers must consider when making decisions. These demands—individual and aggregate—drive consumer tastes. Most consumers do not demand goods that do not provide them with utility or satisfaction.

Consumers must also consider supply and scarcity. Consumers do not always have enough time or money to make their purchases, and this is known as scarcity. **Scarcity** basically means that consumers have to make choices: they cannot always have all the goods they want and participate in all their preferred activities. Likewise, all consumers—individuals, households, businesses, and governments—are bound to the supply chains of goods. At times, the actually goods or services might become scarce, meaning there are not enough products or services to meet consumer demand. As a result, consumers might have to consider alternative options for utility or satisfaction.

When an individual decides between possibilities, that individual is making a choice. Choices allow people to compare opportunity costs. *Opportunity costs* are benefits that a person could have received, but gave up, in choosing another course of action. What is an individual willing to trade or give up for a different choice? For example, if an individual pays someone to mow the lawn because he or she would rather spend that time doing something else, then the opportunity cost of paying someone to mow the lawn is worth the time gained from not doing the job himself or herself.

Individuals earn an income by trading their labor—both mental and physical—for pay. They then budget their money through spending or saving it. As consumers, every choice has an opportunity cost since they must choose which goods and services they want to buy with a limited income. By purchasing one good or service, they give up the chance to purchase another.

Additionally, consumers have the choice to save money when they don't have enough money to purchase what they want, or when they want to utilize a savings account to use during emergencies or periods of economic difficulty. People also choose to save for **retirement**, a time when they will no longer be working and drawing a salary. Saving money by putting it in a bank is considered low-risk—the bank will pay the saver a low interest rate to keep it safe, but it will not increase much in value. A riskier path is investing money through the purchase of valuable items (or **assets**) in the hopes that they will increase in worth over time and yield returns (or **profits**). Assets can include shares in companies, real estate or land investments, or capital such as money, equipment, and structures used to create wealth.

The Economic Interdependence Between Nations

International trade is when countries import and export goods and services. Countries often want to deal in terms of their own currency. Therefore, when importing or exporting goods or services, consumers and businesses need to enter the market using the same form of currency. For example, if the United States would like to trade with China, the U.S. may have to trade in China's form of currency, the *Yuan*, versus the dollar, depending on the business.

The exchange rate is what one country's currency will exchange for another. The government and the market (supply and demand) determine the exchange rate. There are two forms of exchange rates: fixed and floating. Fixed exchange rates involve government interventions (like central banks) to help keep the exchange rates stable. Floating or "flexible" exchange rates constantly change because they rely on supply and demand needs. While each type of exchange rate has advantages and disadvantages, the rate truly depends on the current state of each country's economy. Therefore, each exchange rate may differ from country to country.

Here is a chart displaying the advantages and disadvantages of fixed and floating exchange rates:

Advantages and Disadvantages of Fixed Versus Floating Exchange Rates			
Fixed Exchange Rate: government intervention to help keep exchange rates stable		Floating or "Flexible" Exchange Rate: Supply and demand determines the exchange rate	
Advantages -Stable prices -Stable foreign exchange rates -Exports are more competitive and in turn more profitable	*Disadvantages* -Requires a large amount of reserve funds -Possibly mispricing currency values -Inflation increases	*Advantages* -Central bank involvement is not needed. -Facilitates free trade	*Disadvantages* -Currency speculation -Exchange rate risks -Inflation increases

While each country may have differing economic statuses and exchange rates, countries rely on one another for goods and services. Prices of imports and exports are affected by the strength of another country's currency. For example, if the United States dollar is at a higher value than another country's currency, imports will be less expensive because the dollar will have more value than that of the country selling its good or service. On the other hand, if the dollar is at a low value compared to the currency of another country, importers will tend to defer away from buying international items from that country. However, U.S. exporters to that country could benefit from the low value of the dollar.

How Human, Natural, and Capital Resources are Used in the Production of Goods and Services

Economics are closely linked with the flow of resources, technology, and population in societies. The use of natural resources, such as water and fossil fuels, has always depended in part on the pressures of the economy. A supply of a specific good may be limited in the market, but with sufficient demand the sellers are incentivized to increase the available quantity. Unfortunately, the demand for certain objects can often be unlimited, and a high price or limited supply may prevent consumers from obtaining the product or service. If the sellers succumb to the consumers' demand and continue to exploit a scarce resource, supply could potentially be exhausted.

The resources for most products, both renewable and nonrenewable, are finite. This is a particularly difficult issue with nonrenewable resources, but even renewable resources often have limits: organic products such as trees and animals require stable populations and sufficient habitats to support those populations. Furthermore, the costs of certain decisions can have detrimental effects on other resources. For example, industrialization provides economic benefits in many countries but also has had the negative effect of polluting surrounding environments; the pollution, in turn, often eliminates or harms fish, plants, and other potential resources.

The control of resources within an economy is particularly important in determining how resources are used. While the demand may change with the choices of consumers, the range of supply depends on the objectives of the people producing the goods. They determine how much of their supply they allot for sale, and in the case of monopolies, they might have sole access to the resource. They might choose to limit their use of the resources or instead gather more to meet the demand. As they pay for the products, consumers can choose which sellers they rely on for the supply. In the case of a monopoly, though, consumers have little influence over the company's decision because there is no alternative supplier. Therefore, the function of supply within an economy can drastically influence how the resources are exploited.

The availability of resources, in turn, affects the human population. Humans require basic resources such as food and water for survival, as well as additional resources for healthy lifestyles. Therefore, access to these resources helps determine the survival rate of humans. For much of human existence, economies have had limited ability to extract resources from the natural world, which restricted the growth rate of populations. However, the development of new technologies, combined with increasing demand for certain products, has pushed resource use to a new level. On the one hand, this led to higher living standards that ensured that fewer people would die. However, this has also brought mass population growth. Admittedly, countries with higher standards of living often have lower birthrates. Even so, the increasing exploitation of resources has sharply increased the world's population as a whole to unsustainable levels. The rising population leads, in turn, to more demand for resources that cannot be met. This creates poverty, reduced living conditions, and higher death rates. As a result, economics can significantly influence local and world population levels.

Technology is also intricately related to population, resources, and economics. The role of demand within economies has incentivized people to innovate new technologies that enable societies to have a higher quality of life and greater access to resources. Entrepreneurs expand technologies by finding ways to create new products for the market. The Industrial Revolution, in particular, illustrates the relationship between economics and technology because the ambitions of businessmen led to new infrastructure that enabled more efficient and sophisticated use of resources. Many of these inventions reduced the amount of work necessary for individuals and allowed the development of leisure activities, which in turn created new economic markets. However, economic systems can also limit the growth of technology. In the case of monopolies, the lack of alternative suppliers reduces the incentive to meet and exceed consumer expectations. Moreover, as demonstrated by the effects of economics on resources, technology's increasing ability to extract resources can lead to their depletion and create significant issues that need to be addressed.

Government's Role in Economics and the Impact of Economics on Government

Governments have considerable influence over the flow of economies, which makes it important to understand the relationships between them. When a government has full control over the economic decisions of a nation, it is called a command system. This was the case in many absolute monarchies such as eighteenth-century France; King Louis XIV built his economy on the concept of mercantilism, which believed that the state should manage all resources, particularly by accumulating gold and silver. This system of economics discouraged exports and thereby limited trade.

In contrast, the market system is guided by the concept of capitalism, in which individuals and businesses have the freedom to manage their economic decisions. This allows for private property and increases the opportunities for entrepreneurship and trade. Early proponents of capitalism emphasized **laissez-faire** policies, which means "let it be," and argued that the government should not be involved with the economy at all. They believe the market is guided by the concept of self-interest and that individuals will optimally work for their personal success. However, individuals' interests do not necessarily correlate with the needs of the overall economy. For instance, during a financial recession, consumers may decide to save up their money rather than make purchases; doing so helps them in the short run but further reduces demand in a slumping economy. Therefore, most capitalist governments still assert a degree of control over their economies while still allowing for private business.

Likewise, many command system economies, such as monarchical France, still relied heavily on private businesses maintained by wealthy businessmen. With the end of most absolute monarchies, communism has been the primary form of command system economies in the modern era. Communism is a form of socialism that emphasizes communal ownership of property and government control over production. The high degree of government control gives more stability to the economy, but it also creates considerable flaws. The monopolization of the economy by the government limits its ability to respond to local economic conditions because certain regions often have unique resources and needs. With the collapse of the Soviet Union and other communist states, command systems have been largely replaced with market systems.

The U.S. government helps to manage the nation's economy through a market system in several ways. First and foremost, the federal government is responsible for the production of money for use within the economy; depending on how the government manages the monetary flow, it may lead to a stable economy, deflation, or inflation. Second, state and federal governments impose taxes on individuals, corporations, and goods. For instance, a tariff might be imposed on imports in order to stimulate demand for local goods in the economy. Third, the government can pass laws that require additional regulation or inspections. In addition, the government has passed antitrust laws to inhibit the growth of private monopolies, which could limit free growth in the market system. Debates continue over whether the government should take further action to manage private industries or reduce its control over the private sector.

Just as governments can affect the direction of the economy, the state of the economy can have significant implications on government policies. Financial stability is critical in maintaining a prosperous state. A healthy economy will allow for new developments that contribute to the nation's growth and create jobs. On the other hand, an economic crisis, such as a recession or depression, can gravely damage a government's stability. Without a stable economy, business opportunities plummet, and people begin to lose income and employment. This, in turn, leads to frustration and discontent in the population, which can lead to criticism of the government. This could very well lead to demands for new leadership to resolve the economic crisis.

The dangers of a destabilized economy can be seen with the downfall of the French monarchy. The mercantilist approach to economics stifled French trade. Furthermore, regional aristocracies remained exempt from government taxes, which limited the government's revenues. This was compounded by expensive wars and poor harvests that led to criticism of King Louis XIV's government. The problems persisted for decades, and Louis XIV was forced to convene the Estates-General, a legislative body of representatives from across France, to address the crisis. The economic crises at the end of the eighteenth century were critical in the beginning of the French Revolution. Those financial issues, in turn, at least partially stemmed from both the government's control of the economy through mercantilism and its inability to impose economic authority over local regions.

Fiscal Policy

A fiscal policy is when the government is involved in adjusting spending and tax rates to assist the way in which an economy financially functions. Fiscal policies can either increase or decrease tax rates and spending. These policies represent a tricky balancing act, because if the government increases taxes too much, consumer spending and monetary value will decrease. Conversely, if the government lowers taxes, consumers will have more money in their pockets to buy more goods and services, which increases demand and the need for companies to supply those goods and services. Due to the higher demand, suppliers can add jobs to fulfill that demand. While the increase of supply, demand, and jobs are positive for the overall economy, they may result in a devaluation of the dollar and less purchasing power.

Types of Productive Resources and the Role of Money as a Resource

Productive resources are the means used by a society to succeed and survive. The four types are:

- Natural resources—the raw materials taken from the land, such as corn, beef, lumber, water, oil, and iron.
- Human resources—the human labor, both mental and physical, that are required to produce goods.
- Capital resources—the man-made physical resources used to create products, such as machinery, tools, buildings, and equipment.
- Entrepreneurship—the capability and motivation to cultivate, organize, and oversee the other three resources into a business venture.

Money functions as a method of exchange to obtain goods or services. It replaced the barter system, which was often considered inefficient and disorganized. Economists referred to the barter system as a double coincidence of wants since trades between parties were not always considered equal. Prices of goods are determined by supply and demand. **Inflation** occurs when people have money to spend, but not enough goods can be produced or imported to meet their demand for a product, which causes prices to rise. The amount of money issued by government-controlled central banks and the prices of leading commodities, such as oil, can also affect inflation. **Deflation** is when people save their money and spend less, leaving stores with surplus goods, which causes prices to drop.

Practice Questions

1. Which of the following correctly lists the Thirteen Colonies?
   a. Connecticut, Delaware, Georgia, Maryland, Massachusetts, New Hampshire, New Jersey, New York, North Carolina, Pennsylvania, Rhode Island, South Carolina, Virginia
   b. Carolina, Connecticut, Delaware, Maryland, Massachusetts, New Hampshire, New Jersey, New York, Ohio, Pennsylvania, Rhode Island, Virginia, West Virginia
   c. Connecticut, Delaware, Georgia, Maine, Massachusetts, New Hampshire, New Jersey, New York, North Carolina, South Carolina, Pennsylvania, Vermont, Virginia
   d. Canada, Connecticut, Delaware, Georgia, Florida, Maryland, Massachusetts, New Hampshire, New York, North Carolina, Rhode Island, South Carolina, Virginia

2. Which of the following was NOT an issue contributing to the American Revolution?
   a. Increased taxes on the colonies
   b. Britain's defeat in the French and Indian War
   c. The stationing of British soldiers in colonists' homes
   d. Changes in class relations

3. The election of a presidential candidate from which party led to the Civil War?
   a. Democrat
   b. Whig
   c. Republican Abraham Lincoln
   d. Federalist

4. Which of the following was NOT an important invention in the twentieth century?
   a. Airplanes
   b. Telegraph 1830s
   c. Television
   d. Computers

5. A teacher is working on a lesson describing cause and effect. Which of the following sets might the teacher use as an example using a primary cause and effect of the American Revolution?
   a. A cause was the taxation of the colonies, and an effect was the civil rights movement.
   b. A cause was the Declaration of Independence, and an effect was the Constitution.
   c. A cause was the French and Indian War, and an effect was the Bill of Rights.
   d. A cause was the debate over slavery, and an effect was the Seven Years' War.

6. What are the two main parts of the federal legislative branch?
   a. President and vice president executive
   b. Federal and state
   c. District court and court of appeals Judicial
   d. Senate and House of Representatives

7. What was a concern that George Washington warned of in his Farewell Address?
   a. The danger of political parties
   b. To be prepared to intervene in Europe's affairs
   c. The abolition of slavery
   d. To protect states' rights through sectionalism

8. Fourth graders are brainstorming ideas about responsibilities of citizens of democracy. Which of the following suggested responsibilities is NOT correct and could warrant further discussion as a class?

a. To stay aware of current issues and history
b. To avoid political action
c. To actively vote in elections
d. To understand and obey laws

9. Which of the following statements is true?

a. Times zones are defined by their latitude.
b. Eastern and Western hemispheres are defined by the prime meridian.
c. A place is constant, while a location is changeable with the movement of people.
d. A continent is one of six especially large landmasses in the world.

10. Which of the following statements is true?

a. Water usage has largely shifted from appropriation to riparian.
b. Native Americans lived in harmony with nature by never disrupting it.
c. Cities are fully isolated environments.
d. Invasive species can have catastrophic impacts on ecosystems.

11. A fifth grader wants to know why geography is important to the examination of history. Which of the following are valid reasons that a teacher could share with this student?

I. Historians make use of maps in their studies to get a clear picture of how history unfolded.
II. Knowing the borders of different lands helps historians learn different cultures' interactions.
III. Geography is closely linked with the flow of resources, technology, and population in societies.
IV. Environmental factors, such as access to water and proximity of mountains, help shape the course of civilization.

a. I, II, and III only
b. II, III, and IV only
c. I, II, and IV only ←
d. I, III, and IV only

12. Which of the following statements is true?

a. All Native American tribes are matrilineal.
b. Japan is struggling to manage its high birthrate. china
c. Shi'a Muslims traditionally follow imams. ←
d. Mexico's culture is deeply tied to its Protestant roots.

13. Which of the following advancements was NOT invented by Greek culture?

a. The alphabet
b. The Hippocratic Oath
c. Democratic government
d. Theater

14. Which of the following was an important development in the twentieth century?

a. The United States and the Soviet Union officially declared war on each other in the Cold War.
b. The League of Nations signed the Kyoto Protocol.
c. World War I ended when the United States defeated Japan.
d. India violently partitioned into India and Pakistan after the end of colonialism. ←

15. A second grade teacher is discussing cross-cultural interactions. Which of the following is NOT an example that he or she should share with the class?
   a. Egyptian and Mayan pyramids
   b. The Spanish language
   c. Styles of sushi
   d. Study of Chinese culture

16. Which of the following is true?
   a. The barter system no longer exists.
   b. Economic resources can be divided into four categories: natural, capital, manufactured, and nonrenewable.
   c. Individuals help to determine the scarcity of items through their choices.
   d. According to the law of supply, as the price of a product increases, the supply of the product will decrease.

17. What is NOT an effect of monopolies?
   a. Promote a diverse variety of independent businesses
   b. Inhibit developments that would be problematic for business
   c. Control the supply of resources
   d. Limit the degree of choice for consumers

18. Which method is NOT a way that governments manage economies in a market system?
   a. Laissez-faire
   b. Absolute Monarchy
   c. Capitalism
   d. Self-interest

19. Which of the following nations did NOT establish colonies in what would become the United States?
   a. Italy
   b. England
   c. France
   d. Spain

20. Which of the following statements about the U.S. Constitution is true?
   a. It was signed on July 4, 1776. 1787
   b. It was enacted at the end of the Revolutionary War.
   c. New York failed to ratify it, but it still passed by majority.
   d. It replaced the Articles of Confederation.

21. Which of the following locations was NOT subjected to American imperialism?
   a. Philippines
   b. Puerto Rico
   c. Canada
   d. Guam

22. What is a power that Congress has?
   a. To appoint the cabinet
   b. Right of nullification
   c. To impeach the president
   d. To interpret laws through courts

23. Which of the following is true?
  a. The Emancipation Proclamation ended slavery in the United States.
  b. President Wilson called for the foundation of the United Nations in his Fourteen Points.
  c. The Constitution of 1787 and the Bill of Rights were ratified simultaneously.
  d. The Declaration of Independence was primarily concerned with the colonists' complaints against King George III.

24. *The entire Roman Empire was destroyed in the fifth century A.D.* Is this statement true or false?
  a. True; it was conquered by barbarians in that era.
  b. True; it was destroyed by a civil war during that time period.
  c. False; the western half survived as the Holy Roman Empire.
  d. False; the eastern half, known as the Byzantine Empire, survived until 1453 A.D.

25. Which of the statements about the United Nations is false?
  a. It ensured the continuance of an alliance between the United States and Soviet Union.
  b. It was based on the idea for the League of Nations.
  c. It helps to promote human rights.
  d. It includes many former colonies from around the world.

26. Which of the following gentlemen was not instrumental in leading the charge for discussion at the Constitutional Convention held in Philadelphia in 1787?
  a. George Washington
  b. Alexander Hamilton
  c. Thomas Jefferson
  d. James Madison

27. Which American Indian tribe led a nomadic lifestyle and lived in teepees that were easily moved from place to place?
  a. Plains Tents!
  b. Southwest
  c. Eastern
  d. Northwest

28. A third grade teacher is planning a lesson on life in the United States during WWII. Which of the following would be an applicable primary source to include in the lesson?
  a. A recording of one of FDR's Fireside chats
  b. A picture book about the Treaty of Versailles
  c. A movie about life in Germany under the Nazi regime
  d. A documentary of Eisenhower's Inaugural Address (TOOK OFFICE AFTER WWII

29. What was the controlling act imposed by the British on American colonists that taxed imported lead, glass, paints, paper, and tea, and prompted the colonies to unite against British rule?
  a. The Stamp Act
  b. The Sugar Act
  c. The Currency Act
  d. The Townsend Act

30. Where did the first shot of the American Revolution take place?
    a. At the Boston Massacre
    b. During the Boston Tea Party
    c. On Lexington Green
    d. At the Battle of Trenton

31. The Revolutionary War's final battle took place on October 19, 1781, when British General Lord Cornwallis surrendered to Washington's troops at what location?
    a. Yorktown, Virginia
    b. Valley Forge, Pennsylvania
    c. Trenton, New Jersey
    d. Saratoga, New York

32. What important U.S. structure was burned during the War of 1812?
    a. The Washington Monument
    b. Independence Hall
    c. The White House
    d. The Statue of Liberty

33. Who was elected President of the Confederate States of America during the Civil War?
    a. Robert E. Lee
    b. Jefferson Davis
    c. William T. Sherman
    d. Abraham Lincoln

Because it seemed shiny

34. The period of business and industrial growth from 1876 through the turn of the twentieth century was deemed by author Mark Twain as what?
    a. Manifest Destiny
    b. The Columbian Exchange
    c. The New Deal
    d. The Gilded Age

35. When did World War I begin?
    a. 1915
    b. 1917
    c. 1914
    d. 1918

36. Which of the following countries was a U.S. ally during World War II?
    a. The Soviet Union
    b. Italy
    c. Germany
    d. Japan

37. The North Atlantic Treaty Organization (NATO) was formed between which countries or regions?
    a. Canada, the U.S., and South America
    b. Western Europe, the U.S., and Canada
    c. The U.S., Western Europe, Canada, and the Soviet Union
    d. Asia, the U.S., and Western Europe

38. A fifth grade student is giving a report on events that served as driving forces for the passage of the Civil Rights Act in 1964. She has cited the following four events. As her teacher, upon completion of her report, you acknowledge her successes and then inform her that which of the following was actually NOT a driving force?

a. *Brown vs. the Board of Education*
b. Freedom rides
c. The G.I. Bill
d. The Montgomery bus boycott

39. What program launched by the U.S. government under President Ronald Reagan was designed to shield the U.S. from nuclear attack by the Soviet Union?

a. The Strategic Arms Limitation Talks (SALT I and II)
b. The Strategic Defense Initiative (SDI)
c. The Iran-Contra Affair
d. *Glasnost*

40. After the terrorist attacks initiated by Islamic fundamentalist Osama bin Laden on September 11, 2001, President George W. Bush ordered bombing raids on various locations in what country in an attempt to bring down bin Laden and his al-Qaeda network?

a. Afghanistan
b. Iraq
c. Kuwait
d. Pakistan

41. What are the two largest rivers in the U.S. called?

a. The Mississippi and the Colorado
b. The Mississippi and the Missouri
c. The Missouri and the Ohio
d. The Mississippi and the Ohio

42. What is used to pinpoint location on a map?

a. Scale and longitude
b. Contour lines and scale
c. Latitude and longitude
d. Latitude and contour lines

43. Third grader students are debating what are the obligations of citizens under America's democratic form of government. Which of the following is NOT one of these such obligations?

a. Obey the law
b. Pay taxes
c. Serve on a jury if asked to do so
d. Vote in elections

44. A teacher is preparing a lesson about the dynamic nature of history. Which of the following is a good example of this principle?

a. The fact that GPS technology was first implemented in the 1960s but now is available on smartphones.
b. The fact there are checks and balances built into the various branches of government.
c. The fact that there are contradictory accounts of certain historical events, such as when Europeans first came to America.
d. The fact that there are twenty-seven amendments to the U.S. Constitution

As in constantly changing

45. What is interaction of consumers, households, and companies within individual markets and the relationships between them called?

a. Macroeconomics
b. Microeconomics
c. Boom and bust
d. Economic output

46. What are the types of productive resources used to create products, such as machinery, tools, buildings, and equipment called?

a. Natural resources
b. Human resources
c. Capital resources
d. Entrepreneurship

47. What is the business sector of the economy that provides consumer or business services, including industries such as entertainment, travel and tourism, and banking called?

a. Primary
b. Secondary
c. Tertiary
d. Quaternary

48. Consumers must make choices regarding the goods and services to buy with their limited income. By purchasing one good or service, they are giving up the chance to purchase another. This is referred to as which of the following?

a. The circular flow model
b. Opportunity cost
c. Savings account
d. Assets

49. Which of the following is one way teachers can move beyond traditional direct instruction in the social studies classroom?

a. Textbook work
b. Lectures
c. PowerPoints
d. Field experiences

50. Which of the following geographic tools best allows teachers and students to use satellite technology in the classroom?
   a. Globes
   b. GPS
   c. Timelines
   d. Map projections

51. Which of the following represents the Florida state economy?
   a. It has strong ties to the aerospace industry.
   b. It is a Rust Belt state that has experienced decades-long bouts with deindustrialization.
   c. It has historically relied on ranching.
   d. It has benefitted from the Mexican national period.

52. The following should be implemented in EC-6 social studies classrooms for the benefit of student learning:
   a. Differentiated assessments
   b. Field experiences
   c. Project-based learning
   d. All of the above.

53. What is the difference between a primary source and a secondary source?
   a. Secondary sources are usually fictional, while primary sources are always true.
   b. Primary sources are context-specific, first-hand accounts, and secondary sources usually synthesize primary sources with some historical distance.
   c. Secondary sources are almost always first-hand accounts, while primary sources are second-hand fictional testimonies.
   d. There are no major differences between primary sources and secondary sources.

54. Which of the following is a pre-colonial Native American tribe in Florida?
   a. Seminoles
   b. Karankawas
   c. Witchitas
   d. All of the above

55. Which countries controlled Florida during the era of European colonization?
   a. Spain, France, and the United States
   b. Spain, Mexico, and the United States
   c. Spain, Cuba, and the United States
   d. Spain, Portugal, and the United States

Answer Explanations

1. A: Carolina is divided into two separate states—North and South. Maine was part of Nova Scotia and did not become an American territory until the War of 1812. Likewise, Vermont was not one of the original Thirteen Colonies. Canada remained a separate British colony. Finally, Florida was a Spanish territory. Therefore, by process of elimination, *A* is the correct list.

2. B: Britain was not defeated in the French and Indian War, and, in fact, disputes with the colonies over the new territories it won contributed to the growing tensions. All of the other options were key motivations behind the Revolutionary War.

3. C: Abraham Lincoln was elected president as part of the new Republican Party, and his plans to limit and potentially abolish slavery led the southern states to secede from the Union.

4. B: Out of the four inventions mentioned, the first telegraphs were invented in the 1830s, and did not have as great of an impact during the twentieth century. In contrast, the other inventions had considerable influence over the course of the twentieth century.

5. C: Cause and effect is an important concept in social sciences. The Declaration of Independence occurred during the American Revolution, so it should therefore be considered an effect, not a cause. Similarly, slavery was a cause for the later Civil War, but it was not a primary instigator for the Revolutionary War. Although a single event can have many effects long into the future, it is also important to not overstate the influence of these individual causes; the civil rights movement was only tangentially connected to the War of Independence among many other factors, and therefore it should not be considered a primary effect of it. The French and Indian War (which was part of the Seven Years' War) and the Bill of Rights, on the other hand, were respectively a cause and effect from the American Revolution, making Choice *C* the correct answer.

6. D: The president and vice president are part of the executive branch, not the legislative branch. The question focuses specifically on the federal level, so state government should be excluded from consideration. As for the district court and the court of appeals, they are part of the judicial branch. The legislative branch is made up of Congress, which consists of the House of Representatives and the Senate.

7. A: George Washington was a slave owner himself in life, so he did not make abolition a theme in his Farewell Address. On the other hand, he was concerned that sectionalism could potentially destroy the United States, and he warned against it. Furthermore, he believed that Americans should avoid getting involved in European affairs. However, one issue that he felt was especially problematic was the formation of political parties, and he urged against it in his farewell.

8. B: It is not a responsibility to avoid involvement in political processes such as voting is antithetical to the principles of a democracy. Therefore, the principal responsibility of citizens is the opposite, and they should be steadily engaged in the political processes that determine the course of government.

9. B: Time zones are determined by longitude, not latitude. Locations are defined in absolute terms, while places are in part defined by the population, which is subject to movement. There are seven continents in the world, not six. On the other hand, it is true that the prime meridian determines the border for the Eastern and Western hemispheres.

10. D: Riparian water usage was common in the past, but modern usage has shifted to appropriation. While often practicing sustainable methods, Native Americans used fire, agriculture, and other tools to shape the landscape for their own ends. Due to the importance of trade in providing essential resources to cities, a city is never truly separated from the outside world. However, invasive species are a formidable threat to native environments, making *D* the correct answer.

11. C: I, II, and IV only. Historians make use of maps in their studies to get a clear picture of how history unfolded, knowing the borders of different lands helps historians learn different cultures' interactions, and environmental factors, such as access to water and the proximity of mountains, help determine the course of civilization. The phrase "Geography is closely linked with the flow of resources, technology, and population in societies" is a characteristic of economics.

12. C: While many Native American tribes are matrilineal, not all of them are. Japan is currently coping with an especially low birthrate, not a high one. Mexico's religion, like that of Spain, is primarily Roman Catholic rather than Protestant. On the other hand, Shi'a Islam is based on the view that imams should be honored as Muhammad's chosen heirs to the Caliphate, making *C* correct.

13. A: Although Greeks used the alphabet as the basis for their written language, leading to a diverse array of literature, they learned about the alphabet from Phoenician traders. All the other options, in contrast, were invented in Greece.

14. D: It is important to realize that the Cold War was never an official war and that the United States and the Soviet Union instead funded proxy conflicts. The Kyoto Protocol was signed by members of the United Nations, as the League of Nations was long since defunct. While Japan was a minor participant in World War I, it was not defeated by America until World War II. The correct answer is *D*: India's partition between Hindu India and Islamic Pakistan led to large outbreaks of religious violence.

15. A: Although Egyptian and Mayan civilizations are an interesting subject for comparisons, the two cultures never interacted; therefore, the teacher should not use this as an example of cross-cultural interactions. The other answers are all examples of interactions between different cultures; a study of Chinese culture, for instance, would require examination of the multiple ethnic groups throughout China.

16. C: Although monetary systems were invented to solve problems with barter systems, it is wrong to assume that barter systems have ceased to exist; bartering remains a common practice throughout the world, albeit less common than money. The four main categories for economic resources are land, labor, capital, and entrepreneurship. The law of supply says that supplies will increase, not decrease, as prices increase. The correct answer is *C,* as scarcity is determined by human choice.

17. A: Rather than competition, a monopoly prevents other businesses from offering a certain product or service to consumers.

18. B: Absolute monarchies often use command system economies, but they do not represent a way that governments manage economies. Laissez-faire, capitalism, and self-interest, in contrast, are all fundamental concepts behind the market system.

19. A: England, France, and Spain all established North American colonies that would later be absorbed into the United States, but Italy, despite Christopher Columbus' role as an explorer, never established a colony in America.

20. D: The Constitution was signed in 1787; the Declaration of Independence was signed in 1776. It was successfully ratified by all the current states, including New York. Finally, the Articles of Confederation was established at the end of the American Revolution; the Constitution would replace the articles years later due to issues with the government's structure.

21. C: Although American forces made several early attempts to take Canada from Britain, the United States was never able to successfully seize this territory. On the other hand, the United States did control the Philippines, Puerto Rico, and Guam.

22. C: The executive branch determines the cabinet, while the judicial branch has the responsibility of interpreting the Constitution and laws. Even so, the legislative branch can check the president's power by impeaching him.

23. D: The Emancipation Proclamation only freed slaves in Confederate-held territories; southern states still loyal to the Union kept their slaves for the time being. Although Wilson succeeded in instituting the League of Nations, the United Nations would not emerge until decades later. The Bill of Rights was ratified after the Constitution to provide additional protection for individual liberties. However, it is true that the main body of the Declaration of Independence consisted of grievances that the colonies had against British rule.

24. D: While it is true that Rome fell to barbarians in the fifth century A.D., it would be inaccurate to say the Roman Empire had been completely destroyed. The Byzantine Empire considered itself the heir of the Roman Empire. The western sections, on the other hand, certainly collapsed; the later Holy Roman Empire tried to draw on Rome's past glory but was not a true successor.

25. A: Based on the prior League of Nations, the United Nations included many nations in postcolonial Africa and Asia and worked to support human rights. However, it failed to maintain the World War II alliance between the United States and the Soviet Union, leading to the unofficial Cold War.

26. C: At the time of the Constitutional Convention, Thomas Jefferson was in Paris serving as America's foreign minister to France. George Washington led the meeting, and Alexander Hamilton and James Madison set the tone for debate, rendering *A*, *B*, and *D* incorrect.

27. A: Plains Indians followed the buffalo across the prairies, living in tent-like teepees that were easily moved from place to place. Choice *B* is incorrect because Indians in the Southwest relied on farming for much of their food and built adobes, which are houses made out of dried clay or earth. Indians in the Eastern and Northwest sections of North America survived by hunting, gathering, farming, and fishing, and lived in wooden longhouses, plank houses, or wigwams. Thus, Choices *C* and *D* are incorrect.

28. A: President Franklin Roosevelt is notorious for his Fireside chats during his presidency, particularly surrounding WWII. A recording of one of these radio broadcasts is a good example of a primary source. Primary sources are context-specific, first-hand accounts. They don't have to be in the form of written words, so a radio recording that is a first-hand account of life during that time would be a great example for a third-grade class. Choices *B* and *C* might be useful during WWII lessons, but they are not examples of primary sources. Moreover, Choice *C* is not about life in the United States. Choice *D* is incorrect because Eisenhower took to office after WWII had ended.

29. D: The British issued the Townsend Act in 1767, which taxed imported lead, glass, paints, paper, and tea, and increased the colonists' anger and further strained the relationship between England and the colonies. Choice *A*, the Stamp Act of 1765, taxed printed items, including playing cards and newspapers printed in the colonies. Choice *B*, the Sugar Act of 1764, placed import duties on items such as molasses, sugar, coffee, and wine. Choice *C*, the Currency Act, banned the issuing of paper money in the colonies and mandated the use of gold in business dealings.

30. C: The first shot took place on Lexington Green. When the British heard that colonists were stockpiling weapons, they sent troops to Concord to seize them. However, a group of approximately seventy Minutemen confronted the British soldiers on Lexington green. British troops killed five protesting colonists during the Boston Massacre in 1770, but this is not considered the first shot of the Revolution. Thus, Choice *A* is incorrect. Choice *B* is incorrect because the Boston Tea Party was when colonists dumped 342 chests of expensive tea into the Boston Harbor in defiance of the tea tax. The Revolution had already started when the Battle of Trenton took place on December 25, 1776, making Choice *D* incorrect.

31. A: British General Lord Cornwallis surrendered to Washington's troops at Yorktown, Virginia. No battles occurred at Valley Forge, but Washington's troops suffered major losses as a result of starvation, disease, and exposure to the cold, making Choice *B* incorrect. Choice *C* is incorrect because the Battle of Trenton was the first major battle of the Revolution, which occurred when Washington led his troops across the Delaware River to wage a surprise attack on British and Hessian soldiers stationed in Trenton on December 25, 1776. Choice *D,* Saratoga, New York, was the site of a major victory by General John Burgoyne in October 1777 and prompted European countries to help support the American cause.

32. C: British soldiers burned the White House during the War of 1812. Neither the Washington Monument nor the Statue of Liberty – Choices *A* and *D* – were built at the time, and Philadelphia's Independence Hall, Choice *B*, escaped conflict during this war.

33. B: Jefferson Davis was elected president of the Confederate States of America in November 1861. Choice *A*, General Robert E. Lee, was the leader of the Confederate Army. Choice *C*, William T. Sherman, was a union general famous for his march through Georgia and the burning of Atlanta in 1864. Choice *D*, Abraham Lincoln, was President of the U.S. during the Civil War.

34. D: This period was called the Gilded Age since it appeared shiny and golden on the surface, but was fueled by undercurrents of corruption led by big businessmen known as robber barons. Choice *A*, Manifest Destiny, is the concept referring to the pursuit and acquisition of new lands by the U.S., which led to the purchase of Alaska from Russia in 1867 and the annexation of Hawaii in 1898. The Columbian Exchange, Choice *B*, was an era of discovery, conquest, and colonization of the Americas by the Europeans. The New Deal, Choice *C*, was a plan launched by President Franklin Delano Roosevelt to help rebuild America's economy after the Great Depression.

35. C: World War I began in 1914 when a Serbian assassin killed Archduke Franz Ferdinand of Austria and prompted Austria-Hungary to declare war on Serbia. 1915, Choice *A*, is the year when German submarines sank the passenger ship *Lusitania*, killing 128 Americans and leading many to support U.S. efforts to enter the war. 1917, Choice *B*, is the year the U.S. entered World War I, declaring war on Germany. 1918, Choice *D*, signaled the end of the war when American troops helped defeat the German army that September. Fighting ended in November after Germany signed a peace agreement.

36. A: The Soviet Union was invaded by Germany in 1941 and allied with Britain and subsequently the U.S. President Roosevelt, British Prime Minister Winston Churchill, and Soviet director Joseph Stalin met in 1945 to plan their final assault on Germany and discuss postwar strategies. Germany aligned with Italy and Japan in 1940 to form the Axis Alliance. Their goal was to establish a German empire in Europe and place Japan in control over Asia. Thus, Choices *B*, *C*, and *D* are incorrect.

37. B: The North Atlantic Treaty Organization (NATO) was formed between Western Europe, Canada, and the U.S. in defense of Soviet hostility after the Soviet Union introduced Communism into Eastern Europe. The Soviet Union countered by creating the Warsaw Pact.

38. C: You inform her that the G.I. Bill was a government program started in the 1950s that gave military veterans a free education. In the revolutionary 1954 case, *Brown vs. the Board of Education,* the Supreme Court ruled that school segregation was illegal, thereby setting the Civil Rights Movement in motion, making Choice *A* incorrect. *Freedom Rides*, Choice *B*, and the Montgomery bus boycott, Choice *D*, were among the non-violent protests against segregation that took place in the U.S. in the 1960s.

39. B: President Reagan advocated *peace through strength*, building up the U.S. military and launching the Strategic Defense Initiative (SDI), also called *Star Wars*. Choice *A*, the Strategic Arms Limitation Talks (SALT I and II), negotiated between 1972 and 1979, resulted in limits on nuclear weapons for both the U.S. and Russia. Choice *C*, the Iran-Contra Affair, was a scandal involving the secret sale of weapons to Iran in exchange for American hostages. Choice *D*, *Glasnost*, was a policy of political openness launched by Soviet leader Mikhail Gorbachev.

40. A: Afghanistan was the site of the bombing raids. Bush invaded Iraq, Choice *B*, in 2003 when Iraqi dictator Saddam Hussein defied the terms of the truce agreed upon in 1991 after the Gulf War. Kuwait, Choice *C*, was invaded by Iraq in 1990, sparking the Gulf War. Pakistan, Choice *D*, is where Osama bin Laden was killed by a group of Navy SEALs under orders from President Obama.

41. B: The Mississippi and the Missouri are the two largest rivers in the U.S., winding through the Great Plains in the center of the country. The Colorado and Ohio Rivers are about half the length of the Mississippi and Missouri.

42. C: Latitude – imaginary lines covering the globe from east to west – and longitude – imaginary lines running north to south – are used to pinpoint location on a map. Scale is used to show the relationship between the map measurements and the equivalent distance on the world's surface. Contour lines are used to show detailed elevation on a map.

43. D: Under America's democratic form of government, voting is a *right*, but it is not an *obligation*. U.S. citizens are *obliged* to obey the law, pay taxes, and serve on a jury if asked to do so, making Choices *A*, *B*, and *C* incorrect.

44. D: History is dynamic, meaning that it can change over time. A good example of this is that there are twenty-seven amendments to the U.S. Constitution. The document was not created and then set permanently in stone. It has been changed to reflect changing thoughts and circumstances in the country. The 14th Amendment was adopted in 1868 to abolish slavery. The 18th Amendment was passed in 1919 and prohibited the production and sale of alcoholic beverages, but the 21st Amendment repealed it in 1933. It is true that GPS technology was first implemented in the 1960s and now is available on smartphones, but this is more about improvements in technology and not how the field of history and social sciences itself changes. There are checks and balances built into the various branches of government, but this is an example of balancing power rather than change. Lastly, there are contradictory accounts of certain historical events, such as when Europeans first came to America. This is a good example of considering sources, perspectives, reliability, and circumstances when studying social sciences.

45. **B:** Microeconomics looks at the interplay of consumers, households, and companies within individual markets and the relationships between them. Macroeconomics, Choice *A*, is the study of entire economies. Booms and busts, Choice *C*, are terms used to describe the cyclical nature of economic activity, typically prompted by extreme changes in the economy. Economic output, Choice *D*, is the total amount of goods and services produced by an ***economy.***

46. C: Capital resources are the man-made physical resources used to create products, such as machinery, tools, buildings, and equipment. Natural resources, Choice *A*, are raw materials taken from the land, such as corn, beef, lumber, water, oil, and iron. Human resources, Choice *B*, refer to the human labor—both mental and physical—required to produce goods. Entrepreneurship, Choice *D*, is the capability and motivation to cultivate, organize, and oversee the other three resources into a business venture.

47. C: The tertiary sector provides consumer or business services, including industries such as entertainment, retail sales, and restaurants. The primary sector, Choice *A*, takes raw materials from the Earth, such as coal, timber, copper, and wheat. The secondary sector, Choice *B*, converts raw materials into goods, such as textile manufacturing, food processing, and car manufacturing. The quaternary sector, Choice *D*, provides informational and knowledge services, such as education, business consulting, and financial services.

48. B: Opportunity cost is the term used to describe the choices that determine how consumers spend or save their money. Choice *A*, the circular flow model, is used by economists to describe the movement of supply, demand, and payment between businesses and consumers. A savings account, Choice *C*, is considered low-risk because the bank will pay the saver a low interest rate to keep it safe. Assets, Choice *D*, are valuable items purchased by investors in the hopes that they will increase in worth over time and yield returns or profits.

49. D: Field experiences. The FTCE guide recommends that teachers move beyond traditional, direct instruction to enhance student learning and better prepare students for work in secondary school and college. Field experiences can enhance student learning by exposing them to real-world objects, ideas, and issues. Field experiences prepare students to become young social scientists who can carry out qualitative and quantitative research.

50. B: GPS uses satellite technology to analyze and display geographic features. In an increasingly technological world, students must know how to use GPS technology to their advantage in the classroom. Other tools, such as globes, timelines, and map projections can also be useful, but none of these employ satellite technologies.

51. A: Florida has had long-standing ties to the aerospace industry and has been a hub for NASA. Florida is a Sunbelt state, not a Rust Belt state, so Choice *B* is incorrect. Florida is not traditionally a ranching state, so Choice *C* is also incorrect. Finally, Florida was never under Mexican control, so Choice *D* is also incorrect.

52. D: All of the above. The FTCE guide recommends that differentiated assessments, field experiences, and project-based learning should be implemented in EC-6 social-studies classrooms. Differentiated assessments are crucial for reaching and evaluating all learning types. Through exposure to real-world artifacts, ideas, and issues, field experiences enhance student knowledge. Project-based learning prepares EC-6 social science students for projects in secondary school, college, and the real world.

53. B: Primary sources are context-specific, first-hand accounts, and secondary sources usually synthesize primary sources with some historical distance. Choice *A* is incorrect because both primary and secondary sources can be fictional or realistic. Choice *C* is wrong for two reasons. First, it confuses the fact that primary sources are first-hand accounts and secondary sources can be second-hand testimonies. Second, secondary sources aren't always fictional. Choice *D* is incorrect because primary sources and secondary sources are drastically different in scope and context.

54. A: Seminoles. Seminoles were an indigenous group that lived in Florida during the pre-colonial and colonial eras. Choices *A* (Karankawas) and *B* (Witchitas) are incorrect because these Native Americans didn't live in Florida. Choice *D* is therefore incorrect.

55. A: Spain, France, and the United States all had footholds in the Florida peninsula during the era of European colonization. Spain had the strongest foothold in Florida prior to the U.S. purchase of the Florida territory via the Adams-Onis Treaty of 1819. Spain colonized Florida between the 1500s and 1800s. France also briefly colonized Florida between 1562 and 1565 when a French Huguenot colony was established on the peninsula. Choices *B, C,* and *D* are incorrect because Mexico, Cuba, and Portugal didn't possess colonial control over Florida.

Science

Effective Science Instruction

Developmentally-Appropriate Researched-Based Strategies for Teaching Science Practices

Teachers must be well versed in the different ages and stages of student development, implementing researched-based strategies that account for the age ranges and emotional capacities of the students in their classrooms. Students should be able to engage with materials, activities, and assignments that are just at or slightly above their developmental level. Experts refer to these researched-based activities as **Developmentally-Appropriate Practices (DAP).** It is critical that the science curricula and materials employed in classroom environments meet the age-appropriate and stage-appropriate needs of each student. DAP encourages teachers to combine their knowledge of child development, multiple intelligences, and learning preferences to create a learning environment that differentiates instruction on both general (i.e., age) and individual (i.e., stage) levels. The following questions can help a teacher evaluate whether their classroom employs DAP:

- Does the instruction align with the developmentally-appropriate assessment practices of the classroom?
- Do the activities in the classroom match the general age (i.e., early childhood, elementary school, middle school, and high school) of the classroom?
- Do the activities reflect the age appropriateness embedded within state and national standards for science?
- Do the activities provide differentiated options that acknowledge the different stages of learning (i.e., low achieving, grade level, and high achieving) for each student?
- Do the activities respect individual differences, cultural diversities, and a variety of learning styles in the classroom?
- Are the activities based on what research tells us about how young children learn?
- Are the activities relevant to the children's identities and life experiences?
- Are the activities accounting for each student's current knowledge and linguistic capabilities?
- Do the activities provide students with the opportunity to advance to the next stage of the learning process?

It is critical that the content, materials/textbooks, and activities of every classroom are selected with these questions in mind. The educator must seek to adapt the curricula for a broad audience (i.e., age) while also keeping in mind the needs of each student (i.e., stage). When it becomes clear that one or many students are struggling with a particular activity or topic, then the teacher should take the time to revisit these DAP questions. In general, it is insufficient for schools or teachers to adopt/adapt curricula based solely on the educational grade level of each student. The state standards will guide age-appropriate activities, but local assessments will drive stage-appropriate responses. Consequently, teachers must continue to use a variety of local assessments—diagnostic assessments, formative assessments, and summative assessments—to gain a better understanding of what stage of learning each student is at. In science, these assessments must account for both unique scientific language and subject-specific scientific processes.

Safe and Effective Instructional Strategies to Utilize Manipulatives, Models, Scientific Equipment, Real-World Examples, and Print and Digital Representations to Support and Enhance Science Instruction

Scientific concepts, such as potential and kinetic energy, will remain entirely abstract for a student audience unless a teacher employs safe and effective instructional strategies that reinforces these concepts with manipulatives, models, scientific equipment, real-world examples, and print/digital resources.

Real-world examples allow students to experience abstract concepts, like potential and kinetic energy, beyond the classroom. For example, this abstract notion may become more concrete for students if they witness the forces of potential and kinetic energy at play as a cart sits at the top of a hill and then rolls down the hill. Manipulatives and models also provide students with objects that can be touched and seen in the classroom that make scientific ideas more concrete. For instance, students can build or witness derby cars rolling down a track in the science classroom, to familiarize themselves with potential and kinetic energy. These types of models and manipulatives can be blended with other research-based instructional practices such as collaborative learning or project-based learning; this allows students the opportunity to test hypotheses and share ideas with their classmates. Physical models, such as models of the solar system, can be built and described by student teams in the classroom. More importantly, in the twenty-first century, digital learning environment students can interact with and build virtual models and manipulatives. They can, for example, create computer simulations that analyze the physics behind potential and kinetic energy. They can even use printing and 3-D printing capabilities to help to further visualize the models/manipulatives they created.

Strategies for Formal and Informal Learning Experiences to Provide Science Curriculum that Promotes Students' Innate Curiosity and Active Inquiry

Formal Learning Experiences

Formal learning experiences are typically employed in a teacher-led classroom – they are traditionally structured, compulsory, standardized, curriculum based, and driven by intended outcomes. The goal of formal learning experiences is empirically driven results.

Informal Learning Experiences

Informal learning experiences, while not bound to the classroom environment, typically take place outside the classroom environment—they are usually unstructured, voluntary, noncurricular based (i.e., experientially based or exploratory based), and driven by student choice. The goal of informal learning is not measurable outcomes, but rather positive experiences that might enhance measurable outcomes.

Enhancing Formal Scientific Learning with Informal Scientific Learning

Research supports using informal learning outside the classroom to bolster formal learning inside the classroom. Researchers have suggested that these two modes of learning actually enhance one another. Outdoor science projects and field lessons, for instance, can enhance students' understanding of scientific processes and/or concepts. Thus, these modes of learning should not remain mutually exclusive, but rather they should be aligned and integrated.

Hands-on Learning Experiences

Hands-on learning experiences, both inside and outside the classroom, can help "bridge the gap" between formal and informal learning. Hands-on learning experience may include laboratory activities inside the classroom (i.e., formal learning), or scientific experiments outside the classroom (i.e., informal learning). In both settings, these hands-on learning experiences are characterized by tactile, experiential, and kinesthetic activities.

Active Engagement in the Natural World

Students can only actively engage in the natural world if they are thrust outside the compulsory structures of formal learning environments. Field trips/lessons, service projects, nature walks, and outdoor labs are all examples of ways that students can informally engage with the world around them in order to enhance their classroom experience.

Student Interaction and Collaboration

While student interaction and collaboration can be a component of both formal and informal learning environments, social interactions tend to take precedence in informal learning activities. The social aspects of these activities can be used to create student discourse and ignite student curiosities with diverse perspectives. Most informal learning environments lend themselves to collaborative strategies that help clarify formal science terms and dispel scientific misconceptions.

Collaborative Strategies to Help Students Explain Concepts, Introduce and Clarify Formal Science Terms, and Identify Misconceptions

Collaborative learning in a science course is much like collaborative learning in any course, except with a few content-specific scientific nuances. **Collaborative learning** refers to any instructional strategy that involves students working together to complete an assignment, solve a problem, or create a product. Students can choose their groups, or the teacher can separate them into groups or small teams according to ability, task, or interest. The entire framework is based on the premise that learning is a naturally social act that brings a variety of stakeholders together for a similar cause. Collaborative learning takes place when:

- Students are engaged in an activity process where they assimilate information, relating new information to background knowledge.
- Students are challenged to actively engage with peers in order to synthesize information (rather than simply memorizing or regurgitating information).
- Students are exposed to a diversity of viewpoints via a variety resources, processes, and stakeholders.
- Students are encouraged to participate in a kind "intellectual gymnastics" that allows them to carry out conversations with their peers and create new meaning through discourse.
- Students are challenged both socially and emotionally as they converse with peers, present and defend theories/ideas, exchange values and beliefs, and question the viewpoints of others.
- Students are able to cooperatively explain concepts, introduce and clarify formal, relevant terms, and identify misconceptions.

Defined in this manner, the collaborative learning process can be embedded within a multitude of science-related activities. These activities can include: Socratic seminars, group projects, group laboratory activities, and experiments.

The overall goal of a collaborative learning model is to shift learning from a teacher-centered classroom to a student-centered classroom. Lecturing, notetaking, and other direct instruction approaches might entirely disappear from the classroom as a result of the implementation of collaborative learning activities. Or, collaborative learning activities can enhance or "live alongside" these more traditional classroom strategies.

Appropriate Reading Strategies, Mathematical Practices, and Science-Content Materials to Enhance Science Instruction for Learners at All Levels

Reading Strategies

Science courses should not be much different than English Language Arts (ELA) or reading courses in that their goal should be to employ techniques and strategies that enhance the fluency, comprehension, and writing capabilities of each student. To prepare students for college and career readiness, science educators must first teach them how to construct (and deconstruct) meaning within their science materials. The science classroom, therefore, is a perfect place to teach literacy skills and provide students with skills for constructing/deconstructing content. Like in any other literacy-based class, science teachers must ask the following questions:

- Are students aware of the reason(s) why they are being asked to read a particular text?
- Are students able to identify main ideas and critical arguments within a text?
- Are students engaged in the reading process?
- Are they activating their background knowledge?
- Are they able to sufficiently to have a command over science vocabulary?

These questions, and especially the last question, are crucial for ensuring that every science course is also a literacy-driven course. The only major nuance between ELA and science is vocabulary. Scientific vocabulary can be difficult to grasp—especially for students from special populations—because it is typically laden with specificity. Nevertheless, teaching traditional methods for deconstructing words—such as teaching students about Latin prefixes and suffixes—can provide greater access to scientific vocabulary.

Mathematical Practices

Along with literacy, science classrooms can be great places for providing students with activities and opportunities that build their numeracy skills. Students should come out of science classrooms with an enhanced competence and confidence with mathematics. Science classrooms are the perfect place to build mathematical skills because science and math are so closely intertwined in real-world applications, especially in the growing STEM (science, technology, engineering, and mathematics) fields. The science classroom is perfect for developing the following mathematical skills: computation, sorting, classifying, estimating, graphing, measuring, collecting and analyzing data, recognizing patterns, and presenting statistical findings.

Science-Content Materials

Science-content materials should be selected and vetted with these literacy- and numeracy-based pedagogies in consideration. Written materials must be selected and vetted by classroom teachers and campus leaders with several criteria in mind:

- They must be widely accepted as reasonable by the scientific profession.
- They must incorporate interdisciplinary aspects, bringing in other skills from STEM, the arts, the humanities, and the social sciences.
- They must engage students with real-world relevancy.
- They must promote global, regional, and local experiences, phenomena, and knowledge.

- They must be culturally relevant.
- They must be aligned with assessment and instruction.
- They must already be scaffolded and differentiated, or they must be able to be adapted for scaffolding and differentiation.

Differentiated Strategies in Science Instruction and Assessments Based on Students' Needs

Differentiated instruction in the science classroom is much like differentiated instruction in any classroom. At its core, **differentiated instruction** is about using multiple instructional and assessment strategies to reach multiple intelligences and learning styles in the classroom; it is a way to connect with all students in the classroom. The ultimate goal is to engineer a learning environment that maximizes the potential for success. Flexibility is essential for implementing differentiated instruction in the classroom, so teachers must be open to adapting to their students' needs. Nevertheless, the most effective instructors will plan for differentiation by creating an arsenal of effective teaching and assessment strategies that lend themselves to positive learning outcomes. Differentiated instruction **is** about managing instructional time in a way that meets the stated goals and requirements; however, it is also about "breathing life" in the standards and provides students with challenging, motivating, and meaningful experiences.

Below are some steps teachers can take to implement differentiated strategies in science instruction and assessment in their classrooms. In addition, there are some basic suggestions for building that repertoire of different strategies:

Step 1: Get to Know Your Classroom

Differentiation is a process of getting to know each and every student's intelligence/learning type. Begin with the data that are available in your school. Start by determining the ability of each student and surveying past records of student performance. This data will help determine prior learning experiences, past disciplinary records, past test results, and overall capabilities. This will help to create a profile or baseline of learning for each student. Behavioral tendencies or styles, along with academic performance, should be considered in this process. At times, student grades are a reflection of classroom management, not student ability. Familiarize yourself with all behavioral concerns so that you adequately adapt for the benefit of student learning. In particular, familiarize yourself with the ways in which each student performed and behaved in previous science classrooms. Try surveying former science teachers, if possible, but try to consider all subjects as well.

Besides digging into past records and surveying former teachers, it is important that you get to know your students on a more informal basis. Try surveying student interests by implementing individual interviews/conferences, interest inventories, or learning preference questionnaires. Keep in mind age-appropriateness as you survey your students.

Step 2: Have an Arsenal of Teaching Strategies in the Science Classroom

Differentiated learning is based on the premise that "one size does not fit all." Thus, it is crucial that a variety of teaching strategies are employed in the classroom. We have already discussed collaborative learning models, project-based learning models, and experiential learning models in previous sections. Some other strategies to consider are: 1) Direct Instruction, 2) Inquiry-Based Learning, and 3) Project-Based Learning.

Direct Instruction
Direct instruction is the most widely used teaching strategy. It is a teacher-centered strategy that drives most traditional classrooms. Direct instruction is a common classroom strategy based on the premise that the most efficient way to educate students is through explicit, guided instructions. Direct instruction does not allow for much variation in the classroom; it is focused on strict lesson plans and lectures. While it is an effective strategy supported by research, it typically results in a more passive type of learning. Other strategies such as classroom discussions, workshops, and case studies do not typically fit within a direct instruction framework. Although it has been criticized in recent years, direct instruction still should be a part of every teacher's arsenal because it can be used to cover an extensive amount of material in a short period of time. It also matches some students' preferred learning styles.

Inquiry-Based Learning
Inquiry-based learning refers to utilizing the scientific method and its questioning techniques to develop critical-thinking and problem-solving skills. Unlike direct instruction, it is student centered, requiring students to conduct investigations that are independent of compulsory activities. The teacher acts as a "guide" rather than a "sage on a stage" for this model.

Project-Based Learning
Project-based learning is also a student-centered pedagogy; it typically involves students confronting a real-world problem and capturing their analyses and/or resolutions in a culminating project.

This is by no means a comprehensive list of differentiated frameworks. However, these are three dominant pedagogical trends in the field of education that every educator should understand.

Step 3: Identify a Variety of Instructional Activities Within These Larger Frameworks
Within these larger frameworks, teachers need to create an arsenal of activities that engage students in a variety of ways. These activities can include: jigsaws, debates, labs, experiments, projects, Socratic seminars, etc. The best activities in a science classroom require that students develop and apply knowledge about meaningful and relevant topics.

Step 4: Tier or Scaffold Content and Activities to Meet Different Ability Levels
Once you know your students' profiles and you have an arsenal of frameworks and activities, you have a better chance at keeping students on task. Nevertheless, inevitably some of these activities will have to be tiered or scaffolded for students who are at different stages of learning development. For instance, English Language Learners (ELLs) might need activities that are either bilingual in nature or scaffolded/tiered at a language level that suits their linguistic development.

A differentiated classroom not only differentiates the types of frameworks and activities, but it also differentiates content of the resources.

Step 5: Identify Differentiated Ways to Assess Student Progress
To move away from a "one size fits all" approach, teachers must also differentiate assessment in the classroom. A variety of assessment techniques can include rubrics, performance-based assessments, portfolios, and oral assessments, to name a few. Multiple, differentiated assessments are crucial for educating the "whole child" and creating holistic evaluations of student and classroom success.

Organizing and Managing a Classroom for Safe, Effective Science Teaching that Reflect State Safety Procedures and Restrictions

When conducting experiments and activities in a science classroom, laboratory environment, or field experience, safety should always be the primary concern of a science educator. It is the teacher's responsibility to ensure a safe environment for student learning. Proper direction and supervision greatly reduce the risk of injury. Failure to prepare students with safety precautions and to ensure student safety in the environment can result in the failure to exercise ordinary or reasonable care, or legal negligence. Thus, safety procedures, equipment protocols, directions for disposing of chemicals, rules for complying with mandated classroom layouts, and rules for safely handling living organisms and specimens should be embedded within classroom curricula and routines.

Safety Procedures: Students should be explicitly taught and quizzed on safety procedures in the classroom. Likewise, these procedures should be posted throughout the classroom with adequate cautionary signage. In particular, they should know how to exit in case of an emergency or respond in case of a fire or hazardous spill.

Equipment Protocols: Students must be taught how to properly use all science equipment in the classroom, including, but not limited to: graduated cylinders, Bunsen burners, scales, thermometers, scalpels, safety equipment (i.e., fire extinguishers, fire blankets, and emergency eye-wash stations), microscopes, safety goggles, gloves, storage cabinets for flammable materials, and containers for broken glassware, flammables, corrosives, and wastes.

Storing and Disposing of Chemicals: Chemicals should not be stored near heat sources or in open/active areas of the classroom; all solutions should be disposed of according to local codes and laws; all chemical waste should be disposed of in properly labeled containers and separated from other chemicals.

Compliance with Classroom Layout Rules: Every classroom's spatial layout should be in compliance with local, state, and federal codes; likewise, students should be informed of these safety laws and should understand the function of the spatial layout, the location of emergency accessories, and the procedures for exiting during an emergency.

Safely Handling Living Organisms and Specimens: Biological materials, like chemical materials, should be handled with gloves; biological materials such as living organism and specimens should not be stored near food or water supplies; they should be labeled appropriately and disposed of according to local, state, and federal codes.

Appropriate Technology, Science Tools, and Measurement Units for Students' Use in Data Collection and the Pursuit of Science

Outside of nanotechnology measurements, students will encounter other forms of digital technologies, including various software and hardware that can be used to collect, manipulate, and analyze data in the classroom. These tools include, but are not limited to:

- Internet Search Engines, Online Community Sites, and Social Media Platforms: These online communities and social networks allow students to access, retrieve, consolidate, share, and compare data at an unprecedented pace.

- Word Processors like Microsoft Word and Google Docs: These word processing platforms help students collect, consolidate, and arrange data, specifically text-based data, for lab reports and other documents.
- Digital Spreadsheets such as Microsoft Excel and Google Sheets: These digital spreadsheets assist students with basic tabulations and calculations that can help organize and visualize quantitative data.
- Digital Database Software and Online Databases: These databases can be used to archive or retrieve important data for scientific records.

Beyond computer-based technologies, students now have greater access to other scientific tools to improve their critical-thinking and problem-solving skills. These tools include, but are not limited to:

- Digital Scale: Digitized tool that measures the weight or mass of an object
- Digital Microscope: Digitized device that acts like a traditional optical microscope, but employs digital cameras for better imaging
- Graphing Calculator: Mini, handheld computer that carries out and visualizes calculations that are much more complicated than the calculations of traditional calculators
- Digital Temperature Sensor or Thermometer: Digital device that measures temperatures through electronic signals
- Digital Spectrometer: Digital device that separates different scientific phenomena – such as light particles, atoms, and molecules – into spectral categories for measurement
- Digital Accelerometer: An electromagnetic digital device that can measure the force of acceleration

Essentially, in a twenty-first century classroom all traditional scientific tools—from microscopes to telescopes, from scales to spectrometers—are now digitized, making the collection and storage of data much easier for students. It is up to teachers to ensure that these tools are incorporated and utilized by students in the classroom. Students must encounter these technologies in order to prepare for a rapidly-evolving technological world. Students need to become excited-yet-skeptical consumers of technological tools in the classroom.

Developmentally-Appropriate Diagnostic, Formative, and Summative Assessments to Evaluate Prior Knowledge, Guide Instruction, and Evaluate Student Achievement

Teachers must also be well versed in the different ways to properly assess the different ages and stages of student development, implementing a wide range of assessment protocols that account for the individual and collective capacities in the classroom. There are a variety of assessments and assessment terms that a teacher must be familiar with in the classroom in order to evaluate prior knowledge, guide instruction, and evaluate student achievement. These types of assessments include:

- **Diagnostic Assessments**: Often referred to as "pretests," these assessments evaluate student background knowledge prior to the learning process.
- **Formative Assessments**: These frequent, structured assessments are carried out throughout the learning process; they can be formal or informal, and they help quantify learning and guide instruction.
- **Summative Assessments**: These assessments evaluate learning at the end of the learning process; they are cumulative and can be used to assess the quality of instruction and the progress of student learning.
- **Self-Assessments**: These assessments help students reflect on their own learning, and provide teachers with crucial data for understanding student perceptions and gaps in student perceptions.
- **Standardized Tests/Assessments/Exams**: These assessments – which have national, state, and local variations – create controlled conditions and consistent scoring procedures to evaluate a particular aspect of student learning.
- **Traditional Assessments**: These assessments—which usually take the form of multiple-choice questions, matching questions, true-or-false questions, or mathematical equations—have been traditionally employed as evaluative tools both inside and outside American classrooms; while they have recently been the targets of public criticism, they still remain the most dominant form of testing in the United States.
- **Alternative Assessments**: These assessments attempt to move away from the status quo, departing from the traditional formats of most standardized assessments; they often involve student-centered responses to a particular skill, task, or question, which typically take form as projects or portfolios.
- **Performance Assessments**: These assessments—which typically stem from pre-established rubrics or assessment criteria—involve systematic observations and ratings of student performances; they can be used to evaluate speeches, plays, presentations, and recitals.

A good classroom will not only differentiate the types of assessments, but will also scaffold the structures of assessments. For assessments to be developmentally appropriate, they must account for the age and stage of each student (much like instruction at large). Thus, the following questions can help a teacher evaluate whether their assessments match the developmentally-appropriate practices of their instruction:

- Do the assessments align with the developmentally-appropriate practices of the instruction?
- Do the assessments in the classroom match the general age (i.e., early childhood, elementary school, middle school, and high school) of the classroom?
- Do the assessments reflect the age-appropriateness embedded within state and national standards for science?

- Do the assessments provide differentiated options that acknowledge the different stages of learning (i.e., low achieving, grade level, and high achieving) for each student?
- Do the assessments respect individual differences, cultural diversities, and a variety of learning styles in the classroom?
- Are the assessments based on what research tells us about how young children learn?
- Are the assessments relevant to the children's identities and life experiences?
- Are the assessments accounting for each student's current knowledge and linguistic capabilities?
- Do the assessments provide students with the opportunity to advance to the next stage of the learning process?

It is critical that the assessments are created, selected, and implemented with these questions in mind. Additionally, these assessments must account for both unique scientific language and subject-specific scientific processes.

Choosing Scientifically- and Professionally Responsible Content and Activities that are Socially and Culturally Sensitive

Science classrooms should always account for the personal identities and cultural contexts of the students they serve. These classrooms should not only examine the societal dimensions of scientific issues, they should also be informed by the societal dimensions of scientific issues. Students should therefore be able to examine science through socio-cultural lenses. Moreover, science should be taught in a manner that considers, acknowledges, and respects differing worldviews, beliefs, philosophies, and ethical stances within not only the entire scientific profession, but also the entire community of students. Without undermining scientific objectivity, every science educator should seek to understand the belief systems that drive students and communities. Moreover, every science teacher is expected to present scientific information – via materials and instruction – in an unbiased manner. Every culturally and socially sensitive teacher must be professionally responsible in their interactions by ensuring that the following categories resonate within the instruction and materials of the classroom:

- **Gender Equity**: Science educators should strive to create equitable experiences for the genders in the science classroom, paying close attention to the ways in which different genders are represented in the instruction and materials.
- **Multiculturalism and Racial/Ethnic Diversity**: Science educators should also allow multiculturalism – different racial and ethnic voices and opinions – to be present within the instruction and materials.
- **Socioeconomic Sensitivity**: Science educators should attempt to also account for socioeconomic diversity in instruction and the materials; moreover, they should strive to create scientific opportunities for students regardless of the socioeconomic condition of the school or its community.
- **Respect to Special Populations (ELL and SPED Students)**: With differentiation as a guide, students should ensure that equity and sensitivity are extended to students with disabilities and linguistic barriers.

All of these considerations not only diversify the classroom, but also diversify democratic society at large by exposing a greater diversity of students to high-quality scientific activities and information.

Nature of Science

Science Models, Laws, Mechanisms, and Theories

Theories, models, and laws have one thing in common: *they develop on the basis of scientific evidence that has been tested and verified by multiple researchers on many different occasions*. Listed below are their exact definitions:

- **Theory:** An explanation of natural patterns or occurrences—i.e., the theory of relativity, the kinetic theory of gases, etc.
- **Model:** A representation of a natural pattern or occurrence that's difficult or impossible to experience directly, usually in the form of a picture or 3-D representation—i.e., Bohr's atomic model, the double-helix model of DNA, etc.
- **Law:** A mathematical or concise description of a pattern or occurrence in the observable universe—i.e., Newton's law of gravity, the laws of thermodynamics, etc.

The terms *theory, model,* and *law* are often used interchangeably in the sciences, although there's an essential difference: theories and models are used to explain *how* and *why* something happens, while laws describe exactly *what* happens. A common misconception is that theories develop into laws. But theories and models never become laws because they inherently describe different things.

Observe this chart:

Type	Function	Examples
Theory	To explain how and why something happens	Einstein's Theory of Special Relativity The Big Bang Theory
Model	To represent how and why something happens	A graphical model or drawing of an atom
Laws	To describe exactly what happens	$E = mc^2$ $F = ma$ $PV = nRT$

In order to ensure that scientific theories are consistent, scientists continually gather information and evidence on existing theories to improve their accuracy.

Applying Science and Engineering Practices Through Integrated Process Skills

The scientific method provides the framework for studying and learning about the world in a scientific fashion. The scientific method has been around since at least the 17th century and is a codified way to answer natural science questions. Due to objectivity, the scientific method is impartial and its results are highly repeatable; these are its greatest advantages. There is no consensus as to the number of steps involved in executing the scientific method, but the following six steps are needed to fulfill the criteria for correct usage of the scientific method:

- Ask a question: Most scientific investigations begin with a question about a specific problem.
- Make observations: Observations will help pinpoint research objectives on the quest to answer the question.
- Create or propose a hypothesis: The hypothesis represents a possible solution to the problem. It is a simple statement predicting the outcome of an experiment testing the hypothesis.
- Formulate an experiment: The experiment tests the proposed hypothesis.
- Test the hypothesis: The outcome of the experiment to test the hypothesis is the most crucial step in the scientific method.
- Accept or reject the hypothesis: Using results from the experiment, a scientist can conclude to accept or reject the hypothesis.

Several key nuances of the scientific method include:

- The hypothesis must be verifiable and falsifiable. Falsifiable refers to the possibility of a negative solution to the hypothesis. The hypothesis should also have relevance, compatibility, testability, simplicity, and predictive power.

- Investigation must utilize both deductive and inductive reasoning. Deductive reasoning employs a logical process to arrive at a conclusion using premises considered true, while inductive reasoning employs an opposite approach. Inductive reasoning allows scientists to propose hypotheses in the scientific method, while deductive reasoning allows scientist to apply hypotheses to particular situations.

- An experiment should incorporate an independent, or changing, variable and a dependent, or non-changing, variable. It should also utilize both a control group and an experimental group. The experimental group will ultimately be compared against the control group.

A scientific explanation has three crucial components—a claim, evidence, and logical reasoning. A claim makes an assertion or conclusion focusing on the original question or problem. The evidence provides backing for the claim and is usually in the form of scientific data. The scientific data must be appropriate and sufficient. The scientific reasoning connects the claim and evidence and explains why the evidence supports the claim.

Scientific explanations must fit certain criteria and be supported by logic and evidence. The following represent scientific explanation criteria. The proposed explanation:

- Must be logically consistent
- Must abide by the rules of evidence
- Must report procedures and methods

- Must be open to questions and possible modification
- Must be based on historical and current scientific knowledge

The scientific method encourages the growth and communication of new information and procedures among scientists. Explanations of how the natural world shifts based on fiction, personal convictions, religious morals, mystical influences, superstitions, or authorities are not scientific and therefore irrelevant.

Scientific explanations have two fundamental characteristics. First, they should explain all scientific data and observations gleaned from experiments. Second, they should allow for predictions that can be verified with future experiments.

The Characteristics of Experiments

Hypothesis

Valid experiments must start with a valid hypothesis. There must be one independent variable for any scientific question and a measurable dependent variable that is used to investigate the question. The **hypothesis** is a statement that explains how changing the **independent variable** would affect the dependent variable, and is often stated as an *if (*independent variable plus verb*), then (*dependent variable plus verb*)* sentence. At the early childhood level, before developing a hypothesis, it's important to emphasize valid dependent variables.

Dependent variables must be measurable. Common dependent variables include mass (measured with a balance or scale), length (measured with a ruler), and volume (measured with a graduated cylinder or the more familiar tablespoons, cups, and pints for young students).

It is also important to develop an independent variable with at least two known conditions. The normal condition is called the **control group**, and other conditions different from the control group are called **experimental groups**.

For example, a simple experiment could entail investigating how fertilizer affects plant growth.

Here are examples of valid hypotheses that collect quantitative data:

- If fertilizer is added to the soil, then plant height will increase.
- If fertilizer is added to the soil, then the number of leaves on the plant will increase.

Here are examples of invalid hypotheses:

- If fertilizer is added to the soil, then the plant will grow better.
- If the plant soil changes, then the plant will grow better.

Notice in the valid hypothesis that there's a clear independent variable: the addition of fertilizer to soil. Also, both dependent variable options are quantitative and can be measured. Height can be measured with a ruler, and the number of leaves can be measured by counting.

The invalid hypotheses contain immeasurable changes. "Growing better" isn't specific enough and can't be measured. "Soil changes" isn't specific enough and could involve many different changes, including amount of soil, type of fertilizer, or amount of fertilizer.

Variable Development

After developing a valid hypothesis with specific changes and measurements, the details of the experiment must be confirmed before developing a procedure. That means defining constants, a control group, experimental groups, and measurement methods/devices.

With the proposed hypothesis in mind (*If fertilizer is added to the soil, then plant height will increase),* several constants should be defined. The type of plant is important. Some plants grow faster than others, so all the plants included in the experiment should be of the same type (Wisconsin fast plants are an excellent choice). The brand and amount of soil should be the same; the shape and type of pot should be the same; and the amount of watering and light exposure should be consistent between all test groups. If any one of these factors is different, it will be impossible to tell which factor caused an observable change as opposed to the independent variable. The independent variable (the addition of fertilizer) should be the only changed factor.

A control group is also important to include in all experiments. In this case, the control group would be soil with no added fertilizer. There would be no way to know if the fertilizer was actually helpful unless the experiment included the unaffected condition. Including at least two experimental conditions of the manipulated variable is important if it is desirable to see varying amounts of change. Good options in this case would be to include soil with 5% fertilizer and 10% fertilizer.

The dependent variable should be something easy for young students to measure. In this experiment, a good dependent variable is length. It's important for children to know that the measurement should consist of stretching out the plant and measuring its length with a string, then using the ruler to measure the length of the straightened string. This method of measurement will account for possible drooping and will be more accurate. Discussing with students why such a procedure is important offers an opportunity for students to analyze and come up with the reason for this measuring procedure on their own, enhancing their high-level analysis skills.

Finally, it's important to include multiple trials of each test group—in this case, multiple seeds in each fertilizer condition. Students must be able to have confidence in their results; some experiments inevitably go wrong through forces of nature (such as a dud seed), so this is a critical part of any experiment.

Procedure

Developing a procedure could be a class process. For this particular experiment, several parameters should be kept in mind:

- The experiment should last for at least a week so the plants have a chance to grow.
- Water and light should be a critical part of plant care and should be uniform in all conditions.
- The string/ruler measurement system is important.

Example procedure:

Day 1

1. Place 2 cups of soil without fertilizer (0% fertilizer) * into the pot.

2. Add five seeds in the pattern exemplified below.

3. Pour ½ cup of tap water over seeds.
4. Sprinkle ¼ cup of soil over watered seeds.
5. Place the group name on the pot (label the pot appropriately).
6. Repeat steps #1-5 with:
    a. Low fertilizer mix (5% fertilizer) *
    b. High fertilizer mix (10% fertilizer) *
7. Lastly, put the pots in the light box.

*For young students, percentages are a concept that can be omitted, depending on their level. The purpose of this experiment is teaching the scientific process (not math), so "no fertilizer," "low fertilizer," and "high fertilizer" are sufficient experimental group descriptions.

Days 2-14

Water the plants with 1/3 cup of water every school day.

Day 14

Carefully pull each plant out of the soil. Carefully stretch it out and measure its length with a piece of string. Then measure the piece of string against a ruler and record the value.

At the early elementary level, it's important to know that qualitative data based on the senses (sight, taste, touch, smell, hearing) should be used in investigation as well as quantitative data (numerical data). As a class, discussing data about plants such as color, number and size of leaves, and root structure adds to the learning experience.

Developing the procedure as a class has many benefits. There is opportunity for students to make choices and further discussion. For example, if they want to use only one seed, it's a good opportunity to talk about the importance of multiple trials.

Data Collection and Results

At a young age, students will need guidance with data collection as well as communicating results. A great way to model data collection is having a data table on the blackboard and asking each group to walk up and fill in their data. Teachers should be sure to guide them so they know where to put their numbers. For example:

	Plant height (cm)					
Amount of Fertilizer	**Group 1**	**Group 2**	**Group 3**	**Group 4**	**Group 5**	**Average**
None						
Low						
High						

If students aren't familiar with the concept of averaging, it might be more appropriate to do that for them and instead to place on the board a simplified table like the one below (with mock data):

	Plant Height (cm)*
No fertilizer	5
Medium Fertilizer	12
High Fertilizer	19

*Note that figures are rounded to the nearest integer. Rounding is fine for early childhood experiments and a good point of discussion. More advanced students can write numbers to the tenths place in their data collection.

A concept that students should eventually develop on their own is how to make and present a graph; however, this should be modeled by the teacher for younger students by giving them the actual graph on paper for them to color. For older or more advanced students, an empty graph without the data bars would be sufficient, so students can draw and color the bars themselves. Teachers should emphasize to students that the independent variable should be the x-axis and the dependent variable should be the y-axis so the results are easy to interpret.

Communicating the results with a graph is simple because either the fertilizer affected the plants or it didn't, and the trend in the graph will illustrate the answer.

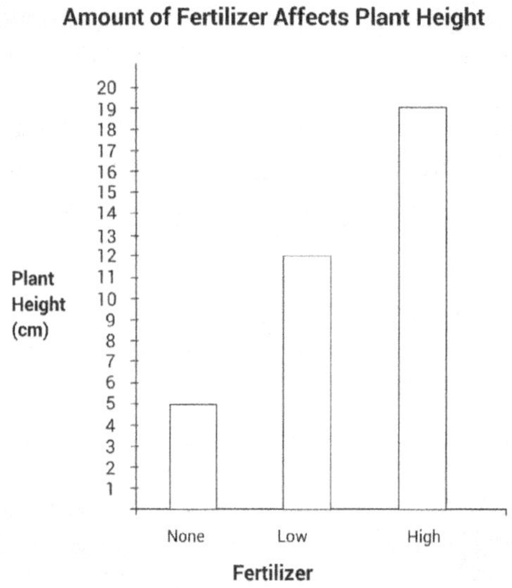

A simple conclusion sentence can be written to wrap up the investigation. Students should decide whether the hypothesis was proven true or false, such as, "*When fertilizer was added to the soil, plant growth increased.*"

Attitudes and Dispositions Underlying Scientific Thinking

Sensitivity has already been mentioned as an attribute of scientific thinking. But there are other traits most scientists share. These traits include curiosity, open-mindedness, skepticism, and cooperation. Mastery of these traits helps science students balance their questions, criticism, ideas, and values.

Curiosity

Curiosity is one of the cornerstones of scientific thinking; it is often overlooked compared to other categories such as skepticism and logical thinking. Past scientists like Copernicus, Newton, Galileo, and Kepler all applied curiosity in their scientific careers. Some of the greatest scientific discoveries in history began with curiosity. That's because curiosity begins with *inquiry-based learning*, a foundational component of the scientific process. Curiosity provides students with the opportunity to acquire knowledge and experiences and ask questions that allow them to better understand the world around them. This type of strategic question and information gathering requires higher-level learning. There is a pedagogical pattern that can be followed by teachers and students to help catalyze this curiosity with scientific reasoning:

- Act upon curiosity
- Develop relevant questions
- Navigate controversies and dilemmas in thought
- Analyze the legitimacy of ideas, problems, and questions
- Develop and test hypotheses
- Draw conclusions
- Find possible solutions
- Target gaps in knowledge and repeat the process

Notice how this pattern begins with curiosity, the inquisitive foundation of all scientific discovery.

Balancing Appropriate Skepticism with an Openness to New Ideas

While curiosity typically inaugurates and guides the scientific process, appropriate skepticism and an openness to new ideas provide an equilibrium to the process. The best scientists are neither wholly skeptical (i.e., cautious and close-minded) nor wholly open-minded (i.e., ungrounded in their thinking). A good scientist allows their mind to vacillate between these two poles of thinking. A good skeptic does not resist change, but rather critiques change, maintaining an openness to new evidence and rational arguments. Likewise, a good scientist who is open to new ideas also evaluates these new ideas with caution, reason, and skepticism. Balance is key to all scientific thinking. Scientists must balance logic and creativity as well as skepticism and openness.

Cooperation/Collaboration

Cooperation and collaboration are also crucial components of the scientific process. Science is an interdisciplinary field built upon the exchange of knowledge and ideas. Science students must learn how to cooperate with the rules and procedures of a science classroom, as well as with their peers. Likewise, they must collaborate with classmates as well as with the discourses present in classroom materials. The entire scientific process is **syncretic**—it fuses the questions, critiques, thought patterns, theories, frameworks, and hypotheses of others together. This takes both interpersonal skills and intertextual awareness. Try to imagine some of the biggest scientific projects in U.S. history, such as the Manhattan Project, without the cooperation or collaboration of the scientists involved. Or try to image NASA sending astronauts to the moon without cooperation and teamwork. Science often gets typecast as a solitary endeavor, but really it is a process of negotiating and balancing solitary passions with collaborative endeavors.

Appropriate Tools, Including Digital Technologies, and Units of Measurement for Various Science Tasks

The use of scientific tools, including digital technologies, can enhance a student's ability to collect data, assess and measure scientific theories, and carry out various scientific tasks. As an extension of previously mentioned safety procedures and precautions, science educators must explicitly teach students appropriate uses for each tool. In general, the types of tools can be broken down into three categories: 1) Observation Tools, 2) Measurement Tools, and 3) Communication Tools. Additionally, as our society becomes increasingly digitized, a new overarching category has emerged: 4) Digital Tools.

Observation Tools: Used to capture or observe scientific phenomena, but not necessarily measure or communicate the findings

- Magnifying Glass: A traditional observation tool that magnifies small things, but not usually microscopic entities
- Microscope: A classic scientific tool that allows students to observe and analyze microscopic compounds and organisms
- Camera: Any device that records visual images or videos for documentation; a camera can be a standalone tool or can be attached to other tools such as microscopes or telescopes
- Telescope: Made famous by astronomers like Galileo, this popular observation tool allows scientists to observe things that are far away, such as stars and planets

Measurement Tools: Scientific tools that assist scientists with accurate and precise measurements of quantity, quality, length, weight, mass, and character

- Ruler: A primitive scientific tool that allows students to measure height, width, and length for mathematical calculations
- Scale: Another simple scientific tool that can help measure the weight or mass of an object by assessing the pull of gravity
- Thermometer: A basic scientific tool that measures temperature

Communication Tools: Help scientists communicate the findings they obtain through observation and measurement

- Writing: Writing is the foundation of all communication – handwritten or digital – in science; students will have to learn how to use writing as a tool to convey their ideas.
- Graphics and Visuals: Sometimes words need to be enhanced with graphics or visuals; these tools include tables, graphs, charts, and maps.

- Conceptual Diagrams or Models: Conceptual diagrams or models are visual representations of complex biological processes or chemical reactions.
- Photographs and Videos: Photographs and videos are the products of cameras, and can be used to communicate findings in a visual manner.
- Social Media and the Internet: In the digital world we live in, students and scholars are now able to communicate information seamlessly in a virtual setting.

Digital Tools: Any type of tool can be a digital tool so long as it uses computer-based technologies to enhance student observation, measurement, and communication. In fact, these digital technologies have led to the development of entirely new units of measurements. Recent developments in nanotechnology instruments, for instance, have enhanced the ways in which science classrooms can measure extremely small units of time, length, and mass. "Nano" means extremely small or dwarf-sized. In past decades, students would be unable to analyze small quantities of time, length, and math. Today, science students have digital nanotechnologies that allow them to measure one billionth of a meter (nanometer), one billionth of a second (nanosecond), and one billionth of a gram (nanogram).

These technologies include, but are not limited to, NanoGauges, electron microscopes, and nanosensors.

- NanoGauge: A device that carries out precision nanometer measurements without any complex procedures
- Electron Microscope: A microscope that produces images of microscopic organisms by using electron beams
- Nanosensor: A term used to describe any device that analyzes the characteristics or behaviors of nanoscale phenomena or particles

These nanotechnology measurement skills prepare students for all fields in science, technology, engineering, and mathematics. As nanotechnologies and telescopic technologies continue to advance, so does our understanding of measurements, which are getting infinitesimally smaller and larger with advancements in technology. Take a look at how the International System of Units (SI System) has been impacted by the changes in technological advancements in measurement over time:

Prefix	Symbol	10^n	Decimal	Short scale	Since
yotta	Y	10^{24}	1,000 000 000 000 000 000 000 000	Septillion	1991
zetta	Z	10^{21}	1,000 000 000 000 000 000 000	Sextillion	1991
exa	E	10^{18}	1,000 000 000 000 000 000	Quintillion	1975
peta	P	10^{15}	1,000 000 000 000 000	Quadrillion	1975
tera	T	10^{12}	1,000 000 000 000	Trillion	1960
giga	G	10^{9}	1,000 000 000	Billion	1960
mega	M	10^{6}	1,000 000	Million	1960
kilo	k	10^{3}	1,000	Thousand	1795
hecto	h	10^{2}	100	Hundred	1795
deca	da	10^{1}	10	Tenth	1795
		10^{0}	1	One	
deci	d	10^{-1}	0.1	Tenth	1795
centi	c	10^{-2}	0.01	Hundreth	1795
milli	m	10^{-3}	0.001	Thousandth	1795
micro	µ	10^{-6}	0.000 001	Millionth	1960
nano	n	10^{-9}	0.000 000 001	Billionth	1960
pico	p	10^{-12}	0.000 000 000 001	Trillionth	1960
femto	f	10^{-15}	0.000 000 000 000 001	Quadrillionth	1964
atto	a	10^{-18}	0.000 000 000 000 000 001	Quintillionth	1964
zepto	z	10^{-21}	0.000 000 000 000 000 000 001	Sextillionth	1991
yocto	y	10^{-24}	0.000 000 000 000 000 000 000 001	Septillion	1991

Interpreting Pictorial Representations, Charts, Tables, and Graphs

Observations made during a scientific experiment are organized and presented as data. Data can be collected in a variety of ways, depending on the purpose of the experiment. In testing how light exposure affects plant growth, for example, the data collected would be changes in the height of the plant relative to the amount of light it received. The easiest way to organize collected data is to use a **data table**.

A data table always contains a title that relates the two variables in the experiment. Each column or row must contain the units of measurement in the heading only. See the below example (note: this is not actual data).

Plant Growth During Time Exposed to Light (130 Watts)	
Time (Hours)	Height (cm)
0	3.2
192	5.0
480	7.9
720	12.1

Data must be presented in a concise, coherent way. Most data are presented in graph form. The fundamental rule for creating a graph based on data is that the independent variable (i.e., amount of time exposed to light) is on the x-axis, and the dependent variable (i.e., height of plant) is on the y-axis.

There are many types of graphs that a person may choose to use depending on which best represents the data.

The **illustrative diagram** provides a graphic representation or picture of some process. Questions may address specific details of the process depicted in the graphic. For example, "At which stage of the sliding filament theory of muscle contraction does the physical length of the fibers shorten (and contract)?"

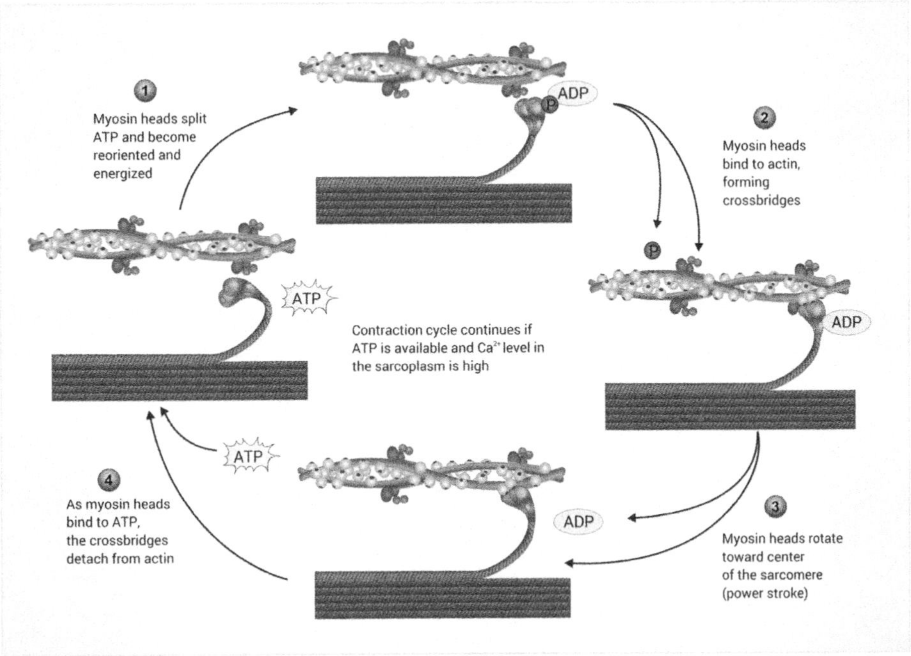

Bar graphs depict the passage data as parallel lines of varying heights. GED bar graphs will be printed in black and white. Data may be oriented vertically or horizontally. Questions may ask, "During the fall season, in what habitat do bears spend the most time?"

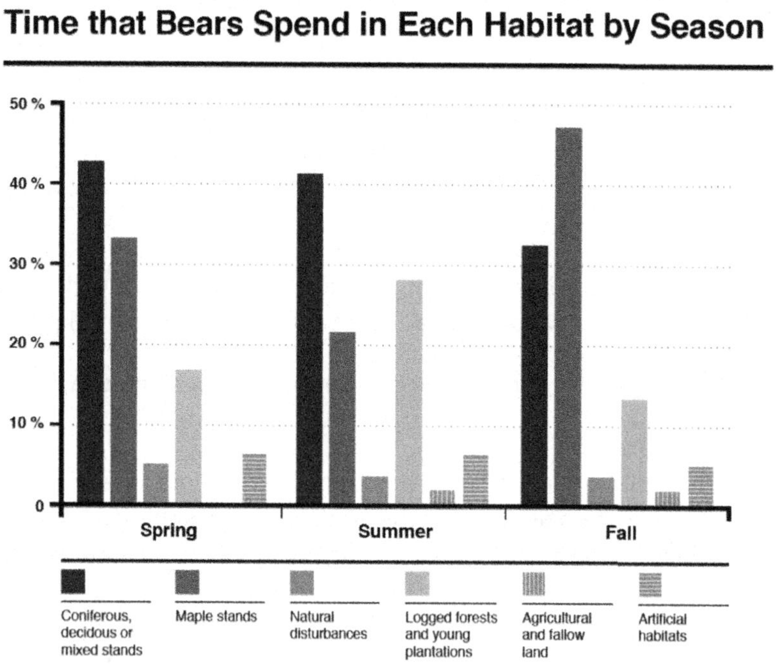

Bar graphs can also be horizontal, like the graph below.

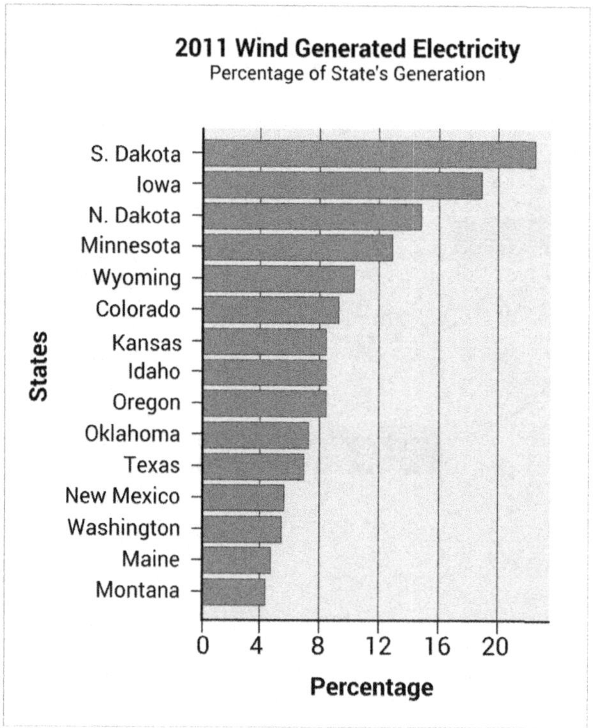

Scatter plots provide a visual representation of the passage data along the x- and y-axes. This representation indicates the nature of the relationship between the two variables. It is important to note that correlation doesn't equal causation. The relationship may be linear, curvilinear, positive, negative, inverse, or there may be no relationship. Questions may ask "What is the relationship between x and y?"

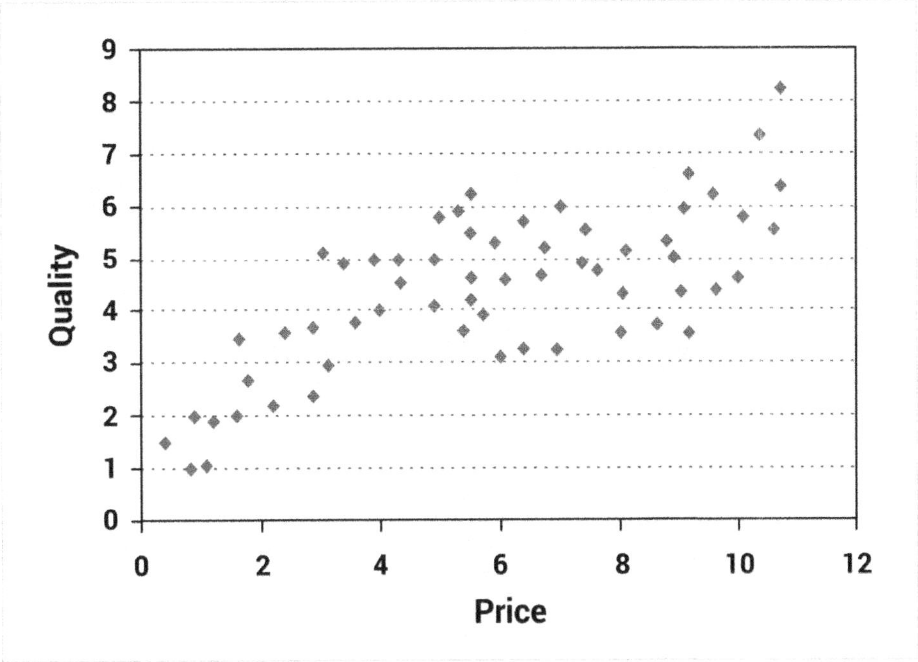

Line graphs are scatter plots that compare and contrast the relationships between two or more data sets. The horizontal axis represents the passage data sets that are compared over time. The vertical axis is the scale for measurement of that data. The scale points are equidistant from one another. There will always be a title for the line graph. Questions related to line graphs might ask," Which of the following conclusions is supported by the provided graph of tropical storms?"

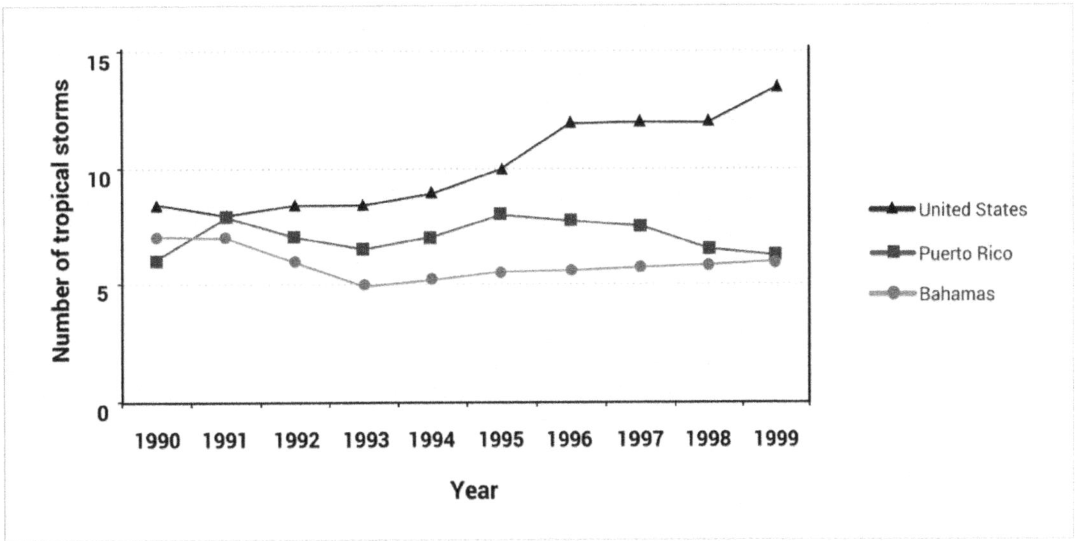

A **region graph** is a visual representation of the passage data set used to display the properties of a given substance under different conditions or at different points in time. Questions relating to this graph may ask, "According to the figure, what is the temperature range associated with liquid nitrogen?"

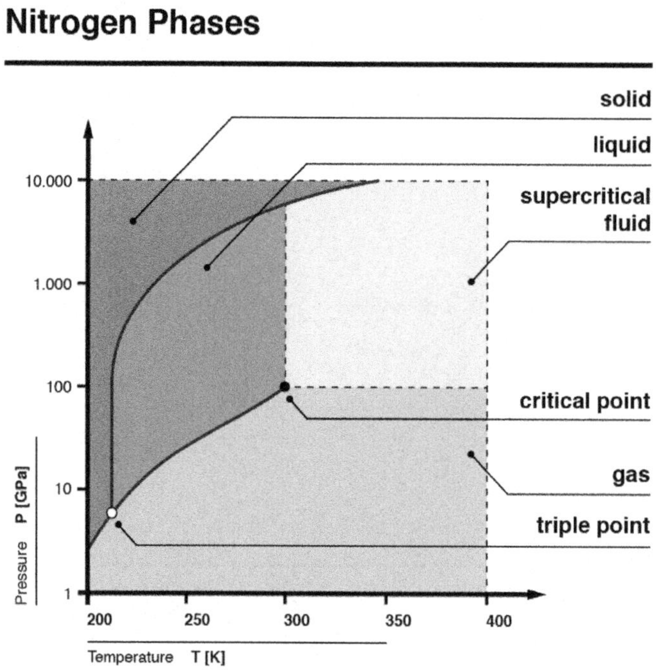

A **pie** or **circle graph** is used when the data sum to 100%, such as the percentage of students in each high school class interested in a trip to a local museum.

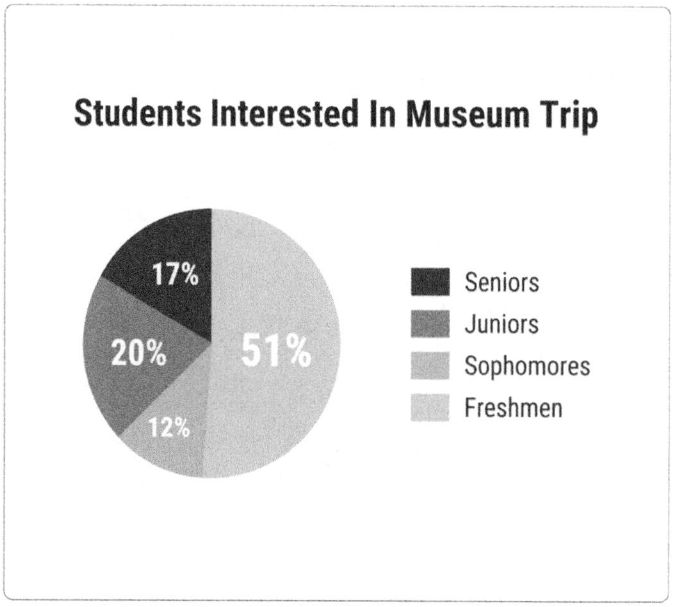

Ways in Which Science is an Interdisciplinary Process and Interconnected to STEM Disciplines

Science, technology, engineering, and mathematics—collectively known as the STEM disciplines—are typically categorized as "different fields" in scholarship but remain inextricably connected in real-world practices. These disciplines, at least in academic terms, can be defined as follows:

- **Science**: The discipline of science focuses on the study of the natural world; scientists—who work in subdisciplines such as biology, physics, and chemistry—analyze the laws, concepts, facts, principles, and conventions associated with living, physical, and chemical components of the universe.
- **Technology**: The discipline of technology refers to the systems, processes, people, and devices that enhance the animate world with inanimate human creations, such as machines, computers, and artificial intelligence.
- **Engineering**: The discipline of engineering focuses on the human-driven design, development, and construction of simple structures and technological structures.
- **Mathematics**: The discipline of mathematics—whether it is applied or theoretical mathematics—focuses on quantitative patterns, numbers, and dimensions.

In simply defining these disciplines, it is hard to imagine one without the other. That's because all of the STEM fields are so closely linked that often we confuse them as one and the same. Because they are so closely connected in the real world, they should remain connected in the science classroom through interdisciplinary pursuits. Scientific inquiry should be driven by an interdisciplinary union of these categories: mathematics should lend its quantitative theories and applications to science, technology, and engineering; technology should both utilize and advance scientific inquiry, engineering practices, and mathematical applications; engineering should be built upon the sturdy foundation of science, technology, and mathematics; and mathematics should come alive in science, technology, and engineering. Students should be exposed to project-based activities and experiential learning environments that encompass all four STEM categories.

The Interactions of Science and Technology with Society

People of all cultures around the world utilize science in order to explore questions and find solutions to problems. The systematic process of designing, conducting, and analyzing experiments is universally known and respected. These processes are time-consuming and require specific knowledge and skills. Therefore, the pursuit of science is its own career path, with many smaller paths for each respective area of study (i.e., life sciences, chemical sciences, physical sciences). Of course, each of those paths splits into even more refined areas and requires much study and dedication. Men and women alike pursue scientific questions; some are driven by pure curiosity and others are compelled by finding a faster, or even a more economical way, of performing a task or producing an object.

Not all ideas, methods, or results are popular or accepted by society. Thus, the pursuit of science is often riddled with controversy. This has been an underlying theme since the early days of astronomical discovery. Copernicus was excommunicated from his religious establishment when he announced the belief that the sun, not the Earth, was the controlling body of the heavens known to humans at the time. Despite his having documented observations and calculations, those opposed to his theory could not be convinced. Copernicus experienced great ridicule and suffering due to his scientific research and assertions. In addition, other scientists have faced adverse scrutiny for their assertions including Galileo, Albert Einstein, and Stephen Hawking. In each case, logical thought, observations, and calculations have been used to demonstrate their ideas, yet opposition to their scientific beliefs still exists.

The possibilities for careers involving science range from conducting research, to the application of science and research (engineering), to academia (teaching). All of these avenues require intensive study and a thorough understanding of the respective branch of science and its components. An important factor of studying and applying science is being able to concisely and accurately communicate knowledge to other people. Many times, this is done utilizing mathematics or even through demonstration. The necessity of communicating ideas, research, and results brings people from all nationalities together. This often lends to different cultures finding common ground for research and investigation, and opens lines of communication and cooperation.

Physical Sciences

Physical Properties of Matter

In the physical sciences, it is important to break things down to their simplest components in order to truly understand why they act and react the way they do. It may seem burdensome to separate out each part of an object or to diagram each movement made by an object, but these methods provide a solid basis for understanding how to accurately depict the motion of objects and then correctly predict their future movements.

Everything around us is composed of different materials. To properly understand and sort objects, we must classify what types of materials they comprise. This includes identifying the foundational properties of each object such as its reaction to chemicals, heat, water, or other materials. Some objects might not react at all and this is an important property to note. Other properties include the physical appearance of the object or whether it has any magnetic properties. The importance of being able to sort and classify objects is the first step to understanding them.

- Matter: anything that has mass and takes up space
- Substance: a type of matter that cannot be separated out into new material through a physical reaction
- Elements: substances that cannot be broken down by either physical or chemical reactions. Elements are in the most basic form and are grouped by identified properties using the Periodic Table. The periodic table groups elements based on similar properties. Metallic elements, inert elements, and transition elements are a few categories used to organize elements on the periodic table. New elements are added as they are discovered or created, and these newer elements tend to be heavier, fall into the metal section of the periodic table, and are often unstable. Examples of elements include carbon, gold, and helium.
- Atoms: the building blocks of all elements. Atoms are the smallest particles of matter that retain their identities during chemical reactions. Atoms have a central nucleus that includes positively charged protons, and neutrons, which carry no charge. Atoms are also surrounded by electrons that carry a negative charge. The amount of each component determines what type of atom is formed when the components come together. For example, two hydrogen atoms and one

oxygen atom can bond together to form water, but the hydrogen and oxygen atoms still remain true to their original identities.

- Mass: the measure of how much of a substance exists in an object. The measure of mass is not the same as weight, area, or volume.

Physical Properties vs. Chemical Changes

Both physical and chemical properties are used to sort and classify objects:

Physical properties: refers to the appearance, mass, temperature, state, size, or color of an object or fluid; a physical change indicates a change in the appearance, mass, temperature, state, size or color of an object or fluid.

Chemical properties: refers to the chemical makeup of an object or fluid; a chemical change refers to an alteration in the makeup of an object or fluid and forms a new solution or compound.

Reversible Change vs. Non-Reversible Change

Reversible change (physical change) is the changing of the size or shape of an object without altering its chemical makeup. Examples include the heating or cooling of water, change of state (solid, liquid, gas), the freezing of water into ice, or cutting a piece of wood in half.

When two or more materials are combined, it is called a mixture. Generally, a mixture can be separated out into the original components. When one type of matter is dissolved into another type of matter (a solid into a liquid or a liquid into another liquid), and cannot easily be separated back into its original components, it is called a solution.

Properties of Matter During Phase Changes

States of matter refers to the form substances take such as solid, liquid, gas, or plasma. Solid refers to a rigid form of matter with a flexed shape and a fixed volume. Liquid refers to the fluid form of matter with no fixed shape and a fixed volume. Gas refers to an easily compressible fluid form of matter with no fixed shape that expands to fill any space available. Finally, plasma refers to an ionized gas where electrons flow freely from atom to atom.

> Examples: A rock is a solid because it has a fixed shape and volume. Water is considered to be a liquid because it has a set volume, but not a set shape; therefore, you could pour it into different containers of different shapes, as long as they were large enough to contain the existing volume of the water. Oxygen is considered to be a gas. Oxygen does not have a set volume or a set shape; therefore, it could expand or contract to fill a container or even a room. Gases in fluorescent lamps become plasma when electric current is applied to them.

Matter can change from one state to another in many ways, including through heating, cooling, or a change in pressure.

Changes of state are identified as:

- Melting: solid to liquid
- Sublimation: solid to gas
- Evaporation: liquid to gas

- Freezing: liquid to solid
- Condensation: gas to liquid

Non-reversible change (chemical change): When one or more types of matter change and it results in the production of new materials. Examples include burning, rusting, and combining solutions. If a piece of paper is burned it cannot be turned back into its original state. It has forever been altered by a chemical change.

Homogenous Mixtures and Heterogeneous Mixtures

When a material can be separated by physicals means (such as sifting it through a colander), it is called a **mixture.** Mixtures are categorized into two types: heterogeneous and homogeneous. **Heterogeneous mixtures** have physically distinct parts, which retain their different properties. A mix of salt and sugar is an example of a heterogeneous mixture. With heterogenous mixtures, it is possible that different samples from the same parent mixture may have different proportions of each component in the mixture. For example, in the sugar and salt mixture, there may be uneven mixing of the two, causing one random tablespoon sample to be mostly salt, while a different tablespoon sample may be mostly sugar.

A **homogeneous mixture,** also called a **solution,** has uniform properties throughout a given sample. An example of a homogeneous solution is salt fully dissolved in warm water. In this case, any number of samples taken from the parent solution would be identical.

Atoms, Elements, Molecules, and Compounds

Everything that takes up space and has mass is composed of **matter.** Understanding the basic characteristics and properties of matter helps with classification and identification.

An **element** is a substance that cannot be chemically decomposed to a simpler substance, while still retaining the properties of the element.

Compounds are composed of two or more elements that are chemically combined. The constituent elements in the compound are in constant proportions by mass.

The basic building blocks of matter are **atoms,** which are extremely small particles that retain their identity during chemical reactions. Atoms can be singular or grouped to form elements. Elements are composed of one type of atom with the same properties.

Molecules are a group of atoms—either the same or different types—that are chemically bonded together by attractive forces. For example, hydrogen and oxygen are both atoms but, when bonded together, form water.

Ions are electrically-charged particles that are formed from an atom or a group of atoms via the loss or gain of electrons.

Potential Energy vs. Kinetic Energy

Potential energy (gravitational potential energy, or PE) is stored energy, or energy due to an object's height above the ground. Kinetic energy (KE) is the energy of motion. If an object is moving, it has some amount of kinetic energy.

Consider a rollercoaster car sitting still on the tracks at the top of a hill. The rollercoaster has all potential energy and no kinetic energy. As it travels down the hill, the energy transfers from potential energy into kinetic energy. At the bottom of the hill, where the car is going the fastest, it has all kinetic energy, but no potential energy. If energy losses to the environment (friction, heat, sound) are ignored, the amount of potential energy at the top of the hill equals the amount of kinetic energy at the bottom of the hill.

Forms of Energy

The term **energy** typically refers to an object's ability to perform work. This can include a transfer of heat from one object to another, or from an object to its surroundings. Energy is usually measured in Joules. There are two main categories of energy: renewable and non-renewable.

> **Renewable**: energy produced from the exhaustion of a resource that can be replenished. Burning wood to produce heat, then replanting trees to replenish the resource is an instance of using renewable energy.
>
> **Non-renewable**: energy produced from the exhaustion of a resource that cannot be replenished. Burning coal to produce heat would be an example of a non-renewable energy. Although coal is a natural resource found in/on the earth that is mined or harvested from the earth, it cannot be regrown or replenished. Other examples include oil and natural gas (fossil fuels).

The study of energy and matter, including heat and temperature, is called **thermodynamics.** There are four fundamental laws of thermodynamics, but the first two are the most commonly discussed.

First Law of Thermodynamics

The first law of thermodynamics is also known as the **conservation of energy.** This law states that energy cannot be created or destroyed, but is just transferred or converted into another form through a thermodynamic process. For example, if a liquid is boiled and then removed from the heat source, the liquid will eventually cool. This change in temperature is not because of a loss of energy or heat, but from a transfer of energy or heat to the surroundings. This can include the heating of nearby air molecules, or the transfer of heat from the liquid to the container or to the surface where the container is resting.

This law also applies to the idea of perpetual motion. A self-powered perpetual motion machine cannot exist. This is because the motion of the machine would inevitably lose some heat or energy to friction, whether from materials or from the air.

Second Law of Thermodynamics

The second law of thermodynamics is also known as the **law of entropy. Entropy** means chaos or disorder. In simple terms, this law means that all systems tend toward chaos. When one or more systems interacts with another, the total entropy is the sum of the interacting systems, and this overall sum also tends toward entropy.

Conservation of Matter in Chemical Systems

The conservation of energy is seen in the conservation of matter in chemical systems. This is helpful when attempting to understand chemical processes, since these processes must balance out. This means that extra matter cannot be created or destroyed, it must all be accounted for through a chemical process.

Kinetic and Potential Energy

The conservation of energy also applies to the study of energy in physics. This is clearly demonstrated through the kinetic and potential energy involved in a system.

The energy of motion is called **kinetic energy**. If an object has height, or is raised above the ground, it has **potential energy**. The total energy of any given system is the sum of the potential energy and the kinetic energy of the subject (object) in the system.

Potential energy is expressed by the equation:

$$PE = mgh$$

Where *m* equals the object's mass, *g* equals acceleration caused by the gravitational force acting on the object, and *h* equals the height of the object above the ground.

Kinetic energy is expressed by the following equation:

$$KE = \frac{1}{2} mv^2$$

Where *m* is the mass of the object and *v* is the velocity of the object.

Conservation of energy allows the total energy for any situation to be calculated by the following equation:

$$KE + PE$$

For example, a roller coaster poised at the top of a hill has all potential energy, and when it reaches the bottom of that hill, as it is speeding through its lowest point, it has all kinetic energy. Halfway down the hill, the total energy of the roller coaster is about half potential energy and half kinetic energy.

Therefore, the total energy is found by calculating both the potential energy and the kinetic energy and then adding them together.

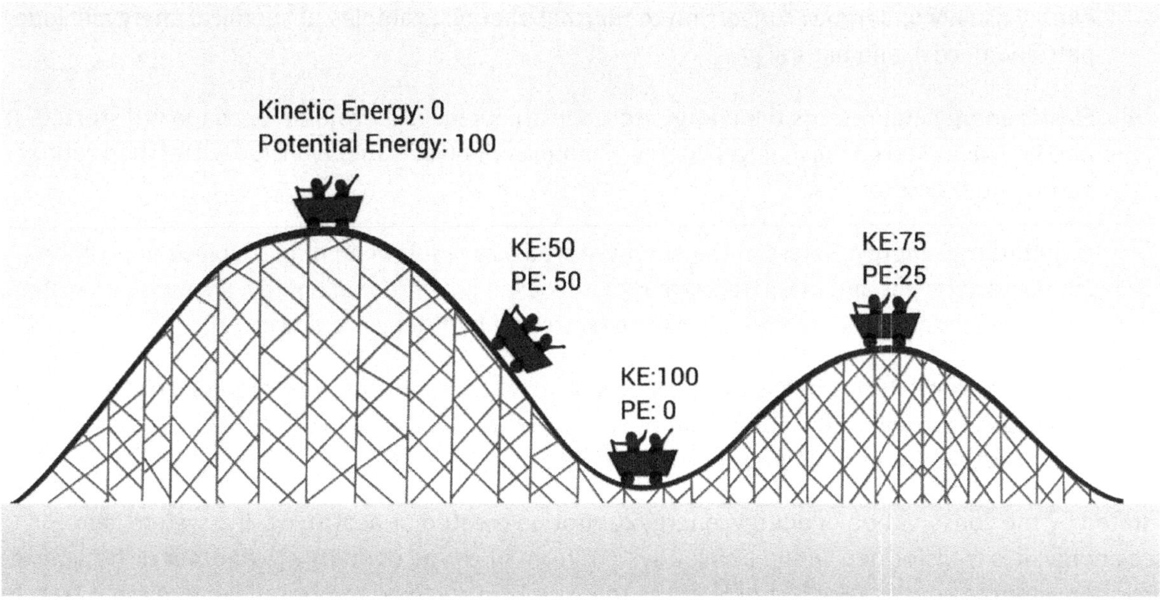

Types of Energy and Transformations Between Different Forms of Energy

Other Forms of Energy

The following are forms of kinetic energy:

- **Radiant energy**: Represents electromagnetic energy, which usually travels in waves or particles. Examples of radiant energy include visible light, gamma rays, X-rays, and solar energy.
- **Thermal energy**: Refers to the vibration and movement of molecules and atoms within a substance. It is also known as heat. When an object is heated, its molecules and atoms move and collide with each other more quickly. Examples of thermal energy include geothermal energy from the Earth, heated swimming pools, baking in an oven, and the warmth of a campfire on a person's skin.
- **Sound energy**: Represents the movement of energy through a substance, such as water or air, in waves. Vibrations cause sound energy. Examples of sound energy include a person's voice, clapping, singing, and musical instruments.
- **Electrical energy**: Utilizes charged particles called electrons moving through a wire. Some examples of electrical energy include lightning, batteries, alternating current (AC), direct current (DC), and static electricity.
- **Mechanical energy**: Represents the energy derived from the movement of objects. It is also called motion energy. Examples of mechanical energy include wind, flight of an airplane, electrons orbiting an atom's nucleus, and running.

The following are forms of potential energy:

- **Chemical energy**: Represents the energy stored in the bonds of molecules and atoms. Chemical energy usually undergoes conversion to thermal energy. Examples of chemical energy include petroleum, coal, and natural gas.
- **Elastic energy**: Represents the energy stored in an object as its volume or shape is distorted. It is also known as stored mechanical energy. Examples of elastic energy include stretched rubber bands and coiled springs.
- **Gravitational energy**: Refers to the energy stored as a result of an object's place or position. Increases in height and mass translate into increased gravitational energy. Examples of systems using gravitational energy include rollercoasters and hydroelectric power.
- **Nuclear energy**: Refers to the energy stored in an atom's nucleus. Vast amounts of energy can be released through the combination or splitting of nuclei. An example of nuclear energy is the nucleus of the element uranium.

As stated by the conservation of energy, energy cannot be created or destroyed. If a system gains or loses energy, it is transformed within a single system from one type of energy to another or transferred from one system to another. For example, if the roller coaster system has potential energy that transfers to kinetic energy, the kinetic energy can then be transferred into thermal energy or heat released through braking as the coaster descends the hill. Energy can also transform from the chemical energy inside of a battery into the electrical energy that lights a train set. The energy released through nuclear fusion (when atoms are joined together, they release heat) is what supplies power plants with the energy for electricity. All energy is transferred from one form to another through different reactions. It can also be transferred through the simple action of atoms bumping into each other, causing a transfer of heat.

Interactions of Energy

There is a fundamental law of thermodynamics (the study of heat and movement) called Conservation of Energy. This law states that energy cannot be created or destroyed, but rather energy is transferred to different forms involved in a process. For instance, a car pushed beginning at one end of a street will not continue down that street forever; it will gradually come to a stop some distance away from where it was originally pushed. This does not mean the energy has disappeared or has been exhausted; it means the energy has been transferred to different mediums surrounding the car. The frictional force from the road on the tires dissipates some of the energy, the air resistance from the movement of the car dissipates some of the energy, the sound from the tires on the road dissipates some of the energy, and the force of gravity pulling on the car dissipates some of the energy. Each value can be calculated in a number of ways including measuring the sound waves from the tires, measuring the temperature change in the tires, measuring the distance moved by the car from start to finish, etc. It is important to understand that many processes factor into such a small situation, but all situations follow the conservation of energy.

As in the earlier example, the rollercoaster at the top of a hill has a measurable amount of potential energy, and when it rolls down the hill, it converts most of that energy into kinetic energy. There are still additional factors like friction and air resistance working on the rollercoaster and dissipating some of the energy, but energy transfers in every situation.

Temperature, Heat, and Heat Transfer

Temperature Scales

There are three main temperature scales used in science. The scale most often used in the United States is the Fahrenheit scale. This scale is based on the measurement of water freezing at 32^0 F and water boiling at 212^0 F. The Celsius scale uses 0^0 C as the temperature for water freezing and 100^0 C for water boiling. The Celsius scale is the most widely used in the scientific community. The accepted measurement by the International System of Units (from the French Système international d'unités), or SI, for temperature is the Kelvin scale. This is the scale employed in thermodynamics, since its zero is the basis for absolute zero, or the unattainable temperature, when matter no longer exhibits degradation.

The conversions between the temperature scales are as follows:

^{0}Fahrenheit to ^{0}Celsius: $^0C = \frac{5}{9}(^0F - 32)$

^{0}Celsius to ^{0}Fahrenheit: $^0F = \frac{9}{5}(^0C) + 32$

^{0}Celsius to Kelvin: $K = {}^0C + 273.15$

Temperature Versus Heat

Temperature should not be confused with heat. Heat is a form of energy: a change in temperature or a transfer of heat can also be a measure of energy. The amount of energy measured by the change in temperature (or a transfer) is the measure of heat.

Transfer of Thermal Energy and Its Basic Measurement

There are three basic ways in which heat energy (thermal energy) is transferred. The first is through **radiation**. Radiation is transmitted through electromagnetic waves and it does not need a medium to travel (it can travel in a vacuum). This is how the sun warms the Earth, and typically applies to large objects with great amounts of heat or objects with a large difference in their heat measurements.

The second form of heat transfer is **convection**. Convection involves the movement of "fluids" from one place to another. (The term *fluid* does not necessarily apply to a liquid, but any substance in which the molecules can slide past each other, such as gases.) It is this movement that transfers the heat to or from an area. Generally, convective heat transfer occurs through diffusion, which is when heat moves from areas of higher concentrations of particles to those of lower concentrations of particles and less heat. This process of flowing heat can be assisted or amplified through the use of fans and other methods of forcing the molecules to move.

The final process is called **conduction.** Conduction involves transferring heat through the touching of molecules. Molecules can either bump into each other to transfer heat, or they may already be touching each other and transfer the heat through this connection. For example, imagine a circular burner on an electric stove top. The coil begins to glow orange near the base of the burner that is connected to the stove because it heats up first. Since the burner is one continuous piece of metal, the molecules are touching each other. As they pass heat along the coil, it begins to glow all the way to the end.

To determine the amount of heat required to warm the coil in the above example, the type of material from which the coil is made must be known. The quantity of heat required to raise one gram of a substance one degree Celsius (or Kelvin) at a constant pressure is called **specific heat**. This measurement can be calculated for masses of varying substances by using the following equation:

$$q = s \times m \times \Delta t$$

Where q is the specific heat, s is the specific heat of the material being used, m is the mass of the substance being used, and Δt is the change in temperature.

A calorimeter is used to measure the heat of a reaction (either expelled or absorbed) and the temperature changes in a controlled system. A simple calorimeter can be made by using an insulated coffee cup with a thermometer inside. For this example, a lid of some sort would be preferred to prevent any escaping heat that could be lost by evaporation or convection.

The Functionality of an Electrical Circuit

A **circuit** is a closed loop through which current can flow. A simple circuit contains a voltage source and a resistor. The current flows from the positive side of the voltage source through the resistor to the negative side of the voltage source. Note that if the switch is open or there is some other disconnected wire or break in continuity in the circuit, there will be no electromotive force; the circuit must be a closed loop to create a net flow of electrons from the voltage source through the wires and system.

Open and Closed Circuits

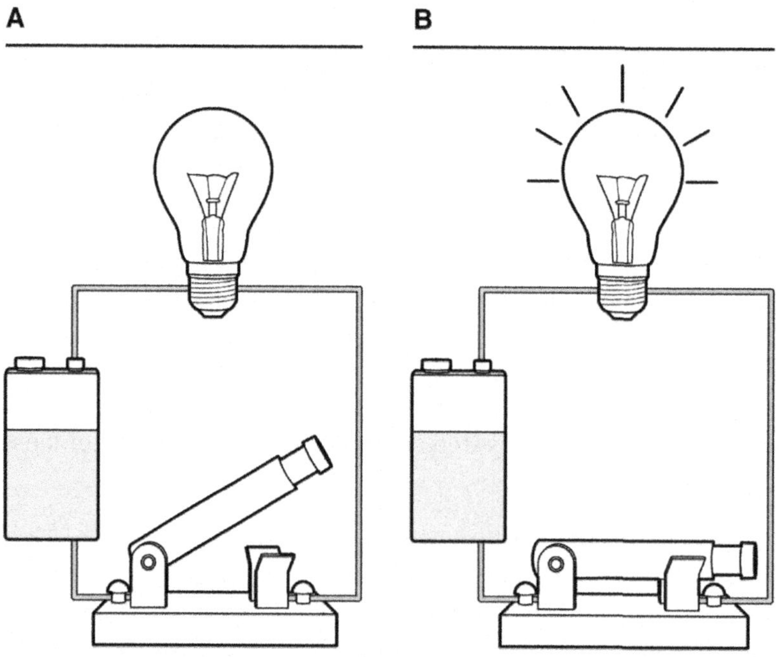

Open Circuit with no electric current

Closed Circuit with electric current flowing

Electrostatics is the study of electric charges at rest. A charge comes from an atom having more or fewer electrons than protons. If an atom has more electrons than protons, it has a negative charge. If an atom has fewer electrons than protons, it has a positive charge. It is important to remember that opposite charges attract each other, while like charges repel each other. So, a negative attracts a positive, a negative repels a negative, and similarly, a positive repels a positive. Just as energy cannot be created or destroyed, neither can charge; charge is transferred. This transfer can be done through touch.

If a person wears socks and scuffs their feet across carpeting, they are transferring electrons to the carpeting through friction. If that person then goes to touch a light switch, they will receive a small shock, which is the electrons transferring from the switch to their hand. The person lost electrons to the carpet, which left them with a positive charge; therefore, the electrons from the switch attract to the person for the transfer. The shock is the electrons jumping from the switch to the person's finger.

Another method of charging an object is through induction. Induction is when a charged object is brought near, but not touched to, a neutral conducting object. The charged object will cause the electrons within the conductor to move. If the charged object is negative, the electrons will be induced away from the charged object and vice versa.

Yet another way to charge an object is through polarization. Polarization can be achieved by simply reconfiguring the electrons on an object. If a person were to rub a balloon on their hair, the balloon would then stick to a wall. This is because rubbing the balloon causes it to become negatively charged and when the balloon is held against a neutral wall, the negatively charged balloon repels all of the wall's electrons, causing a positively charged surface on the wall. This type of charge would be temporary, due to the massive size of the wall, and the charges would quickly redistribute.

Electricity is a form of energy, like heat or movement, that can be harnessed to perform useful work. Electrical energy results from the electric force that exists between atoms and molecules with electrical charge, which is associated with the atomic structure of those substances. Atoms contain various subatomic particles. Protons, which are in the nucleus, carry a +1 charge. Electrons, which surround the outer part of an atom in orbitals or clouds, carry a –1 charge. Net charges of atoms or molecules occur when there is an imbalance in the number of electrons and protons. A net positive charge occurs when there are more protons than electrons, while a net negative charge results when there are more electrons than protons.

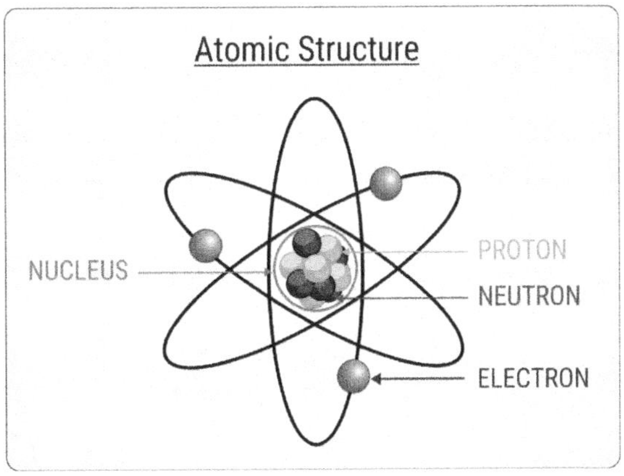

Atoms or molecules with electric charges that are the same experience a force that causes them to repel one another, while those with opposite charges attract each other. Therefore, two positive charges repel one another, two negative charges repel one another, but a positive and a negative charge attract one another. The unit of charge is denoted by C, the coulomb.

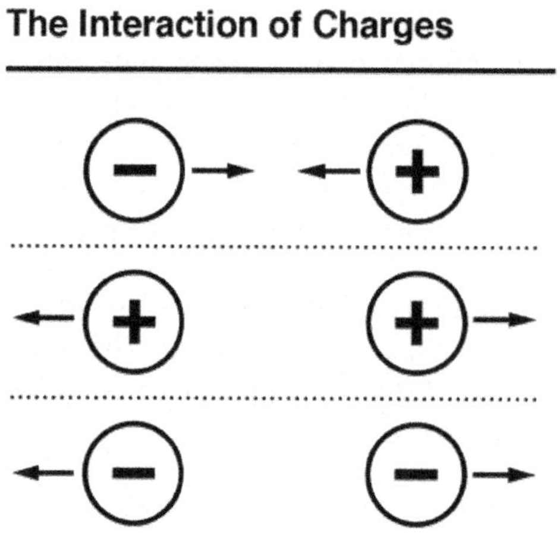

Similar to the Law of Conservation of Energy (which states that energy cannot be created or destroyed, only transferred from one form to another), there is a **conservation of charge** in the universe and in an isolated system. In a given isolated system, individual objects may experience a net loss or gain of charge with the transfer of charge from one object to another from within the system, but the overall charge within the system (or universe) cannot be created or destroyed. Individual positive or negative charges can be created or destroyed, but only in pairs (one positive with one negative), so that the net change in charge is zero.

The properties of any atom vary based on the number and arrangement of electrons in the cloud surrounding the nucleus. For example, electrons in the outer orbitals of metals are relatively free to drift between atoms because they are not pulled in strongly by their atom's own nucleus. These electrons, which carry a negative charge, move through conductive materials, such as other metals, by jumping quickly from atom to atom, creating an electrical flow. This electrical flow is energy that can be harnessed to do work.

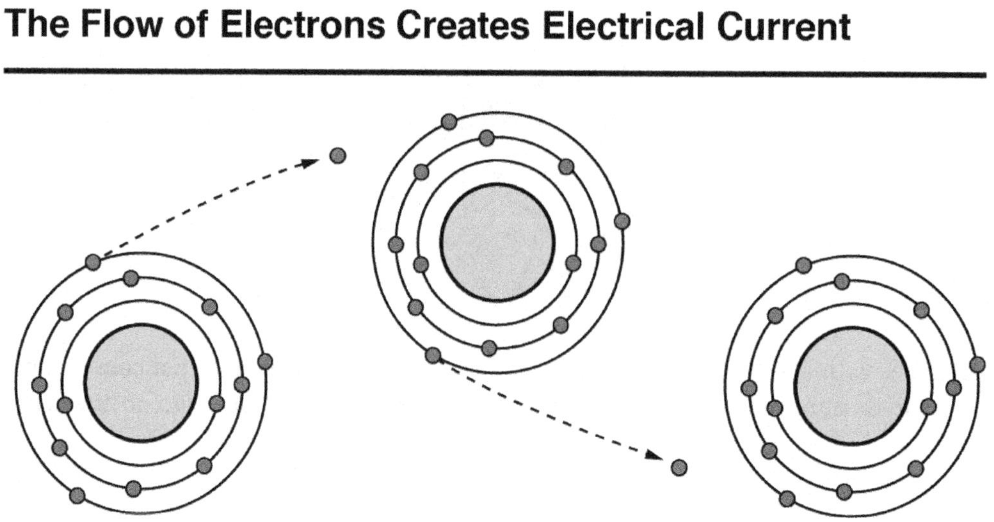

Current is the rate at which the electrical charge—or the number of electrons—flows through a conductive material. It is measured in amperes (A), with each ampere equal to approximately 6.24×10^{18} electrons per second.

Electric current carries energy much like pipes carry water. Water tanks serving an area are often elevated and have various pipes to transport the water down under ground, into each house, and then into smaller pipes leading to each sink, toilet, or shower. The purpose behind elevating the tank is to create pressure in the pipes carrying the water caused by the water above it pushing down. This pressure results in water flow, which can be equated to voltage (akin to pressure) that pushes electrons (the "water") through a circuit. With the water pipes, when the faucet is closed, water does not flow through the pipes, but water flows faster and faster the more the faucet is turned on to allow water in. The rate of water flow is analogous to current—the rate of electron flow through a circuit.

Voltage is the push, or potential, behind electrical work. It is measured in volts (V) and can be thought of as the electromotive potential. Voltage causes current, such that if there is a closed path for electrons and a voltage, current will flow. If there is a suitable path for electrons but no voltage, or voltage in the absence of a viable path, current will cease.

A voltage source is the general term used to describe anything that can be used to generate voltage, such as a battery or generator.

Electrical resistance, measured in ohms (Ω), is the amount of pressure inhibiting the flow of electrical current. Like friction, which slows the rate of movement, resistance dissipates energy and reduces the rate of flow or the movement of current. The amount of resistance that a given object contributes to a circuit depends on the properties of the object, particularly the material. Materials that are inherently more resistant inhibit the ease at which the electrons in the material's atoms can be displaced.

Some circuits have resistors built into them, which are specific electrical components designed to contribute a certain resistance to the circuit.

Resistance is inversely related to conductance, such that a highly conductive material has little resistance, and a material with high resistance has little conductance.

Materials vary in resistance because of the ease (or difficulty) with which electrons in the material's atoms can be displaced. The cross-sectional area and length of a given material also affect the resistance in a predictable relationship. The longer a given conductor is, the greater the resistance it provides; the greater the cross-sectional area (larger material), the less resistance there is. This relationship is quantitatively expressed as $R = \rho \cdot LA$, where ρ is the inherent resistivity of the specific conducting material, L is the length of the material, and A is the cross-sectional area.

The Effects of Forces on Motion

Projectile motion describes the path of an object in the air. Generally, it is described by two-dimensional movement, such as a stone thrown through the air. This activity takes the shape of a parabolic curve. However, the definition of projectile motion also applies to free fall, or the non-arced motion of an object in a path straight up and/or straight down. When an object is thrown horizontally, it is subject to the same influence of gravity as an object that is dropped straight down. The farther the projectile motion, the farther the distance of the object's flight.

Friction is a force that opposes motion. It can be caused by several materials; there are even frictions caused by air or water. Whenever two differing materials touch, rub, or pass by each other, this can create friction, or an oppositional force. To move an object across a floor, the force exerted on the object must overcome the frictional force keeping the object in place. Friction is also why people can walk on surfaces. Without the oppositional force of friction to a shoe pressing on the floor, a person would not be able to grip the floor to walk—similar to the challenges of walking on ice. Without friction, shoes slip and are unable to help people push forward and walk.

When calculating the effects of objects colliding with each other, several things are important to remember. One of these is the definition of **momentum**: the mass of an object multiplied by the object's velocity. It is expressed by the following equation:

$$p = mv$$

Here, p is equal to an object's momentum, m is equal to the object's mass, and v is equal to the object's velocity.

Another important thing to remember is the principal of the **conservation of linear momentum**. The total momentum for objects in a situation will be the same before and after a collision. There are two primary types of collisions: **elastic** and **inelastic**. In an elastic collision, the objects collide and then travel in different directions. During an inelastic collision, the objects collide and then stick together in their final direction of travel. The total momentum in an elastic collision is calculated by using the following formula:

$$m_1v_1 + m_2v_2 = m_1v_1 + m_2v_2$$

Here, m_1 and m_2 are the masses of two separate objects, and v_1 and v_2 are their velocities, respectively.

The total momentum in an inelastic collision is calculated by using the following formula:

$$m_1v_1 + m_2v_2 = (m_1 + m_2)v_f$$

Here, v_f is the final velocity of the two masses after they stick together post-collision.

Example:

> If two bumper cars are speeding toward each other and collide head-on, they are designed to bounce off of each other and head in different directions. This would be an elastic collision.
>
> If real cars were speeding toward each other and collided head-on, there is a good chance their bumpers might get caught together and their subsequent direction of travel would be in the same direction together.

Circular motion takes place around an **axis,** which is an invisible line around which an object can rotate. This type of motion can be observed in the movements of a toy top. There is actually a point (or rod) through the center of a toy top on which the top can be observed as the spinning point for the top. This rod is called the axis.

When objects move in a circle by spinning on their own axis, or from being tethered around a central point (also an axis), they exhibit **circular motion**. In many ways, circular motion is similar to linear (straight line) motion. One difference is, when spinning an object on or around an axis, a force is created that feels like it is pushing out from the center of the circle. In reality, the force is actually pulling into the center of the circle, and the reactionary force is what is creating the feeling of pushing out. The inward force is the real force and is called **centripetal** force. The outward, or reactionary, force is called **centrifugal** force. The reactionary force is not the real force—it just feels like it is there. This has also been referred to as a **fictional** force. The true force is the one pulling inward, or the centripetal force. The terms *centripetal* and *centrifugal* are often mistakenly interchanged.

Example:

> A traditional upright-style washing machine spins a load of laundry to remove the water from the load. The machine spins a barrel with holes in a circle at a high rate of speed. A force is pulling in toward the center of the circle (centripetal force). At the same time, the force reactionary to the centripetal force is pressing the laundry up against the outer sides of the barrel, thus pushing the water through the small holes that line the outer wall of the barrel.

An object moving in a circular motion also has momentum. In a circular motion, this is called **angular momentum**. It is determined by rotational inertia, rotational velocity, and the distance of the mass from the axis of rotation, or center of rotation.

Objects exhibiting circular motion also demonstrate the conservation of angular momentum. This means that the angular momentum of a system is always constant, regardless of the placement of the mass. Rotational inertia can be affected by how far the mass of the object is placed with respect to the center of rotation (axis of rotation). The farther the mass is from the center of rotation, the slower the rotational velocity. Conversely, if the mass is closer to the center of rotation, the rotational velocity increases. A change in one affects the other, thus conserving the angular momentum. This holds true as long as no external forces act on the system.

Example:

> When ice skaters are spinning on one ice skate, they can extend their arms to slow their rotational velocity. However, when skaters bring their arms in close to their bodies (or shorten the distance between the mass and the center of rotation), their rotational velocity increases, and they will spin much faster. Some skaters extend their arms straight above their heads, which causes an extension of the axis of rotation, thus removing any distance between the mass and the center of rotation and maximizing their rotational velocity. In other words, they spin extremely fast.

The center of mass is the point that provides the average location for the total mass of a system. The word "system" can apply to just one object/particle or to many. The center of mass for a system can be calculated by finding the average of the mass of each object and multiplied by its distance from an origin point using the following formula:

$$x_{center\ of\ mass} = \frac{m_1 x_1 + m_2 x_2}{m_1 + m_2}$$

In this case, *x* is the distance from the point of origin for the center of mass and each respective object, and *m* is the mass of each object.

To calculate for more than one object, the pattern can be continued by adding additional masses and their respective distances from the origin point.

Earth and Space

Characteristics of Geologic Formations

Rocks cover the surface of Earth. Igneous rock comes from the molten, hot, liquid magma circulating beneath Earth's surface in the upper mantle. Through vents called volcanoes, magma explodes or seeps onto the Earth's surface. Magma is not uniform; it varies in its elemental composition, gas composition, and thickness or viscosity. There are three main types of volcanoes: shield, cinder, and composite.

Shield volcanoes are the widest because their thin magma flows out of a central crater calmly and quietly, like a gentle fountain. This flowing magma results in layers of solid lava. The slow flow results in a convex hill that spans a wide area.

Like shield volcanoes, **cinder volcanoes** typically have a central crater and thin lava. In contrast to shield volcanoes, they are small, cone-shaped hills with steep sides. They are made of volcanic debris, or cinders. They are often found as secondary volcanoes near shield and composite volcanoes. In cinder volcanoes, the central vent spews lava that shatters into rock and debris and settles around it, resulting in its characteristic cone shape. Cinder volcanoes are surrounded by ashy, loose, magma dust.

Composite volcanoes (also called **stratovolcanoes**) are the most common and the tallest type of volcano. Their thick magma gets stuck at the vent, and as more and more builds up, the volcano eventually explodes and removes the clog. These eruptions generate loose debris, and once the plug has been violently expelled, the thick lava oozes out like a fountain. These volcanoes are the most dangerous with their extremely violent behavior and huge height. Most volcanoes are located around cracks in Earth's lithosphere.

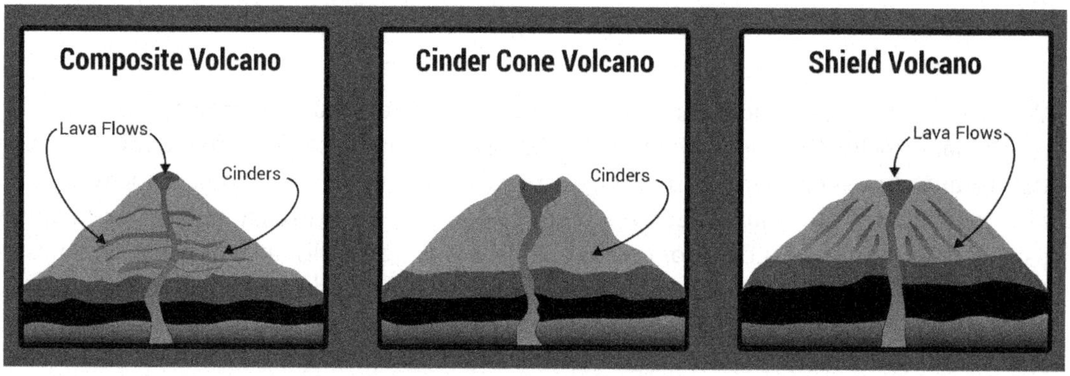

Once magma makes it to the surface, it is called lava. Once it cools, it solidifies into igneous rock. Common examples of igneous rock are obsidian, pumice, and granite. Weathering and erosion result in these rocks becoming soil or sediment and accumulating in layers mostly found in the ocean. These loose sediments settle over time and compress to become a uniform rock in a process called lithification. Examples of sedimentary rock include shale, limestone, and sandstone. As layers are piled atop each other, the bottom rock experiences an intense amount of pressure and transforms into metamorphic rock. Examples of metamorphic rocks are marble and slate. After long periods of time, the metamorphic rock moves closer to the asthenosphere and becomes liquid hot magma. Magma's eventual fate is lava and igneous rock, and the cycle starts anew.

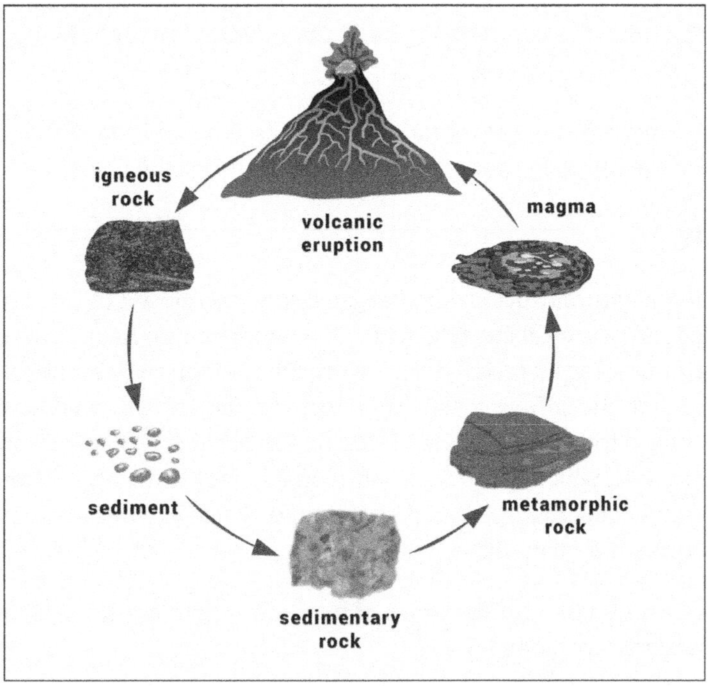

How does magma return to the surface if the lithosphere presses it down? Intense heat from the Earth's core travels to the upper mantle via convection. Convection involves thermal energy (heat) that converts into kinetic energy (movement), resulting in rapidly circulating molecules. Convection moves heat energy through fluids. In a pot of boiling water, the water closest to the burner becomes hot, causing its particles to move faster. Faster-moving molecules have more space between them and become less dense, so they rise. Some will vaporize, and some hit the cool air and slow down, becoming dense and sinking. Likewise, Earth's interior particles undergo convection (the heat source being the nuclear fission from the core), and the rock in the upper mantle will acquire so much kinetic energy that magma will be expelled from underneath Earth to the surface.

There are seven or eight major plates in the lithosphere and several minor plates. These tectonic plates explain the changing topography, or shape, of earth.

There are three types of boundaries between plates: divergent, convergent, and transform. All boundaries can be sites of volcanic activity. A **divergent boundary** occurs when plates separate. Lava fills in the space the plates create and hardens into rock, which creates oceanic crust. In a **convergent boundary,** if one of the plates is in the ocean, that plate is denser due to the weight of water. The dense ocean plate will slip under the land plate, causing a subduction zone where the plate moves underneath. Where plates converge on land, the continental crusts are both lighter with a similar density, and as a result they will buckle together and create mountains.

In **transform boundaries,** adjacent plates sliding past each other create friction and pressure that destroy the edges of the boundary and cause earthquakes. Transform boundaries don't produce magma, as they involve lateral movement.

Just as plates pushing together cause mountains, **canyons** are deep trenches caused by plates moving apart. Weather and erosion from rivers and precipitation run-off also create canyons. **Deltas** form when rivers dump their sediments and water into oceans. They are triangular flat stretches of land that are kind of like a triangular spatula; the handle represents the river and the triangle represents the mouth of a delta.

Sand dunes are another landform caused by wind or waves in combination with the absence of plants to hold sand in place. These are found in sandy areas like the desert or the ocean.

Rocks and Minerals

A **mineral,** such as gold, is a naturally occurring inorganic solid composed of one type of molecule or element that's organized into a crystalline structure. One important physical characteristic of a mineral is its **hardness,** which is defined as its resistance to scratching. When two crystals are struck together, the harder crystal will scratch the softer crystal. The most common measure of hardness is the Mohs Hardness Scale, which ranges from 1 to 10, with 10 being the hardest. Diamonds are rated 10 on the Mohs Hardness Scale, and talc, which was once used to make baby powder, is rated 1. Other important characteristics of minerals include luster or shine, color, and cleavage, which is the natural plane of weakness at which a specific crystal breaks.

Rocks are solid blocks composed of a combination of minerals. There are three different types of rocks: igneous, sedimentary, and metamorphic.

Igneous rocks are formed from magma in the Earth's mantle or lava that has cooled after volcanic eruptions. **Sedimentary rocks** are little pieces of igneous rocks that break off and then they combine in layers many times at the bottom of oceans. **Metamorphic rocks** are the rocks underneath layers and layers of either sedimentary or igneous rocks that meld together and transform due to the pressure of the layers and the heat radiating upward from the Earth's core.

The differences in the appearances of rocks are called their **physical properties**. Some are shiny and some are dull. Others are hard and don't scratch easily, while still others are soft and can be scratched. They come in a range of colors, and some are even metallic. Many rocks can be found every day in houses. Igneous rocks, like granite, are found on many kitchen countertops, and pumice stones are used in foot care. Metamorphic rock, such as marble, is often found in bathroom countertops. Limestone, a sedimentary rock, is commonly found in cement.

See the example below:

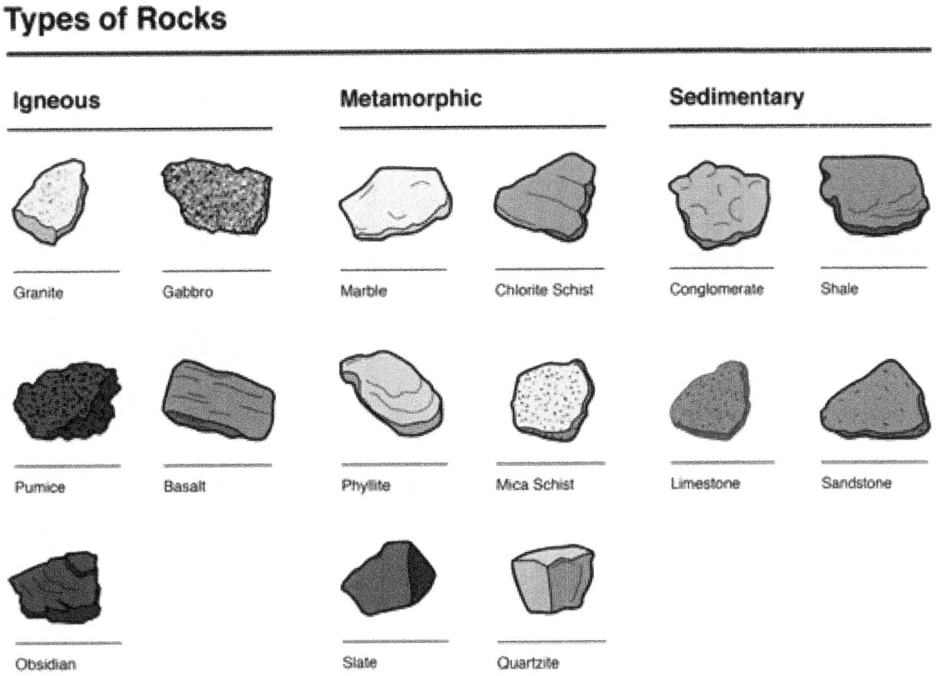

To demonstrate the differences between rocks, activities in the classroom could involve taking qualitative data on the rocks while having a theme of the day. For example, igneous rock formation can be demonstrated by making erupting papier-mâché volcanoes. On that day, the class could be full of igneous rocks. Students can use their senses to record properties of the rocks and the proximity and connection to the volcano will help them remember that igneous rocks come from lava.

In order to connect metamorphic rocks to the concept that they are changed due to heat and pressure, metamorphic rocks can be scattered around the room with a stack of books over each one. Students can temporarily remove the "pressure" and examine the look and feel of the rock, recording qualitative data.

Students can investigate sedimentary rocks by digging for buried sedimentary rocks in a sandbox. The physical properties of the rocks can be recorded, and the proximity to the sand communicates that sedimentary rocks are formed by the erosion of subsequent compression of layers of sediment from other rocks. Precipitation and the water cycle results in the weathering and breakdown of rocks. Erosion involves runoff that carries them away to where they pile up into the layers of sediments that form sedimentary rock.

Fossils show Earth's changing history and are trapped in sedimentary rocks. The lower the fossil, the older the organism because it has been buried deeper and deeper over time.

There is an entire field of science called *paleontology* that specifically studies fossils. Fossils can be completely intact organisms, like the mosquito preserved in the sap in the movie *Jurassic Park*. Fossils can also include remnants of an organism left behind, such as bones and teeth. Structures like these have remained intact due to minerals seeping inside and preserving them like the process that occurs in petrified wood. **Trace fossils** like a footprint are also considered fossils even though they aren't actual remains—they are simply evidence that the organism was there.

Using the sandbox to hunt for fossils will enhance the learning experience. If students also get their hands dirty with soil, the next day, they can compare and contrast soil with sand. While sedimentary rock is the result of erosion and compaction of sediments, soil is the result of weathered rock mixing with decomposing dead organisms to form a loose mix conducive to plant growth. Liquid flows in soil, and air seeps through it as well. Sedimentary rock does not have the same amount of vulnerability to liquids and gases.

The Characteristics of Soil

Soil is a combination of minerals, organic materials, liquids, and gases. There are three main types of soil, as defined by their compositions, going from coarse to fine: sand, silt, and clay. Large particles, such as those found in sand, affect how water moves through the soil, while tiny clay particles can be chemically active and bind with water and nutrients. An important characteristic of soil is its ability to form a crust when dehydrated. In general, the finer the soil, the harder the crust, which is why clay (and not sand) is used to make pottery.

There are many different classes of soil, but the components are always sand, silt, or clay. Below is a chart used by the United States Department of Agriculture (USDA) to define soil types:

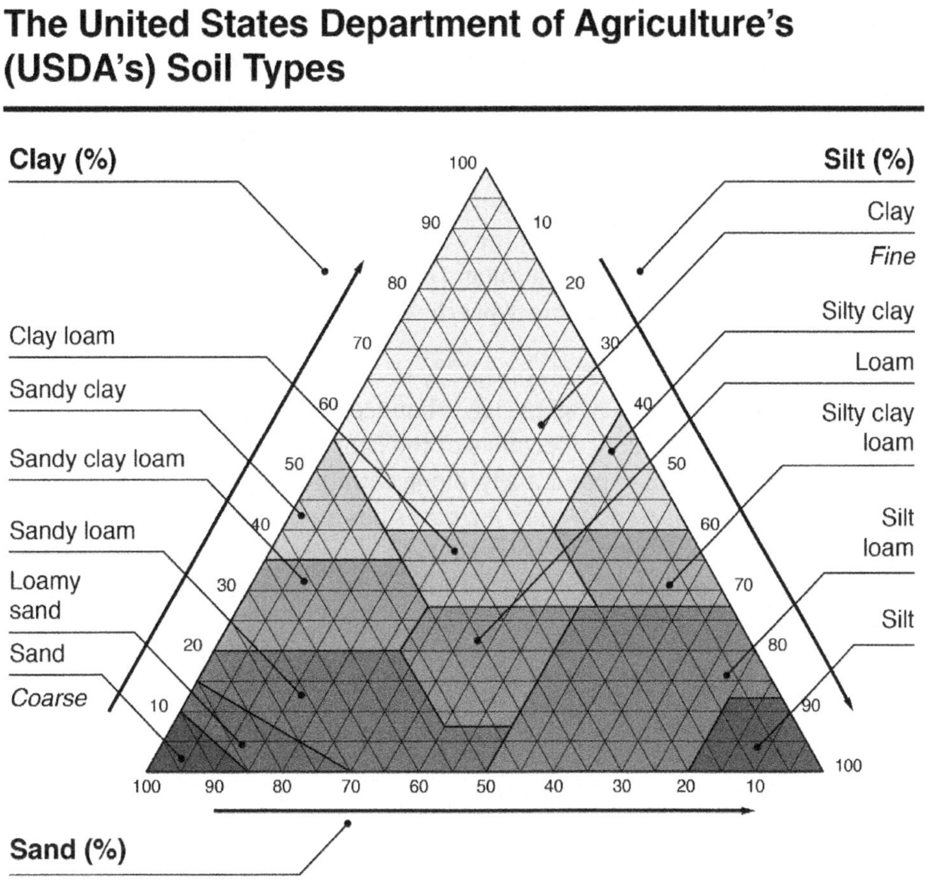

Loam is a term for soil that is a mixture of sand, silt, and clay. It's also the soil most commonly used for agriculture and gardening.

Processes by Which Energy from the Sun is Transferred Through Earth's Systems

Heat energy (thermal energy) can be transferred through the following ways:

Conduction

Conduction is the heating of one object by another through the actual touching of molecules, in order to transfer heat across the objects involved. A spiral burner on an electric stovetop heats from one molecule touching another to transfer the heat via conduction.

Convection

Heat transfer due to the movement/flow of molecules from areas of high concentration to ones of low concentration. Warmer molecules tend to rise, while colder molecules tend to sink. The heat in a house will rise from the vents in the floor to the upper levels of the structure and circulate in that manner, rising and falling with the movement of the molecules. This molecular movement helps to heat or cool a house and is often called convection current.

Radiation

The sun warms the earth through radiation or radiant energy. Radiation does not need any medium for the heat to travel; therefore, the heat from the sun can radiate to the earth across space.

Greenhouse Effect

The sun transfers heat into the earth's atmosphere through radiation traveling in waves. The atmosphere helps protect the earth from extreme exposure to the sun, while reflecting some of the waves continuously within the atmosphere, creating habitable temperatures. The rest of the waves are meant to dissipate out through the atmosphere and back into space. However, humans have created pollutants and released an overabundance of certain gasses into the earth's atmosphere, causing a layer of blockage. So, the waves that should be leaving the atmosphere continue to bounce back upon the earth repeatedly, thus contributing to global warming. This is a negative effect from the extra re-radiation of the sun's energy and causes planetary overheating.

This additional warming is not something easily or quickly reversed. Because the rate of reflection within the atmosphere only multiplies the more a light wave is bounced around, it will take a concerted effort to undue past reflectance and stop future reflectance of the light waves in the earth's atmosphere. Once the re-reflectance occurs, it duplicates exponentially, along with the additional compounding of more waves. Each degree the atmospheric temperature increases has a profound effect on the delicate balance of our planet, including the melting of polar ice caps, the rise of tidal currents—which cause strong weather systems—and the depletion of specific ecosystems necessary to sustain certain species of animals or insects, to name a few.

The Water Cycle, Weather, and Climate

The water cycle is the cycling of water between its three physical states: solid, liquid, and gas. The sun is a critical component of the water cycle because its thermal energy heats up surface liquid water so much that parts of it evaporate. Transpiration is a similar process that occurs when the sun evaporates water from plant pores called stomata. As water vapor rises into the atmosphere through evaporation and transpiration, it eventually condenses and forms clouds heavy with liquid water droplets. The liquid (or solid ice or snow) will precipitate back to Earth, collect on land, and either be absorbed by soil or run-off to the oceans and lakes where it will accumulate, circulate, and evaporate once again.

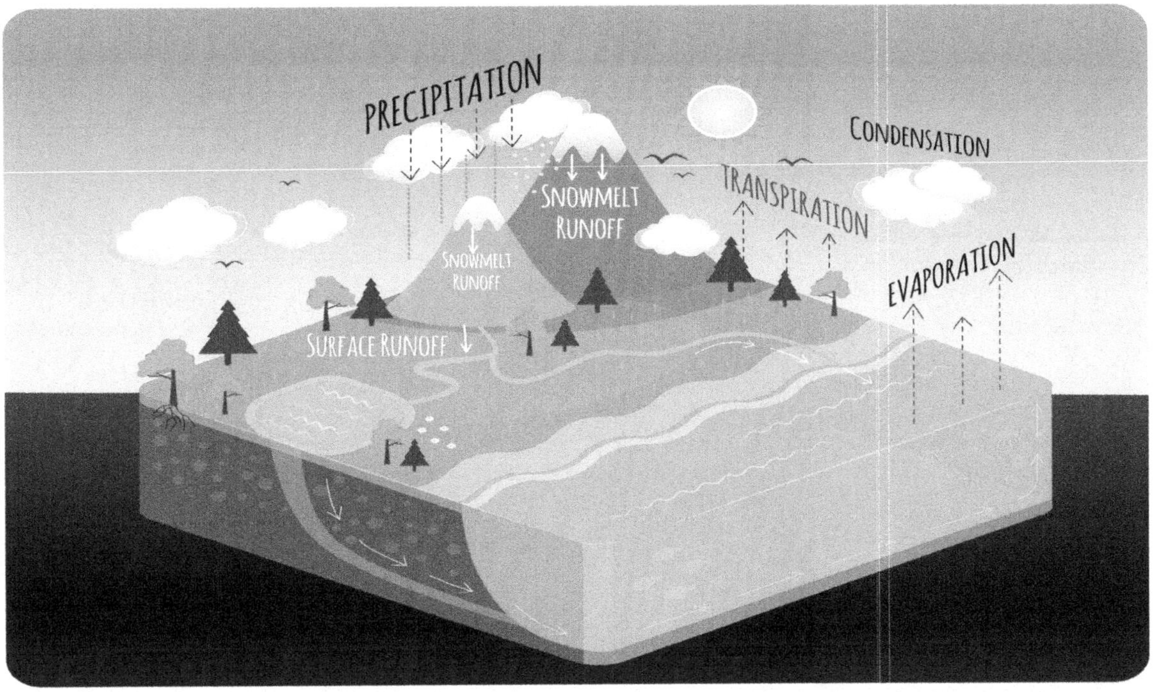

Clouds are condensed water vapor, which is water that has cooled from a gas to liquid, like the droplets on the outside of a glass of lemonade on a hot summer day. That water on the glass is water vapor that cooled enough to slow down the moving particles so that they become denser, forming a liquid. In the sky, water vapor combines in different ways so clouds appear in different forms. Cloud height, shape, and behavior results in a variety of different types:

- High-Clouds
  - Cirrus: wispy and thread-like
  - Cirrostratus: like cirrus clouds, but wider and thicker sheets. They have a halo effect where sunlight and moonlight refract through.
  - Cirrocumulus: a cross between cirrus and cirrostratus clouds. These have rows of round puffs like a cotton-ball stretched out.
  - Contrails: clouds made by jets
- Mid-Clouds
  - Altostratus: thick, stretched clouds that block sunlight and are blue-grayish in color
  - Nimbostratus: a thick altostratus cloud accompanied by rain
  - Altocumulus: layered rolls of clouds

- Low-Clouds

  Cumulus: white, round, puffy clouds
  Stratus: wide, thick, stretched-out, gray clouds that may cause drizzle
  Fog: lazy stratus clouds that have drooped so low that they reach Earth's surface
  Cumulonimbus: the angry cloud that brings thunderstorms, hail, and tornadoes. It looks like a thick mountain.
  Stratocumulus: stretched-out, grayish, puffy, cumulus clouds

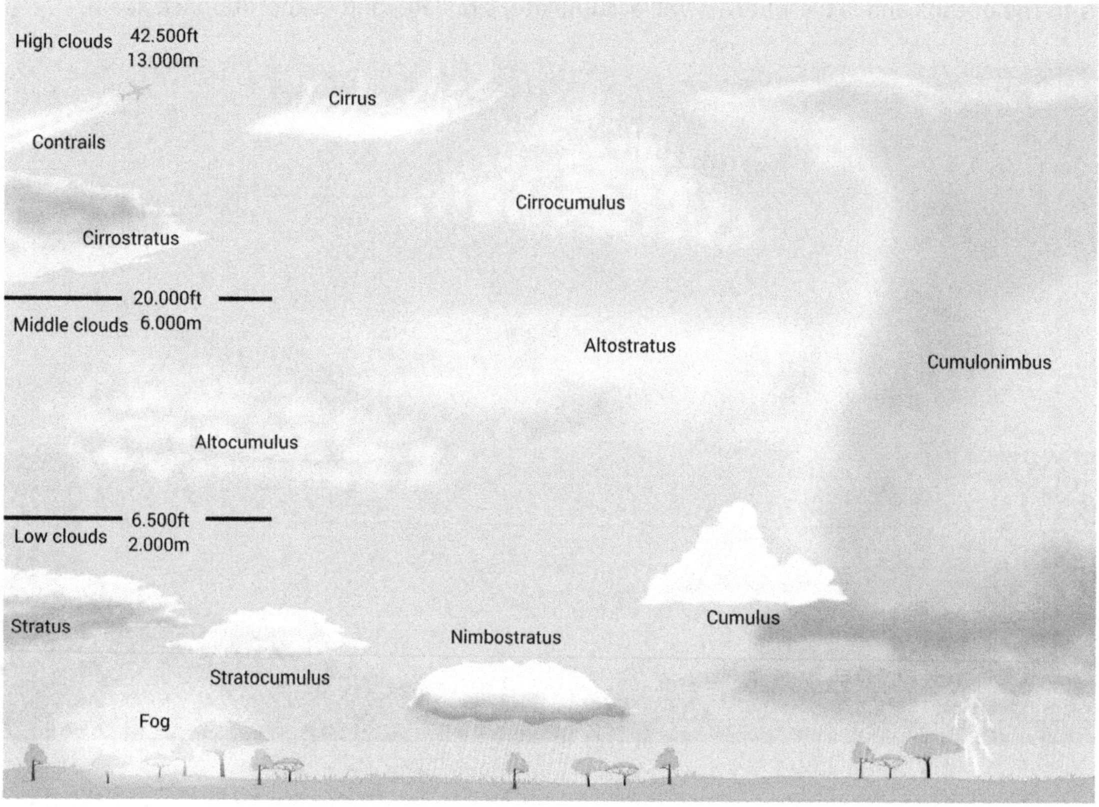

Precipitation comes in many different forms:

- **Rain** occurs due to water vapor condensing on dust particles in the troposphere. As more and more water condenses, the drops will eventually enlarge and accumulate mass, becoming so heavy that they fall to Earth.

- If the temperature is above the freezing point, the water falls as rain. Rain can freeze on the ground if the temperature on Earth's surface is colder than that of the troposphere. Freezing rain causes extremely dangerous driving conditions due to the slickness of the ice.

- **Sleet** freezes on its way down as opposed to freezing upon impact. Sleet starts as ice that melts as it falls through the atmosphere due to hitting spots of warmer temperature, and then it freezes again before hitting the ground.

- **Hail** is precipitation of balls of ice. Hail begins as ice at very cold temperatures in the atmosphere. Instead of precipitating sheets of ice like sleet storms, hailstorms precipitate ice that looks like rocks because hail is formed during thunderstorms. The massive winds throw hail up and down so more and more water vapor condenses and freezes on the original ice. Layer upon layer of ice combine, creating hail sometimes as large as golf balls.

- **Snow** forms as loosely packed ice crystals. Snow is less dangerous than the other frozen forms of precipitation and can produce beautiful snowflakes.

Even though seasons have predictable temperatures, there can be significant differences day to day. In the troposphere, the Sun's heat is trapped by the blanket of greenhouse gases and creates warm, low-pressure air. Because warm gas particles move faster and have less space between them, they are less dense than colder air, and they rise. Cool air moves below the warm air. This atmospheric movement is called general circulation and is the source of wind. Earth's spinning motion also causes wind.

Weather depends in a large part on temperature. Earth's equator is closest to the sun and receives more heat, so this area of earth is significantly warmer than the poles (Arctic and Antarctic). This warm air can form huge bubbles, as can the colder air at the poles. When warm air and cold air meet, the boundary is called a front. Fronts can be the site of extreme weather like thunderstorms, which are caused by water particles in clouds quickly rubbing against each other and transferring electrons, creating positive and negative regions. Lightning occurs when there is a massive electric spark due to the electrical current within a cloud, between two clouds, and even between a cloud and the ground.

While seasons are predictable trends in temperatures over a few months, climate describes the average weather and temperature patterns for a particular area over a long period of time, upwards of thirty years. While **fall** describes a season and **rain** describes weather, **rainforest** describes a climate. The climate of a rainforest, due to its proximity to the equator and oceans, consists of warm temperatures with humid air.

Even more extreme weather includes tornadoes and hurricanes. Tornadoes are spinning winds that can exceed 300 miles per hour and are caused by changing air pressure and quick winds. Hurricanes, typhoons, and tropical cyclones (the same phenomenon with different regional names) are storms with spinning winds that form over the ocean. Hurricanes are caused by warm ocean water quickly evaporating and rising to a colder, lower-pressure portion of the atmosphere. The fast movement of the warm air starts a cyclone around a central origination point (the eye of the storm). Blizzards are also caused by the clash of warm air and cold air. They occur when the cold Arctic air moves toward warmer air and involve massive amounts of snow.

Precipitation and run-off are constantly affecting the surface of Earth, as the run-off weathers rocks or breaks them down from the original bedrock into pieces called regolith. Regolith sizes range from microscopic to large and quickly form either soil or sediment. **Weathering** is the process of breaking rock while **erosion** is the process of moving rock. Weathering can be caused by both physical and chemical changes. Mechanical forces such as roots growing, animal contact, wind, and extreme weather cause weathering. Another cause is the water cycle, which includes flowing water, moving glaciers, and liquid ice seeping into rocks and cracking them as water freezes and expands. Chemical weathering actually transforms the regolith into clay and soft minerals. One consequence of chemical weathering is corrosive acid rain.

The Effectiveness of Conservation Methods to Renewable and Nonrenewable Resources

Recycling and conservation are two important tools for protecting the Earth's resources, but as relatively newer practices, they are not without issues. In general, the practice of **recycling** allows for the **conservation** of Earth's resources by reusing manufactured products, which limits the production and use of raw materials. This reduces landfill use, minimizes waste elimination practices that release greenhouse gas emissions, and is often more cost-effective for manufacturers. However, introducing new recycling centers to an area is often costly in the beginning, as it requires constructing and developing the facility and hiring and training workers. Recycling facilities are often dirty, due to the nature of the items that are recycled, which may have once contained food items, human waste, and other organic materials. These materials quickly rot, may attract vermin, and/or create an overall biological hazard. If the waste from recycled materials is improperly handled, it can cause a pollution problem. Additionally, recycled materials used to create new goods may not be high quality, which can be problematic for the consumer. Finally, recycling is a newer trend that has not yet been adopted on a global scale. Some researchers worry that the amount of recycling that occurs is on a scale that is too small to have a lasting impact, and therefore may be a cost-prohibitive practice.

All presently available energy resources have pros and cons to their utilization. Fossil fuels are a non-renewable resource created from organic sources (such as coal) that developed over millions of years. Two pros for using fossil fuels include the existence of systems that are already in place to use this form of energy, and that a fairly large resource of fossil fuel material still exists. However, burning this resource for energy is a primary contributor to greenhouse gas production and disrupts many ecosystems. Sources are concentrated in certain areas around the globe, which has led to geopolitical conflict and tension. Additionally, the current rate of expenditure is faster than the rate of replenishment. This fact has led to research and development in the alternative energy industry.

Alternative energy sources include any source of energy that protects the environment and can be used as an alternative to fossil fuels. The term usually refers to solar, wind, water, and biomass power, but additional options also exist. In general, alternative energy sources are considered to be sustainable and conserving measures. However, a major con is that the industry is relatively new, and research is ongoing to utilize these sources in the most productive, efficient, and wide-reaching ways. Specific pros and cons of different types of alternative energy sources are listed below.

Nuclear fuel is a renewable resource created by the splitting of uranium atoms. This source greatly limits air pollution, as greenhouse gas emissions are low. Nuclear fuel also enjoys a relatively low production cost. However, upfront costs to build safe facilities are high. Nuclear accidents are also likely to be catastrophic to life, and adequate and safe storage of radioactive waste is another issue yet to resolve.

Hydropower refers to a renewable resource created from fast-flowing water sources that may be natural or man-made. This source is cheap, helps with global irrigation, and can provide drinking water. Disadvantages to hydropower include its inevitable disruption to many ecosystems; facilities are costly and may displace residents; and finally, while the risk of flooding is moderate, the risk of pollution is high.

Wind power refers to a renewable resource created by harnessing air flow. This source is abundant, cheap, clean, and does not require water or large facilities to use. However, wind has to be moving swiftly in order to be harnessed, and it cannot be stored. Commercializing a resource that easily crosses man-made borders can become complicated from legal and business standpoints.

Solar power is a renewable resource that uses the sun's rays for energy. This source is abundant, easily accessible, receives capital funding from both government and private sources, and requires minimal maintenance. However, even with subsidizing, initial production can be costly. It requires land or roof space for cell panels, and utilizes large-scale batteries. These can be a major contributor to waste and pollution.

Finally, **geothermal power** is a renewable resource that uses the Earth's core temperature to generate energy. This resource does not involve combustion (therefore no greenhouse gas emission), yet is three-to-five times more efficient than other sources. It can be used to heat or cool any residential or commercial space. However, utilizing this resource has a high upfront cost. It also requires a large amount of water, and can cause underground and well water damage. Additionally, emergency events, such as geyser eruptions and landslides, have a high risk of being catastrophic to life.

The Use and Extraction of Earth's Resources

Extracting resources from the Earth is inherently damaging in its process. **Mining** for minerals and fossil fuels has vast environmental impacts. Surface damage, unnatural erosion, increases in sinkholes, disruption to ecosystems, unnatural animal migration, and pollution are all side effects of mining. **Deforesting** lands to use the land for commercial or residential use or to use the trees for raw materials significantly disrupts ecosystems, contributes to global warming from reduced carbon dioxide consumption, affects water levels, reduces biodiversity, and endangers wildlife. Many rainforests, such as the Amazon rainforest, are believed to have "tipping points" of damage, where the land will be unable to replenish itself and the overall climate will have changed so drastically that it will set off other climate feedback responses. For example, cutting down trees leads to increased atmospheric carbon dioxide in the area, which leads to higher temperatures, which decreases plant water availability, resulting in less vegetation (and the loop continues). **Land reclamation** often focuses on correcting negative impacts to natural resources (i.e., restoring deforested lands by planting indigenous vegetation, replacing sands near beaches that have eroded, and so forth).

Sun-Earth-Moon System

The heat from the sun as well as the orbit and position of earth cause seasons. As discussed, earth rotates around the sun and spins on an axis. Earth is slightly tilted on its side. An imaginary line around the middle called the equator splits the earth into the northern and southern hemispheres.

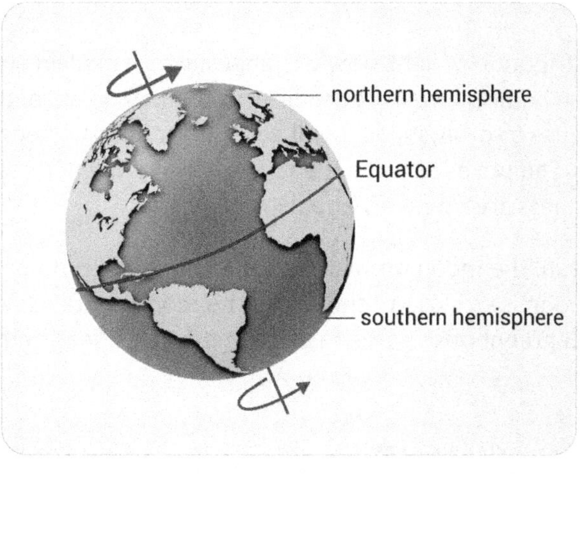

To understand seasons and the heating of the planet, refer to this picture:

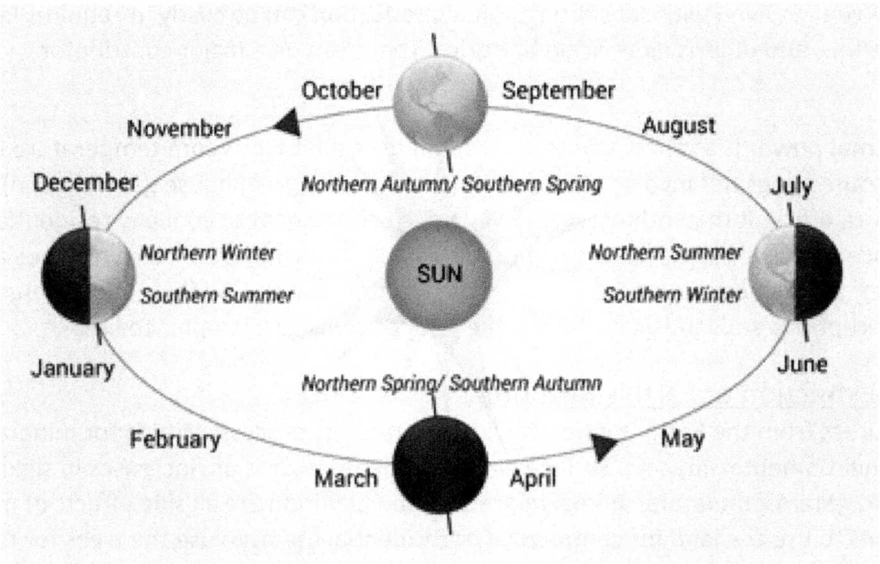

Observing July, these facts are apparent:

- Earth is tilted so that the northern hemisphere is pointing towards the sun. The southern hemisphere is pointed away.
- Because the north is tilted toward the sun, it gets more daylight in July than the southern hemisphere.

These observations explain why in July, the northern hemisphere experiences summer while the southern hemisphere experiences winter.

Notice in December that the opposite is true: the southern hemisphere gets more daylight compared to the northern hemisphere.

In spring and fall, both the north and the south get around the same sun exposure; therefore, those seasons have milder temperatures.

As the earth rotates, the distribution of light slowly changes, which explains why seasons gradually change. In June, the northern hemisphere experiences the summer solstice, the day with the most daylight. As the earth continues to orbit, its days will get shorter and shorter until the winter solstice, the shortest day of the year. Equinoxes occur in the fall and the spring and represent the days when the amount of daylight and darkness are relatively equal.

Just as the earth orbits the sun, the moon orbits the earth. The moon is much closer to earth than the sun. And even though the moon is so close to the earth, the moon contains no life because it lacks water and an atmosphere. Without greenhouse gases to blanket the sun's heat, temperatures on the moon are very low at night.

The moon is visible from the earth because it reflects sunlight at certain points in its orbit. The moon's orbit has a predictable pattern. It has two main phases, waxing and waning. When the moon is waxing, it goes from a new moon to a full moon. Notice that only the left side of the moon is dark during the waxing phase. The waning phase goes from full moon to new moon. Only the right side of the moon is dark when it is waning.

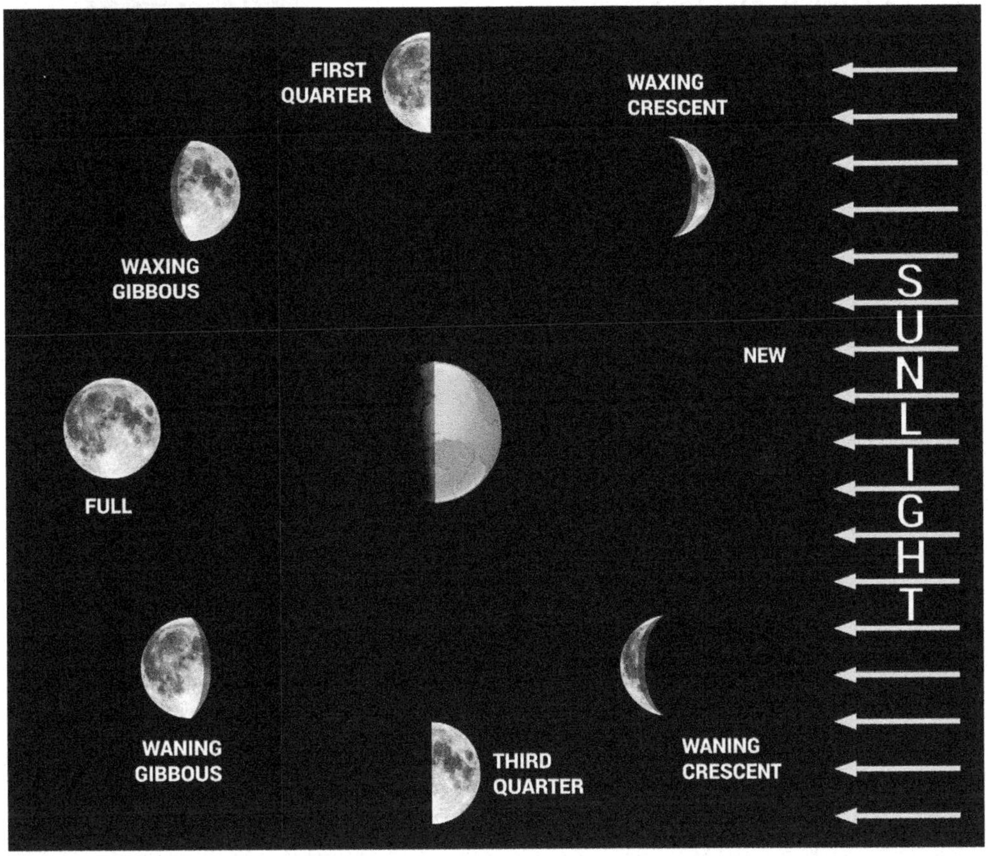

This picture shows that when the moon is behind the earth, then the moon's entire surface is reflected and we see a full moon. When the moon is between the earth and the sun, it is invisible at night, which is called a **new moon**.

Half-moons are visible when the moon and the earth are in a line that is perpendicular to the direction of sunlight. Only half of the moon reflects light to the earth at night, as seen in the figure above.

A moon that looks larger than a half moon is called a **gibbous moon**, and a moon that looks smaller is called a **crescent moon**.

Eclipses occur when the earth, the sun, and the moon are all aligned—the earth blocks the others from seeing each other. If they are perfectly lined up, a total eclipse happens, and if they are only a little lined up, there is a partial eclipse.

There are two types of eclipses: lunar and solar. A lunar eclipse occurs when the earth interrupts the sun's light reflecting off of the full moon. Earth will then cast a shadow on the moon, and particles in earth's atmosphere refract the light so some reaches the surface of the moon, causing the moon to look yellow, brown, or red.

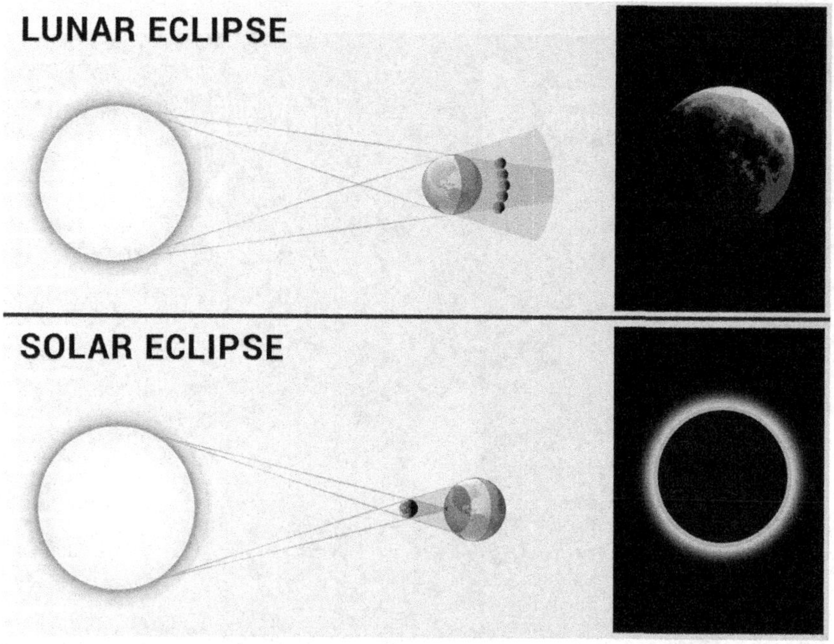

During a new moon, when the moon is between the earth and the sun, the moon will interrupt the sunlight, casting a shadow on earth. This is called a solar eclipse.

The moon also affects ocean tide due to gravity. Earth is much larger than the moon and has a very significant gravitational force that keeps us on the ground even though it is spinning very quickly. The moon is much smaller than earth, but because it is so close, it has a pulling effect on earth's oceans. When it is closest to earth, it pulls the water more, resulting in high tide. When the moon is farthest from earth, it pulls the ocean less and is called low tide.

Relationships in the Solar System and Universe

Earth is part of a solar system that rotates around a star. Our solar system is a miniscule portion of the universe; the Sun is just one star, and there are more stars in the universe than there are grains of sands on Earth. Almost every existing star belongs to a galaxy, clusters of stars, rocks, ice, and space dust. Between galaxies there is nothing, just darkness. There could be as many as a hundred billion galaxies. There are three main types of galaxies: spiral, elliptical, and irregular.

The majority of galaxies are spiral galaxies, with a large, central galactic bulge, which is a cluster of older stars. They look like a disk with arms circulating stars and gas. Elliptical galaxies have no particular rotation pattern. They can be spherical or extremely elongated and do not have circulating arms. Irregular galaxies have no pattern and can vary significantly in size and shape.

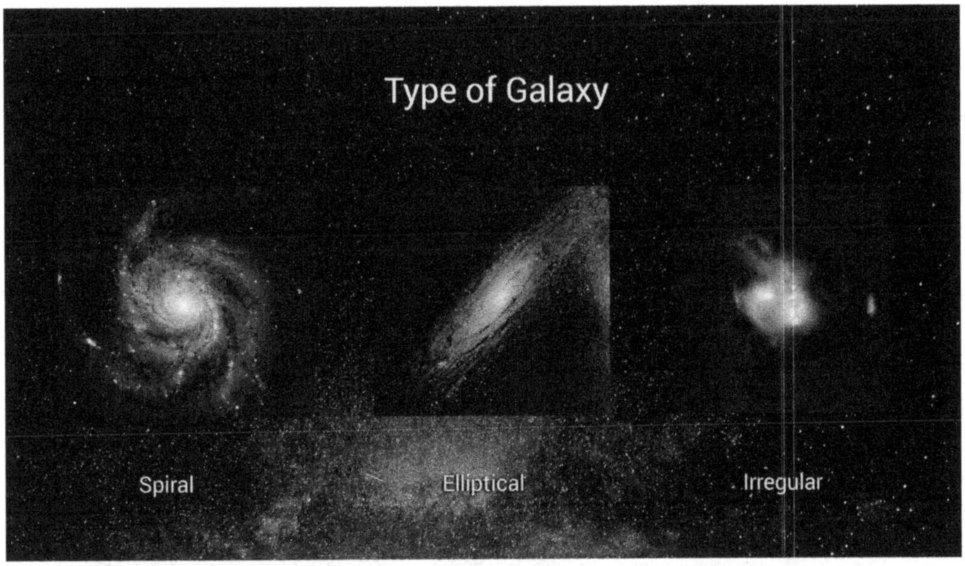

Earth's galaxy, the Milky Way, is a spiral galaxy and contains hundreds of billions of stars.

Pre-stars form from nebulas, clouds of gas and dust that can combine to form two types of small stars: brown and red dwarfs. Stars produce enormous amounts energy by combining hydrogen atoms to form helium via nuclear fusion. Brown dwarfs don't have enough hydrogen to undergo much fusion and fizzle out. Red dwarfs have plenty of gas (hydrogen) to undergo nuclear fusion and mature into white dwarfs. When they use all of their fuel (hydrogen), a burst of energy expands the star into a red giant. Red giants eventually condense into a white dwarf, which is a star approaching the end of its life.

Stars that undergo nuclear fusion will run out of gas quickly and burst in violent explosions called supernovas. This burst releases as much energy in a few seconds as the Sun will release in its entire lifetime. The particles from the explosion will condense into the smallest type of star, a neutron star; this will eventually condense into a black hole, which has such a high amount of gravity that not even light energy can escape.

Earth's sun is currently a red dwarf; it is early in its life cycle. As the center of Earth's solar system, the Sun has planets and space debris (rocks and ice) orbiting around it. The various forms of space debris include:

- Comet: made of rock and ice with a tail due to the melting ice
- Asteroid: a large rock orbiting a star. The asteroid belt lies between Mars and Jupiter and separates the smaller rocky planets (Mercury, Venus, Earth, and Mars) from the larger, gassy planets (Jupiter, Saturn, Uranus, and Neptune). Pluto is not considered a planet anymore due to its small size and distance from the Sun.
- Meteoroid: a mini-asteroid with no specific orbiting pattern

- Meteor: a meteoroid that has entered Earth's atmosphere and starts melting due to the warmth provided by our insulating greenhouse gases. These are commonly known as "falling stars."
- Meteorite: a meteor that hasn't completely burned away and lands on Earth. One is believed to have caused the Cretaceous mass extinction.

Each planet travels around the Sun in an elliptic orbit. The time it takes for one complete orbit is considered a year. The gravity of the massive Sun keeps the planets rotating, and the farther the planets are from the Sun, the slower they move and the longer their orbits. Earth's journey is little bit over 365 days a year. Because Mercury is so close to the Sun, one year for Mercury is actually only 88 Earth days. The farthest planet, Neptune, has a year that is about 60,255 Earth days long. Planets not only rotate around the Sun, but they also spin like a top. The time it takes for a planet to complete one spin is considered one day. On Earth, one day is about 24 hours. On Jupiter, one day is about nine Earth hours, while a day on Venus is 241 Earth days.

Planets may have natural satellites that rotate around them called moons. Some planets have no moons and some have dozens. In 1969, astronaut Neil Armstrong became the first man to set foot on Earth's only moon.

Space Exploration

One of the largest areas of scientific research is space exploration. Of course, people have always wondered about the universe, but the United States didn't make space research a priority until the 1940s and 1950s "space race" with the Soviet Union. In 1957, Russia launched a satellite called Sputnik, which fueled the intense competition between the two countries. In space research, the question that accelerated space exploration was "How can man travel into space safely?" This question fueled the creation of NASA (the National Aeronautics and Space Administration) on October 1, 1958.

NASA research continues today. They observe the sky, launch satellites and telescopes into space, and study the data collected. Currently, there are a multitude of satellites and land vehicles or "rovers" on Mars collecting data with the hope of one day finding a way for humans to live there. In fact, the target date for human occupation on Mars is somewhere in the 2030s.

Life Science

Characteristics of Living and Non-Living Things

There are several common traits among all living organisms, including:

- They are comprised of cells
- The contain DNA, the genetic code of life
- They grow and develop
- They reproduce
- They need food for energy
- They maintain homeostasis
- They react to their surroundings
- They evolve as a population

There are two types of cells that make up living things: simple bacterial cells (prokaryotes) and the complicated cells of protists, fungi, plants, and animals (eukaryotes). All of these have a set of instructions, DNA, which codes for the proteins that allow organisms to grow. In the case of bacteria and single-celled eukaryotes, there is simple development, such as creating structures like DNA, ribosomes (protein factories), and a cell membrane. Bacteria do not have complex development because they simply divide once and make a new organism; however, multicellular organisms develop more complex structures—for examples, humans have hearts, stomachs, brains, etc. A human starts as one cell called a **zygote**. In nine months, that zygote has developed so much that it has all the internal organs needed to support life.

Organisms cannot live without energy to fuel the necessary reactions to grow and develop. They get the energy they need either by making it themselves (if they are producers/autotrophs like plants) or consuming it (like animals and fungi) from an outside source. Not only do organisms use that food to grow and develop, but they also use it to stay healthy and maintain homeostasis. For example, the human body has a constant temperature of 98.6 degrees. If the temperature goes above that, the body starts to sweat to cool off. Much below that temperature, the body will shiver in order to generate energy to heat up. For survival, all organisms must be highly regulated to function, kind of like a car. Every single part has to work together in harmony in order to function properly.

Living things, such as humans, respond to their surroundings. If someone hears a loud noise, his or her head turns toward it. If something gets thrown at one's face, the person blinks. Even plants grow towards sunlight. Living things also evolve as a population. Humans today are nothing like our ancestors of long ago because as a species, humans had to continually adapt to the Earth's changing environment.

An extensive explanation of these characteristics of life is beyond an early childhood curriculum, but it's helpful for the teacher to know them because delineating living and nonliving objects can be tricky. A teacher needs to know why fire, a dead grasshopper, and a robot are not alive, because these are common student misconceptions. Although a fire can grow, it does not have DNA. Although a dead grasshopper is made of cells and has DNA, it can't grow or reproduce. A robot doesn't have DNA and isn't made of cells, although it can react to its environment. Conversely, some students don't believe that plants are alive because they don't walk around. To illustrate that they are alive, simple experiments can be used to show that they can reproduce, develop, and grow, such as planting seeds and using light-boxes to show that plants grow toward light.

Teachers must be able to explain that not all organisms move. Plants are alive because they are made of cells, have DNA, grow independently, and meet all of the other characteristics of life. Tiny germs are alive for the same reasons.

These nuances are complicated, but young students should be able to explain that living things grow and nonliving things don't. They should be able to identify mushrooms, plants, and animals as living, and fire, desks, and robots as nonliving.

Cell Theory

The cell is the main functional and structural component of all living organisms. Robert Hooke, an English scientist, coined the term "cell" in 1665. Hooke's discovery laid the groundwork for the cell theory, which is composed of three principals:

- All organisms are composed of cells.
- All existing cells are created from other living cells.
- The cell is the most fundamental unit of life.

Organisms can be unicellular (composed of one cell) or multicellular (composed of many cells). All cells must be bounded by a cell membrane, be filled with cytoplasm of some sort, and be coded by a genetic sequence.

The cell membrane separates a cell's internal and external environments. It is a selectively permeable membrane, which usually only allows the passage of certain molecules by diffusion. Phospholipids and proteins are crucial components of all cell membranes. The cytoplasm is the cell's internal environment and is aqueous, or water-based. The genome represents the genetic material inside the cell that is passed on from generation to generation.

Plant and Animal Cells

The two main classes of eukaryotes are plants and animals. Animal and plant cells contain many of the same or similar *organelles*, which are membrane enclosed structures that each have a specific function; however, there are a few organelles that are unique to either one or the other general cell type. The following cell organelles are found in both animal and plant cells, unless otherwise noted in their description:

- *Nucleus*: The nucleus consists of three parts: the nuclear envelope, the nucleolus, and chromatin. The **nuclear envelope** is the double membrane that surrounds the nucleus and separates its contents from the rest of the cell. The *nucleolus* produces ribosomes. *Chromatin* consists of DNA and protein, which form chromosomes that contain genetic information. Most cells have only one nucleus; however, some cells, such as skeletal muscle cells, have multiple nuclei.

- *Endoplasmic reticulum (ER)*: The ER is a network of membranous sacs and tubes that is responsible for membrane synthesis. It is also responsible for packaging and transporting proteins into vesicles that can move out of the cell. It folds and transports other proteins to the Golgi apparatus. It contains both smooth and rough regions; the rough regions have ribosomes attached, which are the sites of protein synthesis.

- *Flagellum*: Flagellum are found only in animal cells. They are made up of a cluster of microtubules projected out of the plasma membrane, and they aid in cell mobility.

- *Centrosome*: The centrosome is the area of the cell where **microtubules,** which are filaments that are responsible for movement in the cell, begin to be formed. Each centrosome contains two centrioles. Each cell contains one centrosome.

- *Cytoskeleton*: The cytoskeleton in animal cells is made up of microfilaments, intermediate filaments, and microtubules. In plant cells, the cytoskeleton is made up of only microfilaments and microtubules. These structures reinforce the cell's shape and aid in cell movement.

- *Microvilli*: Microvilli are found only in animal cells. They are protrusions in the cell membrane that increase the cell's surface area. They have a variety of functions, including absorption, secretion, and cellular adhesion. They are found on the apical surface of epithelial cells, such as in the small intestine. They are also located on the plasma surface of a female's eggs to help anchor sperm that are attempting fertilization.

- *Peroxisome*: A peroxisome contains enzymes that are involved in many of the cell's metabolic functions, one of the most important being the breakdown of very long chain fatty acids. Peroxisomes produces hydrogen peroxide as a byproduct of these processes and then converts the hydrogen peroxide to water. There are many peroxisomes in each cell.

- *Mitochondrion*: The mitochondrion is often called the powerhouse of the cell and is one of the most important structures for maintaining regular cell function. It is where aerobic cellular respiration occurs and where most of the cell's adenosine triphosphate (ATP) is generated. The number of mitochondria in a cell varies greatly from organism to organism, and from cell to cell. In human cells, the number of mitochondria can vary from zero in a red blood cell, to 2000 in a liver cell.

- *Lysosome*: Lysosomes are responsible for digestion and can hydrolyze macromolecules. There are many lysosomes in each cell.
- *Golgi apparatus*: The Golgi apparatus is responsible for the composition, modification, organization, and secretion of cell products. Because of its large size, it was actually one of the first organelles to be studied in detail. There are many Golgi apparati in each cell.
- *Ribosomes*: Ribosomes are found either free in the cytosol, bound to the rough ER, or bound to the nuclear envelope. They manufacture proteins within the cell.
- *Plasmodesmata*: The plasmodesmata are found only in plant cells. They are cytoplasmic channels, or tunnels, that go through the cell wall and connect the cytoplasm of adjacent cells.
- *Chloroplast*: Chloroplasts are found only in plant cells. They are responsible for *photosynthesis*, which is the process of converting sunlight to chemical energy that can be stored and used later to drive cellular activities.
- *Central vacuole*: A central vacuole is found only in plant cells. It is responsible for storing material and waste. This is the only vacuole found in a plant cell.
- *Plasma membrane*: The plasma membrane is a phospholipid bilayer that encloses the cell.
- *Cell wall*: Cell walls are only present in plant cells. The cell wall is made up of strong fibrous substances including cellulose and other polysaccharides, and protein. It is a layer outside of the plasma membrane, which protects the cell from mechanical damage and helps maintain the cell's shape.

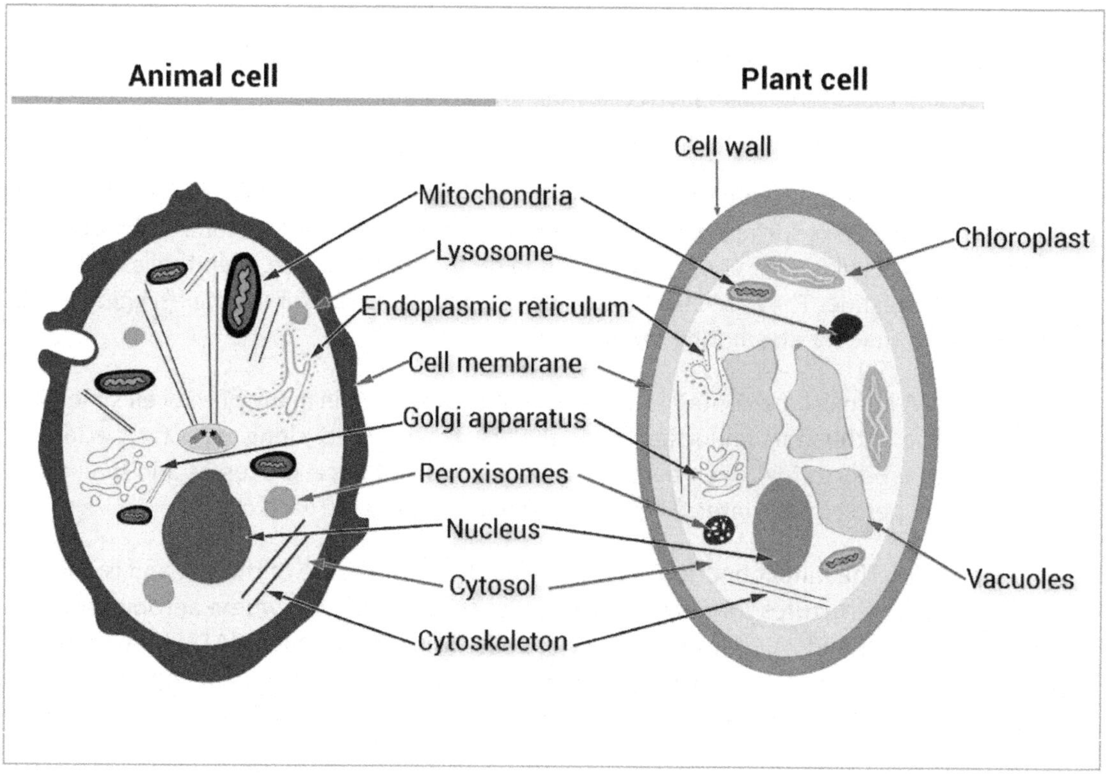

Although a human is noticeably different from a carrot, cells in these organisms have only a few differences. The main differences are the cell structure, appearance, and method of energy production.

Plant cells have a **cell wall** made of cellulose—a strong, fibrous material that adds bulk to stool because it's so hard to break down. This material must be strong in order to prevent the cell from bursting when water enters and increases the intracellular pressure. Animal cells don't have a cell wall. Instead, they have a **cell membrane** composed of several materials (which differ depending on cell type) embedded in a phospholipid bilayer. This bilayer is exactly what it sounds like: two layers of phospholipids stacked tail-to-tail. A **phospholipid** is a molecule with a glycerol (phosphate) head and two fatty acid (lipid) tails. This membrane is much weaker compared a plant's cellulose wall, so animal cells are much more susceptible to bursting from water pressure. And herein lies an important characteristic of the phospholipid bilayer: the tails inside the layer are actually **hydrophobic** (water-repellent) so they are able to prevent too much water from entering and killing the cell.

The shapes and sizes of plant and animal cells are also quite different. Plant cells have a consistent rectangular shape and are generally much larger, ranging from 10–100 micrometers. Animal cells vary in shape and are around 10–30 micrometers. Human liver cells (which are round) look completely different from nerve cells (which have a large cell body and long projections outward). The vacuoles are also different; plant cells tend to have just one large vacuole, while animal cells have several tiny ones.

The most important difference between plants and animals is how they create energy. Animals must consume energy from other living organisms. Plants have the amazing ability to use energy from the sun to power their growth and survival. The little organelles that make this possible are the **chloroplasts** in plants and **mitochondria** in animals. Both use carbon, oxygen, and water. Through photosynthesis, a chloroplast is able to extract carbon from the carbon dioxide (CO_2) in the air and combine it with water (H_2O) to make glucose ($C_6H_{12}O_6$) and oxygen (O_2). Glucose provides energy for animal cells. In the body, mitochondria use the energy embedded inside glucose molecules and combine them with oxygen to create carbon dioxide, water, and ATP (a form of useable energy for physiological processes). This process is called cellular respiration. Memorizing the chemical equations for these reactions may help with understanding these processes:

Photosynthesis: $6\ H_2O + 6\ CO_2 + \text{sunlight} \rightarrow C_6H_{12}O_6 + 6\ O_2$

Six molecules of water and six of carbon dioxide make one glucose molecule and six molecules of oxygen.

Cellular respiration: $C_6H_{12}O_6 + 6\ O_2 \rightarrow 6\ H_2O + 6\ CO_2 + \text{heat (energy)}$

Note that this is basically the reverse of photosynthesis.

Bacterial cells are a completely different story. There are a huge variety of bacteria, and they can actually share characteristics with both plant and animal cells. Some can utilize photosynthesis, some can only perform cellular respiration, and some can even do both or neither!

Classification of Living Things

Due to the speciation that has occurred, the variety of organisms is astronomical. Scientists have identified about 2 million species, and they suspect that there are at least 8 million others out there.

A man named Carolus Linnaeus developed a naming system to try to create some order in classifying all species. For example, the classification of humans through the seven levels, from all-inclusive to the most specific, looks like this:

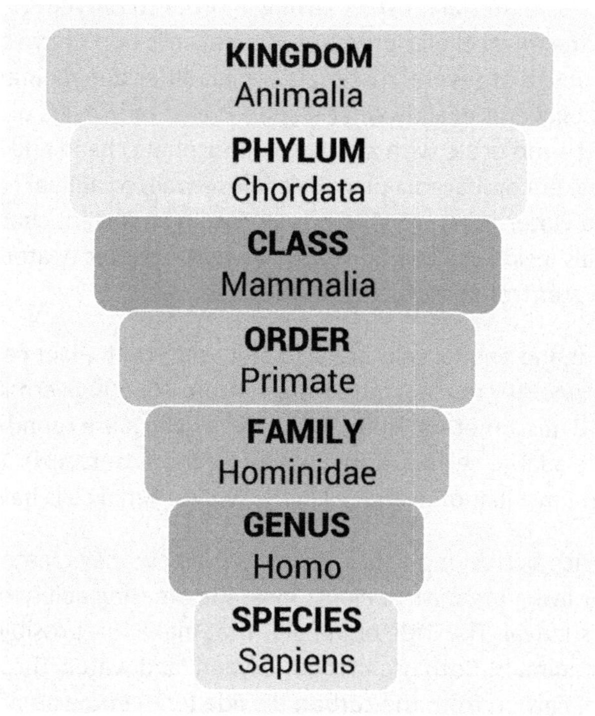

One benefit of this universal naming system is that because some organisms have different common names, like the roly-poly and doodlebug, or the cougar and panther, it allows scientists to have a common language. Due to the sheer magnitude of species, scientists need the seven levels, but when referring to organisms, their official names are just the last two: genus and species. Humans are simply referred to as *Homo sapiens*. This two-name system is called binomial nomenclature.

There are currently six kingdoms, although the prokaryotes (simpler cells) used to be lumped together into one kingdom called Monera. Currently, there are two prokaryotic kingdoms, Archaebacteria and Eubacteria.

Archaebacteria

Prokaryotes that have a cell membrane made of fats. They live in harsh places including extremely hot areas (volcanic vents or hot springs) and extremely salty locations (Utah's Salt Lake). These are the rarest prokaryotes.

Eubacteria

Common bacteria that have a cell membrane made of a protein-carbohydrate blend. They make up the vast majority of existing prokaryotes. An example is staphylococcus.

Protista

This kingdom consists of eukaryotes. Most are unicellular. This kingdom is the most diverse and can be divided into three types: fungus-like (including slime-molds), plant-like (including algae), and animal-like (including amoeba). Some scientists believe that there is so much diversity within the kingdom that they should be split into separate kingdoms, but so far, they remain in one group.

Animal-like protists are heterotrophs (they do not make their own food), and plant-like protists are autotrophs (they make their own food). Fungus-like protists are heterotrophs. Like actual fungi, these organisms externally digest their food by acting as parasites and decomposers. Animal-like protists ingest their food via phagocytosis (cell eating) or by absorbing it.

Depending on the particular protists, some produce asexually via mitosis and others reproduce sexually.

Fungi

Fungi are eukaryotic heterotrophs that digest their food externally. Many of them, including common mushrooms and toadstools, act as decomposers by breaking down dead organisms then absorbing the broken-down nutrients. Other fungi accomplish ingestion as parasites feeding off of living organisms, as in the case of a yeast infection. All fungi are multicellular with one exception—yeast. Fungi have cell walls made of a complex carbohydrate called chitin. Most fungi reproduce sexually and asexually.

Plantae

Plants are multicellular autotrophs like daisies, roses, and pine trees. They are closely related to the aquatic producer, algae, but different in that algae don't contain true roots, stems, or leaves. Plants are photosynthesizers, and their cells have surrounding cell walls made of the starch cellulose.

Animalia

Animals are multicellular heterotrophs, like fungi, except that animals move and internally ingest their food by consuming it. Animals are the only kingdom to not have cells with cell walls due to their flexibility and ability to move. The animal kingdom is very diverse and includes humans, jellyfish, and spiders, as well as all sorts of other organisms.

Cellular Organization and Organ Systems

Prokaryotes contain ribosomes, DNA, cytoplasm, a cell membrane, a cytoskeleton, and a cell wall. Eukaryotes vary between kingdoms but contain all of these structures except a cell wall because animal cells require so much mobility. Large, land-dwelling animals typically compensate with an exoskeleton (like insects) or an endoskeleton (like humans and other mammals, reptiles, and birds) for structure.

All bacterial cells are unicellular (existing as just one cell). Almost all types of protist and some species in fungi kingdom are unicellular, but they still have the complicated organelles of eukaryotes. A few protists, almost all fungi, and all plants and animals are multicellular. Multicellularity leads to development of structures that are perfectly designed for their function.

Cells combine to form tissue. Tissue combines to form organs. Organs combine to form organ systems, and organ systems combine to form one organism. The structures of all of these combinations allow for the maximum functionality of an organism, as demonstrated by the nervous system.

A neuron is a cell in the nervous system designed to send and receive electrical impulses. Neurons have dendrites, which are sensors waiting to receive a message. Neurons also have an axon, a long arm that sends the message to the neighboring neuron. The axon also has insulation known as myelin that speeds the message along. Many neurons combine to form a nerve, the tissue of the nervous system, which is like a long wire. The structure of this nerve is perfect—it is a long cable whose function is to send signals to the brain so the brain can process the information and respond. Nerve tissue combines with other tissue to form the brain, a complex structure of many parts.

The brain also has glands (epithelial tissue) that release hormones to control processes in our body. The brain and spinal cord together form the central nervous system that controls the stimulus/response signaling in our body. The nervous system coordinates with the circulatory system to make our heart beat, the digestive system to control food digestion, the muscular system to move an arm, the respiratory system to facilitate breathing, and all other body systems to make the entire organism functional. Cells are the basic building block in our bodies, and their structure is critical for their function and the function of the tissues, organs, and systems that they comprise.

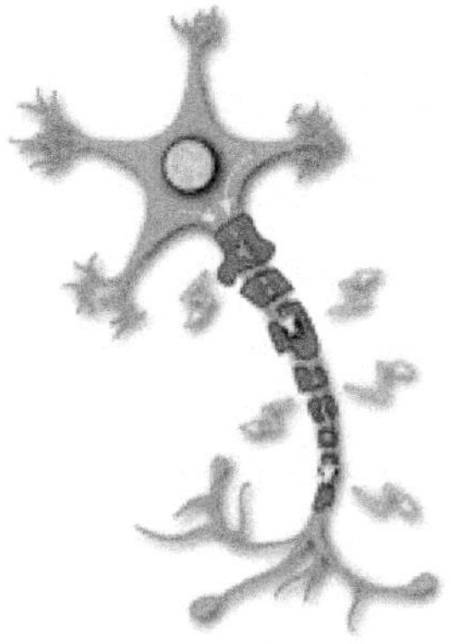

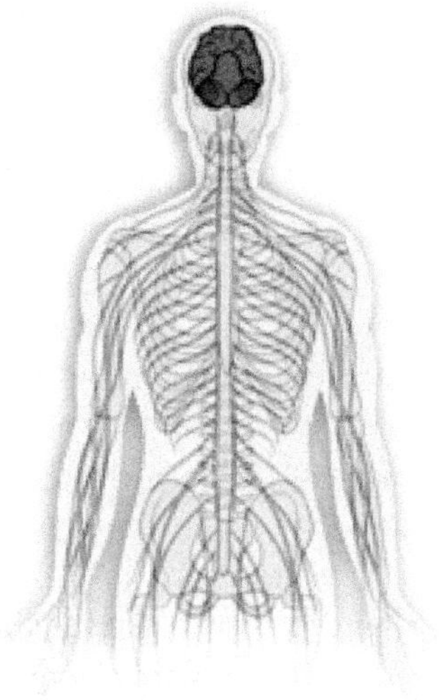

In the graphic above, the left depicts a neuron, and the right depicts the nervous system. A neuron is a nerve cell, and it is the basic building block of the nervous system. Cell, tissue, organ, and organ system structure are critical for function. The following table lists organ systems in the human body:

Name	Function	Main organs
Nervous	Detect stimuli and direct response	Brain and spinal cord
Circulatory	Pump blood to deliver oxygen to cells so they can perform cellular respiration	Heart
Respiratory	Breathe in oxygen (reactant for cellular respiration) and release carbon dioxide waste	Lungs
Muscular	Movement	Heart and muscles
Digestive	Break down food so that glucose can be delivered to cells for energy	Stomach, small intestine, lots of others
Skeletal	Support and organ protection	All sorts of joints, skull, ribcage

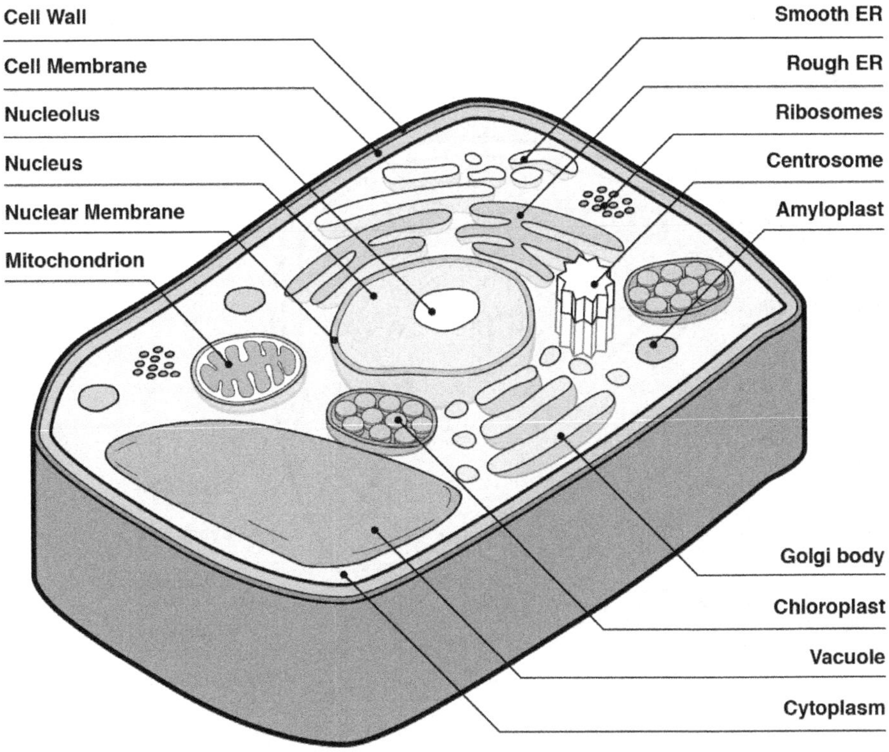

Infectious Agents, Their Transmission, and Their Effects on the Body

Every living organism is made up of cells, and these cells come in various shapes and sizes, depending on the organism. There are two types of cells: prokaryotes and eukaryotes. The big difference between them is that eukaryotes have a nucleus and prokaryotes do not. The structures that will be focused on for this section will be:

Bacteria	Protist, Fungus, Plant, Animal
DNA Ribosomes Cytoplasm Cell Membrane Cell Wall	DNA Ribosomes Cytoplasm Cell Membrane Cell Wall (except animal cells) Unique structures Nucleus Mitochondria Chloroplasts (only autotrophs, or organisms that can produce their own food. Only protists and plants are producers).

Eukaryotic cells are more complex than prokaryotic cells. They make up all the organisms in the kingdoms protist, fungus, plant, and animal. Eukaryotic cells are also larger than prokaryotes and contain a nucleus and other organelles.

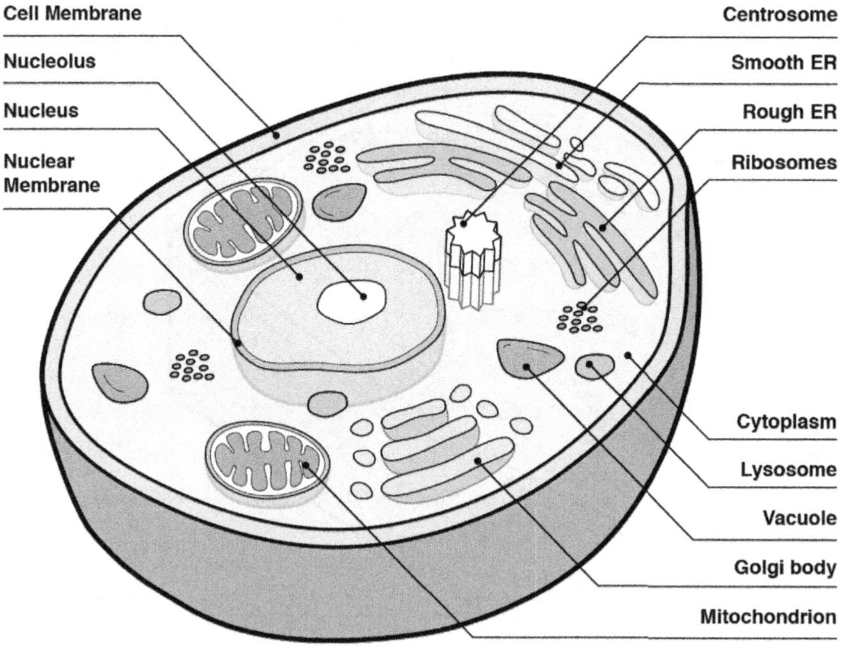

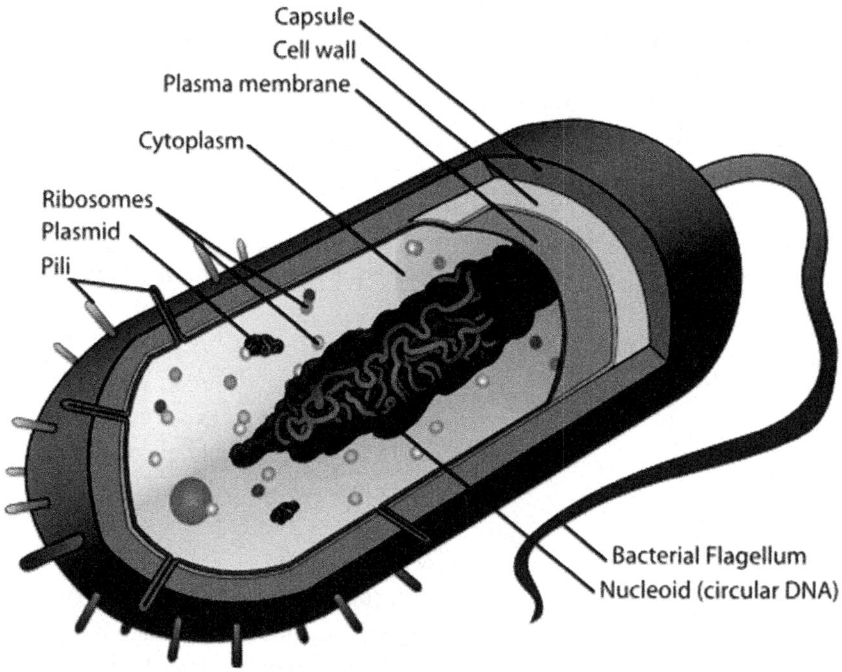

Eukaryotic cells hold their DNA inside a nucleus in pieces called chromosomes. Chromosomes are a cell's way of organizing long strands of DNA in twisted-up bundles. Imagine a room filled with rolls of toilet paper compared to a room that has all of those rolls unraveled and thrown everywhere; it would be a mess!

Other important organelles include chloroplasts and mitochondria. Chloroplasts can be found in cells called autotrophs, which can convert sunlight into energy. Plants are autotrophs. Mitochondria are little energy factories found in almost every type of cell. They use chemical reactions to make little packets of energy that can be used by other parts of the cell.

Like all cells, bacterial cells contain DNA, the genetic material that gives instructions for every single structure and process that the cell undergoes. DNA is a code made up of four letters: A (adenine), T (thymine), G (guanine), and C (cytosine). There are billions of these letters in DNA, and the order of these letters tells a cell exactly what to do and how to do it (just like reading a book of instructions).

Because DNA doesn't do anything on its own, all cells must have a means of decoding DNA and turning it into the structure, which is the function of ribosomes—they are protein-makers. If DNA is like a recipe, then the ribosomes are like the chef.

DNA and ribosomes sit in a fluid called cytoplasm, which contains a cytoskeleton (a network of proteins) that holds them in place. All cells need a covering to contain everything inside—these are called cell membranes in animals or cell walls for plant cells.

Bacteria can also have a capsule and a flagellum, which are all external structures. A capsule is sticky and causes bacteria to cluster with other cells or on food. Only about 50 percent of bacteria can move, and those that do often have a flagellum, which is a whip-like structure like a tadpole's tail.

Viruses are commonly thought of as living organisms, but many scientists argue they aren't for two reasons: (1) they are not cells, and (2) they cannot reproduce by themselves. Both qualities are required for an organism to be considered alive. Viruses are unique in that they require a host in order to make proteins and reproduce, because viruses don't have all of the complex tools of a living cell. When a virus has infected a host, it acts like a living organism—it moves and reproduces—but outside of a host, it does nothing. A virus can survive outside of a host, but it cannot reproduce. Scientists are still trying to properly define a virus, so we can currently say that viruses are not like bacteria or any other living thing.

Heredity, Natural Selection, and Evolution

All living things are a product of their DNA, specifically portions of their DNA called genes that code for different characteristics.

Learned behavior is not affected by DNA and is not hereditable. Changes in appearance like a woman painting her toenails, a bird whose feathers accidentally fall out due to a tornado, or a person getting a scar are also not heritable. Heritable characteristics are those coded by DNA like eye color, hair color, and height.

A man named Gregor Mendel is considered the father of genetics. He was a monk and a botanist, and through extensive experiments with pea plants, he figured out a great deal about heredity.

Our genetic code comes in pairs. Each chromosome contains many genes, and since we have one chromosome from our mom and one chromosome from our dad, we have two copies of each gene. Genes come in different forms called alleles. The two alleles work together, and when the cell reads them and follows their instructions, the way an organism looks or behaves is called a trait. For some traits, there are only two alleles: a dominant allele and a recessive allele. Even though eye color is a bit more complicated, pretend that brown eyes are dominant over blue eyes, and there are the only two alleles:

- B = Brown eyes
- b = blue eyes

A child inherits these alleles from his parents. There are three possible combinations a child can inherit, dependent on his parents' alleles:

- BB (homozygous dominant)
- Bb (heterozygous)
- bb (homozygous recessive)

The combination of genes above will determine the trait in the offspring. If the child gets any combination with a B, the more powerful allele, his eyes will be brown. Only the bb combination will give the child blue eyes. In this example, the combination of alleles is called a genotype, and the actual eye color the child has is called a phenotype.

Evolution

Biological evolution is the concept that a population's gene pool changes over generations. According to this concept, populations of organisms evolve, not individuals, and over time, genetic variation and mutations lead to such changes.

Darwin's Theory of Natural Selection

Charles Darwin developed a scientific model of evolution based on the idea of *natural selection*. When some individuals within a population have traits that are better suited to their environment than other individuals, those with the better-suited traits tend to survive longer and have more offspring. The survival and inheritance of these traits through many subsequent generations lead to a change in the population's gene pool. According to natural selection, traits that are more advantageous for survival and reproduction in an environment become more common in subsequent generations.

Evolutionary Fitness

Sexual selection is a type of natural selection in which individuals with certain traits are more likely to find a mate than individuals without those traits. This can occur through direct competition of one sex for a mate of the opposite sex. For example, larger males may prevent smaller males from mating by using their size advantage to keep them away from the females. Sexual selection can also occur through mate choice. This can happen when individuals of one sex are choosy about their mate of the opposite sex, often judging their potential mate based on appearance or behavior. For example, female peacocks often mate with the showiest male with large, beautiful feathers. In both types of sexual selection, individuals with some traits have better reproductive success, and the genes for those traits become more prevalent in subsequent populations.

Adaptations are Favored by Natural Selection

Adaptations are inherited characteristics that enhance survival and reproductive capabilities in specific environments. Charles Darwin's idea of natural selection explains *how* populations change—adaption explains *why*. Darwin based his concept of evolution on three observations: the unity of life, the diversity of life, and the suitability of organisms for their environments. There was unity in life based on the idea that all organisms descended from common ancestors. Then, as the descendants of the common ancestors faced changes in their environments they moved to new environments. There they adapted new features to help them in their new way of life. This concept explains the diversity of life and how organisms are matched to their environments.

An example of natural selection is found in penguins—birds that cannot fly. Over time, populations of penguins lost the ability to fly but became master swimmers. Their habitats are surrounded by water, and their food sources are in the water. Penguins that could dive for food survived better than those that could fly, and the divers produced more offspring. The gene pool changed as a result of natural selection.

Parameters for Natural Selection

There are three important points to remember about natural selection. Although natural selection occurs due to an individual organism's relationship to its environment, it is a population—not individuals— that change over time. Second, natural selection only affects heritable traits that vary within a population. If all individuals within a population share an identical trait, natural selection cannot occur, and that trait will not be modified. Lastly, which traits are the favored traits is always changing. The environment is an important factor in natural selection, so if the environment changes, a trait that was previously favored may no longer be beneficial. Natural selection is a fluid process that is always at work.

Environmental Change Serve as Selective Mechanisms

The environment constantly changes, which drives selection. Although an individual's traits are determined by their **genotype,** or makeup of genes, natural selection more directly influences **phenotype,** or observable characteristics. The outward appearance or ability of individuals affects their ability to adapt to their environment and survive and reproduce. Phenotypic changes occurring in a population over time are accompanied by changes in the gene pool.

The classic example of this is the peppered moth. It was once a light-colored moth with black spots, though a few members of the species had a genetic variation resulting in a dark color. When the Industrial Revolution hit London, the air became filled with soot and turned the white trees darker in color. Birds were then able to spot and eat the light-colored moths more easily. Within just a few months, the moths with genes for darker color were better able to avoid predation. Subsequent generations had far more dark-colored moths than light ones. Once the Industrial Revolution ended and the air cleared, light-colored moths were better able to survive, and their numbers increased.

Interdependence of Organisms

All organisms work together so that life can exist. An organism represents a specific species, like the fish below, and all organisms serve a particular function. The fish's niche is to eat aquatic producers and excrete waste that acts as fertilizer.

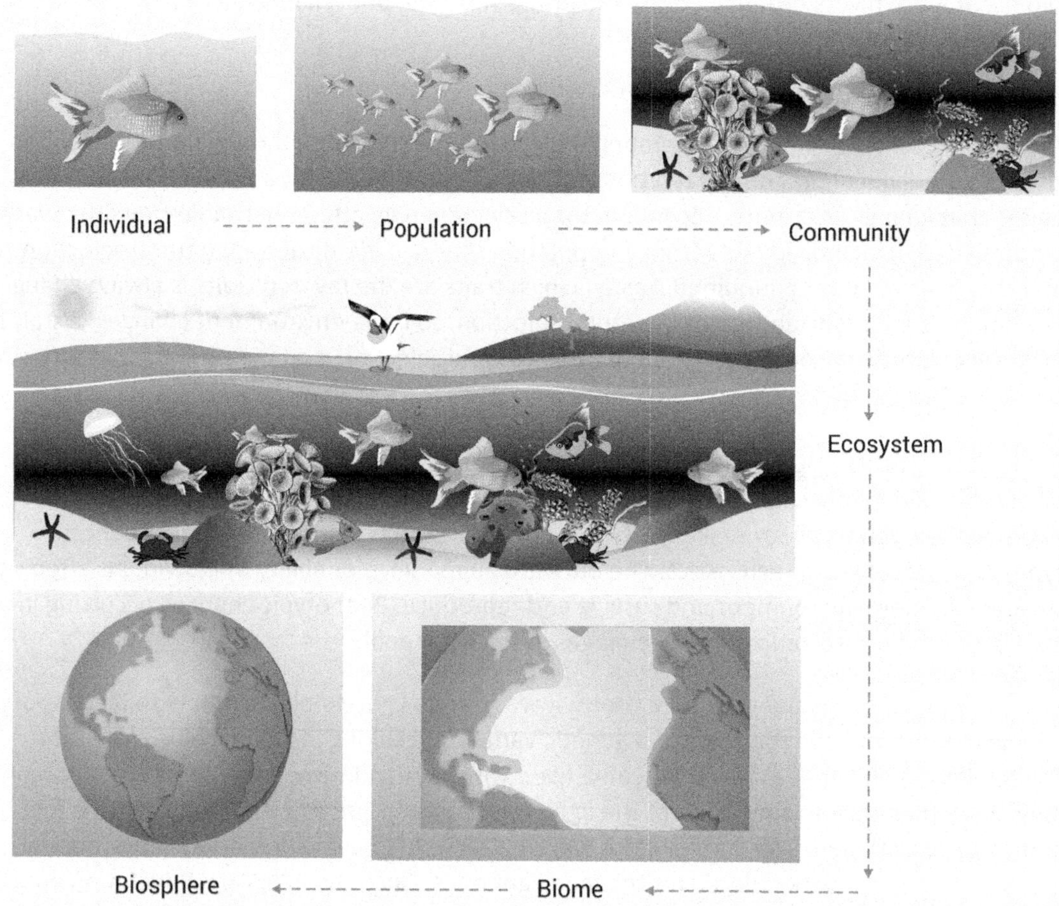

This fish is just one organism within a population. A population represents multiple individuals living in the same habitat. The community includes every biotic factor (living organism) within an ecosystem, in this case, the fish, jellyfish, algae, crab, bacteria, etc. An ecosystem includes all the biotic factors as well as the abiotic, which includes anything non-living—for the fish, that's a rock, a shipwreck, and a nearby glacier. For biomes, add weather and climate into the mix. The biosphere is all of Earth, which is the combination of all biomes.

We already discussed that producers (plants, protists, and even some bacteria) photosynthesize and make the food that provides energy required for all chemical reactions to occur and therefore all life to exist. A non-photosynthesizer must find and eat food, and this feeding relationship can be visualized in food chains.

Consider this food chain:

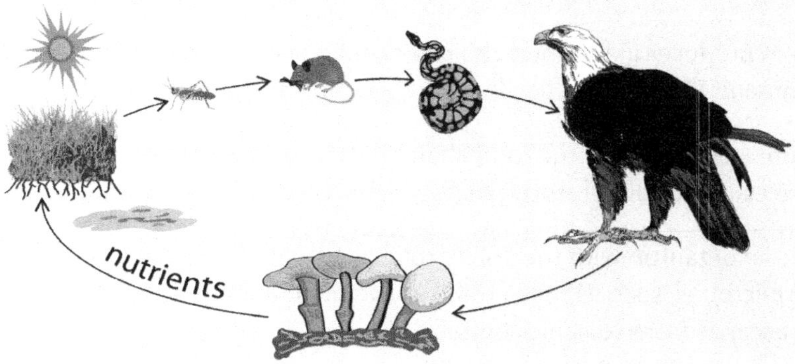

The true source of the energy for every living organism is the sun. Plants absorb the sun's energy to make glucose and are on the first trophic level (feeding level). The grasshopper on the second trophic level is an example of an herbivore and is a primary consumer, as he is the first eater in the food chain. Unfortunately, he receives only 10 percent of the energy that the plant absorbed (this is known as the 10 percent rule) because the other 90 percent of energy was either used by the plant to grow or will be lost as heat. The mouse on the third trophic level is the secondary consumer, or second eater. Food chains are not as inclusive as food webs, which show all feeding relationships in an ecosystem. Looking at this food chain suggests that mice are carnivores (eaters of animals), but mice also eat berries and plants, so they are actually considered omnivores (eaters of both plants and animals). The mouse only gets 10 percent of the energy from the grasshopper, which is actually only 1 percent of the original energy provided by the Sun. The snake on the fourth trophic level is a carnivore, as is the hawk on the highest trophic level.

The arrows in the food chain show the transfer of energy, and fungi as well as bacteria act as decomposers, which break down organic material. Decomposers act at every trophic level because they feed on all organisms; they are non-discriminating omnivores. Decomposers are critical for life, as they recycle the atoms and building blocks of organisms.

In any food chain, producer organisms like grass or algae make up the bottom of the chain, while the top is comprised of apex predators such as lions and tigers. The food chain is useful for depicting the flow of energy, or nutrition, from bottom to top. Terms commonly used while discussing the food chain include:

- **Autotroph**: A producer in the food chain with the ability to produce organic compounds from the environment. Photosynthetic plants are examples of autotrophs.
- **Heterotroph**: A consumer in the food chain that must consume organic materials to thrive. Humans are examples of heterotrophs.
- **Lithotroph**: An organism with the ability to use inorganic material to survive. Lithotrophs are exclusively microbes, such as those that survive deep underwater, where they utilize inorganic sulfur that escapes from volcanic vents.

The study of biological relationships is called **ecology,** which explores how organisms affect one another. These relationships can be defined as either **intraspecific** (within the same species) or **interspecific** (between different species) interactions. For example, a man being friendly to his neighbor can be considered an intraspecific interaction, while a man interacting with a dog is an interspecific interaction. Feeding relationships and predator-prey relationships (hunter-hunted, like the hawk and the rabbit in the food web above) are not the only relationships in an ecosystem. There also can be competition within and between species. For example, in the food chain above, the rabbit and snail both eat grass, showing a relationship called competition, when two organisms want the same thing. Other relationships include the following:

- **Amensalism**: Occurs when an organism harms another, but the organism inflicting harm does not benefit from the interaction.
- **Competition**: This is the basis for Darwin's theory of natural selection and survival of the fittest. Competition occurs when the organisms' interactions are mutually harmful, as they compete with one another in order to benefit themselves.
- **Antagonism**: One individual or species hunts another (inflicting harm) for the benefit of food. The harmed species is not working toward the same goal, differentiating amensalism from competition. Classic examples of antagonism are predation and parasitism.
- **Neutralism**: Occurs when different individuals or species interact with one another and neither species is harmed or benefits from the relationship.
- **Facilitation**: Describes interactions in which one participant benefits without harming the other.
- **Commensalism**: Occurs when only one participant receives benefit from the interaction.
- **Mutualism**: Occurs when both parties benefit from the interaction.
- **Symbiosis**: A close mutualistic relationship between organisms of different species. A popular example is the relationship between a clown fish and a sea anemone. The clown fish cleans the sea anemone, and in return, it is protected from predators by the anemone's stinging arms.

Plant Structures and Photosynthesis, Transpiration, and Reproduction

Any producer must have a chloroplast in order to convert light energy into food, usually in the form of a carbohydrate. Chloroplasts are organelles that look like little green beans because they contain the pigment chlorophyll, which is able to absorb the sunlight's energy in the form of photons, or light rays. Some prokaryotes are also photosynthetic, and although they don't have a chloroplast because they're too simple and don't contain organelles, they have a pigment in order to make their own food.

Plants need water and sunlight to live. Plants suck up water from their roots. The sunlight they need is absorbed by the chlorophyll in chloroplasts, which are clustered and concentrated in their leaves. Interestingly, the chlorophyll actually is able to absorb every color of light except for green, which is why leaves look green: they reflect green light. If the roots take in water and the leaves take in carbon dioxide and sunlight energy, why are stems important? The stems in plants are an example of how structure helps function. The stem is like a skeleton for plants; it holds the leaves high so they can be closer to the sun.

Plants are critical for life on earth because they absorb the energy from the sun and invest it in the bonds that make sugar. Sugar passes through the food chain to provide energy for all living organisms. Plants and other autotrophs can make their own energy, while heterotrophs (which cannot make their own energy) consume the sugar, break it down, and convert it into usable energy with their mitochondria.

Vascular and Nonvascular Plants

Plants that have an extensive vascular transport system are called **vascular plants**. Those plants without a transport system are called **nonvascular plants**. Approximately ninety-three percent of plants that are currently living and reproducing are vascular plants. The cells that comprise the vascular tissue in vascular plants form tubes that transport water and nutrients through the entire plant. Nonvascular plants include mosses, liverworts, and hornworts. They do not retain any water; instead, they transport water using other specialized tissue. They have structures that look like leaves, but are actually just single sheets of cells without a cuticle or stomata.

Structure and Function of Roots, Leaves, and Stems

Roots are responsible for anchoring plants in the ground. They absorb water and nutrients and transport them up through the plant. **Leaves** are the main location of photosynthesis. They contain **stomata,** which are pores used for gas exchange, on their underside to take in carbon dioxide and release oxygen. **Stems** transport materials through the plant and support the plant's body. They contain **xylem**, which conducts water and dissolved nutrients upward through the plant, and **phloem**, which conducts sugars and metabolic products downward through the leaves.

Growth

Germination is the process of a plant growing from a seed or spore, such as when a seedling sprouts from a seed or a sporeling grows from a spore. Plants then grow by **elongation**. Plant cell walls are modified by the hormone auxin, which allows for cell elongation. This process is regulated by light and phytohormones, which are plant hormones that regulate growth, so plants are often seen growing toward the sun.

Uptake and Transport of Nutrients and Water

Plant roots are responsible for bringing nutrients and water into the plant from the ground. The nutrients are not used as food for the plant, but rather to maintain the plant's health so that the plant can make its own food during photosynthesis. The xylem and phloem in the stem help with transport of water and other substances throughout the plant.

Photosynthesis

Photosynthesis refers to the process used by plants, some algae, and some bacteria to convert sunlight into chemical energy. It combines water and carbon dioxide using light energy to produce the sugar glucose and oxygen. Glucose is converted to adenosine triphosphate (ATP) through cellular respiration. ATP is the molecule that provides energy for all cellular activities and can be thought of as a sort of energy currency.

Photosynthesis is the most prolific process to create useable energy for life on Earth. In plants, photosynthesis takes place in chloroplasts, organelles containing photosynthetic structures and chemicals. **Thylakoids,** the structural units of photosynthesis, are found within chloroplasts and use **chlorophyll,** a green pigment, to harness sunlight in photosynthesis.

Photosynthesis has two types of reactions: light-dependent and light-independent. Light-dependent reactions produce ATP and release oxygen into the atmosphere. Light-independent reactions utilize ATP to produce glucose.

In photosynthesis, solar energy is used to fix carbon dioxide into glucose, oxidizing water to oxygen.

$$6CO_2 + 6H_2O + Energy \rightarrow C_6H_{12}O_6 + 6O_2$$

In aerobic respiration, the opposite happens, and glucose and oxygen are broken down into carbon dioxide and water to liberate energy in the form of ATP.

$$C_6H_{12}O_6 + 6O_2 \rightarrow 6CO_2 + 6H_2O + Energy$$

Heterotrophs are organisms that eat other living things to obtain organic compounds. This is usually simplified as the thought of eating other animals for food to gain energy, as most animals are unable to produce their own food. As a result, heterotrophs are completely dependent on autotrophs and other heterotrophs as food sources. All animals are considered heterotrophs.

Autotrophs are able to fix carbon dioxide into useable organic compounds. Most of them produce their own food by harnessing the power of sunlight and employing photosynthesis. As a result, autotrophs are not dependent on other organisms for sources of carbon. All plants are considered autotrophs.

Transpiration

Transpiration is an evaporation-like process that occurs in plants and soil. Water from the stomata of plants and from pores in soil evaporates into water vapor and enters the atmosphere.

Asexual and Sexual Reproduction

Plants can generate future generations through both asexual and sexual reproduction. Asexually, plants can go through an artificial reproductive technique called **budding,** in which parts from two or more plants of the same species are joined together with the hope that they will begin to grow as a single plant.

Sexual reproduction of flowers can happen in a couple of ways. **Angiosperms** are flowering plants that have seeds. The flowers have male parts that make pollen and female parts that contain ovules. Wind, insects, and other animals carry the pollen from the male part to the female part in a process called

pollination. Once the ovules are pollinated, or fertilized, they develop into seeds that then develop into new plants. In many angiosperms, the flowers develop into fruit, such as oranges, or even hard nuts, which protect the seeds inside of them.

Nonvascular plants reproduce by sexual reproduction involving **spores.** Parent plants send out spores that contain a set of chromosomes. The spores develop into sperm or eggs, and fertilization is similar to that in humans. Sperm travel to the egg through water in the environment. An embryo forms and then a new plant grows from the embryo. Generally, this happens in damp places.

The Responses of Plants to Various Stimuli

Because plants have limited mobility, they often respond to stimuli through changes in their growth behavior. **Tropism** is a response to stimuli that causes the plant to grow toward or away from the stimuli:

- *Phototropism*: A reaction to light that causes plants to grow toward the source of the light
- *Thermotropism*: A response to changes in temperature
- *Hydrotropism*: A response to a change in water concentration
- *Gravitropism*: A response to gravity that causes roots to follow the pull of gravity and grow downward, but also causes plant shoots to act against gravity and grow upward

Life Cycles and Development

When we eat a hamburger, we're eating more than carbohydrates; we're also eating proteins and fats. Plants provide more than just carbohydrates when we eat them; they also are able to use the light energy to make proteins, fats, and, of course, their DNA, because if they didn't have DNA, they'd have no instructions to grow. The following organic compounds and their atoms don't magically appear in organisms—life has to either grab the nutrients from soil or seeds or eat them.

- Carbohydrates, proteins, fats, and DNA/RNA have carbon, hydrogen, and oxygen
- DNA, proteins, and fats also have phosphorous
- DNA and proteins also have nitrogen
- Proteins also can have sulfur

Plants need all of these elements to make food. Where do they get them? Remember that earth's atmosphere is a conglomerate of different gases, including nitrogen. Bacteria in the soil are able to convert that nitrogen into a usable form, and the roots of plants absorb the critical nitrogen. Carbon and oxygen get into the plant via photosynthesis (carbon dioxide), as does the element hydrogen, because plants take in water, which contains hydrogen. Phosphorous and sulfur are absorbed in plants through soil. Since heterotrophs cannot make their own food, they have to eat an autotroph (or eat something that ate an autotroph) in order to obtain these critical elements.

Cycles are a recurring pattern in science, and making food is no exception. When living things die, fungi and bacteria act as decomposers and break down the material. That's actually why dead things and rotten meat smell bad; the decomposers have broken them down so much that gases containing carbon, oxygen, phosphorous, nitrogen, and even smelly sulfur are released. Remember that sulfur is heavy in protein, and eggs are protein-rich. It makes sense that rotten eggs have an unpleasant smell as they release sulfur because they're mostly protein. Once living things decompose, all the elements eventually recycle back to the atmosphere or to the soil, and the atoms are available to construct molecules once again.

Human **development** starts when sperm fertilizes an egg to create a zygote, which will develop into an embryo. Pregnant women carry an **embryo** inside their bodies for nine months before giving birth to a live baby. Human reproduction is a concept best left for an older age, but mentioning that babies come from eggs that grow inside a mom is a concept that can be briefly discussed because all the organisms below develop from external eggs.

It will provide a good contrast to emphasize the following life cycles:

Chicken	Hens are female chickens, and they lay about one egg per day. If there is no rooster (male chicken) around to fertilize the egg, the egg never turns into a chick and instead becomes an egg that we can eat. If a rooster is around, he mates with the female chicken and fertilizes the egg. Once the egg is fertilized, the tiny little embryo (future chicken) will start as a white dot adjacent to the yolk and **albumen** (egg white) and will develop for 21 days. The mother hen sits on her clutch of eggs (several fertilized eggs) to incubate them and keep them warm. She will turn the eggs to make sure the embryo doesn't stick to one side of the shell. The embryo continues to develop, using the egg white and yolk nutrients, and eventually develops an "egg tooth" on its beak that it uses to crack open the egg and hatch. Before it hatches, it even chirps to let the mom know of its imminent arrival!
Frog	Frogs mate similar to the way chickens do, and then lay eggs in a very wet area. Sometimes, the parents abandon the eggs and let them develop on their own. The eggs, like chickens', will hatch around 21 days later. Just like chickens, a frog develops from a yolk, but when it hatches, it continues to use the yolk for nutrients. A chicken hatches and looks like a cute little chick, but a baby frog is actually a **tadpole** that is barely developed. It can't even swim around right away, although eventually it will develop gills, a mouth, and a tail. After more time, it will develop teeth and tiny legs and continue to change into a fully-grown frog! This type of development is called **metamorphosis.**
Fish	Most fish also lay eggs in the water, but unlike frogs, their swimming sperm externally fertilize the eggs. Like frogs, when fish hatch, they feed on a yolk sac and are called *larvae*. Once the larvae no longer feed on their yolk and can find their own nutrients, they are called **fry,** which are basically baby fish that grow into adulthood.
Butterfly	Like frogs, butterflies go through a process called **metamorphosis**, where they completely change into a different looking organism. After the process of mating and internal fertilization, the female finds the perfect spot to lay her eggs, usually a spot with lots of leaves. When the babies hatch from the eggs, they are in the larva form, which for butterflies is called a **caterpillar**. The larvae eat and eat and then go through a process like hibernation and form into a **pupa**, or a **cocoon**. When they hatch from the cocoon, the butterflies are in their adult form.
Bugs	After fertilization, other bugs go through **incomplete metamorphosis**, which involves three states: eggs that hatch, nymphs that look like little adults without wings and molt their exoskeleton over time, and adults.

All of these organisms depend on a proper environment for development, and that environment depends on their form. Frogs need water, caterpillars need leaves, and baby chicks need warmth in order to be born.

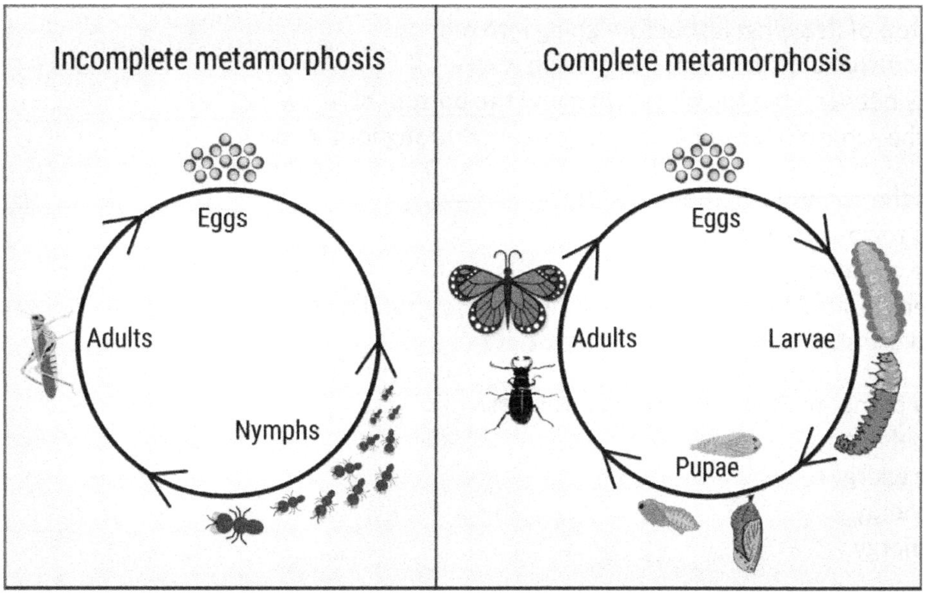

Engaging ways to introduce the life cycle are books like *Rainbow Fish* by Marcus Pfister and *The Very Hungry Caterpillar* by Eric Carle.

Practice Questions

1. At what point in its swing does a pendulum have the most mechanical energy?
   a. At the top of its swing, just before going into motion
   b. At the bottom of its swing, in full motion
   c. Halfway between the top of its swing and the bottom of its swing
   d. It has the same amount of mechanical energy throughout its path

The given energy at any point!

Not potential energy!

2. What does the scientific method describe?
   a. How to review a scientific paper
   b. How to organize a science laboratory
   c. The steps utilized to conduct an inquiry into a scientific question
   d. How to use science to earn money in society

3. The energy of motion is also referred to as what?
   a. Potential energy
   b. Kinetic energy
   c. Solar energy
   d. Heat energy

4. Burning a piece of paper is what type of change?
   a. Chemical change
   b. Physical change
   c. Sedimentary change
   d. Potential change

It can't be returned to its original form.

5. A ramp leading up to a loading dock would be considered which type of simple machine?
   a. Screw
   b. Lever
   c. Inclined plane
   d. Pulley

6. Who is credited for simplifying the laws of motion?
   a. Einstein
   b. Hawking
   c. Copernicus
   d. Newton

3 basic rules of motion!

7. The heat transfer due to the movement of gas molecules from an area of higher concentration to one of lower concentration is known as:
   a. Conduction
   b. Convection
   c. Solarization
   d. Radiation

Convection oven

8. Which of the following is true of an object at rest on earth?
   a. It has no forces acting upon it. ← If its on Earth, gravity is "acting" upon it.
   b. It has no gravity acting upon it.
   c. It is in transition.
   (d.) It is in equilibrium.

9. A third grade class is beginning a research project. The teacher explains that when researching a problem in science, not all sources are equal. The teacher explains that the best sources are which of the following?
   a. People you have seen on television
   b. Anyone with a Ph.D.
   (c.) Accredited laboratories and universities
   d. Any source with an internet webpage

10. What is a change in state from a solid to a gas called? ←
   a. Evaporation - Liquid to Gas
   b. Melting - Solid to liquid
   c. Condensation - Gas to liquid
   (d.) Sublimation - Solid to gas

11. The forces acting upon an object can be illustrated using what?
   a. A Venn diagram
   b. A periodic table
   (c.) A force diagram
   d. A stress-strain diagram (Engineering)

12. Which is not a form of Energy?
   a. Light
   b. Sound
   c. Heat
   (d.) Mass - quantity of an object

13. A projectile at a point along its path has 30 Joules of potential energy and 20 Joules of kinetic energy. What is the total mechanical energy for the projectile?
   (a.) 50 Joules
   b. 30 Joules
   c. 20 Joules
   d. 10 Joules

* Mechanical energy is the sum of the potential & kinetic energy.

14. What factors can prompt scientific inquiry and progress?
   a. Curiosity
   b. Competition
   c. Greed - Humans, pfft!
   (d.) All of the above

15. Which of the following is considered a force?
   (a.) Weight = Force
   b. Mass
   c. Acceleration
   d. Gravity

16. Why would a pencil appear to bend at the water line in a glass of water?
   a. The wood of the pencil becomes warped from being in the water.
   b. It appears to bend because of the refraction of light traveling from air to water.
   c. The pencil temporarily bends because of its immersion into separate mediums.
   d. The reflection of the light from water to a human's pupil creates the illusion of a warping object.

17. Which of the following is NOT one of Newton's three laws of motion?
   a. Inertia: an object at rest tends to stay at rest, and an object in motion tends to stay in motion
   b. $E = mc^2$
   c. For every action there is an equal and opposite reaction
   d. $F = ma$

18. The law of the conservation of energy states which of the following?
   a. Energy should be stored in power cells for future use.
   b. Energy will replenish itself once exhausted.
   c. Energy cannot be created or destroyed.
   d. Energy should be saved because it can run out.

19. Which of the following is true regarding magnets?
   a. Opposite charges attract
   b. Like charges attract
   c. Opposite charges repel
   d. Like charges do not repel or attract

20. Running electricity through a wire generates which of the following?
   a. A gravitational field
   b. A frictional field
   c. An acoustic field
   d. A magnetic field

21. When an ice skater spins on one skate in a circle, what happens if they extend their arms out like the letter "T"?
   a. They spin faster.
   b. They spin slower.
   c. They stop spinning.
   d. Nothing changes.

22. For circular motion, what is the name of the actual force pulling toward the axis of rotation?
   a. Centrifugal force
   b. Gravity
   c. Centripetal force
   d. No force is acting.

23. Students are conducting experiments about how to transfer electrostatic charge. Which of the following is NOT an effective method?
   a. Polarization
   b. Touch
   c. Election
   d. Induction

24. What does the re-radiation of solar waves trapped in the earth's atmosphere contribute to?
    a. Global warming
    b. Greenhouse effect
    c. Climate change
    d. All of the above

25. Velocity is a measure of which of the following?
    a. Speed with direction
    b. The change in position over the change in time
    c. Meters covered over seconds elapsed
    d. All of the above

26. Which of the following sources of energy are non-renewable?
    a. Wind energy
    b. Solar energy
    c. Fossil fuel energy
    d. Geothermal energy

Use the following image to answer question 27.

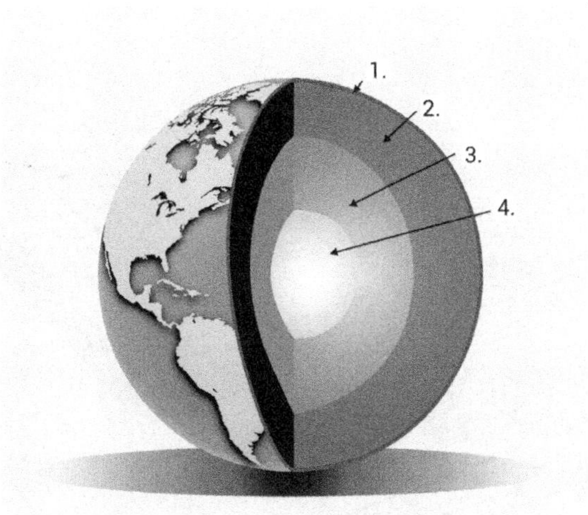

27. A second grade teacher has prepared the following model. Which choice describes the label he should use for layer 4?
    a. Inner core: solid
    b. Inner core: liquid
    c. Outer core: solid
    d. Outer core: liquid

28. Which type of rock accumulates in layers at the bottom of the ocean due to run-off?
    a. Igneous
    b. Sedimentary
    c. Metamorphic
    d. Minerals

29. The water cycle involves phase changes. Which example below is evaporation?
   a. Clouds forming in the sky
   b. Rain, snow, or ice storms
   c. River water flowing to the ocean
   d. Sunlight's effect on morning dew

30. Which of the following is NOT directly caused by tectonic plate movement?
   a. Spreading of the ocean floor
   b. Earthquakes
   c. Mountain formation
   d. Precipitation

31. A formative assessment is given to third grade students during an earth science unit. Which of the following statements does the teacher flag to correct and discuss with the class?
   a. Magma circulates in the upper mantle.
   b. All volcanoes have explosive eruptions.
   c. Igneous rocks are formed by crystallized lava.
   d. Igneous rocks recycle and form magma.

Use the following image to answer questions 32 and 33.

32. Which fossil is the oldest?
   a. Dinosaur head
   b. Seashell
   c. Skeleton
   d. Grass

33. The fossils in the figure are embedded in which type of rock?
   a. Metamorphic
   b. Igneous
   c. Sedimentary
   d. Magma

Use the following image to answer question 34.

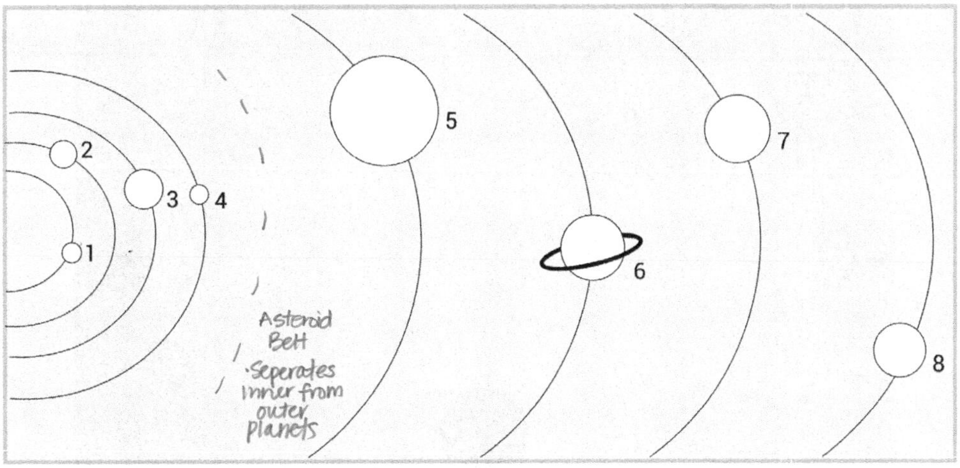

34. Where is the asteroid belt located in the figure above?
    a. Between structures #2 and #3
    b. Between structures #3 and #4
    c. Between structures #4 and #5
    d. Between each planet

35. Why is a year on Mars shorter than a year on Jupiter?
    a. Mars is much smaller than Jupiter.
    b. Mars is a rocky planet, while Jupiter is made of gas.
    c. Mars has a smaller orbit around the Sun.
    d. Mars is inside the asteroid belt.

Use the following image to answer question 36.

36. The figure above illustrates earth's orbit around the sun. What season is it where the dot is located?
    a. Summer
    b. Winter
    c. Fall
    d. Spring

37. Which statement(s) are true about the phases of the moon?
    a. Full moons are farther away from the sun than new moons.
    b. Crescent moons are smaller than half-moons.
    c. Gibbous moons are larger than half-moons.
    d. All of the above are true.

38. A fifth grade student wants to know why greenhouse gases are important. Her teacher could begin the discussion by giving which of the following reasons?
    a. They allow UV rays to penetrate the troposphere.
    b. They insulate earth and keep it warm.
    c. They reflect light so that the sky looks blue.
    d. They form clouds and directly participate in the water cycle.

39. How is a theory different from a hypothesis?
    a. Theories are predictions based on previous research, and hypotheses are proven.
    b. Hypotheses can change, while theories cannot.
    c. Theories are accepted by scientists, while hypotheses remain to be proven.
    d. Hypotheses are always wrong, while theories are always true.

40. Which scientist is correctly paired with what he or she studies?
    a. Paleontologist: earth's crust
    b. Meteorologist: fossils
    c. Seismologist: earthquakes
    d. Geologist: weather

41. What part of most plants performs photosynthesis?
   a. Root
   b. Stem
   c. Leaf
   d. Flower

42. Which definition describes an ecosystem?
   a. One individual organism
   b. Rocks, soil, and atmosphere within an area
   c. All the organisms in a food web
   d. All living and nonliving things in an area

Use the following image to answer questions 43 and 44.

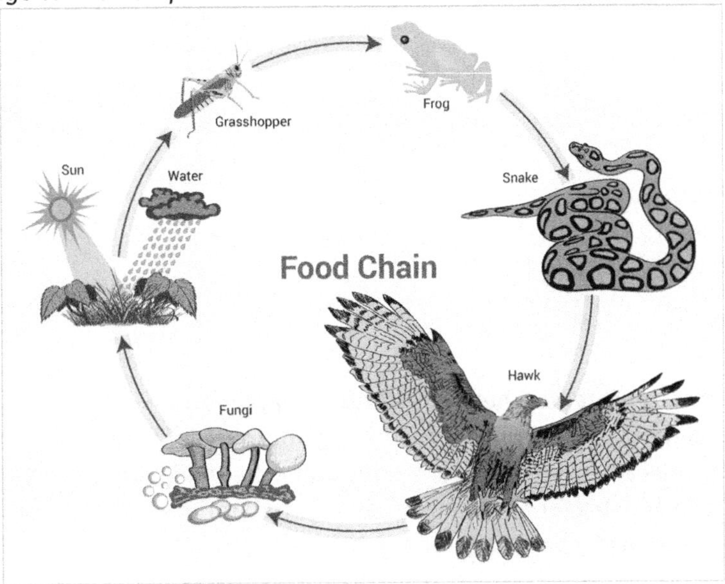

43. Which is the decomposer in the food chain above?
   a. Sun
   b. Grass
   c. Frog
   d. Fungi

44. Which is the herbivore in the food chain above?
   a. Grass
   b. Grasshopper
   c. Frog
   d. Fungi

45. What is a product of photosynthesis?
   a. Water
   b. Sunlight
   c. Oxygen
   d. Carbon Dioxide

46. What is cellular respiration?
    a. Making high-energy sugars
    b. Breathing
    c. Breaking down food to release energy
    d. Sweating

47. Which is true regarding DNA?
    a. It is the genetic code.
    b. It provides energy.
    c. It is single-stranded.
    d. All of the above.

it is double-stranded

48. Which one of the following can perform photosynthesis?
    a. Mold
    b. Ant
    c. Mushroom
    d. Algae

49. What happens at stomata?
    a. Carbon dioxide enters.
    b. Water exits due to transpiration.
    c. Oxygen exits.
    d. Glucose exits.

stomata: pores at the bottom of a leaf.

50. Which of the following represents a helpful inherited adaptation?
    a. A male elephant defending his territory by chasing another elephant away.
    b. A female dog that has a permanent strong odor that other male dogs tend to avoid.
    c. A male moose born with bigger horns that enable him to reduce competition for mating.
    d. A monkey learning to peel a banana after several tries.

a, d: experience
b: If males avoid her she won't mate.

51. Esther is left-handed. Hand dominance is a genetic factor. If being right-handed is a dominant trait over being left-handed, which of the following cannot be true about Esther's parents?
    a. Her parents are both right-handed.
    b. Her parents are both left-handed.
    c. Only one parent is right-handed.
    d. All of the above can be true.

52. What structures are made by the body's white blood cells that fight bacterial infections?
    a. Antibodies
    b. Antibiotics
    c. Vaccines
    d. Red blood cells

53. Cell → _______ → _______ → organ system → organism
Fill in the blanks with the correct structures and a possible example in the circulatory system.
    a. Tissue → organ
    b. Organ → blood vessel
    c. Organ → heart
    d. Tissue → blood vessel

Use the following image to answer question 54.

54. Ants and aphids are organisms commonly found in nature. The ant doesn't eat the aphid, nor does the aphid eat the ant, so they have a different type of relationship than predator-prey. When aphids feed on plants, they simultaneously secrete a sugary substance that ants like to snack on. Ants in return protect the aphids from predators. What kind of relationship do the ant and the aphid demonstrate?

a. Competition
b. Parasitism
c. Mutualism - Both Benefit (mutual benefits)
d. Commensalism

55. Jackson wants to open a dog-training business. He wants to see which dog treat is most effective in training dogs to sit. If he wants to design an experiment testing twenty dogs to figure out which treats to use, what would be a good dependent variable?

a. Type of food (independent variable)
b. Time in seconds the dogs sit
c. How many times the dog wags its tail
d. Shape of food (independent variable)

Answer Explanations

1. D: It has the same amount of mechanical energy throughout its path. Mechanical energy is the total amount of energy in the situation; it is the sum of the potential energy and the kinetic energy. The amount of potential and kinetic energy both vary by the position of an object, but the mechanical energy remains constant.

2. C: The scientific method refers to how to conduct a proper scientific inquiry, including recognizing a question/problem, formulating a hypothesis, making a prediction of what will happen based on research, experimenting, and deciding whether the outcome confirmed or denied the hypothesis.

3. B: Kinetic energy is energy an object has while moving. Potential energy is energy an object has based on its position or height. Solar energy is energy that comes from the sun. Heat energy is the energy produced from moving atoms, molecules, or ions, and can transfer between substances.

4. A: A chemical change alters the chemical makeup of the original object. When a piece of paper burns it cannot be returned to its original chemical makeup because it has formed new materials. Physical change refers to changing a substance's form, but not the composition of that substance. In physical science, "sedimentary change" and "potential change" are not terms used to describe any particular process.

5. C: An inclined plane is a simple machine that can make it easier to raise or lower an object in height. Simple machines offer a mechanical advantage to performing tasks. While a screw, a level, and a pulley are also simple machines, they would be used to offer a mechanical advantage in other situations.

6. D: Sir Isaac Newton simplified the laws of motion into three basic rules, based upon his observations in experimentation and advanced mathematical calculations. Albert Einstein was known for his theories involving electricity and magnetism, relativity, energy, light, and gravitational waves. Stephen Hawking is known for his theories and studies of space, dark matter, black holes, and relativity. Copernicus was known for his observations and theories regarding the movements of the planets in our universe; specifically, that the sun was the center of our solar system, not earth.

7. B: Convection is the transfer of heat due to the movement of molecules from an area of higher concentration to that of lower concentration; this is also how heat can travel throughout a house to warm each room. Conduction is the transfer of energy from one molecule to another molecule through actually touching or making contact with each other. Radiation is how the sun warms the earth; no medium is needed for this type of transfer.

8. D: An object at rest has forces acting upon it, including gravitational, normal, and frictional forces. All of these forces are in balance with each other and cause no movement in the object's position. This is equilibrium. An object in constant motion is also considered to be in equilibrium or a state of balanced forces.

9. C: When conducting scientific research, it is best to rely on sources that are known for honest, ethical, and unbiased research and experimentation. Most laboratories and universities must have their work validated through independent means in order to publish or claim results. Anyone can publish things on the Internet—it does not mean their work has been validated, and therefore, their work may not be correct.

10. D: Sublimation is a change in state from a solid to a gas. Evaporation is a change in state from a liquid to a gas, melting is a change in state from a solid to a liquid, and condensation is a change in state from a gas to a liquid.

11. C: A force diagram shows all of the forces acting upon an object in a situation. The direction of arrows pointing around the object shows the direction of each force. A Venn diagram is used to show mathematical sets, a periodic table shows how the elements are categorized, and a stress-strain diagram is used in engineering.

12. D: Mass refers to the amount or quantity there is of an object. Light, sound, and heat are all forms of energy that can travel in waves.

13. A: The mechanical energy is the total (or sum) of the potential energy and the kinetic energy at any given point in a system.

$$ME = PE + KE$$

$$50\,Joules = 30\,Joules + 20\,Joules$$

14. D: Scientific inquiry can be prompted by simple curiosity as to how or why something works. As seen in the race to enter outer space, scientific progress can be driven by competition. Many inventors are motivated by the idea of finding a better, faster, or more economical way of doing or producing something so that they can prosper from their discovery.

15. A: Using Newton's equation for motion, $F = ma$, and substituting gravity in for acceleration (a), the weight, or force could be calculated for an object having mass (m). Weight is a force, mass is the amount of a substance, and acceleration and gravity are rate of speed over time.

16. B: It appears to bend because of the refraction of light traveling from air to water. When light travels from one material to another it can reflect, refract, and go through different materials. Choice *A* is incorrect, as the pencil does not actually become warped but only *appears* to be warped. Choice *C* is incorrect; although the pencil appears to bend because of its immersion into separate mediums where speed is different, the pencil does not become temporarily warped—it only appears to be warped. Choice *D* is incorrect; it is the refraction of light, not reflection. The latter happens within the same medium, which makes the answer choice incorrect.

17. B: While this is Einstein's application of Newton's theory to that of light, it is not one of Newton's original three laws of motion. Newton's three laws are $F = ma$, the law of inertia, and for every action there is an equal and opposite reaction.

18. C: This is a fundamental law of thermodynamics. Energy can only transfer, transform, or travel. The amount of energy in a system is always the same.

19. A: The ends (or poles) of a straight magnet are different charges. One end is positive and one end is negative. Therefore, the positive end of magnet #1 would attract the negative end of magnet #2 and repel magnet #2's positive end.

20. D: When electricity is run through a wire, it is carrying current, and current has a charge. Therefore, there is a charge running down the wire, which creates a magnetic field that can attract and repel just like any magnet.

21. B: The ice skater is demonstrating the conservation of angular momentum. This means that the amount of momentum for the situation will remain the same. If the skater is redistributing the mass (their arms), then the angular speed will compensate for that alteration. In this case, the mass is extended out away from the axis of rotation, so the rate of rotation is slowed down. If their arms were brought back in near their body, then the rate of rotation would increase, making the skater spin faster.

22. C: This is the actual force recognized in a rotational situation. The reactive force acting opposite of the centripetal force is named the centrifugal force, but it is not an actual force on its own. A common mistake is to interchange the two terms. But, the real force acting in a rotational situation is pulling in toward the axis of rotation and is called the centripetal force.

23. C: Electric charge can be transferred through touch of one physical object to another, induction by bringing a charged object near another object, and polarization, or the forcing of one charge to the end of an object in a centralized area.

24. D: The solar waves from the sun warm the earth. Many of the waves are meant to reflect back off of the atmosphere to keep the earth warm, and the rest of the waves are meant to reflect back out into space through the atmosphere. This is known as the greenhouse effect. However, when the atmosphere has become too dense (polluted by gases), the waves meant to escape are trapped and re-radiate in the earth's atmosphere, causing an overall warming of the climate, known as global warming.

25. D: Velocity is a measure of speed with direction. To calculate velocity, find the distance covered and the time it took to cover that distance; change in position over the change in time. A standard measurement for velocity is in meters per second (m/s).

26. C: Fossil fuel energy. Wind energy from turbines, solar energy from sun panels, and geothermal energy are all considered renewable and preferable alternatives to fossil fuel, of which there is a limited supply.

The following image is the answer to question 27.

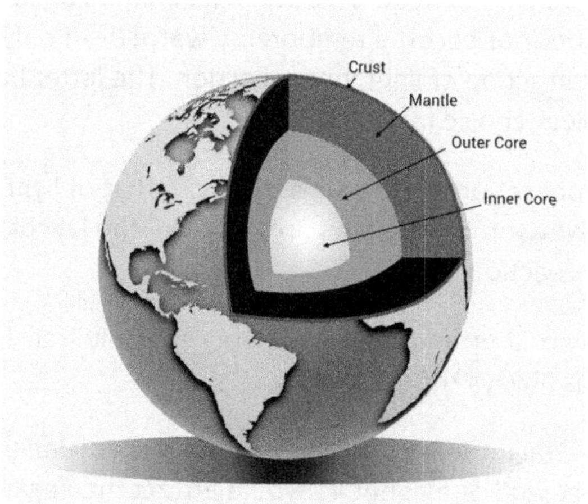

27. A: Inner core: solid. Layer 4 is the inner core; therefore, Choices *C* and *D* are incorrect. The inner core is solid due to the intense pressure upon it, making Choice *B* incorrect.

28. B: Sedimentary. Choice *A* (igneous) is incorrect, because that is crystallized magma found on land. Choice *C* (metamorphic) is incorrect, because that is unified, solid rock close to earth's mantle. Choice *D* (minerals) isn't a type of rock, but what composes rock.

29. D: Sunlight evaporates dew from plants. Choice *A* is incorrect because cloud formation is condensation. Choice *B* is incorrect because rain, snow, and ice storms are different forms of precipitation. Choice *C* is incorrect because rivers flowing into the oceans are examples of run-off.

30. D: Precipitation. Precipitation has nothing to do with plate tectonic theory. Plate movement causes ocean floor spreading, mountain formation, and earthquakes; therefore, all other answer choices are correct.

31. B: Formative evaluation are helpful in gauging students' understanding and shape further instruction. It is not true that all volcanoes have explosive eruptions. Shield volcanoes have thin magma that oozes out gently. Therefore, the teacher should discuss this concept again with the class if several students' assessment responses indicate confusion. Choice *A* is correct because magma circulates in the upper mantle. Choice *C* is correct because igneous rock is cooled lava. Choice *D* is correct because igneous rock goes through the rock cycle and will eventually become magma again.

The following image is for questions 32 and 33.

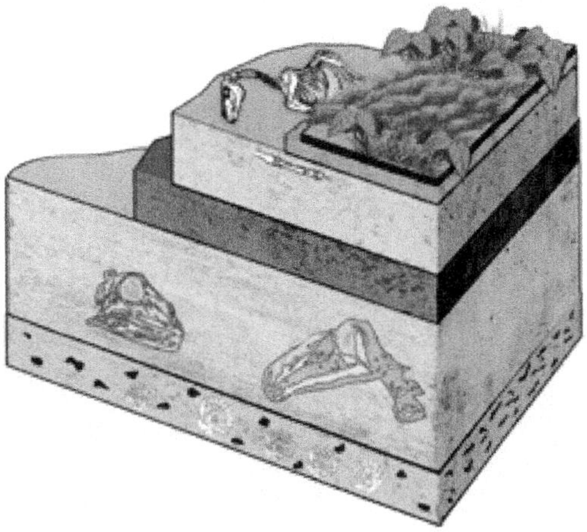

32. B: Seashells. The oldest rock layer is on the bottom. Choice *D* doesn't show a fossil—the grass is a living organism. Choices *A* and *C* show fossils in higher layers, so these are not the correct answers.

33. C: Sedimentary rock. Fossils are only found in sedimentary rock. Igneous rock, metamorphic rock, and liquid magma don't contain fossils, so Choices *A*, *B*, and *D* are incorrect.

The following image is for question 34.

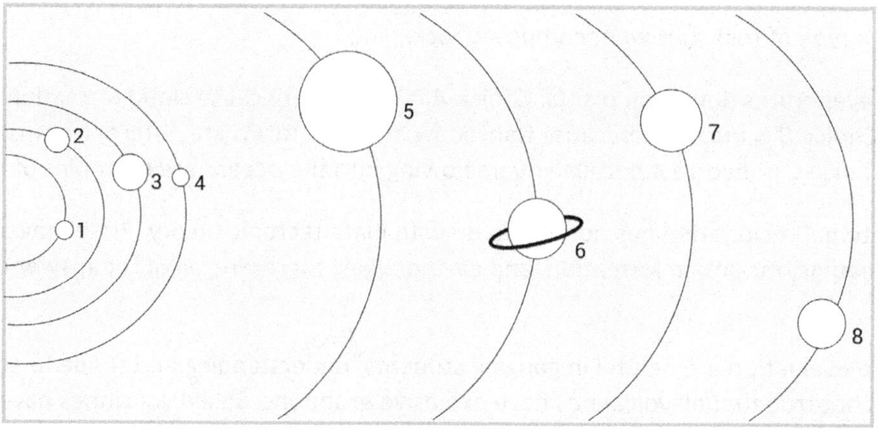

34. C: Between structures #4 and #5. The asteroid belt is rock orbiting between the inner, solid planets and the outer, gassy planets. More precisely, it is between Mars (planet #4) and Jupiter (planet #5). It is not Choice *A* (between Venus and Earth), nor is it Choice *B* (between Earth and Mars). Choice *D* is incorrect since it is not between every planet.

35. C: Mars has a smaller orbit around the Sun. This question requires critical thinking because every answer choice is true, but only one of them has to do with orbiting time. A year is the time it takes a planet to orbit the Sun, and because Mars is closer to the Sun and has a smaller orbit, its year is significantly shorter than a year on Jupiter.

The following image is for question 36.

36. B: Winter. Students must identify the lateral equator and know the difference between North and South. They should recognize that because the top hemisphere is tilted away from the Sun; it would be winter at that time. Spring and fall (Choices *D* and *C*) are incorrect because both hemispheres have the same exposure to the sun, and summer (Choice *A*) is incorrect since the top hemisphere is tilted toward the sun.

37. D: All of the above. All choices are correct. New moons are closest to the sun and full moons are farthest (Choice *A*). Crescent moons are smaller than half-moons (Choice *B*), and gibbous moons are larger than half-moons (Choice *C*).

38. B: They insulate earth and keep it warm. Greenhouse gases serve as a blanket and allow earth to exist at livable temperatures. Choice *D* is incorrect because greenhouse gases do not form clouds; clouds are formed by condensed water vapor. Choice *C* is incorrect because while it is true that particles in the atmosphere reflect light so that the sky appears blue, this isn't an important function of the particles in the troposphere. The blue appearance is just cosmetic. Choice *A* is incorrect because ozone in the stratosphere actually prevents UV rays from passing.

39. C: Theories are accepted by scientists, while hypotheses remain to be proven. Choice *A* is incorrect because theories are far more than predictions; they are actually highly supported and accepted as truth. Choice *B* is incorrect because theories can change with new technology and understanding. Choice *D* is also incorrect because theories may not always be true and can change. Also, hypotheses can be and often are supported.

40. C: Seismologist: earthquakes. All other choices have been mixed up. Paleontologists study fossils, meteorologists study weather, and geologists study the earth's crust.

41. C: Leaf. Leaves are the part of the plant that contain chloroplast (due to their green appearance), thus they are the parts that perform photosynthesis. Roots (Choice *A*) suck up water. Seeds and flowers are reproductive structures (Choices *B* and *D*).

42. D: All living and nonliving things in an area. Choice *C* (all the organisms in a food web) describes feeding relationships and not symbiosis. Choice *B* (rocks, soil, and atmosphere in an area) includes nonliving factors in an ecosystem. Choice *A*, one organism, is too small to be considered an ecosystem.

The following image is for questions 43 and 44.

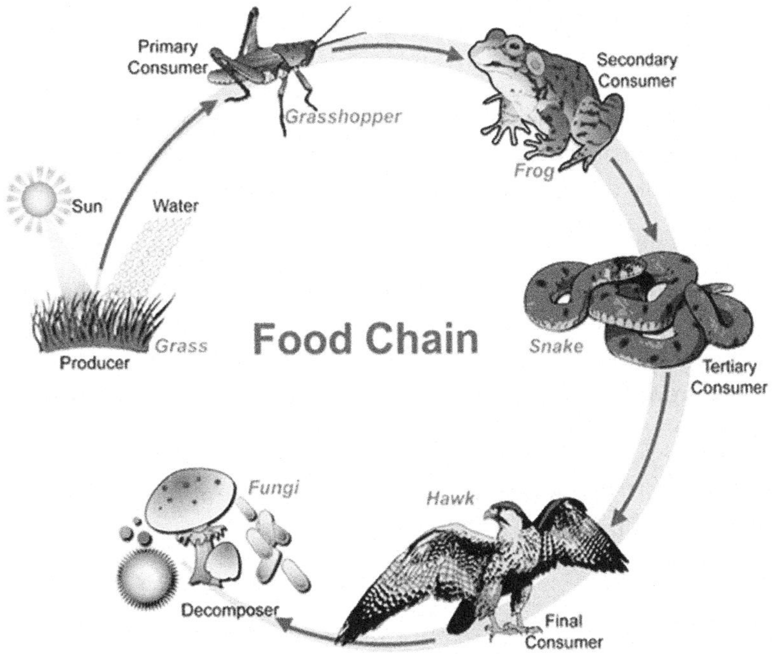

43. D: Fungi. Choice *A* (the sun) is not even a living thing. Grass (*B*) is a producer, and the frog (*C*) is a consumer. The fungi break down dead organisms and are the only decomposer shown.

44. B: Grasshopper. An herbivore is an organism that eats only plants, and that's the grasshopper's niche in this particular food chain. Grass (*A*) is a producer, the frog (*C*) is a consumer, and the fungi (*D*) is a decomposer.

45. C: Oxygen. Water (*A*) is a reactant that gets sucked up by the roots. Carbon dioxide (*D*) is a reactant that goes into the stomata, and sunlight (*B*) inputs energy into the reaction in order to create the high-energy sugar.

46. C: Breaking down food to release energy. Breathing (*B*) is not cellular respiration; breathing is an action that takes place at the organism level with the respiratory system. Making high-energy sugars (*A*) is photosynthesis, not cellular respiration. Perspiration (*D*) is sweating, and has nothing to do with cellular respiration.

47. A: It is the genetic code. Choice *B* is incorrect because DNA does not provide energy—that's the job of carbohydrates and glucose. Choice *C* is incorrect because DNA is double-stranded. Because Choices *B* and *C* are incorrect, Choice *D*, all of the above, is incorrect.

48. D: Algae can perform photosynthesis. One indicator that a plant is able to perform photosynthesis is the color green. Plants with the pigment chlorophyll are able to absorb the warmer colors of the light spectrum, but are unable to absorb green. That's why they appear green. Choices *A* and *C* are types of fungi, and are therefore not able to perform photosynthesis. Fungi obtain energy from food in their environment. Choice *B*, ant, is also unable to perform photosynthesis, since it is an animal.

49. D: Glucose exits. The stomata are pores at the bottom of the leaf, and carbon dioxide enters (it is a reactant for photosynthesis) and oxygen exits (it is a product for photosynthesis), so Choices *A* and *C* are correct. Water exits through the stomata in the process of transpiration, so Choice *B* is correct as well. Glucose is the sugar that is either broken down by the plant for its own energy usage or eaten by other organisms for energy.

50. C: A male moose with horns that enable him to reduce competition for mating. Choices *A* and *D* (elephant and monkey) are not caused by genes. These are learned behaviors from other animals. Choice *B* (smelly dog) is actually a detriment because the dog will be less likely to mate, so she will not pass on her smelly genes.

51. D: All of the above. Let's label *R* as the right-handed allele and *r* as the left-handed allele. Esther has to have the combination rr since she's left-handed. She had to get at least one recessive allele from each parent. So, mom could either be Rr or rr (right-handed or left-handed), and dad can also be Rr or rr. As long as each parent carries one recessive allele, it is possible that Esther is left-handed. Therefore, all answer choices are possible.

52. A: Antibodies. Antibiotics (*B*) fight bacteria, but the body does not make them naturally. White blood cells, not red blood cells (*D*) are the blood cells produced that fight the bacteria. Vaccines (*C*) are given to create antibodies and prevent future illness.

53. A: Tissue → organ. The first blank is tissue and the second blank is organ, so Choices *B* and *C* are automatically incorrect. Blood vessels (*B and D*) are a type of smooth muscle and connective tissue while the heart is an organ.

The following image is for question 54.

54. C: Mutualism. In the ant-aphid case, both organisms benefit, as the ants are getting food and the aphids are getting protection. Competition (*A*) is when organisms want the same thing (food, water, shelter, space), which is clearly not the case here. Parasitism (*B*) involves one organism getting hurt in the relationship at the expense of the other, while commensalism (*D*) involves an organism that is benefited connected to an indifferent party.

55. B: Time in seconds the dogs sit. This is a better choice than Choice *C* (tail wagging) because it is a measurable, meaningful, and relevant dependent variable. Tail wagging, although quantitative, is not a valid measure of anything. Choices *A* and *D* could be independent variables in the experiment.

Mathematics

Student Thinking and Instructional Practices

Mathematical Concepts to Evaluate Student Solutions

One of the first concepts in elementary mathematics that needs to be mastered is the ability to subitize. Once mastered, the student is able to know how many there are of a quantity without counting each individual piece. They use patterns recognition to do so. For example, they can count by 5s or 10s, group small quantities together, or split up numbers such as knowing 7 can be thought of as the sum of 6 and 1. For example, adding 7 + 9 + 20 might be rethought as 6 + (1+9) + 20 = 36. Secondly, transitivity is a property used to build arguments with both equality and inequality. The property of equality states that if a = b and b = c, then a = c. A transitivity property of inequality is if a > b and b > c, then a > c.

An iteration is a repetition of a process. In mathematics, it refers to a mathematical operation applied to the result of a previous operation. For example, an output of a function can be plugged back into the function to obtain another output. Again, this output can be plugged in as well. The repetition would be an iterative process. Finally, a tiling exists when individual shapes are placed to fill a flat space with no gaps or overlapping. A tiling is also known as a tessellation. Some can have repeating patterns and some do not. If they repeat, they are known as a periodic tiling. Some can also be symmetric because if it is folded over a line of symmetry, the pattern represents two mirror images.

In the classroom, these concepts should be part of the students' problem-solving abilities. The teacher should recognize when each concept is applicable to a concept, and also recognize when they are being used in their students' solutions.

Problem Structures with Unknowns in All Positions

Traditional methods do not always have to apply when introducing operations in the classroom. For example, there are multiple problem structures when working with multiplication. Consider 6×8. If student did not have the multiplication table memorized, he or she could use the put-together/take-apart method. This involves breaking up the problem into multiplication that is known. In this problem, 8 can be written as the sum of two 4's, or $4 + 4$. The student should know that $6 \times 4 = 24$, and therefore because there are two 4's, the result is found by adding 24 two times. This results in 48. The put-together/take-apart method can also be used in addition. For example, 325 + 417 could be rewritten as individual addition problems within each place value. Therefore, the problem would be the same as 300 + 400 + 20 + 10 + 5 + 7 = 700 + 30 + 12 = 742, which might be easier for some students than the traditional approach of adding vertically by digit. A similar methodology can be used for subtraction. Consider 642 – 165. First, subtract 100 from 642 to obtain 542. Then, 60 is subtracted from 542 to obtain 482. Finally, this amount is reduced by 5. The final answer is 477.

An array/area model is a method that can be used instead of the traditional multiplication techniques. Each number is broken up by place value, and individual multiplication problems are completed within each combination. Here is the problem 65×29 using an area/array model:

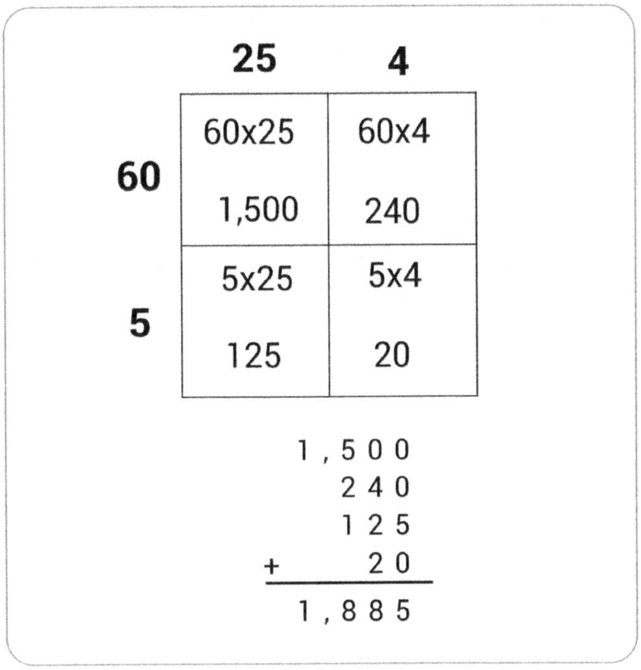

Area models can also be used within division problems. It involves multiplication and subtraction. Here is an example of such a model being used to compute the problem $8580 \div 55 = 156$.

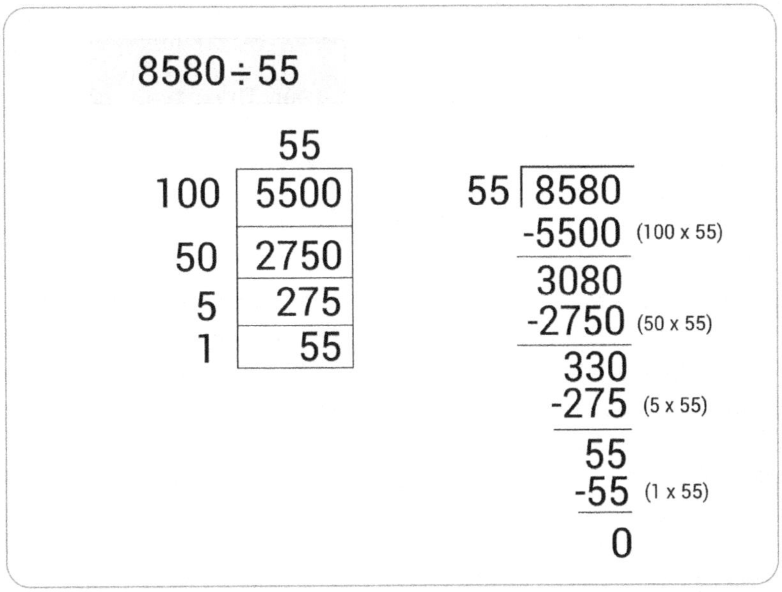

It is up to the teacher to highlight the advantages and disadvantages of the new methods and the traditional methods, and distinguish amongst all the different solving mechanisms to develop students understanding of operations in the most appropriate manner.

Validity of a Student's Mathematical Model

Even though there could be more than one correct approach to solving math problems, there are approaches that are deemed to be either valid and invalid. A standard algorithm refers to the traditional way of doing something. For example, in addition, if the sum of 345 and 746 needed to be found, the standard algorithm would involve adding the ones place, the tens place, and then the hundreds place in the traditional sense. An inventive strategy involves any other strategy besides the traditional approach. In the case of the same addition problem, the numbers could be estimated or decomposed to obtain a result.

For example, grouping by 5s, 10s, and 100s would be a nontraditional approach that would result in the same answer. Within the inventive strategies, students are focused more on place value in this example and less on the actual addition of digits. There are many benefits to using inventive strategies, but both techniques must be taught. Inventive strategies might be able to help the students understand the concepts more because they are breaking the problem down further instead of just repeating a process over and over. It might take more time in the classroom to introduce inventive strategies rather than the standard algorithms, but research shows that these methods are less likely to be retaught. Teachers will decide when the students need to use inventive strategies and standard algorithms, and be able to see which type of method was used and if it was valid or not.

Interpreting Individual Student Mathematics Assessment Data

Throughout each school year, teachers can use assessments to guide their lecture, assist in creating their lesson plans, and adapt instructional techniques. Diagnostic tests are given at the beginning of the year. They are used to test each student's skill level before new material is introduced, and teachers can use this information to their advantage. They can use the results to determine if any review of previous material is necessary and determine the skill level of the overall class. Balance is the difficult part of this process. If some students are way behind, it does not benefit those that are advanced to spend a ton of time with review. It is up to teachers to find a good balance at the beginning of the year.

Secondly, formative assessments are used throughout the year. These types of assessments can be in the form of quizzes and tests. For example, a chapter test is an example of a formative assignment. They are used to monitor how well the new material is being understood and retained. They are usually scheduled at regular intervals, and teachers can use their results to determine if any concepts need to be reinforced.

Finally, progress monitoring is a technique teachers can use to evaluate their own teaching effectiveness. They measure the student's effectiveness on all of the skills needed to master that year at regular intervals in the school year. They differ from formative assessments in that the measurement is on an entire skill set, and not just a single unit or chapter from the textbook.

Structured Experiences

Depending on the complexity of the mathematical concept being discussed, group activity might be used as a method of instruction. Group activities allow students to develop skills that are crucial in the real-world, such as time management, communication skills, and working with feedback. Whether to use small or large group activities depends on the cognitive complexity of the task. Cognitive complexity is defined in psychology to be how well people perceive concepts, and in the mathematics classroom this concept would relate to how intricate the students' critical thinking skills are.

For a situation that involves brainstorming or discussing a question or a problem, a small group might be the best option. A small group ensures that each student has an opportunity to voice his or her own opinion. In this situation, students do not have to have clearly defined roles, and the general goal of the task is just a discussion. Larger groups work better for more complex project-based assignments. In order for a large group to work best, roles must be clearly defined within the project or problem. For example, one student can be in charge of keeping time, another one can be the recorder, etc. All students will play an integral role in developing the answer to the problem, but the more organized the process is the better. The larger projects allow this scenario to happen. In either case, it is important to organize the classroom in the best way so that each group member is able to see each other.

Analyzing Learning Progressions

Learning progressions are plans that lay out a specific sequence of math skills that students are expected to master as they progress throughout the school year. Given a time frame, such as midyear fifth grade, there is a set of corresponding learning standards. The standards summarize all the topics each student should have mastered at that point in time, and such standards are based on the traditional structure of teaching mathematics. Learning progressions have been developed so that students are working on material that is not too hard or not too easy while preparing them for harder topics that will be taught at the next level. Unless students are in an accelerated class, learning progressions are a structured way to ensure students are getting what they need in the classroom. Each standard builds on the previous one, showing how progression is made as each student masters the concepts being taught.

For example, consider the topic of fractions. In third grade, students should be able to know what a fraction means, graph them on a number line, and compare their quantities. However, they should not be expected to find equivalent fractions, convert to decimals, and add or subtract with common denominators. In fifth grade, they should be able to add or subtract with different denominators, and multiply and divide fractions. As each year is summarized, there is a progression that is seen. Each topic builds on each other, and each student's understanding of fractions develops as time progresses and more concepts are introduced.

Components of Math Fluency

In order to be fluent in math, one must be able to retrieve facts from memory and apply them to processes in a quick, effective, and accurate manner. For a student to be accurate, the concepts applied must be correct and precise. Another component of math fluency is automaticity, which is related to speed. If a student is able to recall the mathematical facts at a rapid pace, he or she has automaticity of the concept. For example, if a student is able to quickly recall the correct multiplication tables, he or she is both accurate and automatic when recalling such information. Each year, there is a different benchmark that a student must maintain given a concept. For example, in first grade, let's say a student is able to complete 10 addition problems in a minute at the beginning of the year. Together, the student and teacher could work towards computing 50 addition problems in a minute midyear and 75 addition problems in a minute at the end of the year. Each amount per minute is known as the rate of completion. As each operation is learned, more benchmarks can be introduced. For example, second grade can focus more on subtraction, and fourth grade can focus more on multiplication and division. Teachers should pass out problem lists with more problems than a student could possibly compute in an allotted time so that a correct amount can be counted. Not only do the problems need to be completed, but they also need to be accurate.

Students demonstrate flexibility throughout critical thinking in the classroom. They need to not just memorize the concepts being discussed, but also to learn how to use the concepts in multiple scenarios. An important part of math fluency is to work with numbers and concepts in different ways, without just recalling and stating concepts. For example, a student will memorize multiplication tables, but there is more to the process that just knowing the answers. Flexibility involves knowing when multiplication is necessary to solve a problem. Consider the area of a rectangle. The multiplication tables would be used to find the area of a rectangle that had a length of 6 inches and width of 9 inches. However, a student needs to understand that multiplication connects the problem to the answer. The memorization of the tables is not useful unless it can be applied to tangible scenarios.

Operations, Algebraic Thinking, Counting and Number in Base Ten

Interpreting and Extending Multiple Representations of Patterns and Functional Relationships

Patterns within a sequence can come in 2 distinct forms: the items (shapes, numbers, etc.) either repeat in a constant order, or the items change from one step to another in some consistent way. The core is the smallest unit, or number of items, that repeats in a repeating pattern. For example, the pattern oo▲oo▲o… has a core that is oo▲. Knowing only the core, the pattern can be extended. Knowing the number of steps in the core allows the identification of an item in each step without drawing/writing the entire pattern out. For example, suppose the tenth item in the previous pattern must be determined. Because the core consists of three items (oo▲), the core repeats in multiples of 3. In other words, steps 3, 6, 9, 12, etc. will be ▲ completing the core with the core starting over on the next step. For the above example, the 9th step will be ▲ and the 10th will be o.

The most common patterns in which each item changes from one step to the next are arithmetic and geometric sequences. An arithmetic sequence is one in which the items increase or decrease by a constant difference. In other words, the same thing is added or subtracted to each item or step to produce the next. To determine if a sequence is arithmetic, determine what must be added or subtracted to step one to produce step two. Then, check if the same thing is added/subtracted to step two to produce step three. The same thing must be added/subtracted to step three to produce step four, and so on. Consider the pattern 13, 10, 7, 4 . . . To get from step one (13) to step two (10) by adding or subtracting requires subtracting by 3. The next step is checking if subtracting 3 from step two (10) will produce step three (7), and subtracting 3 from step three (7) will produce step four (4). In this case, the pattern holds true. Therefore, this is an arithmetic sequence in which each step is produced by subtracting 3 from the previous step. To extend the sequence, 3 is subtracted from the last step to produce the next. The next three numbers in the sequence are 1, -2, -5.

A geometric sequence is one in which each step is produced by multiplying or dividing the previous step by the same number. To determine if a sequence is geometric, decide what step one must be multiplied or divided by to produce step two. Then check if multiplying or dividing step two by the same number produces step three, and so on. Consider the pattern 2, 8, 32, 128 . . . To get from step one (2) to step two (8) requires multiplication by 4. The next step determines if multiplying step two (8) by 4 produces step three (32), and multiplying step three (32) by 4 produces step four (128). In this case, the pattern holds true. Therefore, this is a geometric sequence in which each step is produced by multiplying the previous step by 4. To extend the sequence, the last step is multiplied by 4 and repeated. The next three numbers in the sequence are 512; 2,048; 8,192.

Although arithmetic and geometric sequences typically use numbers, these sequences can also be represented by shapes. For example, an arithmetic sequence could consist of shapes with three sides, four sides, and five sides (add one side to the previous step to produce the next). A geometric sequence could consist of eight blocks, four blocks, and two blocks (each step is produced by dividing the number of blocks in the previous step by 2).

Using an Input-Output Table to Generate a Number Pattern that Follows a Given Rule

Patterns are an important part of mathematics. Identifying and understanding how a group or pattern is represented in a problem is essential for being able to expand this process to more complex problems. A simple input-output table can model a pattern that pertains to a specific situation or equation. These can then be utilized in other areas in math, such as graphing.

For example, for every 1 parakeet the pet store sells, it sells 5 goldfish. Using the following equation to model this situation, fill in numbers missing in the input-output table, to show the total number of pets sold by the store.

Equation:

Total number of pets sold (*t*) = number of parakeets (*p*) + number of parakeets (*p*) × 5 goldfish

$$t = p + (p \times 5)$$
$$t = 6p$$

p	t
1	6
2	12
3	
4	24
5	

The missing numbers are 18 and 30.

This can also be shown by using an equation. If 3 is put in for *p*, it would look as follows:

$$t = 6 \times 3$$

$$t = 18$$

If 5 is put in for *p*, it would look as follows:

$$t = 6 \times 5$$

$$t = 30$$

The completed table would appear as follows:

p	t
1	6
2	12
3	18
4	24
5	30

By looking at the completed table, the numeric patterns between consecutive *p* and *t* values (from one row to the next) can be seen. The *p*-values increase by 1, and the *t*-values increase by 6.

Conjectures, Predictions, or Generalizations Based on Patterns

An arithmetic or geometric sequence can be written as a formula and used to determine unknown steps without writing out the entire sequence. (Note that a similar process for repeating patterns is covered in the previous section.) An arithmetic sequence progresses by a **common difference**. To determine the common difference, any step is subtracted by the step that precedes it. In the sequence 4, 9, 14, 19 . . . the common difference, or *d*, is 5. By expressing each step as a_1, a_2, a_3, etc., a formula can be written to represent the sequence. a_1 is the first step. To produce step two, step 1 (a_1) is added to the common difference (*d*):

$$a_2 = a_1 + d$$

To produce step three, the common difference (*d*) is added twice to a_1:

$$a_3 = a_1 + 2d$$

To produce step four, the common difference (*d*) is added three times to a_1:

$$a_4 = a_1 + 3d$$

Following this pattern allows a general rule for arithmetic sequences to be written. For any term of the sequence (a_n), the first step (a_1) is added to the product of the common difference (*d*) and one less than the step of the term ($n - 1$):

$$a_n = a_1 + (n - 1)d$$

Suppose the 8th term (a_8) is to be found in the previous sequence. By knowing the first step (a_1) is 4 and the common difference (*d*) is 5, the formula can be used:

$$a_n = a_1 + (n - 1)d \rightarrow a_8$$

$$4 + (7)5 \rightarrow a_8 = 39$$

In a geometric sequence, each step is produced by multiplying or dividing the previous step by the same number. The *common ratio*, or (*r*), can be determined by dividing any step by the previous step. In the sequence 1, 3, 9, 27 . . . the common ratio (*r*) is 3($\frac{3}{1} = 3$ or $\frac{9}{3} = 3$ or $\frac{27}{9} = 3$). Each successive step can be expressed as a product of the first step (a_1) and the common ratio (*r*) to some power. For example:

$$a_2 = a_1 \times r; a_3 = a_1 \times r \times r$$

or

$$a_3 = a_1 \times r^2; a_4 = a_1 \times r \times r \times r$$

or

$$a_4 = a\_1 \times r^3$$

Following this pattern, a general rule for geometric sequences can be written. For any term of the sequence (a_n), the first step (a_1) is multiplied by the common ratio (*r*) raised to the power one less than the step of the term ($n - 1$):

$$a_n = a_1 \times r^{(n-1)}$$

Suppose for the previous sequence, the 7th term (a_7) is to be found. Knowing the first step (a_1) is one, and the common ratio (*r*) is 3, the formula can be used:

$$a_n = a_1 \times r^{(n-1)}$$

$$a_7 = (1) \times 3^6$$

$$a_7 = 729$$

Corresponding Terms of Two Numerical Patterns

When given two numerical patterns, the corresponding terms should be examined to determine if a relationship exists between them. Corresponding terms between patterns are the pairs of numbers that appear in the same step of the two sequences. Consider the following patterns 1, 2, 3, 4 . . . and 3, 6, 9, 12 . . . The corresponding terms are: 1 and 3; 2 and 6; 3 and 9; and 4 and 12. To identify the relationship, each pair of corresponding terms is examined and the possibilities of performing an operation (+, −, ×, ÷) to the term from the first sequence to produce the corresponding term in the second sequence are determined. In this case:

$1 + 2 = 3$ or $1 \times 3 = 3$

$2 + 4 = 6$ or $2 \times 3 = 6$

$3 + 6 = 9$ or $3 \times 3 = 9$

$4 + 8 = 12$ or $4 \times 3 = 12$

The consistent pattern is that the number from the first sequence multiplied by 3 equals its corresponding term in the second sequence. By assigning each sequence a label (input and output) or variable (*x* and *y*), the relationship can be written as an equation. If the first sequence represents the inputs, or *x*, and the second sequence represents the outputs, or *y*, the relationship can be expressed as: $y = 3x$.

Consider the following sets of numbers:

a	2	4	6	8
b	6	8	10	12

To write a rule for the relationship between the values for *a* and the values for *b*, the corresponding terms (2 and 6; 4 and 8; 6 and 10; 8 and 12) are examined. The possibilities for producing *b* from *a* are:

$2 + 4 = 6$ or $2 \times 3 = 6$

$4 + 4 = 8$ or $4 \times 2 = 8$

$6 + 4 = 10$

$8 + 4 = 12$ or $8 \times 1.5 = 12$

The consistent pattern is that adding 4 to the value of *a* produces the value of *b*. The relationship can be written as the equation $a + 4 = b$.

Selecting the Representation of an Algebraic Expression, Equation, or Inequality that Models a Real-World Situation

Addition and subtraction are "inverse operations." Adding a number and then subtracting the same number will cancel each other out. This results in the original number, and vice versa. For example,$8 + 7 - 7 = 8$ and $137 - 100 + 100 = 137$.

Multiplication and division are also **inverse operations**. So, multiplying by a number and then dividing by the same number results in the original number. For example:

$$8 \times 2 \div 2 = 8$$

and

$$12 \div 4 \times 4 = 12$$

Inverse operations are used to work backwards to solve problems. In the case that 7 and a number add to 18, the inverse operation of subtraction is used to find the unknown value $(18 - 7 = 11)$. If a school's entire 4th grade was divided evenly into 3 classes each with 22 students, the inverse operation of multiplication is used to determine the total students in the grade $(22 \times 3 = 66)$. More scenarios involving inverse operations are listed in the tables below.

Word problems take concepts you learned in the classroom and turn them into real-life situations. Some parts of the problem are known and at least one part is unknown. There are three types of instances in which something can be unknown: the starting point, the change, or the final result. Any of these can be missing from the information they give you.

For an addition problem, the change is the quantity of a new amount added to the starting point.

For a subtraction problem, the change is the quantity taken away from the starting point.

Regarding addition, the given equation is $3 + 7 = 10$.

The number 3 is the starting point. 7 is the change, and 10 is the result from adding a new amount to the starting point. Different word problems can arise from this same equation, depending on which value is the unknown. For example, here are three problems:

- If a boy had 3 pencils and was given 7 more, how many would he have in total?
- If a boy had 3 pencils and a girl gave him more so that he had 10 in total, how did she give to him?
- A boy was given 7 pencils so that he had 10 in total. How many did he start with?

All three problems involve the same equation. Finding out which part of the equation is missing is the key to solving each word problem. The missing answers would be 10, 7, and 3, respectively.

In terms of subtraction, the same three scenarios can occur. Imagine the given equation is $6 - 4 = 2$.

The number 6 is the starting point, 4 is the change, and 2 is the new amount that is the result from taking away an amount from the starting point. Again, different types of word problems can arise from this equation. For example, here are three possible problems:

- If a girl had 6 quarters and 2 were taken away, how many would be left over?
- If a girl had 6 quarters, purchased a pencil, and had 2 quarters left over, how many did she pay with?
- If a girl paid for a pencil with 4 quarters and had 2 quarters left over, how many did she start with?

The three question types follow the structure of the addition word problems. Finding out whether the starting point, the change, or the final result is missing is the goal in solving the problem. The missing answers would be 2, 4, and 6, respectively.

The three addition problems and the three subtraction word problems can be solved by using a picture, a number line, or an algebraic equation. If an equation is used, a question mark can be used to show the number we don't know. For example, $6 - 4 = ?$ can be written to show that the missing value is the result. Using equation form shows us what part of the addition or subtraction problem is missing.

Key words within a multiplication problem involve *times, product, doubled*, and *tripled.* Key words within a division problem involve *split, quotient, divided, shared, groups*, and *half*. Like addition and subtraction, multiplication and division problems also have three different types of missing values.

Multiplication consists of a certain number of groups, with the same number of items within each group, and the total amount within all groups. Therefore, each one of these amounts can be the missing value.

For example, the given equation is $5 \times 3 = 15$.

5 and 3 are interchangeable, so either amount can be the number of groups or the number of items within each group. 15 is the total number of items. Again, different types of word problems can arise from this equation. For example, here are three problems:

- If a classroom is serving 5 different types of apples for lunch and has 3 apples of each type, how many total apples are there to give to the students?
- If a classroom has 15 apples with 5 different types, how many of each type are there?

- If a classroom has 15 apples total with 3 of each type, how many types are there to choose from?

Each question involves using the same equation to solve. It is important to decide which part of the equation is the missing value. The answers to the problems are 15, 3, and 5, respectively.

Similar to multiplication, division problems involve a total amount, a number of groups having the same amount, and a number of items within each group. The difference between multiplication and division is that the starting point in a division problem is the total amount. This then gets divided into equal amounts.

For example, the equation is $48 \div 8 = 6$.

48 is the total number of items, which is being divided into 8 different groups. In order to do so, 6 items go into each group. Also, 8 and 6 are interchangeable. So, the 48 items could be divided into 6 groups of 8 items each. Therefore, different types of word problems can arise from this equation. For example, here are three types of problems:

- A boy needs 48 pieces of chalk. If there are 8 pieces in each box, how many boxes should he buy?
- A boy has 48 pieces of chalk. If each box has 6 pieces in it, how many boxes did he buy?
- A boy has partitioned all of his chalk into 8 piles, with 6 pieces in each pile. How many pieces does he have in total?

Each one of these questions involves the same equation. The third question can easily utilize the multiplication equation $8 \times 6 = ?$ instead of division. The answers are 6, 8, and 48.

Properties of Equality and Operations

Properties of operations exist that make calculations easier and solve problems for missing values. The following table summarizes commonly used properties of real numbers.

Property	Addition	Multiplication
Commutative	$a + b = b + a$	$a \times b = b \times a$
Associative	$(a + b) + c = a + (b + c)$	$(a \times b) \times c = a \times (bc)$
Identity	$a + 0 = a;\ 0 + a = a$	$a \times 1 = a;\ 1 \times a = a$
Inverse	$a + (-a) = 0$	$a \times \frac{1}{a} = 1;\ a \neq 0$
Distributive	$a(b + c) = ab + ac$	

The **cumulative property of addition** states that the order in which numbers are added does not change the sum. Similarly, the **commutative property of multiplication** states that the order in which numbers are multiplied does not change the product. The **associative property** of addition and multiplication state that the grouping of numbers being added or multiplied does not change the sum or product, respectively. The commutative and associative properties are useful for performing calculations. For example, $(47 + 25) + 3$ is equivalent to $(47 + 3) + 25$, which is easier to calculate.

The **identity property of addition** states that adding zero to any number does not change its value. The **identity property of multiplication** states that multiplying a number by 1 does not change its value. The **inverse property of addition** states that the sum of a number and its opposite equals zero. Opposites are numbers that are the same with different signs (ex. 5 and -5; $-\frac{1}{2}$ and $\frac{1}{2}$). The **inverse property of multiplication** states that the product of a number (other than 0) and its reciprocal equals 1. **Reciprocal numbers** have numerators and denominators that are inverted (ex. $\frac{2}{5}$ and $\frac{5}{2}$). Inverse properties are useful for canceling quantities to find missing values (see algebra content). For example, $a + 7 = 12$ is solved by adding the inverse of 7 (which is -7) to both sides in order to isolate a.

The **distributive property** states that multiplying a sum (or difference) by a number produces the same result as multiplying each value in the sum (or difference) by the number and adding (or subtracting) the products. Consider the following scenario: You are buying three tickets for a baseball game. Each ticket costs $18. You are also charged a fee of $2 per ticket for purchasing the tickets online. The cost is calculated: $3 \times 18 + 3 \times 2$. Using the distributive property, the cost can also be calculated $3(18 + 2)$.

Determining Whether Two Algebraic Expressions are Equivalent by Applying Properties of Operations or Equality

Algebraic expressions are made up of numbers, variables, and combinations of the two, using mathematical operations. Expressions can be rewritten based on their factors. For example, the expression $6x + 4$ can be rewritten as $2(3x + 2)$ because 2 is a factor of both $6x$ and 4. More complex expressions can also be rewritten based on their factors. The expression $x^4 - 16$ can be rewritten as $(x^2 - 4)(x^2 + 4)$. This is a different type of factoring, where a difference of squares is factored into a sum and difference of the same two terms. With some expressions, the factoring process is simple and only leads to a different way to represent the expression. With others, factoring and rewriting the expression leads to more information about the given problem.

In the following quadratic equation, factoring the binomial leads to finding the zeros of the function:

$$x^2 - 5x + 6 = y$$

This equations factors into $(x - 3)(x - 2) = y$, where 2 and 3 are found to be the zeros of the function when y is set equal to zero. The zeros of any function are the x-values where the graph of the function on the coordinate plane crosses the x-axis.

Factoring an equation is a simple way to rewrite the equation and find the zeros, but factoring is not possible for every quadratic. Completing the square is one way to find zeros when factoring is not an option. The following equation cannot be factored: $x^2 + 10x - 9 = 0$. The first step in this method is to move the constant to the right side of the equation, making it $x^2 + 10x = 9$. Then, the coefficient of x is divided by 2 and squared. This number is then added to both sides of the equation, to make the equation still true. For this example, $\left(\frac{10}{2}\right)^2 = 25$ is added to both sides of the equation to obtain:

$$x^2 + 10x + 25 = 9 + 25$$

This expression simplifies to $x^2 + 10x + 25 = 34$, which can then be factored into:

$$(x + 5)^2 = 34$$

Solving for x then involves taking the square root of both sides and subtracting 5. This leads to two zeros of the function:

$$x = \pm\sqrt{34} - 5$$

Depending on the type of answer the question seeks, a calculator may be used to find exact numbers.

Given a quadratic equation in standard form— $ax^2 + bx + c = 0$—the sign of a tells whether the function has a minimum value or a maximum value. If $a > 0$, the graph opens up and has a minimum value. If $a < 0$, the graph opens down and has a maximum value. Depending on the way the quadratic equation is written, multiplication may need to occur before a max/min value is determined.

There are also properties of numbers that are true for certain operations. The **commutative** property allows the order of the terms in an expression to change while keeping the same final answer. Both addition and multiplication can be completed in any order and still obtain the same result. However, order does matter in subtraction and division. The **associative** property allows any terms to be "associated" by parenthesis and retain the same final answer. For example:

$$(4 + 3) + 5 = 4 + (3 + 5)$$

Both addition and multiplication are associative; however, subtraction and division do not hold this property. The **distributive** property states that $a(b + c) = ab + ac$. It is a property that involves both addition and multiplication, and the *a* is distributed onto each term inside the parentheses.

The expression $4(3 + 2)$ is simplified using the order of operations. Simplifying inside the parenthesis first produces 4×5, which equals 20. The expression $4(3 + 2)$ can also be simplified using the distributive property:

$$4(3 + 2)$$

$$4 \times 3 + 4 \times 2$$

$$12 + 8 = 20$$

Consider the following example: $4(3x - 2)$. The expression cannot be simplified inside the parenthesis because 3*x* and -2 are not like terms and therefore cannot be combined. However, the expression can be simplified by using the distributive property and multiplying each term inside of the parenthesis by the term outside of the parenthesis: $12x - 8$. The resulting equivalent expression contains no like terms, so it cannot be further simplified.

Consider the expression:

$$(3x + 2y + 1) - (5x - 3) + 2(3y + 4)$$

Again, there are no like terms, but the distributive property is used to simplify the expression. Note there is an implied one in front of the first set of parentheses and an implied -1 in front of the second set of parentheses. Distributing the 1, -1, and 2 produces:

$$1(3x) + 1(2y) + 1(1) - 1(5x) - 1(-3) + 2(3y) + 2(4)$$

$$3x + 2y + 1 - 5x + 3 + 6y + 8$$

This expression contains like terms that are combined to produce the simplified expression $-2x + 8y + 12$.

Algebraic expressions are tested to be equivalent by choosing values for the variables and evaluating both expressions. For example, $4(3x - 2)$ and $12x - 8$ are tested by substituting 3 for the variable x and calculating to determine if equivalent values result.

Evaluating Expressions with Parentheses, Brackets, and Braces

When reviewing calculations consisting of more than one operation, the order in which the operations are performed affects the resulting answer. Consider $5 \times 2 + 7$. Performing multiplication then addition results in an answer of 17 ($5 \times 2 = 10; 10 + 7 = 17$).

However, if the problem is written $5 \times (2 + 7)$, the order of operations dictates that the operation inside the parenthesis must be performed first. The resulting answer is 45 ($2 + 7 = 9$, then $5 \times 9 = 45$).

The order in which operations should be performed is remembered using the acronym PEMDAS. PEMDAS stands for parenthesis, exponents, multiplication/division, and addition/subtraction. Multiplication and division are performed in the same step, working from left to right with whichever comes first. Addition and subtraction are performed in the same step, working from left to right with whichever comes first.

Consider the following example: $8 \div 4 + 8(7 - 7)$. Performing the operation inside the parenthesis produces:

$$8 \div 4 + 8(0)$$

or

$$8 \div 4 + 8 \times 0$$

There are no exponents, so multiplication and division are performed next from left to right resulting in: $2 + 8 \times 0$, then $2 + 0$. Finally, addition and subtraction are performed to obtain an answer of 2. Now consider the following example:

$$6x3 + 3^2 - 6$$

Parentheses are not applicable. Exponents are evaluated first:

$$6 \times 3 + 9 - 6$$

Then multiplication/division forms $18 + 9 - 6$. At last, addition/subtraction leads to the final answer of 21.

Essentially, parentheses separate different parts of an equation, and operations within them should be thought of as taking place before the outside operations take place. Practically, this means that the distinction between what is inside and outside of the parentheses decides the order of operations that the equation follows. Failing to solve operations inside the parentheses before addressing the part of the equation outside of the parentheses will lead to incorrect results.

For example, let's analyze $5 - (3 + 25)$. The addition operation within the parentheses must be solved first. So $3 + 25 + 28$, leaving:

$$5 - (28) = -23$$

If this was solved in the incorrect order of operations, the solution might be found to be $5 - 3 + 25 = 2 + 25 = 27$, which would be wrong.

Equations often feature multiple layers of parentheses. To differentiate them, square brackets [ ] and braces { } are used in addition to parentheses. The innermost parentheses must be solved before working outward to larger brackets. For example, in:

$$\{2 \div [5 - (3 + 1)]\}$$

solving the innermost parentheses (3 + 1) leaves $\{2 \div [5 - (4)]\}$. $[5 - (4)]$ is now the next smallest, which leaves $\{2 \div [1]\}$ in the final step, and 2 as the answer.

Strategies to Solve Multistep Word Problems

In solving multi-step problems, the first step is to line up the available information. Then, try to decide what information the problem is asking to be found. Once this is determined, construct a strip diagram to display the known information along with any information to be calculated. Finally, the missing information can be represented by a **variable** (a letter from the alphabet that represents a number) in a mathematical equation that the student can solve.

For example, Delilah collects stickers and her friends gave her some stickers to add to her current collection. Joe gave her 45 stickers, and Aimee gave her 2 times the number of stickers that Joe gave Delilah. How many stickers did Delilah have to start with, if after her friends gave her more stickers, she had a total of 187 stickers?

In order to solve this, the given information must first be sorted out. Joe gives Delilah 45 stickers, Aimee gives Delilah 2 times the number Joe gives (2 × 45), and the end total of stickers is 187.

A strip diagram represents these numbers as follows:

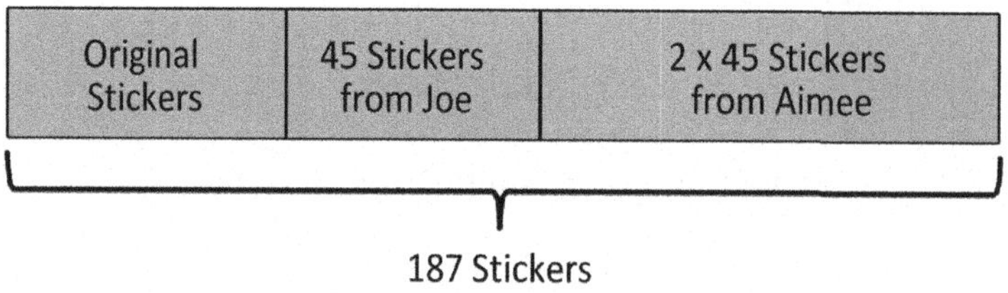

The entire situation can be modeled by this equation, using the variable s to stand for the original number of stickers:

$$s + 45 + (2 \times 45) = 187.$$

Solving for s would give the solution, as follows:

$$s + 45 + 90 = 187$$

$$s + 135 = 187$$

$$s + 135 - 135 = 187 - 135$$

$$s = 52 \text{ stickers.}$$

Word problems take concepts you learned in the classroom and turn them into real-life situations. Some parts of the problem are known and at least one part is unknown. There are three types of instances in which something can be unknown: the starting point, the change, or the final result. These can all be missing from the information they give you.

For solving problems with unknown factors, it is often easiest to set up an array to visualize the grouping of the information. In these problems, set up the initial numbers in uniformly sized groups, so the solution can be determined by inspection of the grouping.

Find the missing number (?) in the following equation:

$$? \times 5 = 35$$

Knowing that one of the factors is to be multiplied is 5 allows the groupings to be made in sets of five columns. In this case, there 5 columns of items are created, until the desired number (35) is reached.

Here, the number of 35 is reached with the seventh row of items. Therefore, the missing factor is 7.

$$5 \times 7 = 35$$

The same problem could be demonstrated with the equation:

$$5 \times ? = 35$$

This would simply require the information to be grouped into five rows, and items added evenly until the desired number (35) is reached.

Again, the solution is:

$$5 \times 7 = 35.$$

This demonstrates the commutative property of multiplication by showing the missing factor could be the number of rows or the number of columns, and yet result in the same solution.

Problem Situations for Operations

Addition and subtraction are **inverse operations.** Adding a number and then subtracting the same number will cancel each other out, resulting in the original number, and vice versa. For example, $8 + 7 - 7 = 8$ and $137 - 100 + 100 = 137$. Similarly, multiplication and division are inverse operations. Therefore, multiplying by a number and then dividing by the same number results in the original number, and vice versa. For example, $8 \times 2 \div 2 = 8$ and $12 \div 4 \times 4 = 12$. Inverse operations are used to work backwards to solve problems. In the case that 7 and a number add to 18, the inverse operation of subtraction is used to find the unknown value $(18 - 7 = 11)$. If a school's entire 4th grade was divided evenly into 3 classes each with 22 students, the inverse operation of multiplication is used to determine the total students in the grade $(22 \times 3 = 66)$. Additional scenarios involving inverse operations are included in the tables below.

There are a variety of real-world situations in which one or more of the operators is used to solve a problem. The tables on the following pages display the most common scenarios.

Addition & Subtraction

	Unknown Result	Unknown Change	Unknown Start
Adding to	5 students were in class. 4 more students arrived. How many students are in class? $5 + 4 = ?$	8 students were in class. More students arrived late. There are now 18 students in class. How many students arrived late? $8 + ? = 18$ Solved by inverse operations $18 - 8 = ?$	Some students were in class early. 11 more students arrived. There are now 17 students in class. How many students were in class early? $? + 11 = 17$ Solved by inverse operations $17 - 11 = ?$
Taking from	15 students were in class. 5 students left class. How many students are in class now? $15 - 5 = ?$	12 students were in class. Some students left class. There are now 8 students in class. How many students left class? $12 - ? = 8$ Solved by inverse operations $8 + ? = 12 \rightarrow 12 - 8 = ?$	Some students were in class. 3 students left class. Then there were 13 students in class. How many students were in class before? $? - 3 = 13$ Solved by inverse operations $13 + 3 = ?$
	Unknown Total	**Unknown Addends (Both)**	**Unknown Addends (One)**
Putting together/ taking apart	The homework assignment is 10 addition problems and 8 subtraction problems. How many problems are in the homework assignment? $10 + 8 = ?$	Bobby has $9. How much can Bobby spend on candy and how much can Bobby spend on toys? $9 = ? + ?$	Bobby has 12 pairs of pants. 5 pairs of pants are shorts, and the rest are long. How many pairs of long pants does he have? $12 = 5 + ?$ Solved by inverse operations $12 - 5 = ?$
	Unknown Difference	**Unknown Larger Value**	**Unknown Smaller Value**
Comparing	Bobby has 5 toys. Tommy has 8 toys. How many more toys does Tommy have than Bobby? $5 + ? = 8$ Solved by inverse operations $8 - 5 = ?$ Bobby has $6. Tommy has $10. How many fewer dollars does Bobby have than Tommy? $10 - 6 = ?$	Tommy has 2 more toys than Bobby. Bobby has 4 toys. How many toys does Tommy have? $2 + 4 = ?$ Bobby has 3 fewer dollars than Tommy. Bobby has $8. How many dollars does Tommy have? $? - 3 = 8$ Solved by inverse operations $8 + 3 = ?$	Tommy has 6 more toys than Bobby. Tommy has 10 toys. How many toys does Bobby have? $? + 6 = 10$ Solved by inverse operations $10 - 6 = ?$ Bobby has $5 less than Tommy. Tommy has $9. How many dollars does Bobby have? $9 - 5 = ?$

Multiplication and Division

	Unknown Product	Unknown Group Size	Unknown Number of Groups
Equal groups	There are 5 students, and each student has 4 pieces of candy. How many pieces of candy are there in all? $5 \times 4 = ?$	14 pieces of candy are shared equally by 7 students. How many pieces of candy does each student have? $7 \times ? = 14$ Solved by inverse operations $14 \div 7 = ?$	If 18 pieces of candy are to be given out 3 to each student, how many students will get candy? $? \times 3 = 18$ Solved by inverse operations $18 \div 3 = ?$
	Unknown Product	**Unknown Factor**	**Unknown Factor**
Arrays	There are 5 rows of students with 3 students in each row. How many students are there? $5 \times 3 = ?$	If 16 students are arranged into 4 equal rows, how many students will be in each row? $4 \times ? = 16$ Solved by inverse operations $16 \div 4 = ?$	If 24 students are arranged into an array with 6 columns, how many rows are there? $? \times 6 = 24$ Solved by inverse operations $24 \div 6 = ?$
	Larger Unknown	**Smaller Unknown**	**Multiplier Unknown**
Comparing	A small popcorn costs $1.50. A large popcorn costs 3 times as much as a small popcorn. How much does a large popcorn cost? $1.50 \times 3 = ?$	A large soda costs $6 and that is 2 times as much as a small soda costs. How much does a small soda cost? $2 \times ? = 6$ Solved by inverse operations $6 \div 2 = ?$	A large pretzel costs $3 and a small pretzel costs $2. How many times as much does the large pretzel cost as the small pretzel? $? \times 2 = 3$ Solved by inverse operations $3 \div 2 = ?$

Remainders in Division Problems

If a given total cannot be divided evenly into a given number of groups, the amount left over is the remainder. Consider the following scenario: 32 textbooks must be packed into boxes for storage. Each box holds 6 textbooks. How many boxes are needed? To determine the answer, 32 is divided by 6, resulting in 5 with a remainder of 2. A remainder may be interpreted three ways:

- Add 1 to the quotient
  How many boxes will be needed? Six boxes will be needed because five will not be enough.

- Use only the quotient
  How many boxes will be full? Five boxes will be full.

- Use only the remainder
  If you only have 5 boxes, how many books will not fit? Two books will not fit.

The Reasonableness of Results

When solving math word problems, the solution obtained should make sense within the given scenario. The step of checking the solution will reduce the possibility of a calculation error or a solution that may be *mathematically* correct but not applicable in the real world. Consider the following scenarios:

A problem states that Lisa got 24 out of 32 questions correct on a test and asks to find the percentage of correct answers. To solve the problem, a student divided 32 by 24 to get 1.33, and then multiplied by 100 to get 133 percent. By examining the solution within the context of the problem, the student should recognize that getting all 32 questions correct will produce a perfect score of 100 percent. Therefore, a score of 133 percent with 8 incorrect answers does not make sense and the calculations should be checked.

A problem states that the maximum weight on a bridge cannot exceed 22,000 pounds. The problem asks to find the maximum number of cars that can be on the bridge at one time if each car weighs 4,000 pounds. To solve this problem, a student divided 22,000 by 4,000 to get an answer of 5.5. By examining the solution within the context of the problem, the student should recognize that although the calculations are mathematically correct, the solution does not make sense. Half of a car on a bridge is not possible, so the student should determine that a maximum of 5 cars can be on the bridge at the same time.

Estimating

Estimation is finding a value that is close to a solution but is not the exact answer. For example, if there are values in the thousands to be multiplied, then each value can be estimated to the nearest thousand and the calculation performed. This value provides an approximate solution that can be determined very quickly.

Rounding is the process of either bumping a number up or down, based on a specified place value. First, the place value is specified. Then, the digit to its right is looked at. For example, if rounding to the nearest hundreds place, the digit in the tens place is used. If it is a 0, 1, 2, 3, or 4, the digit being rounded to is left alone. If it is a 5, 6, 7, 8 or 9, the digit being rounded to is increased by one. All other digits before the decimal point are then changed to zeros, and the digits in decimal places are dropped. If a decimal place is being rounded to, all subsequent digits are just dropped. For example, if 845,231.45 was to be rounded to the nearest thousands place, the answer would be 845,000. The 5 would remain the same due to the 2 in the hundreds place. Also, if 4.567 was to be rounded to the nearest tenths place, the answer would be 4.6. The 5 increased to 6 due to the 6 in the hundredths place, and the rest of the decimal is dropped.

Sometimes when performing operations such as multiplying numbers, the result can be estimated by rounding. For example, to estimate the value of 11.2×2.01, each number can be rounded to the nearest integer. This will yield a result of 22.

Rounding numbers helps with estimation because it changes the given number to a simpler, although less accurate, number than the exact given number. Rounding allows for easier calculations, which estimate the results of using the exact given number. The accuracy of the estimate and ease of use depends on the place value to which the number is rounded.

Rounding numbers consists of:

- determining what place value the number is being rounded to
- examining the digit to the right of the desired place value to decide whether to round up or keep the digit, and
- replacing all digits to the right of the desired place value with zeros.

To round 746,311 to the nearest ten thousand, the digit in the ten thousands place should be located first. In this case, this digit is 4 (746,311). Then, the digit to its right is examined. If this digit is 5 or greater, the number will be rounded up by increasing the digit in the desired place by one. If the digit to the right of the place value being rounded is 4 or less, the number will be kept the same. For the given example, the digit being examined is a 6, which means that the number will be rounded up by increasing the digit to the left by one. Therefore, the digit 4 is changed to a 5. Finally, to write the rounded number, any digits to the left of the place value being rounded remain the same and any to its right are replaced with zeros. For the given example, rounding 746,311 to the nearest ten thousand will produce 750,000. To round 746,311 to the nearest hundred, the digit to the right of the three in the hundreds place is examined to determine whether to round up or keep the same number. In this case, that digit is a 1, so the number will be kept the same and any digits to its right will be replaced with zeros. The resulting rounded number is 746,300.

Rounding place values to the right of the decimal follows the same procedure, but digits being replaced by zeros can simply be dropped. To round 3.752891 to the nearest thousandth, the desired place value is located (3.752891) and the digit to the right is examined. In this case, the digit 8 indicates that the number will be rounded up, and the 2 in the thousandths place will increase to a 3. Rounding up and replacing the digits to the right of the thousandths place produces 3.753000 which is equivalent to 3.753. Therefore, the zeros are not necessary and the rounded number should be written as 3.753.

When rounding up, if the digit to be increased is a 9, the digit to its left is increased by 1 and the digit in the desired place value is changed to a zero. For example, the number 1,598 rounded to the nearest ten is 1,600. Another example shows the number 43.72961 rounded to the nearest thousandth is 43.730 or 43.73.

Mental math should always be considered as problems are worked through, and the ability to work through problems in one's head helps save time. If a problem is simple enough, such as $15 + 3 = 18$, it should be completed mentally. The ability to do this will increase once addition and subtraction in higher place values are grasped. Also, mental math is important in multiplication and division. The times tables multiplying all numbers from 1 to 12 should be memorized. This will allow for division within those numbers to be memorized as well. For example, we should know easily that $121 \div 11 = 11$ because it should be memorized that $11 \times 11 = 121$.

Here is the multiplication table to be memorized:

x	1	2	3	4	5	6	7	8	9	10	11	12	13	14	15
1	1	2	3	4	5	6	7	8	9	10	11	12	13	14	15
2	2	4	6	8	10	12	14	16	18	20	22	24	26	28	30
3	3	6	9	12	15	18	21	24	27	30	33	36	39	42	45
4	4	8	12	16	20	24	28	32	36	40	44	48	52	56	60
5	5	10	15	20	25	30	35	40	45	50	55	60	65	70	75
6	6	12	18	24	30	36	42	48	54	60	66	72	78	84	90
7	7	14	21	28	35	42	49	56	63	70	77	84	91	98	105
8	8	16	24	32	40	48	56	64	72	80	88	96	104	112	120
9	9	18	27	36	45	54	63	72	81	90	99	108	117	126	135
10	10	20	30	40	50	60	70	80	90	100	110	120	130	140	150
11	11	22	33	44	55	66	77	88	99	110	121	132	143	154	165
12	12	24	36	48	60	72	84	96	108	120	132	144	156	168	180
13	13	26	39	52	65	78	91	104	117	130	143	156	169	182	195
14	14	28	42	56	70	84	98	112	126	140	154	168	182	196	210
15	15	30	45	60	75	90	105	120	135	150	165	180	195	210	225

The values along the diagonal of the table consist of **perfect squares**. A perfect square is a number that represents a product of two equal integers.

Number Theory Concepts

Prime and Composite Numbers

Whole numbers are classified as either prime or composite. A prime number can only be divided evenly by itself and one. For example, the number 11 can only be divided evenly by 11 and one; therefore, 11 is a prime number. A helpful way to visualize a prime number is to use concrete objects and try to divide them into equal piles. If dividing 11 coins, the only way to divide them into equal piles is to create 1 pile of 11 coins or to create 11 piles of 1 coin each. Other examples of prime numbers include 2, 3, 5, 7, 13, 17, and 19.

A composite number is any whole number that is not a prime number. A composite number is a number that can be divided evenly by one or more numbers other than itself and one. For example, the number 6 can be divided evenly by 2 and 3. Therefore, 6 is a composite number. If dividing 6 coins into equal piles, the possibilities are 1 pile of 6 coins, 2 piles of 3 coins, 3 piles of 2 coins, or 6 piles of 1 coin. Other examples of composite numbers include 4, 8, 9, 10, 12, 14, 15, 16, 18, and 20.

To determine if a number is a prime or composite number, the number is divided by every whole number greater than one and less than its own value. If it divides evenly by any of these numbers, then the number is composite. If it does not divide evenly by any of these numbers, then the number is prime. For example, when attempting to divide the number 5 by 2, 3, and 4, none of these numbers divide evenly. Therefore, 5 must be a prime number.

Odd and Even Numbers

Even numbers are all divisible by the number 2. **Odd numbers** are not divisible by 2, and an odd quantity of items cannot be paired up into groups of 2 without having 1 item leftover. Examples of even numbers are 2, 4, 6, 20, 100, 242, etc. Examples of odd numbers are 1, 3, 5, 27, 99, 333, etc.

Factors, Multiples, and Divisibility

The **Fundamental Theorem of Arithmetic** states that any integer greater than 1 is either a prime number or can be written as a unique product of prime numbers. Factors can be used to find the combination of numbers to multiply to produce an integer that is not prime. The factors of a number are all integers that can be multiplied by another integer to produce the given number. For example, 2 is multiplied by 3 to produce 6. Therefore, 2 and 3 are both factors of 6. Similarly, $1 \times 6 = 6$ and $2 \times 3 = 6$, so 1, 2, 3, and 6 are all factors of 6. Another way to explain a factor is to say that a given number divides evenly by each of its factors to produce an integer. For example, 6 does not divide evenly by 5. Therefore, 5 is not a factor of 6.

Essentially, **factors** are the numbers multiplied to achieve a product. Thus, every product in a multiplication equation has, at minimum, two factors. Of course, some products will have more than two factors. For the sake of most discussions, assume that factors are positive integers.

To find a number's factors, start with 1 and the number itself. Then divide the number by 2, 3, 4, and so on, seeing if any divisors can divide the number without a remainder, keeping a list of those that do. Stop upon reaching either the number itself or another factor.

Let's find the factors of 45. Start with 1 and 45. Then try to divide 45 by 2, which fails. Now divide 45 by 3. The answer is 15, so 3 and 15 are now factors. Dividing by 4 doesn't work, and dividing by 5 leaves 9. Lastly, dividing 45 by 6, 7, and 8 all don't work. The next integer to try is 9, but this is already known to be a factor, so the factorization is complete. The factors of 45 are 1, 3, 5, 9, 15 and 45.

A **common factor** is a factor shared by two numbers. Let's take 45 and 30 and find the common factors:

> The factors of 45 are: 1, 3, 5, 9, 15, and 45.
> The factors of 30 are: 1, 2, 3, 5, 6, 10, 15, and 30.
> The common factors are 1, 3, 5, and 15.

The **greatest common factor** is the largest number among the shared, common factors. From the factors of 45 and 30, the common factors are 3, 5, and 15. Thus, 15 is the greatest common factor, as it's the largest number.

Multiples of a given number are found by taking that number and multiplying it by any other whole number. For example, 3 is a factor of 6, 9, and 12. Therefore, 6, 9, and 12 are multiples of 3. The multiples of any number are an infinite list. For example, the multiples of 5 are 5, 10, 15, 20, and so on. This list continues without end. A list of multiples is used in finding the **least common multiple**, or **LCM,** for fractions when a common denominator is needed. The denominators are written down and their multiples listed until a common number is found in both lists. This common number is the LCM.

If two numbers share no factors besides 1 in common, then their least common multiple will be simply their product. If two numbers have common factors, then their least common multiple will be their product divided by their greatest common factor. This can be visualized by the formula $LCM = \frac{x \times y}{GCF}$, where *x* and *y* are some integers and LCM and GCF are their least common multiple and greatest common factor, respectively.

Prime factorization breaks down each factor of a whole number until only prime numbers remain. All composite numbers can be factored into prime numbers. For example, the prime factors of 12 are 2, 2, and 3 ($2 \times 2 \times 3 = 12$). To produce the prime factors of a number, the number is factored, and any composite numbers are continuously factored until the result is the product of prime factors only. A factor tree, such as the one below, is helpful when exploring this concept.

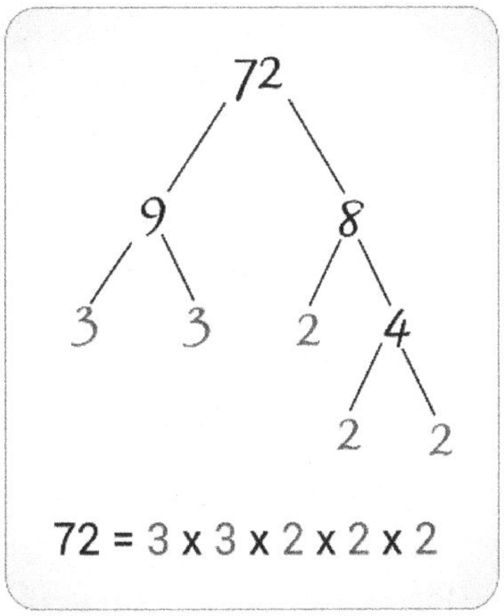

Let's break 129 down into its prime factors. First, the factors are 3 and 43. Both 3 and 43 are prime numbers, so we're done. But if 43 was not a prime number, then it would also need to be factorized until all of the factors are expressed as prime numbers.

Strategies Based on Place Value to Perform Multidigit Arithmetic

In accordance with the base-10 system, the value of a digit increases by a factor of ten each place it moves to the left. For example, consider the number 7. Moving the digit one place to the left (70), increases its value by a factor of 10 ($7 \times 10 = 70$). Moving the digit two places to the left (700) increases its value by a factor of 10 twice ($7 \times 10 \times 10 = 700$). Moving the digit three places to the left (7,000) increases its value by a factor of 10 three times ($7 \times 10 \times 10 \times 10 = 7{,}000$), and so on.

Conversely, the value of a digit decreases by a factor of ten each place it moves to the right. (Note that multiplying by $\frac{1}{10}$ is equivalent to dividing by 10). For example, consider the number 40. Moving the digit one place to the right (4) decreases its value by a factor of 10 ($40 \div 10 = 4$). Moving the digit two places to the right (0.4), decreases its value by a factor of 10 twice:

$$(40 \div 10 \div 10 = 0.4)$$

or

$$(40 \times \frac{1}{10} \times \frac{1}{10} = 0.4)$$

Moving the digit three places to the right (0.04) decreases its value by a factor of 10 three times

$$(40 \div 10 \div 10 \div 10 = 0.04)$$

or

$$(40 \times \frac{1}{10} \times \frac{1}{10} \times \frac{1}{10} = 0.04)$$

and so on.

Rounding Multi-Digit Numbers

Rounding numbers changes the given number to a simpler and less accurate number than the exact given number. Rounding allows for easier calculations which estimate the results of using the exact given number. The accuracy of the estimate and ease of use depends on the place value to which the number is rounded.

Rounding numbers consists of:

- Determining what place value the number is being rounded to
- Examining the digit to the right of the desired place value to decide whether to round up or keep the digit
- Replacing all digits to the right of the desired place value with zeros

To round 746,311 to the nearest ten thousands, the digit in the ten thousands place should be located first. In this case, this digit is 4 (7<u>4</u>6,311). Then, the digit to its right is examined. If this digit is 5 or greater, the number will be rounded up by increasing the digit in the desired place by one. If the digit to the right of the place value being rounded is 4 or less, the number will be kept the same. For the given example, the digit being examined is a 6, which means that the number will be rounded up by increasing the digit to the left by one. Therefore, the digit 4 is changed to a 5. Finally, to write the rounded number, any digits to the left of the place value being rounded remain the same and any to its right are replaced with zeros. For the given example, rounding 746,311 to the nearest ten thousand will produce 750,000. To round 746,311 to the nearest hundred, the digit to the right of the three in the hundreds place is examined to determine whether to round up or keep the same number. In this case, that digit is a one, so the number will be kept the same and any digits to its right will be replaced with zeros. The resulting rounded number is 746,300.

Rounding place values to the right of the decimal follows the same procedure, but digits being replaced by zeros can simply be dropped. To round 3.752891 to the nearest thousandth, the desired place value is located (3.75<u>2</u>891) and the digit to the right is examined. In this case, the digit 8 indicates that the number will be rounded up, and the 2 in the thousandths place will increase to a 3. Rounding up and replacing the digits to the right of the thousandths place produces 3.753000 which is equivalent to 3.753. Therefore, the zeros are not necessary and the rounded number should be written as 3.753.

When rounding up, if the digit to be increased is a 9, the digit to its left is increased by 1 and the digit in the desired place value is changed to a zero. For example, the number 1,598 rounded to the nearest ten is 1,600. Another example shows the number 43.72961 rounded to the nearest thousandth is 43.730 or 43.73.

Addition

Addition is the combination of two numbers so their quantities are added together cumulatively. The sign for an addition operation is the + symbol. For example, 9 + 6 = 15. The 9 and 6 combine to achieve a cumulative value, called a **sum**.

There are set columns for addition: ones, tens, hundreds, thousands, ten-thousands, hundred-thousands, millions, and so on. To add how many units there are total, each column needs to be combined, starting from the right, or the ones column.

THOUSANDS	HUNDREDS	TENS	ONES

Every 10 units in the ones column equals one in the tens column, and every 10 units in the tens column equals one in the hundreds column, and so on.

Example: The number 5432 has 2 ones, 3 tens, 4 hundreds, and 5 thousands. The number 371 has 3 hundreds, 7 tens and 1 one. To combine, or add, these two numbers, simply add up how many units of each column exist. The best way to do this is by lining up the columns:

$$\begin{array}{r} 5\;4\;3\;2 \\ +\quad 3\;7\;1 \\ \hline \end{array}$$

The ones column adds 2 + 1 for a total (sum) of 3.

The tens column adds 3 + 7 for a total of 10; since 10 of that unit was collected, add 1 to the hundreds column to denote the total in the next column:

$$\begin{array}{r} 1\quad\;\; \\ 5\;4\;3\;2 \\ +\quad 3\;7\;1 \\ \hline 0\;3 \end{array}$$

When adding the hundreds column this extra 1 needs to be combined, so it would be the sum of 4, 3, and 1.

$$4 + 3 + 1 = 8$$

The last, or thousands, column listed would be the sum of 5. Since there are no other numbers in this column, that is the final total.

The answer would look as follows:

$$\begin{array}{r} 5\,4\,3\,2 \\ +\quad 3\,7\,1 \\ \hline 5\,8\,0\,3 \end{array}$$

Find the sum of 9,734 and 895.

Set up the problem:

$$\begin{array}{r} 9\,7\,3\,4 \\ +\quad 8\,9\,5 \\ \hline \end{array}$$

Total the columns:

$$\begin{array}{r} 9\,7\,3\,4 \\ +\quad 8\,9\,5 \\ \hline 1\,0\,6\,2\,9 \end{array}$$

In this example, another column (ten-thousands) is added to the left of the thousands column, to denote a carryover of 10 units in the thousands column. The final sum is 10,629.

When adding using all negative integers, the total is negative. The integers are simply added together and the negative symbol is tacked on.

$$(-12) + (-435) = -447$$

Subtraction

Subtraction is taking away one number from another, so their quantities are reduced. The sign designating a subtraction operation is the – symbol, and the result is called the **difference**. For example, 9 - 6 = 3. The number *6* detracts from the number *9* to reach the difference *3*.

Unlike addition, subtraction follows neither the commutative nor associative properties. The order and grouping in subtraction impact the result.

$$15 = 22 - 7 \neq 7 - 22 = -15$$

$$3 = (10 - 5) - 2 \neq 10 - (5 - 2) = 7$$

When working through subtraction problems involving larger numbers, it's necessary to regroup the numbers. Let's work through a practice problem using regrouping:

$$\begin{array}{r} 3\,2\,5 \\ -\ 7\,7 \\ \hline \end{array}$$

Here, it is clear that the ones and tens columns for 77 are greater than the ones and tens columns for 325. To subtract this number, borrow from the tens and hundreds columns. When borrowing from a column, subtracting 1 from the lender column will add 10 to the borrower column:

$$\begin{array}{rrr} 3-1 & 10+2-1 & 10+5 \\ - & 7 & 7 \\ \hline \end{array} = \begin{array}{rrr} 2 & 11 & 15 \\ - & 7 & 7 \\ \hline 2 & 4 & 8 \end{array}$$

After ensuring that each digit in the top row is greater than the digit in the corresponding bottom row, subtraction can proceed as normal, and the answer is found to be 248.

Addition and Subtraction with Negative Integers

When adding mixed-sign integers, determine which integer has the larger absolute value. Absolute value is the distance of a number from zero on the number line. Absolute value is indicated by these symbols: | |.

Take this equation for example:

$$12 + (-435)$$

The absolute value of each of the numbers is as follows:

$$|12| = 12$$

$$|-435| = 435$$

Since -435 is the larger integer, the final number will have its sign. In this case, that sign is negative. Now, subtract the smaller integer from the larger one. If you work out the equation, it will look like this:

$$12 + (-435) = -423$$

Mathematically, the equation looks like the one above, but practically speaking you will be doing it like this:

$$435 - 12 = 423$$

(then add the negative sign)

When using subtraction with negative integers, every unmarked integer is assumed to have a positive sign unless it is clearly marked as a negative integer. Subtracting an integer is the same as adding a negative integer.

Example:

-3 - 4
-3 + (-4)
-3 + (-4) = -7

Subtracting a negative integer is the same as adding a positive integer.

Example

-3 - (-4)
-3 + 4
-3 + 4 = 1

Multiplication

Multiplication involves adding together multiple copies of a number. It is indicated by an × symbol or a number immediately outside of a parenthesis. For example:

$$5(8-2)$$

The two numbers being multiplied together are called **factors**, and their result is called a **product**. For example, $9 \times 6 = 54$. This can be shown alternatively by expansion of either the 9 or the 6:

$$9 \times 6 = 9+9+9+9+9+9 = 54$$

$$9 \times 6 = 6+6+6+6+6+6+6+6+6 = 54$$

For larger-number multiplication, how the numbers are lined up can ease the process. It is simplest to put the number with the most digits on top and the number with fewer digits on the bottom. If they have the same number of digits, select one for the top and one for the bottom. Line up the problem, and begin by multiplying the far right column on the top and the far right column on the bottom. If the answer to a column is more than 9, the ones place digit will be written below that column and the tens place digit will carry to the top of the next column to be added after those digits are multiplied. Write the answer below that column. Move to the next column to the left on the top, and multiply it by the same far right column on the bottom. Keep moving to the left one column at a time on the top number until the end.

Example:

Multiply 37×8

Line up the numbers, placing the one with the most digits on top.

$$\begin{array}{r} 3\ 7 \\ \times \quad 8 \\ \hline \end{array}$$

Multiply the far right column on the top with the far right column on the bottom (7 x 8). Write the answer, 56, as below: The ones value, 6, gets recorded, the tens value, 5, is carried.

$$\begin{array}{rrr} & {}^{+5} & \\ & 3 & 7 \\ \text{X} & & 8 \\ \hline & & 6 \end{array}$$

Move to the next column left on the top number and multiply with the far right bottom (3 x 8). Remember to add any carry over after multiplying: 3 x 8 = 24, 24 + 5 = 29. Since there are no more digits on top, write the entire number below.

$$\begin{array}{rrr} & {}^{+5} & \\ & 3 & 7 \\ \text{X} & & 8 \\ \hline 2 & 9 & 6 \end{array}$$

The solution is 296

If there is more than one column to the bottom number, move to the row below the first strand of answers, mark a zero in the far right column, and then begin the multiplication process again with the far right column on top and the second column from the right on the bottom. For each digit in the bottom number, there will be a row of answers, each padded with the respective number of zeros on the right. Finally, add up all of the answer rows for one total number.

Example: Multiply 512×36.

Line up the numbers (the one with the most digits on top) to multiply.

Begin with the right column on top and the right column on bottom (2×6).

$$\begin{array}{rrrr} & 5 & 1 & 2 \\ \text{X} & & 3 & 6 \\ \hline \end{array}$$

Move one column left on top and multiply by the far right column on the bottom (1×6). Add the carry over after multiplying: $1 \times 6 = 6, 6 + 1 = 7$.

$$\begin{array}{rrrr} & & {}^{+1} & \\ & 5 & 1 & 2 \\ \text{x} & & 3 & 6 \\ \hline & & 7 & 2 \end{array}$$

Move one column left on top and multiply by the far right column on the bottom (5×6). Since this is the last digit on top, write the whole answer below.

$$\begin{array}{rrrr} & 5 & 1 & 2 \\ \text{X} & & 3 & 6 \\ \hline 3 & 0 & 7 & 2 \end{array}$$

Now to the second column on the bottom number. Starting on the far right column on the top, repeat this pattern for the next number left on the bottom (2×3). Write the answers below the first line of answers; remember to begin with a zero placeholder on the far right.

$$\begin{array}{r} 512 \\ \times \quad 36 \\ \hline 3072 \\ 60 \end{array}$$

Continue the pattern (1×3).

$$\begin{array}{r} 512 \\ \times \quad 36 \\ \hline 3072 \\ 360 \end{array}$$

Since this is the last digit on top, write the whole answer below.

$$\begin{array}{r} 512 \\ \times \quad 36 \\ \hline 3072 \\ 15360 \end{array}$$

Now add the answer rows together. Pay attention to ensure they are aligned correctly.

$$\begin{array}{r} 512 \\ \times \quad 36 \\ \hline 3072 \\ 15360 \\ \hline 18432 \end{array}$$

The solution is 18,432.

Division

Division and multiplication are inverses of each other in the same way that addition and subtraction are opposites. The signs designating a division operation are the ÷ and / symbols. In division, the second number divides into the first.

The number before the division sign is called the **dividend** or, if expressed as a fraction, the **numerator**. For example, in $a \div b$, a is the dividend, while in $\frac{a}{b}$, a is the numerator.

The number after the division sign is called the **divisor** or, if expressed as a fraction, the **denominator.** For example, in $a \div b$, b is the divisor, while in $\frac{a}{b}$, b is the denominator.

Like subtraction, division doesn't follow the commutative property, as it matters which number comes before the division sign, and division doesn't follow the associative or distributive properties for the same reason. For example:

$$\frac{3}{2} = 9 \div 6 \neq 6 \div 9 = \frac{2}{3}$$

$$2 = 10 \div 5 = (30 \div 3) \div 5 \neq 30 \div (3 \div 5) = 30 \div \frac{3}{5} = 50$$

$$25 = 20 + 5 = (40 \div 2) + (40 \div 8) \neq 40 \div (2 + 8) = 40 \div 10 = 4$$

If a divisor doesn't divide into a dividend an integer number of times, whatever is left over is termed the remainder. The remainder can be further divided out into decimal form by using long division; however, this doesn't always give a quotient with a finite number of decimal places, so the remainder can also be expressed as a fraction over the original divisor.

Example:

Divide $1050/42$ or $1050 \div 42$.

Set up the problem with the denominator being divided into the numerator.

$$42\overline{)1050}$$

Check for divisibility into the first unit of the numerator, 1.

42 cannot go into 1, so add on the next unit in the denominator, 0.

42 cannot go into 10, so add on the next unit in the denominator, 5.

42 can be divided into 105, two times. Write the 2 over the 5 in 105 and multiply 42 x 2. Write the 84 under 105 for subtraction and note the remainder, 21 is less than 42.

$$\begin{array}{r} 2 \\ 42\overline{)1050} \\ -84 \\ \hline 21 \end{array}$$

Drop the next digit in the numerator down to the remainder (making 21 into 210) to create a number 42 can divide into. 42 divides into 210 five times. Write the 5 over the 0 and multiply 42×5.

$$\begin{array}{r} 25 \\ 42\overline{)1050} \\ -84 \\ \hline 210 \end{array}$$

Write the 210 under 210 for subtraction. The remainder is 0.

$$
\begin{array}{r}
25 \\
42\overline{)1050} \\
-84 \\
\hline
210 \\
-210 \\
\hline
0
\end{array}
$$

The solution is 25.

Example:

Divide $375/4$ or $375 \div 4$.

Set up the problem.

$$
4\overline{)375}
$$

4 cannot divide into 3, so add the next unit from the numerator, 7. 4 divides into 37 nine times, so write the 9 above the 7. Multiply $4 \times 9 = 36$. Write the 36 under the 37 for subtraction. The remainder is 1 (1 is less than 4).

$$
\begin{array}{r}
9 \\
4\overline{)375} \\
-36 \\
\hline
1
\end{array}
$$

Drop the next digit in the numerator, 5, making the remainder 15. 4 divides into 15, three times, so write the 3 above the 5. Multiply 4×3. Write the 12 under the 15 for subtraction, remainder is 3 (3 is less than 4).

$$
\begin{array}{r}
93 \\
4\overline{)375} \\
-36 \\
\hline
15 \\
-12 \\
\hline
3
\end{array}
$$

The solution is 93 remainder 3 or 93 ¾ (the remainder can be written over the original denominator).

Fractions, Ratios, and Integers

Comparing and Ordering Fractions, Integers, and Exponents

A **rational number** is any number that can be written as a fraction or ratio. Within the set of rational numbers, several subsets exist that are referenced throughout the mathematics topics. **Counting numbers** are the first numbers learned as a child. Counting numbers consist of 1,2,3,4, and so on. **Whole**

numbers include all counting numbers and zero (0,1,2,3,4,...). **Integers** include counting numbers, their opposites, and zero (...,-3,-2,-1,0,1,2,3,...). **Rational numbers** are inclusive of integers, fractions, and decimals that terminate, or end (1.7, 0.04213) or repeat ($0.136\overline{5}$).

A **number line** typically consists of integers (...3,2,1,0,-1,-2,-3...), and is used to visually represent the value of a rational number. Each rational number has a distinct position on the line determined by comparing its value with the displayed values on the line. For example, if plotting -1.5 on the number line below, it is necessary to recognize that the value of -1.5 is .5 less than -1 and .5 greater than -2. Therefore, -1.5 is plotted halfway between -1 and -2.

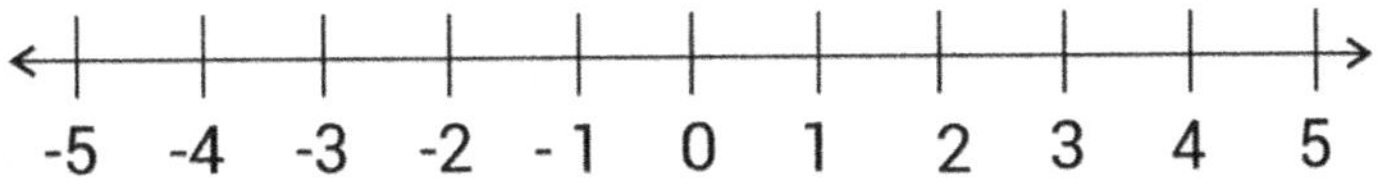

The number system that is used consists of only ten different digits or characters. However, this system is used to represent an infinite number of values. The **place value system** makes this infinite number of values possible. The position in which a digit is written corresponds to a given value. Starting from the decimal point (which is implied, if not physically present), each subsequent place value to the left represents a value greater than the one before it. Conversely, starting from the decimal point, each subsequent place value to the right represents a value less than the one before it.

The names for the place values to the left of the decimal point are as follows:

...	Billions	Hundred-Millions	Ten-Millions	Millions	Hundred-Thousands	Ten-Thousands	Thousands	Hundreds	Tens	Ones

*Note that this table can be extended infinitely further to the left.

The names for the place values to the right of the decimal point are as follows:

Decimal Point (.)	Tenths	Hundredths	Thousandths	Ten-Thousandths	...

*Note that this table can be extended infinitely further to the right.

When given a multi-digit number, the value of each digit depends on its place value. Consider the number 682,174.953. Referring to the chart above, it can be determined that the digit 8 is in the ten-thousands place. It is in the fifth place to the left of the decimal point. Its value is 8 ten-thousands or 80,000. The digit 5 is two places to the right of the decimal point. Therefore, the digit 5 is in the hundredths place. Its value is 5 hundredths or $\frac{5}{100}$ (equivalent to .05).

In accordance with the **base-10 system**, the value of a digit increases by a factor of ten each place it moves to the left. For example, consider the number 7. Moving the digit one place to the left (70), increases its value by a factor of 10 ($7 \times 10 = 70$). Moving the digit two places to the left (700) increases its value by a factor of 10 twice:

$$(7 \times 10 \times 10 = 700)$$

Moving the digit three places to the left (7,000) increases its value by a factor of 10 three times:

$$(7 \times 10 \times 10 \times 10 = 7{,}000)$$

and so on.

Conversely, the value of a digit decreases by a factor of ten each place it moves to the right. (Note that multiplying by $\frac{1}{10}$ is equivalent to dividing by 10). For example, consider the number 40. Moving the digit one place to the right (4) decreases its value by a factor of 10 ($40 \div 10 = 4$). Moving the digit two places to the right (0.4), decreases its value by a factor of 10 twice:

$$(40 \div 10 \div 10 = 0.4)$$

or

$$(40 \times \frac{1}{10} \times \frac{1}{10} = 0.4)$$

Moving the digit three places to the right (0.04) decreases its value by a factor of 10 three times:

$$(40 \div 10 \div 10 \div 10 = 0.04)$$

or

$$(40 \times \frac{1}{10} \times \frac{1}{10} \times \frac{1}{10} = 0.04)$$

and so on.

Exponents

Exponents are used in mathematics to express a number or variable multiplied by itself a certain number of times. For example, x^3 means *x* is multiplied by itself three times. In this expression, x is called the **base**, and 3 is the **exponent.** Exponents can be used in more complex problems when they contain fractions and negative numbers.

Fractional exponents can be explained by looking first at the inverse of exponents, which are **roots.** Given the expression x^2, the square root can be taken, $\sqrt{x^2}$, cancelling out the 2 and leaving *x* by itself, if *x* is positive. Cancellation occurs because $\sqrt{x}$ can be written with exponents, instead of roots, as $x^{\frac{1}{2}}$. The numerator of 1 is the exponent, and the denominator of 2 is called the **root** (which is why it's referred to as a **square root**). Taking the square root of x^2 is the same as raising it to the $\frac{1}{2}$ power. Written out in mathematical form, it takes the following progression:

$$\sqrt{x^2} = (x^2)^{\frac{1}{2}} = x$$

From properties of exponents, $2 \times \frac{1}{2} = 1$ is the actual exponent of *x*. Another example can be seen with $x^{\frac{4}{7}}$. The variable *x*, raised to four-sevenths, is equal to the seventh root of *x* to the fourth power: $\sqrt[7]{x^4}$. In general,

$$x^{\frac{1}{n}} = \sqrt[n]{x}$$

and

$$x^{\frac{m}{n}} = \sqrt[n]{x^m}$$

Negative exponents also involve fractions. Whereas y^3 can also be rewritten as $\frac{y^3}{1}$, y^{-3} can be rewritten as $\frac{1}{y^3}$. A negative exponent means the exponential expression must be moved to the opposite spot in a fraction to make the exponent positive. If the negative appears in the numerator, it moves to the denominator. If the negative appears in the denominator, it is moved to the numerator. In general, $a^{-n} = \frac{1}{a^n}$, and a^{-n} and a^n are reciprocals.

Take, for example, the following expression:

$$\frac{a^{-4}b^2}{c^{-5}}$$

Since *a* is raised to the negative fourth power, it can be moved to the denominator. Since *c* is raised to the negative fifth power, it can be moved to the numerator. The *b* variable is raised to the positive second power, so it does not move.

The simplified expression is as follows:

$$\frac{b^2c^5}{a^4}$$

In mathematical expressions containing exponents and other operations, the order of operations must be followed. **PEMDAS** states that exponents are calculated after any parenthesis and grouping symbols but before any multiplication, division, addition, and subtraction.

Ordering Numbers

A common question type asks to order rational numbers from least to greatest or greatest to least. The numbers will come in a variety of formats, including decimals, percentages, roots, fractions, and whole numbers. These questions test for knowledge of different types of numbers and the ability to determine their respective values.

Before discussing ordering all numbers, let's start with decimals.

To compare decimals and order them by their value, utilize a method similar to that of ordering large numbers.

The main difference is where the comparison will start. Assuming that any numbers to left of the decimal point are equal, the next numbers to be compared are those immediately to the right of the decimal point. If those are equal, then move on to compare the values in the next decimal place to the right.

For example:

Which number is greater, 12.35 or 12.38?

Check that the values to the left of the decimal point are equal:

$$12 = 12$$

Next, compare the values of the decimal place to the right of the decimal:

12.3 = 12.3

Those are also equal in value.

Finally, compare the value of the numbers in the next decimal place to the right on both numbers:

12.3**5** and 12.3**8**

Here the 5 is less than the 8, so the final way to express this inequality is:

$$12.35 < 12.38$$

Comparing decimals is regularly exemplified with money because the "cents" portion of money ends in the hundredths place. When paying for gasoline or meals in restaurants, and even in bank accounts, if enough errors are made when calculating numbers to the hundredths place, they can add up to dollars and larger amounts of money over time.

Now that decimal ordering has been explained, let's expand and consider all real numbers. Whether the question asks to order the numbers from greatest to least or least to greatest, the crux of the question is the same—convert the numbers into a common format. Generally, it's easiest to write the numbers as whole numbers and decimals so they can be placed on a number line. Follow the examples on the next page to understand this strategy.

1) Order the following rational numbers from greatest to least:

$$\sqrt{36}, 0.65, 78\%, \frac{3}{4}, 7, 90\%, \frac{5}{2}$$

Of the seven numbers, the whole number (7) and decimal (0.65) are already in an accessible form, so concentrate on the other five.

First, the square root of 36 equals 6. (If the test asks for the root of a non-perfect root, determine which two whole numbers the root lies between.) Next, convert the percentages to decimals. A percentage means "per hundred," so this conversion requires moving the decimal point two places to the left, leaving 0.78 and 0.9. Lastly, evaluate the fractions:

$$\frac{3}{4} = \frac{75}{100} = 0.75\,; \frac{5}{2} = 2\frac{1}{2} = 2.5$$

Now, the only step left is to list the numbers in the request order:

$$7, \sqrt{36}, \frac{5}{2}, 90\%, 78\%, \frac{3}{4}, 0.65$$

2) Order the following rational numbers from least to greatest:

$$2.5, \sqrt{9}, -10.5, 0.853, 175\%, \sqrt{4}, \frac{4}{5}$$

$$\sqrt{9} = 3$$

$$175\% = 1.75$$

$$\sqrt{4} = 2$$

$$\frac{4}{5} = 0.8$$

From least to greatest, the answer is:

$$-10.5, \frac{4}{5}, 0.853, 175\%, \sqrt{4}, 2.5, \sqrt{9}$$

Converting Among Standard Measurement Units Within and Between Measurement Systems

The U.S. Customary and Metric Systems of Measurement

Measurement is how an object's length, width, height, weight, and so on, are quantified. Measurement is related to counting, but it is a more refined process.

The United States customary system and the metric system each consist of distinct units to measure lengths and volume of liquids. The U.S. customary units for length, from smallest to largest, are: inch (in), foot (ft), yard (yd), and mile (mi). The metric units for length, from smallest to largest, are: millimeter (mm), centimeter (cm), decimeter (dm), meter (m), and kilometer (km). The relative size of each unit of length is shown below.

U.S. Customary	Metric	Conversion
12in = 1ft	10mm = 1cm	1in = 254cm
36in = 3ft = 1yd	10cm = 1dm(decimeter)	1m ≈ 3.28ft ≈ 1.09yd
5,280ft = 1,760yd = 1mi	100cm = 10dm = 1m	1mi ≈ 1.6km
	1000m = 1km	

The U.S. customary units for volume of liquids, from smallest to largest, are: fluid ounces (fl oz), cup (c), pint (pt), quart (qt), and gallon (gal). The metric units for volume of liquids, from smallest to largest, are: milliliter (mL), centiliter (cL), deciliter (dL), liter (L), and kiloliter (kL). The relative size of each unit of liquid volume is shown below.

U.S. Customary	Metric	Conversion
8fl oz = 1c	10mL = 1cL	1pt ≈ 0.473L
2c = 1pt	10cL = 1dL	1L ≈ 1.057qt
4c = 2pt = 1qt	1,000mL = 100cL = 10dL = 1L	1gal ≈ 3.785L
4qt = 1gal	1,000L = 1kL	

The U.S. customary system measures weight (how strongly Earth is pulling on an object) in the following units, from least to greatest: ounce (oz), pound (lb), and ton. The metric system measures mass (the quantity of matter within an object) in the following units, from least to greatest: milligram (mg), centigram (cg), gram (g), kilogram (kg), and metric ton (MT).

The relative sizes of each unit of weight and mass are shown below.

U.S. Measures of Weight	Metric Measures of Mass
16oz = 1lb	10mg = 1cg
2,000lb = 1 ton	100cg = 1g
	1,000g = 1kg
	1,000kg = 1MT

Note that weight and mass DO NOT measure the same thing.

Time is measured in the following units, from shortest to longest: second (sec), minute (min), hour (h), day (d), week (wk), month (mo), year (yr), decade, century, millennium. The relative sizes of each unit of time is shown below.

- 60sec = 1min
- 60min = 1h
- 24hr = 1d
- 7d = 1wk
- 52wk = 1yr
- 12mo = 1yr
- 10yr = 1 decade
- 100yrs = 1 century
- 1,000yrs = 1 millennium

Some units of measure are represented as square or cubic units depending on the solution. For example, perimeter is measured in units, area is measured in square units, and volume is measured in cubic units.

Also, be sure to use the most appropriate unit for the thing being measured. A building's height might be measured in feet or meters while the length of a nail might be measured in inches or centimeters. Additionally, for SI units, the prefix should be chosen to provide the most succinct available value. For example, the mass of a bag of fruit would likely be measured in kilograms rather than grams or milligrams, and the length of a bacteria cell would likely be measured in micrometers rather than centimeters or kilometers.

Problems that involve measurements of length, time, volume, etc. are generally dependent upon understanding how to manipulate between various units of measurement, as well as understanding their equivalencies.

Identifying and utilizing the proper units for the scenario requires knowing how to apply the conversion rates for money, length, volume, and mass. For example, given a scenario that requires subtracting 8 inches from $2\frac{1}{2}$ feet, both values should first be expressed in the same unit (they could be expressed $\frac{2}{3}$ft & $2\frac{1}{2}$ft, or 8in and 30in). The desired unit for the answer may also require converting back to another unit.

Consider the following scenario: A parking area along the river is only wide enough to fit one row of cars and is $\frac{1}{2}$ kilometers long. The average space needed per car is 5 meters. How many cars can be parked along the river? First, all measurements should be converted to similar units: $\frac{1}{2}$km = 500m. The operation(s) needed should be identified. Because the problem asks for the number of cars, the total space should be divided by the space per car. 500 meters divided by 5 meters per car yields a total of 100 cars. Written as an expression, the meters unit cancels, and the cars unit is left: $\frac{500m}{5m/car}$ the same as $500m \times \frac{1\,car}{5m}$ yields 100 cars.

For an example manipulating time, Maria is scheduled to take a 90-minute test for her English class. It takes her 25 minutes to get ready and 40 minutes to ride the bus to school. If she begins to get ready at 1:10 p.m., what time will she be finished taking the test?

To find the ending time, all of the elapsed minutes must be totaled and then converted to hours.

$$25 + 40 + 90 = 155 \text{ minutes}$$

The conversion necessary for this problem is that 1 hour = 60 minutes.

The total number of minutes must be converted into hours and minutes, by dividing the total number of minutes by 60.

$$155 \div 60 = 2\,R\,35$$

The remainder is stated as minutes. So, the total elapsed time is 2 hours and 35 minutes. If Maria begins to get ready at 1:10 p.m., 2 hours from that time is 3:10 p.m., and an additional 35 minutes would add up to 3:45 p.m. Maria can expect to be finished with everything 2 hours and 35 minutes later, at 3:45 p.m.

When measuring length, choosing the right tool to perform the measurement requires determining whether United States customary units or metric units are desired, and having a grasp of the approximate length of each unit and the approximate length of each tool. The measurement can still be performed by trial and error without the knowledge of the approximate size of the tool.

For example, to determine the length of a room in feet, a United States customary unit, various tools can be used for this task. These include a ruler (typically 12 inches/1-foot-long), a yardstick (3 feet/1-yard-long), or a tape measure displaying feet (typically either 25 feet or 50 feet). Because the length of a room is much larger than the length of a ruler or a yardstick, a tape measure should be used to perform the measurement.

Converting Units of Measurement

Converting measurements in different units between the two systems can be difficult because they follow different rules. The best method is to look up an English to Metric system conversion factor and then use a series of equivalent fractions to set up an equation to convert the units of one of the measurements into those of the other. The table below lists some common conversion values that are useful for problems involving measurements with units in both systems:

English System	Metric System
1 inch	2.54 cm
1 foot	0.3048 m
1 yard	0.914 m
1 mile	1.609 km
1 ounce	28.35 g
1 pound	0.454 kg
1 fluid ounce	29.574 mL
1 quart	0.946 L
1 gallon	3.785 L

Consider the example where a scientist wants to convert 6.8 inches to centimeters. One method for converting units is to write and solve a proportion. The arrangement of values in a proportion is extremely important. The table above is used to find that there are 2.54 centimeters in every inch, so the following equation should be set up and solved:

$$\frac{6.8\ in}{1} \times \frac{2.54\ cm}{1\ in} = 17.272\ cm$$

Notice how the inches in the numerator of the initial figure and the denominator of the conversion factor cancel out. (This equation could have been written simply as $6.8\ in \times 2.54\ cm = 17.272\ cm$, but it was shown in detail to illustrate the steps). The goal in any conversion equation is to set up the fractions so that the units you are trying to convert from cancel out and the units you desire remain.

For a more complicated example, consider converting 2.15 kilograms into ounces. The first step is to convert kilograms into grams and then grams into ounces. Note that the measurement you begin with does not have to be put in a fraction.

So, in this case, 2.15 kg is by itself although it's technically the numerator of a fraction:

$$2.15\ kg \times \frac{1000g}{kg} = 2150\ g$$

Then, use the conversion factor from the table to convert grams to ounces:

$$2150g \times \frac{1\ oz}{28.35g} = 75.8\ oz$$

Now suppose that a problem requires converting 20 fluid ounces to cups. To do so, a proportion can be written using the conversion rate of 8fl oz = 1c with *x* representing the missing value. The proportion can be written in any of the following ways:

$$\frac{1}{8} = \frac{x}{20} \left(\frac{c\ for\ conversion}{fl\ oz\ for\ conversion} = \frac{unknown\ c}{fl\ oz\ given} \right)$$

$$\frac{8}{1} = \frac{20}{x} \left(\frac{fl\ oz\ for\ conversion}{c\ for\ conversion} = \frac{fl\ oz\ given}{unknown\ c} \right)$$

$$\frac{1}{x} = \frac{8}{20} \left(\frac{c\ for\ conversion}{unknown\ c} = \frac{fl\ oz\ for\ conversion}{fl\ oz\ given} \right)$$

$$\frac{x}{1} = \frac{20}{8} \left(\frac{unknown\ c}{c\ for\ conversion} = \frac{fl\ oz\ given}{fl\ oz\ for\ conversion} \right)$$

To solve the proportion, the ratios are cross-multiplied and the resulting equation is solved. When cross-multiplying, all four proportions above will produce the same equation: $(8)(x) = (20)(1) \rightarrow 8x = 20$. Dividing by 8 to isolate the variable *x*, the result is *x* = 2.5. The variable *x* represented the unknown number of cups. Therefore, the conclusion is that 20 fluid ounces converts (is equal) to 2.5 cups.

Sometimes converting units requires writing and solving more than one proportion. Suppose an exam question asks to determine how many hours are in 2 weeks. Without knowing the conversion rate between hours and weeks, this can be determined knowing the conversion rates between weeks and days, and between days and hours. First, weeks are converted to days, then days are converted to hours. To convert from weeks to days, the following proportion can be written:

$$\frac{7}{1} = \frac{x}{2} \left(\frac{days\ conversion}{weeks\ conversion} = \frac{days\ unknown}{weeks\ given} \right)$$

Cross-multiplying produces: $(7)(2) = (x)(1) \rightarrow 14 = x$. Therefore, 2 weeks is equal to 14 days. Next, a proportion is written to convert 14 days to hours:

$$\frac{24}{1} = \frac{x}{14} \left(\frac{conversion\ hours}{conversion\ days} = \frac{unknown\ hours}{given\ days} \right)$$

Cross-multiplying produces: $(24)(14) = (x)(1) \rightarrow 336 = x$. Therefore, the answer is that there are 336 hours in 2 weeks.

Operations Involving Fractions, Decimals, and Percent Using Visual Models and Equations

Fractions

A **fraction** is a part of something that is whole. Items such as apples can be cut into parts to help visualize fractions. If an apple is cut into 2 equal parts, each part represents ½ of the apple. If each half is then cut into two parts, the apple now is cut into quarters. Each piece now represents ¼ of the apple. In this example, each part is equal because they all have the same size. Geometric shapes, such as circles and squares, can also be utilized to help visualize the idea of fractions. For example, a circle can be drawn on the board and divided into 6 equal parts:

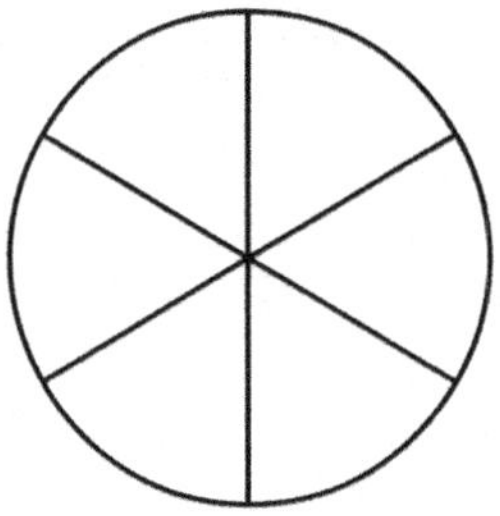

Shading can be used to represent parts of the circle that can be translated into fractions. The top of the fraction, the **numerator,** can represent how many segments are shaded. The bottom of the fraction, the **denominator,** can represent the number of segments that the circle is broken into. A pie is a good analogy to use in this example. If one piece of the circle is shaded, or one piece of pie is cut out, $^1/_6$ of the object is being referred to. An apple, a pie, or a circle can be utilized in order to compare simple fractions. For example, showing that ½ is larger than ¼ and that ¼ is smaller than $^1/_3$ can be accomplished through shading. A **unit fraction** is a fraction in which the numerator is 1, and the denominator is a positive whole number. It represents one part of a whole—one piece of pie.

Imagine that an apple pie has been baked for a holiday party, and the full pie has eight slices. After the party, there are five slices left. How could the amount of the pie that remains be expressed as a fraction? The numerator is 5 since there are 5 pieces left, and the denominator is 8 since there were eight total slices in the whole pie. Thus, expressed as a fraction, the leftover pie totals $\frac{5}{8}$ of the original amount.

Fractions come in three different varieties: proper fractions, improper fractions, and mixed numbers. **Proper fractions** have a numerator less than the denominator, such as $\frac{3}{8}$, but **improper fractions** have a numerator greater than the denominator, such as $\frac{15}{8}$. **Mixed numbers** combine a whole number with a proper fraction, such as $3\frac{1}{2}$. Any mixed number can be written as an improper fraction by multiplying the integer by the denominator, adding the product to the value of the numerator, and dividing the sum by the original denominator. For example:

$$3\frac{1}{2} = \frac{3 \times 2 + 1}{2} = \frac{7}{2}$$

Whole numbers can also be converted into fractions by placing the whole number as the numerator and making the denominator 1. For example, $3 = \frac{3}{1}$.

The bar in a fraction represents division. Therefore $^6/_5$ is the same as $6 \div 5$. In order to rewrite it as a mixed number, division is performed to obtain $6 \div 5 = 1\ R1$. The remainder is then converted into fraction form. The actual remainder becomes the numerator of a fraction, and the divisor becomes the denominator. Therefore $1\ R1$ is written as $1\frac{1}{5}$, a mixed number. A mixed number can also decompose into the addition of a whole number and a fraction.

For example:

$$1\frac{1}{5} = 1 + \frac{1}{5} \text{ and } 4\frac{5}{6} = 4 + \frac{1}{6} + \frac{1}{6} + \frac{1}{6} + \frac{1}{6} + \frac{1}{6}$$

Every fraction can be built from a combination of unit fractions.

One of the most fundamental concepts of fractions is their ability to be manipulated by multiplication or division. This is possible since $\frac{n}{n} = 1$ for any non-zero integer. As a result, multiplying or dividing by $\frac{n}{n}$ will not alter the original fraction since any number multiplied or divided by 1 doesn't change the value of that number. Fractions of the same value are known as equivalent fractions. For example, $\frac{2}{8}, \frac{25}{100}$, and $\frac{40}{160}$ are equivalent, as they are all equal $\frac{1}{4}$.

Like fractions, or **equivalent fractions**, are the terms used to describe these fractions that are made up of different numbers but represent the same quantity. For example, the given fractions are $^4/_8$ and $^3/_6$. If a pie was cut into 8 pieces and 4 pieces were removed, half of the pie would remain. Also, if a pie was split into 6 pieces and 3 pieces were eaten, half of the pie would also remain. Therefore, both of the fractions represent half of a pie. These two fractions are referred to as like fractions. **Unlike fractions** are fractions that are different and do not represent equal quantities. When working with fractions in mathematical expressions, like fractions should be simplified. Both $^4/_8$ and $^3/_6$ can be simplified into $^1/_2$.

Comparing fractions can be completed through the use of a number line. For example, if $^3/_5$ and $^6/_{10}$ need to be compared, each fraction should be plotted on a number line. To plot $^3/_5$, the area from 0 to 1 should be broken into 5 equal segments, and the fraction represents 3 of them. To plot $^6/_{10}$, the area from 0 to 1 should be broken into 10 equal segments and the fraction represents 6 of them.

It can be seen that $\frac{3}{5} = \frac{6}{10}$

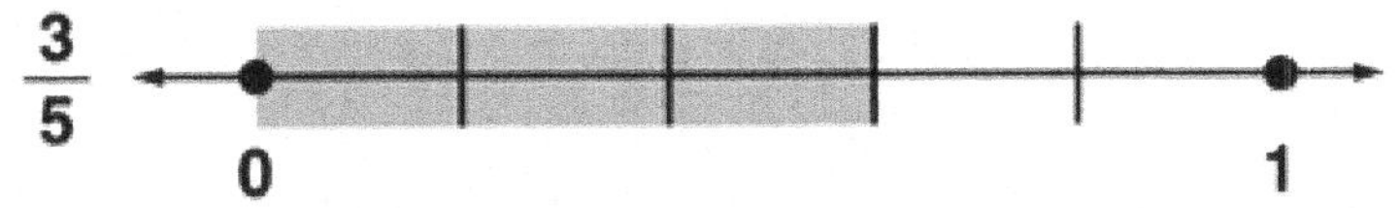

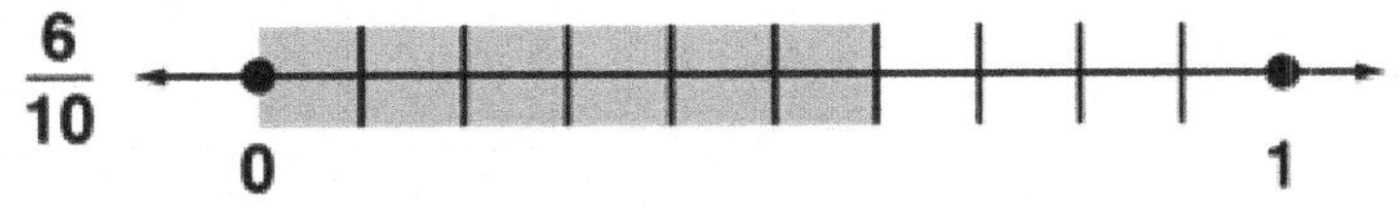

Like fractions are plotted at the same point on a number line. Unit fractions can also be used to compare fractions. For example, if it is known that:

$$\frac{4}{5} > \frac{1}{2}$$

and

$$\frac{1}{2} > \frac{4}{10}$$

then it is also known that:

$$\frac{4}{5} > \frac{4}{10}$$

Also, converting improper fractions to mixed numbers can be helpful in comparing fractions because the whole number portion of the number is more visible.

Adding and subtracting mixed numbers and fractions can be completed by decomposing fractions into a sum of whole numbers and unit fractions. For example, the given problem is:

$$5\frac{3}{7} + 2\frac{1}{7}$$

Decomposing into

$$5 + \frac{1}{7} + \frac{1}{7} + \frac{1}{7} + 2 + \frac{1}{7}$$

This shows that the whole numbers can be added separately from the unit fractions. The answer is:

$$5 + 2 + \frac{1}{7} + \frac{1}{7} + \frac{1}{7} + \frac{1}{7} = 7 + \frac{4}{7} = 7\frac{4}{7}$$

Although many equivalent fractions exist, they are easier to compare and interpret when reduced or simplified. The numerator and denominator of a simple fraction will have no factors in common other than 1. When reducing or simplifying fractions, divide the numerator and denominator by the greatest common factor. A simple strategy is to divide the numerator and denominator by low numbers, like 2, 3, or 5 until arriving at a simple fraction, but the same thing could be achieved by determining the greatest common factor for both the numerator and denominator and dividing each by it. Using the first method is preferable when both the numerator and denominator are even, end in 5, or are obviously a multiple of another number. However, if no numbers seem to work, it will be necessary to factor the numerator and denominator to find the GCF. Let's look at examples:

1) Simplify the fraction $\frac{6}{8}$:

Dividing the numerator and denominator by 2 results in $\frac{3}{4}$, which is a simple fraction.

2) Simplify the fraction $\frac{12}{36}$:

Dividing the numerator and denominator by 2 leaves $\frac{6}{18}$. This isn't a simple fraction, as both the numerator and denominator have factors in common. Dividing each by 3 results in $\frac{2}{6}$, but this can be further simplified by dividing by 2 to get $\frac{1}{3}$. This is the simplest fraction, as the numerator is 1. In cases like this, multiple division operations can be avoided by determining the greatest common factor (12, in this case) between the numerator and denominator.

3) Simplify the fraction $\frac{18}{54}$ by dividing by the greatest common factor:

First, determine the factors for the numerator and denominator. The factors of 18 are 1, 2, 3, 6, 9, and 18. The factors of 54 are 1, 2, 3, 6, 9, 18, 27, and 54. Thus, the greatest common factor is 18. Dividing $\frac{18}{54}$ by 18 leaves $\frac{1}{3}$, which is the simplest fraction. This method takes slightly more work, but it definitively arrives at the simplest fraction.

Adding and Subtracting Fractions

Adding and subtracting fractions that have the same denominators involves adding or subtracting the numerators. The denominator will stay the same. Therefore, the decomposition process can be made simpler, and the fractions do not have to be broken into unit fractions.

For example, the given problem is:

$$4\frac{7}{8} - 2\frac{6}{8}$$

The answer is found by adding the answers to both

$$4 - 2 \text{ and } \frac{7}{8} - \frac{6}{8}$$

$$2 + \frac{1}{8} = 2\frac{1}{8}$$

A common mistake would be to add the denominators so that $\frac{1}{4} + \frac{1}{4} = \frac{1}{8}$ or to add numerators and denominators so that $\frac{1}{4} + \frac{1}{4} = \frac{2}{8}$. However, conceptually, it is known that two quarters make a half, so neither one of these are correct.

If two fractions have different denominators, equivalent fractions must be used to add or subtract them. The fractions must be converted into fractions that have common denominators. A **least common denominator** or the product of the two denominators can be used as the common denominator. For example, in the problem $\frac{5}{6} + \frac{2}{3}$, either 6, which is the least common denominator, or 18, which is the product of the denominators, can be used. In order to use 6, $\frac{2}{3}$ must be converted to sixths. A number line can be used to show the equivalent fraction is $\frac{4}{6}$. What happens is that $\frac{2}{3}$ is multiplied by a fractional form of 1 to obtain a denominator of 6. Hence:

$$\frac{2}{3} \times \frac{2}{2} = \frac{4}{6}$$

Therefore, the problem is now:

$$\frac{5}{6}+\frac{4}{6}=\frac{9}{6}$$

which can be simplified into $\frac{3}{2}$. In order to use 18, both fractions must be converted into having 18 as their denominator. $\frac{5}{6}$ would have to be multiplied by $\frac{3}{3}$, and $\frac{2}{3}$ would need to be multiplied by $\frac{6}{6}$. The addition problem would be:

$$\frac{15}{18}+\frac{12}{18}=\frac{27}{18}$$

which reduces into $\frac{3}{2}$.

It is always possible to find a common denominator by multiplying the denominators. However, when the denominators are large numbers, this method is unwieldy, especially if the answer must be provided in its simplest form. Thus, it's beneficial to find the **least common denominator** of the fractions—the least common denominator is incidentally also the **least common multiple**.

Once equivalent fractions have been found with common denominators, simply add or subtract the numerators to arrive at the answer:

1) $\frac{1}{2}+\frac{3}{4}=\frac{2}{4}+\frac{3}{4}=\frac{5}{4}$

2) $\frac{3}{12}+\frac{11}{20}=\frac{15}{60}+\frac{33}{60}=\frac{48}{60}=\frac{4}{5}$

3) $\frac{7}{9}-\frac{4}{15}=\frac{35}{45}-\frac{12}{45}=\frac{23}{45}$

4) $\frac{5}{6}-\frac{7}{18}=\frac{15}{18}-\frac{7}{18}=\frac{8}{18}=\frac{4}{9}$

Multiplying and Dividing Fractions

Of the four basic operations that can be performed on fractions, the one which involves the least amount of work is multiplication. To multiply two fractions, simply multiply the numerators, multiply the denominators, and place the products as a fraction. Whole numbers and mixed numbers can also be expressed as a fraction, as described above, to multiply with a fraction.

Because multiplication is commutative, multiplying a fraction by a whole number is the same as multiplying a whole number by a fraction. The problem involves adding a fraction a specific number of times. The problem $3 \times \frac{1}{4}$ can be translated into adding the unit fraction three times:

$$\frac{1}{4}+\frac{1}{4}+\frac{1}{4}=\frac{3}{4}$$

In the problem $4 \times \frac{2}{5}$, the fraction can be decomposed into $\frac{1}{5}+\frac{1}{5}$ and then added four times to obtain $\frac{8}{5}$. Also, both of these answers can be found by just multiplying the whole number by the numerator of the fraction being multiplied.

The whole numbers can be written in fraction form as:

$$\frac{3}{1} \times \frac{1}{4} = \frac{3}{4}$$

$$\frac{4}{1} \times \frac{2}{5} = \frac{8}{5}$$

Multiplying a fraction by a fraction involves multiplying the numerators together separately and the denominators together separately. For example:

$$\frac{3}{8} \times \frac{2}{3} = \frac{3 \times 2}{8 \times 3} = \frac{6}{24}$$

This can then be reduced to $^1/_4$.

Dividing a fraction by a fraction is actually a multiplication problem. It involves flipping the divisor and then multiplying normally. For example:

$$\frac{22}{5} \div \frac{1}{2} = \frac{22}{5} \times \frac{2}{1} = \frac{44}{5}$$

The same procedure can be implemented for division problems involving fractions and whole numbers. The whole number can be rewritten as a fraction over a denominator of 1, and then division can be completed.

A common denominator approach can also be used in dividing fractions. Considering the same problem, $\frac{22}{5} \div \frac{1}{2}$, a common denominator between the two fractions is 10. $\frac{22}{5}$ would be rewritten as $\frac{22}{5} \times \frac{2}{2} = \frac{44}{10}$, and $\frac{1}{2}$ would be rewritten as:

$$\frac{1}{2} \times \frac{5}{5} = \frac{5}{10}$$

Dividing both numbers straight across results in:

$$\frac{44}{10} \div \frac{5}{10} = \frac{^{44}/_5}{^{10}/_{10}} = \frac{^{44}/_5}{1} = {}^{44}/_5$$

Many real-world problems will involve the use of fractions. Key words include actual fraction values, such as *half, quarter, third, fourth*, etc. The best approach to solving word problems involving fractions is to draw a picture or diagram that represents the scenario being discussed, while deciding which type of operation is necessary in order to solve the problem. A phrase such as "one fourth of 60 pounds of coal" creates a scenario in which multiplication should be used, and the mathematical form of the phrase is $\frac{1}{4} \times 60$.

Decimals

The **decimal system** is a way of writing out numbers that uses ten different numerals: 0, 1, 2, 3, 4, 5, 6, 7, 8, and 9. This is also called a "base ten" or "base 10" system. Other bases are also used. For example, computers work with a base of 2. This means they only use the numerals 0 and 1.

The **decimal place** denotes how far to the right of the decimal point a numeral is. The first digit to the right of the decimal point is in the **tenths'** place. The next is the **hundredths'** place. The third is the **thousandths'** place.

So, 3.142 has a 1 in the tenths place, a 4 in the hundredths place, and a 2 in the thousandths place.

The **decimal point** is a period used to separate the **ones'** place from the **tenths'** place when writing out a number as a decimal.

A **decimal number** is a number written out with a decimal point instead of as a fraction, for example, 1.25 instead of $\frac{5}{4}$. Depending on the situation, it may be easier to work with fractions, while other times, it may be easier to work with decimal numbers.

A decimal number is **terminating** if it stops at some point. It is called **repeating** if it never stops but repeats a pattern over and over. It is important to note that every rational number can be written as a terminating decimal or as a repeating decimal.

Addition with Decimals

To add decimal numbers, each number in columns needs to be lined up by the decimal point. For each number being added, the zeros to the right of the last number need to be filled in so that each of the numbers has the same number of places to the right of the decimal. Then, the columns can be added together. Here is an example of 2.45 + 1.3 + 8.891 written in column form:

$$\begin{array}{r} 2.450 \\ 1.300 \\ \underline{+\ 8.891} \end{array}$$

Zeros have been added in the columns so that each number has the same number of places to the right of the decimal.

Added together, the correct answer is 12.641:

$$\begin{array}{r} 2.450 \\ 1.300 \\ \underline{+\ 8.891} \\ 12.641 \end{array}$$

Subtraction with Decimals

Subtracting decimal numbers is the same process as adding decimals. Here is 7.89 – 4.235 written in column form:

$$\begin{array}{r} 7.890 \\ -\ \underline{4.235} \\ 3.655 \end{array}$$

A zero has been added in the column so that each number has the same number of places to the right of the decimal.

Multiplication with Decimals

The simplest way to multiply decimals is to calculate the product as if the decimals are not there, then count the number of decimal places in the original problem. Use that total to place the decimal the same number of places over in your answer, counting from right to left. For example, 0.5 x 1.25 can be rewritten and multiplied as 5 x 125, which equals 625. Then the decimal is added three places from the right for .625.

The final answer will have the same number of decimal places as the total number of decimal places in the problem. The first number has one decimal place, and the second number has two decimal places. Therefore, the final answer will contain three decimal places:

0.5 x 1.25 = 0.625

Division with Decimals

Dividing a decimal by a whole number entails using long division first by ignoring the decimal point. Then, the decimal point is moved the number of places given in the problem.

For example, $6.8 \div 4$ can be rewritten as $68 \div 4$, which is 17. There is one non-zero integer to the right of the decimal point, so the final solution would have one decimal place to the right of the solution. In this case, the solution is 1.7.

Dividing a decimal by another decimal requires changing the divisor to a whole number by moving its decimal point. The decimal place of the dividend should be moved by the same number of places as the divisor. Then, the problem is the same as dividing a decimal by a whole number.

For example, $5.72 \div 1.1$ has a divisor with one decimal point in the denominator. The expression can be rewritten as $57.2 \div 11$ by moving each number one decimal place to the right to eliminate the decimal. The long division can be completed as $572 \div 11$ with a result of 52. Since there is one non-zero integer to the right of the decimal point in the problem, the final solution is 5.2.

In another example, $8 \div 0.16$ has a divisor with two decimal points in the denominator. The expression can be rewritten as $800 \div 16$ by moving each number two decimal places to the right to eliminate the decimal in the divisor. The long division can be completed with a result of 50.

Percentages

Think of percentages as fractions with a denominator of 100. In fact, **percentage** means "per hundred." Problems often require converting numbers from percentages, fractions, and decimals.

The basic percent equation is the following:

$$\frac{is}{of} = \frac{\%}{100}$$

The placement of numbers in the equation depends on what the question asks.

Example 1

Find 40% of 80.

Basically, the problem is asking, "What is 40% of 80?" The 40% is the percent, and 80 is the number to find the percent "of." The equation is:

$$\frac{x}{80} = \frac{40}{100}$$

Solving the equation by cross-multiplication, the problem becomes 100x = 80(40). Solving for x gives the answer: x = 32.

Example 2
What percent of 90 is 20?

The 20 fills in the "is" portion, while 90 fills in the "of." The question asks for the percent, so that will be x, the unknown. The following equation is set up:

$$\frac{20}{90} = \frac{x}{100}$$

Cross-multiplying yields the equation 90x = 20(100). Solving for x gives the answer of 22.2%.

Example 3
30% of what number is 30?

The following equation uses the clues and numbers in the problem:

$$\frac{30}{x} = \frac{30}{100}$$

Cross-multiplying results in the equation 30(100) = 30x. Solving for x gives the answer x = 100.

Conversions

Decimals and Percentages

Since a percentage is based on "per hundred," decimals and percentages can be converted by multiplying or dividing by 100. Practically speaking, this always involves moving the decimal point two places to the right or left, depending on the conversion. To convert a percentage to a decimal, move the decimal point two places to the left and remove the % sign. To convert a decimal to a percentage, move the decimal point two places to the right and add a "%" sign. Here are some examples:

65% = 0.65
0.33 = 33%
0.215 = 21.5%
99.99% = 0.9999
500% = 5.00
7.55 = 755%

Fractions and Percentages

Remember that a percentage is a number per one hundred. So a percentage can be converted to a fraction by making the number in the percentage the numerator and putting 100 as the denominator:

$$43\% = \frac{43}{100}$$

$$97\% = \frac{97}{100}$$

Note that the percent symbol (%) kind of looks like a 0, a 1, and another 0. So, think of a percentage like 54% as 54 over 100.

To convert a fraction to a percent, follow the same logic. If the fraction happens to have 100 in the denominator, you're in luck. Just take the numerator and add a percent symbol:

$$\frac{28}{100} = 28\%$$

Otherwise, divide the numerator by the denominator to get a decimal:

$$\frac{9}{12} = 0.75$$

Then convert the decimal to a percentage:

$$0.75 = 75\%$$

Another option is to make the denominator equal to 100. Be sure to multiply the numerator by the same number as the denominator. For example:

$$\frac{3}{20} \times \frac{5}{5} = \frac{15}{100}$$

$$\frac{15}{100} = 15\%$$

Changing Fractions to Decimals

To change a fraction into a decimal, divide the denominator into the numerator until there are no remainders. There may be repeating decimals, so rounding is often acceptable. A straight line above the repeating portion denotes that the decimal repeats.

Example: Express 4/5 as a decimal.

Set up the division problem.

$$5\overline{)4}$$

5 does not go into 4, so place the decimal and add a zero.

$$5\overline{)4.0}$$

5 goes into 40 eight times. There is no remainder.

$$\begin{array}{r} 0.8 \\ 5\overline{)4.0} \\ -\ 4.0 \\ \hline 0 \end{array}$$

The solution is 0.8.

Example: Express 33 1/3 as a decimal.

Since the whole portion of the number is known, set it aside to calculate the decimal from the fraction portion.

Set up the division problem.

$$3\overline{)1}$$

3 does not go into 1, so place the decimal and add zeros. 3 goes into 10 three times.

$$\begin{array}{r} 0.3 \\ 3\overline{)1.0} \end{array}$$

This will repeat with a remainder of 1.

$$\begin{array}{r} 0.333 \\ 3\overline{)1.000} \\ \underline{-9} \\ 10 \\ \underline{-9} \\ 10 \end{array}$$

So, we will place a line over the 3 to denote the repetition. The solution is written $0.\overline{3}$.

Changing Decimals to Fractions

To change decimals to fractions, place the decimal portion of the number—the numerator—over the respective place value—the denominator—then reduce, if possible.

Example: Express 0.25 as a fraction.

This is read as twenty-five hundredths, so put 25 over 100. Then reduce to find the solution.

$$\frac{25}{100} = \frac{1}{4}$$

Example: Express 0.455 as a fraction

This is read as four hundred fifty-five thousandths, so put 455 over 1000. Then reduce to find the solution.

$$\frac{455}{1000} = \frac{91}{200}$$

There are two types of problems that commonly involve percentages. The first is to calculate some percentage of a given quantity, where you convert the percentage to a decimal, and multiply the quantity by that decimal. Secondly, you are given a quantity and told it is a fixed percent of an unknown quantity. In this case, convert to a decimal, then divide the given quantity by that decimal.

Example: What is 30% of 760?

Convert the percent into a useable number. "Of" means to multiply.

$$30\% = 0.30$$

Set up the problem based on the givens, and solve.

$$0.30 \times 760 = 228$$

Example: 8.4 is 20% of what number?

Convert the percent into a useable number.

$$20\% = 0.20$$

The given number is a percent of the answer needed, so divide the given number by this decimal rather than multiplying it.

$$\frac{8.4}{0.20} = 42$$

Representing Fractions

A **fraction** is a part of something that is whole. Items such as apples can be cut into parts to help visualize fractions. If an apple is cut into 2 equal parts, each part represents ½ of the apple. If each half is cut into two parts, the apple now is cut into quarters. Each piece now represents ¼ of the apple. In this example, each part is equal because they all have the same size. Geometric shapes, such as circles and squares, can also be utilized in the classroom to help visualize the idea of fractions.

For example, a circle can be drawn on the board and divided into 6 equal parts:

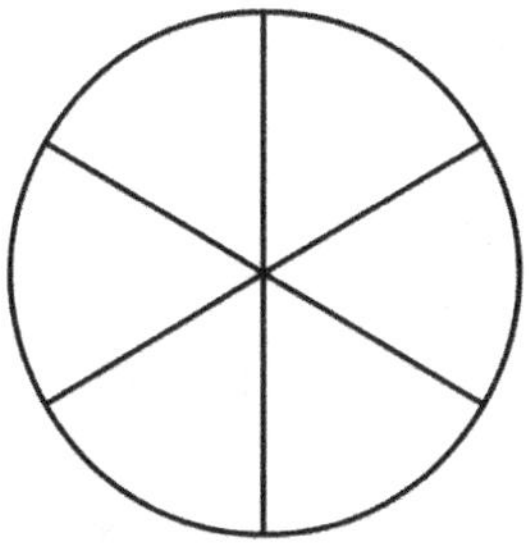

Shading can be used to represent parts of the circle that can be translated into fractions. The top of the fraction, the **numerator,** can represent how many segments are shaded. The bottom of the fraction, the **denominator,** can represent the number of segments that the circle is broken into. A pie is a good analogy to use in this example. If one piece of the circle is shaded, or one piece of pie is cut out, $^1/_6$ of the object is being referred to. An apple, a pie, or a circle can be utilized in order to compare simple fractions. It's also beneficial to view a shape before and after it is shaded, to demonstrate the variation in the entire shape; this helps in understanding the representation of the size of different fractions.

A **unit fraction** is a fraction in which the numerator is 1, and the denominator is a positive whole number. It represents one part of a whole—one piece of pie. A unit fraction is sometimes symbolized mathematically by $1/b$, where *b* can be any positive or negative number (called an **integer**). For now, it makes sense to just consider positive whole numbers like 2, 3, 4, or 10. Examples of unit fractions are $\frac{1}{2}$ or $\frac{1}{8}$. Essentially, a unit fraction is a fraction in which the numerator is 1, and the denominator is a positive whole number. It represents one part of a whole—one piece of pie.

When shading in a unit fraction, just one piece gets filled in. However, not all fractions are unit fractions. What happens when more than one piece is desired? For example, a week has seven days so the unit fraction—what each day represents mathematically—is $\frac{1}{7}$. But what happens when you want to express how many days a week you go to school? If, like most students, you go to school on Monday, Tuesday, Wednesday, Thursday, and Friday, you attend school 5 days a week or $\frac{5}{7}$ of the week. A fraction a/b, like $\frac{5}{7}$, is a multiple of the unit fraction 1/b, or in this case, $\frac{1}{7}$. It is 5 times the unit fraction. Written as an equation, $\frac{5}{7} = 5 \times \frac{1}{7}$.

Let's look at some representations of multiples of unit fractions. For example, Marion's parents said she could eat 2 out of 6 pieces of a small pizza. How could this be illustrated by shading the following figure? What fraction of the pizza is Marion allowed to eat?

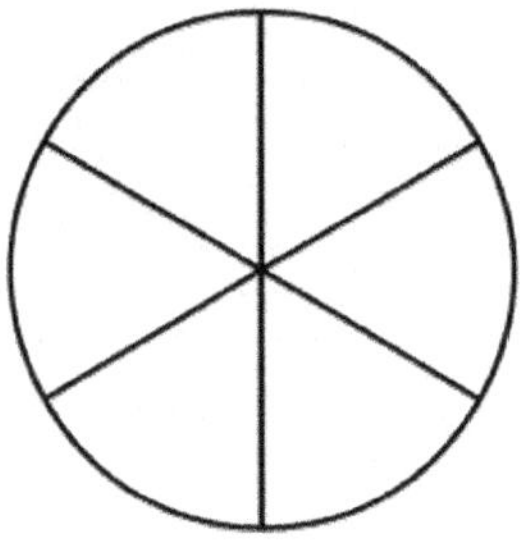

Solution:

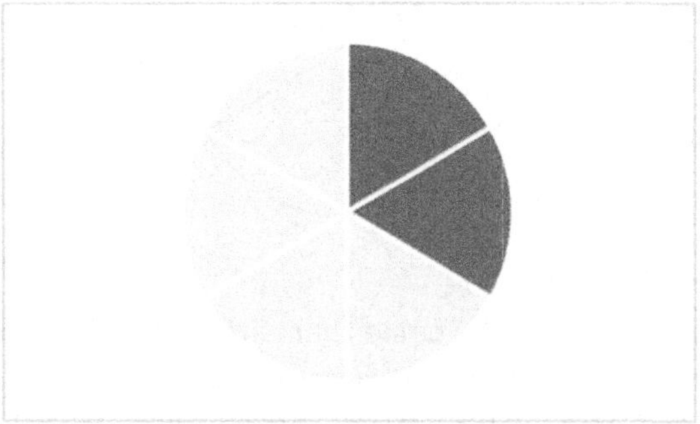

As seen in the solution, 2 out of the 6 total pieces are shaded, which represents $\frac{1}{3}$ of the entire pizza.

In another example, Marty wants to shade $\frac{3}{4}$ of this strip. How would this be represented?

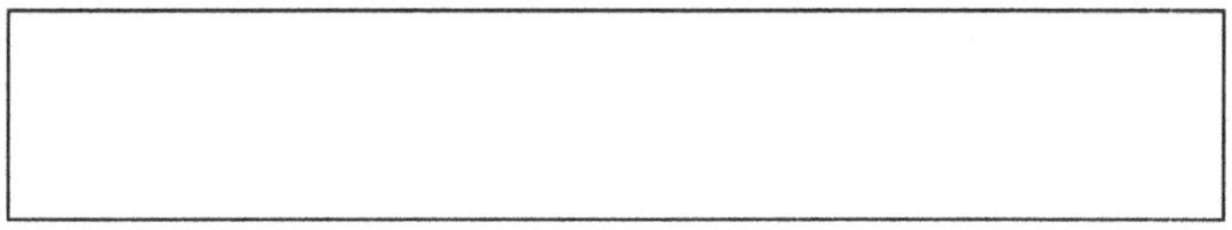

In order to show this, Marty would need to divide the strip up into 4 equal parts, and then shade 3 of those 4 parts, as follows:

This shading represents the fraction $\frac{3}{4}$.

When representing fractions, it is important to remember the meaning of the word *fraction*. The number is a fraction, or portion, of a whole. The whole, or 1, is the number on the bottom part of the fraction, the denominator. For example, the fraction $\frac{2}{5}$ represents a number of portions (the numerator, 2) of how many it would take to make a whole (the denominator, 5). So, $\frac{2}{5}$ represents 2 portions out of the 5 it would take to make a whole.

This could also be represented with blocks, as follows:

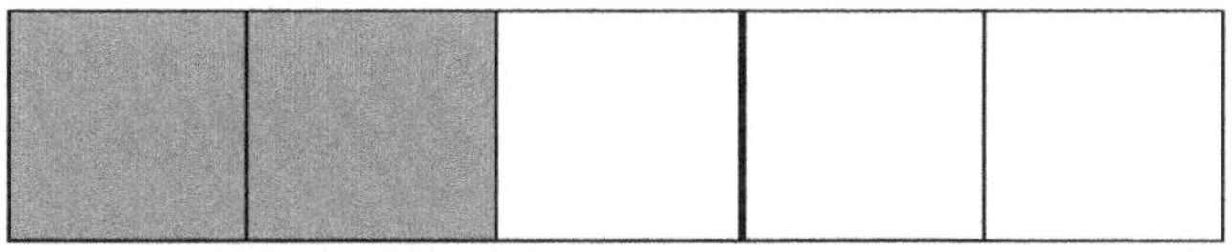

5 blocks = 1 whole, so only 2 of the 5 are shaded.

This method could also be used to represent fractions with a higher number in the numerator than in the denominator.

What does the fraction $\frac{6}{5}$ look like with the block method?

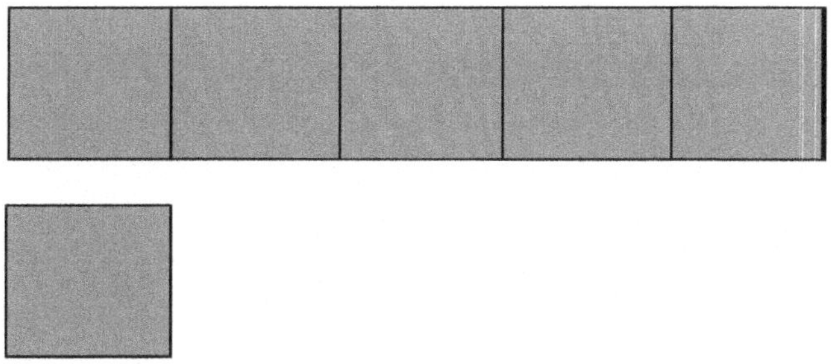

To represent fractions and decimals as distances beginning at zero on a number line, it's helpful to relate the fraction to a real-world application. For example, a charity walk covers $\frac{3}{10}$ of a mile. How could this distance be represented on a number line?

First, divide the number line into tenths, as follows:

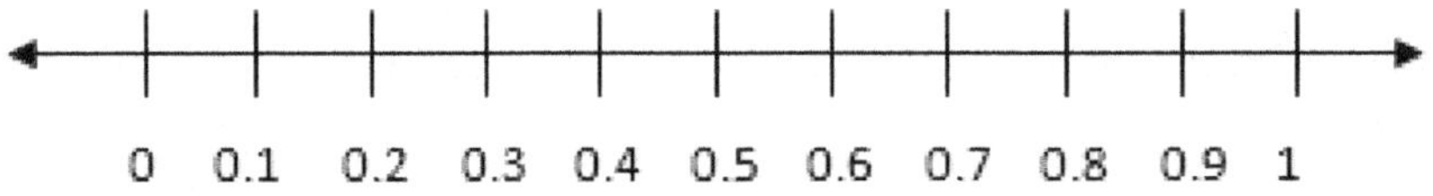

If each division on the number line represents one-tenth of one, or $\frac{1}{10}$, then representing the distance of the charity walk, $\frac{3}{10}$, would cover 3 of those divisions and look as follows:

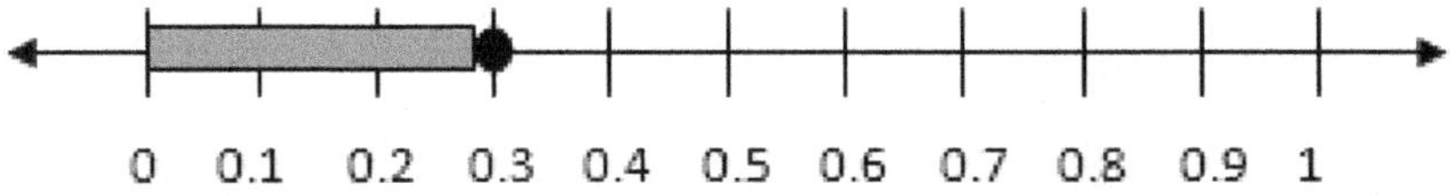

So, the fraction $\frac{3}{10}$ is represented by covering from 0 to 0.3 (or 3 sections) on the number line.

Like fractions, or **equivalent fractions**, represent two fractions that are made up of different numbers, but represent the same quantity. For example, the given fractions are $^4/_8$ and $^3/_6$. If a pie was cut into 8 pieces and 4 pieces were removed, half of the pie would remain. Also, if a pie was split into 6 pieces and 3 pieces were eaten, half of the pie would also remain. Therefore, both of the fractions represent half of a pie. These two fractions are referred to as like fractions. **Unlike fractions** are fractions that are different and cannot be thought of as representing equal quantities. When working with fractions in mathematical expressions, like fractions should be simplified. Both $^4/_8$ and $^3/_6$ can be simplified into $^1/_2$.

Comparing fractions can be completed through the use of a number line. For example, if $\frac{3}{5}$ and $\frac{6}{10}$ need to be compared, each fraction should be plotted on a number line. To plot $\frac{3}{5}$, the area from 0 to 1 should be broken into 5 equal segments, and the fraction represents 3 of them. To plot $\frac{4}{10}$, the area from 0 to 1 should be broken into 10 equal segments and the fraction represents 6 of them.

It can be seen that $\frac{3}{5} = \frac{6}{10}$

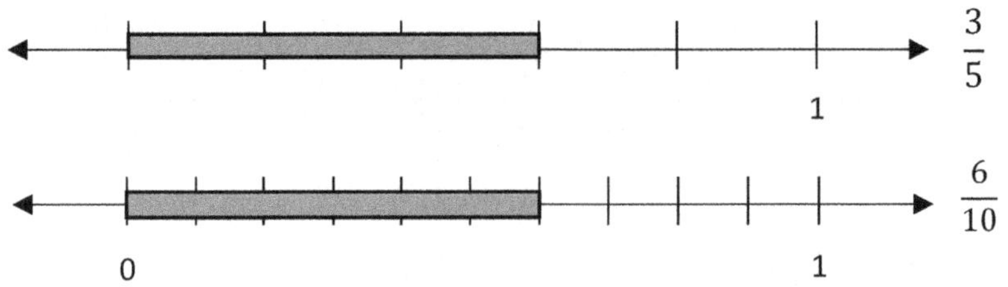

Like fractions are plotted at the same point on a number line.

Solving Real-World Problems Involving Ratios and Proportions

Ratios are used to show the relationship between two quantities. The ratio of oranges to apples in the grocery store may be 3 to 2. That means that for every 3 oranges, there are 2 apples. This comparison can be expanded to represent the actual number of oranges and apples. Another example may be the number of boys to girls in a math class. If the ration of boys to girls is given as 2 to 5, that means there are 2 boys to every 5 girls in the class. Ratios can also be compared if the units in each ratio are the same. The ratio of boys to girls in the math class can be compared to the ratio of boys to girls in a science class by stating which ratio is higher and which is lower.

Rates are used to compare two quantities with different units. **Unit rates** are the simplest form of rate. With unit rates, the denominator in the comparison of two units is one. For example, if someone can type at a rate of 1000 words in 5 minutes, then his or her unit rate for typing is $\frac{1000}{5} = 200$ words in one minute or 200 words per minute. Any rate can be converted into a unit rate by dividing to make the denominator one. 1000 words in 5 minutes has been converted into the unit rate of 200 words per minute.

Computing Unit Rates

Unit rate word problems will ask to calculate the rate or quantity of something in a different value. For example, a problem might say that a car drove a certain number of miles in a certain number of minutes and then ask how many miles per hour the car was traveling. These questions involve solving proportions. Consider the following examples:

1) Alexandra made $96 during the first 3 hours of her shift as a temporary worker at a law office. She will continue to earn money at this rate until she finishes in 5 more hours. How much does Alexandra make per hour? How much will Alexandra have made at the end of the day?

This problem can be solved in two ways. The first is to set up a proportion, as the rate of pay is constant. The second is to determine her hourly rate, multiply the 5 hours by that rate, and then add the $96.

To set up a proportion, put the money already earned over the hours already worked on one side of an equation. The other side has x over 8 hours (the total hours worked in the day). It looks like this: $\frac{96}{3} = \frac{x}{8}$. Now, cross-multiply to get $768 = 3x$. To get x, divide by 3, which leaves $x = 256$. Alternatively, as x is the numerator of one of the proportions, multiplying by its denominator will reduce the solution by one step. Thus, Alexandra will make $256 at the end of the day. To calculate her hourly rate, divide the total by 8, giving $32 per hour.

Alternatively, it is possible to figure out the hourly rate by dividing $96 by 3 hours to get $32 per hour. Now her total pay can be figured by multiplying $32 per hour by 8 hours, which comes out to $256.

2) Jonathan is reading a novel. So far, he has read 215 of the 335 total pages. It takes Jonathan 25 minutes to read 10 pages, and the rate is constant. How long does it take Jonathan to read one page? How much longer will it take him to finish the novel? Express the answer in time.

To calculate how long it takes Jonathan to read one page, divide the 25 minutes by 10 pages to determine the page per minute rate. Thus, it takes 2.5 minutes to read one page.

Jonathan must read 120 more pages to complete the novel. (This is calculated by subtracting the pages already read from the total.) Now, multiply his rate per page by the number of pages. Thus, $120 \times 2.5 = 300$. Expressed in time, 300 minutes is equal to 5 hours.

3) At a hotel, $\frac{4}{5}$ of the 120 rooms are booked for Saturday. On Sunday, $\frac{3}{4}$ of the rooms are booked. On which day are more of the rooms booked, and by how many more?

The first step is to calculate the number of rooms booked for each day. Do this by multiplying the fraction of the rooms booked by the total number of rooms.

Saturday: $\frac{4}{5} \times 120 = \frac{4}{5} \times \frac{120}{1} = \frac{480}{5} = 96$ rooms

Sunday: $\frac{3}{4} \times 120 = \frac{3}{4} \times \frac{120}{1} = \frac{360}{4} = 90$ rooms

Thus, more rooms were booked on Saturday by 6 rooms.

4) In a veterinary hospital, the veterinarian-to-pet ratio is 1:9. The ratio is always constant. If there are 45 pets in the hospital, how many veterinarians are currently in the veterinary hospital?

Set up a proportion to solve for the number of veterinarians: $\frac{1}{9} = \frac{x}{45}$

Cross-multiplying results in $9x = 45$, which works out to 5 veterinarians.

Alternatively, as there are always 9 times as many pets as veterinarians, is it possible to divide the number of pets (45) by 9. This also arrives at the correct answer of 5 veterinarians.

5) At a general practice law firm, 30% of the lawyers work solely on tort cases. If 9 lawyers work solely on tort cases, how many lawyers work at the firm?

First, solve for the total number of lawyers working at the firm, which will be represented here with x. The problem states that 9 lawyers work solely on torts cases, and they make up 30% of the total lawyers at the firm. Thus, 30% multiplied by the total, x, will equal 9. Written as equation, this is: $30\% \times x = 9$.

It's easier to deal with the equation after converting the percentage to a decimal, leaving $0.3x = 9$. Thus, $x = \frac{9}{0.3} = 30$ lawyers working at the firm.

6) Xavier was hospitalized with pneumonia. He was originally given 35mg of antibiotics. Later, after his condition continued to worsen, Xavier's dosage was increased to 60mg. What was the percent increase of the antibiotics? Round the percentage to the nearest tenth.

An increase or decrease in percentage can be calculated by dividing the difference in amounts by the original amount and multiplying by 100. Written as an equation, the formula is:

$$\frac{new\ quantity - old\ quantity}{old\ quantity} \times 100$$

Here, the question states that the dosage was increased from 35mg to 60mg, so these are plugged into the formula to find the percentage increase.

$$\frac{60 - 35}{35} \times 100 = \frac{25}{35} \times 100 = .7142 \times 100 = 71.4\%$$

Using Ratio Reasoning to Convert Rates

Ratios and rates can be used together to convert rates into different units. For example, if someone is driving 50 kilometers per hour, that rate can be converted into miles per hour by using a ratio known as the **conversion factor**. Since the given value contains kilometers and the final answer needs to be in miles, the ratio relating miles to kilometers needs to be used. There are 0.62 miles in 1 kilometer. This, written as a ratio and in fraction form, is $\frac{0.62\ miles}{1\ km}$. To convert 50km/hour into miles per hour, the following conversion needs to be set up:

$$\frac{50\ km}{hour} \times \frac{0.62\ miles}{1\ km} = 31\ miles\ per\ hour$$

Proportional Relationships

Much like a scale factor can be written using an equation like $2A = B$, a **relationship** is represented by the equation $Y = kX$. X and Y are **proportional** because as values of X increase, the values of Y also increase. A relationship that is **inversely proportional** can be represented by the equation $Y = \frac{k}{X}$, where the value of Y decreases as the value of x increases and vice versa.

Proportional reasoning can be used to solve problems involving ratios, percentages, and averages. Ratios can be used in setting up proportions and solving them to find unknowns. For example, if a student completes an average of 10 pages of math homework in 3 nights, how long would it take the student to complete 22 pages? Both ratios can be written as fractions. The second ratio would contain the unknown.

The following proportion represents this problem, where x is the unknown number of nights:

$$\frac{10\ pages}{3\ nights} = \frac{22\ pages}{x\ nights}$$

Solving this proportion entails cross-multiplying and results in the following equation: $10x = 22 \times 3$. Simplifying and solving for x results in the exact solution: $x = 6.6\ nights$. The result would be rounded up to 7 because the homework would actually be completed on the 7th night.

The following problem uses ratios involving percentages:

If 20% of the class is girls and 30 students are in the class, how many girls are in the class?

To set up this problem, it is helpful to use the common proportion: $\frac{\%}{100} = \frac{is}{of}$. Within the proportion, % is the percentage of girls, 100 is the total percentage of the class, *is* is the number of girls, and *of* is the total number of students in the class. Most percentage problems can be written using this language. To solve this problem, the proportion should be set up as $\frac{20}{100} = \frac{x}{30}$, and then solved for x. Cross-multiplying results in the equation $20 \times 30 = 100x$, which results in the solution $x = 6$. There are 6 girls in the class.

Problems involving volume, length, and other units can also be solved using ratios. For example, a problem may ask for the volume of a cone to be found that has a radius, $r = 7m$ and a height, $h = 16m$. Referring to the formulas provided on the test, the volume of a cone is given as:

$$V = \pi r^2 \frac{h}{3}$$

where r is the radius, and h is the height. Plugging $r = 7$ and $h = 16$ into the formula, the following is obtained:

$$V = \pi(7^2)\frac{16}{3}$$

Therefore, volume of the cone is found to be approximately 821m^3. Sometimes, answers in different units are sought. If this problem wanted the answer in liters, 821m^3 would need to be converted. Using the equivalence statement 1m^3 = 1000L, the following ratio would be used to solve for liters:

$$821\text{m}^3 \times \frac{1000L}{1m^3}$$

Cubic meters in the numerator and denominator cancel each other out, and the answer is converted to 821,000 liters, or 8.21×10^5 L.

Other conversions can also be made between different given and final units. If the temperature in a pool is 30°C, what is the temperature of the pool in degrees Fahrenheit? To convert these units, an equation is used relating Celsius to Fahrenheit. The following equation is used:

$$T_{°F} = 1.8T_{°C} + 32$$

Plugging in the given temperature and solving the equation for T yields the result:

$$T_{°F} = 1.8(30) + 32 = 86°F$$

Both units in the metric system and U.S. customary system are widely used.

Here are some more examples of how to solve for proportions:

1) $\frac{75\%}{90\%} = \frac{25\%}{x}$

To solve for x, the fractions must be cross multiplied: $(75\%x = 90\% \times 25\%)$. To make things easier, let's convert the percentages to decimals: $(0.9 \times 0.25 = 0.225 = 0.75x)$. To get rid of x's co-efficient, each side must be divided by that same coefficient to get the answer $x = 0.3$. The question could ask for the answer as a percentage or fraction in lowest terms, which are 30% and $\frac{3}{10}$, respectively.

2) $\frac{x}{12} = \frac{30}{96}$

Cross-multiply: $96x = 30 \times 12$

Multiply: $96x = 360$

Divide: $x = 360 \div 96$

Answer: $x = 3.75$

3) $\frac{0.5}{3} = \frac{x}{6}$

Cross-multiply: $3x = 0.5 \times 6$

Multiply: $3x = 3$

Divide: $x = 3 \div 3$

Answer: $x = 1$

You may have noticed there's a faster way to arrive at the answer. If there is an obvious operation being performed on the proportion, the same operation can be used on the other side of the proportion to solve for x. For example, in the first practice problem, 75% became 25% when divided by 3, and upon doing the same to 90%, the correct answer of 30% would have been found with much less legwork. However, these questions aren't always so intuitive, so it's a good idea to work through the steps, even if the answer seems apparent from the outset.

Solving Ratio and Percent Problems

Questions dealing with percentages can be difficult when they are phrased as word problems. These word problems almost always come in three varieties. The first type will ask to find what percentage of some number will equal another number. The second asks to determine what number is some percentage of another given number. The third will ask what number another number is a given percentage of.

One of the most important parts of correctly answering percentage word problems is to identify the numerator and the denominator. This fraction can then be converted into a percentage, as described above.

The following word problem shows how to make this conversion:

A department store carries several different types of footwear. The store is currently selling 8 athletic shoes, 7 dress shoes, and 5 sandals. What percentage of the store's footwear are sandals?

First, calculate what serves as the 'whole', as this will be the denominator. How many total pieces of footwear does the store sell? The store sells 20 different types (8 athletic + 7 dress + 5 sandals).

Second, what footwear type is the question specifically asking about? Sandals. Thus, 5 is the numerator.

Third, the resultant fraction must be expressed as a percentage. The first two steps indicate that $\frac{5}{20}$ of the footwear pieces are sandals. This fraction must now be converted into a percentage:

$$\frac{5}{20} \times \frac{5}{5} = \frac{25}{100} = 25\%$$

Measurement, Data, and Statistics

Statistics of Variability and Central Tendency

A set of data can be described in terms of its center, spread, shape and any unusual features. The center of a data set can be measured by its mean, median, or mode. The spread, or variability, of a data set refers to how far the data points are from the center (mean or median). The spread can be measured by the range or the quartiles and interquartile range. A data set with data points clustered around the center will have a small spread. A data set covering a wide range will have a large spread.

When a data set is displayed as a **histogram** or frequency distribution plot, the shape indicates if a sample is normally distributed, symmetrical, or has measures of skewness or kurtosis.

When graphed, a data set with a **normal distribution** will resemble a bell curve.

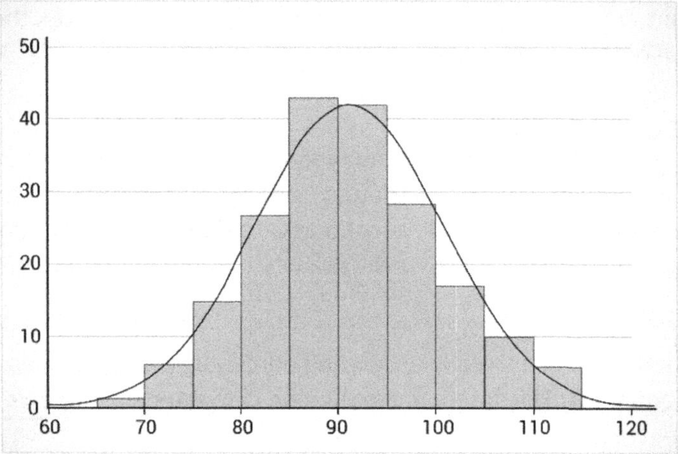

If the data set is symmetrical, each half of the graph when divided at the center is a mirror image of the other. If the graph has fewer data points to the right, the data is **skewed right**. If it has fewer data points to the left, the data is **skewed left**.

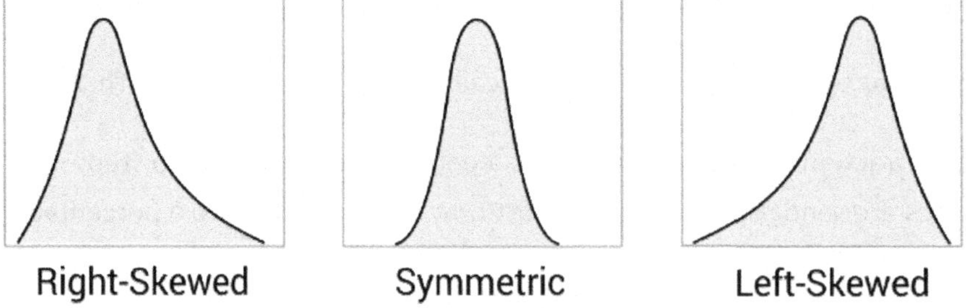

Kurtosis is a measure of whether the data is heavy-tailed with a high number of outliers, or light-tailed with a low number of outliers.

A description of a data set should include any unusual features such as gaps or outliers. A **gap** is a span within the range of the data set containing no data points. An **outlier** is a data point with a value either extremely large or extremely small when compared to the other values in the set.

The **range** of a data set is the difference between the highest and the lowest values in the set. The range can be considered to be the span of the data set. To determine the range, the smallest value in the set is subtracted from the largest value. The ranges for the data sets A, B, and C above are calculated as follows: A: $14 - 7 = 7$; B: $51 - 33 = 18$; C: $173 - 151 = 22$.

The **center** of a set of data (statistical values) can be represented by its mean, median, or mode. These are sometimes referred to as **measures of central tendency**.

Mean

Suppose that you have a set of data points and some description of the general properties of this data need to be found.

The first property that can be defined for this set of data is the **mean**. This is the same as average. To find the mean, add up all the data points, then divide by the total number of data points. For example, suppose that in a class of 10 students, the scores on a test were 50, 60, 65, 65, 75, 80, 85, 85, 90, 100. Therefore, the average test score will be:

$$\frac{50 + 60 + 65 + 65 + 75 + 80 + 85 + 85 + 90 + 100}{10} = 75.5$$

The mean is a useful number if the distribution of data is normal (more on this later), which roughly means that the frequency of different outcomes has a single peak and is roughly equally distributed on both sides of that peak. However, it is less useful in some cases where the data might be split or where there are some **outliers**. Outliers are data points that are far from the rest of the data. For example, suppose there are 10 executives and 90 employees at a company. The executives make $1000 per hour, and the employees make $10 per hour.

Therefore, the average pay rate will be:

$$\frac{\$1000 \times 10 + \$10 \times 90}{100} = \$109 \text{ per hour}$$

In this case, this average is not very descriptive since it's not close to the actual pay of the executives or the employees.

Median

Another useful measurement is the **median**. In a data set, the median is the point in the middle. The middle refers to the point where half the data comes before it and half comes after, when the data is recorded in numerical order. For instance, these are the speeds of the fastball of a pitcher during the last inning that he pitched (in order from least to greatest):

90, 92, 93, 93, 95, 96, 97, 97, 97

There are nine total numbers, so the middle or median number in the 5th one, which is 95.

In cases where the number of data points is an even number, then the average of the two middle points is taken. In the previous example of test scores, the two middle points are 75 and 80. Since there is no single point, the average of these two scores needs to be found. The average is:

$$\frac{75+80}{2} = 77.5$$

The median is generally a good value to use if there are a few outliers in the data. It prevents those outliers from affecting the "middle" value as much as when using the mean.

Since an outlier is a data point that is far from most of the other data points in a data set, this means an outlier also is any point that is far from the median of the data set. The outliers can have a substantial effect on the mean of a data set, but usually do not change the median or mode, or do not change them by a large quantity. For example, consider the data set (3, 5, 6, 6, 6, 8). This has a median of 6 and a mode of 6, with a mean of $\frac{34}{6} \approx 5.67$. Now, suppose a new data point of 1000 is added so that the data set is now (3, 5, 6, 6, 6, 8, 1000). This does not change the median or mode, which are both still 6. However, the average is now $\frac{1034}{7}$, which is approximately 147.7. In this case, the median and mode will be better descriptions for most of the data points.

The reason for outliers in a given data set is a complicated problem. It is sometimes the result of an error by the experimenter, but often they are perfectly valid data points that must be taken into consideration.

Mode

One additional measure to define for *X* is the **mode.** This is the data point that appears most frequently. If two or more data points all tie for the most frequent appearance, then each of them is considered a mode. In the case of the test scores, where the numbers were 50, 60, 65, 65, 75, 80, 85, 85, 90, 100, there are two modes: 65 and 85.

A data set may have a single mode, multiple modes, or no mode. If different values repeat equally as often, multiple modes exist. If no value repeats, no mode exists. Consider the following data sets:

- A: 7, 9, 10, 13, 14, 14
- B: 37, 44, 33, 37, 49, 44, 51, 34, 37, 33, 44
- C: 173, 154, 151, 168, 155

Set A has a mode of 14. Set B has modes of 37 and 44. Set C has no mode.

The range of a data set is the difference between the highest and the lowest values in the set. The range can be considered the span of the data set. To determine the range, the smallest value in the set is subtracted from the largest value. The ranges for the data sets A, B, and C above are calculated as follows: A: $14 - 7 = 7$; B: $51 - 33 = 18$; C: $173 - 151 = 22$.

Changing all values of a data set in a consistent way produces predictable changes in the measures of the center and range of the set. A linear transformation changes the original value into the new value by either adding a given number to each value, multiplying each value by a given number, or both. Adding (or subtracting) a given value to each data point will increase (or decrease) the mean, median, and any modes by the same value. However, the range will remain the same due to the way that range is calculated. Multiplying (or dividing) a given value by each data point will increase (or decrease) the mean, median, and any modes, and the range by the same factor.

Consider the following data set, call it set *P*, representing the price of different cases of soda at a grocery store:

$4.25, $4.40, $4.75, $4.95, $4.95, $5.15

The mean of set *P* is $4.74. The median is $4.85. The mode of the set is $4.95. The range is $0.90. Suppose the state passes a new tax of $0.25 on every case of soda sold. The new data set, set *T*, is calculated by adding $0.25 to each data point from set *P*. Therefore, set *T* consists of the following values: $4.50, $4.65, $5.00, $5.20, $5.20, $5.40. The mean of set *T* is $4.99. The median is $5.10. The mode of the set is $5.20. The range is $.90. The mean, median and mode of set *T* is equal to $0.25 added to the mean, median, and mode of set *P*. The range stays the same.

Now suppose, due to inflation, the store raises the cost of every item by 10 percent. Raising costs by 10 percent is calculated by multiplying each value by 1.1. The new data set, set *I*, is calculated by multiplying each data point from set *T* by 1.1. Therefore, set *I* consists of the following values: $4.95, $5.12, $5.50, $5.72, $5.72, $5.94. The mean of set *I* is $5.49. The median is $5.61. The mode of the set is $5.72. The range is $0.99. The mean, median, mode, and range of set *I* is equal to 1.1 multiplied by the mean, median, mode, and range of set *T* because each increased by a factor of 10 percent.

Analyzing and Interpreting Data Through the Use of Frequency Tables and Graphs

A set of data can be visually displayed in various forms allowing for quick identification of characteristics of the set. **Histograms**, such as the one shown below, display the number of data points (vertical axis) that fall into given intervals (horizontal axis) across the range of the set. Suppose the histogram below displays IQ scores of students. Each rectangle represents the number of students with scores between a given ten-point span. For example, the furthest bar to the right indicates that two trees are 90 feet tall. Histograms can describe the center, spread, shape, and any unusual characteristics of a data set.

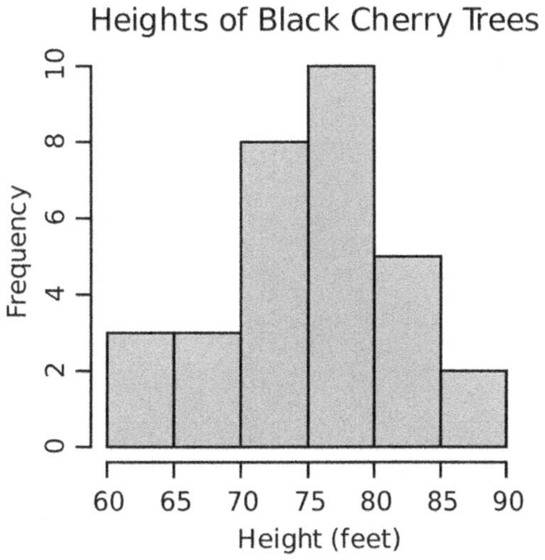

A **picture graph** is a diagram that shows pictorial representation of data being discussed. The symbols utilized can represent the quantity of the objects being discussed. By using the key, it should be determined that each fruit symbol in the following graph represents a count of two fruits. One drawback of picture graphs is that they can be less accurate if each symbol represents a large number.

For example, if each banana symbol represented ten bananas, and students consumed 22 bananas, it may be challenging to draw and interpret two and one-fifth bananas as a frequency count of 22.

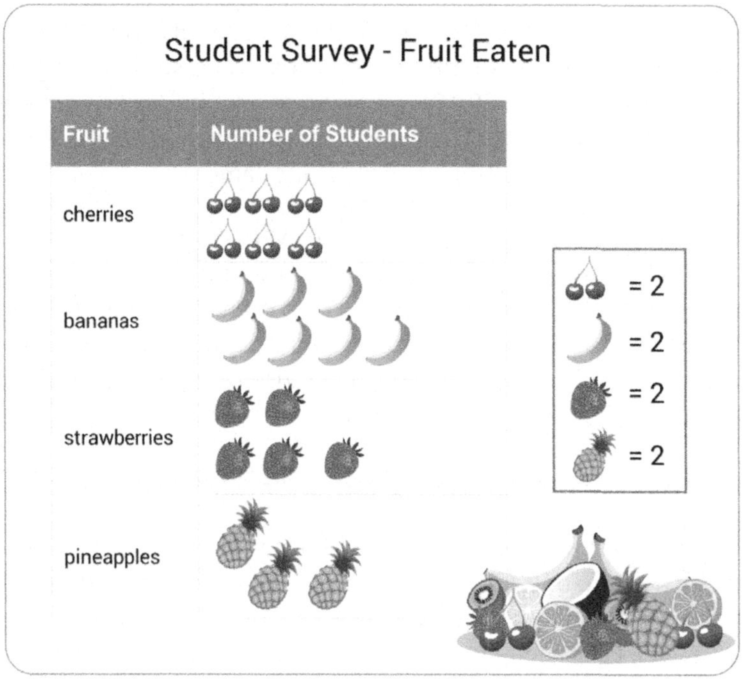

A **bar graph** is a diagram in which the quantity of items within a specific classification is represented by the height of a rectangle. Each type of classification is represented by a rectangle of equal width. Here is an example of a bar graph:

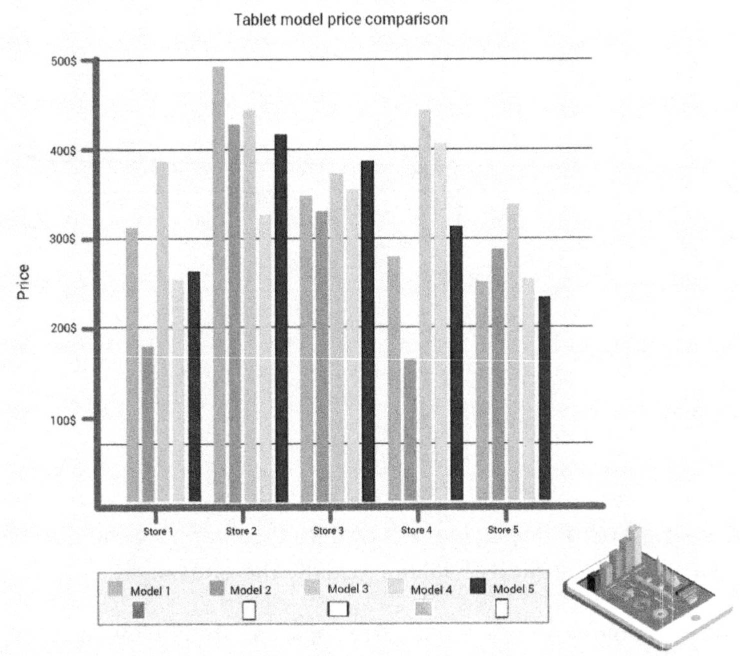

A **circle graph**, also called a **pie chart**, shows categorical data with each category representing a percentage of the whole data set. To make a circle graph, the percent of the data set for each category must be determined. To do so, the frequency of the category is divided by the total number of data points and converted to a percent. For example, if 80 people were asked what their favorite sport is and 20 responded basketball, basketball makes up 25% of the data ($\frac{20}{80}$ =.25=25%). Each category in a data set is represented by a **slice** of the circle proportionate to its percentage of the whole.

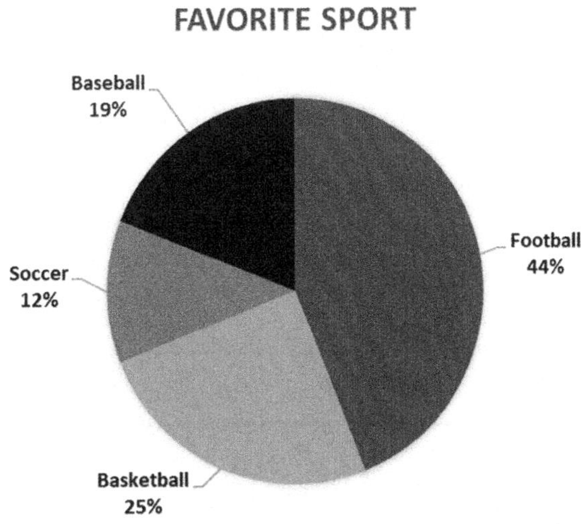

A **line plot**, also called **dot plot**, displays the frequency of data (numerical values) on a number line. To construct a line plot, a number line is used that includes all unique data values. It is marked with x's or dots above the value the number of times that the value occurs in the data set.

A **stem-and-leaf plot** is a method of displaying sets of data by organizing the numbers by their stems (usually the tens digit) and the different leaf values (usually the ones digit).

For example, to organize a number of movie critic's ratings, as listed below, a stem and leaf plot could be utilized to display the information in a more condensed manner.

Movie critic scores: 47, 52, 56, 59, 61, 64, 66, 68, 68, 70, 73, 75, 79, 81, 83, 85, 86, 88, 88, 89, 90, 90, 91, 93, 94, 96, 96, 99.

	Movie Ratings
4	7
5	2 6 9
6	1 4 6 8 8
7	0 3 5 9
8	1 3 5 6 8 8 9
9	0 0 1 3 4 6 6 9
Key	6 | 1 represents 61

Looking at this stem and leaf plot, it is easy to ascertain key features of the data set. For example, what is the range of the data in the stem-and-leaf plot?

Using this method, it is easier to visualize the distribution of the scores and answer the question pertaining to the range of scores, which is $99 - 47 = 52$.

Another way to represent data is with a **frequency table**. These can display the number of times specific answers are given, in order to provide a clearer overall picture of information. The following is the data representing the scores gathered on a patient satisfaction survey, visualized on a frequency dot table.

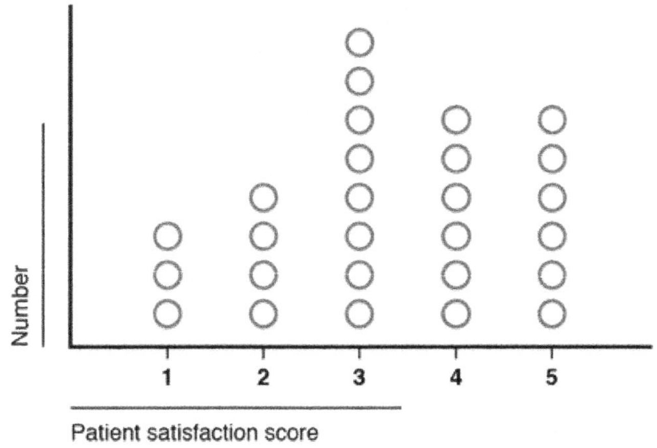

It is clear that the majority of the scores are in the middle, and higher at 2.0 and 2.5.

A **tally chart** is a diagram in which tally marks are utilized to represent data. Tally marks are a means of showing a quantity of objects within a specific classification. Here is an example of a tally chart:

Number of days with rain	Number of weeks
0	||
1	𝍸
2	𝍸
3	𝍸
4	𝍸 𝍸 𝍸 ||||
5	𝍸 |
6	𝍸 |
7	||||

Data is often recorded using fractions, such as half a mile, and understanding fractions is critical because of their popular use in real-world applications. Also, it is extremely important to label values with their units when using data. For example, regarding length, the number 2 is meaningless unless it is attached to a unit. Writing 2 cm shows that the number refers to the length of an object.

Solving Problems Using Frequency Data

Multi-step problems can be solved using information displayed in a stem-and-leaf plot. For example, the following graph shows the data collected regarding snowfall on top of specific mountains in the Alps.

It can be used to answer the following questions regarding the data.

February		April
	0	2, 4, 9
8	1	
9, 5, 2	2	2, 4, 7, 8
6, 2	3	1, 3
9, 6, 2	4	0, 3, 6, 8, 9
8, 7, 6, 6, 5	5	0
4	6	2

On the left side, 6 |4 means 4.6 in. On the right side, 4 | 6 means 4.6 in.

1. Which month had the largest collective snowfall, February or April?
2. How much larger was this snowfall?
3. How many mountains reported more than 4.0 inches of snowfall in February?
4. What is the difference between the lowest reported snowfall in February and the lowest reported snowfall in April?
5. What was the total for the three highest snowfalls in April?

The solution involves adding up the total amount of snowfall in both months individually and finding that February reported more snowfall than April with a total of 64.5 inches. This total was more than the April snowfall by 12.7 inches. There are 9 data points that are higher than 4.0 inches in February. The lowest reported snowfall in February is 1.8 inches, and the lowest reported snowfall in April is 0.2 inches. The difference between the two points is 1.6 inches. The three highest snowfalls in April are 6.2, 5.0, and 4.9. The total of these is 16.1 inches.

Let's try another problem. This time, we will use the dot plot below:

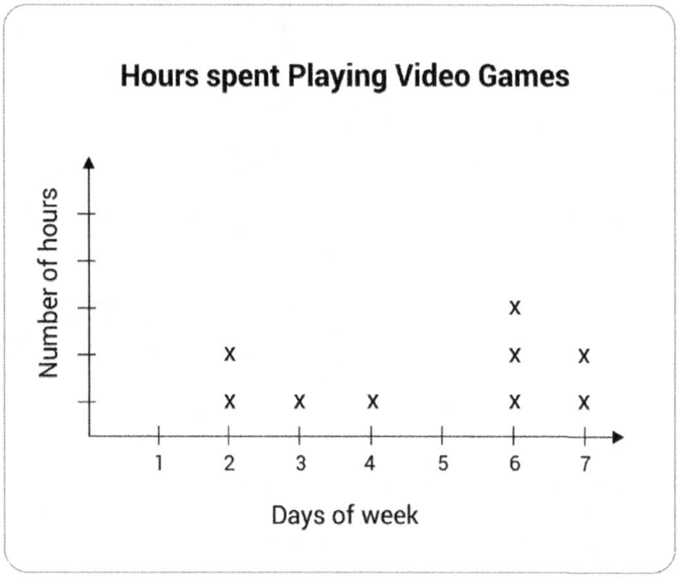

On which day of the week, did the person spend the most time playing video games?

By looking for the highest stack of x's, it can easily be seen that the most time was spent playing video games on the sixth day.

Selecting Appropriate Measurement Units to Solve Problems Involving Estimates and Measurements

Measurement is the process by which an object's length, width, height, weight, and so on, are quantified. Measurement is related to counting, but it is a more refined and descriptive process. At this point, students are aware of length, weight, temperature, and time, and it is up to the teacher to develop these skills further. It is also up to the teacher to move the understanding of measurement from a physical sense to a more theoretical sense. This process will ensure success in the real-world application problems that appear so frequently in mathematics classes, and it will ensure success in real-world situations in which measurement is required.

Identifying, Classifying, Describing, and Comparing the Measurable Attributes of Objects

The United States units of measure are utilized within these age ranges. Standard units of length are *inches*, *feet*, and *yards*. Weight units can vary, based on whether the substance being measured is a liquid or a solid. Standard units of weight to measure liquids include *ounces*, *pints*, *quarts*, and *gallons*. Occasionally, solids can also be measured using pints and quarts. For example, both milk and berries can be measured in pints. Other units of weight for solids are *pounds* and *tons*.

An introduction to the **metric system** is also important in this age group. Units of mass within the metric system are *milligrams*, *grams*, and *kilograms*. Units of volume within the metric system are *milliliters* and *liters*. Finally, units of length within the metric system are *centimeters*, *meters*, and *kilometers*. Some other measures that are important in real-life settings are found in baking terminology, such as *teaspoons*, *tablespoons*, and *cups*, and temperature measures in *Celsius* and *Fahrenheit*. All of these units can be used to compare two objects within the classroom. Conclusions can be made that state an item is taller or heavier than another object, for example. Making sure students can utilize the proper units in order to talk about measurements is crucial. They should also use the appropriate units when making measurements or estimates, for example, when discussing body weight, pounds or kilograms should be used, not ounces or grams.

Telling time is another important measurement and real-world application that needs to be introduced in this age group. Units of time such as *seconds, minutes*, *hours*, *days*, and *years*, etc., need to be familiarized. Again, measurements and estimates need to be in the correct units. For example, nightly sleep length should be measured or estimated in hours (not minutes), while the length of time needed to tie one's shoes is better represented by seconds. Clocks should be shown in the classroom, and the hour and minute hands should be used in order to tell the correct time. An analog clock can also help teach angle measurement.

Converting units within either the United States units of measure or the metric system is important in real-world application problems. It is important to make sure that all values are converted to the same units before any operations are performed. If two lengths are added that have different units, the answer would not make sense mathematically. Common length conversions within the U.S. system are that 1 foot is 12 inches, 1 yard is 3 feet, and 1 mile is 5,280 feet. Common length conversions within the metric system are that 1 centimeter is 10 millimeters, 1 meter is 100 centimeters, and 1 kilometer is

1,000 meters. In terms of volume, 1 liter is 1,000 milliliters. A meter stick is a good classroom tool to show students how to relate feet and meters.

There is a difference between an exact answer and an estimation. Sometimes answering a question with an estimate is good enough; however, an exact answer is often required. Also, using an estimate as a ballpark to tell if an exact answer is reasonable is sometimes a good technique to use as well. For example, consider the situation if a student has to buy lunch at school, and they only have $5 to do so. A sandwich is $2.29, a piece of fruit is $0.75, and a drink is $1.25. An estimate might be enough to tell if he or she had enough money. A good estimate would be to round each cost to whole dollar amounts. Therefore, the estimate would be that lunch would cost $2.00 for the sandwich, $1.00 for the fruit, and $1.00 for the drink, which adds up to $4.00. The estimate would be that $5.00 is enough to pay for lunch. The exact amount is $4.29, so the estimate does the trick. However, sometimes estimation could steer someone in the wrong direction. Consider a situation where the sandwich was $2.45, the fruit was $1.25, and the drink was $1.35. Rounding to the nearest dollar would still result in an estimate of $4.00; however, the exact amount in this scenario is $5.05. Therefore, the student would not have enough money. Perhaps rounding to the nearest $0.50 would be a better estimation process. Exact calculations are usually the best, but estimations are useful if they are done correctly.

Choosing Measures of Center and Variability

Measures of central tendency, namely mean, median, and mode, describe characteristics of a set of data. Specifically, they are intended to represent a *typical* value in the set by identifying a central position of the set. Depending on the characteristics of a specific set of data, different measures of central tendency are more indicative of a typical value in the set.

When a data set is grouped closely together with a relatively small range and the data is spread out somewhat evenly, the mean is an effective indicator of a typical value in the set. Consider the following data set representing the height of sixth grade boys in inches: 61 inches, 54 inches, 58 inches, 63 inches, 58 inches. The mean of the set is 58.8 inches. The data set is grouped closely (the range is only 9 inches) and the values are spread relatively evenly (three values below the mean and two values above the mean). Therefore, the mean value of 58.8 inches is an effective measure of central tendency in this case.

When a data set contains a small number of values, with one either extremely large or extremely small when compared to the other values, the mean is not an effective measure of central tendency. Consider the following data set representing annual incomes of homeowners on a given street: $71,000; $74,000; $75,000; $77,000; $340,000. The mean of this set is $127,400. This figure does not indicate a typical value in the set, which contains four out of five values between $71,000 and $77,000. The median is a much more effective measure of central tendency for data sets such as these. Finding the middle value diminishes the influence of outliers, or numbers that may appear out of place, like the $340,000 annual income. The median for this set is $75,000 which is much more typical of a value in the set.

The mode of a data set is a useful measure of central tendency for categorical data when each piece of data is an option from a category. Consider a survey of 31 commuters asking how they get to work with results summarized below.

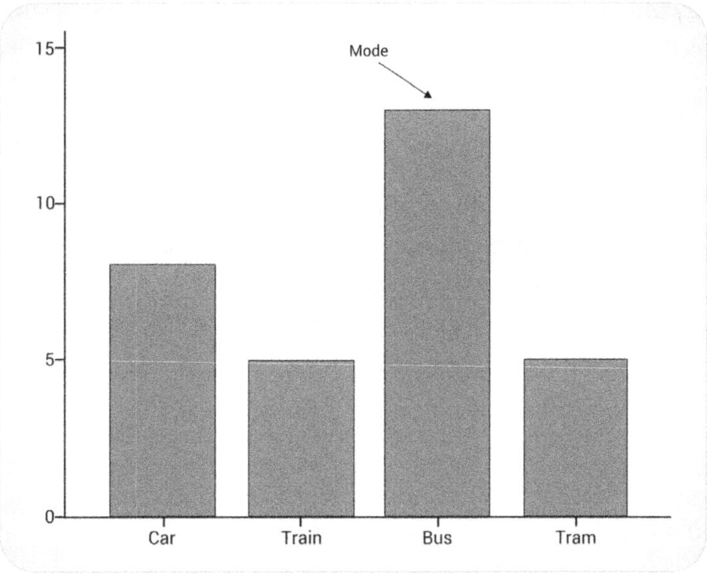

The mode for this set represents the value, or option, of the data that repeats most often. This indicates that the bus is the most popular method of transportation for the commuters.

Effects of Changes in Data

Changing all values of a data set in a consistent way produces predictable changes in the measures of the center and range of the set. A linear transformation changes the original value into the new value by either adding a given number to each value, multiplying each value by a given number, or both. Adding (or subtracting) a given value to each data point will increase (or decrease) the mean, median, and any modes by the same value. However, the range will remain the same due to the way that range is calculated. Multiplying (or dividing) a given value by each data point will increase (or decrease) the mean, median, and any modes, and the range by the same factor.

Consider the following data set, call it set *P*, representing the price of different cases of soda at a grocery store: $4.25, $4.40, $4.75, $4.95, $4.95, $5.15. The mean of set *P* is $4.74. The median is $4.85. The mode of the set is $4.95. The range is $0.90. Suppose the state passes a new tax of $0.25 on every case of soda sold. The new data set, set *T*, is calculated by adding $0.25 to each data point from set *P*. Therefore, set *T* consists of the following values: $4.50, $4.65, $5.00, $5.20, $5.20, $5.40. The mean of set *T* is $4.99. The median is $5.10. The mode of the set is $5.20. The range is $.90. The mean, median and mode of set *T* is equal to $0.25 added to the mean, median, and mode of set *P*. The range stays the same.

Now suppose, due to inflation, the store raises the cost of every item by 10 percent. Raising costs by 10 percent is calculated by multiplying each value by 1.1. The new data set, set *I*, is calculated by multiplying each data point from set *T* by 1.1. Therefore, set *I* consists of the following values: $4.95, $5.12, $5.50, $5.72, $5.72, $5.94. The mean of set *I* is $5.49. The median is $5.61. The mode of the set is $5.72. The range is $0.99. The mean, median, mode, and range of set *I* is equal to 1.1 multiplied by the mean, median, mode, and range of set *T* because each increased by a factor of 10 percent.

Solving Problems Involving Distance, Time, Liquid Volume, Mass, and Money

Problems that involve measurements of length, time, volume, etc. are generally dependent upon understanding how to manipulate between various units of measurement, as well as understanding their equivalencies. They also require determining which operations (addition, subtraction, multiplication, and division) should be performed, and using and/or converting the proper unit for the scenario.

The following table lists key words that can be used to indicate the proper operation:

Addition	Sum, total, in all, combined, increase of, more than, added to
Subtraction	Difference, change, remaining, less than, decreased by
Multiplication	Product, times, twice, triple, each
Division	Quotient, goes into, per, evenly, divided by half, divided by third, split

Problems Involving Time

Time is measured in units such as *seconds, minutes, hours, days*, and *years*. For example, there are 60 seconds in a minute, 60 minutes in each hour, and 24 hours in a day.

When dealing with problems involving elapsed time, break the problem down into workable parts. For example, suppose the length of time between 1:15pm and 3:45pm must be determined. From 1:15pm to 2:00pm is 45 minutes (knowing there are 60 minutes in an hour). From 2:00pm to 3:00pm is 1 hour. From 3:00pm to 3:45pm is 45 minutes. The total elapsed time is 45 minutes plus 1 hour plus 45 minutes. This sum produces 1 hour and 90 minutes. 90 minutes is over an hour, so this is converted to 1 hour (60 minutes) and 30 minutes. The total elapsed time can now be expressed as 2 hours and 30 minutes.

To illustrate time intervals, a clock face can show solutions.

For example, Ani needs to complete all of her chores by 1:50 p.m. If she begins her chores at 1:00 p.m., can she finish the following? Vacuuming (15 minutes), dusting (10 minutes), replacing light bulbs (5 minutes), and degreasing the garage floor (25 minutes).

A blank clock face is useful in illustrating the time lapse necessary for all of Ani's tasks.

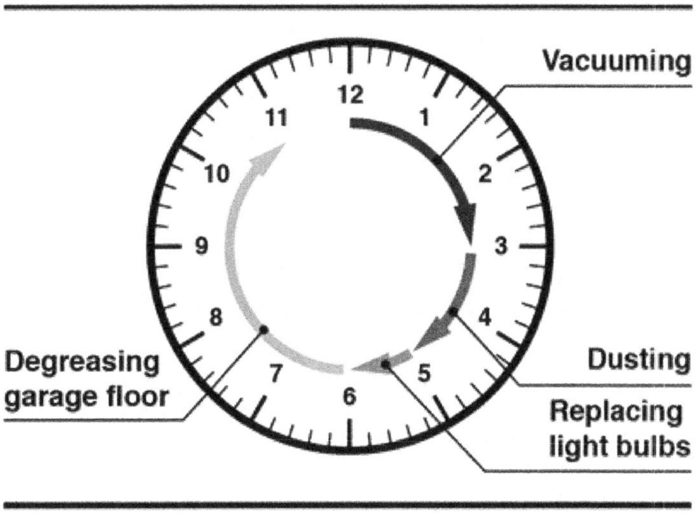

It is easy to see that the chores will span beyond 50 minutes after the hour, so no, Ani could not complete the chores in the given time frame.

When dealing with problems involving elapsed time, breaking the problem down into workable parts is helpful. For example, suppose the length of time between 1:15pm and 3:45pm must be determined. From 1:15pm to 2:00pm is 45 minutes (knowing there are 60 minutes in an hour). From 2:00pm to 3:00pm is 1 hour. From 3:00pm to 3:45pm is 45 minutes. The total elapsed time is 45 minutes plus 1 hour plus 45 minutes. This sum produces 1 hour and 90 minutes. 90 minutes is over an hour, so this is converted to 1 hour (60 minutes) and 30 minutes. The total elapsed time can now be expressed as 2 hours and 30 minutes.

Problems Involving Volume

Volume is how much space something occupies. That "something" can be liquid or solid. Essentially, volume is a measurement of capacity. Whereas area is calculated by counting squares within a two-dimensional object, volume is calculated by counting cubes within a three-dimensional object. It is a measure of the space a figure occupies. Volume is measured using cubic units, such as cubic inches, feet, centimeters, or kilometers. Centimeter cubes can be utilized in the classrooms in order to promote understanding of volume.

For instance, if 10 cubes were placed along the length of a rectangle, with 8 cubes placed along its width, and the remaining area was filled in with cubes, there would 80 cubes in total, which would equal a volume of 80 cubic centimeters. Its area would equal 80 square centimeters. If that shape was doubled so that its height consists of two cube lengths, there would be 160 cubes, and its volume would be 160 cubic centimeters. Adding another level of cubes would mean that there would be $3 \times 80 = 240$ cubes. This idea shows that volume is calculated by multiplying area times height. The actual formula for volume of a three-dimensional rectangular solid is $V = l \times w \times h$, where *l* represents length, *w* represents width, and *h* represents height. Volume can also be thought of as area of the base times the height.

The base in this case would be the entire rectangle formed by *l* and *w*. Here is an example of a rectangular solid with labeled sides:

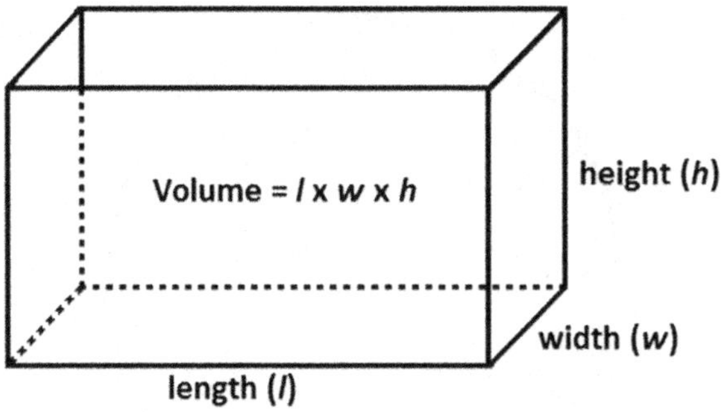

A **cube** is a special type of rectangular solid in which its length, width, and height are the same. If this length is s, then the formula for the volume of a cube is $V = s \times s \times s$.

The U.S. customary units for volume of liquids, from smallest to largest, are: fluid ounces (fl oz), cup (c), pint (pt), quart (qt), and gallon (gal). The metric units for volume of liquids, from smallest to largest, are: milliliter (mL), centiliter (cL), deciliter (dL), liter (L), and kiloliter (kL.).

A problem involving liquid volume would be: If Mart needed 2 quarts of liquid for a recipe and only has a measuring cup, how could he measure out 2 quarts?

The solution would involve Mart measuring out 2 quarts by filling the cup 8 times.

Problems Involving Money

Let's consider a problem involving change. Gwen wants to purchase a number of items at the school supply store. Prices are as follows:

Erasers = \$0.05
Highlighters = \$0.20
Pencils = \$0.10
Pens = \$0.15

Gwen wants to buy 1 highlighter, 5 erasers, 2 pencils, and 3 pens. Would she be able to use the following coins, and if so, what are possible combinations Gwen could use?

To begin, add the total value of the coins:

2 quarters + 5 dimes + 2 nickel

$$(2 \times \$0.25) + (5 \times \$0.10) + (2 \times \$0.05) = \$1.10$$

Then calculate the total cost of the items Gwen wants to purchase:

Erasers = $0.05
Highlighters = $0.20
Pencils = $0.10
Pens = $0.15

Gwen wants to buy 1 highlighter, 5 erasers, 2 pencils, and 3 pens.

1 highlighter + 5 erasers + 2 pencils + 2 pens

$$\$0.20 + (5 \times \$0.05) + (2 \times \$0.10) + (2 \times \$0.15)$$

$$\$0.20 + \$0.25 + \$0.20 + \$0.30 = \$0.95$$

Gwen has enough money to purchase all of the items, and there is only one combination that would provide the correct amount of $0.95: 2 quarters, 4 dimes, and 1 nickel.

Here is another example of a problem involving money that is a bit more difficult:

A store is having a spring sale, where everything is 70% off. You have $45.00 to spend. A jacket is regularly priced at $80.00. Do you have enough to buy the jacket and a pair of gloves, regularly priced at $20.00?

There are two ways to approach this.

Method 1:

Set up the equations to find the sale prices: the original price minus the amount discounted.
$80.00 - ($80.00 (0.70)) = sale cost of the jacket.
$20.00 – ($20.00 (0.70)) = sale cost of the gloves.
Solve for the sale cost.
$24.00 = sale cost of the jacket.
$6.00 = sale cost of the gloves.
Determine if you have enough money for both.
$24.00 + $6.00 = total sale cost.
$30.00 is less than $45.00, so you can afford to purchase both.

Method 2:

Determine the percent of the original price that you will pay.
100% – 70% = 30%
Set up the equations to find the sale prices.
$80.00 (0.30) = cost of the jacket.
$20.00 (0.30) = cost of the gloves.
Solve.

$24.00 = cost of the jacket.
$6.00 = cost of the gloves.
Determine if you have enough money for both.
$24.00 + $6.00 = total sale cost.
$30.00 is less than $45.00, so you can afford to purchase both.

Problems Involving Length

The length of an object can be measured using standard tools such as rulers, yard sticks, meter sticks, and measuring tapes. The following image depicts a yardstick:

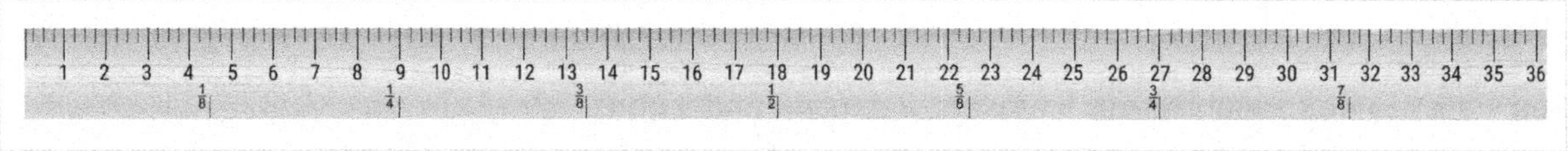

Choosing the right tool to perform the measurement requires determining whether United States customary units or metric units are desired, and having a grasp of the approximate length of each unit and the approximate length of each tool. The measurement can still be performed by trial and error without the knowledge of the approximate size of the tool.

For example, to determine the length of a room in feet, a United States customary unit, various tools can be used for this task. These include a ruler (typically 12 inches/1-foot-long), a yardstick (3 feet/1-yard-long), or a tape measure displaying feet (typically either 25 feet or 50 feet). Because the length of a room is much larger than the length of a ruler or a yardstick, a tape measure should be used to perform the measurement.

When the correct measuring tool is selected, the measurement is performed by first placing the tool directly above or below the object (if making a horizontal measurement) or directly next to the object (if making a vertical measurement). The next step is aligning the tool so that one end of the object is at the mark for zero units, then recording the unit of the mark at the other end of the object. To give the length of a paperclip in metric units, a ruler displaying centimeters is aligned with one end of the paper clip to the mark for zero centimeters.

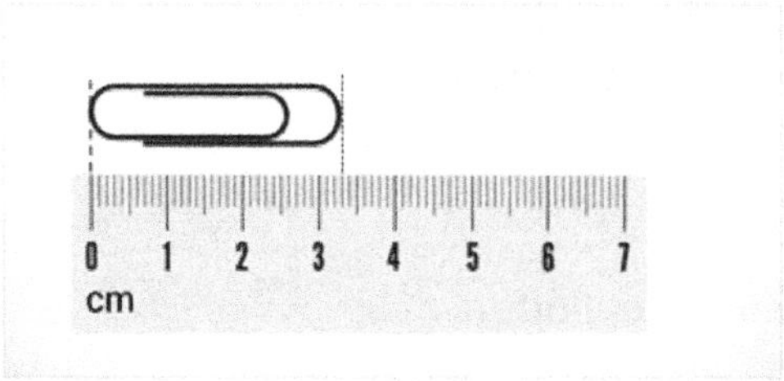

Directly down from the other end of the paperclip is the mark that measures its length. In this case, that mark is two small dashes past the 3-centimeter mark. Each small dash is 1 millimeter (or .1 centimeters). Therefore, the length of the paper clip is 3.2 centimeters.

To compare the lengths of objects, each length must be expressed in the same unit. If possible, the objects should be measured with the same tool or with tools utilizing the same units. For example, a ruler and a yardstick can both measure length in inches. If the lengths of the objects are expressed in different units, these different units must be converted to the same unit before comparing them. If two lengths are expressed in the same unit, the lengths may be compared by subtracting the smaller value from the larger value. For example, suppose the lengths of two gardens are to be compared. Garden A has a length of 4 feet, and garden B has a length of 2 yards. 2 yards is converted to 6 feet so that the measurements have similar units. Then, the smaller length (4 feet) is subtracted from the larger length (6ft): 6ft – 4ft = 2ft. Therefore, garden B is 2 feet larger than garden A.

Identifying and utilizing the proper units for the scenario requires knowing how to apply the conversion rates for length. For example, given a scenario that requires subtracting 8 inches from $2\frac{1}{2}$ feet, both values should first be expressed in the same unit (they could be expressed $\frac{2}{3}$ft & $2\frac{1}{2}$ft, or 8in and 30in). The desired unit for the answer may also require converting back to another unit.

Consider the following scenario that involves length: A parking area along the river is only wide enough to fit one row of cars and is $\frac{1}{2}$ kilometers long. The average space needed per car is 5 meters. How many cars can be parked along the river? First, all measurements should be converted to similar units: $\frac{1}{2}$km = 500m. The operation(s) needed should be identified. Because the problem asks for the number of cars, the total space should be divided by the space per car. 500 meters divided by 5 meters per car yields a total of 100 cars. Written as an expression, the meters unit cancels and the cars unit is left: $\frac{500m}{5m/car}$ the same as $500m \times \frac{1\,car}{5m}$ yields 100 cars.

Problems Involving Mass

The metric system measures **mass**, which is the quantity of matter within an object. Mass and weight do not measure the same thing. **Weight** is affected by gravity, and deals with how strongly Earth is pulling on an object.

The following is an example of a problem involving mass:

A piggy bank contains 12 dollars' worth of nickels. The mass of a nickel is 5 grams, and the empty piggy bank has a mass of 1050 grams. What is the total mass of the full piggy bank?

A dollar contains 20 nickels. Therefore, if there are 12 dollars' worth of nickels, there are $12 \times 20 = 240$ nickels. The mass of each nickel is 5 grams. Therefore, the mass of the nickels is $240 \times 5 = 1{,}200$ grams. Adding in the mass of the empty piggy bank, the mass of the filled bank 2,250 grams.

Geometric Concepts

Solving Problems Involving Perimeter, Area, Surface Area, and Volume

Perimeter and Area of Geometric Shapes

Perimeter is the measurement of a distance around something or the sum of all sides of a polygon. Think of perimeter as the length of the boundary, like a fence. In contrast, **area** is the space occupied by a defined enclosure, like a field enclosed by a fence.

When thinking about perimeter, think about walking around the outside of something. When thinking about area, think about the amount of space or **surface area** something takes up.

Square

The perimeter of a square is measured by adding together all of the sides. Since a square has four equal sides, its perimeter can be calculated by multiplying the length of one side by 4. Thus, the formula is $P = 4 \times s$, where s equals one side. For example, the following square has side lengths of 5 meters:

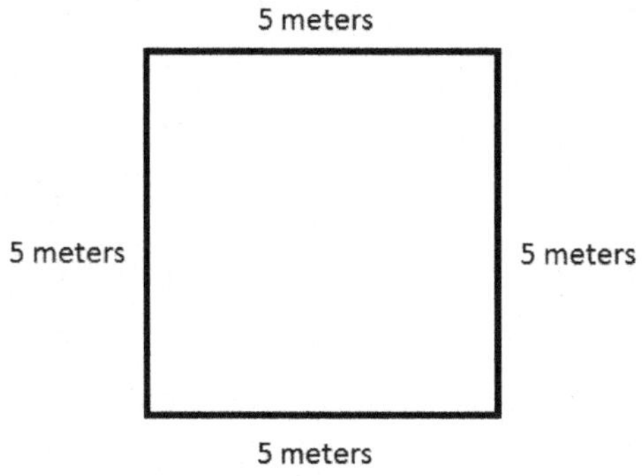

The perimeter is 20 meters because 4 times 5 is 20.

The area of a square is the length of a side squared. For example, if a side of a square is 7 centimeters, then the area is 49 square centimeters. The formula for this example is $A = s^2 = 7^2 = 49$ square centimeters. An example is if the rectangle has a length of 6 inches and a width of 7 inches, then the area is 42 square inches:

$$A = lw = 6(7) = 42 \text{ square inches}$$

Rectangle

Like a square, a rectangle's perimeter is measured by adding together all of the sides. But as the sides are unequal, the formula is different. A rectangle has equal values for its lengths (long sides) and equal values for its widths (short sides), so the perimeter formula for a rectangle is:

$$P = l + l + w + w = 2l + 2w$$

l equals length
w equals width
The area is found by multiplying the length by the width, so the formula is $A = l \times w$.

For example, if the length of a rectangle is 10 inches and the width 8 inches, then the perimeter is 36 inches because:

$$P = 2l + 2w = 2(10) + 2(8) = 20 + 16 = 36 \text{ inches}$$

Triangle

A triangle's perimeter is measured by adding together the three sides, so the formula is $P = a + b + c$, where a, b, and c are the values of the three sides. The area is the product of one-half the base and height so the formula is:

$$A = \frac{1}{2} \times b \times h$$

It can be simplified to:

$$A = \frac{bh}{2}$$

The base is the bottom of the triangle, and the height is the distance from the base to the peak. If a problem asks to calculate the area of a triangle, it will provide the base and height.

For example, if the base of the triangle is 2 feet and the height 4 feet, then the area is 4 square feet. The following equation shows the formula used to calculate the area of the triangle:

$$\mathrm{A} = \frac{1}{2}\mathrm{bh} = \frac{1}{2}(2)(4) = 4 \text{ square feet}$$

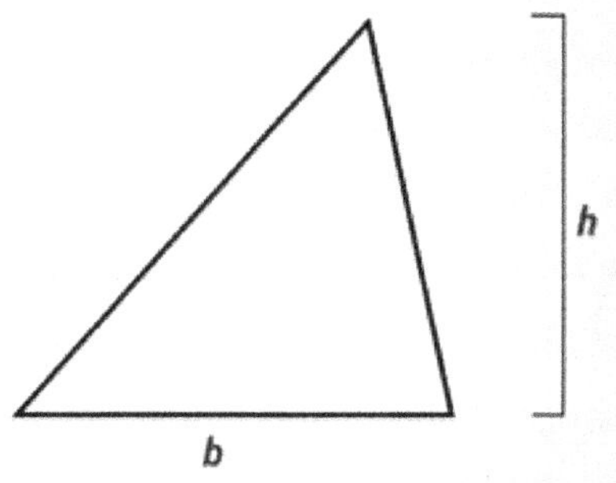

Circle
A circle's perimeter—also known as its circumference—is measured by multiplying the diameter by π.

Diameter is the straight line measured from one end to the direct opposite end of the circle.

π is referred to as pi and is equal to 3.14 (with rounding).

So the formula is $\pi \times d$.

This is sometimes expressed by the formula:

$$C = 2 \times \pi \times r$$

where r is the radius of the circle. These formulas are equivalent, as the radius equals half of the diameter.

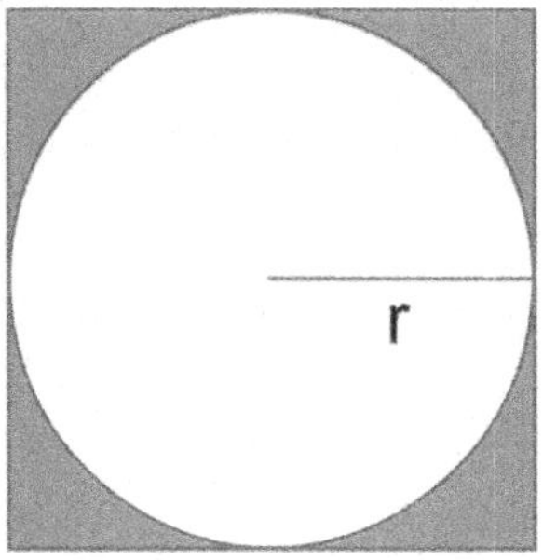

The area of a circle is calculated through the formula:

$$A = \pi \times r^2$$

The test will indicate either to leave the answer with π attached or to calculate to the nearest decimal place, which means multiplying by 3.14 for π.

Surface Area and Volume of Geometric Shapes

The area of a two-dimensional figure refers to the number of square units needed to cover the interior region of the figure. This concept is similar to wallpaper covering the flat surface of a wall. For example, if a rectangle has an area of 8 square inches (written 8 in^2), it will take 8 squares, each with sides one inch in length, to cover the interior region of the rectangle. Note that area is measured in square units such as: square feet or ft^2; square yards or yd^2; square miles or mi^2.

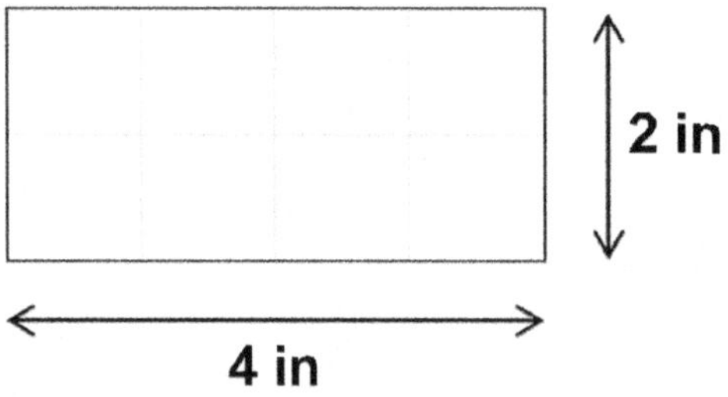

The surface area of a three-dimensional figure refers to the number of square units needed to cover the entire surface of the figure. This concept is similar to using wrapping paper to completely cover the outside of a box. For example, if a triangular pyramid has a surface area of 17 square inches (written $17in^2$), it will take 17 squares, each with sides one inch in length, to cover the entire surface of the pyramid. Surface area is also measured in square units.

Many three-dimensional figures (solid figures) can be represented by nets consisting of rectangles and triangles. The surface area of such solids can be determined by adding the areas of each of its faces and bases. Finding the surface area using this method requires calculating the areas of rectangles and triangles. To find the area (*A*) of a rectangle, the length (*l*) is multiplied by the width:

$$(w) \rightarrow A = l \times w$$

The area of a rectangle with a length of 8cm and a width of 4cm is calculated:

$$A = (8cm) \times (4cm) \rightarrow A = 32cm^2$$

To calculate the area (*A*) of a triangle, the product of $\frac{1}{2}$, the base (*b*), and the height (*h*) is found

$$A = \frac{1}{2} \times b \times h$$

Note that the height of a triangle is measured from the base to the vertex opposite of it forming a right angle with the base. The area of a triangle with a base of 11cm and a height of 6cm is calculated:

$$A = \frac{1}{2} \times (11cm) \times (6cm) \rightarrow A = 33cm^2$$

Consider the following triangular prism, which is represented by a net consisting of two triangles and three rectangles.

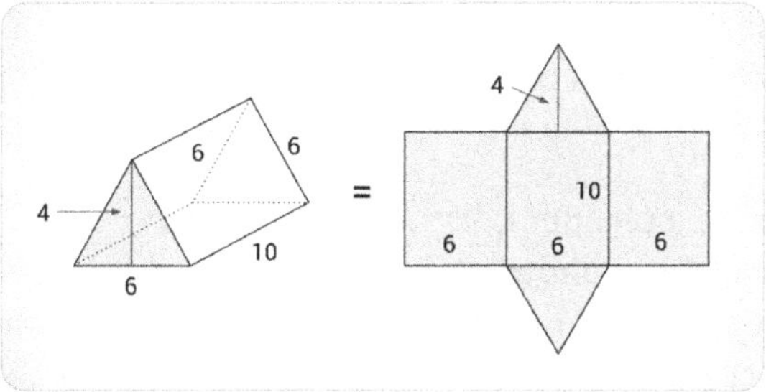

The surface area of the prism can be determined by adding the areas of each of its faces and bases. The surface area (*SA*) = area of triangle + area of triangle + area of rectangle + area of rectangle + area of rectangle.

$$SA = \left(\frac{1}{2} \times b \times h\right) + \left(\frac{1}{2} \times b \times h\right) + (l \times w) + (l \times w) + (l \times w)$$

$$SA = \left(\frac{1}{2} \times 6 \times 4\right) + \left(\frac{1}{2} \times 6 \times 4\right) + (6 \times 10) + (6 \times 10) + (6 \times 10)$$

$$SA = (12) + (12) + (60) + (60) + (60)$$

$$SA = 204 \textit{ square units}$$

Volume is the measurement of how much space an object occupies, like how much space is in the cube. Volume is useful in determining the space within a certain three-dimensional object. Volume can be calculated for a cube, rectangular prism, cylinder, pyramid, cone, and sphere. By knowing specific dimensions of the objects, the volume of the object is computed with these figures. The units for the volumes of solids can include cubic centimeters, cubic meters, cubic inches, and cubic feet.

Cube
The cube is the simplest figure for which volume can be determined because all dimensions in a cube are equal. In the following figure, the length, width, and height of the cube are all represented by the variable *a* because these measurements are equal lengths.

The volume of any rectangular, three-dimensional object is found by multiplying its length by its width by its height. In the case of a cube, the length, width, and height are all equal lengths, represented by the variable *a*. Therefore, the equation used to calculate the volume is $(a \times a \times a)$ or a^3. In a real-world example of this situation, if the length of a side of the cube is 3 centimeters, the volume is calculated by utilizing the formula $(3 \times 3 \times 3) = 9$ cm^3.

Rectangular Prism
The dimensions of a rectangular prism are not necessarily equal as those of a cube. Therefore, the formula for a rectangular prism recognizes that the dimensions vary and use different variables to represent these lengths. The length, width, and height of a rectangular prism are represented with the variables *a, b*, and *c*.

The equation used to calculate volume is length times width times height. Using the variables in the diagram above, this means $a \times b \times c$. In a real-world application of this situation, if *a*=2 cm, *b*=3 cm, and *c*=4 cm, the volume is calculated by utilizing the formula $3 \times 4 \times 5 = 60$ cm^3.

Cylinder
Discovering a cylinder's volume requires the measurement of the cylinder's base, length of the radius, and height. The height of the cylinder can be represented with variable *h*, and the radius can be represented with variable *r*.

The formula to find the volume of a cylinder is $\pi r^2 h$. Notice that πr^2 is the formula for the area of a circle. This is because the base of the cylinder is a circle. To calculate the volume of a cylinder, the slices of circles needed to build the entire height of the cylinder are added together. For example, if the radius is 5 feet and the height of the cylinder is 10 feet, the cylinder's volume is calculated by using the following equation: $\pi 5^2 \times 10$. Substituting 3.14 for π, the volume is 785.4 ft^3.

Pyramid
To calculate the volume of a pyramid, the area of the base of the pyramid is multiplied by the pyramid's height by $\frac{1}{3}$. The area of the base of the pyramid is found by multiplying the base length by the base width.

Therefore, the formula to calculate a pyramid's volume is $(L \times W \times H) \div 3$.

Cone
The formula to calculate the volume of a circular cone is similar to the formula for the volume of a pyramid. The primary difference in determining the area of a cone is that a circle serves as the base of a cone. Therefore, the area of a circle is used for the cone's base.

The variable *r* represents the radius, and the variable *h* represents the height of the cone. The formula used to calculate the volume of a cone is $\frac{1}{3}\pi r^2 h$. Essentially, the area of the base of the cone is multiplied by the cone's height. In a real-life example where the radius of a cone is 2 meters and the height of a cone is 5 meters, the volume of the cone is calculated by utilizing the formula:

$$\frac{1}{3}\pi 2^2 \times 5 = 21$$

After substituting 3.14 for π, the volume is 785.4 ft^3.

Sphere
The volume of a sphere uses π due to its circular shape.

The length of the radius, *r*, is the only variable needed to determine the sphere's volume. The formula to calculate the volume of a sphere is $\frac{4}{3}\pi r^3$. Therefore, if the radius of a sphere is 8 centimeters, the volume of the sphere is calculated by utilizing the formula:

$$\frac{4}{3}\pi(8)^3 = 2{,}143\ cm^3$$

Locating Ordered Pairs in All Four Quadrants of a Rectangular Coordinate System

The coordinate plane, sometimes referred to as the Cartesian plane, is a two-dimensional surface consisting of a horizontal and a vertical number line. The horizontal number line is referred to as the *x*-axis, and the vertical number line is referred to as the *y*-axis. The *x*-axis and *y*-axis intersect (or cross) at a point called the origin. At the origin, the value of the *x*-axis is zero, and the value of the y-axis is zero. The coordinate plane identifies the exact location of a point that is plotted on the two-dimensional surface. Like a map, the location of all points on the plane are in relation to the origin. Along the *x*-axis (horizontal line), numbers to the right of the origin are positive and increasing in value (1,2,3, . . .) and to the left of the origin numbers are negative and decreasing in value (-1,-2,-3, . . .). Along the *y*-axis (vertical line), numbers above the origin are positive and increasing in value and numbers below the origin are negative and decreasing in value.

The *x*- and *y*-axis divide the coordinate plane into four sections. These sections are referred to as quadrant one, quadrant two, quadrant three, and quadrant four, and are often written with Roman numerals I, II, III, and IV.

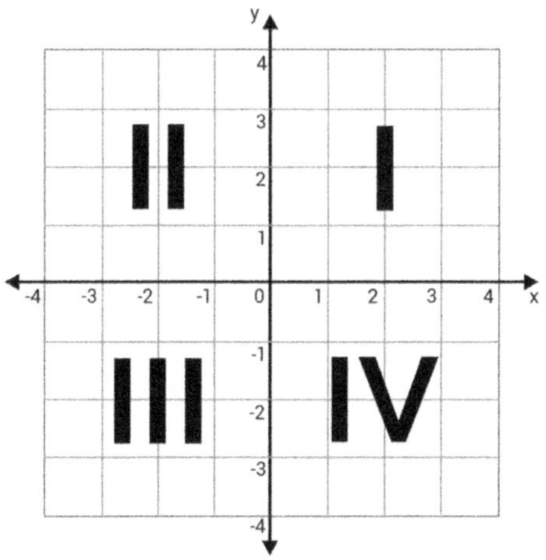

The upper right section is Quadrant I and consists of points with positive *x*-values and positive *y*-values. The upper left section is Quadrant II and consists of points with negative *x*-values and positive *y*-values. The bottom left section is Quadrant III and consists of points with negative *x*-values and negative *y*-values. The bottom right section is Quadrant IV and consists of points with positive *x*-values and negative *y*-values.

Any point within the plane can be defined by a set of **coordinates** (x, y). The coordinates consist of two numbers, x and y, which represent a position on each number line. The coordinates can also be referred to as an **ordered pair,** and (0, 0) is the ordered pair known as the **vertex**, or the origin, the point in which the axes intersect. Positive x-coordinates go to the right of the vertex, and positive y-coordinates go up. Negative x-coordinates go left, and negative y-coordinates go down.

Here is an example of the coordinate plane with a point plotted:

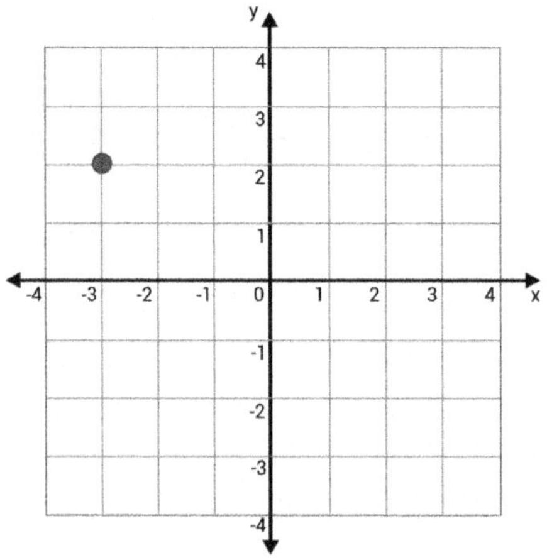

In order to plot a point on the coordinate plane, each coordinate must be considered individually. The value of x represents how many units away from the vertex the point lies on the x-axis. The value of y represents the number of units away from the vertex that the point lies on the y-axis.

The points on the coordinate plane are labeled based on their position in relation to the origin. If a point is found 4 units to the right and 2 units up from the origin, the location is described as (4, 2). These numbers are the *x*- and *y*-coordinates, always written in the order (*x*, *y*). This point is also described as lying in the first quadrant. Every point in the first quadrant has a location that is positive in the *x* and *y* directions. The following figure shows the coordinate plane with examples of points that lie in each quadrant:

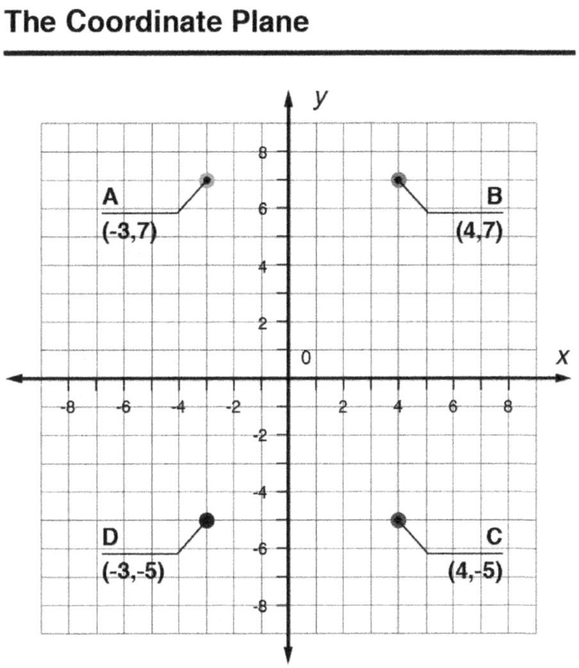

Point B lies in the first quadrant, described positive *x*- and *y*-values, above the *x*-axis and to the right of the *y*-axis. Point A lies in the second quadrant, where the *x*-value is negative and *y*-value is positive. This quadrant is above the *x*-axis and to the left of the *y*-axis. Point D lies in the third quadrant, where both the *x*- and *y*-values are negative. Below the *x*-axis, and to the left of the *y*-axis, is how this quadrant is described. Point C is in the fourth quadrant, where the *x*-value is positive and the *y*-value is negative.

Graphing on the Coordinate Plane Using Mathematical Problems, Tables, and Patterns

Data can be recorded using a coordinate plane. Graphs are utilized frequently in real-world applications and can be seen in many facets of everyday life. A relationship can exist between the *x*- and *y*-coordinates that are plotted on a graph, and those values can represent a set of data that can be listed in a table. Going back and forth between the table and the graph is an important concept, and defining the relationship between the variables is the key that links the data to a real-life application.

For example, temperature increases during a summer day. The *x*-coordinate can be used to represent hours in the day, and the *y*-coordinate can be used to represent the temperature in degrees. The graph would show the temperature at each hour of the day. Time is almost always plotted on the *x*-axis and utilizing different units on each axis, if necessary, is important. Labeling the axes with units is also important.

Within the first quadrant of the coordinate plane, both the x and y values are positive. Most real-world problems can be plotted in this quadrant because most real-world quantities, such as time and distance, are positive. Consider the following table of values:

X	Y
1	2
2	4
3	6
4	8

Each row gives a coordinate pair. For example, the first row gives the coordinates (1,2). Each *x*-value tells you how far to move from the origin, the point (0,0), to the right, and each *y*-value tells you how far to move up from the origin. Here is the graph of the points listed above in the table in addition to the origin:

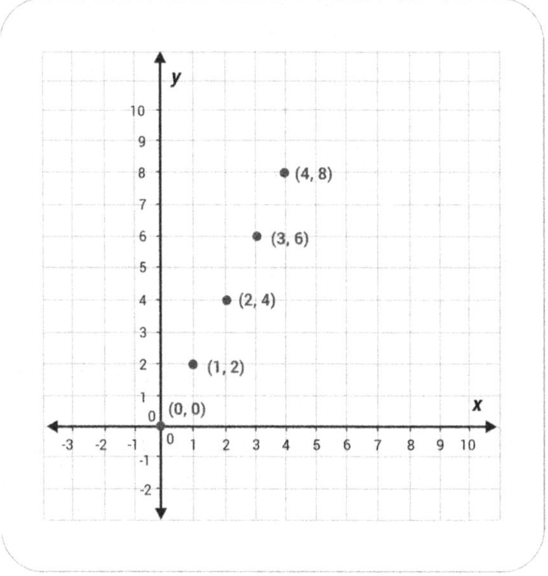

Notice that each *y*-value is found by doubling the *x*-value that forms the other portion of its coordinate pair.

Properties of Three-Dimensional Shapes

A solid is a three-dimensional figure that encloses a part of space. Common three-dimensional shapes include spheres, prisms, cubes, pyramids, cylinders, and cones.

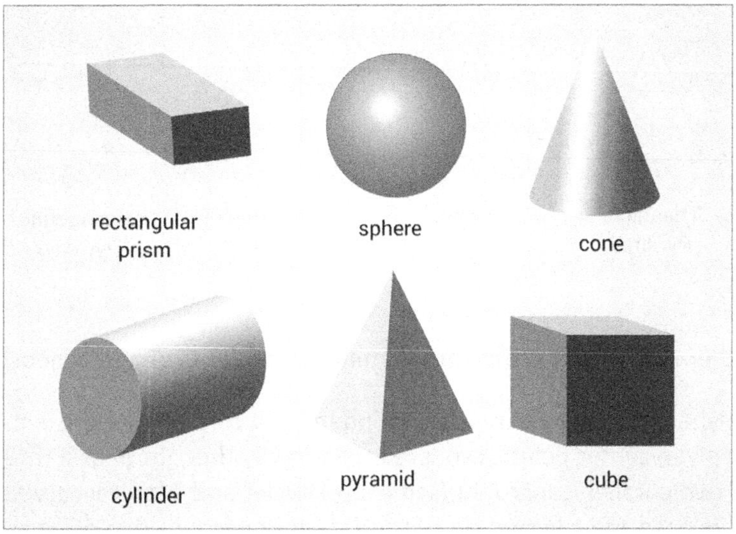

Solids consisting of all flat surfaces that are polygons are called polyhedrons. The two-dimensional surfaces that make up a polyhedron are called faces. Types of polyhedrons include prisms and pyramids. A prism consists of two parallel faces that are congruent (or the same shape and same size), and lateral faces going around (which are parallelograms). A prism is further classified by the shape of its base, as shown below:

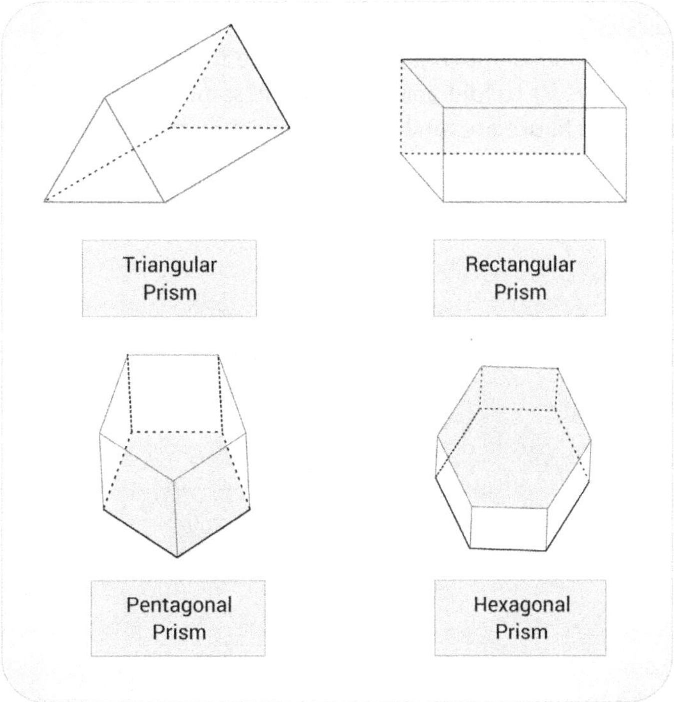

A pyramid consists of lateral faces (triangles) that meet at a common point called the vertex and one other face that is a polygon, called the base. A pyramid can be further classified by the shape of its base, as shown below.

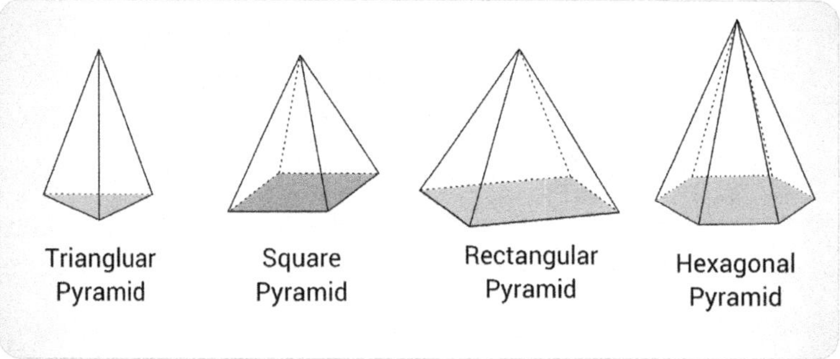

A tetrahedron is another name for a triangular pyramid. All the faces of a tetrahedron are triangles.

Solids that are not polyhedrons include spheres, cylinders, and cones. A sphere is the set of all points a given distance from a given center point. A sphere is commonly thought of as a three-dimensional circle. A cylinder consists of two parallel, congruent (same size) circles and a lateral curved surface. A cone consists of a circle as its base and a lateral curved surface that narrows to a point called the vertex.

Similar polygons are the same shape but different sizes. More specifically, their corresponding angle measures are congruent (or equal) and the length of their sides is proportional. For example, all sides of one polygon may be double the length of the sides of another. Likewise, similar solids are the same shape but different sizes. Any corresponding faces or bases of similar solids are the same polygons that are proportional by a consistent value.

Three-Dimensional Figures with Nets

A net is a construction of two-dimensional figures that can be folded to form a given three-dimensional figure. More than one net may exist to fold and produce the same solid, or three-dimensional figure. The bases and faces of the solid figure are analyzed to determine the polygons (two-dimensional figures) needed to form the net.

Consider the following triangular prism:

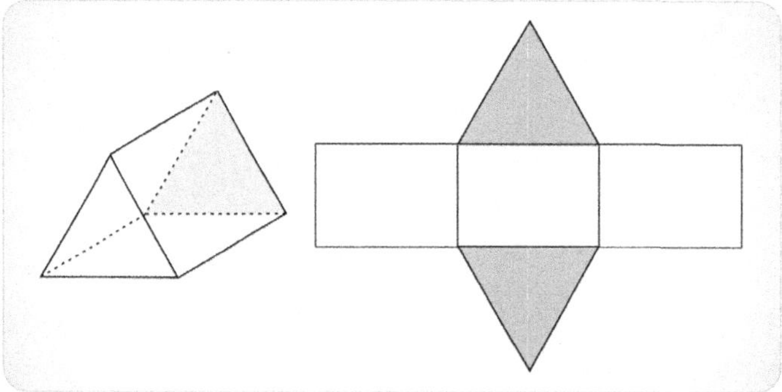

The surface of the prism consists of two triangular bases and three rectangular faces. The net beside it can be used to construct the triangular prism by first folding the triangles up to be parallel to each other, and then folding the two outside rectangles up and to the center with the outer edges touching.

Consider the following cylinder:

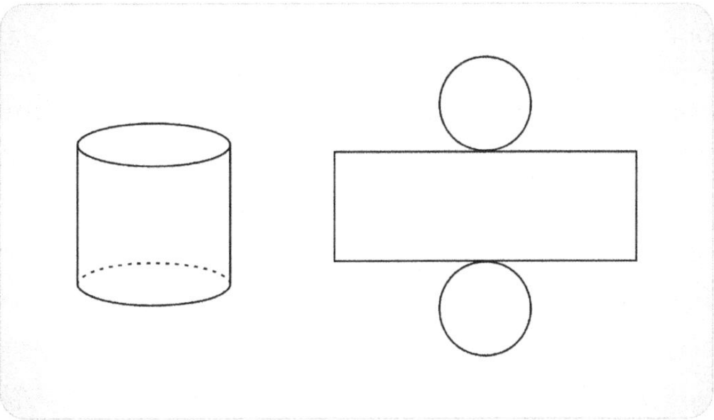

The surface consists of two circular bases and a curved lateral surface that can be opened and flattened into a rectangle. The net beside the cylinder can be used to construct the cylinder by first folding the circles up to be parallel to each other, and then curving the sides of the rectangle up to touch each other. The top and bottom of the folded rectangle should be touching the outside of both circles.

Consider the following square pyramid below on the left. The surface consists of one square base and four triangular faces. The net below on the right can be used to construct the square pyramid by folding each triangle towards the center of the square. The top points of the triangle meet at the vertex.

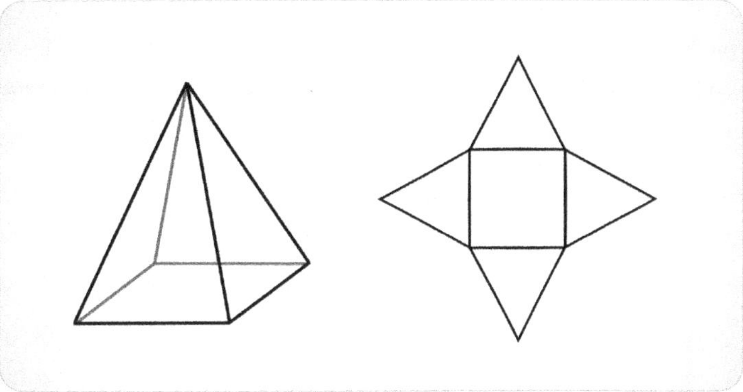

Classifying Two-Dimensional Figures

A **polygon** is a closed geometric figure in a plane (flat surface) consisting of at least 3 sides formed by line segments. These are often defined as two-dimensional shapes. Common two-dimensional shapes include circles, triangles, squares, rectangles, pentagons, and hexagons. Note that a circle is a two-dimensional shape without sides.

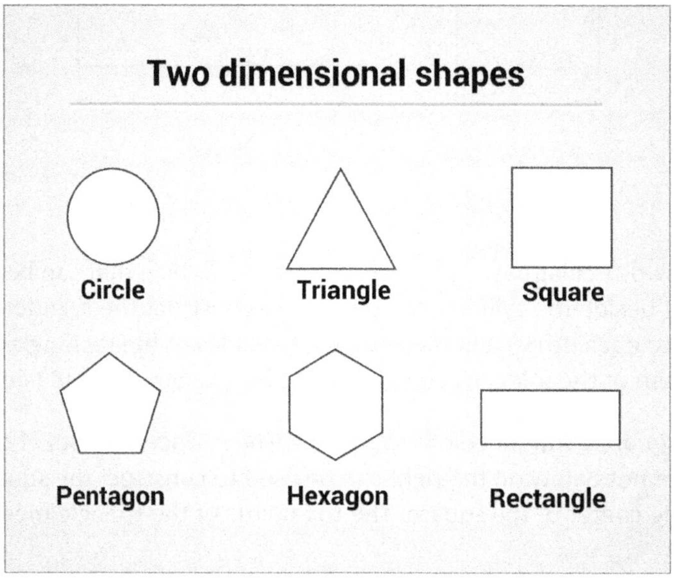

Polygons can be either convex or concave. A polygon that has interior angles all measuring less than 180° is convex. A concave polygon has one or more interior angles measuring greater than 180°. Examples are shown below.

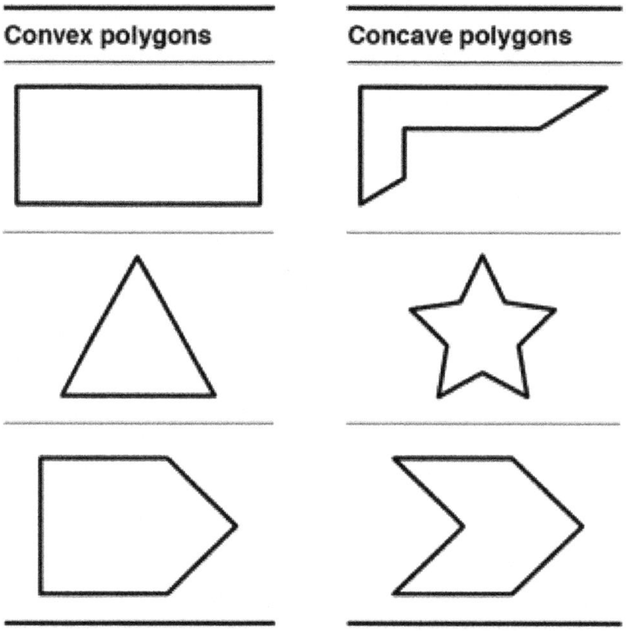

Polygons can be classified by the number of sides (also equal to the number of angles) they have. The following are the names of polygons with a given number of sides or angles:

# of sides	3	4	5	6	7	8	9	10
Name of polygon	Triangle	Quadrilateral	Pentagon	Hexagon	Septagon (or heptagon)	Octagon	Nonagon	Decagon

Equiangular polygons are polygons in which the measure of every interior angle is the same. The sides of equilateral polygons are always the same length. If a polygon is both equiangular and equilateral, the polygon is defined as a regular polygon.

Triangles can be further classified by their sides and angles. A triangle with its largest angle measuring 90° is a right triangle. A triangle with the largest angle less than 90° is an acute triangle. A triangle with the largest angle greater than 90° is an obtuse triangle. Below is an example of a right triangle.

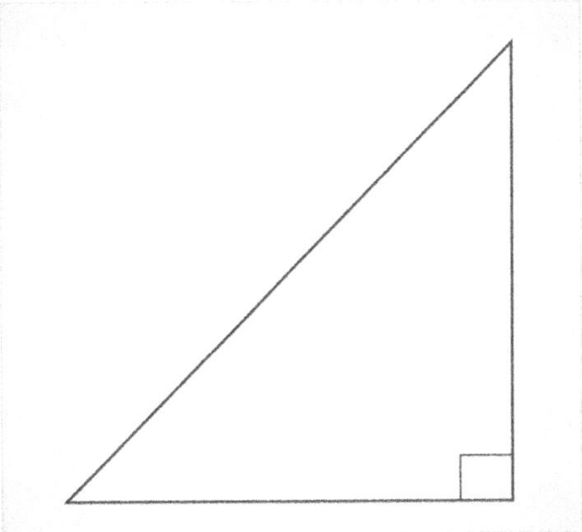

A triangle consisting of two equal sides and two equal angles is an isosceles triangle. A triangle with three equal sides and three equal angles is an equilateral triangle. A triangle with no equal sides or angles is a scalene triangle.

Isosceles triangle:

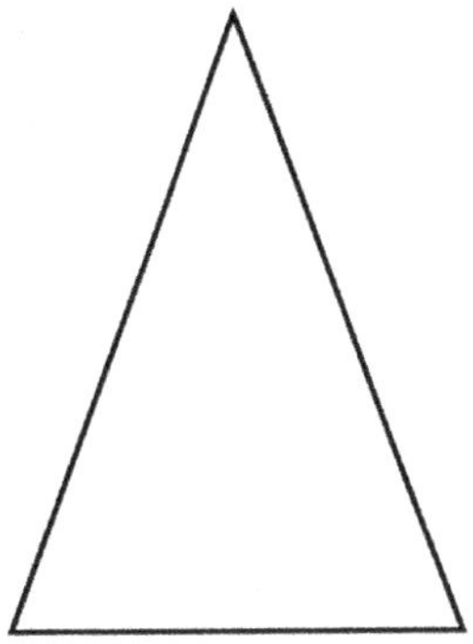

Equilateral triangle:

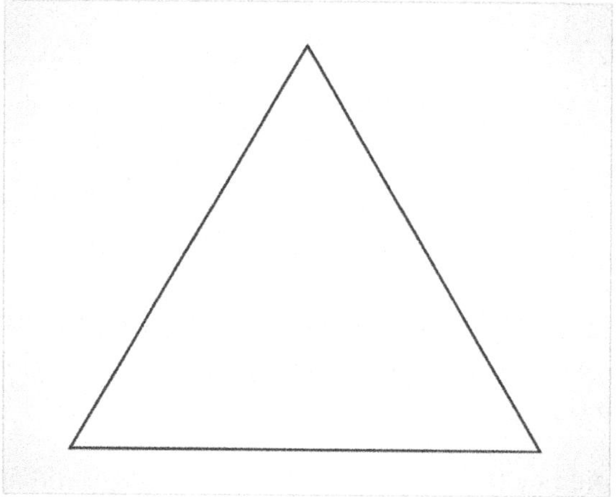

Scalene triangle:

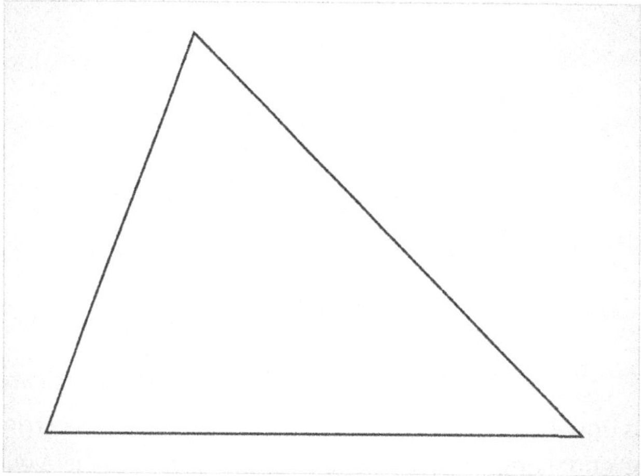

Quadrilaterals can be further classified according to their sides and angles. A quadrilateral with exactly one pair of parallel sides is called a trapezoid. A quadrilateral that shows both pairs of opposite sides parallel is a parallelogram. Parallelograms include rhombuses, rectangles, and squares. A rhombus has four equal sides. A rectangle has four equal angles (90° each). A square has four 90° angles and four equal sides. Therefore, a square is both a rhombus and a rectangle.

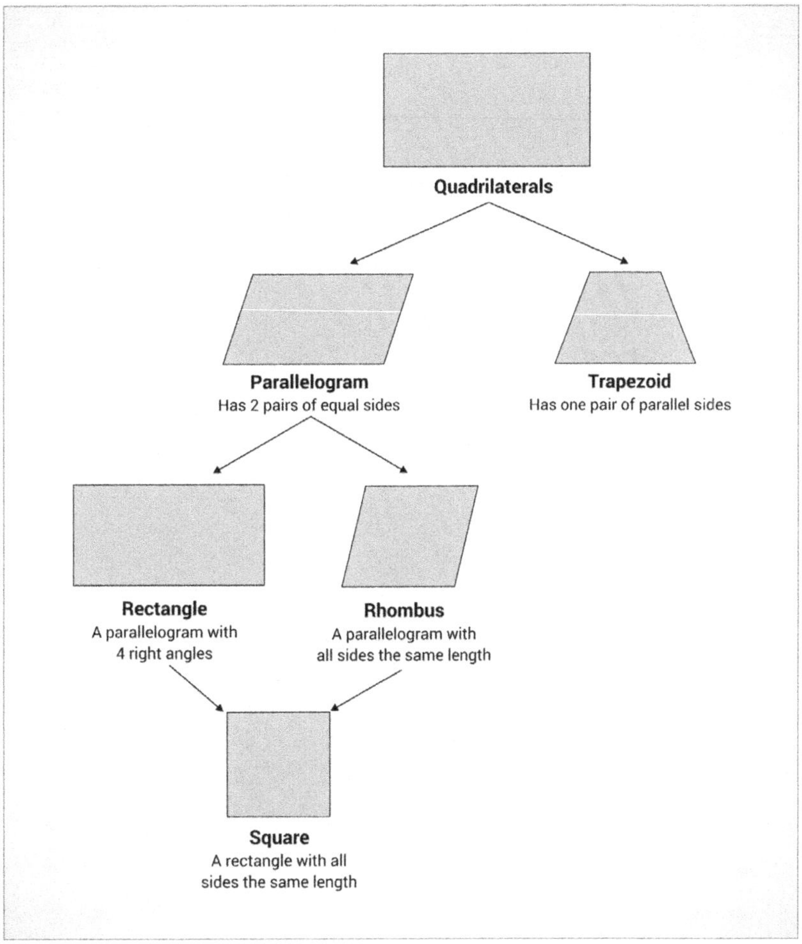

Angles and Diagonals

Diagonals are lines (excluding sides) that connect two vertices within a polygon. **Mutually bisecting diagonals** intersect at their midpoints. Parallelograms, rectangles, squares, and rhombuses have mutually bisecting diagonals. However, trapezoids don't have such lines. **Perpendicular diagonals** occur when they form four right triangles at their point of intersection. Squares and rhombuses have perpendicular diagonals, but trapezoids, rectangles, and parallelograms do not. Finally, **perpendicular bisecting diagonals** (also known as **perpendicular bisectors**) form four right triangles at their point of intersection, but this intersection is also the midpoint of the two lines. Both rhombuses and squares have perpendicular bisecting angles, but trapezoids, rectangles, and parallelograms do not. Knowing these definitions can help tremendously in problems that involve both angles and diagonals.

Polygons with More than Four Sides

A **pentagon** is a five-sided figure. A six-sided shape is a **hexagon**. A seven-sided figure is classified as a **heptagon**, and an eight-sided figure is called an **octagon**. An important characteristic is whether a polygon is regular or irregular. If it's **regular,** the side lengths and angle measurements are all equal. An

irregular polygon has unequal side lengths and angle measurements. Mathematical problems involving polygons with more than four sides usually involve side length and angle measurements. The sum of all internal angles in a polygon equals $180(n - 2)$ degrees, where n is the number of sides. Therefore, the total of all internal angles in a pentagon is 540 degrees because there are five sides so $180(5 - 2)$ = 540 degrees. Unfortunately, area formulas don't exist for polygons with more than four sides. However, their shapes can be split up into triangles, and the formula for area of a triangle can be applied and totaled to obtain the area for the entire figure.

Practice Questions

1. Which of the following could be used in the classroom to show $\frac{3}{7} < \frac{5}{6}$ is a true statement?
   a. A bar graph
   b. A number line
   c. An area model
   d. Base 10 blocks

2. A teacher is showing students how to evaluate $5 \times 6 + 4 \div 2 - 1$. Which operation should be completed first?
   a. Multiplication
   b. Addition
   c. Division
   d. Subtraction

3. What is the definition of a factor of the number 36?
   a. A number that can be divided by 36 and have no remainder
   b. A number that 36 can be divided by and have no remainder
   c. A prime number that is multiplied times 36
   d. An even number that is multiplied times 36

4. Which of the following is the definition of a prime number?
   a. A number that factors only into itself and 1
   b. A number greater than one that factors only into itself and 1
   c. A number less than 10
   d. A number divisible by 10

5. What is the next number in the following series: $1, 3, 6, 10, 15, 21, \ldots$?
   a. 26
   b. 27
   c. 28
   d. 29

6. Which of the following is the correct order of operations that could be used on a difficult math problem that contained grouping symbols?
   a. Parentheses, Exponents, Multiplication, Division, Addition, Subtraction
   b. Exponents, Parentheses, Multiplication, Division, Addition, Subtraction
   c. Parentheses, Exponents, Addition, Multiplication, Division, Subtraction
   d. Parentheses, Exponents, Division, Addition, Subtraction, Multiplication

7. If Danny takes 48 minutes to walk 3 miles, how long should it take him to walk 5 miles maintaining the same speed?
   a. 32 min
   b. 64 min
   c. 80 min
   d. 96 min

8. Rewriting mixed numbers as improper fractions can help students perform operations on mixed numbers. Which of the following is a mixed number?

a. $16\frac{1}{2}$
b. 16
c. $\frac{16}{3}$
d. $\frac{1}{4}$

9. If a teacher was showing a class how to round 245.2678 to the nearest thousandth, which place value would be used to decide whether to round up or round down?

a. Ten-thousandth
b. Thousandth
c. Hundredth
d. Thousand

10. Carey bought 184 pounds of fertilizer to use on her lawn. Each segment of her lawn required $12\frac{1}{2}$ pounds of fertilizer to do a sufficient job. If a student were asked to determine how many segments could be fertilized with the amount purchased, what operation would be necessary to solve this problem?

a. Multiplication
b. Division
c. Addition
d. Subtraction

11. Students should line up decimal places within the given numbers before performing which of the following?

a. Multiplication
b. Division
c. Subtraction
d. Exponents

12. Which of the following expressions best exemplifies the additive and subtractive identity?

a. $5 + 2 - 0 = 5 + 2 + 0$
b. $6 + x = 6 - 6$
c. $9 - 9 = 0$
d. $8 + 2 = 10$

13. Which of the following is an equivalent measurement for 1.3 cm?

a. 0.13 m
b. 0.013 m
c. 0.13 mm
d. 0.013 mm

14. Using the following diagram, calculate the total circumference, rounding to the nearest decimal place:

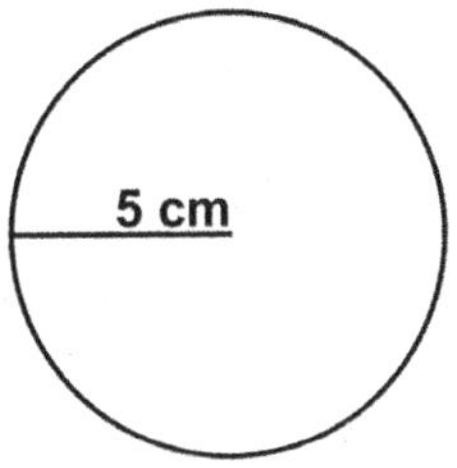

a. 25.0 cm
b. 15.7 cm
c. 78.5 cm
d. 31.4 cm

15. Which four-sided shape is always a rectangle?
a. Rhombus
b. Square
c. Parallelogram
d. Quadrilateral

16. A rectangle was formed out of pipe cleaner. Its length was $\frac{1}{2}$ feet and its width was $\frac{11}{2}$ inches. What is its area in square inches?
a. $\frac{11}{4}$ inch^2
b. $\frac{11}{2}$ inch^2
c. 22 inch^2
d. 33 inch^2

17. A teacher cuts a pie into 6 equal pieces and takes one away. What topic would she be introducing to the class by using such a visual?
a. Decimals
b. Addition
c. Fractions
d. Measurement

18. Which item taught in the classroom would allow students to correctly find the solution to the following problem: A clock reads 5:00 am. What is the measure of the angle formed by the two hands of that clock?
a. Each time increment on an analog clock measures 90 degrees.
b. Each time increment on an analog clock measures 30 degrees.
c. Two adjacent angles sum up to 180 degrees.
d. Two complementary angles sum up to 180 degrees.

19. Which of the following represent one hundred eighty-two billion, thirty-six thousand, four hundred twenty-one and three hundred fifty-six thousandths?

a. 182,036,421.356
b. 182,036,421.0356
c. 182,000,036,421.0356
d. 182,000,036,421.356

20. A solution needs 5 mL of saline for every 8 mL of medicine given. How much saline is needed for 45 mL of medicine?

a. $\frac{225}{8}$ mL
b. 72 mL
c. 28 mL
d. $\frac{45}{8}$mL

21. What other operation could be utilized to teach the process of dividing 9453 by 24 besides division?

a. Multiplication
b. Addition
c. Exponents
d. Subtraction

22. What unit of volume is used to describe the following 3-dimensional shape?

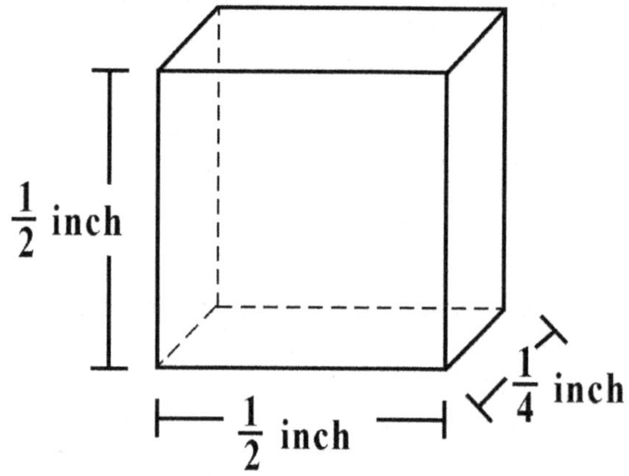

a. Square inches
b. Inches
c. Cubic inches
d. Squares

23. Which common denominator would be used to evaluate $\frac{2}{3}+\frac{4}{5}$?

a. 15
b. 3
c. 5
d. 10

24. What operation are students taught to repeat to evaluate an expression involving an exponent?
 a. Addition
 b. Multiplication
 c. Division
 d. Subtraction

25. Which of the following formulas would correctly calculate the perimeter of a legal-sized piece of paper that is 14 inches long and $8\frac{1}{2}$ inches wide?
 a. $P = 14 + 8\frac{1}{2}$
 b. $P = 14 + 8\frac{1}{2} + 14 + 8\frac{1}{2}$
 c. $P = 14 \times 8\frac{1}{2}$
 d. $P = 14 \times \frac{17}{2}$

26. Which of the following are units that would be taught in a lecture covering the metric system?
 a. Inches, feet, miles, pounds
 b. Millimeters, centimeters, meters, pounds
 c. Kilograms, grams, kilometers, meters
 d. Teaspoons, tablespoons, ounces

27. Which important mathematical property is shown in the expression: $(7 \times 3) \times 2 = 7 \times (3 \times 2)$?
 a. Distributive property
 b. Commutative property
 c. Associative property
 d. Multiplicative inverse

28. A grocery store is selling individual bottles of water, and each bottle contains 750 milliliters of water. If 12 bottles are purchased, what conversion will correctly determine how many liters that customer will take home?
 a. 100 milliliters equals 1 liter
 b. 1,000 milliliters equals 1 liter
 c. 1,000 liters equals 1 milliliter
 d. 10 liters equals 1 milliliter

29. If a student evaluated the expression $(3 + 7) - 6 \div 2$ to equal 2 on an exam, what error did she most likely make?
 a. She performed the operations from left to right instead of following order of operations.
 b. There was no error. 2 is the correct answer.
 c. She did not perform the operation within the grouping symbol first.
 d. She divided first instead of the addition within the grouping symbol.

30. What is the solution to $(2 \times 20) \div (7 + 1) + (6 \times 0.01) + (4 \times 0.001)$?
 a. 5.064
 b. 5.64
 c. 5.0064
 d. 48.064

31. A cereal box has a base 3 inches by 5 inches and is 10 inches tall. Another box has a base 5 inches by 6 inches. What formula is necessary for students to use to find out how tall the second box would need to be in order to hold the same amount of cereal?

a. Area of a rectangle
b. Volume of a rectangular solid
c. Volume of a cube
d. Perimeter of a square

32. An angle measures 54 degrees. In order to correctly determine the measure of its complementary angle, what concept is necessary?

a. Two complementary angles sum up to 180 degrees.
b. Complementary angles are always acute.
c. Two complementary angles sum up to 90 degrees.
d. Complementary angles sum up to 360 degrees.

33. The diameter of a circle measures 5.75 centimeters. What tool could be used in the classroom to draw such a circle?

a. Ruler
b. Meter stick
c. Compass
d. Yard stick

34. A piggy bank contains 12 dollars' worth of nickels. A nickel weighs 5 grams, and the empty piggy bank weighs 1050 grams. What is the total weight of the full piggy bank?

a. 1,110 grams
b. 1,200 grams
c. 2,250 grams
d. 2,200 grams

35. $\frac{3}{4}$ of a pizza remains on the stove. Katie eats $\frac{1}{3}$ of the remaining pizza. In order to determine how much of the pizza is left, what topic must be introduced to the students?

a. Converting fractions to decimals
b. Subtraction of fractions with like denominators
c. Addition of fractions with unlike denominators
d. Division of fractions

36. Last year, the New York City area received approximately $27\frac{3}{4}$ inches of snow. The Denver area received approximately 3 times as much snow as New York City. How much snow fell in Denver?

a. 60 inches
b. $27\frac{1}{4}$ inches
c. $9\frac{1}{4}$ inches
d. $83\frac{1}{4}$ inches

37. Joshua has collected 12,345 nickels over a span of 8 years. He took them to bank to deposit into his bank account. If the students were asked to determine how much money he deposited, for what mathematical topic would this problem be a good introduction?

a. Adding decimals
b. Multiplying decimals
c. Geometry
d. The metric system

38. Which of the following would be an instance in which ordinal numbers are used in the classroom?

a. Katie scored a 9 out of 10 on her quiz.
b. Matthew finished second in the spelling bee.
c. Jacob missed 1 day of school last month.
d. Kim was 5 minutes late to school this morning.

39. What is the solution to $9 \times 9 \div 9 + 9 - 9 \div 9$?

a. 0
b. 17
c. 81
d. 9

40. A student answers a problem with the following fraction: $\frac{3}{15}$. Why would this be considered incorrect?

a. It is not expressed in decimal form.
b. It is not simplified. The correct answer would be $\frac{1}{5}$.
c. It needs to be converted to a mixed number.
d. It is in the correct form, and there is no problem with it.

41. Which of the following statements is true about the two lines below?

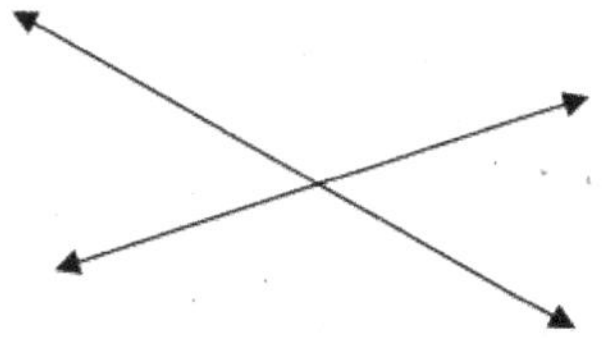

a. The two lines are parallel but not perpendicular.
b. The two lines are perpendicular but not parallel.
c. The two lines are both parallel and perpendicular.
d. The two lines are neither parallel nor perpendicular.

42. Which of the following figures is not a polygon?

a. Decagon
b. Cone
c. Triangle
d. Rhombus

43. What is the area of the regular hexagon shown below?

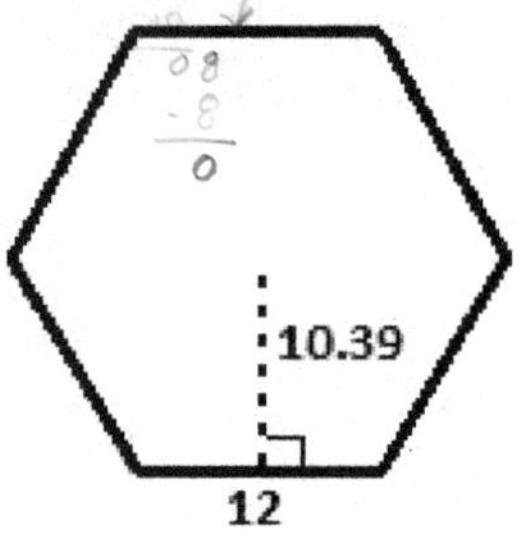

a. 72
b. 124.68
c. 374.04
d. 748.08

44. The area of a given rectangle is 24 square centimeters. If the measure of each side is multiplied by 3, what is the area of the new figure?
a. 48 cm^2
b. 72 cm^2
c. 216 cm^2
d. 13,824 cm^2

45. What are the coordinates of the point plotted on the grid?

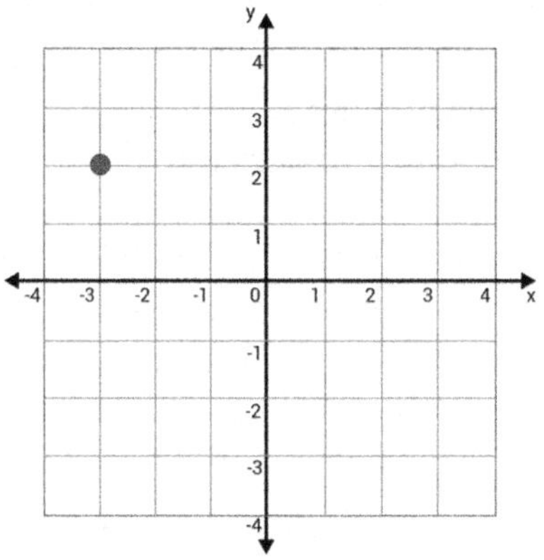

a. (-3, 2)
b. (2, -3)
c. (-3, -2)
d. (2, 3)

46. The perimeter of a 6-sided polygon is 56 cm. The length of three sides are 9 cm each. The length of two other sides are 8 cm each. What is the length of the missing side?
a. 11 cm
b. 12 cm
c. 13 cm
d. 10 cm

47. Katie works at a clothing company and sold 192 shirts over the weekend. $^1/_3$ of the shirts that were sold were patterned, and the rest were solid. Which mathematical expression would calculate the number of solid shirts Katie sold over the weekend?

a. $192 \times \frac{1}{3}$

b. $192 \div \frac{1}{3}$

c. $192 \times (1 - \frac{1}{3})$

d. $192 \div 3$

48. Which measure for the center of a small sample set is most affected by outliers?

a. Mean
b. Median
c. Mode
d. None of the above

49. Given the value of a given stock at monthly intervals, which graph should be used to best represent the trend of the stock?

a. Box plot
b. Line plot
c. Line graph
d. Circle graph

50. What is the probability of randomly picking the winner and runner-up from a race of 4 horses and distinguishing which is the winner?

a. $\frac{1}{4}$

b. $\frac{1}{2}$

c. $\frac{1}{16}$

d. $\frac{1}{12}$

Answer Explanations

1. B: This inequality can be seen with the use of a number line. $\frac{3}{7}$ is close to $\frac{1}{2}$. $\frac{5}{6}$ is close to 1, but less than 1, and $\frac{8}{7}$ is greater than 1. Therefore, $\frac{3}{7}$ is less than $\frac{5}{6}$.

2. A: Using the order of operations, multiplication and division are computed first from left to right. Multiplication is on the left; therefore, the teacher should perform multiplication first.

3. B: A factor of 36 is any number that can be divided into 36 and have no remainder. $36 = 36 \times 1, 18 \times 2, 9 \times 4, \text{and } 6 \times 6$. Therefore, it has 7 unique factors: 36, 18, 9, 6, 4, 2, and 1.

4. B: A number is prime because its only factors are itself and 1. Positive numbers (greater than one) can be prime numbers.

5. C: Each number in the sequence is adding one more than the difference between the previous two. For example:

$$10 - 6 = 4, 4 + 1 = 5$$

Therefore, the next number after 10 is $10 + 5 = 15$.

Going forward:

$$21 - 15 = 6, 6 + 1 = 7$$

The next number is $21 + 7 = 28$. Therefore, the difference between numbers is the set of whole numbers starting at 2: 2, 3, 4, 5, 6, 7….

6. A: Order of operations follows PEMDAS—Parentheses, Exponents, Multiplication and Division from left to right, and Addition and Subtraction from left to right.

7. C: 80 min. To solve the problem, a proportion is written consisting of ratios comparing distance and time. One way to set up the proportion is:

$$\frac{3}{48} = \frac{5}{x} \left(\frac{distance}{time} = \frac{distance}{time} \right)$$

where *x* represents the unknown value of time. To solve a proportion, the ratios are cross-multiplied:

$$(3)(x) = (5)(48) \rightarrow 3x = 240$$

The equation is solved by isolating the variable, or dividing by 3 on both sides, to produce $x = 80$.

8. A: A mixed number contains both a whole number and either a fraction or a decimal. Therefore, the mixed number is $16\frac{1}{2}$.

9. A: The place value to the right of the thousandth place, which would be the ten-thousandth place, is what gets used. The value in the thousandth place is 7. The number in the place value to its right is greater than 4, so the 7 gets bumped up to 8. Everything to its right turns to a zero, to get 245.2680. The zero is dropped because it is part of the decimal.

10. B: This is a division problem because the original amount needs to be split up into equal amounts. The mixed number $12\frac{1}{2}$ should be converted to an improper fraction first.

$$12\frac{1}{2} = \frac{(12 * 2) + 1}{2} = \frac{23}{2}$$

Carey needs to determine how many times $\frac{23}{2}$ goes into 184. This is a division problem: $184 \div \frac{23}{2} = ?$ The fraction can be flipped, and the problem turns into the multiplication:

$$184 \times \frac{2}{23} = \frac{368}{23}$$

This improper fraction can be simplified into 16 because $368 \div 23 = 16$. The answer is 16 lawn segments.

11. C: Numbers should be lined up by decimal places before subtraction is performed. This is because subtraction is performed within each place value. The other operations, such as multiplication, division, and exponents (which is a form of multiplication), involve ignoring the decimal places at first and then including them at the end.

12. A: The additive and subtractive identity is 0. When added or subtracted to any number, 0 does not change the original number.

13. B: 100 cm is equal to 1 m. 1.3 divided by 100 is 0.013. Therefore, 1.3 cm is equal to 0.013 m. Because 1 cm is equal to 10 mm, 1.3 cm is equal to 13 mm.

14. D: To calculate the circumference of a circle, use the formula $2\pi r$, where r equals the radius or half of the diameter of the circle and $\pi = 3.14 \ldots$. Substitute the given information, $2\pi 5 = 31.4 \ldots$, answer *D*.

15. B: A rectangle is a specific type of parallelogram. It has 4 right angles. A square is a rhombus that has 4 right angles. Therefore, a square is always a rectangle because it has two sets of parallel lines and 4 right angles.

16. D: Area = length x width. The answer must be in square inches, so all values must be converted to inches. $\frac{1}{2}$ ft is equal to 6 inches. Therefore, the area of the rectangle is equal to:

$$6 \times \frac{11}{2} = \frac{66}{2} = 33 \text{ square inches}$$

17. C: The teacher would be introducing fractions. If a pie was cut into 6 pieces, each piece would represent $\frac{1}{6}$ of the pie. If one piece was taken away, $\frac{5}{6}$ of the pie would be left over.

18. B: Each hour on the clock represents 30 degrees. For example, 3:00 represents a right angle. Therefore, 5:00 represents 150 degrees.

19. D: There are no millions, so the millions period consists of all zeros. 182 is in the billions period, 36 is in the thousands period, 421 is in the hundreds period, and 356 is the decimal.

20. A: Every 8 ml of medicine requires 5 mL. The 45 mL first needs to be split into portions of 8 mL. This results in $\frac{45}{8}$ portions. Each portion requires 5 mL. Therefore:

$$\frac{45}{8} \times 5 = \frac{45 \times 5}{8} = \frac{225}{8} \text{ mL is necessary}$$

21. D: Division can be computed as a repetition of subtraction problems by subtracting multiples of 24.

22. C: Volume of this three-dimensional figure is calculated using length x width x height. Each measure of length is in inches. Therefore, the answer would be labeled in cubic inches.

23. A: A common denominator must be found. The least common denominator is 15 because it has both 5 and 3 as factors. The fractions must be rewritten using 15 as the denominator.

24. B: A number raised to an exponent is a compressed form of multiplication. For example:

$$10^3 = 10 \times 10 \times 10$$

25. B: The perimeter of a rectangle is the sum of all four sides. Therefore, the answer is:

$$P = 14 + 8\frac{1}{2} + 14 + 8\frac{1}{2}$$

$$14 + 14 + 8 + \frac{1}{2} + 8 + \frac{1}{2}$$

$$45 \text{ square inches}$$

26. C: Inches, pounds, and baking measurements, such as tablespoons, are not part of the metric system. Kilograms, grams, kilometers, and meters are part of the metric system.

27. C: It shows the associative property of multiplication. The order of multiplication does not matter, and the grouping symbols do not change the final result once the expression is evaluated.

28. B: $12 \times 750 = 9{,}000$. Therefore, there are 9,000 milliliters of water, which must be converted to liters. 1,000 milliliters equals 1 liter; therefore, 9 liters of water are purchased.

29. A: According to order of operations, the operation within the parentheses must be completed first. Next, division is completed and then subtraction. Therefore, the expression is evaluated as:

$$(3 + 7) - 6 \div 2$$

$$10 - 6 \div 2$$

$$10 - 3 = 7$$

In order to incorrectly obtain 2 as the answer, the operations would have been performed from left to right, instead of following PEMDAS.

30. A: Operations within the parentheses must be completed first. Then, division is completed. Finally, addition is the last operation to complete. When adding decimals, digits within each place value are added together. Therefore, the expression is evaluated as:

$$(2 \times 20) \div (7 + 1) + (6 \times 0.01) + (4 \times 0.001)$$

$$40 \div 8 + 0.06 + 0.004$$

$$5 + 0.06 + 0.004 = 5.064$$

31. B: The formula for the volume of a rectangular solid would need to be used. The volume of the first box is:

$$V = 3 \times 5 \times 10 = 150 \text{ cubic inches}$$

The second box needs to hold cereal that would take up the same space. The volume of the second box is:

$$V = 5 \times 6 \times h = 30 \times h$$

In order for this to equal 150, *h* must equal 5 inches.

32. C: The measure of two complementary angles sums up to 90 degrees. $90 - 54 = 36$. Therefore, the complementary angle is 36 degrees.

33. C: A compass is a tool that can be used to draw a circle. The circle would be drawn by using the length of the radius, which is half of the diameter.

34. C: A dollar contains 20 nickels. Therefore, if there are 12 dollars' worth of nickels, there are:

$$12 \times 20 = 240 \text{ nickels}$$

Each nickel weighs 5 grams. Therefore, the weight of the nickels is:

$$240 \times 5 = 1{,}200 \text{ grams}$$

Adding in the weight of the empty piggy bank, the filled bank weighs 2,250 grams.

35. B: Katie eats $\frac{1}{3}$ of $\frac{3}{4}$ of the pizza. That means she eats:

$$\frac{1}{3} \times \frac{3}{4} = \frac{3}{12} = \frac{1}{4} \text{ of the pizza}$$

Therefore:

$$\frac{3}{4} - \frac{1}{4} = \frac{2}{4} = \frac{1}{2} \text{ of the pizza remains}$$

This problem involves subtraction of fractions with like denominators.

36. D: 3 must be multiplied times $27\frac{3}{4}$. In order to easily do this, the mixed number should be converted into an improper fraction.

$$27\frac{3}{4} = \frac{27 \times 4 + 3}{4} = \frac{111}{4}$$

Therefore, Denver had approximately $\frac{3x111}{4} = \frac{333}{4}$ inches of snow. The improper fraction can be converted back into a mixed number through division.

$$\frac{333}{4} = 83\frac{1}{4}\text{ inches}$$

37. B: Each nickel is worth $0.05. Therefore, Joshua deposited:

$$12{,}345 \times \$0.05 = \$617.25$$

Working with change is a great way to teach decimals to children, so this problem would be a good introduction to multiplying decimals.

38. B: Ordinal numbers represent a ranking. Placing second in a competition is a ranking among the other participants of the spelling bee.

39. B: According to the order of operations, multiplication and division must be completed first from left to right. Then, addition and subtraction are completed from left to right. Therefore:

$$9 \times 9 \div 9 + 9 - 9 \div 9$$

$$81 \div 9 + 9 - 9 \div 9$$

$$9 + 9 - 9 \div 9$$

$$9 + 9 - 1 = 18 - 1 = 17$$

40. B: When giving an answer to a math problem that is in fraction form, it always should be simplified. Both 3 and 15 have a common factor of 3 that can be divided out, so the correct answer is:

$$\frac{3 \div 3}{15 \div 3} = \frac{1}{5}$$

41. D: The two lines are neither parallel nor perpendicular. Parallel lines will never intersect or meet. Therefore, the lines are not parallel. Perpendicular lines intersect to form a right angle (90°). Although the lines intersect, they do not form a right angle, which is usually indicated with a box at the intersection point. Therefore, the lines are not perpendicular.

42. B: Cone. A polygon is a closed two-dimensional figure consisting of three or more sides. A decagon is a polygon with 10 sides. A triangle is a polygon with three sides. A rhombus is a polygon with 4 sides. A cone is a three-dimensional figure and is classified as a solid.

43. C: 374.04. The formula for finding the area of a regular polygon is $A = \frac{1}{2} \times a \times P$ where *a* is the length of the apothem (from the center to any side at a right angle), and P is the perimeter of the figure.

The apothem *a* is given as 10.39, and the perimeter can be found by multiplying the length of one side by the number of sides (since the polygon is regular):

$$P = 12 \times 6 \rightarrow P = 72$$

To find the area, substitute the values for *a* and *P* into the formula:

$$A = \frac{1}{2} \times a \times P$$

$$A = \frac{1}{2} \times (10.39) \times (72)$$

$$A = 374.04$$

44. C: 216cm. Because area is a two-dimensional measurement, the dimensions are multiplied by a scale that is squared to determine the scale of the corresponding areas. The dimensions of the rectangle are multiplied by a scale of 3. Therefore, the area is multiplied by a scale of 3^2 (which is equal to 9):

$$24\ cm \times 9 = 216\ cm$$

45. A: (-3, 2). The coordinates of a point are written as an ordered pair (*x*, *y*). To determine the *x*-coordinate, a line is traced directly above or below the point until reaching the *x*-axis. This step notes the value on the *x*-axis. In this case, the *x*-coordinate is -3. To determine the *y*-coordinate, a line is traced directly to the right or left of the point until reaching the y-axis, which notes the value on the *y*-axis. In this case, the *y*-coordinate is 2. Therefore, the ordered pair is written (-3, 2).

46. C: Perimeter is found by calculating the sum of all sides of the polygon. $9 + 9 + 9 + 8 + 8 + s = 56$, where *s* is the missing side length. Therefore, 43 plus the missing side length is equal to 56. The missing side length is 13 cm.

47. C: $\frac{1}{3}$ of the shirts sold were patterned. Therefore, $1 - \frac{1}{3} = \frac{2}{3}$ of the shirts sold were solid. Anytime "of" a quantity appears in a word problem, multiplication should be used. Therefore:

$$192 \times \frac{2}{3} = \frac{192 \times 2}{3} = \frac{384}{3} = 128 \text{ solid shirts were sold}$$

The entire expression is:

$$192 \times \left(1 - \frac{1}{3}\right)$$

48. A: Mean. An outlier is a data value that is either far above or far below the majority of values in a sample set. The mean is the average of all the values in the set. In a small sample set, a very high or very low number could drastically change the average of the data points. Outliers will have no more of an effect on the median (the middle value when arranged from lowest to highest) than any other value above or below the median. If the same outlier does not repeat, outliers will have no effect on the mode (value that repeats most often).

49. C: Line graph. The scenario involves data consisting of two variables, month and stock value. Box plots display data consisting of values for one variable. Therefore, a box plot is not an appropriate choice. Both line plots and circle graphs are used to display frequencies within categorical data. Neither can be used for the given scenario. Line graphs display two numerical variables on a coordinate grid and show trends among the variables.

50. D: $\frac{1}{12}$. The probability of picking the winner of the race is:

$$\frac{1}{4}\left(\frac{number\ of\ favorable\ outcomes}{number\ of\ total\ outcomes}\right)$$

Assuming the winner was picked on the first selection, three horses remain from which to choose the runner-up (these are dependent events). Therefore, the probability of picking the runner-up is $\frac{1}{3}$. To determine the probability of multiple events, the probability of each event is multiplied:

$$\frac{1}{4} \times \frac{1}{3} = \frac{1}{12}$$

Dear FTCE Elementary Education Test Taker,

We would like to start by thanking you for purchasing this study guide for your FTCE Elementary Education exam. We hope that we exceeded your expectations.

Our goal in creating this study guide was to cover all of the topics that you will see on the test. We also strove to make our practice questions as similar as possible to what you will encounter on test day. With that being said, if you found something that you feel was not up to your standards, please send us an email and let us know.

We would also like to let you know about another book in our catalog that may interest you.

FTCE General Knowledge

This can be found on Amazon: amazon.com/dp/1628457465

We have study guides in a wide variety of fields. If the one you are looking for isn't listed above, then try searching for it on Amazon or send us an email.

Thanks Again and Happy Testing!
Product Development Team
info@studyguideteam.com

FREE Test Taking Tips DVD Offer

To help us better serve you, we have developed a Test Taking Tips DVD that we would like to give you for FREE. **This DVD covers world-class test taking tips that you can use to be even more successful when you are taking your test.**

All that we ask is that you email us your feedback about your study guide. Please let us know what you thought about it – whether that is good, bad or indifferent.

To get your **FREE Test Taking Tips DVD**, email freedvd@studyguideteam.com with "FREE DVD" in the subject line and the following information in the body of the email:

a. The title of your study guide.

b. Your product rating on a scale of 1-5, with 5 being the highest rating.

c. Your feedback about the study guide. What did you think of it?

d. Your full name and shipping address to send your free DVD.

If you have any questions or concerns, please don't hesitate to contact us at freedvd@studyguideteam.com.

Thanks again!

Made in the USA
Las Vegas, NV
13 July 2021

26393181R00216